What people said about Chris Searle's la

CW01663139

"None of the many individual pieces tak
minutes to read, but any of them could l
satisfying listening. So a final caution: don't be tempted to adopt this as a bedside book, unless you are prepared for chronic sleep deprivation." *Jon Turney, UK Jazz News*

"The great strength of Left jazz criticism is that it places the music in a social context, rather than treating it like the ivory-tower conservatoire art it is not. Chris Searle, for nearly three decades the jazz correspondent of the Morning Star is always worth reading for this reason." *Chris May, All About Jazz*

"Most of the pieces come in at about a page and a half of reading and many have accompanying gig reviews to give a fuller picture. Searle is a great enthusiast for the music with a great fondness for the British free scene centred on Dalston's Café Oto, though his articles range far and wide; his enthusiasm is best reflected at the end of many of the articles in his urging the reader to buy this album or go to that gig. It's immensely readable though." *Dave Sayer, Bebop Spoken Here*

"As to the quality of the writing, it is simultaneously committed, insightful and elegant. The uncommitted reader will be pleased at the absence of anything resembling political dogma or theory herein. Searle's focus is always on the music and on the artists themselves." *Duncan Heining, All About Jazz*

"Talking The Groove is worth reading for its focus on British jazz and jazz seen from a British perspective. Despite the free-flowing and unhindered positivity, it comes not unexpectedly with a generosity of spirit missing from more jaundiced surveys." *Nigel Jarrett, Jazz Journal*

"... all are short and to the point, often containing real insights, but also making for ideal 'dip in' reading. Importantly, what comes across in this collection is Searle's passion for, and connection with, the music; he understands the importance of the artist's struggle for creative (and often, social and political) freedom as a crucial driving force in jazz." *Kevin Whitlock, Jazzwise*

GLOBAL GROOVE

WORDS OF A JAZZ COSMOS

Cover photographs

1. Mark Sanders
(England/Belize)
© *Pete Woodman*

2. Annie Whitehead
(England)
© *Pete Woodman*

3. Neil Charles
(England/Grenada)
© *Pete Woodman*

4. George Adams
(USA)
© *John Thurlow*

5. Bint Mbareh
(Palestine)
© *Nelly Rodriguez*

6. Peter Somuah
(Ghana)
© *Patrick Kenawy*

7. Bokani Dyer
(Botswana/South Africa)
© *Mac Creative Lines*

8. Melissa Aldana
(Chile)
© *Eduardo Pavez Goye*

9. Sun-Mi Hong
(South Korea)
© *Pete Woodman*

CHRIS SEARLE

978-1-0683644-2-6

First published 2026 by Jazz in Britain Ltd

Compiled and edited by John Thurlow

Cover design by Chris Searle and Pete Woodman

Note: the year in brackets in the heading of each piece
is the year it was written.

Printed by Biddles Books Ltd, Kings Lynn, Norfolk, UK

JAZZ IN BRITAIN

jazzinbritain.org
admin@jazzinbritain.org

Acknowledgements

This book would not exist without the labours of two outstanding lovers and artisans of the music, the creators of Jazz In Britain, John Thurlow and Pete Woodman. Their hard and original work has meant that many otherwise unknown beautiful sounds would not be available for our ears, and writers like me would never have seen their work in book form.

They consistently demonstrate that the urge to make and preserve such music does not go hand-in-glove with the counter-urge to hear these sounds as a means of lucre; that the superb artistry of the world's groove can sustain our imagination, pleasure and consciousness without the constant drive for profit – power to their work!

My thanks too go to those who produce and publicise the recordings of this music: to Mike Gavin and the late John Jack of Cadillac Records, Hazel Miller of Ogun, the late Martin Davidson of Emanem, Martin Archer of Discus, Bill Trythall of Discovery, Kris Davis of Pyroclastic, Ann Braithwaite and Tom Fletcher: and to Oliver Weindling and friends at the Vortex and Fielding Hope and Mo Dafa of Café Oto.

Finally my thanks to the pianist and keyboards virtuoso Pat Thomas, for his generous words of introduction. I have heard him playing live countless times and have always been deeply moved by his startling technique and the way his music embodies a love of the jazz tradition (Ellington, Monk, Joe Harriott, Ornette and Derek Bailey) with astonishing reinvention and surprise spilling from his every note. The sound of his Antiguan heritage radiates from his fingers, and I can hear the ancestral voices of Africa and the Antilles lapping rhythmically as he plays, reminding me of the voices of Caribbean genius that never leave me: of Bishop, Creft, James, Brathwaite, Carter, Rodney, Marley, Hodge, Lamming, Guillen, Claudia and Fanon all resonating from the soul of his hands.

Chris Searle, December 2025

Contents

© *Pete Woodman*

Preface

It is a great honour to be asked to write about this remarkable book by Chris, in my view the most profound writer on the subject of Jazz and related musics in the country today. His love and dedication to the music pours out from every letter. Each review opens a new horizon on the variety of Jazz in the world today.

This art form rooted in African-American cultural aesthetics has become the impetus for globalization, but in a positive sense, with people creating new approaches through cultural exchange, not exploitation. Chris is not afraid to see that justice has always been crucial to the message of Jazz, created in the worst conditions possible by a people who overcame inhumane brutality and horrific torture; people who were regarded as barely human, yet through their art have shown the triumph of the human spirit. This is a great book!

Pat Thomas, December 2025

Introduction

This book encompasses three decades of writing about jazz, a music which began in the street parades, dance halls, backstairs venues and Jim Crow ambiance of New Orleans, was first recorded over a century ago, and which in now-times has exploded as a true music of the world, the sound of the cosmos in rapid change. There is the artistry and passion of musicians from over a hundred nations and heritages within these pages: from Korea to Toronto, from the Philippines to Trinidad, from Chile to Afghanistan, from Sweden to Peru, from Brooklyn to Damascus, from Mexico to Palestine, from Greece to Ghana, from Cape Town to Beijing, Sao Paulo to Copenhagen. And because the writer is English there are many English virtuosi, youth and veterans, interviewed and reviewed, musicians whom I have regularly heard and seen express their astonishing creativity. There are many writings too from the birthplace of jazz, from copious locations from the great nation of Louis Armstrong, Duke Ellington, Charles Mingus, Max Roach and John Coltrane, which is presently being debased and besmirched by the appalling, cruel and crude leadership of an imperial regime which enacts every day the contrary of all which the freedom, cosmopolitan and justice-loving soul of jazz stands for.

Almost all of these writings first found print in Europe's only daily socialist newspaper, the Morning Star, for which I have been the jazz correspondent for almost 30 years. I thank its journalists, editorial staff and readers for all they have done to support the paper's decades-long championing of jazz, a truly critical, discovering and revolutionary music. I have also been lucky to have been an ardent attender and listener at some of the most challenging and audacious venues in London, particularly the true creative hubs of London's free improvising, the Café Oto and Vortex in Dalston, East London, while also staying a regular at the more long-established West End venues like Ronnie Scott's and the Pizza Express.

When I wrote in my review of Daniel Spicer's biography of the German saxophonist Peter Brotzmann that 'as a musical revolutionary he was a profoundly committed internationalist and there were no barriers of genre, nation or tradition that would obstruct the untrammelled liberation of his sound', I am also writing about musicians from all over the world who strive to create something holding a kindred meaning. Descriptions of many of them will be found in the pages that follow, and I feel proud to have heard and responded to them in words, whether live or on record.

One last point: I make no apologies for being a jazz eclectic. I can regularly savour the most outrageously free improvising sounds at Café Oto, then come home and the next morning very happily play my records of the New Orleans joys of Armstrong, Joe 'King' Oliver and George Lewis, the passionate horn artistry of Coleman Hawkins, Roy Eldridge and Lester Young, the orchestral brilliance of Ellington, Basie and Westbrook and the audacity of

Charlie Parker or Ornette. My school days were full of the New Orleans to London sound of Ken Colyer, Monty Sunshine and Acker Bilk, which is why you will also find in this book words describing Crescent City heroes like Kid Thomas Valentine and Buster Wilson.

There are 70 years of listening to and loving the multisonic sounds of jazz within these pages, written by an Essex boy who grew up with the echoes of New Orleans blowing in his ears. Yet for me now, into my 80s, more than ever, jazz is a music of cosmopolitan unity, the free notes of the world as one, and the true soundscape of the hopes and liberties of all our futures. Writing these words in my front room, I am also listening to Coltrane's Cosmos from his Live in Seattle album, (he played one of his few English concerts in the Granada Cinema, Walthamstow, just up the road from where I live.) I think too of the John Donne poem The Good Morrow, that I have always loved so much from my first teenage reading of its wisdom and beauty, how the love he feels 'makes one little room an everywhere'. I feel the same now with Coltrane's notes seething in my ears and in my blood, knowing that his sound, and that of all those who strive to make such music all over the world, are joining him in one united anthem of hope.

Chris Searle, December 2025

Rez Abbasi (Pakistan/USA) Acoustic Quintet
Sound Remains
(2025)

As soon as you hear the opening notes of the New York City-recorded album by guitarist Rez Abbasi's Acoustic Quintet, Sound Remains, you know you are hearing sounds that were only partly birthed in America, for Abbasi was born in Karachi, Pakistan in 1969, and came to live in Los Angeles as a boy, starting on guitar at 11.

His superfine, fleeting runs which sprint through the album's opening track, Presence, have a unique edge, supplemented by bassist Stephan Crump, drummer Eric McPherson, with percussionist Hasan Bakr and Bill Ware on vibes.

'Sound Remains' is an assertive title of a musician 'wrestling with the reality of impermanence' after the loss of his mother. Everything passes, except the waxed music - as he says in his sleeve notes, 'the only 'voice' that remains is sound'.

Guitar and vibes make a quietly beautiful duo on the track called You Are, with McPherson's restless drums and crump's heartbeat bass igniting their rhythmic fire behind the mollifying melodic improvisation of Abbasi and Ware. There is something deeply poetic about this album, as if Andrew Marvell and his 'time's winged chariot' were watching over the session like a ghostly studio engineer, for all musicians are seizing and swinging the time, as if it were fast running out and only the music will be left.

Strange thoughts perhaps for a listener engrossed by a guitarist from Pakistan and his American confreres, but such are the idiosyncrasies provoked by their music. Just listen to their playing of Coltrane's Lonnie's Lament. It's a bass-emphatic excursion of quietude, an elegiac rhapsody of human feeling that took me back to 'Speak...', a poem by the great Pakistani laureate Faiz Ahmad Faiz, another assertion of sheer human creativity: 'Speak there is little time/But little though it is/It is enough/Time enough/Speak - truth still lives/Say what you have/To say.'

Abbasi's guitar and his bandmates' instruments all speak their very human truthful song - melodic and fulsome in Meet the Moment, which is all the finest musicians can ever do, and they do with an emotive brilliance.

(Sound Remains is available on Whirlwind Recordings)

Muhal Richard Abrams (USA) - The sounds of an unlatched future

Levels and Degrees of Light, Young at Heart/Wise in Time
& Things to Come from Those now Gone
(2003)

'To cultivate young musicians and to create music of a high artistic level for the general public through the presentation of programmes designed to magnify the importance of creative music!' Such was the first tenet of the Chicago black community-based Association for the Advancement of Creative Musicians (AACM), founded in May 1965 by the Shytown-born pianist Muhal Richard Abrams and also emphasising musical self-reliance, local and original performance and 'high moral standards for musicians.'

Abrams was the AACM's first president, and by 1967, when the album Levels and Degrees of Light was recorded in his home city, there were 30-plus avant- garde spirits working and performing alongside him. Levels includes some of those who were to become leaders in their own right and creators of some of the most audacious and free-spirited jazz of the next three decades: altoist Anthony Braxton, violinist Leroy Jenkins, and tenorist Kalaparusha Maurice McIntyre. Levels was also Muhal's first record for the Chicago-based Delmark label, eclectic in its philosophy, loyal to local musicians and risk-taking in its outlook. This was free and assertive Windy City music at its most fiery and innovative, and it was coming from the heart of the city.

The title track begins with a haunting wordless vocal by Penelope Taylor and Thurman Barker's splashing percussion. Abrams's cawing clarinet enters, soaring high then dipping into low register, a bird gliding lonesomely over Lake Michigan launching its song. The Bird Song continues this avian theme, but music and poetry fuse with David Moore's words evoking birds flying over 'the ruins of a cursed land.' Braxton's wailing alto creates a sound that only he could manifest and when Kalaparusha's tenor bursts in during the 13th minute the ensemble lets rip with freedom.

The paired basses of Charles Clark and Leonard Jones and Muhal's lightning piano preface My Thoughts Are My Future - Now and Forever. Kalaparusha blows out a rampaging solo, Barker's drums stoke burning rhythmic fuel, Braxton's notes take myriad directions and the basses challenge each other in a twanging twosome. The blues-soaked south side had never seen the like.

In July/August 1969, Muhal returned to the same Sound Studios to record the Young at Heart/Wise in Time album. Young at Heart is a 29-minute piano solo, daring enough for any pianist, but for Muhal, exposing himself as an architect of the new music, it took particular nerve and courage. From the outset his keyboard sounds as if it is a mile long, with some notes very close to the ears and others chiming from a distant, faraway place. 'It just flowed from the way I lived,' Muhal said. Its amalgam of harmony and dissonance, quiet and rhythmic freedom with unstinting surprise and invention perhaps summarised his creative life. Wise in Time brought Muhal together with Lester Lashley, old bass confrere of the 1961 Experimental Band, with revolutionary hornmen Henry Threadgill on alto saxophone making his first recording and the trumpeter from Leland, Mississippi, Leo Wadada Smith. Barker's drums are on hand again. The suspirations of Smith's breathy, eventually rasping horn begin the piece. Suddenly the bass beat moves apace, Barker's drums crash and Threadgill's spiky alto breaks ahead with relentless motion. Muhal's speed catches him and his solo patterns are spurred by Baker and Lashley urging him on in a chase of beauty until Baker's gong strikes a cessation.

In 1972 Muhal recorded the album Things to Come from Those Now Gone, with different personnel for each of the seven tracks. Ballad for New Souls is a reflective duo between Muhal and flautist Wallace McMillan, who picks up his alto for the fleet, frantic and free title tune alongside fellow altoist Edwin Daugherty and paired drummers Steve McCall and Wilbur Campbell. In Retrospect features Muhal, the gripping tenorist Ari Brown and a throbbing Rufus Reid on bass - a harsh trio beauty here. And in 1 and 4 plus 2 and 7 Muhal plays piano and synthesiser, with the path-finding free percussionist McCall provoking new sonic discoveries. All Chicago men, AACM musicians were made in and inspired by Chicago and aimed directly at its people, in particular its youth.

'Ah, pioneers!' somebody once wrote. They could say it again about Muhal, his confreres and these ear-opening albums of over four decades ago, full of the sounds of an unlatched future.

(Levels and Degrees of Light, Young at Heart/Wise in Time & Things to Come from Those now Gone are available on Delmark)

Muhal Richard Abrams (USA) - An eternally unquiet world
SoundDance
(2016)

There's no doubt that due to his incessant organising and music-making, Muhal Richard Abrams has been one of the most powerfully significant figures in jazz development over the last half century, and one who despite his modesty and low profile has contributed a vitally original and influential seam to the music.

Born in Chicago in 1930, Abrams was mainly self-taught, his piano playing originally stimulated by the bop brilliance of Bud Powell. Always an experimenter, he formed the briefly lived Experimental Band in 1961, and in 1965 alongside other musical risk-takers of the Windy City, he formed and became the first president of the groundbreaking Association for the Advancement of Creative Musicians (AACM) which emphasised musical self-reliance, creative innovation and educating and mobilising the Chicago community in support of its new music. Beginning with his first album for the local Chitown label Delmark, Levels and Degrees of Light, Blu Blu Blu and Hearing a Suite which combined unpredictable ensemble passages with startling solo work from musicians such as trumpeter Jack Walrath, trombonist Craig Harris, cellist Abdul Wadid, drummer Andrew Cyrille and reedman Marty Erlich.

At almost 80, in 2009-10 Muhal made a double album in New York with two fellow veterans and luminaries of the Chicago free jazz scene, trombonist George Lewis (who in the mid-70s had a spell in the Count Basie Orchestra) and the fellow AACM founder, proprietor of the legendary Velvet Lounge jazz venue and titanic tenor saxophonist, the Louisiana-born Fred Anderson. Muhal duets with each on the two separate albums, both turning back and turning on the years. The Muhal-Anderson duo is sealed by so much mutual empathy that it seems like one human being is playing two instruments and the notes are the sound of centuries. Muhal caresses, romps along and pounds the keys like a sound griot playing piano, while Anderson leads and follows, initiates and responds in a colloquy of wisdom, taste and sheer experience. It is a rare amalgam indeed and one baked in the rural and urban blues, from Monroe, Louisiana to Chicago, Illinois.

Their performance is in four parts and entitled Focus ThruTime... Time and with more than 150 years between them, Time is an apt enough theme, so apt that it was for Anderson, who died in 2010, a final recorded performance. The harmonies of this duo seem uncannily woven, like the sequence in Part 3 where both masters soar upwards towards crescendoed flights, then pause, reflect and create on, as if no force can countermand or stop them, so huge is their shared musical authority, and so much have they given to the sonic culture of their city and its people over all those years of struggle, hope and achievement.

The acoustic glory of the Muhal-Anderson performance is very different to the union with Lewis, who for the last decade has used interactive computer sounds alongside his dextrous and roaring trombone. This too is recorded in an AACM concert in New York, a city far from his home, but Muhal, all through his musical life has been up for anything and the new technology is but another challenge, as the performers' peak of laughter, following the opening applause, suggests. Muhal's dark chords mesh immediately with the electronic whispers and cadences as if he were a man veering into a new, unimagined and eternally unquiet world. As Lewis picks up his trombone his slide artistry jags over Muhal's grounding phrases in an angry storm of notes which are given electronic reinforcement by the computer's low wails, which turn to sheer birdsong and suspiration as Muhal lays out.

Part 3 has Muhal gently striking his keys alongside a technological netherworld undreamed of when he first began organising and making new sounds more than half a century ago in Chicago. Or perhaps those faraway dreams were always there, inchoate and unformed, in the crowded streets and jazz venues like the Velvet Lounge, rampant in the free sounds of the improvised music.

It is this Muhal-Lewis performance that is called SoundDance and its very title reminds us that jazz was born in New Orleans as a music of parade and dance - and even in the century-later epoch of electronic and computer communication its notes still gyrate and swing through the breath and hands of these veterans.

(SoundDance is available on Pi Recordings)

George Adams (USA) – The sonic beauty of a sax master

The Complete Remastered Recordings on Black Saint and Soul Note (2013)

If you want some authentic idea of the true tenor saxophone glory of George Adams you could turn to YouTube and trace his sublime duet performance of What a Wonderful World with his long-time piano partner Don Pullen, recorded live at a Japanese jazz festival. Then you could go directly to this combined box set of his complete Black Saint and Soul Note albums, recorded between 1980 and 1983 with several of his ex-confreres of the Charles Mingus groups that he played with.

Adams was born in Covington, Georgia, in 1940, started on piano as a boy but by 1961 he was playing tenor in soul and funk bands, including the one which accompanied Sam Cooke. He moved to Ohio, playing in organ combos before switching to New York in 1968, where he joined bands led by drummers Art Blakey and Roy Haynes and the Gil Evans Orchestra before becoming a part of Mingus's Jazz Workshop from 1973-6. By 1979, the year Mingus died, Adams and Pullen had assembled a hot quartet - all four of them Mingus alumni - to record the album Don't Lose Control. Mingus's ex- drummer and close musical comrade Dannie Richmond became a fixture with Adams, as did the Canadian bassist Cameron Brown, who had been brought into Jazz Workshop to replace the ailing Mingus while he was convalescing in Mexico shortly before his death.

Adams begins with a filigreeing flute at the start of the opener Autumn Song before his big tenor sound takes over, warbling hugely over Pullen's chimes. The album's title song gives Adams a gruff blues vocal with Pullen stomping beside him before his adenoidal tenor growls and hoots its way through the chorus. The pianist's tune Remember is slow and reflective at its outset and as bass, drums and finally tenor enter, Pullen's keys crash and echo like memories that never leave while Adams' horn talks of four lives in amalgam.

The 15 minutes of Double Arc Jake include some Cameron bass that would have excited Mingus and Pullen playing piano like a many-keyed drum with Richmond's splashing cymbals beside him. Adams's flute sings over the percussion like a wounded bird and it is his roaring tenor which brings the foursome home.

Nineteen-eighty brought a quintet album, Hand to Hand, with Adams and Richmond again, but this time with another Mingus man, trombonist Jimmy Knepper, and pianist Hugh Lawson with Mike Richmond on bass. The Cloocker begins the session with some splurging Adams tenor chased by a romping Lawson and Knepper's slides in eloquent fettle. Yamani's Passion follows, with Adams marking out its melodic centre, Lawson's muscular notes and the marvellously deft Knepper winding all round the theme. The closer is Joobulie, begun by Mike Richmond's throbbing bassline. Knepper's solo is racked with thought and invention and Adams's tenor almost bursts with emotive sound before Richmond's resonant bass brings forward the close. A sublime track, this.

The same stellar quintet recorded another album, Gentleman's Agreement, in 1983. Adams's growling beauty dominates More Sightings, he turns pleading balladeer in Don't Take Your Love From Me, all members flourish on the enigmatic Symphony for Five, Adams blows with astonishing speed and invention and Knepper's short solo catches the stars on Prayer For a Jitterbug. The closer, Ripp-Off exudes the funk and blowout of Adams's early horn days.

The two volumes of Live at the Village Vanguard were recorded on the night of August 1983 at New York's prime jazz venue. It was the Adams-Pullen-Richmond- Brown quartet again, and how they groove through the almost two hours of boiling music. Pullen's stomping tune The Necessary Blues (Thank You Very Much, Mr Monk) moves with tremendous life with the pianist in rampaging spirit and Adams's unaccompanied introduction to Ellington's Solitude is sheer sonic excitation and beauty.

The second volume opens with Pullen's Saturday Night in the Cosmos with Adams's flute a-fluttering. He said of his tune City Gates, which follows, 'Every city has gates to it, and many things come out and go into many city gates.' These four musicians come in, throbbing and pulsating with astonishing sounds, making the city theirs, and Adams's mighty horn blows all its walls down - just hear him blast through Pullen's Big Alice.

Pullen wrote his moving lament for Adams - Ah George, We Hardly Knew Ya - shortly after the hornman's death in 1992, and the wonderful Pullen was to permanently leave the bandstand himself in 1995. They both surge on with their comrades in this apex of boxed sets.

(George Adams - The Complete Remastered Recordings are available on Black Saint/Soul Note)

Pepper Adams (USA) - A dash of Pepper

Pepper Adams and Jimmy Knepper - Pepper-Knepper Quintet (2014)

I remember well the first time that I heard the rampant baritone saxophone of Pepper Adams. It was a Saturday in the early '70s when I used to do an afternoon cruise up Charing Cross Road. Collett's London Bookshop with all its socialist tomes on one side and, right opposite, my other emporium of delight, Dobell's jazz record shop - particularly its second-hand basement.

I recall once walking into Dobell's and being hit by the grumbling, swinging hard bop notes of a surging baritone horn. It sounded straight from the urban canyons of the US, a deeper, more delving pitch than the great tenorists like Coleman Hawkins and Chu Berry, with more vibrato than Harry Carney, Ellington's pioneer baritonist who had set the instrument's standard for me when I first heard him with the Duke at the Leeds Grand Theatre in 1964.

I looked at the sleeve displayed on Dobell's counter and, seeing a speckled white face, I marvelled that a white man could play with such skyward fire and earthen weight. But Pepper had come to jazz fruition in Detroit alongside black second-generation boppers like trumpeter Donald Byrd, pianists Tommy Flanagan and Barry Harris, drummer Elvin Jones and guitarist Kenny Burrell and was totally attuned to their sound.

Park 'Pepper' Adams was born in Highland Park, Illinois, in 1930 and moved to Detroit when he was 16. He took up the baritone and soon became part of Motown's flourishing jazz scene, eventually moving to New York in 1958, cutting a host of albums and playing regularly with Byrd, Charles Mingus (1959-63), becoming a long-time member of the Thad Jones/Mel Lewis Big Band (1965-78). He died in 1986.

On the Pepper-Knepper Quintet album his front-line partner is another white hornman admired by black jazz virtuosi, Mingus's favourite trombonist Jimmy Knepper, born in Los Angeles in 1927, who as a young man gained experience in the big bands of Charlie Barnet, Woody Herman and Claude Thornhill before becoming a Mingus regular between 1957 and 1962. Like Pepper, he played with the Jones/Lewis Band, from 1968-74. Yet the powerhouse of this 1958 quintet is the stellar rhythm section, with Elvin Jones, shortly to be the drummer of the John Coltrane Quartet, bassist Paul Chambers of Pittsburgh and the Jamaica-born pianist Wynton Kelly, who a year later was to play Freddie Freeloader on Miles Davis's Kind Of Blue, one of the most sublime albums in jazz history. From the outset of the fast-moving opener Minor Catastrophe, Pepper is well on the mark with a rumbling chorus. Kelly and Chambers make their signature solos and Knepper is all artistry and passion.

All Too Soon moves into Ellingtonia with a beautiful Carney-inspired performance by Pepper, his long, lingering notes filled with a serene sadness. Kelly adds a thoughtful interlude and Knepper's horn lifts the balladic theme towards the planets. Kelly romps ahead in his intro to Beaubien, Knepper is note-brilliant and racked with invention and Pepper dances in with his big horn, its depth no impediment to sheer facility and speed. Jones instigates a call and response with both horns and Chambers is not to be outdone as he breaks into a twanging solo.

Adam's In The Apple is just that. Pepper seems more than pleased to be there and New York pounds with him. Knepper's authority over his slides is astonishing, inspiring Pepper for a swinging stroll through the streets. One of them, Riverside Drive, gets a tune for itself, with Pepper full of zest and verve, exploring every metropolitan metre. It's back to Ellington for the love tune I Didn't Know About You, with Pepper in lyrical mode, Knepper in tender orbit and Kelly playing a belligerent organ. The closer is the trombonist's own Primrose Path led by Pepper's jaunty solo, a coolly swinging chorus from Kelly and some marvellous slidework from the composer.

The reissue's three concluding tracks are from a session a year earlier with the same miracle-working sounds of another Detroiter, the altoist Sonny Red, who sounds fiery on Watkins Production and levitating on the Fats Navarro tune Stop. But Pepper is there to keep him grounded, along with Jones's stomping drums. The final track is the altoist's opus, Redd's Head, where the two horns lock in an unbridled jam, with Sonny's ups and Pepper's downs dancing inside of each other in joyous and uproarious notes. You'll love it.

(Pepper-Knepper Quintet is available on American Jazz Classics)

Faradena Afifi (Afghanistan)

In Afghanistan no women or girls have access to education - by playing music I am playing for the people who can't

(2024)

As she was about to enter an east London studio in November 2022 to create the album which eventually became bee Reiki, violinist and vocalist Faradena Afifi had an unusual meeting.

'A white-tailed bumblebee was the first being I encountered before going into the studio to record with Steve Beresford and Paul Khimasia Morgan. I was warming up outside, doing some T'ai Chi and I noticed the poor bee lying in a puddle. I ended up doing a reiki treatment and witnessing her flying off to the blue sky. It put me in a very good mood and my joy influenced everybody there. The bee became a folk song and I turned into its mood - definitely not something I would come up with on my own.'

Born in Greenwich in 1975, her mother teaches singing and her father was a doctor from Kabul, Afghanistan, 'who liked to sing Afghan songs and songs from the charts. I was playing piano since I could crawl and I would also play cardboard boxes, rubber bands and cutlery, and sing sometimes in my sleep. When my dad worked at Glasgow Royal Infirmary when I was a baby, I'd go to the airport and spend hours listening to and watching the planes.'

She told me that as a schoolgirl she loved listening to 'classical baroque music - Bach, Buxtehude, Vivaldi and 20th-century composers like Berg, Bartok and Ligeti. Also Afghan and Indian folk music and whatever pop music was being played on the school bus.'

'I developed a liking for birdsong as my grandfather knew all the birds and he passed that on to me. I also loved to listen to the rain, thunderstorms, the wind through the trees and reed beds, and the sounds of building sites (especially cement mixers), trains, markets and traffic. I loved going to nature reserves and other green spaces as a child.'

This natural, utilitarian and metropolitan music of the world, nature-made and human-made, was supplemented by her playing of piano, violin and viola in a youth orchestra, although 'my reading of music was and still is severely limited because of dyslexia, and I prefer to learn by ear.'

By her late 20s she was taken by jazz. 'I went to a Cecil Taylor concert and thought it was brilliant, never having heard that kind of free music before. I went to gigs at Café Oto and by the London Improvisation Workshop run by Eddie Prevost, and other workshops by Maggie Nicols and Keith Tippett, and Community Music sessions using John Stevens's free techniques.'

During lockdown she played online gigs with Maggie Nicols, the Glasgow Improvisers' Orchestra and Caroline Kraabel. Then on Zoom she met septuagenarian pianist, electronics wizard and toy instrument virtuoso Beresford and Morgan, playing amplified acoustic guitar body. They promised each other they would record together as a trio after lockdown.

The result was the bee Reiki album. I asked her, what is reiki? 'It is one of the moving forces of energy healing that has been around for millennia. It comes from Japan. I do a combination of T'ai Chi, massage, reiki and music with recorded birdsong, listening to and discovering natural rhythms, connecting myself with others. The healing energy is already there.'

What about the creative energy of the trio? 'We connected with one another, listened deeply, gave each other plenty of space and enjoyed each other's humanity and humour. Steve has a real sense of playfulness and spontaneity, like watching an enthusiastic toddler explore possibilities with a spoon and bowl. Paul is considered yet unexpected, at points I couldn't tell who was playing what. It was like a three-person dawn chorus.'

Certainly, they make powerful and tender sounds as a trio that reflect the timbres of city, countryside and cosmos. 'Even in the busiest street you can hear wind, the oak trees and there is usually a pigeon, fox, robin, blackbird. sparrow, gull or jackdaw flying around. For me, music is a form of freedom and empowerment. It has been banned from being played in Afghanistan and no women or girls have access to education. So by playing music I am countering that. I am playing for the people who can't.'

As a listener, you remember all this through her album, and you remember at its jazz heart is a trapped bee - released and flying, its sister or brother beautifully photographed on the sleeve, free again to help sustain and sweeten the world.

(Faradena Afifi with Steve Beresford and Paul Khimasia Morgan - bee Reiki, is available on Discus Music)

Naseem Alatrash (Palestine) - Because of the Second Intifada and lack of violin teachers the cello became an alternative

Jazz cellist Naseem Alatrash (Palestine) of the IZE Trio (2024)

It's quite an album this, by the cosmopolitan IZE trio. Just consider its four titles, with the first track called Break G4S 'On Capitalism'; the second, Resurrecting The Amber Sky 'On Environmentalism'; the third All Loved 'On Immigration'; and the fourth Elemeno, 'On Education'.

The trio are San Diego, California-born pianist Chase Morrin, Cyprus-born percussionist George Lernis and Palestinian cellist, Naseem Alatrash. I asked Naseem about his life in music and the story behind the trio's album, The Global Suites.

'I was born in 1991 in Beit Sahour, a town next to Bethlehem. I spent all my childhood there until college. My parents are dentists, but they liked music and supported me and my siblings in our music.

'The Palestinian musical tradition was the first genre that shaped my musical identity. Before the internet I had limited exposure to Western music as a child. I heard music of Palestine and the Levant and Arab world generally, performed at concerts, weddings and social gatherings, and played on the radio or cassettes and records that we had at home. I was also introduced to Greek music as my dad went to college in Greece and had lots of Greek records.

'As a teenager I listened to all kinds: classical, Western and Arab music, and Arabian and American pop. At aged 11 I wanted to learn an instrument, at first violin. I had no idea what a cello was. Because of the Second Intifada and lack of violin teachers the cello became an alternative. I fell in love with it at first listen. I also picked up the lute-like oud, which my brother plays.

'My earliest musical education was at the Edward Said National Conservatory in Palestine, after in Lubeck, Germany, and then, in 2010, at Berklee College of Music in Boston. I had years of training in classical Arab music and global jazz, where I learned structure, technique as well as the openness of improvisation and cultural dialogue between genres.'

At Berklee, Naseem was mentored by the great Panamanian pianist, Danilo Perez, with whom he studied, recorded and toured. This led to performing with the Turtle Island Quartet and the renowned radical trumpeter, Terence Blanchard. It was at Berklee too that he met Morrin. 'We quickly discovered our connections and continually exchanged ideas. Then I met George on the Boston music scene,' and the IZE Trio was complete.

'Chase is a brilliant pianist and composer, deeply immersed in jazz and classical music. He's one of the most creative and curious musicians I've ever met. George is a solid percussionist, a master orchestrator who always finds the right percussion instruments for any piece.

'We recorded the album as we were coming out of the pandemic, when we had lots of time to think differently about the world. And George and I are both immigrants and have experienced the challenges that brings.'

So, how does his Palestinian heritage affect his music? 'As Palestinians we are proud of our culture and that is apparent in every aspect of our personal and professional lives. We were forced out of Palestine and scattered all over the world, and we brought our culture and education with us. We're known for our high level of education, and as I travel all over the Arab world for concerts, I'm told how Palestinians were a big source of education when we arrived as refugees. And wherever we went, we developed our music.'

Does he aspire to perform one day in a free Palestine? 'Of course!' he replies. 'That would be the most important performance of my entire life. I hope to live long enough to see it.'

The IZE Trio declare themselves with four essential verbs: ImprovIZE; HumanIZE, HarmonIZE; EmpathIZE, and their album spans the world with these prerogatives. How does he categorize the trio, or does he prefer to describe them as Duke Ellington described the best of all music, as 'beyond category'? 'Unfortunately the music business dictates the need to label music. 'Beyond category' is a great way to describe us. We don't think much about genre. We aim to create music that comes from deep within our human DNA. Folk music is as close as we can get to that.'

The world reaches in and reaches out of The Global Suites. Listen and you will hear of its wrongs, its dreams and its achievements played by three troubadours of freedom. Naseem's cello melodises and improvises alongside Morrin's rhapsodic keys and Lernis's scuttling and defiant percussion. Their music expresses four essential themes of the future in the present and, with all their dedication to a better world, in a key album of our times.

(The Global Suites is available on Izetrio.com Records)

Melissa Aldana (Chile) - Jubilant reedsong from a master

Melissa Aldana and Crash Trio
(2015)

Her grandfather Enrique Aldana was one of Chile's pioneer tenor saxophonist virtuosi and she inherited his instrument at the age of 16. Her father Marcos Aldana became a renowned jazz saxophonist at the Club de Jazz de Santiago. And now his daughter Melissa, under his tutelage, has become her country's most celebrated jazz expert, having been introduced to the Berklee College of Music by the Panamanian pianist Danilo Perez, and won the Thelonius Monk International Jazz Saxophone Competition in 2013 - the first South American and the first woman ever to do so.

After her prodigious teenage years leading bands and sessions in her home city, the leap to the US jazz scene was a formidable challenge. But her friendships with the great tenorist George Coleman and the contemporary altoist Greg Osby helped her through her introductory years and she was soon performing around the New York jazz scene with masters like Christian McBride, Kevin Hayes and Jeff 'Tain' Watts, as well as recording two albums for Osby's label Inner Circle Music.

By 2014 she had cut her first album with her Crash Trio, with Chilean bassist Pablo Menares and the drummer from Bayamo, Cuba, Francisco Mela, both musicians being powerful composers as well as masters of their instruments. But it is Aldana's compositional skills that open the album with M and M, which perhaps refers to her bandmates. Certainly Crash is a trio of equal compadres and not a star horn plus two accompanists and that is clear from the off, where Menares and Mela establish a scintillating stop-time rhythmic propulsion and Melissa's notes weave and twine around their sound with a sense of lightness and buoyancy that is almost like levitation.

Aldana also wrote the virtually quiescent Turning, with Menares's pulsating beat close to the earth and Mela's butterfly drums and cymbals sprinkling his bandmates with a dappled sound. Aldana travels low on her horn and then ascends in steps, showing the artistry which so impressed the judges of the Monk prize - saxophonists as eminent as Wayne Shorter, Jimmy Heath, Bobby Watson and Branford Marsalis, not exactly a mediocre bunch.

Melissa shows that she is no mean balladeer on the songbook standard You're My Everything. Her unaccompanied opening gives no guess of the melody, which comes like a gradual revelation. M and M come in as she begins this narrative and, as she continues, her light sounds and occasional serpentine turns remind me a little of another tenorist who grew up within a Latin musical context and turned to jazz, the Cape Verde-born Ellingtonian, Paul Gonsalves. Yet as her reedsong begins to skip and dance through the jubilant Bring Him Home, with Mela's rustling drums and Menares's bass hopping beneath her, it is as if her sound and its quasi-weightlessness is like no other.

A solo Menares begins his own composition Tirapie, full of polyrhythmic delight. Mela enters on bongos and Melissa narrates the theme as if she were telling a children's story. Peace, Love and Music by Mela begins with a drums charge straight from Havana before Melissa's ascendant notes come singing in, anchored by Menares's plunging basslines.

Menares played at jazz festivals and venues all over South America before he moved to New York in 2009, and there is more evidence of his artistry in the trio's performance of his tune Perdon. His bass, sometimes almost subterranean, is everywhere. Melissa's featherweight tenor wanders through her own piece, New Points, playing over the rhythmic breaks and changes like a veteran. As for Mela's tune, Dear Joe, it has a strong Caribbean and calypso lilt and is the kind of theme Sonny Rollins - one of Melissa's girlhood heroes whose joyous sound caused her to change from alto to tenor sax - loved to play to listeners all over the world. She plays it like his sonic shadow.

Perhaps it is fitting that the album's last track is Melissa's solo rendition of Monk's Ask Me Now, all the way up to the great pianist's home city from the cone of South America. How he would have nourished and loved its beauty in Chilean breath - as we, lucky listeners, can.

(Melissa Aldana and Crash Trio is available on Concord)

Melissa Aldana (Chile) - Connecting with Kahlo

The jazz saxophonist Melissa Aldana talks about the influence of the Mexican artist on her new album 'Visions' (2019)

Born in the Chilean capital Santiago in 1988, Melissa Aldana has saxophone music in her blood. Both her father and grandfather were eminent Chilean saxophonists and Aldana grew up listening to the records of Sonny Rollins, Charlie Parker and Cannonball Adderley. She took up the horn aged six and by her early teens was already a working musician as a tenor saxophonist. By 2009, having moved to the US and graduated from top jazz academy Berklee, she won the Thelonious Monk International Jazz Saxophone Award at the age of just 24.

'I just knew at some point I was ready to leave Chile and come to New York,' she tells me. 'If I wanted to be the best as a musician and keep learning, New York is the city that pushes you to do that. It's a hard place to live but it keeps you moving and growing. I have the freedom to be myself and do what I love and, thankfully, I get recognition for that - which doesn't happen to everyone.'

Her quintet now plays around the world but her new album Visions takes her back to her young days in Chile when she was deeply affected by the communist Mexican artist Frida Kahlo. 'Frida to me was an artist who embraced who she was through her art. She talks about beauty, ugliness, being a female, religion, politics, love affairs and sexuality but mostly accepting herself as an individual. This is a big part of how she engendered me to write this music,' she explains.

Her record, she says, reflects Kahlo's struggles: 'The album became a path for my own identity and expression, experimenting both harmonically and rhythmically with moments of frantic movement interspersed with order and structure. This is how I conjure the messiness, struggles and heartbreaking contradictions present in those visions of identity and self-worth.' Her horn sounds create new elements, based on Kahlo's own visions, which respond to the challenging questions which bubbled up while she was immersed in her paintings. 'I felt connected to her personal struggles on an intuitive level - opposing forces in Kahlo's life that have had a direct impact on my own music, my own self-identity.'

As soon as her album begins, with Sam Harris's rolling piano, Pablo Menares's bass, Tommy Crane's sprinkling drums and Joel Ross's vibes, you can sense that deep connection with Kahlo in a charged empathy with the Americas. The track La Madrina is Aldana's sonic reincarnation of Kahlo's choice of 'either living with inescapable pain due to childhood polio and a horrific bus accident, gangrene and miscarriages or dying and finding peace,' she says. 'To capture the complexity of our life choices, I've written layers of tension and resolution into the music. There are tightly arranged sections but also extended improvisation.'

It's a unique musical excursion into the mind of a sister artist, with Aldana's beautifully fluid sound sometimes floating, elsewhere delving into the Mexican artist's consciousness with a keening insight and intimacy. And it's an album which shows that Aldana, despite her global achievements, has never artistically left Latin America. 'I usually go back to Chile every year,' she says. 'People there are very supportive and proud of me. I have always felt that since day one.'

(Visions is released on Motema)

Gabriel Alegria (Peru) - It's about resistance and hope

El Muki by Gabriel Alegria and the Afro-Peruvian Sextet (2025)

Have you heard the rampant sound of the Afro-Peruvian Sextet, led by trumpeter/composer Gabriel Alegria? Their new album is called El Muki, a celebration of the mythical protector of the Andes miners.

Alegria announces in his sleeve notes: 'Our mission is to preserve the essence of music created by human hands. We are here as defenders of a living art form, resisting the encroachment of technology that seeks to overshadow the unique human experience of creation.' Alegria fuses the earth and rock of Peru and his nation's mountains with his commute to the concrete and steel of New York in both sound and rhythm. 'El Muki is about resistance and hope,' he declares, 'a reminder that music is most powerful when it speaks from lived experience, from a place of humanity.' Amen to that!

The album's musicianship carries the power of two continents. The melodic mysticism of the track about fireflies, Luciernagas, has Laura Andrea Leguia's serpentine saxophone in full fettle while the folkloric festejo dance grooves of Mala Senal gives the high note horn of Alegria a potent eloquence alongside the percussion of Hugo Alcazar and Freddy 'Huevito' Lobaton. Panabe is the story of the Amazonian river dolphin, a track of grace and strength featuring Alegria and the fleeting guitar of Jocho Velasquez.

Ausencia is one of four compositions by Leguia, and the saddening sense of absence radiates from the opening ensemble before more Velasquez lyricism and a beautifully burnished Alegria solo and a short chorus by cellist Marco Lucioni.

The album is full of the people's life-contrasts. La Zafra is a tune inspired by the sugar harvest, radiating a sense of sweetness and joy emboldened by Alegria's dancing solo above the spirited drums and guitar. But there is also a unity of sound and image. As you admire Jesus Ruiz Durand's expressive sleeve art work while listening to the music, the Muki symbolism is, as he says for generations of mining and ex-mining families everywhere from the Andes to Durham to South Africa, 'the connection of a community with its resources, a cultural and ecological defense, reminding us that the mine is a living entity that demands respect and community.'

The planet, its nature, its earth, rock and minerals, its art and its endless sounds: they all arise full of flesh and music from this empowering record.

(El Muki is available on Saponegro Records)

Joe Alexander Quintet (USA) - Blue Jubilee
(2014)

The history of jazz is full of stories of missed opportunities, racist exclusion, passed-over brilliance and unsung musicians who with a little more luck, notice or being in the right place at the right time could have clambered out of obscurity and enjoyed success and recognition many times over.

When you listen to the forty minutes or so of the 1960 album Blue Jubilee and you look at the names of the two featured hornmen, tenorist Joe Alexander and trumpeter John Hunt, you first of all wonder whatever happened to them in subsequent years. You might even think of the line from the Victorian poet Francis Palgrave: 'We see them born from darkness, and into darkness go.'

The same could never be said of the other three men who accompanied them on that June day in New York City 53 years ago. On piano was Philly man Bobby Timmons (1933 - 74), who found fame with the Cannonball Adderley Quintet in 1959 with his gospelised notes and hit tune This Here followed by another, Dat Dere - having already done something similar with Art Blakey's Jazz Messengers in 1958 with his hard-bop anthem Moanin'. The bassist was the wizard Sam Jones from Jacksonville, Florida, who between 1957 and 1966 was the pulse of bands and trios led by Dizzy Gillespie, Monk, Adderley and Oscar Peterson while leading some memorable sessions for the Riverside label, The Chant and Down Home included. On drums was the youngest of the Heath brothers, Tootie, who along with bassist Percy and tenorist Jimmy lit up thousands of live and studio performances for decades.

So what of the much lesser-known front line partners? Alexander was from Birmingham, Alabama, had played with the piano trio The Blue Sounds and was living out of the way of jazz prominence in Cleveland, Ohio. Hunt was playing with jazz and blues eminence Ray Charles before this session, but in a supportive, unfeatured role. So this was the day of the sidemen, when the artisans blew centre-studio like those of the jazz pantheon with a rhythm section to dream of. Orrin Keepnews, the record producer who wrote the sleeve notes, calls Alexander and Hunt 'brisk, long-limbed swingers', and how they get to it in the opening title tune, with Tootie's drums crashing all around them. Joe's chorus is confident, sure-footed and patterned with melodic lines, while Hunt shows a beautifully-poised pitch and is unafraid to seek the heights. He soars skywards before Timmons' churchy piano digs earthwards for the music's roots.

The next track is Norris Austin's Brown's Town and over Jones' dancing bass Alexander's tenor skips and tumbles loose-jointedly and agilely, and as Hunt enters he soon finds top pitch and his notes cascade blithely over his confreres. If this is the town of the great trumpeter Clifford Brown, then Brownie has found a true brass companion with the dextrous Hunt. A ballad next, and it is the sumptuous I'll Close My Eyes. Alexander weaves melody with a soulful beauty and Hunt's trickling cadences and flickering phrases give a sound that is paradoxically contrary and complementary.

Jones' running bassline introduces the fast Terri's Blues, and this is the album's apex. Alexander's solo is superbly lithe and swinging, rising and falling in gushing streams with Timmons' prompting and urging him ever forwards. Hunt's solo is featherweight, technically accomplished, full of surprise and eloquence. When the two horns exchange sentences in colloquy over Heath's showering drums, they are indeed brothers in sound.

The closing track is Hank Crawford's Weird Beard, fast-paced and fiery, with Hunt's opening solo full of allusion and movement, Timmons in romping mood and the testifying Alexander telling his southern story during an era when his Birmingham co-citizens were on the streets marching for their civil rights. He sounds as if he were with them.

A marvellously-chosen reissue this, a 1960 gem picked from the bottom of the pile. The sleeve photo shows the two hornmen relaxing between takes, with Joe sucking his bottom lip, his saxophone hanging from his neck with his slim tie and suit, while the peak-capped John coolly smokes. They were truly two of the forgotten promises of jazz. Fifty two years later we might ask, 'what kind of a half-century was it for them?' Who can tell us?

(Blue Jubilee is available on Fresh Sound Records)

Monty Alexander (Jamaica) – Jazz and Dub across the Gulf

Monty Alexander Septet: Stir It Up! and Monty Alexander Trio at Ronnie Scott's (2000)

From the very first notes of Jammin', with the pianist hovering then plunging between the notes of Monk and Marley, you knew that you were in for a session of astonishing music. Monty Alexander is from Kingston, Jamaica, born in 1944 on the island of mento, ska and reggae. And yet, as with other musical compatriots like Wynton Kelly, Joe Harriott and Dizzy Reece, he turned brilliantly to jazz. After some youthful Kingston exuberance with Monty and the Cyclones, Alexander migrated to the US and found his music with players like Milt Jackson, Ray Brown and other stellar figures. Yet he always proclaimed his Jamaican roots.

A contemporary of Bob Marley (they were both born in the same year), he feels that the lion of reggae is 'part of my musical subconscious. He touched the sky. He touched our lives.' Stir It Up - also recorded on Telarc - is his presentation of Marley's music. He brings together his US rhythm section (Troy Davis, drums from Louisiana and Hassan Shakur, an LA bassman), with a Jamaican-dub backing group. Four young Kingston men - Chris McDonald (keyboards), Robert Browne (reggae bass), Michael Fletcher (reggae bass) and Desmond Jones (drums) bring reggae to bop with a subliminal verve and excitement in a series of Marley's most beloved and enduring tunes.

The naked nobility of Redemption Song - which Alexander played unaccompanied - and No Woman, No Cry - which he played with his trio - opened the session after Jammin'. But after some rollicking piano choruses of I Shot The Sheriff, which Alexander introduced as a narrative of Marley's 'altercation with the authorities,' on came the Kingston reggae virtuosos changing the sound completely and creating beautiful interplays between the bop and dub rhythm sections. Fletcher's electric bass threw out a challenge to Shakur's acoustic, producing deep soundings which ended in empathy and unity.

The two drummers faced each other, Louisiana to Jamaica, during a pounding and bloodraising Could You Be Loved? as if they were reaching toward each other and emulating their disparate histories across the Gulf of Mexico. These were weaving, fusing and historical moments of music which seemed to make a diaspora whole again. And all through it, the subtleties and eloquence of Alexander's piano, taking inspiration from Caribbean and black

US traditions, bringing them together in an amalgam of the unity of the many Americas.

Alexander declared that Marley 'brought to the world some messages to make a difference.' So did these Caribbean and mainland Americans. By continuing his story and struggle they moved into a new chapter.

(Stir It Up! and Monty Alexander Trio at Ronnie Scott's are available on Telarc)

The L'Antidote Trio (Iran/Albania/Lebanon)
King's Place, London
(2025)

The L'Antidote Trio are true as their words: 'We aim to pit the healing powers of breath and life of music against the poisons of the present day.' Cosmopolitan to the core, their percussionist, Bijan Chemirani, is of Iranian heritage from a family of drummers. His father, Djamchid (1942 - 2025) was a master of the Iranian zarb or tombak drum, born in Tehran, who came to live in Marseilles with his family; the astonishing Albanian cellist Redi Hasa was born in Tirana in 1979, and the strident Lebanese pianist Rami Khalife was born in Beirut in 1981 and is a long-time resident of Paris.

As soon as they began, Khalife made the King's Place Steinway grand chime lucidly like a Levantine bell, Hasa's bow was bouncing, spring-like from the strings of his cello and Chemirani's artistry in polyrhythmic pulses, mostly hand-drummed on his zarb, set his trio-mates searching for new rhythms of their own. As Hasa stood and plucked and stroked his strings with his muscled fingers he sounded like the most accomplished of bass players - like Ray Brown, Dave Holland or Barry Guy, but suddenly he was sitting on a stool with his cello over his knees, strumming and picking like a skiffle guitarist while Chemirani sang what sounded like a scat in Farsi while he pummelled his zarb and drummed the buzzing edges of the large, circular bendir in front of his knees. In one dramatic solo stretch Khalife's piano went from virtual quietude to a rampant crescendo, and with an artist's gradual reach, back again to quietude.

The captivated audience fully understood when Khalife announced: 'What unites us is our love for freedom and light; we hope we are an antidote to darkness.' As they played on into improvised free melodies instantaneously composed and performed with a powerfully inventive musicianship and as it sometimes seemed that a whole orchestra, not just three musicians were playing, we began to realise how light shines so strong in such a beautiful complexity and cosmos of geographical sounds.

amere3 (England) – New noise afoot in Liverpool
Trees & Aplicate
(2013)

The three grizzled faces on the sleeve of amere3's new album Aplicate aren't the musicians but a detail from Hieronymus Bosch's 1515 picture Christ Carrying The Cross. Two of the musicians were born in Leeds in 1959. Phil Hargreaves carries a tenor and soprano saxophone and Simon H. Fell his acoustic bass. The youngest, Rob Dainton, Bolton-born in 1976, carries his drums into a Liverpool studio. Hargreaves describes Aplicate as a 'three-way conversation,' which, Fell adds, 'Remains non-hierarchical throughout,' without the horn in a commandist role.

Fell commends Hargreaves as having a 'unique and extremely personal voice on the saxophone, one which allows him to contribute freely without ever dominating or railroading the ensemble by sheer physical power.' amere3 are not a new formation. They made their first album Trees in 2000. The cover photograph shows a barren, blasted-out glade, but the sleeve notes seem to allude to urban trees, 'desperate and unloved, with a foothold in the shabby brickwork.'

And the opener Deodar, with Dainton's scuttling drums, Fell's hurrying, searching bass and Hargreaves's muttering, irascible tenor, seems somehow to sonically depict a shattered and ruinous cityscape. But every created note is evidence of an astonishing co-operative sound.

When Fell says that over the years the trio have sought and striven 'to find a language,' as a listener you feel firstly that you can work and succeed to understand it, and secondly that the three musicians have forged sounds as words which are completely mutually understood - one of the achievements of jazz's century of history and defying all internal categories from Armstrong's Hot Five and the Ellington Orchestra to Ornette Coleman's Quartet to the Spontaneous Music Ensemble. It is always a new language to those who listen and imagine.

Hear the track Gean, where Hargreaves's soprano bursts into birdsong above Fell's grounded trunk and the branches, twigs and fluttering foliage of Dainton's life of percussion. Or the two furious parts of Katsura, with Fell's relentless deep murmurs, Hargreaves's forest of quiet grunts and the insects frantically tapping Dainton's cymbals and skins.

In Hiba Hargreaves's flute is almost breathless, while Dainton's rumbles at the end suggests some other cessation·. The opening two minutes of virtual quietude of Coigue, almost noiseless and broken suddenly by the pounding first notes of Madrona, manifest the interior contrasts of amere3's conception of music - surprise in artistry all the way.

Surprise continued some decade later in Aplicate, produced by Fell's pioneering label Bruce's Fingers, which has been at the heart of British free jazz for well over two decades. From the outset with the first track Yesterday's Filth the musicians' empathy seems so natural that it is almost as if this is a one-man trio at work after 10 years of sound communion. When the pace slows right down with Fell's bow stroking and scraping his strings next to Dainton's crackling drums and Hargreaves's sucking and spitting tenor, there is startling new noise afoot in Liverpool.

Metamorphisis (it is amere3's spelling) begins with some extraordinary bass and drums, with Hargreaves's warbling tenor gradually taking fire. If you sit in a park, a garden or a countryside venue, you may hear around you the groundings of these sounds, metamorphosed to free jazz studio performance. In this sense, nothing could be closer to the real world than this music, which is perhaps why, with Fell's huge striding bowed sounds, the next track is aptly called Something About Exactitude And Truth. No wonder Fell declared of Hargreaves's sound engineering: 'Phil, who recorded this music, has excellently captured the acoustic sound of my bass.'

Hargreaves's soprano almost whistles in The Far Corner above Dainton's world of drums and his tenor carries a Leeds and Liverpool blues timbre throughout Between Throat And Chin, with his bandmates in full unison. Levitation seems to be the place of At What Height Do You Hover? with Fell's springing bass the primary means of leverage.

As for Bruce Fingers, Hargreaves wrote to me: 'It's a pleasure and a privilege to be part of that canon. All props to Simon for curating and playing with it, and here's to its survival and flourishing in these uncertain times.' Not half.

(Trees & Aplicate are available on Bruce's Fingers)

Fred Anderson (USA) – International Velvet

A Chicago hornman's swansong collection

(2012)

What images do the nightclub name The Velvet Lounge spark in your brain? A luxurious venue full of glamorous waitresses and the softest of chairs? Plush surroundings in a dimly lit US playboy nest swimming with cocktails and dressed up dandies? Not true at all if it was Fred Anderson's Velvet Lounge in Chicago's South Side. Squeezed between two shuttered storefronts strewn with debris, tiny, spartan and full of free jazz, this was a true liberated zone of new music.

Frequently throbbing with the enormous sound of Anderson's tenor saxophone urging his listeners to move further and further out with his golden improvising horn - and for years targeted by police because of its strong and proud black profile - the Lounge was, as the prime soprano saxophonist Steve Lacy described it, a temple of jazz discovery.

Born in Monroe, Louisiana, in 1929, Anderson was a migrant to the Windy City like thousands of other jazz-loving and jazz-playing southerners. A founding member of the Association for the Advancement of Creative

Musicians in the early '60s, he was as much influenced by Ornette Coleman's sounds blowing from the west coast as he was by his avant garde Chicagoan comrades of music. He stayed fast in his adopted city and was rarely recorded until the final two decades of his life before his death in 2010.

Anderson worked as a barman in the Velvet Lounge before he became its proprietor in 1981, and gave Chicago's free music an established home and nursery. He became a griot of the saxophone, his sound embedded with the narratives of all the great horns of his lifespan from Lester Young to John Coltrane. As he put it, 'I've got all these melodies in my head that I just kind of put together. The story keeps going on and on. I got that from listening to Lester, who was one of the greatest storytellers.'

The opening years of this present millennium at last gave Anderson the opportunity to record profusely from his home ground on the Chicago-based Delmark label. The album On The Run, cut in 2000, put Anderson alongside his close drum confrere of 25 years and another arrivant from Louisiana, Hamid Drake, of whom Anderson said: 'We've gotten to the point in our playing where the other person is going on a subconscious level. We could probably play together in our sleep.'

The Japanese-American and founder of the Chicago Asian-American Jazz Festival, Tatsu Aoki, is the bassist. The Lounge had a throbbing groove that night. Anderson hurls his horn into the title track with Drake's brimming skins and Aoki's subtle yet booming undertow. Smooth Velvet has a more echoing sound, with Aoki's shaking heartbeat especially prominent and Anderson, slow and ruminative, every note a discovery. But as he erupts in the heart of the performance, creating an instinctive empathy with his confreres, the listener's ears reach bursting point. A dark bass rumbling begins Tatsu's Groove and Anderson's early riffs become rhapsodies as his inventive genius ignites and burns, on and on. The album's closer, Hamid's On Fire is exactly that, with Drake in perfect percussive musicianship, yet wild, free and brilliant, Aoki stirring a subterranean storm and Anderson's roaring lyricism in shuddering fettle.

In 2002, Delmark and Anderson were Back At The Velvet Lounge with Aoki and Chicago stalwart Harrison Bankhead sharing bass duties, guitarist Jeff Parker, drummer Chad Taylor and the tempestuous 22-year-old trumpeter Maurice Brown, 52 years Anderson's junior at the time. Fred sounds lithely agile, even acrobatic, on the opener Fougeux, and Brown unleashes his notes with a rare and rapid power. Olivia is a ballad, and Anderson begins it with a long and lyrical cappella appeal, but the crux of the album is Job Market Blues, as relevant to British listeners as it is to Chicagoans, with Parker's edgy guitar sounds full of indignation and Anderson's deep, deep phrases radiating anger too, profound urban anger.

Anderson is back with Drake and Bankhead on the Timeless trio album of 2005. Seventy- eight years behind him and still blowing with huge energy and conviction, Anderson finds musical union with his two lifelong comrades and plays like a a real and beautiful dream. Ode To Tip remembers his old boss at the Lounge and radiates a common human connection in a powerful jazz message, while Flashback holds a compendium of jazz history.

Sometimes you hear snatches of Coltrane in Anderson's narrative, other times it is Rollins, Hawkins and his beloved Lester Young. All present, all breathing life in Anderson's enormous kaleidoscopic cry and the soundscapes of Drake and Bankhead too in a great life-driven story of jazz.

(On The Run: Live At The Velvet Lounge, Back At The Velvet Lounge & Timeless: Live At The Velvet Lounge are available on Delmark)

Art Ensemble Of Chicago (USA) - New from the old

Tribute to Lester - Live at the Jazz Café, London (2006)

One of the great jazz innovations lies inside the music of the Art Ensemble of Chicago, a living creation of the Advancement of Creative Musicians (AACM) which sprang up in the Windy City in the late 1960s.

Originally composed of reedmen Roscoe Mitchell of Chicago and Joseph Jarman of Pine Bluff, Arkansas, Maryland-born trumpeter Lester Bowie, Chicagoan Malachi Favors on bass and, after 1969, drummer Famoudou Don Moye from Rochester, New York state, they lived out Bowie's stirring credo of making 'great black music' for more than three decades.

Even now, with the recent deaths of Bowie and Favors, they continue to shake jazz foundations with their musical originality and concoctions of everything from brass band, gutbucket, gospel, bop, post-bop, blues, funk, carnival and circus bands, pre-jazz Africanisms and the free-est of free jazz.

Reduced lo a trio of Mitchell, Favors and Moye, the ensemble recorded their salute to the incomparable Bowie and his extraordinarily vocalised brass sound, album Tribute to Lester, in 2003. Mitchell plays alto, tenor, soprano, sopranino and bass saxophones plus flute and whistles. Moye has congas, bongos, counsel drums, bells, gongs, chimes and more whistles in addition to his drums. Favors has his bass, bells, gongs, bells and yet more whistles.

You hear the percussive heart of the group from the very first sounds of the opening track Sangaredi, with Favor's bass springing and sawing with his bow out of the drums, chimes, gong and bells. Mitchell's bass saxophone rumbles in and the percussion continues, unperturbed and unabated. Mitchell's mournful alto begins Suite for Lester and, as he switches to flute, he provokes a poised, classical-sounding solo besides Favor's thudding bassline. A roll from Moye and Mitchell re-enters on bass saxophone, then straight into Zero on tenor in a sequence of boppish choruses with Favors and Moye playing more traditional trio roles.

Favors's invocation of the boy king Tutankhamun begins with more of Mitchell's growling bass sax, but sounding agile and athletic, before the bassist's licks vibrate in the Egyptian night and Moye 's earnest drums wake the desert. Mitchell returns with a marvellously wrought and aspish alto solo. As Clear as the Sun begins with a bass and drums-cymbals duet which is exactly that, before Mitchell's sopranino comes in with an extraordinary half-wailing, half-mewing solo lasting for 11 minutes, dancing like a tiny twig on a fast-running brook, as if moving forever.

Whether He Speaks to Me Often in Dreams is Bowie's after-effects on his confreres, it brings a version of hypnosis on the ears. The bells, tambourine, triangle, whistles and congas make the trance-like setting before Mitchell's shuddering alto enters briefly with a cry. The echoing gongs signal long soprano notes and the rest is clattering percussion and the very soul of ancestral music, concluding an album profound in its simplicity, almost instrumentally vocal in its musicality.

The Jazz Café in London on March 20 was a chance to see and hear another, larger version of the Art Ensemble of Chicago, including the return of the long-absent Jarman, plus the presence of bassist Jaribu Shahid, replacing the departed Favors. Also playing was the young trumpeter Corey Wilkes, who blew on Mitchell's 2001 album Song for My Sister.

An extraordinary array of reed instruments, drums, percussion items, mutes, bells and whistles were laid out on the Jazz Café stage as these three old men and two newcomers climbed down the stairs to the platform. Jarman and Moye had their faces made up with black and red stripes and Mitchell's neck was hung by yet more flutes and saxophones. Here was a veteran threesome of the avant-garde of jazz's avant-garde and have been so since the end of the '60s. Every breath that Mitchell and Jarman breathed into their horns and on every thud of Moye's tight skins was a search for new sounds, fresh combinations of noise emerging from the past sufferings and glories of African-American peoples, the first authors of jazz.

We were witness to the heaven and hell of the Ensemble's music. Heaven because of its burning, raw lucidity, its eternal creative clarity and daring. Hell because of the stories that it told of the diasporas history of black music, its brutal scattering and epic journeys to recreate itself through the pain of 400 years of imperial and racist outrage. All that was deeply felt, even in a crushed room in Camden Town. Moye started rapping his congas. Jarman was playing a long, bent bass flute, Mitchell a tiny one, less than a foot long, while Wilkes's rasping muted notes sawed out beyond them.

Then Moye walked to his drum set, thumped out a frantic marching rhythm on his snares and we heard 10 astonishing minutes of Mitchell's guttural soprano cries and wails, punctuated by Jarman's backing of a host of whistles – from large metal tubes to those used by football referees lo a plastic slide-whistle and finally a fragile-looking mouth piano with a plastic tube to blow through, like those used by scuba divers. This is the first long soprano saxophone aria by Mitchell, while Jarman played a more supportive role throughout the set, clinking and clashing his bells or bass dish and wooden pestle, urging his band mates on. When he came in hard with his sopranino saxophone, it sounded agonised, like some unknown animal's fused cry of pain, elation and defiance.

And the dreadlocked Wilkes showed that relative youth is not to be outdone in this jazz ceremonial. With the bell of his horn embracing the microphone, he created shaking, quivering brass sounds, cawing and kissing howls, almost as if his trumpet was another percussion instrument. And, all through his solos, Jarman turned to the side table beside him, selecting from his miniature orchestra of bells, whistles and wooden objects to strike, rub and caress out their primeval sounds.

Wilkes spoke and howled into his mouthpiece and made an unheard language. He picked up his flugelhorn and played it with the right side of his lips while blowing into the trumpet on his left side, as Mitchell and Jarman played their altos each side of him and Shahid plucked his mountainous bass and Moye's eternally restless drums rattled behind them all.

What music is it? Its roar and its rawness told of the Earth and a long history. It was real music of audacity and brimming adventure obeying no rules, following no patterns, bowing to no masters, emulating no models. It is as jazz ought to be, void of the mercenary or smooth, the predictable and the practised, the saccharine and the easy listening. It's out there, maybe somewhere where we are all going or somewhere we have all come from. But it is huge, beautiful, worrisome and free with its own incorrigible artistry - our lives in notes of the past, present and the future.

Art Ensemble of Chicago (USA) - Joyful ensemble bridges continents

Nice Guys, Full Force, Urban Bushmen & The Third Decade (2013)

'Great Black Music' was the collective that Lester Bowie, trumpeter of the Art Ensemble of Chicago gave in the mid-'60s not only to their own sounds but to those of the evolving tradition of jazzmakers, from the New Orleans veterans to the nascent genius of John Coltrane, Ornette Coleman and Albert Ayler. The term stuck, particularly with the often wild and incendiary performances of the Art Ensemble of Chicago, which grew directly from the free directions of the Association for the Advancement of Creative Musicians, launched in the Windy City in the early '60s by a group of powerful innovators led by pianist Muhal Richard Abrams and including original members of the ensemble, saxophonists Joseph Jarman and Roscoe Mitchell.

With bassist Malachi Favors they became a co-operative drummerless quartet when they relocated to Paris in 1969. By 1970 Don Moye joined them on drums although their shared multi-instrumentalism made percussionists of them all - with gongs, bells and congas and a plethora of pipes, whistles, conch shells, horns and kazoos continuously sounding off from their midst as they blew and struck from all the eras of the jazz canon, from street marches, church routines, rock, punk, soul and the avant garde, with masks, face paint, African and carnival garb, full of humour, hokum and panache.

From 1978 they began to record for the Munich-based ECM label with their first album, ambiguously titled Nice Guys, with Jarman adopting a fey and playful Jamaican accent on his vocal in the opener Ja. Bowie plays some raucous half-toned trumpet and the fivesome split apart with sonic ambivalence and timbral laughter. Folkus emulates birdsong, insect-song, traffic-song and a bizarre mesh of the rural and the very urban, Moye's drums are rampant on 597-59 with Jarman's free riffing alto chorus and Favor's pulsating bassline. Mitchell's tune Cyp has a braying Bowie and some ghostly woodwind and the 12 minutes of Dreaming Of The Master opens like a Mingus small-group piece with Bowie's muted horn lying back on a bluesy saxophone ensemble followed by some unleashed soaring Mitchell. Altogether a very arresting record.

The year 1980 brought the album Full Force. Opener Magg Zelma with its whistles, cowbells, chicken sounds and echoes of rustic domesticity before Favor's cavernous undertow and Mitchell's bellowing tenor lead into a triad of whirling horns. Who Charlie M is remains a mystery, but the piece named after him has a bass saxophone basement, a tightly squeezed solo from Bowie and Favors's emphatic heart beat never stops throbbing. Old Time Southside Street Dance, begun by Jarman's lightning alto, is as quick as possible, while the denouement title tune has Moye's hand-drums, hooting-owl flutes and a virtual cacophony of outlandish horns.

A more ambitious double CD project was born in May 1980 called Urban Bushmen, with a high degree of self-realisation in an African past and a New York present. Starting from the Malian annals of Cote Bamako and with Moye's balafon and other instruments of Sun Percussion, the Bush Magic moves onto Urban Magin, with, as Jarman tells in his sleeve notes, 'flowers blooming through concrete in our urban savannahs, as we stroll down hi-stepping and prancing,' for here history comes to nowtimes - and hear Bowie's sauntering horn celebrate it on the Warm Night Blues Stroll beside Moye's leaping drums and the two reedmen scintillating their way Down The Walkway. As the steps are retraced by 1980 South Africa in Sun Condition Two and Moye's solo drums present the Soweto Messenger, the defiance of racism and apartheid moves between two continents and the track Entering The City can speak of New York, Johannesburg or Birmingham, Alabama.

The second CD begins with Bowie's aching New York Is Full Of Lonely People, where his horn moans out its alienated testimony above Favors's profoundly rooted bass. A historical memory of Africa resides at the centre of all the ensemble's music, but hear them swing out, almost Kansas City-style, in the final track Odwalla, as if the fused heritage of two great continents is rising in their blood and in their notes.

Urban Bushmen is doubtlessly their most powerful and thematic achievement, but The Third Decade of 1984 has its moments too. The bluesy-folk of Prayer For Jimbo is dedicated to Jimbo Kwesi, the first black officer to serve and die in the British army, killed by his own side who thought he was the enemy, with Jarman's synthesizer playing a long salute over Moye's swinging drums. Or Walking In The Moonlight, inspired by a youthful love poem by Mitchell and what Bowie called 'avant pop' at its most sublime.

'The music, the joy, the wonderful happiness that our lives are all about,' is how Jarman saw the work of the ensemble. The adventurousness, daring and one-off brilliance too - it's all there in these records.

(Nice Guys, Full Force, Urban Bushmen & The Third Decade are available on ECM)

Dorothy Ashby (USA) - A new sound in the jazz galaxy

(2016)

Dorothy Ashby (1932-86) called one of her albums Hip Harp, and it wasn't easy to encourage her very volatile instrument to become 'hip.' But she did it, and the proof is here in this marvellous reissue, a box set of three records which take in almost her complete recordings. Dorothy was a Detroiter who studied piano at Wayne State University. She switched to harp in 1952, recognised its jazz potential and by 1956 she had cut her first album, appeared on television, and played at concerts with Louis Armstrong and Woody Herman, becoming a true jazz pioneer.

The first track of her first album, The Jazz Harpist, Rogers and Hart's Thou Swell, has her comping behind Frank Wess's flute before her harp breaks out assuredly into sparkling solo fire with Eddie Jones's bass and Ed Thigpen's drums lifting her sound as if it were levitating. Stella by Starlight is slow, picked out and beautiful, as if a new sound has entered the jazz galaxy, as of course, it had. Dancing on the Ceiling begins an evocative duet between Jones's bowed bass and Ashby's multiplicity of strings before Wess blows in with the theme. The last four tunes are all Ashby's with Thigpen's brushes sweeping a keen rhythm on Aeolian Groove, Ashby's sweet melodic lyricism on Quietude, Wess's flute stomping on Spicy and the cutting Latin edge of Lamentation.

Six months later Ashby was back in the same New Jersey studio in March 1958 to cut Hip Harp, with Wess again, but with fellow Detroiter and bassist Herman Wright and the arch-bopper Art Taylor on drums. She begins with her own very lively Pawky, picking up the creative camaraderie with Wess as if they had never been away from each other. They swing amiably though Back Talk and the romanticism seeps out of Moonlight in Vermont. It's a pity that Wess, one of Count Basie's most powerful post-war tenor saxophonists, never picked up his tenor to play with Ashby over three albums - it would have created a very different soundscape.

The third, In a Minor Groove, has Wright again but with the rampaging Roy Haynes on drums, who adds his own spirit of extra excitation to the session. Rascality is Ashby's tune, and after Wess's opening solo she plucks out a dynamic piece of improvised and sharply etched stringwork. She surges through her chorus on You'd Be So Nice to Come Home To, and her solos and colloquy with Wess on It's a Minor Thing are brilliantly played out. Bohemia After Dark is another rampant swinger with both Wright and Haynes pulsating, and Margarita Lecuona's Cuban tune Taboo has a breathless Havana feel, with Haynes on fire and the ever-inventive Ashby in prime fettle.

Dan Bronstein's expressive photograph of Ashby's plucking fingers and concentrated face graces the sleeve of the 1961 trio album Dorothy Ashby, a Chicago studio gig with Wright and drummer John Tooley, an ex-accompanist of Billie Holiday. Ashby is more exposed on this album and her artistry resonates. She zips through Secret Love, has her Ellington moments in Satin Doll and finds a Basie groove in L'il Darlin'. There are two of her own compositions. On John R her harp sounds like a many-stringed acoustic guitar over Wright's springing bass, and in the brief Booze she finds speed and an improvised zest which signals some of her best playing on record.

The cover of her fifth album, recorded in August 1961, Soft Wings, has the blurred lines of four shadowy, blue-tinted musicians silhouetted in a studio setting, two of them women with their Afros picked out and distinct. They are Ashby with her harp and her Detroit sister Terry Pollard on vibes. Washingtonian Jimmy Cobb, of Miles Davis's Kind of Blue fame, plays drums, and Wright returns again. The strong sonic bond between the two women, made a Motown threesome by Wright, is powerful in the slow and emotive Wild is the Wind and the Kurt Weill tune My Ship, where they create a beautiful melodism and in Ashby's With Strings Attached they move with apparent ease into a buoyant swing.

In the '70s Ashby moved to the West Coast, where she became very much a studio musician. Yet her half-decade of audaciously original recordings between 1957-61 established her temperamental instrument as an unlikely voice of jazz - a signal achievement.

(The reissue albums are available on Fresh Sounds)

Mulatu Astatke (Ethiopia) - Embrace across cultures

Sketches of Ethiopia
(2013)

One of the first direct encounters between jazz and Ethiopia was in 1940, when Duke Ellington's renowned trumpeter Rex Stewart led a band of Ellingtonians including the mighty Duke on piano, in his recording of Menelik. It was jazz's act of musical solidarity with the Ethiopian people, invaded by 120,000 Mussolini fascists in 1935, and recalled the Ethiopian victory of 1896 when the warrior emperor Menelik led the Ethiopian forces to defeat three invading Italian brigades at the northern town of Adwa.

Now in 2013 we have an album recorded by an orchestra led by the Ethiopian vibraphonist, conga drummer and pianist Mulatu Astatke, comprising Ethiopian and Europe-based musicians cut in studios in Addis Ababa, London and Avignon. Members of Astatke's band Step Ahead, they include one of Britain's prime free bassists, John Edwards, the stomping young pianist and organist Alex Hawkins, trumpeter Byron Wallen and drummer Tom Skinner who play together in Wallen's London-based band, cellist Danny Keane and tenorist and flautist James Arben. As for the veteran Astatke, known as the father of 'Ethio-jazz,' his long-time immersion in multiple musical traditions is a life commitment to integrate the traditional sounds of his homeland into jazz.

Born in 1943 in Jinna, western Ethiopia, as a youth his parents sent him to Wales to study engineering. He was tempted towards music though, and found his way into the Trinity College of Music in London before moving to the US in the early '60s and becoming the first African student at Boston's Berklee College of Music. He soon became an enthusiast of Latin American jazz and his first two records, Afro-Latin Soul Volumes I-II, were cut in New York City in 1966. In the early '70s he returned to Ethiopia, introducing 'Ethio-jazz' to his people. In 1973, during Ellington's tour of Ethiopia, Astatke was featured in the Duke's orchestral concerts as guest vibraphonist. His music was revived in France during the 1990s and appreciation of his transoceanic brilliance grew across both Europe and the US, culminating in being awarded an honorary doctorate at Berklee in 2012.

Sketches of Ethiopia begins with the fierce rhythmic foray of Azmari, with Edwards's bass, well used to African musical genius as a member of South African drummer Louis Moholo-Moholo's band, seething through the percussive undertow. Gamo gives power to the horn ensemble and lead vocalist Tesfaye, with scope to Jean-Baptiste Saint-Martin's chinking guitar. Hawkin's piano sound dominates the opening of the traditional Hager Fiker before Astatke's mallets come dancing in above the surging drum-beaten earth. Gambella begins devoid of the relentless beat, as if it is gradually discovering its own true rhythm, but beneath Tesfaye's words and a unison of horns it finds its own route. Astatke's vibes take a chorus before Arben's serpentine tenor saxophone brings the flow of African rivers to Assosa Derache, while Wallen's piping trumpet calls out to the sky. The complex orchestration of Astatke's music is fully evinced in this track as if his Ethiopian encounter with Ellington brought the master's genius to his own very complex heart-sound on his own continent.

The tribal echoes of the Gumuz people radiate into the next track, simply called Gumuz, with Tesfaye's expressive vocal bringing the sounds of the African village into the blood of jazz, in a way reminiscent of many Abdullah Ibrahim South African tunes. Motherland Abay gives Keane his moment on the album as the track's first section gives his cello its full scope of beauty, there in the mix of Astatke's African soundscape. The fragility of Wallen's London trumpet, its notes so close to breaking point, add a mood of vulnerability creating an amalgam of sounds which only a much-travelled and migratory jazz brain could conceive - a true syncretism of continents.

The finale is Surma, led by Fatoumata Diawara's vocal, blooming from the forest of percussion and horns, and reasserting as Astatke's entire album, does that jazz starts and finishes as the music of ensemble and unity, of peoples and cultures mixing and embracing, teaching and learning - the giving and exchanging of civilisations from the large and small centres of the living Earth.

(Sketches of Ethiopia is available on Jazz Village)

Gilad Atzmon (Israel) - Sonic visionary
In Loving Memory of America
(2009)

Between 1949 and 1952 the nonpareil bop altoist Charlie 'Bird' Parker recorded his Charlie Parker with Strings sessions in New York. Bird plays with his customary exuberant brilliance and assurance, his imagination and powers of improvisation flare, his blues impulse is rampant and fecund - even through the most maudlin Hollywood and Tin Pan Alley tunes such as Dancing in the Dark, What Is this Thing Called Love? and Temptation. But what a contrast with the strings that accompany him - saccharine, insipid and implausible, contrasting with and lacking the intensity of Parker's phenomenal tone and boundless invention.

So when I first saw Gilad Atzmon's new album In Loving Memory of America, recorded with the Sigamos String Quartet more than half a century on from Parker's sessions, but including some of the same tunes as one alto saxophonist's emulative tribute to the instrument's master, I had a slight sense of a strange foreboding: what was going to happen here? How was the Levantine beauty of Atzmon's Palestinian cry going to reflect Bird's soaring blues-song? And how were Atzmon's notes going to mesh with the strings and themes of the American Song Book's subliminal mawkishness?

I shouldn't have been nervous, for the album is a work of beauty, power and intense sonic vision. The plucked string intro of the opener, Everything Happens to Me, prefaces Atzmon, playing straight melody with a cascading blues undertone. One cadence falls as if from a dizzying height and you wonder if the song, born as a love-ballad but as ironically played by Atzmon, seemingly enfold the Palestinian life, for there is the sound of exile, loss, occupation and defiance absorbed in all his notes and even more so in the insurgent-sounding drums that begin If I Should Lose You. As for the strings, there is no syrup or sentiment with their sound. They are entirely with Atzmon, gelling with his tone and carrying his strength and narrative with them. Especially so in his own composition and theme tune for an earlier album, Musik. Here the dark melody leads through their measured composure.

Atzmon soars - at one moment he reminds you of Sidney Bechet's mountainous breath, until he returns with the theme's vulnerability before a final truculent coda.

What are the children's voices at the closure of a virtual marching What Is this Thing Called Love? Are they of Palestinian or US children - for what unity could be theirs, prevented by the neocon Creed within the following track, called expressively Call Me Stupid, Ungrateful, Vicious And Insatiable.

I Didn't Know What Time it Was moves close to Parker, with Yaron Stavi's bass emphatic. Yet it is redrawn by Atzmon, given a contemplative, ponderous blowing as if the world doesn't know either. His own tune In the Small Hours sustains the sense of concentrated thought in the midst of a bombarded Gaza community, more sonic beauty and more Parkeresque licks. Tu Tu Tango begins quietly, but half-way through throws out a Latino challenge, as if the people of the south American cone, up through Argentina, Bolivia, Ecuador and Venezuela are casting an alternative to the cruel policies of the titan of the north.

The album's title tune comes as the penultimate track and carries neither bitterness nor malice. Instead, we hear ordinary US voices and street scat, with Atzmon's alto an almost distant sound, fused with the vibrant and ever-changing speech of a diverse people, the true humanity of the US on whom much of the future's potency will depend.

Finally there is Refuge, embodying a theme set forth in Atzmon's 2007 album, with one of the tracks called The Burning Bush. Now that Bush's rule is gone, much counts too on the intentions and will of his successor. This Refuge is a gleeful klezmer-style romp, with Atzmon's horn and the strings in a question and answer colloquy, radiating sheer optimism and joy. Is this a future US? As in all jazz, the listener listens, the ear hearkens and the brain interprets. So hear Bird first and Atzmon next and take stock of the messages: the US is there, Palestine is there and the story telling hornman is there. What is he saying to us? Only he and the listener know.

(In Loving Memory Of America is available on Enja-Tiptree)

Behdad Babaei (Iran/Qatar) and other 'Persian Jazz' events – Nourished by the truth

London Jazz Festival, Rich Mix
(2025)

Some of the more intriguing sessions of the 2025 London Jazz Festival were to be found at the 'Persian Jazz' evenings held at Rich Mix, at the top of Brick Lane in East London. My only previous connection with jazz and Iran was and is marvelling at Johnny Hodges' sublime alto saxophone solo on the Ellington Orchestra's Isfahan, a musical study of Iran's holy city from the maestro's felicitous Far East Suite of 1966.

So to hear three bands in two nights of Iran-inspired music so close to London's Banglatown was quite a revelation. First was a trio calling themselves 'Insanity Route', led by the Iranian lute-like shurangiz virtuoso Behdad Babaei, born in Doha, Qatar in 1974, with fellow shurangiz master Vahid Taremi, and hand percussionist Navid Afghah, born in Shiraz, Iran in 1970, playing the tombak drum.

These three troubadours had more than a little jazz in their souls, as they melodised and improvised with powerful flourish and excitation. Both Babaei and Taremi provoked extraordinary passages of free notes with their liberated riffs, followed by Afghah's empathetic tombak obligatos. On Babaei's long solo beginning to the trio's unnamed third piece, was that a Persian blues I was hearing, with echoes of Big Bill Broonzy's or Lonnie Johnson's guitar? What stories of his homeland was he telling at this far London crossroads of Brick Lane and Bethnal Green Road, as his mirror-varnished shurangiz reached deep, deep into the tantalising notes of his improvisation? When Afghah answered in the blur of his drumming fingers, could I hear Baby Dodds, Max Roach or Han Bennink? For he sounded like a band of drums drumming, so broad and multisonic were his pummelling fingers.

The next night it was the eclectic guitar fusion of Persian jazz, gypsy swing and Indian Karnatic rhythms of Kourosh Kanani, of Iranian/Irish parentage, playing with the London drummer Matt Davies. Listening close you could hear some of the dense and often ultra-fast patterns of Babaei and Taremi transformed to Kanani's electric strings, and Davies' stop-time full drumset echoing Afghah's single tombak.

This was explicitly secular music. The slow, haunting theme of Kanani's Dream 28, with its caustic phrases, made you wonder what the other 27 were like, as Davies' booming bass drum gained speed at a worrisome rate. Then the young woman Egyptian singer Amena was announced, who sang a beautifully-voiced Kurdish lullaby. The final tune was an Armenian folk song about a young woman who throws her hair ribbon into the sea. It was simplicity beautified, with Kanani's lucid notes as clear as the voice itself, ending a complete set of rampant and tender syncretism.

The final band was a composite of three Iranians and two Spaniards. Led by electric bassist Arin Keshishi of Armenian roots, with drummer Shayan Fathi and vocalist Delaram Kafashzadeh, both from Tehran. With them were alto saxophonist Robert Nieva from Avila and Xavi Torres from Barcelona.

A young band this, their unity of traditions creating a very different timbre to the Babaei trio, much closer to a conventional jazz sound, but none the less arresting. Nieva wasn't a Hodges, but the lyricism of his saxophone still soared through the Spitalfields night. Delaram's wordless, rhythmic, floating instrumental singing made you think that if Norma Winstone had been born in Tehran rather than up the road in Bow, this how she might have sounded, and Torres' Catalan piano choruses made you remember his late, great compatriot, Tete Montoliu.

Three bands with Iranian foundations, yet as with the inevitable jazz infusion, their realities springing everywhere, nourished by the truth of cosmopolitan East London.

Derek Bailey (England)/Sabu Toyozumi (Japan)
Breath Awareness
(2025)

I grew up in the immediate postwar years where in the British media and public discourse there was a deep antipathy towards the Japanese state and its people. Paperbacks such as Russell Braddon's The Naked Island or films like The Bridge on the River Kwai documented the horrific experiences of British and Australian prisoners of war in Japanese POW camps in Singapore or Malaya, while images of the mass nuclear death, devastation and undiminished cruelty of Hiroshima and Nagasaki were a teenage nightmare which prompted a whole generation's anti-war consciousness.

Derek Bailey (1930 - 2005) and Sabu Toyozumi (born 1943) lived through those years, with Bailey's boyhood in Sharrow, Sheffield and Toyozumi's in Tsurumi, Yokohama. As soon as the first track of their 1987 session Breath Awareness (on the Lithuanian NoBusiness label) begins, you can feel on your senses the duo's bond, as if war, empire and fascism were eras well passed for both musicians, with the only focus creative union. My Jimny, the opening half-hour piece is called, and the partners launch into it with astonishing attack and gusto, as if the said Jimny were a beloved car as close to the both of them as their own flesh and blood.

Bailey's percussive guitar shudders with life like an eternal drum, and as Toyozumi's own drumset rolls, thuds, jumps, and rattles, they are two drummers from two ends of the Earth bringing their artistry together in a unity which eradicates the war and horror of erstwhile, yet only too recent, generations. Of all the sessions I have heard which carry an implicit anti-war message, few could compare with this duo's sustained improvising brilliance, making their message a summative rejection of conflict, and the welcoming of a new era of fellowship, sharing, dexterity and peace.

(Breath Awareness is available on NoBusiness Records)

Duck Baker (USA) - Jazz was created for and by the African-American community and was always political by its very nature
Duck Baker Plays Monk
(2024)

'Thelonious Monk is not only our greatest genius, no-one else is even close.' Thus declares guitarist Richard Royall 'Duck' Baker in the sleeve notes of his album Duck Baker Plays Monk, a powerfully original and intriguing interpretation of the pianist's music.

Baker was born in Washington DC in 1949, the son of an Episcopalian minister and a housewife who played piano for her enjoyment. 'As a teenager liked Rock and RnB music,' he tells me. 'My big favourite was Ray Charles. I started guitar when I was 14 and was soon playing in a rock band, and also seriously fingerpicking folk and blues. 'We fledgling rockers felt that jazz was over our heads. I was more into blues, until I decided to try Monk as a 16-year-old. I didn't understand a note of it, but just loved it!'

By the late 1950s the family was living in Richmond, Virginia. 'It was the former capital of the Confederacy. I grew up in a segregated racist environment, not including my immediate family, but most people, including almost all the kids I knew. I realised at 13 that this was all wrong. Certainly the protest songs of Bob Dylan and others affected me greatly, as did the attitudes of the college kids I was meeting in local coffee houses.'

'I hated school and didn't want to go to university. My first jobs were all manual - in factories and construction sites. I worked up to being a carpenter and made a bit of extra money playing in local rock and blues bands. I expanded to ragtime and early jazz tunes and was developing an approach to free jazz.'

'My political education was provided by Uncle Sam when I was a draft resister during the Vietnam war, eventually moving to Canada for a year. We were old enough to be cannon fodder before we were old enough to vote. 'Many of the 1960s folkies were real lefties, as were most of the free jazzers. Archie Shepp was a huge favourite and I agreed 100 per cent with what he said about his music being folk music.'

'Jazz was created for and by the African-American community and was always political by its very nature. But black and white folk music were never segregated, especially not in the South. I hear the same cry in Ornette Coloman that I hear in an Appalachian singer like Roscoe Holcomb. That idea of always being a folk musician and all of it being a political act was central to my approach.'

'I moved with my wife and daughter to San Francisco in 1973, also playing bluegrass, trad and swing jazz. In 1974 I signed with Kicking Mule Records and started touring as a soloist.' I ask him about his attachment to Monk. 'He reached me in an immediate way, like Ray Charles. It seemed very deep and direct and his playing had a rawness to it like that I loved in real blues, like Robert Johnson and Doc Watson. Fingerpickers like me keep an independent bass line under the melody, and applying this to Monk is a different starting place. I loved the wry humour in his tunes, the way he added a dash of bitter to the sweet standards, and his sparer voicings, more than most jazz pianists, is a big plus for guitarists.'

What other jazz musicians have made their own brilliance out of Monk? 'The influence of Steve Lacy, the great soprano saxophonist, is all over my record especially in the single note playing. And trombonist Roswell Rudd opened up some of Monk's mysteries to me. But Monk has influenced almost every modern musician I love, and they all do different things with his compositions.'

Which Monk tune on his album gave him most challenges? 'Off Minor is so far out! Its first chord change is from Mars, goes off to Jupiter in the B section - and keeping the bass line going on Bemsha Swing and developing the melody over it was a big challenge too.'

What is his relationship with Britain? 'I lived in London from 1978-82 because I was getting more work in Europe than Stateside. I moved back to England in 2003 because the USA had gotten so insane. I'd gotten into British free musicians like Evan Parker and Derek Bailey in the 1970s. But the music I listened to most often was traditional Irish and the great Irish players near where I lived in Fulham.'

I told him how when I was teaching in east London in the early 1970s, John Stevens and Trevor Watts had visited our school and had taught the 12-year-old students Blue Monk while I was teaching poetry in the classroom next door. All together, they blew and tapped it out beautifully. Wasn't there a brilliantly childlike quality of wisdom and simplicity in Monk's music, like Blake's Songs of Innocence?

'I never thought of it in that way, but I like the comparison,' he replies. 'Monk appeals to many people who can't get on with other forms of music. I think Blake would have loved him too.'

(Duck Baker plays Monk is released by Fulica Records)

Ginger Baker (England) shows us why he's unforgotten

Ginger Baker – Why?
(2017)

Who remembers Ginger Baker? The legendary British drummer born in Lewisham in 1939 set the music world alight in the '60s as part of threesome Cream with Eric Clapton and Jack Bruce. But Baker was then and now essentially a drummer of the blues and of jazz, who began with the blues-drenched Graham Bond Organisation in 1964. He was inspired by the greatest of British jazz drummers, Phil Seaman of Burton-on-Trent, and counted as his friends and 'uncles' three legendary jazz drumming giants - Max Roach, Art Blakey and Elvin Jones, who he befriended in the US.

And beyond jazz for Baker was the drumming of Africa. It stretched back to 1970 when a visit to Nigeria sparked a fascination with the country's music, prompting him to establish a recording studio in Lagos and make records with Fela Kuti. Living in Colorado in the '90s, Baker established a powerful jazz outfit with the trumpeter Ron Miles called the Denver Jazz

Quintet-to-Octet (DJQ2O) which in 1998 waxed fine jazz record Coward of the County with the mighty tenor saxophonist James Carter as guest.

In February 2014, he recorded the album Why? with a new band called Jazz Confusion by Baker - a quartet comprising Baker, Ghanaian percussionist Abass Dodoo on drums, US saxophonist 'Pee Wee' Ellis and English bassist Alec Dankworth.

Baker's quizzical album title reveals a strongly elegiac session with many allusions to times, tunes and people past, referred to sometimes obliquely, sometimes directly - beginning with Ginger Spice, written by his old trumpet confrere Ron Miles and recorded on Coward of the County. Straight away the percussive unity between Ginger and Abass impresses and Ellis's depth of tone and gurgling notes add to the combustion. Dankworth's solo is full of the earth. Twelve and More Blues shows clearly and doubtlessly where Baker's musical roots are, although strangely in this context you still hear snatches of Cream, Blind Faith and Airforce pounding through his drums. Dankworth's sound is again huge and resonating and when the two drummers create a palaver following his solo, it is the sound of a fiercely beautiful concord.

Cyril Davis remembers another British blues hero of the '60s and Ellis's wailing tenor finds the memories and sense of loss with a keening eloquence. Dankworth, from another generation, also offers a pulsating homage. Wayne Shorter's classic tune Footprints follows with Dankworth's perennial twang pressing the melody forward under Ellis's lucid narrative and the eternal drums, their wake leading directly back to Africa.

Baker's tune, Ain Temouchant, again expresses how inseparable are these drums and drummers, London and Africa unified in a Wiltshire studio. There's no grandstanding, no attempt to draw these drums apart - it is as if a percussion amalgam has founded and inspired the music. So when Sonny Rollins' melody of his parents' Virgin Islands birthplace St Thomas begins to rock through the studio with Ellis's horn in dancing pulse and Dankworth's beat swinging over the ocean to the Caribbean, there is a sudden joy in the sound and a blithe parading in its impact. Then, suddenly, the Atlantic is crossed again and the Nigerian folk tune Aiko Biaye rocks from the grooves with the drums in full and jubilant life still pounding as one.

The final, enigmatic title track is based around the spiritual Wade in the Water that the Graham Bond Organisation once made their own in their frantic and dissolute tours around the cities of Britain. Bond's own blues-aching life ended prematurely and tragically in 1974 and Ellis's painful saxophone narrative - Bond was himself a fine but underachieving alto saxophonist as well as an organist - tells of his life and all the sadnesses of other broken lives that Baker has worked with and known in a full life of music.

This album tells of that life in the truth of a very special and unique way of jazz, Africa and the blues and is a musical experience not to be missed.

(Why? is available on Motema Music)

Lucian Ban (Romania) and Alex Harding (USA) - An unlikely pairing; Romanian folk and Motor City blues combine for some stonking jazz

Somethin' Holy, Premonition & Tuba Project (2015)

A singular and unlikely pairing they are: a baritone saxophonist born in Detroit in 1967 when the sounds of Tamla Motown were at their apex, and a pianist from the Transylvanian village of Seaca in agricultural Romania, born in 1969, where he grew up listening to the folk music played by his family at weddings, birthdays and festivals.

Alex Harding started his musical life playing drums, then heard Grover Washington on the radio and switched to tenor saxophone at high school. He gained a musical scholarship from the University of Massachusetts, then migrated to New York in 1993 and toured with a Haitian band before hugely influential stints with Muhal Richard Abrams, Lester Bowie, Oliver Lake and David Murray's big band. In 1994 he was a part of Julius Hemphill's latest album At Dr King's Table, playing his adopted baritone in a saxophone sextet. A proud Detroiter, he continues to marvel at the sheer volume and quality of 'artists, musicians, writers who come out of the blue-collar working-class culture' of his city.

Lucian Ban studied classical music at the Bucharest Music Academy (1992-95) before arriving in New York in 1999, where his musicianship had a powerful effect upon Harding, whose first two tracks on his debut album Freeflow (2001) were compositions by the Romanian. Harding spoke so enthusiastically of him to CIMP label producer Bob Rusch that, after contacting Ban and hearing tapes of his work, the record boss invited Harding and Ban to record together. The first result was the 2002 duo album Somethin' Holy. The album is marked by both musicians' tribute to the great bassist Wilber Morris (born in Los Angeles in 1937), veteran of many a CIMP session, who during this recording was struggling against his final illness. Invocation to Wilber is played with a hymnal, deeply reflective beauty and Driftin', which follows, shows Harding alternatively breathy and guttural and as if he were organically a part of Ban's lucid, narrative notes.

Their partnership is powerfully empathetic, just as intensely so when Harding turns to bass clarinet in Resonance, with Ban striding up and down his keys. Time for Trane/Night on Earth is a homage to the monumental tenorist lasting almost 20 minutes, composed by Ban with a moving melodic centre and the weight of Harding's sound creating a Paul Robeson-like timbre, as if contrariness were at the heart of their uncanny unity. This amalgam of the lyrical and the visceral is forged through African Blutopia and Duke Ellington's African Flower, with Ban's sublime subtlety inside every one of his lines.

The very next day the twosome became a quintet for the album Premonition, with the addition of altoist Erik Torrente, bassist Chris Dahlgren and drummer Damion Reid. The latter wrote that Ban's compositions on the session 'gave me a chance to cry without words.'

The pianist hits a groove from the outset of opener Harmology and Harding's deep notes swing potently beside Dahlgren's dynamic pulse. Reid's drums are as structured thunder on Serenade for Andrew, where Harding's solo matches his storm. Torrente, on his first recording, plays with a lucid radiance on the ballad At Last, in a colloquy with Harding. Mutiny sounds as if all pillars are shaking with Harding's rumbling fanfare and far-throated cries, the becalmed beauty of Chakra causes both horns to sing quiescently and Ban's soft touch creates a bed of sound. The album finishes with the up-tempo Collision Theory, where Reid's muscled drums drive both Torrente and Harding to super-combustive blowing.

The 2005 album Tuba Project brings the virtuoso tuba man Bob Stewart, born in 1945 in South Dakota's Sioux Falls, into the Ban-Harding mix, alongside Detroit tenorist JD Allen III and San Francisco drummer Derrek Phillips. As they start off with Cajun Stomp, Stewart's bouncing bass pulse gives a rampaging momentum. Allen leads the congregation for Hymn, Ban flies in Muhal' Song and Harding goes even further skyward with his old maestro, while the 16 minutes of Bluesness Suite give all members solo freedoms. Veteran Stewart is in the lower depths of brilliance, making rousing subterranean partnership with Harding's dark profundity. The baritonist testifies eloquently with soulmate Allen through the church-like resonance of Spirit Take My Hand and Hieroglyphics sets the three horns loose above Reid's dancing drumset and Ban's springing keys.

This is a deep, delving album of many earthen beauties, a conjunction of the US and Romania entirely unexpected, powerfully surprising.

(Somethin' Holy, Premonition & Tuba Project are available on CIMP)

Billy Bang (USA) - Music from the film 'Lucky Man'

(xxxx)

In 1967 a 19 year old black American named William Walker (1947 - 2011) from Mobile, Alabama, was drafted into the US Army, and like thousands of his young compatriots, was sent to fight in Vietnam. There, he endured appalling conditions on the Vietnam/Cambodia borderlands, becoming a 'tunnel rat' in the most exposed areas of conflict and jeopardy. It was an experience that scarred him mentally for life, and as a veteran he lived through nightmares, flashbacks, horrific stress, psychological anguish and torture. Turning to music and his prowess as a violinist, he became Billy Bang, a giant of the jazz avant-garde whose live appearances and albums set the music on fire.

By 2002 he decided to return to Vietnam and to meet its people again, this time not through bullets but through his music, and accompanied by film maker Markus Hansen, he travelled through the liberated nation seeking reconciliation and life-restoring redemption. As he proclaims in the introductory track of the album of the film called Lucky Man, speaking of his first tenure in Vietnam: 'I should not have done what I did. I was wrong! I was wrong! I was wrong!' What he found was a people showing the warmest of friendship and love to him through their music, into which he was invited to take part and shine. 'They treated me so beautifully,' he exclaimed, 'and so naturally.'

The album is an extraordinarily compelling listening experience of real, living music, and all through, as he plays with village troubadours from the Banhar Gong Group of the mountains of Kuntum province or the Phu Dong Family Band of Ho Chi Minh City, or finally as soloist alongside the Hanoi Symphony Orchestra in their joint rendition of the Mystery of the Mekong, his music becomes many versions of a cosmopolitan anthem of peace by people who in most of our lifetimes knew in their blood the brutality of war.

Bang had recorded two previous albums which told of his first Vietnam experiences: Vietnam: The Aftermath (2001) and Vietnam Reflections (2004) with fellow Vietnam veterans including saxophonist Frank Lowe, trumpeter Ted Daniel, drummer Michael Carvin and conductor Butch Morris, but the Lucky Man tracks, in particular the field recordings are truly something else, as he finds companionship and intense fellowship among the musicians and their families of a people which his imperial nation had once invaded and slaughtered. As you listen to tracks like Jungle Lullaby with the Sax n' Art Band of Ho Chi Minh City or the New Saigon Phunk with the Phu Dong Family Band, you realise music is the rendezvous, catalyst and true redemption of international friendship between peoples who have decided they will never become prisoners of history.

Each note seems to be calling out Wilfred Owen's 1918 trench words from his poem Strange Meeting: 'I am the enemy you killed, my friend.' And as Bang, however briefly, plays solo his tune Moments for the KIAMA (meaning those killed in action or missing in action) in his hotel lobby before he leaves, as you listen you hear unambiguously and with simple serenity, the message of the folly of war, as throughout the album you imbibe its warm humanity of the beauty and solace of peace.

(Music from the film 'Lucky Man' is available on BBE Music)

Nikola Bankov (Slovakia)
Everwanted
(2025)

He's a whirling, deeply melodic alto saxophonist, born in Slovakia in 1995, based in Copenhagen where his new album, Everwanted, waxed with four young Danes, comes from his summative desire: 'To create music with my close friends and favourite musicians, tp play around the world, to feel happy and blessed, to be surrounded by peace and love is all I ever wanted.'

Not a bad starting point, and this album exemplifies it powerfully. With a haunting, unified backcloth of Frederik Bak's bass, Jonas Gravlund's guitar, Jacob Hedegaard's drums and August Korsgaard's keyboards he maps out a distinctive melody on the opener, Everything I Have, before blowing into colloquial improvising timbre which signals a confessional mode of soaring leaps and cadences. Deliberately seeking to 'compose songs with a large compositional form where the solos sound like part of the composition', the thrusting Hedegaard drums and Gravlund guitar of 5A.M., or Bak's plucked electric notes of What's Next? search out their own rhythmic and fusion assertions alongside Bankov's strident phrases.

On Repeat is slower, surrounded by running waterish sounds and Bankov dives in with emphatic confidence, attacking his notes with a soulful verve, while Eleven Eleven gives pianist Korsgaard defiant solo space and Bankov's coda is sudden and breathless.

The most intriguing track is the shorter Peace of Mind, recorded with the Massachusetts bassist Tim Lefebvre. Terse, fully statemented with the two musicians in full accord, it creates a trans-Atlantic duo of cogent substance.

(Everwanted is available on AMP Records)

Denys Baptiste (England/St Lucia)
Eastside Jazz Club, Leytonstone
(2025)

His notes rise and fall steeply like the Pitons on his ancestral island, St Lucia. Denys Baptiste's tenor saxophone sounds grow more solid and life-telling with his years, plangent yet marked by a delving joy. Here, with the streets of Leytonstone outside, they sound somehow like the chronicles of the people who pass by with their bags: past Iceland and Poundland, KFC and the local library, as Hitchcock once did, and Kenny Wheeler too, surmising his notes as he walked through the station tunnel with his trumpet case.

Baptiste is the featured saxophonist of the Jonathan Gee Quartet, and as they opened with Monk's Straight, No Chaser, his husky Charlie Rouse-like phrases made me think of 'up and down, up and down, I will lead them up and down', even though this was no Shakespearian horn, with Gee's galloping solo on the Eastside Jazz Club's shining upright, some strident solo bass work from Mikele Montolli and Tristan Mailot's swinging drums, as Baptiste's rampant exchanges with his quartet-mates rocked the venue.

Coat of Gold included a wordless vocal of Leytonstone scat from Gee, a deft Montolli solo and a succession of crescendos and cadences from Baptiste's lithe horn. It led directly to Paul McCartney's Michelle, which I had never heard played as a jazz standard before. Baptiste turned its melodic poignancy inside out, overcame its sentimentality even for an old Sixties' geezer like me, and with Gee's digging choruses they made a three-minute long song on a distant LP a beautiful jazz essay.

From Liverpool to Cuba, here in East London as the quartet strode into Gonzalo Rubalcaba's Looking in Retrospect, which they'd first rehearsed in the afternoon to play in the evening. It was a Caribbean adventure, with Baptiste's Windward and rhythmic roots strongly to the fore.

Then a Guys and Dolls standard to extend an eclectic musical mix. If I Were a Bell was a good choice of tune for Gee's tolling piano, tolling like a bell for all of us - for who shall know for whom the bell tolls - including the storming Baptiste, whose solo started quietly and gradually built up pace, sound and emotive invention, with only the naked rhythm of bass and drums behind him: poetry in musical action, all the way up the Central Line.

Harry Beckett (Barbados/England), Harry Miller (South Africa) & Louis Moholo-Moholo (South Africa) - Caressed into synthesis

Beckett/Miller/Moholo & Elton Dean's Ninesense Suite (2012)

In April 1982 during the bitter years of the struggle against apartheid, a black South African drummer from Cape Town, Louis Moholo-Moholo, and a white South African bassist from Johannesburg whose grandparents had arrived in the continent from Lithuania, Harry Miller - both in exile from that accursed system - united with the Barbadian trumpeter resident in London, Harry Beckett, to make an epochal recording in Berlin.

It was one solitary track lasting 37 minutes and it was called Natal, after the eastern province of the country fully at war with the racist deformity of apartheid. From the very first notes of Natal, Miller's sound is epic, as if it were forged deep in the African earth, resonating from the midst of the veldtlands. Louis's drums are everywhere, creating, clattering, orating and entering every conceivable space, generating unity.

When he plays as a duo with Miller, the latter's vibrating buzz and scintillating hum inside the drummer's relentless cymbals make you think that there is a single musician performing. As for Beckett, born not in a great continent but on a small Anglophone island, it is the sheer musical breathiness of his sounds which makes you imagine as you listen that his lungs have come back to Africa, the great domicile of his forebears.

There is a moment when Louis's drums are silent and Miller's bass whines, thuds and moans, before a hint of Beckett's horn precedes a marching rhythm from the drums. It is the sound of resistance and the people's struggle, every day, every hour and every life and it captures an age and its courage like few other sonic messages.

Natal is the second long track on this album. The first was recorded a year before in Berlin, and Beckett, Miller and Moholo-Moholo are there again, but this time part of a nonet, led by the British reed-man Elton Dean and called

Ninesense. Also present are tenorist Alan Skidmore, trumpeter Marc Charig, trombonists Nick Evans and Radu Malfatti, with the Bristolian pianist Keith Tippett. Ninesense was a unique combination of audacious jazz spirits, some of whom had crossed over into advance pop contexts.

Miller had originally arrived in England as part of Manfred Mann's band; Dean and Charig had played with Soft Machine and Tippett had guested with Crimson. So their collective ground was a powerful and expressive amalgam of musical experience.

The free opening ensemble of the Ninesense Suite heralds much to come, with Dean playing his piercing saxello, the trumpeters soaring in high register, the two trombonists blowing a cauldron, Tippett rampaging along his keys above the fire down below stoked up by Miller and Louis. The succession of solos are never quite solos, where there is always something happening alongside or behind them so they never completely move out of an ensemble setting.

When Skidmore takes the lead and the suite is well advanced, Tippett is rampaging along his keyboard. A few minutes later Beckett moves into a low suspiring spirit and Dean and Skidmore are chantering diversely behind him. As Tippett rocks into his solo Dean's caustic notes boil around him and Miller is digging deep into the sonic soil, far beneath and the jumping chords become a springboard for Charig and Beckett at opposite pitch-ends. A trombone growls belligerently and Charig gradually moves into the timbral stratosphere, aeons beyond Louis's eternally reverberating drums.

And so it continues - free, unified, yet each new series of sounds is the initiative of an individual message immediately joined, added to, modified and collectivised - the true communal spirit of jazz from Africa, Europe and the Americas, blown, struck, plucked and caressed into a synthesis.

Much was happening on that June day in Berlin, an apt venue for such musical unity, in a city which in these musicians' lifetimes had known fascist proscription, silencing and banishment. Now there was the creative fervour and joy of Ninesense to signal a world of change.

(Beckett/Miller/Moholo & Elton Dean's Ninesense Suite are available on Jazzwerkstatt)

Harry Beckett (Barbados/England) –
His sonic signature was all-embracing
The Many Faces Of Harry Beckett by John Thurlow
(2025)

There are many strands of motivation for writing a book on jazz or a particular jazz musician. I have read many of them over the years, but none has been so much stimulated by ostensible feelings of love for its protagonist as John Thurlow's book on the music of Barbados-born trumpeter Harry Beckett (1923

- 2010), echoing the words of guitarist Ray Russell, who wrote in its foreword: 'We all loved Harry. His sonic signature was all-embracing, and to be part of the soundscape he provided, can only be counted as a privilege.'

Certainly not a biography, neither a work of musical criticism, yet Thurlow's pages open up Beckett's artistry and hugely broad musical scope in an exemplary way. From his boyhood in Bridgetown, Barbados where his mother was chief cook in the island police force barracks and where he was given a free cornet to play in the Salvation Army band, he found his way to a luminous life in jazz in London, where he arrived in 1954, and settled in Stoke Newington, just to the north of Dalston in East London, which has become - almost like an unconscious tribute to Beckett - the new and audacious centre of London's jazz avant-garde jazz scene, in such now-times venues as The Vortex and Café Oto

Thurlow's thorough and devoted scholarship takes us through all the phases of Beckett's musical life in exactitude and detail. All the musicians and bands he played with, every record he made as leader or sideman, a host of his live appearances across Britain and Europe are described by long extracts, commentaries and photographs, sleeve notes, flyers and reviews from The Guardian, The Times and journals such as Melody Maker, The Wire, Jazz Monthly and Jazz Journal - I even found a quotation from myself, writing for the Morning Star - which show how Beckett was admired and revered by listeners, fellow musicians, writers and critics all. In this way Thurlow's book becomes a quasi-paean to Beckett's musicianship, not in a worshipful way, but a collective expression of dedication and love to a profoundly protean, original and eternally roving jazz troubadour.

The different 'faces' of his music are shown to be an amalgam of musical excellence. 'I enjoy working with a lot of different people and I guess I'm going to go on doing just that', he once declared. From Small Faces to Manfred Mann to Georgie Fame and Alexis Korner, from Scaffold to Memphis Slim and Eddy Grant to Jah Wobble, Thurlow's work shows how Beckett's horn on stage and in studio, bestrode and unified a succession of musical and political eras, beginning with Percy Green's Orchestra in colonial Barbados, playing at a tribute to the great West Indies batsman Everton Weekes in 1951, his early London years with Ambrose Campbell's West African Rhythm Brothers, the 1961 film with Charles Mingus in London - 'All Night Long' when the renowned bass man told him, 'Don't try to play like Gillespie or Miles or anyone like that, just do your Harry Beckett thing!'

Then to the years with Graham Collier's innovative ensembles and the series of brilliant records as featured soloist. For Collier he was 'the man who has given me more listening pleasure than almost anyone. What a great talent he is!' Just listen to him on albums like Songs for My Father, Darius, Symphony of Scorpions or Mosaics for testimony of that. Or his playing with the South African arrivants from Apartheid; Chris McGregor, Johnny Dyani and Dudu Pukwana in large free-blowing outfits like Brotherhood of Breath and the Dedication Orchestra or smaller bands like Claude Deppa's Horns Unlimited or Zila, and his love of Africa and its urgent dreams in outstanding albums like Dyani's Angolian Cry. Other combinations enrichened his listeners' ears like his records with saxophonist Elton Dean's Ninesense and Cape Town drummer Louis Moholo-Moholo and multisonic trombonist Paul Rutherford.

Thurlow describes a life which was a true amalgam of musical breadth and excellence, of sheer and shared artistic achievement. Yet Beckett never copied, never simply imitated those who inspired him, but forged out his own Antillean path like other great trumpeters of the Caribbean, Shake Keane of St. Vincent, Dizzy Reece of Jamaica, or during now-times, Byron Wallen of Belizean parentage. As his trombonist friend Annie Whitehead said: 'Harry always sounds like himself, never anybody else, and he doesn't try to.' Long live his music and his memory, provoked into perpetuity by Thurlow's scrupulous book.

(The Many Faces Of Harry Beckett is published by Jazz in Britain)

Majid Bekkas (Morocco)/Nguyen Le (France/Vietnam) and Hamid Drake (USA)
Jazz At Berlin Philharmonic XVII
(2025)

An astonishing amalgam of jazz internationalism here: Moroccan Majid Bekkas, virtuoso of the lute-like guembri and oud; drummer Hamid Drake from Louisiana and Franco-Vietnamese guitarist Nguyen Le played a succession of tunes on November 10, 2024 at the Berlin Philharmonic, including John Lee Hooker's Boom Boom, Jimi Hendrix's Purple Haze, the traditional Gnawa Moroccan timbre of Mrahba and the South East Asian flavour of Le and Bekkas' Ascending Dragon. To create an even more cosmopolitan foursome, Swedish pianist Joel Lyssarides joins them on the album's final track, Sidi Bouganga.

The plangent opening notes of the first track, Gore Blues, with wordless vocal underscoring, soon takes rhythmic pace with Drake's empathetic drums and Le's quicksilver, romping phrases. This is an all-percussive trio and the traditional Moroccan Mrahba gives Drake, the drummer from the Deltalands, a powerful thrust, as if his true home is the Atlas Mountains, with Le's fleeting guitar taking a solo of poised and stomping speed.

Those of us with long enough memories of the Sixties will remember when Boom Boom was a top-twenty hit with Lee Hooker's promise to knock his listeners 'right off of our feet' and get us dancing. Sixty years later here come Bekkas, Le and Drake to do the same, even in the heart of Berlin. But this is much more than nostalgia, as Bekkas' bass-like guembri takes it all over and the audience love it.

Le's echoing, sublime guitar and winnowing voice radiate through Ascending Dragon, as if it were a far eastern visitation, a complete contrast to

Hooker's blues-laden riffs. Having these two tracks in such close proximity and played with such sublime and nonpareil skill, is yet another manifestation of how far jazz has journeyed from its New Orleans roots. It is a true cosmopolis of sounds magnified even more by Hendrix's Purple Haze where the trio, like the tune's outrageous creator, truly 'kiss the sky', making a fiction of genre and category.

In the Bekkas tune Tair, his oud and voice eke out a Moroccan lament-like blues, taking jazz back, as Randy Weston and Ornette Coleman did with their performances with superfine Gnawa musicians, to its African percussive roots which have never been lost, and now as this album shows, spring all over the world.

(Jazz At Berlin Philharmonic XVII is available on Act Records)

Gregg Bendian (USA) - After Chomaklou was a desert

The Gregg Bendian Project - Counterparts (2025)

It was an Adult Education student of mine in Sheffield in 2005, Diana, who first educated me about the Armenian Genocide of 1915-17. In her beginners' asylum-seeking English she wrote a poem about her beloved country, so historically beset by its Turkish occupiers: 'I am Armenian/My country is Armenia/It is beautiful/ With friendly people/We speak Armenian/Our language is sweet./On 24th. April 1915/The Ottoman government/ Wanted to destroy our folk/They attacked our country/They slaughtered our poor people/They killed over 1,500,000 of us/Babies, young men and women/Everybody who knew nothing of war...'

She carried on to tell about ethnic cleansing and forced death marches into the Syrian desert, and how Armenians were compelled to 'Walk thirsty and hungry/Without shoes, without anything/Without fathers or mothers/Poor people/Without any crime.'

So when I was sent for review the Gregg Bendian Project album Counterparts, with its 15 minute track After Chomaklou Was a Desert, a 'threnody to the victims of the Armenian Genocide', I thanked the absent Diana for what she had taught me and I could listen to the record with an empathy and basic understanding.

With drummer Bendian are trumpeter Paul Smoker, bassist Mark Dresser and clarinet virtuoso Vinny Golia, who recorded the album in January 1996 in The Spirit Room studio in Rossie, upper New York State. They're a hot quartet indeed, with Smoker's dancing horn skipping through the opener, Current, Golia's sopranino clarinet running curlicues, Bendian's pounding drums and Dresser's delving, jumping bass. Golia's twirling sopranino is at the centre of Riff(t)s, which sets the Spirit Room on fire with its fleeting notes before a muted Smoker cools the pace with Bendian's thumping volleys.

An estimated 800,000 Armenians were arrested and force-marched into the Syrian desert between 1915 and 1916, deprived of food and water and incarcerated in purpose-built concentration camps. A Christian people, predominantly peasant farmers from Anatolian villages like Chomaklou, thousands were coercedly converted to Islam, their children removed from them and adopted by Muslim families.

The solo drums opening of After Chomaklou is followed by anguished notes by the horns. Golia's mournful bass clarinet paints the tragedy while Smoker's elegiac brass stretches upwards in weeping timbre, desperate and lonely, before Dresser's bass notes reach a crescent of sound with Smoker's delicate, muted phrases and Bendian's undercurrents express a grief which haunts the ears as the lamentation fades to silence.

Here are four freely-inspired and far-flung American musicians - Bendian from New Jersey, Dresser from Los Angeles, Golia from The Bronx and Smoker from Indiana, playing in trans-Atlantic solidarity with those who suffered so immensely in a Caucasian genocide. Yet their album is not all solemnity and grief; far from it when you hear tracks like the bouncing Herald Days with its urgently colloquial hornplay or the album finale, Running, where Smoker blows a storm, Golia's clarinet explores every corner of the Spirit Room, Bendian's omnipresent drums boom and shudder and Dresser's heartbeat bass ploughs the most fertile of rhythmic earth.

Their music manifests the sheer artistry of musical solidarity, moving thousands of miles to the struggling historical plight of the people of Armenia. I thank them for their music and their teaching, and my student Diana too, wherever she and her family are, from whom I learned so much.

(Counterparts is available on CIMP records)

Evan Parker (England), Louis Moholo-Moholo (South Africa), Steve Beresford (England) and John Edwards (England)
Second to naan – a timeless international quartet

Foxes Fox & Naan Tso
(2012)

Strange how in jazz, as in any other theme of life, sheer serendipity can intervene to have a profound creative impact. In early 1998, the Bristolian saxophonist Evan Parker was performing at the Vortex in Dalston with epochal Cape Town drummer of the Blue Notes, Louis Moholo-Moholo, and the brilliant John Edwards, a doyen among British bassists. Edwards felt ill during the trio's second set, so Parker called up the pianist Steve Beresford from the audience to deputise for him. This new formation created such a vibrant amalgam - particularly with the addition of Edwards - that a new quartet was born, quizzically called Foxes Fox, with Parker and Moholo-Moholo renewing a musical bond forged in the early '70s with the Brotherhood of Breath and other Anglo-South African bands that blasted open new jazz directions.

In July 1999 Emanem producer Martin Davidson brought the foursome to London's Gateway Studios, and Foxes Fox was cut, releasing 78 minutes of riveting music. Wood on Wood starts it off, a duet of Edwards with finessing and twanging bow and Moholo-Moholo with tapping, echoing drums. When the complete quartet finds its full sound for the 22 minutes of Amoebic Mystery, Parker's tenor breathes fire and menace at its centre, Beresford ambles and springs along his keys, Edwards delves into echoing caverns and Louis's clicking, throbbing skins hold the collective sound close to the earth in an uncanny union.

There is discomforting urban birdsong from Parker's tenor, as if its maker were trapped inside Bird with a Shell, and in the Beresford/Edwards duet Snail Kite, only the listener's keening imagination will begin to decipher which is which - or if both are both - with the pianist's stepping chords and Edwards's deep, deep vibrating strings.

Parker's huge guttural broadside begins his duet with a rampaging Moholo-Moholo on Fox's Fox, while the quartet's Foxes Fox belies or exemplifies the play on titular words with some profoundly serious music, in which Parker plays soprano and its 17 minutes move between trio, duet and quartet. Parker breathes fire while Edwards and Moholo-Moholo dialogue through the earth beneath their continents with some astonishing soundscapes, then Beresford finally enters with crushing chords and a pounding colloquy with Parker.

Some five years later the same quartet reassembled in the same studio to record the album Naan Tso, which became a musical goodbye to Moholo -Moholo, who was finally returning to his home city to live after four decades of inspiring musicianship in London during the worst and most degrading years of apartheid, through which his universal drums helped to keep exiled hope thriving. Yet Naan Tso means 'here it is' in Xhosa, and the glory of its sound is neither elegaic nor valedictory, although it made me think of the 1964 Mingus band recording of So Long, Eric, when they were playing goodbye to their great alto saxophonist Eric Dolphy, who was relocating to Europe.

In the album's sleeve notes Parker writes: 'The great Moholo made London his home during the apartheid period and our lives were the richer for it. We made this record to mark his return home and to say goodbye. Don't forget us, Tebugo.'

The 31 minutes of the title improvisation are truly something else. Its power and message of collectivism are superbly balanced by the individual musicianship. Parker's tenor is as a fanfare of freedom and hope, ever grounded by Moholo-Moholo restless and relentlessly unfettered African drums.

Beresford stamps, marches, sprints and saunters intermittently along his keys and Edward's creative and everchanging heartbeat gives the foundation of a life that never relaxes its transience.

There is reflection, memory and excitation, and every note carries invocations of future meeting places for music and the humans who create it, all concentrated and sustained in half an hour's making. After such an upsurge, what can follow? Three more quartet rhapsodies of sublime foxiness is the answer, prefaced by Parker's gut-wrenching tenor on Slightly Foxed and concluding with Renard Pale.

As for the Cape fox Moholo-Moholo, dwelling in such a remote land has not distanced him irreconcilably from his British musical comrades, as his 70th birthday performance with Edwards and other local contenders at the 2010 London Jazz Festival showed. Long live the testimony of endless freedom, sparking and pounding from his drums.

(Foxes Fox & Naan Tso are available on Emanem)

Steve Beresford (England) - Beguiling pianos, toys, music and noise

Andy Hamilton's biography of the idiosyncratic 'enfant terrible' of modern British music

(2021)

In his story of the life and musical times of the protean soundmaker Steve Beresford, Andy Hamilton has developed an audacious and innovative method of conceiving and writing biography – a 260-page series of conversations with his subject, including commentaries by many with whom he inspired, played, affected and changed. As such, it is a book which continually entertains, educates, reflects, informs and chronicles cultural history.

Beresford, now a septuagenarian, has been a constant presence on the experimental musical scene for five decades. Pianist, electronics wizard, film and TV composer, player of an assortment of toy instruments, musical pundit, producer and comedian. His influence within the world of free improvising is ubiquitous –not only as a performer but as a relentless listener, always critically hearing and grooving with every new sound that he absorbs. I have seen him dozens of times within the audience at every jazz and improvising venue – large, small, obscure and prestigious –from the South Bank's Queen Elizabeth Hall to Dalston's Vortex and Café Oto.

Hamilton asserts that "Beresford's work is marked by irreverence, humour, virtuosity, anti-virtuosity and playfulness." A Shropshire man, he moved to London in 1974 and threw himself into the minority world of improvised music, forming bonds with brilliant and pioneering musicians like guitarist Derek Bailey, saxophonists Evan Parker, Lol Coxhill and Tony Coe, and drummer John Stevens. He later made a kind of living with part-time teaching at Westminster University, and has been driven by a continuous life tension and contradiction between the absolutely serious and the glory of being anti-serious. Hamilton catches him pronouncing: "But the point is, we should all be paid for doing things we like – the whole world should be doing what it likes, and getting paid for it."

His book is a profoundly stimulating read – a kind of 21st-century Boswell's Life of Johnson – and difficult to turn aside from, whether its protagonist is talking about Ornette Coleman's harmolodics, Morecambe and Wise's comic genius, John Cage's avant-garde composing or the ineffectiveness of British cardboard milk cartons. It is a biography that never bores its readers and is perpetually alive with music and humanity, humour and narrative.

Hamilton has found a witty, always surprising and digestible way of describing a life and its cultural era. But ohhhh, the price! £90 admission is totally at odds with and a betrayal of Beresford's spirit and message. Bloomsbury – get the cheap paperback out as fast as you can.

(Pianos, Toys, Music And Noise: Conversations With Steve Beresford by Andy Hamilton is published by Bloomsbury Academic)

Free improving pianist Steve Beresford (England)
Album with violinist Mandhira De Saram (Sri Lanka)
and John Edwards (England)
(2025)

Born in Wellington, Shropshire in 1950. Steve Beresford's mother kept house and his father worked for an electronics firm, driving a truck all round Wales, delivering electronic parts to local shops. Steve remembers with fondness going with him, sitting next to him in the cab. Home was full of music. His grandfather 'was a rather out-of-tune violinist' and there was a wind-up gramophone playing 78s of Ellington and Basie. His parents were regular ballroom dancers and his father 'something of a crooner', also singing in church choirs. In all this, Steve learned piano.

In 1968 he began at York University, studying Music. He wasn't inspired by the course, but finished it and went to London, but soon returned to York, and with two young Americans formed an improvising trio (piano, guitar and drums) called Bread and Cheese. Many of the gigs had no piano, so, serendipitously in light of his lifelong fascination for small and toy instruments, he would play whatever was at hand. Hearing musicians like Cecil Taylor, Paul Bley and Steve Lacy on the radio inspired his love of free improvisation, although his earliest and greatest inspiration was Thelonious Monk - particularly he remembers the Monk's Dream album: 'It was always, always Monk!' he exclaimed.

Returning to London, he worked for an off-Oxford Street record distributor and at Dillon's Bookshop in Bloomsbury. He met saxophonist Evan Parker and guitarist Derek Bailey. 'They encouraged me enormously.' he says, 'and I made my first record with Derek on his Incus label, Tea Time, in 1974.'

What about his lifelong love of free improvisation? ' Anybody who can play music can improvise if they want to,' he told me. 'Although schooled musicians often find it more difficult. At the beginning, many saw the whole idea as impossible - how do you play music when you're not in the same key, the same rhythm? But we do! And it's usually really good. It's difficult to understand how it works, but when it works, it works! For me, the late Louis Moholo-Moholo exemplifies it in his drums. Freedom in music and freedom for South Africa and an end to Apartheid! For him, they were in elision, in fusion, in unity. He was always a huge influence on me.'

Despite the gulf of years and genres between them - or perhaps because of that, Steve and the Sri Lanka-born violinist Mandhira de Saram who came to England when she was twelve, are kindred musical spirits. Her background is in classical and Karnatic chamber music, and she was a creator of the Llegeti String Quartet. She loves improvising with Steve. 'He is legendary in the free improvising world,' she says. 'With Steve I feel completely free - I never know what's coming up next.'

The record that they made in January 2025 with the force-of-nature archbassist, John Edwards, is living confirmation of this. In a unique chamber improvisation session they create a cosmos of astonishing sounds. 'I'm playing with two of my favourite musicians, so I'm very happy. From second to second, minute to minute we just carried on, playing and enjoying every moment.'

What does he see as the special qualities of Mandhira and Edwards? 'John is my absolute favourite bass player. He's a stand-out group player, a brilliantly ego-less musician. As for Mandhira she too is a superb group player, and with all her long classical experience I never know when she is calling on it. It's all a part of her; whole, complete. I adored Duke Ellington, and his declaration that the greatest musicians are beyond category certainly applies to John and Mandhira. No question!'

Now, as a true veteran free improviser, how does he see the music's future? 'When I hear younger players - and there are many of them, new generations playing newer and newer sounds and never stopping, then I know for certain that it will just keep going, and going, and going....'

(De Saram/Beresford/Edwards is available on FSR records)

David Binney (USA) - Tribute to the Lakota Sioux

Lifted Land

(2017)

On December 29,1890 at Wounded Knee Creek on the Pine Ridge Reservation in South Dakota, the US 7th Cavalry surrounded the encampment of the besieged Lakota Sioux. When they began their onslaught with Hotchkiss machine guns, it was the cue for the slaughter of 150 men, women and children in the bitter cold.

Looking back at the massacre at the end of his life, survivor and Lakota medicine man Black Elk remembered: 'When I look back from this high hill of my old age, I can still see the butchered women and children lying heaped and scattered all along the crooked gulch as plain as when I saw them with eyes young.'

Some 121 years later at the Rubin Museum of Art in New York, the Miami-born and California-bred alto-saxophonist David Binney brought his quartet to perform his As Snow Before a Summer Sun, an extended composition dedicated to those murdered in the Wounded Knee massacre.

In 2012 a shortened version of the piece was included in Lifted Land, his album with the Minneapolis-born pianist Craig Taborn, Norwegian bassist Elvind Opsvik and Tyshawn Sorey of Newark, New Jersey on drums. Lifted Land, with its emblematic title, is a powerfully reflective album exposing four jazzmen of immense musicianship. The opener, Fanfare for Basu, includes overdubbed saxophones and synthesiser with some pacy Binney and The Road to Your House, he describes as 'a Japanese garden, a roadway in the country, some sort of road to something,' played by the hornman with soft, succulent tones with a wondrously light-touch solo by Taborn.

The narrative of North American genocide begins to resonate in As Snow Before a Summer Sun. Opsvik's ominous sawn bow-strokes, Sorey's mournful gong-strikes radiate the frigidity of the of the deathly Dakota winter and every wavering note that Binney blows speaks of the aftermath of a merciless militarism, and the quietude of Taborn's phrases seem to echo the pain of Black Elk's testimony.

Opsvik's springing preface to The Blue Whale is the beginning of a homage to a live jazz venue in Los Angeles. Full of zest and artistry with Binney's seething upward runs, Sorey's restless drums and Taborn in rampant mood, the music seems unstoppable. The same freedom runs through Curious About Texas, which Binney tells us was his attempt to put his 'discovery' of the Lone Star State into sonic form, which he accomplishes with the whole world of his living saxophone.

In his sleeve notes Binney reminds us that the title Lifted Land comes from Dee Brown's classic history Bury My Heart at Wounded Knee, and of course it applies to US imperial crimes still resonating in so many places in the world. The tune is simple, built on a riff, repeated countless times like the outrages themselves.

Losing the Central Valley is a grim reality in Binney's home state of California, where its great valley's water resources are being 'so polluted from pesticides that the most fertile land in the world is being lost.' It is a quiet, simple melody, lyrical yet elusive with Sorey's deep tapping, the restrained harmonies of Opsvik and Taborn, and Binney's lucid tunefullness.

Red Cloud was chief of the Oglala Lakota Sioux, a war leader who led a successful campaign against the US Cavalry in 1866-68 in what became known as Red Cloud's war, over the control of the Powder River Country in Wyoming and Montana. Red Cloud is Taborn's composition, played as a solo piano tribute to a brave warrior of resistance. It begins with single notes like a call to arms, yet is played throughout with a beautiful calmness, building through its three dramatic minutes to an apex moment, before falling back to a reflective cadence, perhaps with visions of the 'lifted land' all around.

Taborn's rejection of excess and histrionics and the quiet determination of his improvised beauty is a mark of the whole album - a jazz intervention into the real world, of a history and a worrisome present - and a music which feeds and explores both.

(Lifted Land is available on Criss Cross)

Nat Birchall (England) - An ancient and serpentine ritual

Invocations

(2016)

To hear the essence of a real musician is to be seized by the mind and spirit simultaneously, and Nat Birchall, the tenor saxophonist from Glossop, radiates this in the manner of a Coltrane, an Ayler, a Tchicai, a John Gilmore or of the survivor Pharoah Sanders. None of these masters were born English or lived in a Derbyshire town below the Pennines like Birchall, so his message is materially different, but the sounds of his horns enter your blood, bones and consciousness directly from nature and social reality like no other British hornplayer.

Referring to the legacy of Coltrane and his contemporaries, Birchall says: 'Music seems to me to display this connection to whatever this higher source, this higher energy might be. It seems to connect to it the most, more like other music.'

Coltrane's 'higher source,' like that of Blake or Shelley or Morris, has always seemed to me to be an intimation of a better world, of human endeavour matched to common weal, of a universe of fellowship, work and love. You can hear this too pouring from Birchall's saxophone in his new album Invocations - far, far from the commercial formulaic routine music of instant money-making dreams that surrounds and threatens to despoil our ears and circumscribes our lives.

There are but five tracks on this 47-minute album, but they tell enough of Birchall's singular artistry and the subliminal human achievement of his musical context, of a Pennine world of nature transformed by epic work, of every yard of dry stone walling across endless miles of slopes, valleys and hills, communally organised, communally humanised. That to me is the essence of Birchall's musical spirit and it teems from his notes: the labour of history peals through his horn.

With him is his regular piano confrere Adam Fairhall, with Johnny Hunter on drums, bassist Tim Fairhall and Christian Weaver on congas and other hand drums which go back to the hornman's early passion for reggae and the grounding drummer Count Ossie, now integral to his music. All but one of the compositions are by Birchall, worked out on his piano, and a strange, entirely organic amalgam comes streaming from his saxophone: rural, rolling northern England, the proud freedom-seeking drums of Jamaica and the spiritual cosmos of Coltrane's eternal message.

The first and longest track is Song to the Divine Mother, provoked by Weaver's drums. Birchall's horn sounds processional ancient and beautiful, and the music flows with a serpentine sense of ritual above Adam Fairhall's almost Nilotic piano. The other Fairhall's bass dredges the current of the music, which, with Weaver's Caribbean-inspired rampaging beat creates a sense of trans-oceanic unity, even there in a recording studio in Manchester, England.

Fairhall's bass plunges first into Invocation as the piano rolls forward, before Birchall's tenor enters like a blessing, and you feel the primeval Pennines and its worn stone banking up his horn. Fairhall's long piano solo has an echoing, subterranean timbre before Birchall returns, faster, then higher, then deeper, yet more transcendant in his sonic story. The centrepiece track is Coltrane's To Be - from his last session on the Expression album - Birchall's long, exploratory and path-seeking notes voyage out over the earthen drums of Hunter and Weaver; Fairhall's piano is full of searching and softly-chiming phrases and when the horn returns it is marked by assurance, as if it has found a way. Coltrane lives, and in Manchester too.

The final two tracks are full of Africa. Njozi (Vision) is real enough music. Fairhall strikes his keys hard and Hunter's drumset rolls alongside him as Birchall's testimony sets itself down in powerful sound. Power too, is the key of the album's finale, A Luta Continua. I heard this slogan thousands of times during my years as a teacher in revolutionary Mozambique during the mid '70s every morning from my students before classes began or scribed on every naked wall. Now musical tidings via Ossie's Jamaica, Coltrane's Philadelphia, Birchall's Derbyshire, an elision of the worlds of sounds, revolution, north, south, the Americas and the founding earth of Africa find a unified and cosmic syncretism in a Manchester room: Viva!

(Invocations is available on Jazzman)

Nat Birchall (England) - I aim for a sound that conjures up vistas of sunrises and wide-open landscapes
(2024)

When Chorley, Lancashire-born tenor saxophonist Nat Birchall brought his septet, the Unity Ensemble, to the Café Oto in the teeming, cosmopolitan heart of Hackney, it was as if he had brought the ancient majesty and mystery of the Pennines in the beauty of his horn, so much is the rural north of England endemic to his sound. With fellow Coltrane-loving veteran hornman Alan Skidmore supplementing pianist Adam Fairhall, thunderous drummer Paul Hession, bassist Michael Bardon and percussionists Mark Wastell and Lascelle Gordon, they played live the music on their serene, almost hymnal new album, New World, to hugely receptive London listeners. In its own way, it was a southern annunciation of northern-based musicians of real and unique quality, who only rarely find invitations to perform in London venues.

Birchall lived as a child in the small Lancashire village of Brinscall, where his father was a 'tree cutter' and his mother worked in the weaving mills. 'Home wasn't musical except for an old wind-up gramophone and a few 78 records. There was a wireless in the kitchen/living room and Elvis singing Devil in Disguise with my mum singing along while doing the housework. That's as far as the music went,' he tells me. When he left school he became a poultry farm worker, then worked in a woodyard and as a landscape gardener.

'In 1973 I bought a pair of African drums after hearing Count Ossie and the Mystic Revelation's triple album, Grounation. A couple of years later I gave my cousin's husband £2 for his guitar. Its strings used to make my fingers bleed! Then in 1979, when I was 21, I spotted an old silver saxophone in the back room behind the counter of a record shop. I paid the shop owner £20 and took it home. I had to buy a mouthpiece, reeds and a strap before I could try it. But it stirred something deep inside me, something really special that a guitar never could. I became aware of reggae and started to investigate it. I scoured record shops for Jamaican music. One shop didn't have any, so instead I bought Coltrane's Blue Train. I knew that many of the Jamaican musicians I loved were originally jazz players - Tommy McCook, Roland Alphonso and Cedric Brooks - so it felt like the right way to go. Grounation and its follow-up album Tales of Mozambique were fantastic albums of Jamaican jazz.'

'I soon realised that Coltrane's sound spoke to me in a deeper and honestly more soulful way than any other saxophonist. His Afro-Blue Impressions got to me in a big way and his solo on My Favourite Things is so full of joy, it's incredible! I got a job as a saxophone repairman in Manchester. I never intended to be a professional musician or imagined that I could be. But I was learning my instrument, avoiding getting another day job and eating dirt for a few years while I was 'in the woodshed,' practising all day and half the night, trying to make up for lost time.'

I asked him about the Coltrane influence in his playing. 'Most listeners hear that,' he says, 'but they don't hear the Cedric Brooks or Tommy McCook influence because they're not familiar with Jamaican music. The spirit of the hills and the Pennine open spaces are undoubtedly a part of my psyche, but it's not a conscious invocation. I aim for a sound that conjures up vistas of sunrises and wide-open landscapes and mountains around where I live, or also the beginning of a long journey of adventure.'

What about his use of melody, seemingly ancestral at times in New World? 'I believe in the strength of simplicity. Some of the greatest melodies, with the profundity and beauty of moving from one note to another and the emotion that conveys on a single-note instrument like the saxophone, is central. I always say melody is king!'

The New World album was instigated after a Coltrane celebration with Skidmore and Wastell at Café Oto. 'Having Skid on board made the music sound stronger and deeper and the three percussionists deepen the sound even more. I'm a big lover of percussion. The drum speaks to me on a profound level. The sound of a hand or stick hitting the skin resonates with me as the sound of the saxophone does. I'm sure if I hadn't become a saxophonist, I'd have been a drummer. It goes right back to hearing that first Count Ossie album.'

The seven musicians play superbly on the New World album. How do they achieve this level of mutual empathy and communal heart song? 'To play this music successfully you have to be confident yet selfless, only playing whatever makes the music blossom. You can't have anyone showing off their technique. All members must be good listeners aware of everything going on all the time and being immersed in the music of the moment. What I write often only requires the briefest of musical notation, so it's also partly down to having the ability to almost make something out of nothing.'

I ask him about the much fewer opportunities of gigs, recordings and recognition faced by northern musicians. 'Oh, yes, undoubtedly,' he replies, 'that's always been the case, but I try not to let that bother me too much. You could be forgiven for thinking that if it doesn't happen in London, then it doesn't happen at all!'

With its spiritual alignment of Coltrane, Jamaican, African and Pennine drums and the soul of the Peaks, New World is the closest sound in British jazz to A Love Supreme. Let your ears hear it and your heart give its answer.

(New World with Unity ensemble is available on Ancient Archive of Sound Records)

Ingi Bjarni (Iceland)
Farfuglar (migratory Birds)
(2024)

Jazz and Iceland may not come to mind simultaneously, but the Icelandic pianist Ingi Bjarni may change all that.

His new album Farfuglar (Migratory Birds), with a Scandinavian quintet of Norwegian trumpeter Jakob Eri Myhre and drummer Tore Ljokelsoy, Swedish bassist Daniel Andersson plus Estonian guitarist Merje Kagu, create a special sound of nature and lyricism.

The quintet create music in flight, notes with wings. Kagu picks her strings like feathers and Andersson's bass seems to resonate deep in the air while Myhre's horn flies abreast with Bjarni's plucked-out pianism on Bjogun a dugon (Distortion of daybreak).

Their sound is icily beautiful, yet strangely warm and full of melancholic melody as in Pad Sem Er (That Is) where Myhre blows a starkly evocative solo. All the compositions are Bjarni's. It's a long way from New Orleans, but how far and how superbly the music travels, as north as north goes.

(Farfuglar is available on NXN Recordings)

Art Blakey (USA) - Incendiary musical commitment

Art Blakey and the Jazz Messengers, Free Trade Hall, Manchester, 1961 (2017)

How many jazz-loving Mancunians remember a night in May 1961 when Art Blakey's thunderous drums, with one of the most luminous versions of his Jazz Messengers, set on edge the atmospherics of the Free Trade Hall.

The young and fiery Philadelphia trumpeter Lee Morgan, only 22 at the time, a wondrous tenor saxophonist and musical director Wayne Shorter, born in Newark, New Jersey in 1933 and still playing now with a long life's brilliance, the gospel-inspired pianist Bobby Timmons born in 1935 and bassist Jymie Merritt, both Philly boys too, were the other four of the rampaging five-some.

Blakey, an ex-steelworker born in Pittsburgh in 1919 and already a veteran with Mary Lou Williams, Fletcher Henderson and Billy Eckstine, formed the Jazz Messengers with Horace Silver in 1955 and the band became the birthing space of a host of seminal post-bop pathfinders from Freddie Hubbard to Bobby Watson, from Cedar Walton to Wynton Marsalis.

This 1961 European tour climaxed on May 13 with a famous Paris concert at the Olympia, but the Messengers were also building up to cutting one of their epochal Blue Note albums, The Freedom Rider, on May 27. Its title and theme tune was a direct reference to the civil rights struggle being waged in the south and through their incendiary musical commitment, these musicians were messengers of resistance and racial justice as their sounds carried through the halls and streets of the cities of Europe where black men and women were also deeply engaged in their own struggles against racism - in Manchester too in the brick canyons of Moss Side and Hulme.

The quintet pace themselves with the opening Harold Arlen ballad It's only a Paper Moon with a clapping and whistling Manchester throng before them. Morgan is away with the theme, while Shorter's quizzical tenor takes up the solo message. Morgan's horn is edgy and defiant before Timmons rolls out his notes with Blakey's racing beat behind him. And then it's onto Timmons's funky classic Dat Dere, which defined the sound of the Messengers and hard bop itself for a generation. Shorter opens the solos with his enigmatic tone, Morgan's ear-splitting notes continue the message and the composer relaxes contentedly into his own creation before Blakey's pounding skins take the tune home.

Next it's Are You Real? written by a former Messengers tenorist and musical director, Benny Golson. Shorter finds his Manchester groove, Morgan's notes search out the Pennines, Timmons rocks loosely on his stool and Blakey exchanges fierce rolls with the horns.

Dizzy Gillespie was Morgan's first maestro when he was a teenager, so the Gillespie-penned A Night in Tunisia held a precious bond for him. Shorter begins the solos with a strange, stuttering chorus before Morgan cracks the theme open and Merritt, a rare soloist, and Blakey share rhythmic pulses. Morgan's high-rise coda is a tribute to the era-defining Dizzy.

Shorter wrote The Summit and it is he who ploughs a solo tenor furrow to open the track. Morgan follows ardently and Timmons is eloquently laid-back while the horns riff on behind him. Blakey is in jocular mood as he introduces his bandmates, or 'the members of the aggravation' as he calls them, referring to Shorter as a new 'star on the jazz horizon' who has been 'there for quite some time already and Morgan who has topped the jazz polls in every magazine from Downbeat to the Melody Maker to the Ladies Home Journal!'

A little piece of balladry follows with Like Someone in Love with Morgan's fluency leading the way, some lyrical Shorter and gentle phrases from Timmons. Then it is Morgan's own Kozo's Waltz, prompted by a Blakey drum-storm, which pounds out of the Free Trade Hall over Ancoats and Ardwick, Longsight and Burnage, Cheetham Hill to Blackley and Moss Side.

1961 it was and the heart of America beat in Manchester that night with the great and eternal drums of Art Blakey and the message of his comrades-in-music.

Terence Blanchard (USA) - The day the levees broke

A Tale of God's Will (a Requiem for Katrina)
(2008)

New Orleans was the birthplace of jazz and, within its provenance, religion had a central place. Just think of the hymnal tunes and spirituals that became the great anthems of the Crescent City marching bands, from Just a Closer Walk with Thee to Glory Land, from The Old Rugged Cross to Lord, You Sure Been Good to Me. The invocation of Christian myths and symbols were at the core.

Terence Blanchard's requiem for his native city following the appalling tragedy of Hurricane Katrina is called A Tale of God's Will. The listener may or may not detect irony in this title, particularly as he tells in the sleeve notes: 'The faulty levees that the federal government had built col-lapsed, allowing the flood-waters in.' A tale of government will, then, or lack of government will to protect the people of New Orleans, in particular the poor and the black, among them the families of the musicians.

Blanchard is a monumental modern New Orleans trumpeter of astonishing abilities. Among the great Delta City horn men, it is Henry 'Red' Allen who is his true progenitor. He has inherited all Red's ability to soar in the higher register and to bend notes around every conceivable corner, as well as blow them with a tender and moving blues lyricism. His band too are no slouches, with New Orleans tenorist Brice Winston, pianist Aaron Parks, bassist Derrick Hodge and drummer Kendrick Scott, all backed up by the 40-member orchestral might of the Northwest Sinfonia.

Blanchard has written the scores for several Spike Lee films, including Mo' Better Blues, The 25th Hour and Malcolm X and, most recently, for Lee's documentary of the New Orleans floods When the Levees Broke - some of which is included within this present album. The trumpeter's intention is 'to show the calm before the storm that you can hear in the string arrangement and the interlude is when the storm comes and the levees break. The second section is when people are on their roofs, poor people, begging for food, dying from lack of water.'

The opener Ghost of Congo Square remembers the African-American slave gatherings at the square, where drummers were allowed but where the severed heads of rebel slaves were also exhibited, where an amalgam of joy and cruelty was manifest, where tragedy was rife. Blanchard's simmering notes expose its history.

During a track called Levees is when the trumpeter is at his most superb. The agonised tone, the bent and fractured sound, the notes of extended pain and sustained suffering, the blues of a city and its poor, the destruction of their few and precious possessions. All is here in Blanchard's haunting choruses.

Winston's In Time of Need evokes the sufferings of his own family 'as well as the countless people affected by human ineptitude.' Not God's agency here, but huge corrupting and authoritarian human agency. 'I was so frustrated and in rage, I wanted the trumpet to scream on every track,' said Blanchard. 'I had to contain myself.'

The album's harrowing climax is Dear Mom, where Blanchard remembers Lee's filming of his mother's first return with her son to her house crushed by the flood. 'My mother is crying. I am trying not to. I am telling her that these are just things, things that can be rebuilt or repaired or rebought. I know this is not true. Nothing will be as it was.' And he plays like a miracle, as he does with full orchestral backing in Over There, like a messenger of human pain and renewal with the whole New Orleans tradition and history in his melodious, beautiful breath.

(A Tale of God's Will (a Requiem for Katrina) is available on Blue Note)

Celine Bonacina (France) - A horn of plenty

Way of Life/Open Heart

(2017)

When you watch the slight frame of the French baritone saxophonist Celine Bonacina in full sound you might think that here is a woman wrestling with an Amazonian horn, but when you listen you marvel how her sheer virtuosity makes her bulky yet, in her hands, lithe instrument leap and soar into a deep and swinging melodism and improvisation.

Bonacina had a rich musical apprenticeship. She studied in conservatories in Belfort, Besancon and Paris before teaching music in Reunion Island in the Indian Ocean for seven years. She returned to France in 2005 and cut her first album Vue d'en Haut, before joining the Act label and recording Way of Life with the Malagasy drummer Hary Ratsimbazafy and the French bassist Nicolas Garnier in 2010.

Also contributing to the album on four tracks is the French guitarist of Vietnamese roots Nguyen Le whose music had been a powerful inspiration to Bonacina. In his sleeve notes to Way of Life he writes that he has 'never stopped admiring the vitality and beauty of Celine's music,' and both are immediately apparent on the album's opener ZigZag Blues, where her first solo notes throb with power and authority and in Course Pour Suite her 'elephantine' horn (as Nguyen calls it) growls and rumbles through her choruses, still blithe and agile.

Nguyen joins her for Ra Bentr'ol with Ratsimbazafy in particular percussive fettle and Bonacina blowing as if in a joyous dance. Nguyen's solo is stunning - like lightning on the strings. In Wake Up it is as if her horn is doing just that - the arousal of a soundscape, and the two adjacent tracks Free Woman and Travel Story are like chapters of the Bonacina autobiography, so full are they of reflective moods and narrative tension. In Free Woman it is as if she is playing on the very edge of her own invented sound.

Ekena is full of baritone verve with another startling guitar solo from Nguyen and on Deep Red, Bonacina's assured sonic beauty reminds me of the renowned pioneer master of her instrument, Ellington's confrere Harry Carney, playing Sono on the celebrated Jazz Scene album of 1949.

In Jungle Nguyen and Bonacina combine with very powerful calls and answers and the spectral Entre Deux Reves begins like an otherworldly colloquy between the pair, as if their sounds are creating new meanings that they must tell all of us - an astonishing track. In Circle Dance her lightness of touch is unusually nimble for the baritone's profundity and as she saunters forward alongside Paganotti's wordless voice an uncanny union is born.

From the first notes of Wild World with two drummers in pulsing palaver, Bonacina's horn dances with an almost menacing step. In Bayrum the amalgam of vibes, voice and saxophone creates a surprising sonic texture and Bonacina's solo is a sequence of poise and beauty.

Her obligatos to Paganotti's words in So Close So Far are sad responses until she rocks into a faster and more joyous rhythm before Schumacher's sprightly vibes chorus and in Reveyrand's lonely ballad Pierrot she explores the full depth of her horn with an aching and blues-sodden tone.

In Desert she turns to soprano saxophone beside Ratsimbazafy's and Cinelu's pervasive drums.

All through the album she plays a talking horn, with every note a naked word, testifying gently and passionately, telling of a life already brimming with cosmopolitan and musical fullness.

(Way of Life and Open Heart are available on Act)

Graham Bond (England) - The rebellion of sound

Wade In The Water: Classics, Origins And Oddities (2013)

Strange it is sometimes, being a reviewer. When Ivan Beavis, musical pundit as well as Star Fund organiser, sent on to me the new box set of Graham Bond Organization classics from the early 1960s, Wade In The Water, I knew I would be grooving to an early British blues legend as well as a homeboy of mine from Romford, who went to the rival school, The Royal Liberty Grammar, and mastered the Hammond organ and alto sax - unlike his more typical schoolmates I knew who played classical violin and cello.

Yet hearing him growling through his laryngitis on his 1964 recording of Muddy Waters's harmonica, Ginger Baker's rattling drums and Dick Heckstall-Smith's hooting tenor sax, I thought: 'Did this sound really come from the same Essex suburbs where I grew up?' Uncannily, it did, and as I got further into the four CDs, I felt that more than ever I could understand the rebellion of his sound, so different from that made by the thousands of City commuters stepping to Romford and Gidea Park stations to catch the early morning trains to Liverpool Street. Perhaps, in the context of all this, Bond felt, as the lyrics of the song he recorded in 1964 proclaimed, that he was only 'half a man.'

Among these 96 tracks, many of them aimed primarily at the '60s pop market, there are bound to be some mishaps, like the mawkish effort at Tammy or the lifelessly maudlin What Am I Living For? But other tracks are full of energy and verve. Hear Bond's filigreeing organ chorus of Version 1 of Green Onions or the guttural Heckstall-Smith blowing a storm on High-Heeled Sneakers.

On some of the early tracks Bond is playing with two renowned guitarists. He's a part of Ernest Ranglin and The GBs on an April 1964 session and the Jamaican ace and guitar mentor of Bob Marley stacks up many a groove on one of his performing visits to Ronnie Scott's. Hear him solo beside Bond's stinging organ riffs of SO-HO. And on Untitled Abbey Road Blues

Instrumental, it's John McLaughlin's guitar licks that follow another rasping chorus from Bond's organ.

Disc three includes 18 tracks from the Bond/Baker/Bruce/Heckstall-Smith quartet. The performances remixed from the Organization's 1965 album There's A Bond Between Us stand out, in particular Ray Charles's What'd I Say? where Heckstall-Smith lets himself loose, and Have You Ever Loved A Woman? where Bond's soulful vocal is the prelude to more blues-baked Heckstall-Smith and another earthy organ chorus. Two sides of the tenorist emerge on these tracks - a tender, love-toned solo on Bond's ballad Baby, Can It Be True? and his horn raucous and plangent on his own feature, Dick's Instrumental.

Baker stokes up a fire on his own feature - the enigmatically titled Camels And Elephants, with more than an intimation of what was to come half a decade later with Bruce and Eric Clapton in Cream. He sings a desperate vocal of the pains of addiction and incarceration on Cold Rain, enduring '90 days in jail with my backside to the wall,' and Bruce wails on his harmonica on the two versions of Positive aka HHCK Blues.

The final disc brings a little of Bond the alto saxophonist to the fore, but not before a springing trio performance of Wade In The Water, with organ, drums and Bruce plucking acoustic bass. The last nine tracks are live, from autumn 1964. Heckstall-Smith and Bond go head to head on their horns on Queen Of Hearts, with Baker's drums crashing, and despite the low-grade recording quality, the performance is full of skill and spirit. Bruce's voice and harmonica are featured on The First Time I Met The Blues and Bond pulls out a specially gravelly vocal and some powerful Hammond patterns on Little Girl.

When Graham Bond died in 1974 after years of the primal opposites of innovation and addiction, he left almost a mythopoeic story. A story of an insurgent boy living in the superficial calm of the Essex suburbs who strove to play and sing the blues and live the damaged life of the wandering bluesman across the cities of post-war England. Some of those whom he played with survived and others like Bruce, Baker and McLaughlin found world renown - migrating to the US, recording with jazz eminences like Miles Davis and creating amalgams of genres which astonished millions. As for the Romford boy, we have his records like these to tell a different but still potent story.

(Wade In The Water: Classics, Origins And Oddities is available on Repertoire)

Benjamin Boone (USA) - Musical feast in the emerald light

Confluence: The Ireland Sessions

(2025)

How does an alto saxophonist named Benjamin Boone, born in 1963 in Statesville, a small textile town in North Carolina, with an Anglo-German ancestry (and a descendant of John Milton, no less) find himself in Limerick, Ireland, after previous musical forays in Ghana and Moldova, playing with a vibrant group of Irish musicians and making an album with a beautifully melodic opener called On the Banks of the River Shannon?

Boone's father was a glue salesman, his mother a housekeeper turned tutor. As a boy he listened to the Beatles, Carol King, Glenn Miller, Earth, Wind and Fire and Count Basie. 'I started piano at seven, saxophone around thirteen. Then I discovered jazz and wanted to learn how to improvise more than anything. Coltrane, Ben Webster, Monk, Miles and Metheny inspired me the most.'

Mentored by the brilliant Jerry Cohen at the University of Tennessee, 'he modelled to me how to become a compassionate teacher.' Boone's musical life has fused the classics with jazz. 'It's been hard to balance all that,' he told me, 'but the pay-off is I still get excited by what is around the corner, because it's probably something new and exciting.' He became a Music professor in 2000 and now teaches at the University of California at Fresno. His classical compositions have been performed in 38 countries.

He went to Limerick's Irish World Academy of Music and Dance in 2022, as part of its globally-centred curriculum. Did he share the Irish love of melody? 'As a kid I sang in a choir and I play a single-line instrument, so yes I'm foremost a melody person. Ancient Irish melodies are captivating and indescribingly haunting, and I'm fascinated that Irish traditional music and jazz have such commonalities, like a 'swing' rhythmic subdivision.'

What about his bandmates on the album - guitarist Joe O'Callaghan, drummer John Daly, bassists Dan Bodwell and Rory Murphy, pianist James Miley, percussionist Rodrigo Dally and vocalist JaYne? 'They're outstanding, compassionate and great fun. There was no posturing, just connection. Just listen, for example, to Joe O'Callaghan on Confluence, Stern Warning or Clash of the Ash.'

What are his own favourite tracks? 'Maybe She Moved through the Fair. It was hard to arrange since Sinead O'Connor, Led Zeppelin, Wayne Shorter and countless others have covered it. Also Clash of the Ash, since listeners can hear the finesse, pile-ups, athleticism and excitement of a hurling match. And Confluence, because it's so funky.'

I asked him about the new Trump era, how will musicians react and resist? 'The Arts and Education will be on the chopping block, as will real news outlets that support the arts. And will the U,S,A, remain a functioning democracy? We have to keep telling our truths loud and clear, protest and exert political pressure as best we can and not become complacent. It's a dark, disturbing and anxiety-riddled time.'

And is his internationalism the key to his music? 'Indeed. If our government says another country is the 'enemy' we must learn more about that country and its culture, play its music and commission works from its composers so that its people are known and no longer 'the other'. It's imperative to connect and understand, not retract and withdraw.'

So where is he taking his music in the near future? 'I'm going back to Ireland, then there's a European tour with a Viennese group and our New

Global Ensemble with U.S., Irish, Mexican, Ghanaian and German musicians. We'll tour in support of our debut album in North Africa, Asia, India, hopefully England ... so many places to play in and explore.' Or as his forebear Milton wrote in the last line of his pastoral elegy Lycidas:' Tomorrow to fresh woods and pastures new.'

But for now we have Confluence, Irish sessions full of life, humanity, cultural pride, excitation and melodic lyricism - a musical feast in the emerald light.

(Confluence: The Ireland Sessions is available on Origin Records)

Gary Boyle (England/India) - His music has been the true soundbeat of his political heart

(2024)

Of all the albums that the multiple formations of the Mike Westbrook bands have made from duos, trios, to full orchestras and his present 'Band of Bands,' the Live, 1972 album, now reissued, gives us the freest expression of Westbrook's music. Over half a century on, its power and liberated sounds create an uncanny unity with the free improvisation much more common in now-times.

The guitarist on the 1972 album was the outstanding Gary Boyle, whose soloing throughout the album's seven long tracks radiates the influences of Ornette Coleman, a strong dose of the blues, and if you listen closely on such tracks as Spaces, you can hear the far echoes of the sitar and his Indian birthplace.

Born in Patna, India, in 1941, his father worked on the Indian railways. 'I was a child of colonialism,' he quips. 'They called us Anglo-Indians.' Coming to London in 1949, he lived in Fulham, then Lewisham. 'I grew up in the skiffle era,' he tells me. 'I began to play guitar at 16, and as a teenager we used to play our guitars and sing in West End coffee bars. When I left school I had a job turning the lathes in a metal factory in Blackheath.'

The 1960s took him towards pop group professionalism. 'We did the Germany circuit. I remember we played in Hamburg at the same time as the Beatles. They were playing just a street away.' Later he toured with Millie (of My Boy Lollipop fame), Dusty Springfield and Brian Auger and Julie Driscoll's Trinity. But jazz was his primary love. He had heard Coltrane's only English concert at the Granada, Walthamstow, in 1961, and as the power of his music sank in, he knew it was what he wanted to play.

He joined Westbrook in 1972 and toured with the five-piece band in that same year. 'We played very free music,' he remembers, 'even though it wasn't what we listened to. But that became quite common. I was listening to and being excited by Miles Davis and Coltrane, yet what we played on that tour was much freer. I think that it was the only time I was ever recorded playing as free as that.'

'The 1970s were a key political time for all of us: support for the people in South Africa, opposition to the US war in Vietnam, and the Civil Rights Movement were all a part of my political awakening. All the universities and art colleges we played at were alive with politics and the music we played fully supported those struggles. We may not have gone on many marches because we were so busy, but we played our music to support them.' And Marching Song, on the record, a free echo of the section of Westbrook's 1969 similarly titled orchestral suite, crystallises in sound that era of protest and resistance.

What about his four bandmates? 'Westie was so laid back as a leader, he was never dogmatic about the music. Although he was a musician who wrote so creatively and often structurally, he was always very non-prescriptive and never constrained us.' Tenor saxophonist and flutist George Khan he described as 'a completely off-the-wall, brilliantly anarchic musician with a big, free sound,' and drummer Alan Jackson 'was lovely to play with, unfettered and always responsive.' The bassist, the late Butch Potter, 'was a very solid player who really underpinned the rest of us.'

As for Boyle, he plays throughout the album as if playing so free was totally natural and normal to him, even though it was not his usual style. The five play truly like a prophecy of the music to come half a century later, sounds you might hear of free improvisation at present-day sessions at venues like Café Oto or the Vortex. As such it is a unique album driven by the future in the 1972 present.

Living in rural West Yorkshire now as an octogenarian, Boyle remains an activist, helping to organise the pro-Palestinian movement in his area, as if his music has been the true soundbeat of his political heart, expressed in those extraordinary sessions five decades ago.

(Mike Westbrook: Live 1972 is available on Cadillac Records)

Anouar Brahem (Tunisia) - Four minds meet as one in joyful synthesis of Arab music and jazz

Blue Maqams

(2018)

Blue Maqams is a brilliant amalgam of the Arab and jazz musical traditions, made by four veteran virtuosi who, despite or by virtue of the diversity of their origins, were born to make music together. The quartet consists of oud player Anouar Brahem from Tunisia, Chicago-born drummer Jack DeJohnette, bassist Dave Holland, who hails from Wolverhampton, and Django Bates from Beckenham.

Brahem, writing about his first youthful encounters with jazz, emphasises its syncretic power. 'Jazz was an extraordinary field for experimental possibilities and fruitful ground for intermixing and crossbreeding. It was also a language naturally open to different cultures where I could find my place.' And how Blue Maqams manifests that desire. On the first track, Opening Day, Brahem's lute-like oud begins in solitude before Holland and DeJohnette provide him with rhythmic company and Bates's gently running notes sound like a Pennine stream beside Holland's deep, dancing strings.

Bates and Brahem find a beautiful harmony in La Nuit and the title track forges a trans-Atlantic solidarity between the emotive reality of the maqam - the melodic mode used as a springboard for improvisation in Arabic, Persian and Turkish music, often the vessel of love, sadness or pain - and the US loneliness and critical muscle of the blues. Here, it is one music of shared concord and skill as if the entire world were one, as DeJohnette's Southern and Chicago roots, Holland's Black Country blues and Bates's London laments fuse across oceans and continents. Sometimes, when you hear Brahem's oud, it's as if you're hearing the Louisiana guitar of Lonnie Johnson or Muddy Waters's Mississippi strings.

More so at the outset of Bahia, where Brahem's oud is accompanied by a wordless, grunting vocal, before Holland and DeJohnette add swinging vitality. Brahem's sheer fleetness of note-making is astonishing and the snapping of DeJohnette's snares are in absolute empathy with him. Bates's gentle notes form the opening of La Passante and, as Brahem joins him, there's the sense of a lovers' tryst. There are moments in Bom Dia Rio where Holland's bass has so much levitation that it is as if all four musicians are yards above the floor of their New York studio.

Translucent dreams of the ancients are spun from Brahem's strings in Persepolis's Mirage and Bates's opening steps of The Recovered Road to Al-Sham radiate that very lyricism that impresses Brahem so much. He writes that, as a young man, 'jazz was associated with ideas of transgression and freedom for me.' Now, it seems that the same is true for all four of these veteran masters. Together, a new and unified music is born.

(Blue Maqams is available on ECM)

Vibes virtuoso Patricia Brennan (Mexico)
Breaking Stretch
(2025)

A Mexican arrivant in the US from the throbbing musical hub of Veracruz, vibes virtuoso Patricia Brennan brought the heart of her city's sounds with her with love and artistry in her new album, Breaking Stretch. Her parents were both computer engineers. Her father was a Latin percussionist and her paternal grandmother a concert pianist who would practise in their home. 'I was introduced at a very early age to music from classical to salsa', she told me: 'my home town music was heavily influenced by Afro-Cuban traditions.'

'After beginning on piano at three, by six years old I began on mallet percussion, which is how I came to vibraphone. I was always interested in improvisation and in 2004, by which time I was in college in Philadelphia, I was drawn into jazz by listening to the Sixties' Blue Note albums, particularly those by the great vibes player Bobby Hutcherson, and especially Eric Dolphy's Out to Lunch. I was also deeply influenced by the records of pianist Geri Allen, but always my memories of the vibrancy of Veracruz's music still inspire me every day as a core element of my artistic process.'

'My experience of migration was certainly a challenge. It required much work, studying the language for years and aspiring to be the best I could be through music. I went through work visas, artist visas, green card renewals and the culmination of my journey was citizenship in 2024.'

Breaking Stretch is her second Pyroclastic album. 'With it I'm seeking to push sonic boundaries, while staying true to the inherent nature of my music. The title Breaking Stretch distils this inspiration, pushing the sonic and technical limits of each instrument to their breaking point, past their normal expectations within the ensemble. 'Stretch' is a function that makes a graph narrower or wider. The music goes through several stages of expansion and contraction, and is rhythmically driven like salsa ensembles and Seventies' wind and brass rock groups like Earth, Wind and Fire and Chicago. The sleeve illustrations envisage the essence of the music, with the 'breaking' and 'stretching' expressed by volcanic images. The astro images also represent the concept of expansion, and the human spirit of exploration.'

Why does she love the vibes so much? 'I was from childhood drawn to mallet percussion, which combines the rhythm of percussion with the melodic and harmonic qualities of piano. The tone of the vibraphone is unique in its ability to sustain its sound: its liquid quality and etherealness are captivating to me.'

What about her bandmates on the album whose sounds seem to be at their utmost? 'Firstly the saxophonists: Jon Irabagon is a wizard on all his instruments and incredibly creative, while Mark Shim has unmatchable sounds of depth and wisdom. Trumpeter Adam O'Farrill is inventive and always ahead of his time. Kim Cass is a master bassist with limitless sonic and rhythmic capabilities while drummer Marcus Gilmore has a one-and-only talent and musical mind whose creativity and inventiveness transcend his instrument. Maurice Herrera is one of the most innovative percussionists of our time who carries the past into the future.'

I asked her about the particularly evocative track, Suenos de Coral Azul. 'It's a reflection of an immigrant's journey - the uncertainty, excitement for a fresh start, the pain of leaving loved ones, the hopes for new relationships and the dream of one day reuniting with the people from the place you still love and call home. The music's hope is to find a space of healing and reflection.'

Finally, there is the powerfully summative track, Earendel. 'It takes its name from the oldest and most distant star we have yet discovered - 29 billion light years from Earth. We try to explore the concept of constant expansion, the elasticity of the universe and our never-ending travel through space into infinity.'

Well, Sun Ra would have loved it, stars in the galaxies and stars like Patricia and her septet-mates definitely here on Earth. Listen and travel the solid earthways and farthest spaceways with them.

(Breaking Stretch is available on Pyroclastic Records)

Olie Brice (England) - All It Was
(2025)

The new album by London bassist Olie Brice's Quartet is both deeply moving and beautifully played, telling of 'the grief and pain of losing my father tangled and fused with horror and despair at the genocide in Palestine.'

The elision of the personal, the political and the universal is the heartsong of true music, and shared by tenor saxophonist Rachel Musson, pianist Alexander Hawkins and drummer Will Glaser. Musson plays with a dancing, tuneful edge with every invented phrase a line of sonic poetry, and Brice with a plunging heartbeat and an inspired, committed zest in life from the very first notes of his pandemic-written opener, Listening Intently to Raptors, dedicated to fellow bassist, the American John Lindberg. Hawkins is Hawkins, all through the album it is as if he can't help himself making melody in the midst of all his improvisation, while Glaser's nuanced percussive flair, full of rhythmic subtlety is everywhere, across every track.

To me, the most memorable track is the elegiac Morning Mourning - emotion moulded as sound - a listener's true lasting gift, while we consider Elizabeth Caney's fleeting sleeve artwork, portraying the sheer boldness of this album's trapeze-catching music, fusing pictorial form with the quartet's unique soundworld.

The summative final track is And We Dance on the Firm Earth, the title a line from the great Caribbean laureate, Edward Brathwaite of Barbados. Artistry of words, sounds and image mesh in a unity of hope, the signature of the entire album.

(All It Was is available on West Hill Records)

Peter Brötzmann (Germany): The Free-Jazz Revolution and The Politics Of Improvisation
by Daniel Spicer
(2025)

As soon as I began to read this riveting biography of the German saxophonist Peter Brötzmann (1941 - 2023), I went straight to his first blistering annunciation of March, 1968, 'Machine Gun', recorded at the same Frankfurt music festival as 'Fuck de Boere'. Here were German musicians performing alongside fellow British and Dutch iconoclastic horns Evan Parker and Willem Breuker, blasting out their solidarity with the people of Vietnam and South Africa in complete and scorning rejection of the nazism of previous German generations. At their centre was the unprecedented raucous and uniquely scorching saxophone-song of the sonic arch-rebel Brötzmann.

Spicer's biography is also a history of European free improvisation, of which Brötzmann was hierophant and instigator. I deliberately don't use the word 'leader' because such a hierarchical concept was anathema. In the words of Spicer, this was 'a music without leaders, in which every participant was engaged in a collective, communal endeavour.' It is what is heard almost every night at London venues like Dalston's Café Oto: the pursuit of musical excellence and freedom in an entirely cooperative setting, where siblings of improvisation aim never to play the same sound constructs and inventive sequences twice.

Brötzmann was born when fascism and resistance to it were rampant across Europe. His infancy was spent when his country's government was murdering millions across the continent. It was a measure of his audacity in a postwar Germany, that he devised a sound that was a signal of the Sixties, when young people were rising up across Europe and the new imperialist behemoth - the USA- in rebellion against wars in Africa, Asia and the Americas. For a section of them in Europe, Brötzmann's rasping saxophone became their heartsong, as part of the relatively little-known sound of the music he and his world-travelling free improvising musicians created at the very edge of blasting sound.

The Sixties were an era when the word 'freedom' meant many things. I remember hearing the extraordinary Texas voice of Janis Joplin singing at the Carousel Ballroom in San Francisco in the summer of 1968, at the same time that Brötzmann created his 'Machine Gun' in Frankfurt. She sang with something of a similar cyclonic timbre as Brötzmann's volcanic horn, but her message was very different. 'Freedom is another word for nothing else to lose!' she chorused, Brötzmann's interpretation of freedom was 'Never again! Never again! Never again!'

Not only would his musical, improvising, soul ever allow him to play exactly the same eruption of notes again; they stood anthemically as a lifetime's defiance that would never allow fascism to despoil our lives again, not in his own country nor anywhere else where he played. Although as he got older, he lost his close links with the revolutionary left, his music continued with its utmost insurgency, never compromising. But his was not only a continuous blast of freedom (one of his most successful bands was called 'Full Blast') – he could play with a tenderness that would very often be born from some of his most outrageous solos. I remember hearing one of his latter-day sessions at Café Oto, playing with Brooklyn bassist William Parker and the Louisiana drummer Hamid Drake – two of the nonpareils of U.S. free music. After a jaw-breaking volley of caustic and rampaging overblown sound, he played a sequence of such gentleness that seemed almost lullaby-like in its mollifying beauty. In their session a German played his riposte to the crimes of Nazism, and every note of two black Americans defied centuries of slavery and racism. As a trio, they too were calling out their freedom songs with their defining message: 'Never again!'

One of the strengths of Spicer's book is the way in which he sees Brötzmann's life in music as the creative protagonist who inspired those who played with him, from the Americans in the Chicago Tentet, to Scandinavians and English free virtuosi like bassist John Edwards and drummer Steve Noble. He would play everywhere and with everyone carrying his freedom message. I've got an album of him playing in San'aa, Yemen with Yemeni classical musicians who had never heard anything close to his like before. As a musical revolutionary he was a profoundly committed internationalist, there were no barriers of genre, nation or tradition that would obstruct the untrammelled liberation of his sound.

Secondly, Spicer knew Brötzmann as a person as well as a musician, and his book is full of his words, letters and moments of personal closeness. But his love of Brötzmann's music becomes explicit in many evocative and powerful descriptions of his live sessions and those of his compadres with whom he played: drummer Han Bennink, bassist Peter Kowald, pianist Fred van Hove and many others. His eloquent words and vivid pile-ups of adjectives make their music come alive on the page, as well as in the ears. His book is a true and memorable testimony to Brötzmann's dissonant, cacophonic genius, a sound of rampant beauty still throbbing through all his recordings, but one we will never hear live in our ears again. Get hold of his albums, and keep Spicer's book close at hand while you listen to them.

(Peter Brötzmann: The Free-Jazz Revolution And The Politics Of Improvisation is published by Repeater Books)

Peter Brötzmann (Germany)
Live at Café Oto
(2025)

Café Oto in Dalston was truly German free saxophonist Peter Brötzmann 's London home from home. He was loved there by its audiences, management and all who played with him. His final two concerts there, in February 2023, are now available on a double CD, recorded with three of his favourite musicians: Englishmen John Edwards and Steve Noble on bass and drums, and vibraphonist Jason Adasiewicz from Wichita, Kansas.

The four long tracks, each a whole set in its own right, exude Café Oto's powerful atmospherics and you can feel the intensity in every live sound. The first track opens quietly enough, in a blues mode with Adasiewicz sprinkling his notes over Brötzmann 's gradually more rasping phrases and Noble's thunderous scuttle of drums.

This is an unconscious valediction, but Brötzmann's death a few months later, makes it all the more moving as we listen to it now. His horn speaks, its intonation as lucid as words, telling of his life in music all over the world. It's a life-sound, full of storytelling notes from a musical revolutionary, not a Machine Gun of those earliest years, but still a narrative of freedom. When Edwards comes in to make his solo notes, you can feel them breathing and sounding messages of respect and love. As his quartet-mates ground-call Brötzmann to carry on with his story, he lets rip with his cry of life, as if he is releasing and echoing all those holding in their stories in the streets outside, walking up and down Kingsland Road or Dalston Lane, with its library named after another genius raconteur and freedom-lover, C.L.R. James.

The third track has a reflective beginning with vibes and Edwards' booming bass in close palaver beside Noble's rumbling drums and Brötzmann's melodic opening turning to fierce declamation, showing again how he could change sound, form and mood in an instant. What becomes clear one more time is how closely and intuitively these four musicians know each other's artistry and humanity, how every change is anticipated in a fraction of a second and how collectively and unitedly they create in the crucible of improvisation.

As the old Brötzmann returns in the final minutes, urged on by Noble's drums earthquake and Edwards' pounding strings, someone from the audience gives a momentary whistle. It becomes as a signal for Brötzmann's final anthemic blasts, belches and raucous, explosive visceral respirations, giving way to summative notes of quasi-quietude, Edwards' last bass heartbeats and a final farewell of Brötzmann's talking breath.

(The Quartet is available on Roku Records)

Ray Brown (USA) & Christian McBride (USA) - Musical trail to the Limehouse Blues

The Ray Brown Trio and the Christian McBride Quartet, The Barbican, London (2001)

Much has happened in and out of jazz within the difference of years between the two virtuoso bass men who played the same bill at the Barbican last weekend. There's half a century between them.

Ray Brown, the elder, who was born in Pittsburgh in 1926 announced that he made his first musical visit to London in 1948. Christian McBride, a 28-year-old from Philadelphia, is a prodigy of the last decade and a bass dynamo who is the direct inheritor of the veteran.

When the beefy, square-bodied McBride stood on the stage for his first selection, Egad, suddenly, dark bass thunder spoke out and you wondered how this instrument could have been neglected for so many years as a solo force. McBride had been in demand by almost every contemporary jazz leader - and played superbly on albums by Bobby Watson, Benny Golson, Freddie Hubbard and Roy Hargrove, before his own first pathbreaking CD, Gettin' To It, was recorded in 1995. His present quartet is a powerful enough amalgam.

On McBride's Lullaby For A Lady Bug, the soothing chords of pianist Geoff Keezer prompted a humming bowed bass solo that was beautifully sable and melodic. Camille Gainer's empathetic and carefully listening drumming led on to the solitary horn of the evening, that of Ron Black and his serpentine flourishes on soprano sax. Whether on tenor or soprano, his solos were endlessly and passionately inventive, particularly in the futuristic Sci Fi, with McBride on electric bass, which finished the first set.

The spectacle of Ray Brown, standing over the shoulders of his confrere guitarist Russell Malone and the phenomena! Jamaican pianist Monty Alexander like some vigilant grandfather, was but a prelude to a sublimely swinging session of trio jazz. Brown appeared on the New York jazz scene in 1945, played with Dizzy Gillespie, Charlie Parker and Bud Powell in historic bop sessions and became a luminary of the Jazz At The Philharmonic world roadshow, before spending 15 years with Oscar Peterson.

After the booming McBride, the old master's touch across the bass strings seemed light, almost aery, plucking them like a grey-haired Mercury. The musicians performed close to each other, with an intimacy that ran through their music and out again as Brown playfully flicked Malone's ear and Alexander's eyes were fixed on the old bass man, in gestures displaying beaming admiration. In But Not For Me Malone's crystalline notes and the pianist's rumbustious brilliance were all founded in Brown's dazzling subliminal lines. But, suddenly, they were playing one for the Morning Star! An unhurried, real bluesy Limehouse Blues, played slowly as a real blues.

The conversations between Alexander's wit and feeling. Malone's felicitous chordal then finger-picking solo and Brown's swinging poise made it a timeless effort, worthy of all the humanity, power and insight coming out of those offices straight across from St Anne's, Limehouse, and making a musical trail in the London air all the way from the Barbican to Commercial Road.

Jaimeo Brown (USA) - Tradition, change and struggle in new notes

Transcendence/Work Songs
(2016)

'Politically, this music is a warning to our generation. Global corporations and banks are destroying local cultures throughout the world. The same spirituals that gave strength to our ancestors need to give us strength today as we consider the very real possibility of modern global slavery and look in earnest for ways to avoid that unacceptable state.' Not words you'd expect to find within the sleeve notes of modern jazz albums but Transcendence and Work Songs are unique and imperishable records, the eventual outcome of a master's thesis by the New York-based drummer Jaimeo Brown.

While gathering research for his thesis, How the Black Church Affected Jazz, Brown came across the recordings of the Gee's Bend Quilters of Alabama, who sang spirituals while threading quilts. Their renditions deeply affected Brown and inspired him to work with saxophonist J D Allen and guitarist Chris Sholar to create the album Transcendence which combines Brown's contemporary sounds and reflections with evocative sampling of the music of the Gee's Bend quilt-makers. In doing so, he makes history speak to the present and the future from a rural southern location to the cosmopolis of New York City.

From the first lines of This World is a Mean World to Live In, sung by an anonymous quilt-weaver and interpolated by Allen's blues-drenched notes and Brown's crashing drums, the fusion radiates deep emotive meaning and moves through the haunting wordless vocal of Somebody's Knocking.

Power of God brings in the Detroit pianist Geri Allen to find unison with her Alabama forebears. As their voices fade, her keys talk on, fired by their company and the messages of their sound in a long and deeply moving coda. History's memory of Africa is in the very blood of this record. Brown was in Ghana a week before it was made and his Accra, where this thunderous drums leave their storm across New York, precedes the album's last two tracks of the Gee's Bend choir. In You Needn't Mind Me Dyin', Allen's horn blows potent obligatos to their words and in This World Ain't My Home, Brown, Sholar and Allen are deeply and inseparably inside their singing.

In November 2014, three years after the recording of Transcendence, the trio were back in New York to cut Work Songs, using the songs of southern prisoners, coalminers, stonemasons, labourers, collected by the pioneer musicologist Alan Lomax. On several tracks they are joined by the young alto saxophonist of the Mingus Big Band, Jaleel Shaw.

On the opener, Hidden Angel, we hear the voices of Parchman Farm prisoners singing Stewball with Shaw's sad-toned alto in the foreground.

Sholar's surging guitar accompanies the words of inland ship workers on Mississippi.

Allen's tenor combines with Virginian workers singing the spiritual Lazarus, then suddenly there are the sister voices of Japanese safflower pickers and Shaw's alto chorus ringing through Safflower as if the wings of his notes had taken him across continents and oceans. The exhaustion of the Parchman prisoners hollers through I'll Be So Glad When the Sun Goes Down, before Allen's pulsating chorus adds his compadres' witness of 21st-century yearning and struggle. For Brown, singers like those of Gee's Bend and Parchman Farm bring 'a timeless message of hope.'

They are 'a microcosm of a much larger universal community that had to use the highest forms of human ingenuity to survive and create.'

An attestation of the soul and brain of jazz of modern times too: tradition, change and struggle in new notes.

(Transcendence and Work Songs are available on Motema)

Marion Brown (USA) and Dave Burrell (Hawaii/USA) – Creative juices flow as black musicians confer

Live at the Black Musicians' Conference, 1981 (2019)

Would the founding pioneers of jazz in New Orleans at the turn of the 19th century ever have thought that a future nucleus of their music would be created in Vilnius, Lithuania, more than a century later? That is where No Business, one of the music's hottest labels is based and among their newest releases is a marvellous 1981 encounter between alto saxophonist Marion Brown and Hawaiian pianist Dave Burrell at a black musicians' conference.

It was opened by Archie Shepp with a lecture on revolutionary concepts in African-American music, a theme which Burrell and Brown develop with the utmost commitment.

This jewel of a previously unreleased session begins with the Brown composition Gossip/Fortunado, prefaced by a beautifully toned unaccompanied Brown before Burrell's single chimes create an improvised colloquy. Brown's rhythm and pace are accentuated with repeated riffs and Burrell explores the moment while exchanging invented, newly born melodies with Brown's soft-toned horn.

The Mexican edge is explicit on his La Placita, as if there is no kind of wall between these musicians and the people beyond the southern frontier. He plays the melody with a quivering gentleness and his improvisation seethes with vibrato above Burrell's comping keys.

Then it is on to the first of two Billy Strayhorn tunes, My Little Brown Book, played by the duo as if the melody itself is enough. There are moments here when Brown's saxophone seems to be weeping, so emotively does he inhabit Strayhorn's evocative phrases.

Burrell's tune Punaluu Peter follows, named after a pitch-black beach in Hawaii. It's a stomping theme, begun by solo piano before Brown enters. He squeezes his notes as if talking to the sea, while Burrell strides over the sand. Pua Mae Ole is another Burrell tune with a Hawaiian tinge but this time with a beautiful and elegiac sense of lyricism.

On the final track, Strayhorn's narrative ballad Lush Life, the melody sounds as pristine as if these two masters are reinventing it, so moving and authentic does it resonate. At one dramatic point Brown almost croaks its refrain and Burrell plays like Ellington would have played his dear friend's tune, all the way from Lithuania. Who would have thought it?

(Live at the Black Musicians' Conference, 1981 is available on NoBusiness Records)

Bruise (England) - A night on the bruise

Bruised & Bruised with Derek Bailey and We Packed Are Bags (2011)

Jazz has famously been dubbed 'the sound of surprise,' but the improvising band Bruise - with their astonishing combination of diverse sounds in one rampaging quintent - truly create the sound of incredulity. A bass saxophone blown with booming fire by a man from Aylesbury, Bucks, Tony Bevan. A fleet and brilliant British bassist, John Edwards, attuned to playing in a host of improvising contexts including the band of the epochal South African drummer Louis Moholo-Moholo. The pulsing free British drummer Mark Sanders and the fizzing electronicist Ashley Wales of Springheel Jack. And finally the London-born vibraphonist, steel drummer and percussionist of Caribbean roots - Orphy Robinson, who made two Blue Note albums in the early '90s and who has changed his emphasis to free jazz throughout this millennium.

Quite a fivesome this - quite an amalgam. In 2005 they cut their first album, simply called Bruised. The resonating, plunging strings of Edwards's bass and Robinson's skittering pans open its first track Sunhouse. Bevan's tenor steals in then blasts out of Wales's extra-terrestrial soundscapes before Edwards's arco bass leads the quintet to rest.

The second track is Leviathan, with a menacingly subdued beginning like droplets of water on a subterranean lake, preluding the quasi-agonised groans of Bevan's bass saxophone arousing from the percussion and bass ensemble. Sanders's brushes awaken Tempranillo and Bevan's gruff, howling tenor awakes too to make a colloquy with Robinson's echoing vibes. The title track features the bass saxophone again, a rare enough instrument in British jazz, its previous virtuoso being east London Dixielander Harry Gold, his bass horn with its home in a famous pub along the Gray's Inn Road. Bevan makes its sound entirely new, ever plummeting, exploring, constantly reflecting - while soundbuilding.

In 1939 the Count Basie Orchestra recorded the huge swing and cry of Taxi War Dance in the wake of the New York cab drivers' strike. Bruise's Taxi Dance, coming from London some seven decades later, is a sonic commentary on a different urban world, and you wonder what event provoked it as Bevan's tenor carps across the percussive waves, and Robinson's Caribbean pans chime out below.

On an August night in 2004 Bruise became a sextet with the addition of the Sheffield-born free guitarist Derek Bailey at a live performance at the 291 Gallery along the Hackney Road, close to the veteran guitarist's flat. Bailey died in 2005, so this was one of his last recordings. Bevan dedicates the album to his 'dear friend Derek,' reminding listeners that 'search, locate and destroy' was Derek's motto, and the three long tracks carry the titles of these verbs.

Robinson adds to his array of percussive instruments by playing trumpet. Bailey's atonal, acerbic chordings introduce Search, with Bevan's deep, deep horn responses creating a once-made dialogue. The percussion shuffles and embeds the sounds while Bevan's saxophone utters and reverberates like nothing else in jazz. Locate rests and comes alive upon its startling electronicity which sparks out between Edward's heartbeats, Bailey's deft patterns and Sanders's more earthbound and streetbound drums. Pain and grotesquerie fuse with moments of weird lyricism and a new 21st century beauty is born.

In 2007 Bruise recorded again at the 291 Gallery and the Red Rose on Seven Sisters Lane. They called their album We Packed Are Bags, from a child's story which continues: 'And went on our way. We saw a loin and made me sick.' The album sleeve is beautifully designed from a child's drawing and the record itself radiates certain childlike qualities that would have heartened Blake. Could you imagine children playing its first track Big Paws, for example, with its tapping, shaking, rattling, cascading sounds and Edwards's sawing bass groaning behind Robinson's pan? Or the eerier second track Long Face, beginning like a free improvising percussive blues before Bevan's tenor comes wailing in?

But then Bruise are anything but a facile listen, and the hearer cannot rest easily, having to hear, work and imagine hard. But they make a unique sonic message, forging true jazz in the making from the eastern heart of London.

(Bruised & We Packed Are Bags are available on Foghorn)

Ray Bryant (USA) - Memories of a jazz piano master
The Ray Bryant Trio - Con Alma/Little Susie
(2013)

I remember it was the summer of 1976 and I had found my way to the Capital Jazz Festival at Alexandra Palace. Half way up the grassy slopes to the Victorian vestige I came virtually face to face with a pianist playing a solo All the Things You Are on an improvised wooden stage. He was a burly, black, moustachioed middle-aged man deeply engrossed in the music that was spinning off his fingers. It was Ray Bryant, one of the great swing-to-bop eclectics of the jazz piano who was just as at ease accompanying the pioneer of the tenor saxophone Coleman Hawkins or the Basie-ite drummer Jo Jones as he was playing with prime boppers and post-boppers like Charlie Parker and Miles Davis, Sonny Rollins and Jackie McLean. So to both hear of his death in 2011 and see a reissue of a single CD of two of his finest early trio albums filled me with memories and sadness at the loss of such a huge talent.

Born in Philadelphia in 1931, Bryant was born also into music. His mother was an accomplished pianist and tutored him from an early age, and he was surrounded by the sounds of the gospel church. So much so that by his early twenties he was house pianist at Philly's Blue Note, accompanying luminous hornmen like Parker, Lester Young and Davis, and by 1955 he was making his studio debut on the latter's Quintet/Sextet album with jazz eminences like McLean and Milt Jackson.

The trio album Little Susie was Bryant's first album for the giant Columbia label, recorded in December and January 1959-60. Named after his young daughter, the title tune was a bestseller as a single and the album's repertoire was made up of Bryant originals and familiar standards. Ray's brother Tommy was on bass. Gus Johnson played drums on four titles and Eddie Locke on the other four.

The trio rip into Little Susie as if they are three musicians in one, with Johnson's rattling snares providing powerful rhythmic impetus and Bryant striking hard and clear, leaping up and down his keys, with Tommy's walking bass hurrying to catch up with his striding brother. By Myself is more reflective, slower but still jaunty and radiating Bryant's rolling energy. The subject of Blues for Norine must have been a formidable woman, for there is everything strong and potent about her characterisation in this piece, played with an uncompromising forward groove that contrasts with the confident way Bryant sits back on his notes all through his rendition of Erroll Garner's Misty.

Bryant is back to his own creations in Big Buddy, a sprinting performance which gives Tommy a short solo before Ray comes leaping back to show his full virtuosity at breakneck speed. He follows this by two American songbook classics, first Willow Weep for Me played with a strong dose of the blues and Cole Porter's So in Love, made into a keyboard stomp, full of joy and surprise.

In December 1960 Bryant recorded Con Alma, his second Columbia album, this time with Bill Lee and Arthur Harper alternating on bass, and drummer Mickey Roker. The title tune was a Dizzy Gillespie original taken from his Afro-Cuban mode and the album also includes Bryant's own Cubano Chant, in the full wake of the Cuban revolution the year before. Bryant gives Con Alma's cadences a quasi-marching rhythm beside Roker's rhythmic rimshots whereas his version of Ellington's C Jam Blues which follows is pumped out of his keys with a swinging verve. His own composition Nuts and Bolts, full of sudden corners, also shows Roker's impressive percussive skills and the call to action of Cubano Chant makes you think of Fidel and Che and all the other heroes moving through the Sierra Maestra.

The album ends with works from three other great contemporaries. Monk's Round Midnight is revealed in all its beautiful complexity, Miles's Milestones hurtles along beside Roker's brushes and powered by Bryant's startling note clarity, and as the album plays out with John Lewis's evocative and loving tribute: to the great Gypsy guitarist Django.

I still can't get the picture of Ray Bryant's brilliance on the grass in front of Ally Pally out of my mind.

(Con Alma/Little Susie is available on Fresh Sound)

Jane Bunnett (Canada) - Key discoveries

Jane Bunnett With Strings, Ontario Science Centre - Toronto Red Dragonfly (2005)

There have been a series of key moments in Jane Bunnett's Canadian life as a jazz musician. Born in Toronto in 1955 and trained as a child as a classical pianist, tendonitis forced her to scuttle her dream. Then, while travelling in the US as a young woman, she heard Charles Mingus in California and was swept into the world of jazz, opting for the flute and soprano saxophone and, eventually, cutting some fine recordings with major jazz figures like Dewey Redman and Don Pullen.

While visiting Cuba in the late 1980s, in another epiphanous moment, she met the beauty and energy of Cuban music and some of its greatest virtuosi and another fire was ignited within her. Her 1991 album, Spirits of Havana cemented this new artistic union. She has done much to educate Canadian music lovers to the Cuban sound and many Cuban musicians have come to perform and study in Canada as a result of her frequent visits and musical forays to the island. So it is not surprising to learn that, on her new album, in which her regular quintet performs with the Penderecki String Quartet - Red Dragonfly, there are three Cuban tunes among a cosmic selection of folk themes, stretching from Quebec and the Appalachians to Japan and from South Africa to Brazil.

At a lunchtime concert organised by the Toronto radio station, JAZZ FM91, the Bunnett and Strings combination play the tunes from the CD, including Heaven's Gate, a Bunnett composition. It is the albums only new melody and features the muted trumpet of Larry Cramer playing alongside soprano, as the strings filigree in and out of the theme. The piano of Santiago de Cuba-born David Virelles adds an engrossing solo before the two horns return.

Familiar north American folk themes like Black is The Colour Of My True Love's Hair or Un Canadien Errant are given leaping arrangements and run like rivers thought Bunnett's horn, with drummers Mark Mclean and the bass of Kieran Overs providing the rhythmic current. The late Native American Jim Pepper's adaptation of the Navajo peyote chant, Witchi Tia To is one of the album's gems. Bunnett plays with a sublime melodic flow and has a crystalline tone which is powerfully distinctive, and has a way of making her sound surge up through her horn to make an effervescent delivery of gushing notes. The same is true in her performance of the beautiful 1930s Cuban tune of Ernesto Lecuona, Mario La O, arranged for her by the Cuban piano genius, Hilario Duran.

Another Cuban melody, Rabo De Nube, entered the jazz canon when first recorded by Charlie Haden's Liberation Music Orchestra and includes a solo by Dewey Redman. Bunnett's swirling notes emulate her mentor, her improvisational - power potently empathetic while the strings echo her musical pathways.

Virelles's piano chimes against the strings as he introduces his arrangement of the South African resistance anthem, composed in 1897 by Enoch Sontonga, Nkosi Sikelel'I Afrika. "I dedicate this arrangement to the South African jazz master, Abdullah Ibrahim,' Virelles' writes in the sleeve notes. Halfway through, the tempo quickens as if the end of the struggle against apartheid is approaching, and Bunnett re-enters with some rhapsodic phrases over McLean's drums.

She blows out the melody of the Japanese tune Moon Over Ruined Castle with a pointed clarity, while Red Dragonfly itself, the song of an old man conjuring his past with a theme reminiscent of Shenandoah, is a fusion of Virelles's solo piano, Bunnett's chirping saxophone, Overs's relentless beat and McLean's soothing brushwork with the string quartet's shadowy, dusk-like backdrop. A rare album this, combining the universal folksong with jazz adventurousness and an amalgam of classical strings. But such is to be expected of a liberation musician like Bunnett and her discovering jazz comrades.

(Toronto Red Dragonfly is available on Blue Note)

Jaki Byard (USA) - An exceptionally brilliant eclecticism
Sunshine of My Soul/A Matter of Black and White/The Late Show (2018)

The most eclectically brilliant and versatile pianist of a century of jazz, Jaki Byard - born in Worcester, Massachusetts, in 1922 - could play everything, in every piano style or genre, from blues, gospel and stride to post-bop and the avant garde. As a young man, and later in the US army, he played a host of instruments - piano, trumpet, guitar, drums, trombone, as well as tenor saxophone on which he was excellent. He played in jump bands like that of Earl Bostic and the big bands of Herb Pomeroy and Maynard Ferguson, before crossing over to join the Charles Mingus Band in 1962, where he found himself alongside fellow free and discovering spirits like Mingus himself, Eric Dolphy, Roland Rahsaan Kirk, Booker Ervin and Sam Rivers.

Many of his years were spent teaching, particularly in the New England Conservatory of Music where he had a huge effect upon his students, even developing a big band among them (the Apollo Stompers) which made several albums. He died in 1999, murdered in his home in Queen's, in still unsolved circumstances.

One of his students, the eminent pianist Fred Hersch said of his mentor: 'He was one of the all-time great solo players and one of the best pure musicians I have ever met' and three new albums never before issued, of recordings of Byard playing solo at The Keystone Corner in San Francisco in 1978-9 attest to his astonishing solo virtuosity.

Perhaps the most memorable track of the first Keystone album Sunshine of My Soul is Byard's Mingus Medley. He includes the lampoon of Governor Orval Faubus of Arkansas, who stood in the doorway of Central High School in Little Rock in September 1957 with members of the National Guard to block the entry of nine black children. Fables of Faubus became a musical parable and Byard plays it with both humour and verve, and follows it with a stomping version of Mingus's Peggy's Blue Skylight, which he so often played with the Mingus Sextet on the 1964 European tour.

There is also a homage to the great stride pianists of New York like James P Johnson and Willie 'The Lion' Smith in Tribute to the Ticklers, an acknowledgement to complex Latin rhythms in his version of the Mexican Consuelo Gonzalez's Besame Mucho, references to the huge Biblical canvas of jazz in his Excerpts from Songs of Proverbs and an intensely moving reading of the songbook ballad originally sung by Johnny Mathis, Two Different Worlds: in musical terms, Byard knew and played hundreds of them.

The second album is called A Matter of Black and White and, like the first, it becomes a narrative of jazz history. There is a Billie Holiday tribute, including God Bless the Child and Lover Man, which radiates her amalgam of triumph and agony, a beautifully lyrical rendition of Byard's own composition, Seasons, and a powerful nod to one of his brilliant contemporaries, Thelonious Monk, in 'Round Midnight. He sounds quasi-orchestral on the ballad Hello Young Lovers and in his honouring of Duke Ellington and Billy Strayhorn in interpretations of Lush Life, Day Dream and Johnny Come Lately, he plays their melodies after a wave-live introduction, as if they have risen from the sea.

The third album is The Late Show, where Byard's introductory remarks before his performances are included, to both comic and educative effect, as his cost-of-living jokes show before he plays his own Family Suite. In his preamble to European Episode he remembers the succession of cities he played 'one-nighters' in before evocative and rumbustious piano portraits of them, and in GEB Piano Roll he uses his reinvented grasp of stride to remember three of his brilliant ex-bandmates who died far too young: bassist George Tucker, altoist Eric Dolphy and trumpeter Booker Little.

He plays an astonishing Byardisation of the old ragtime classic Sweet Georgia Brown and finishes with a preciously subdued version of For All We Know (We Might Never Meet Again). We meet him again on these three records, and to be alone with such an artist for their three hours is to hear a true griot of jazz, one of its great creators but also one of its most vibrant historians. All through these records the story of jazz tells its tales with Byard's brilliance and love. Don't miss them.

(Sunshine of My Soul, A Matter of Black and White & The Late Show are available on High Note)

Don Byron (USA) & Dave Holland (England) - The best of US jazz

Don Byron & Dave Holland Big Band, The Barbican, London (2005)

Some of the most accomplished musicians of the US jazz scene show their chops at a powerful concert at London's Barbican. First on stage is a quartet led by a New Yorker who studied classical clarinet at the New England Conservatory. Yet there is nothing sombre about the jazz of Don Byron. If ever a musician radiated a sense of sheer enjoyment as well as virtuosic artistry about the music he makes, it is him - particularly when he is playing with such astonishingly vivacious confreres as the glorious drum veteran Billy Hart, ex-Jazz Messenger and unique bass stylist Lonnie Plaxico and piano dramatist George Colligan.

In an opening version of Charlie Parker's Donna Lee. Byron takes off for a 10-minute boiling solo, including two spirited howls, before Colligan takes the lead, with Hart stoking up a fire, dropping bombs and clattering his snares. Plaxico embraces a cello-length bass so thin that it resembles a pregnant washing-line pole. Colligan's piano leaps with keyboard shouts of life and elation throughout - particularly on an ebullient Somebody Loves Me where Byron turns to tenor with a spinning solo and Hart's crashing drums next to him, while Plaxico plays what is almost a cello solo in Ray Brown fashion.

As Colligan begins a slow, unaccompanied ballad-like feature, with tender notes, Byron's entry is like ferocious birdsong. Sometimes the only comparison with the strength of his sound is his instrument's first jazz master, Sidney Bechet of New Orleans. Now, happily, we have Don Byron of New York, playing with such verve that you'd that think he could blow London away too.

Dave Holland's 13-piece Big Band has a sound of its own. Piano-less, the vibes and marimbas of Steve Nelson, Holland's bass glory and the pounding drums of Nate Smith give a unique percussive foundation, upon which the 10 horns blow layer upon layer of sound and colour.

Holland's new album Overtime provides much of the concert material - although with slightly different personnel. At the concert, tenorist Mark Turner replaces Chris Potter on the record and drummer Smith replaces Holland regular Billy Kilson. The album itself provides a surging amalgam of multiplex sound and individual artistry and, live, the band comes at your ears like a great engine of beauty. On Last Minute Man, Nelson's opening marimba chords give little hint of what is to come in Duane Eubanks's crackling trumpet chorus, crystalline and soaring like Booker Little of old.

Triple Dance gives baritonist Gary Smulyan his heroic moment as he romps away, earthbound and altoist Antonio Hart starts his solo with a quirky eccentricity before springing upwards, met in a final skybound conversation with Russian Alex Sipiagin's soaring trumpet as the band explodes behind them. Holland's Ario, dedicated to the Brazilian city, is a sumptuous tribute, with altoist Mark Gross emblazoning the passion, desperation and extremes of a city marked by its wealth and criminalising poverty.

But it is the Monterey Suite from the Overtime album that stays with you and reverberates in your ears on the late tube home. In the first movement, it is Turner's quivering tenor then Robin Eubanks's blistering trombone, but, in the second movement Free For All, it is Holland's imperturbable bass. Nelson's long inventive solo and more serpentine licks from Turner's tenor - all grounded by Smith's thunderous drums - that make such a climax. No uncontrolled musical egoism here. No individual bandsman, despite all their brilliance, have more than two solos throughout the performance.

Collective artistry and disciplined virtuosity and some of the music's finest players, led coolly and modestly by a bassist from the Black Country, a Wolverhampton boy spotted at Ronnie Scott's in 1968 by Miles Davis, who is now writing, arranging and playing jewels of the greatest music of the Americas.

Alina Bzhezhinska (Ukraine) and Tony Kofi (Ghana/England)
Eastside Jazz Club, Leytonstone, London
(2025)

It's an extraordinary jazz rendezvous: a Ukrainian harpist and a Ghanaian/British saxophonist from Nottingham, flourishing in a musical tryst in Leytonstone, East London. But Alina Bzhezhinska and Tony Kofi made beautiful harmonies at an ex-centre for British Army veterans, now called the Eastside Jazz Club: guns and bayonets turned into horns and strings, marches and parades into melodies and improvisations.

As I left home to find the bus, on the newsreels Putin's drones were flying and his bombs were falling on Kyiv and right across Ukraine as far as the Polish frontier. But here in Leytonstone these two protean musicians with roots in different continents were playing Whispers of Rain, the title of Alina's new album, sound-poems to her love of the natural world, all of them.

She introduced Kofi as her 'magic man', turning his powers to tenor saxophone, flute, djembe drum and electronics, while her harp with the serpentine flow of her own magic strings, began the performance with some Alice Coltrane tunes and Pharoah Sanders' The Creator has a Master Plan. Kofi's rasping saxophone frequently changed to sheer lyricism as the duo played tracks from Bzhezinska's 2024 album Altera Vita.

It was musical companionship of contrast and compatibility. with Kofi's caustic cadences somehow fusing with the rhapsody of Bzhezinska's mollifying waves of harpsong: oxymorons of intense sonic unity. The audience were enraptured: a full house. They loved this concord and solidarity of sound, so different, it seemed to the world outside: Trump's arrival in London, his egocentric ravings and the U.N. pronouncements on genocide in Gaza. The Autumn air was cooling fast as I walked back through the Hitchcock mosaics in the station underpass to wait for my bus.

Daniel Carter (USA) - An album of pure jazz luminescence
Daniel Carter, Steve Swell, Tom Abbs and David Brandt
– The Transcendentalists: Real Time Messengers
Daniel Carter and Reuben Radding – Luminescence
(2017)

When I was a student of English at Leeds University half a century ago, we studied a course on the 'American Renaissance' in literature of the mid-1900. Among the prescribed oracles of this era were the 'Transcendentalists' - writers from Ralph Waldo Emerson to Henry David Thoreau, and to Herman Melville and Walt Whitman.

I loved their idealism and conviction to humanity; their belief in union; freedom and democracy; their optimism and lack of fear for the future; their faith in the spontaneous and their ambition, as Emerson had put it in almost jazz terms, to 'mount to paradise, by the stairway of surprise,' or as Whitman earnestly declared: 'I will not make poems with reference to parts. But I will make poems, songs, thoughts, with reference to ensemble.' Looking back to those grey Yorkshire days and boozy nights with so few 'leaves of grass' around, I can see now why I loved these writers so much and five decades onwards, how much their words relate to music.

This was a realisation prompted by listening to the powerful improvising album on the CIMP label The Transcendentalists: Real Time Messengers by an astonishing quartet of hornmen, of saxophones, clarinet, flute and trombone and ex-street and subway virtuoso Daniel Carter, born in Wilkinsburg, Pennsylvania, in 1944; free trombonist Steve Swell born in Newark, New Jersey, in 1954, the Seattle-born bassist Tom Abbs and the drummer from Palo Alto, California, Daniel Brandt.

They came together on this album recorded in rural New York state at the Spirit Room studio in February 2002, a few months before the 'shock and awe' in Iraq, with a purpose, as Swell wrote in his sleeve poem to 'stop the violence in real time, feed the hungry in real time, pray for the clarity of thought for all in real time, once and for all, for all time' - quite an intention for an improvising quartet.

The opening track, The Nowness of Pure Potentiality with Swell's growling slides, Carter's keening alto saxophone and Abbs and Brandt in full communion, manifests the American heart of this recording, and Carter's alto full of joyous cadences in The Spirit of Aspirations Beyond has the essence of exultant birdsong. With Brandt's drums are the relentless rhythms of the Long Island surf that Whitman would hear as he wrote his long, tidal lines, composing on the beach. Carter plays some sizzling trumpet in a brass colloquy with Swell's powerful declamations on The Effects of Right Effort and an almost spectral clarinet through The Effects of Selfless Giving - with Abbs's bass pulsating through the Earth. The Final track, The Moment of Being the Sound, is a momentary 16 minutes of improvising testimony that shows that the impetus and truth of the quartet of Emerson, Thoreau, Melville and Whitman still reverberate.

As the label founder Robert D Rusch describes this 21st-century foursome: 'It is the music of possibilities and, for the listener who connects, the realisation of the best of life.' Mutual understanding, the deepest connection and sheer sonic invention and beauty - the transcendentalists would have a recognised an immediate comradeship here.

The Marvellous Carter makes a duo with the Washington DC-born bassist Reuben Radding on the 2001 album Luminescence, recorded in Seattle shortly after the catastrophe of September 11, 2001. Security baggage restrictions meant that Carter could only take his alto on the plane from New York which curtailed his phenomenal multi-instrumentalism. The first track, You And I Are Disappearing, and its successor are slow, with a mournful beauty, perhaps reflecting contemporary events. Carter's naked melodism floats over Radding's deep twang, his buoyant lyricism like a song of love and loss, almost a levitation. In Refracted Light and Grace, Carter swings with suppleness and agility and Radding's sawing bow brings it all back to the real ground.

Carter's alto sometimes reflects the geometric corners of his namesake of an earlier generation, Benny, and in the album's penultimate track, Qualcosa Verso Azzurro, he seems to be climbing Emerson's 'stairway of surprise' in a way that the old transcendentalists could only have dreamed. 'Do not the great always live extempore?' he once mooted, a century before Carter was born. Yet he was anticipating his very American sound and what Radding calls 'the audible light that emanated from within when he played.' Hear it here and savour its pure luminescence.

(The Transcendentalists: Real Time Messengers is available on CIMP and Luminescence is available on AUM Fidelity)

Daniel Carter (USA) – Carter makes his point with a virtuoso display

Zero Point with Daniel Carter

(2017)

The soaring multi-instrumentalism of Daniel Carter, born in Williamsburg, Pennsylvania, in 1944, found a London landfall in Dalston this week with the other much younger members of the quartet Zero Point, guitarist Marius Duboule, bassist Michael Bates and drummer Deric Dickens. This potent meeting of generations, an amalgam of free musical talents, is jelled by the artistry of the veteran Carter, playing only alto sax and piano this time round.

A singularly modest and reticent virtuoso, Carter's long life in music has never sought leadership or limelight bravado. Yet, when you listen to the power and beauty of his notes, you know immediately the extent and originality of his sonic stature, forged over the years with some of the music's most innovative creators, from William Parker to Roy Campbell and Matthew Shipp to Denis Charles.

As soon as he begins to blow, the breath-laden sounds, buoyant and lyrical, and instant, fluid melodies stream from his horn. Above Dickens's sprightly drums and Bates's earthen bass, they grow into a rhapsodic climax then settle back to softness as Duboule's plectrum picks out its scissoring lines.

Before the performance, I ask Carter which instrument he most enjoys playing - saxophone, flute, piano or trumpet? 'I love them all,' he says. 'It's like asking a percussionist which drum in his drum set he likes most. He has the same feeling for them all - every drum, every cymbal. He loves and needs them all in unity.' That's clear when he goes to the piano and caresses its keys gently as Duboule's guitar takes a solo, then he returns to his alto sax, increasing its pace and raising its pitch with some tumbling cadences. What a sound!

Daniel Carter (USA), William Parker (USA) and Matthew Shipp (USA) – Seraphic Light
(2025)

In April 2017 a concert and discussion session was held at Tufts University, Massachusetts, under the title 'Art, Race and Politics in America'. Three of the speakers and musical virtuosi were improvising musicians, Bronx-born bassist William Parker, the pianist from Wilmington Delaware, Matthew Shipp and multi-reedman and trumpeter Daniel Carter from Wilksburg, Pennsylvania. The speaking part of the event done and a strong bond having been created with their listeners, the three veterans turned to their music - a 55 minute three-part suite which they called Seraphic Light, thus integrating discourse, the sonic and the brilliantly visual in one memorable performance.

Carter is an artist of many tongues and played flute, trumpet, clarinet, soprano, alto and tenor saxophones during the trilogy. He begins with a filigreeing preface on flute, with Shipp delving into the concert grand of Tufts' Distler Performance Hall with bold aplomb and Parker plummeting and dancing deep on his throbbing bass. It is as if the palaver between the musicians is still at full pelt, but now the voices are transformed to the free lyricism of their instruments.

Carter turns to his trumpet while Shipp's keys stamp and run beside him, and you remember that this recording was made just four months before the 'Unite the Right' white supremacist and Ku Klux Klan rally in Charlottesville, Virginia, composed of backward bigots referred to by Trump as 'very fine people'. It is as if Carter's prophesying horns, Parker's plunging strings and Shipp's defiantly-struck, passionate piano chimes and audacious keyboard runs are invoking the mass anti-racist opposition counter-protest that hugely outnumbered the supremacists. Whole lives as well as notes and phrases of militant surprise sounded out of this trio's inventiveness that night, every sound a critique of Trumpery and the dehumanising forces it is feeding and unleashing.

At the outset of the second movement, Shipp's piano pace is fleeting, with Carter's tenor like a sonic shadow behind him and Parker's rapid plucking almost subterranean. It is a colloquy that they are having, there in Massachusetts where a ship called the Mayflower found landfall more than four centuries ago, where indigenous peoples were attacked and massacred, their lands seized and captives dispatched to the Caribbean to be exchanged for enslaved and transported Africans. As these three musicians create and improvise, you wonder at the history in their unified notes, and the life-and-death struggles of the past that they express in their sounds, and in now-times too.

There is a beautiful lucidity to Carter's solo alto at the beginning of the last movement, before Shipp's galloping piano and Parker's twanging strings join him. The three of them, all vastly experienced free improvisation troubadours and messengers, play like griots, as if they can predict and foretell every unknown note of each other and how those notes hold the future in the present. For as a listener, you know that this is the only time that they will play exactly like this, with these unique sound-patterns and musical dispatches. All are assertions of the brilliance of their art, their portraiture of black American freedom and their conviction of a better world for us all in the very heart of backwardness.

(Seraphic Light is available on AUM Records)

Tereza Catarov (Bulgaria/Romania)
Koren
(2025)

The Bulgarian/Romanian singer Tereza Catarov sings in the insurgent language of her grandmother: the Bulgarian dialect, Palkensiki. She sings stories of a key, brutal word which summarises the world of women in that language - Nevesta. She explains in her liner notes: 'More than just a term for a bride, it marks a woman's transition into another family, where she renounces her identity and takes her husband's name. From that moment on, she is 'nevesta' - wife, daughter-in-law, sister-in-law, a woman defined in relation to others. The word holds echoes of an archaic mentality, shaping her destiny as subordinate not only to her husband but also to his family.'

When you hear Tereza's voice, how much are you reminded of Bessie Smith, Ma Rainey, Clara Smith, Ida Cox and the great tradition of Southern women blues singers? Her respiring, huskily-lucid voice, accompanied by Yiorgos Bereris' empathetic piano and the echoing reach of Christos Stylianides' trumpet create a gripping Balkan blues-sound which makes you wonder how such music could emerge in parts of Europe where you might have thought jazz was rare. Yet it has, and it has done so with melody, melancholia, defiance and beauty, just as Tereza tells us her beloved grandmother sang it and taught it to her. It shows us, yet again, that the migration of the jazz sound in all its syncretism, is everywhere.

'The idea for Koren began after video calls with my grandmother, an incredible folk-singer who carries hundreds of traditional songs in her memory. She showed me a notebook left by her late mother, filled with lyrics of her favourite songs. She sang a few of them to me, including some she had written herself. I reminded her, captivated by stories of women's struggles - stories I knew, but felt much more deeply through song.' Her words took me back a century to 1927 and Clara Smith's Struggling Woman Blues: 'But I'll keep on struggling, always struggling,/With my heavy load,' sang Clara: 'I may find a happy home, /But far down the road.'

Du-te Dor has Billy Pod's strident drumming and piercing clarinet from Alex Simu with Erdogan Cem Eviv's pure Balkan blues guitar solo, before Tereza comes back for a wordless chorus, while Hadvate is an argument between bride and groom's families over a richly-threaded, golden wedding dress. The bride's wishes count for nothing. 'Koren' means 'root' in Palkensiki, and these are songs of deep folk provenance like those of the Delta blues. Duslo-j vreme tells a story of young, fourteen year old brides compulsorily married to unknown suitors, another narrative of force and oppression.

It's a beautiful album expressing a universal theme, and listening to its sad yet audacious beauty, I wondered what Clara, Bessie, Ma and Ida would have made of it, a hundred years after their own poignant blues-sounds.

(Koren is available on PKmusik)

Neil Charles (England/Grenada) - Dark Days
(2025)

'I took the book everywhere; I became obsessed by Baldwin's words. Travelling between gigs, when I was at home or away, I'd highlight lines and passages. Always in my pocket, I'd refer to it all the time.'

This is bassist Neil Charles talking about James Baldwin's stories Dark Days, now re-created by four prime musicians: pianist Pat Thomas, vocalist Cleveland Watkiss, drummer Mark Sanders and Charles himself. 'Baldwin's sentences start and finish, words like notes - reading it was like I was listening to music. I found so much poignancy in the words, I felt I could almost make a symphony from them.'

Charles was born near Handsworth in Birmingham to an NHS nurse mother and a mechanic father. His boyhood was spent partly in Birmingham, and partly in the Grenadine island of Carriacou, where his parents came from, and where he was first exposed to the percussive intensity of Big Drum, an African heritage passed down directly from Kromantin, Ibo and Mandingo ancestors.' I relate directly to that. That substance is always there, even more so now: so acoustic, so big, so percussive. For me it is always: percussive first! I remember too the Cuckoo and Callaloo Band of guitars in Carria when I was a boy: it was all percussive!'

At secondary school in Birmingham he began on guitar, inspired by an aunt who played 12-bar blues 'with her friend Mr. Kelly from New Orleans'. He was only eight when he first started on double bass. 'I had to stand on a stool or a table to play it!' he told me, 'until they found me a quarter-size bass.' He did well enough though, to later play in regional orchestras and enter Trinity College of Music in Marylebone, London, where he studied and learned classical bass.

After college, he found getting professional work difficult and worked in the HMV Piccadilly record store. 'One night I was very tired and got the Victoria line train in the wrong direction. Instead of going north to Walthamstow, I found myself going south to Brixton. I got off the train there and saw a black man carrying a double bass out of the station. I started talking to him and it was the jazz bassist Gary Crosby. He told me about his young musicians' initiative, Tomorrow's Warriors, so I started going every Wednesday to their sessions in Hackney. That's how I started in jazz.' Serendipity rules again!

'I began to listen to the great jazz bassists - Jimmy Blanton, Wilbur Ware, Charlie Haden, Charles Mingus and especially the tremendous harmonies and rhythm of Ray Brown. Later I played with saxophonist Jason Yarde's much freer band, Acoustastic Bombastic, and rehearsed with the great U.S. tenor saxophonist David Murray. Then Mark Sanders invited me to play a free gig at the Vortex with Pat Thomas and baritone saxophonist Alan Wilkinson.'

The Dark Days quartet are all musicians of commitment, broad experience and consummate skill. I asked Neil for a summary of the special qualities of each of them. 'Pat is an orchestrator, pianist, influencer and groover so deep and powerful. He wastes nothing. All the time he's thinking of his playing, and all the time I'm thinking: wow! Where did that come from?'

'Mark is a creative cooperator, unpredictable and technically brilliant. I remember him telling me when I first played with him: 'How hard do you want to throw a pebble, a stone or a brick to create ripples and find spaces to play within the ripples?' He's so good at hearing what I don't hear. As for Cleveland, he's a storyteller. He'll find another door to walk through as well as the one you're showing him. His voice is like the petals on a stem, each one slightly different to the others.'

Neil says in Dark Days he is striving to forge the balance between the music and the storytelling. What does the music say about the dark days of 1965 compared to now-times, and how different and relevant are the arguments and descriptions Baldwin makes about then compared to the racism, homophobia, misogyny and hard times in Trump's MAGA America? Neil says wait until after the album's first release to see what impact it makes when its true meanings really get inside its listeners: that's when its influence can be more accurately assessed. Will it take long? We shall see.

(Dark Days is available on Jazz Now/Jazz in Britain)

Neil Charles (England/Grenada) - One Caribbean!

Neil Charles Dark Days Quartet - Tribute to James Baldwin, Café Oto, Dalston London (2024)

I remember being immersed in reading the first explosive 100 pages of James Baldwin's epochal novel, Another Country, as I rode on a Greyhound bus to take part in the massive Poor People's Campaign demonstration in Washington DC in July 1968, shortly after the assassination of Martin Luther King.

Baldwin's words about racist oppression and the life and suicide of the jazz drummer, Rufus Scott, were a profound message of their times. So I was determined, now in 2024, to hear Neil Charles's Dark Days Quartet in Dalston's Café Oto, celebrating Baldwin's centenary.

With bassist Charles were vocalist Cleveland Watkiss, drummer Mark Sanders and pianist Pat Thomas, with their heritage in Grenada, Jamaica, Belize and Antigua respectively. How Baldwin would have loved to have known that his works were being remembered in such unity by this pan-Caribbean quartet in the heart of London.

The soulful depth and delving brilliance of Charles's bass; the subtly rampant and mollifying drums, blocks, gong and cymbals of Sanders's artistry and the musical genius of Thomas's ear-breaking keyboard power and sudden blues lyricism gave the most relevant and meaningful soundscape to Baldwin's choric words, sung with Watkiss's time-worn voice with so much now-times purpose. The first words, 'dark days' were repeated, sung, scatted and thundered by Watkiss so intensely and timelessly with Thomas's chords, Charles's plunging strings and Sanders's gong-blows; and the change to Thomas's poignant blues came with the reminder that 'the record is there for all to read/It's certainly not freedom.'

Deep within the notes, words and revolutionary timbre of this superfine quartet, I heard too the Caribbean prophet Maurice Bishop calling out with all his heart and brain: 'One Caribbean!' And walking out into the Dalston night, among the milling cosmos of London people, I imagined him arm-in-arm with Baldwin, and knew again that the liberating words of both men of the 20th-century Americas were unassailably true: for us, true for Gaza and Lebanon too.

Annie Chen (China) - My band are global guardians, determined to protect the environment

Annie Chen – Guardians
(2024)

It's not usual for a jazz album to have a portrait of a jellyfish as its sleeve design, but Beijing-born Annie Chen is a musician who constantly surprises and educates. With her seven-piece cosmopolitan band of musicians from Brazil, Malaysia, Switzerland, Japan and the US she has recorded her Guardians Suite, an impassioned call to love, respect and protect the natural world, that is being assailed and destroyed all around us, so that what were jellyfish are now in reality poisonous plastics polluting the world's seas. The album is an expression of extraordinary cultural cohesion, an amalgam of Polish musical storytelling, Chinese opera, Turkish and Brazilian melody all fused in a jazz spirit of internationalist improvisation, creating a wish that 'our children will grow up sweet and strong and help to make a better world.'

Born in 1983, her father was an English translator, her mother worked in Beijing's Department of Water Resources. She grew up with music: both her parents were classical singers and she learned piano as a child, later entering Beijing's Central Conservatory. 'I also liked jazz and funk!' she says, 'and my father loved jazz and brought back so many records from his business trips between China and the US. Sarah Vaughan's album with Clifford Brown, Carmen McCrae Sings Monk and Betty Carter's Round Midnight album were my first inspirations. I listened to them hundreds of times. And Abbey Lincoln's 'no-fear' spirit of singing was such a big influence - particularly her duos with Max Roach's drums: speechless, amazing! I came to the US in 2010, to New York for a six months jazz study, and then again in 2012 for a jazz performance in Queen's College.'

The album Guardians was provoked by a winter visit to Acadia National Park in Maine. 'It made me think of the damage of climate change and environmental destruction.' When I asked her whether musicians have a responsibility to make music which exposes the jeopardy facing our polluted planet, she exclaimed: 'That's a big YES! As an artist you must send warning messages to your audience. That's the power of art!'

She is proud to be working with such a cosmopolitan group of musicians. 'With our different backgrounds and sounds I try to make my compositions have unique colours. My band are global guardians, determined to protect the environment.' Japanese percussionist Satoshi Takeshi 'has explosive energy and artistic taste'; Swiss-French guitarist Marius Duboule creates 'exciting arrangements and emotional, sensitive expression in his playing'; Malaysian violinist Fung Chern Hwei 'expresses a deep and energetic understanding of Chinese traditional culture'; US flutist and saxophonist Alex LoRe's playing 'is as agile and breathy as a fox - flexible, rational and passionate simultaneously'; Brazilian Vitor Goncalves is 'so beautiful, dreamy and melodic on piano and accordion and bassist Mathew Muntz also plays the meh, a Croatian bagpipe.' When I asked her whether she thought her album has had an impact, making her listeners think more deeply and actively, she says: 'Yes, I do think so! In China too!'

And why make the jellyfish a symbol of environmental guardianship? 'Jellyfish are one of my favourite ocean species. I wanted to use their image, pictorially and in sound, to warn the people, like I do in my lyrics: 'Tell me, where do I live and stay?' You can see this jellyfish has some brown, reddish part. That means they're very depressed, bleeding and dying with all the white plastic bags polluting the ocean. Many listeners have told me the story has impressed them.'

She thinks the suite's second movement, dedicated to whales, is the album's most powerful section, along with the opener Rozpacz (Despair), written by the Polish jazz composer, Zbigniew Namyslowski. It is an essential part of her universal sonic vision that Rozpacz connects to the Beijing classical opera Farewell My Concubine, where a king is surrounded by his enemies, like humanity of now-times is besieged by possible environmental catastrophe.

That such connections can be made are a message of the wondrous syncretism of jazz, conjured by a Chinese woman singing in the heart of New York. As her voice rings out, prophetic and shamanic: 'Under the world, the bridge to the sky was broken/ There's a tearing bloodless moon, hanging where the ocean died/ Holding shadows of my end, losing light of the land.'

(Guardians is available on JZ Music)

Gerald Cleaver (USA), William Parker (USA) and Craig Taborn (USA) – Harvesting sounds of Earth's beauty

Farmers by Nature & Out of This World's Distortions (2013)

'Farmers by nature,' they call themselves, forging furrows of notes, sowing seeds of outrageous harmony, harvesting the sounds of improvised brilliance - quite a threesome of jazz virtuosity. From the earth of their first album its title became the trio's baptismal name on their second, as if the magic itself comes before everything and writes out its makers' life-giving function and name - as, of course, it does.

Gerald Cleaver is a drummer of Detroit born in 1963, and a University of Michigan companion of the pianist Craig Taborn, born in Minneapolis in 1970 with a youth also spent in Motown and a keyboard collaborator with some of his era's great horns, beginning with multi-reedman James Carter in the mid-'90s. And finally the nonpareil of contemporary bass, William Parker, born in 1952 in the Bronx and featured on hundreds of recorded sessions since the '70s, truly one of jazz's great heartbeats.

These are the farmers and their sonic agriculture is produced by three equals of the soil of sound. There are no mere 'accompanists' here, neither bass nor drums are being led by a star pianist or take any lesser role than the piano in the making of the music. Although it was Cleaver who convened the trio, co-operation is all and as the sessions progress it is clear that leadership is in a constant process of enactment, exchange, initiative and integration, taking and giving in a continuous threefold act of creation and surprise.

The first eponymous album was recorded live at The Stone in New York City in June 2008. You can hear every iota of sound from the off, every jot. The texture and echo of a real venue, the muttering, the whispers, the taps, the human clues, the timbre of musical message and witness in every second. The pluck of the deep strings, the tap and strike of keys, skin and metal in sheer discovery of every succeeding note.

Taborn's hard chords pace through The Night shadowed by Parker's beating blood and Cleaver's relentless flickering blows, until the track segues into the almost 17 minutes of Cranes, where Parker's bow jerks out another sonic pattern of worrisome and dark birdsong and Taborn's atonal steps move forward to sunder oblivion. It is sheer improvisation of resonating power and invention, which when the pace quickens with Taborn's sudden break it is as if these birds have become fugitives.

In organic sequence, the following track Not Unlike Number 10 is born from the levitating sound of Cranes, with Cleaver's fluttering clicks stemming from the pecking of birds across dried earth. Taborn's keyboard runs are mesmeric above Parker's humming bass and as Cleaver's sticks clash and boom on his drums the orchestra of nature comes alive through three master improvisers, and their farm becomes untamed again with what is cultivated lost to a wild freedom as the notes reach out and up again to the succeeding track In Trees.

Out of This World's Distortions came two years later, this time in a Brooklyn studio setting, with the trio in Cleaver's sleeve words 'bearing witness to certain very specific, essential truths that can be spoken of in an infinite number of ways and sounded in an amazingly singular way.' A part of that truth is how the Earth still rises 'magnificent, graceful, elegant' from all the 'gross, horrific, dreadful evil' that the world visits upon it. This is the trio's tribute to that profound 'indomitableness of Earth,' through their own never-ending, always-open, always improvising music. And it begins with a tribute to the mighty Chicago saxophonist and musical organiser Fred Anderson, ever a ploughman of the undiscovered note. Parker's quivering, mourning bow is hugely beautiful, beside Taborn's spacious chords.

The full title of the album's lead track is Out of This World's Distortions Grow Aspens and Other Beautiful Things, true words matched with the truest of sounds with Parker's fleeting fingers plucking such messages of faith and optimism. The satirical edge of Sir Snacktray Speaks seems to be these farmers' lampoon of all which threatens their sustenance. Cleaver's slashing snares are to the fore. Its antithesis is Mud, Mapped, sounding moist within the resourceful earth through Cleaver's repeated grounding rhythm and the astonishing high pitch of Parker's shimmering strings.

Jazz and the Earth's continuing fullness, calibrated together in this extraordinary album.

(Farmers by Nature & Out of This World's Distortions are available on AUM)

Chris Laurence (England), bassist and bandmate of saxophonist Tony Coe (England)

The Buds of Time and Les Voix d'Itxassou (2025)

'With Tony there was no dividing line between any genre of music. He loved jazz, he loved the classics. He proved in The Buds of Time that the twain could always meet.'

These words, about the unique artistry of saxophonist, clarinetist and composer Canterbury-born Tony Coe (1934 - 2023), are those of his longtime bandmate Chris Laurence - himself an eminent jazz and classical music bassist, who played with Coe on the 1979 recording of The Buds of Time (co-written by Robert Cornford who had been taught by Vaughan Williams and collaborated with Benjamin Britten), now at last released on the Jazz in Britain label.

Coe was an astonishingly protean musician who had been a featured soloist with post-war British jazz maestros like Johnny Dankworth and Humphrey Lyttelton, played in the Kenny Clarke/Francy Boland Orchestra, and blew the tenor sax theme melody of Henry Mancini's The Pink Panther. Laurence remembers Coe playing snatches of Debussy and Ravel on his clarinet as they drove between gigs in Germany. 'He was fanatical about the clarinet and would only play clarinets made of boxwood. He was always experimenting and drilled extra holes in them and drove the repairers mad!'

The Buds of Time features his brilliant improvising clarinet in a seven-piece ensemble. 'It's a prime example of mixing and blending jazz and the classics,' said Laurence. 'With Tony and Bob Cornford, it seemed like an easy fit. It worked a treat.'

With The Buds' theme of growth and potential its sound radiates the future: 'Listening to it now, it's full of optimism, like a gradual, developing growth - you can see and feel the buds eventually blossoming, becoming flowers, coming to fruition, lifting people up. That was how Tony saw music.'

Laurence also played on a startling Coe album of 1990, Les Voix d'Itxassou, named after a Basque village in the French Pyrenees, one of the true glories of internationalist jazz. Coe brought together outstanding instrumentalists like Australian altoist Ray Warleigh, British trombonist Malcolm Griffiths, Malian guitarist Ali Farka Toure with singers Dominic Behan, Maggie Bell, Marianne Faithfull. Aura Msang-Lewis and Violeta Ferrer to perform songs of freedom from Palestine, the Spanish Civil War, South Africa, the Irish struggle and Cuba, to sing Bella Ciao, Nkosi Sikelel'i Afrika, The Patriot Game, Hasta Siempre Comandante, Wounded Knee and Buenaventuri Durruti: it was like the whole struggling world on one single record.

Coe's orchestrations, the soloists' eloquence and the singers' multilingual words are beautifully and cogently wrapped in cosmopolitanism and freedom, very close to the spirit of the Charlie Haden/Carla Bley albums of the Liberation Music Orchestra.

Laurence remembers Coe telling him: 'Music frees people! I want people to be free!' He said that Coe had rented a flat in Paris, near the Bastille, and the album's opening and closing tune is a song of the Paris Commune, Le Temps des Cerises. For Laurence, making the recording in the now demolished London Lansdowne studios was 'exciting and beautiful. Anything Tony did had meaning. He found the right musicians to play and sing together all through the album.' Laurence remembered well Buenaventura Durruti when I asked him about particular tracks. 'Beautiful, it's beautiful! Full of excitement!' he exclaimed.

And what was his summation of Coe's artistry? 'As a musician he was a total individual, a one-off. A great saxophonist, of course, but on clarinet he was a master, the greatest clarinetist I ever played with. He was never a clone of anyone. He only had to play a few notes and almost straight away you recognised his sound, you knew for certain it was him. He had all the musical skills while being free as a bird.'

(The Buds of Time is available on Jazz in Britain and Les Voix d'Itxassou on NATO Records)

Xhosa Cole (England)/Liberty Styles (USA)
On A Modern Genius: Vol.1
(2025)

Thelonious Monk (1917 - 82) in Birmingham, England: that's the arrival of the brilliantly original interpretation of the master's music, On a Modern Genius: Vol. 1.

The instigator is the young Birmingham saxophonist Xhosa Cole, who first became 'infatuated' by Monk's music as a youth, at a workshop run by the pianist Hans Koller. 'I heard Monk's tunes Played Twice, then Reflections, Criss Cross and I Mean You, and I was hugely impressed by his care, divergence and sense of melody in his composing, and the architecture of his music. From my earliest musical beginnings, pianist Monk and saxophonist Sonny Rollins became my pillars.'

And the album radiates sparkling music too from his bandmates. 'Guitarist Steve Saunders is a dedicated musician - his playing is full of accuracy; bassist Josh Vadiveloo has an inherently musical instrumental voice, he understands exactly how it all fits together, and Nathan England-Jones is a brilliantly supportive drummer. It's like a homecoming every time we play together.'

'Liberty Styles' tap dancing has exactly the same language as the other players, fitting with Monk's own percussive piano approach. It's like playing with another drummer.'

And why does he include Ellington's great anthem, Come Sunday, as the album's finale? 'I had to include it after I heard Heidi Vogel singing it beautifully at the Proms. Ellington was a parallel genius to Monk, a complementary, yet also a counterpoint.'

Why does he think that Monk's music is so vital for our times? ' It persuades us to look inwardly at our own shortcomings,' he told me, 'as we try to find internal peace during these times of turbulence, and our own directions.'

Certainly the album does that with a tremendous unity and zest. The bass, tap and drums' exchanges, bouncing and clattering alongside Xhosa's fleeting horn and Saunders' felicitous guitar on Trinkle Tinkle and Rhythm-a-

Ning, prompts the closest of listening and makes the listener long to see the dance, while the call-and-response structure of Criss Cross, followed by Liberty's drumming feet in full duet with Xhosa's tenor saxophone, prefaces a moving saxophone sequence on Round Midnight and the rapping tap solo at the outset of Bright Mississippi.

I asked Liberty about her own musical life. Born in 1993 in rural Massachusetts, her Mum a social worker, her Dad a journalist, growing up she was much influenced by local grunge and new wave bands. 'I listened to a lot of flamenco and blues as a teenager, and became a flamenco dancer. I played drums in a high school garage band and started tap dancing at 19, when I moved to New York City.'

'I remember loving Monk's music in college - Ruby My Dear and Monk's Dream. I danced to these over and over again - Monk taught me a lot about improvisation. I love how his music is so sophisticated, yet it doesn't take itself too seriously - there's a real sense of humour in his music and phrasing. His accents, the way his body moves, the silences he leaves in. I love the way his music listens.'

I asked her how she sees tap as an expression of musical artistry. 'First and foremost I see it as an instrument, but not exactly the same as a drumkit. It can be super-melodic and other times functional as a percussive section. It brings a fresh physical and visual energy into the music and its rhythms are simultaneously heard AND seen, which is why I love tap dance as a dance form.'

And what about jazz as a form of cultural resistance, as it has always been. 'In jazz, our voices, instruments and bodies are the tools of storytelling. As a gender non-conforming woman living in a Trump America, I can definitely say that it is a very deep thing to be able to use my body to express myself in the moment, be seen, heard (and perhaps even be understood) by people.'

'To be able to communicate with others through music is a radical thing to do. The language of jazz is a code for what it means to be alive. In these times it serves us to be even more explicit about these implied meanings about who we are and what kind of present and future our music is fighting for. I want to be a part of creating a more gender-inclusive and anti-racist world through the music I make.'

Amen, Liberty! Amen, Xhosa! Amen, Ellington! Amen, Monk!

(On A Modern Genius: Vol.1 is available on Stoney Lane Records)

Ornette Coleman - Still flying after all these years

Ornette Coleman, Barbican, London

(2001)

Tomorrow is the Question, the Shape of Jazz To Come, the Change of the Century – these were titles of the albums that burst across the jazz landscape in the last years of the 1950s. They featured the pianoless quartet of an audaciously original ex-rhythm and blues alto saxophonist from Fort Worth, Texas, who played a plastic instrument - Ornette Coleman.

There had been nothing like Coleman's sound before in jazz. He called it 'harmolodics' - a word which collapsed harmony, melody and rhythm into one neologism. His music was condemned and applauded with equal fervour. On one famous occasion in New York, he was paid not to play! But his musical influence has been profound and deeply innovatory and, at the age of 70, he is back for the first time in five years, playing at the Barbican.

Coleman's old musical comrades, such as Charlie Haden. Don Cherry, Ed Blackwell, Billy Higgins and Charles Moffett, still speak through his horn but his present trio manifest a different brilliance of generations. The drummer is his son Denardo, who has been playing and recording with his father for 30 years. Denardo's deftness and speed of movement is astonishing. He can rap the blocks like Baby Dodds, while moving lightly through his own drum and cymbal universe with the touch of Tony Willams.

The bassist Charnett Moffett is the son of Charles who was one of Ornette's old drummers. His strings quiver with excitement, exuding a rhythmic tension compounded by his dynamic bow work, by turns drawing out powerful, long mellow notes and striking the strings with the back of the bow, rapping out sharp percussive phrases.

As for Ornette, his playing still sings with a haunting beauty above the rhythms. He plays a series of unannounced separate pieces, with some soaked in the blues and others lyrical like birdsong. His melodic lucidity remains as sharp as ever, with soaring crescendos billowing skywards as free as wings. As he begins each selection with unaccompanied flights of notes. Denardo and Charnett. positioned behind him, stare at each other, bending as if at the starting blocks, signalling with their eyes, crouched backs behind their drums and bass strings for their point of entry into the bluesy purity of Ornette's notes.

In the programme notes, Coleman is quoted as saying: 'When I finished high school and I went down to college to enrol. I saw these little black kids that was on welfare. One thing that 1 remember in my growing up was that I was always hungry. I started playing the saxophone to eat. When I grew up, I realised that I wasn't growing up to beat anyone up or change or be different. I was trying to grow up so I could live the way I liked to believe.'

Keats would have heard the beauty and truth of this black Texan's bird-like song from a white alto saxophone. And so would Africa too. For, when Coleman toured Portugal in the '60s with his quartet, they defied the right-wing government at a concert in Lisbon, by dedicating their music to the liberation fighters of the MPLA in Angola, FRELIMO in Mozambique and the PAIGC in Guinea-Bissau.

And Ornette's internationalism still thrives in his cosmopolitan performances. At the Barbican, he performs with classical singer Silvie Jenson. He declares: 'What she was singing was exactly what we was playing.'

As his alto weaves in and out of Jenson's strident, piercing, beautiful sound, you can see what he means. But the world plays on the stage with Ornette's Global Expressions. Indian classical singer Prabhakar Karekar, Pakistani tabla virtuoso Badal Roy and the Chinese erhu player Guowei Wang, all join the trio later in the programme.

Coleman's music forges a universal note and. in his solos, throughout the performance. you could hear the history of US music and that of many other places too. Listening carefully, you can hear snatches of melodies from We Shall Not Be Moved. Let's Fall In Love, My Old Kentucky Home to London Bridge, Pease Pudding Hot and Greensleeves.

What a journey he has taken. In the '50s and '60s, many jazz people complained that his music was so avant-garde as to be incomprehensible and meaningless. Yet he has always played his saxophone for the world – and all its people and their meanings and he is still doing it, for all those that want to hear.

Ornette Coleman (USA) - The shaper of jazz to come

Ornette Coleman: The Territory and the Adventure by Maria Golia (2021)

'How do you try to turn emotion into knowledge? That's what I try to do with my horn.' Thus was the testimony of the revolutionary alto saxophonist Ornette Coleman.

He was born in Fort Worth, Texas, in 1930, and the titles of his early albums reveal his intentions and musical trajectory: Change of the Century, The Shape of Jazz to Come, Tomorrow Is the Question, Free Jazz. These were epochal recordings with fellow musical subversives such as trumpeter Don Cherry, bassist Charlie Haden, drummers Billy Higgins and Ed Blackwell.

In New York in 1959 they set pre-existing jazz patterns on fire and provoked both vituperation and admiration. 'Ornette's music was conceived to hit you right between the eyes,' declared trumpeter Bobby Bradford, while John Coltrane exclaimed: 'Well, that must be the answer!' after hearing Ornette's quartet at the Five Spot venue.

Maria Golia's book describes the Ornette phenomenon with insight and eloquence. It's laden with musical and social insights, and she is particularly strong in her finely written first section. She describes Ornette's early years in Hillside, a poor black neighbourhood in segregated Fort Worth, a 'hardscrabble town' where he grew to musicianship within a musical church-going family. His father was a mechanic, his mother a hotel maid and his elder sister Truvenza sang the blues. Golia tells how Ornette's early musical years in the 1950s were spent around New Orleans and Baton Rouge, where a group of Jim Crow listeners beat him and mashed up his saxophone, and later Los Angeles, where he befriended the great tenor saxophonist Sonny Rollins. They would play duets on the Pacific shoreline, with the pounding waves as their rhythm section.

The author provides an acute analysis of the sources of Coleman's 'harmolodics,' the structure of musical and social-cultural ideas that drove his sound. 'There are as many unisons as there are stars in the sky,' he said, and dreamed, in music as in life, of everyone in the world singing and all of those voices getting together in unison.

Golia describes Coleman's time in Morocco in 1972 and his meeting with the musicians of the Joujouka community, who inspired him for the rest of his life: 'The voices of the individual and the collective were so closely bound, they could scarcely be told apart,' she writes. That's exactly how I remember the last time I heard Coleman, accompanying the Joujouka virtuosi with his saxophone, trumpet and violin at the Royal Festival Hall in 2009. 'I don't try to please when I play,' he asserted. 'I try to cure.' He was uncompromising about releasing the power of music: 'Sound is as free as the gas that passes through your gut,' he insisted. 'In music, the only requirement is for it to be heard.'

Yet in her final chapter Golia tells how Coleman's city, a decade after his death, has been appropriated by some of the most backward figures of the Trump era, entirely contrary to everything about his message. The Fort Worth-based Bass family, whose oil and gas fortunes made them one of the richest and most powerful in America, sold their interests to ex-secretary of state Rex Tillerson, CEO of Exxon Oil, with Steve Bannon manager of their downtown properties.

Coleman's insurgent and prophetic notes still signal and forewarn of the best and worst of America and 90 years after his birth, the sound of that truth still lives on. Play the Tomorrow Is the Question album to remind yourself of it.

(The Territory and the Adventure by Maria Golia is published by Reaktion Books)

John Coltrane (USA) - Rediscovered 1963 recordings a revelatory treasure from a momentous year

John Coltrane - Both Directions at Once: The Lost Album (2021)

At the beginning of March in 1963 the John Coltrane Quartet - Coltrane on soprano and tenor sax, McCoy Tyner on piano, Jimmy Garrison playing bass and Elvin Jones on drums - recorded 14 tracks in New Jersey. Unknown and unissued for 55 years, and only existing on a reference tape Coltrane brought home from the studio before he left to play an evening session at the Birdland jazz club in Manhattan, those tracks were recorded at a momentous time.

This was the year of the Kennedy assassination and also when the civil rights resistance was boiling in the US south, particularly in Birmingham, Alabama, and in August 250,000 people marched on Washington. Eighteen days later, Birmingham's Sixteenth Street Baptist Church was bombed by racists and four girls were killed as they changed into their choir robes. The

Coltrane Quartet responded with the memorial Alabama as part of their Live at Birdland album. Throughout that March 'lost' session, there's a sense of social and musical ferment. Fellow tenor saxophonist Wayne Shorter remembers Coltrane describing this inner tumult as 'starting a sentence in the middle and then going to the beginning and the end of it at the same time ... both directions at once.'

His soprano saxophone surges on opener Untitled Original 11383 before Garrison's inspired solo, first with his bow, then with his fingers. Tyner lays out on piano, with Jones's drums ascendant on Nature Boy and, through Untitled Original 11386, Coltrane's soprano dances and leaps, his notes blithe and full of felicitous life, impacting on Tyner's sweeping solo. Coltrane seizes the melody of Franz Lehar's Vilia from the operetta The Merry Widow and transforms it into an unlikely frolic of black freedom, with Elvin's drums buoyant with joy. Slow Blues is a reflective and cogent essay, with the quartet in powerful accord with every phrase of Coltrane's restless horn. What is in his head as his saxophone reaches out? Is it Birmingham or the campaign against police brutality in Albany, Georgia? Or is it the words of Martin Luther King? 'We must rise above our fears. There is nothing to be afraid of if you believe and know that the cause for which you stand is right.' Those words and their context resonate through 'Trane's sound.

One Up, One Down has a walking bass solo by Garrison and Jones's crashing drums alongside Coltrane's rampaging tenor and there are four different takes of the classic Coltrane opus Impressions, each one seething with its life and times and the second take especially animated. Coltrane sounds low-down and very bluesy and guttural on take six of One Up, One Down, which concludes this double album, undertaking an earnest drums-horn colloquy with Elvin before Tyner comes in for a sprinting solo. Beneath it all pounds the eternity of Garrison's pulsating bass heartbeat - an ending which has no end.

Any retrieval of the music of John Coltrane's greatest quartet is a precious find. His tenor saxophone contemporary Sonny Rollins likened the discovery of these recordings to 'finding a new room in the Great Pyramid.' Quite a hyperbole, perhaps, but not for old jazz-geezers like me.

(Both Directions at Once: The Lost Album is available on Impulse!)

Ray Draper (USA) - Capacity for artistry and sheer beauty

The Complete Ray Draper Quintet Sessions with John Coltrane (2015)

The tuba has not been a common component of the jazz soundscape, but there have been some remarkable virtuosi of the instrument who have gone far beyond the sonic ballast effect which has frequently been its role in marching bands and brass ensembles. Its capacity for artistry and sheer beauty has been shown by musicians from Howard Johnson - who led a tuba-emphatic band called Gravity, recording two throbbing albums for the Verve label in the 1990s, Right Now and Gravity - to Bob Stewart, who held the tuba chair in Lester Bowie's band, Brass Fantasy. In Britain too, tuba specialists George Smith and Andy Grappy have made powerful contributions to Mike Westbrook albums like Marching Song (1969) and Westbrook-Rossini (1986), and the outstanding Orel Marshall is a former key brass element of the contemporary quartet Sons of Kemet, who now have the rampaging Theon Cross as their tuba dynamo.

But there has been no-one else like Ray Draper, born in New York in 1940 and a graduate of the Manhattan School of Music, who was the truly pioneering bop exponent of the tuba and who played and recorded with some of the stellar pathfinders of his time from Max Roach and Jackie McLean to Donald Byrd and Archie Shepp. He also made two albums in 1957 and 1958 when he was still a teenager, with the mighty John Coltrane, and these have been brought together in a marvellous 'twofer' on the Acrobat label.

The first was called The Ray Draper Quintet featuring John Coltrane, and with them were pianist Gil Coggins, bassist Jimmy 'Spanky' DeBrest with Larry Ritchie on drums, and as soon as the opener, Draper's own Clifford Kappa, gets into its mettle with Coltrane striding over the rhythm with his tidal sound, you know this is going to be an exceptional session. Draper's sonorous wind is also agile and spry, the weight of his sound belying its nimbleness. Filidia, another Draper composition, shows Ritchie's drum prowess before Coltrane's tenor steams into motion with beautiful authority before Draper's rocking solo, blowing tumbling cadences, levitates over DeBrest's earthy bass and Coggins's angular solo. Two Sons makes a trio of consecutive Draper tunes and Coggins's leaping notes are a prelude to a lithe, vaulting chorus. Can a tuba skip and frolic? Draper's can, out of and then back into the depths of sound with prodigious skill. Sonny Rollins, clearly a Draper favourite, wrote Paul's Pal and the fivesome lap it up lovingly with Coggins leading the way before Coltrane's horn sprays its notes all over Rudy Van Gelder's New Jersey studio and Draper huffs and swings in delight, as he does too on Under Paris Skies, prefacing a solo with Coltrane in awesome power.

In November 1958 the same quintet (with John Mayer replacing Coggins) were back recording another album, Ray Draper: A Tuba Jazz, which begins with another Draper tune, Essii's Dance, in which he sounds even more assured and endlessly inventive, inspiring the inspiration as Coltrane soars into new skies of beauty. Their living breath of innovation blows through the side-by-side Rollins anthems, Doxy and Oleo. An unlikely foray into Lerner and Loewe's ballad I Talk to the Trees, and two more American Songbook items, Yesterdays and Angel Eyes, transform the mood. Draper's huge horn sounds almost winsome before Coltrane's tenor glory, making unsung words take on a new melodic serenity.

Draper's vast talent never really prospered. He was jailed on drugs charges in the late 1960s but later beat his addiction and made a living playing fusion (including with Jimi Hendrix) before being killed by a 13-year-old mugger on a New York street in 1982. Another jazz tragedy among many more of his generation. So I give a thousand thanks for recording studios and the jewels they made, like this one.

(The Complete Ray Draper Quintet Sessions with John Coltrane is available on Acrobat)

The Cookers (USA) - Luminous sounds from seven prolific warriors of jazz

The Cookers – Warriors
(2015)

What a band! The pick of the post-bop brilliance, all of the septet are leaders in their own right and veterans of many a prime session. 'The Cookers' is right: their sound is the food of jazz tastiness from many a context over the past five decades. For between them are over 250 years of luminous musicianship and more than 1,000 recordings.

First the horns: Billy Harper, born in Houston in 1943, he arrived in The Apple with his tenor in 1966, found work with Art Blakey, Max Roach and Gil Evans and soon became famed for his harsh, gospel-rooted Texan sound. His long-time bandmate, the crackling Eddie Henderson (born 1940), combines his trumpet power with psychiatry and owes his birth on the horn to a stay Miles Davis made at his parents' house in the 1950s, and much of his early exposure to his work with the Herbie Hancock Sextet of the early 1970s. Then Craig Handy of Oakland, CA, who plays alto saxophone and flute on this album. Another Blakey Jazz messenger alumnus and ex-bandmate of Roy Haynes, Elvin Jones and Abdullah Ibrahim, I remember him playing with Freddie Hubbard's last band to tour England in 1997, alongside New Yorker David Weiss who did most of the arranging for that band and who has also achieved a remarkable amalgam by assembling The Cookers.

The pianist is George Cables, born in 1944 in Brooklyn, a superb solo and trio performer, but who was also renowned for his accompanying some of the great saxophonists from Sonny Rollins and Joe Henderson to Art Pepper and Dexter Gordon. On bass is Cecil McBee, born in Tulsa, Oklahoma in 1935, his beat as delving and authoritative as any in jazz, and an anchor of bands led by Jackie McLean, Wayne Shorter, Charles Lloyd and Yusef Lateef. And finally, the consummate drummer born in Washington DC in 1940, Billy Hart, a part of the sound of fellow masters from Jimmy Smith, Wes Montgomery and McCoy Tyner. All together, quite a sevensome. And this is how Weiss characterises them and their records: 'This CD is called 'Warriors' because this is how I look at these great men. They came up at a time when this music was at its most vital and exciting and was part of something epic and historic yet they are still going strong with the same freedom, passion and intensity.'

The earthy riff which begins the opener, Hubbard's opus The Core, leads into some forceful Henderson before Harper's carping chorus tears up the theme. Weiss is more burnished for his solo and Cables sprints through his notes, along spirited sonic pathways before Hart's crashing drums lead into the denouement. Spookerella is a Cables tune, an outing for the birdsong of Handy's keening flute and the composer's own weaving keys. Close To You Alone is a ballad by McBee - all these musicians are skilled tune-writers too - lent to Handy's tender alto, and blown with a strongly gentle lyricism.

Harper wrote Priestess for a 1977 Gil Evans orchestral album of the same name. The track lasted for 20 minutes and featured saxophone solos by Arthur Blythe and David Sanborn. This time it is Harper himself, fiercely beautiful in full Texan mettle, and Handy's alto adds its own gentle lyricism. Her Soul is Cables's waltz from his Sweet Rita Suite, featuring Handy's flute before Henderson enters with piercing, transcendent phrases and Cables guides Handy back to the serenity of his theme. In 1973 Harper led his first solo album session for the independent Strata East label, Capra Black. He reprises the title theme here with a long, gutteral chorus of excitation riding over the other horns, his sound roaring for freedom. Weiss reaches skyward with a crystalline eloquence and Cables's solo notes leap and dance from his keys, propelled by Hart's springing skins.

The final two tunes are McBee's own. Ladybugg is Henderson's track, his muted horn full of the blues, aching and resonant, followed by the composer's cavernous twang. The more upbeat U Phoria has a testifying chorus from an earnest Harper, Cables scuttling through his solo with improvising fire and Hart's drums pounding these formidable warriors' album to a final, and hopefully temporary, jazz peace.

(Warriors is available on JLP)

Paul Cornish (USA)
You're Exaggerating
(2025)

Houston, Texas has produced a succession of the finest contemporary jazz pianists: Jason Moran, Robert Glasper and now the prodigious Paul Cornish. I interviewed him the morning after his resonant performance at Ronnie Scott's, a launch for his new Blue Note album: 'You're Exaggerating'.

Born in 1996, he grew up in a Christian home, and despite his childhood love for the drums, his mother steered him towards the piano, starting lessons at five. His older brothers became professional musicians while Paul attended Houston's High School for the Performing and Visual Arts. where its Director, Dr. Henry Morgan, had tutored both Moran and Glasper and created an enduring musical ambiance. Moving to Los Angeles, he met and formed lasting musical unions with bassist and drummer on his album, Joshua Crumbly and Jonathan Pinson - 'my ying and yang. I just feed off their artistry' - and his bassist at Ronnie's, Logan Kane, a fellow freshman at college and 'an incredible creative genius; there's nothing he can't play.'

Hearing Paul play a stirring version of Coltrane's Giant Steps at Ronnie's, it was soon obvious of his loving attachment to the jazz tradition, but his own composition Queen Geri showed what a huge exemplar the late Detroit pianist Geri Allen is to him. 'She had an unlimited imagination and I wish I could tell her now, 'everything I'm trying to do. you're already doing it!' Listening to her has given me the courage to be the best that I can be and never to be scared of going forward.'

On the album he plays the tune with a galloping speed and gusto, as if he were trying to catch up with Geri's genius, but at Ronnie's his version was much closer to elegy with Californian drummer Savannah Harris playing with a hushed quietude on her cymbals, as if the trio were playing a mellow folk song. Then suddenly the melody of 'Misty' emerges, beautifully, almost mysteriously. 'Geri was researching the music of 'Misty's' composer, the great Erroll Garner, shortly before she died, and Savannah would play it with her.' As the melody develops, there is a seemingly subconscious, deeply moving union between Harris and Cornish, almost as if they are sharing Geri's soulfulness.

I asked him how the murder of George Floyd, another Houston man, had affected him and his musical colleagues. 'It was very heavy,' he said thoughtfully. 'It's continuous and has been for a long time, black men the victims of police brutality. Each generation has their own set of challenges and they have to decide how they're going to rise up. It's a privilege to be an artist and find a way to combat the obstacles that confront us - to add to the empowerment and encourage our generation like the musicians that came before us: Nina Simone, Max Roach, Charles Mingus.'

I asked him what it was like for him to perform at Ronnie Scott's, where so many of the great U.S. musicians of the jazz century had performed. 'These were people who gave their lives to the music. The venue itself speaks to the music's power.'

His album has many engaging and original compositions, all written by Cornish. In the very percussive Queinxiety it is as if within the trio there are three drummers drumming, while in Star is Born the mutual anticipation of each trio member makes it seem as if one whole, unified musician is playing three instruments in one. The heavy-stepping Dinosaur Song portrays some being even weightier and more dire and desperate than even the notes can take - is it Trump, or Vance, or Musk? As for the album title, Paul described it as 'a quote from myself to myself. It's an invitation to question so much of what is in front of us and to ask myself, 'What is real? Where is the truth? Where is the humanity?''

His music, like the form of every fine artist, asks these questions. I hope he's back in England again soon, so we can listen to him asking them again.

(You're Exaggerating is available on Blue Note Records)

Chris Corsano (USA) - Drumming of some consequence
Chris Corsano, Café Oto, Dalston, London
(2022)

The touring US improvising drummer Chris Corsano, born in Englewood, New Jersey in 1975, played a quartet of gigs at the Café Oto in Dalston, with several groups of outstanding British-based musicians. His performance with Evan Parker, John Edwards and Pat Thomas was a sonic cauldron.

Every note from Thomas's piano was like a separate droplet of lucid rain, combining into a timbral cataract, while Corsano's lean torso and shaven head leaned into his drums, becoming his own multiplicities by turns of thunderous, gentle and always subtle sounds.

Edwards' bass throbbed into deep tunnels of sound as he danced with its seemingly living body, his bow fostering periods of dark quietude, while Parker's tenor saxophone made universal hornsound like musical memory, as you heard echoes of the past masters in his every note, from Coleman Hawkins to Sonny Rollins, from Coltrane to Ornette. It was as if their notes were all spilling from his horn.

The next night it was Corsano, Edwards and the alto saxophone of Caroline Kraabel and the heaving breathiness of her sound, its squawks, squalls and groans fused with her wordless vocal chuntering, filling this one Dalston chamber like the sounds of tomorrow already heard tonight, with Corsano the sorcerer of percussion and Edwards' heart of strings setting all ears afire.

Gustavo Cortinas (Mexico/Uruguay) - The Crisis Knows No Borders
(2025)

This record's illuminating message is in its title, The Crisis Knows No Borders, created by a quartet of superfine musicians with provenances in Mexico, Uruguay, the Philippines and across the USA via the birthplace of jazz, New Orleans, where the foursome's instigator studied music, at Loyola University. As in Max Roach's epochal 1960 album of Civil Rights, We Insist!, the album's sleeve illustration by Honduran artist Alexy Lanza, depicts its theme with a signal brilliance - a mass demonstration for life, water, the earth and the best use of our natural resources. What could be more urgent, coming from the belly of Trump's version of America, with its opening track called 'The Basic Economic Farsity', expressing 'the prioritizing of the luxurious wants of the few over the essential needs of the many'.

The quartet's leader is the Mexico-born drummer, Gustavo Cortinas, his father a Uruguayan university professor, his mother a Mexican elementary teacher. He moved from New Orleans to Chicago, the city of violinist Mark Feldman - who has made 200 studio recordings and played in the symphony orchestra of Nashville, Tennessee. The guitarist is Dave Miller from Little Rock, Arkansas, with his blood mixed with the blues, and the urgently inventive saxophonist Jon Irabagon, whose parents were from the Philippines: quite a worldspan is here.

I asked Cortinas about the genesis of the album. 'When we talk about climate justice there is no status quo, but actually a regression on the part of world leaders (political and corporate) to lean into a worldview and practices that are simply unsustainable and an existential threat to our society and humanity. The climate crisis is one that knows no borders, its consequences are real and felt all around the world. At the same time the competitive edge of the capitalist system leads these 'leaders' to ignore this call to action in the name of economic growth.'

'The music of this album also transcends borders and you could say it is genre-defying. It puts together influences of jazz, rock. punk, classical music, renaissance counterpoint, Latin American folkloric, Aztec music, M-base and beyond. It is my hope that all these strands come together to tell a cohesive story without any desire to delineate the differences between these styles, but rather to bring them together and show that music, like our world, is many and one at the same time.'

Hear Feldman's dramatic solo violin, his caustic bow-work and pizzicato on the opener, or how Miller's blues-baked guitar and Feldman's agonising notes 'ultimately erupt into the unpredictability of free improvisation' on The Growth Imperative, expressing the menacing demand for perpetual growth without sustainability. Or the track called Skepticism, involving a palaver between Irabagon's deep, worrisome sounds and his exchanges with Feldman's spiky violin. Or in Sea Level Rising were the two of them play as if they were exchanging instruments with supercharged energy, before Miller's chinking guitar continues in the same ominous mood: four virtuosi voicing in diverse unity the same intuitive messages.

Cortinas said of his bandmates: 'It is an honour to work with these three humans. Jon is a master musician whose energetic creativity is bound to no one style and is ever-curious and ever-explorative. Mark is literally one of the trailblazers for bridging classical music and jazz. He brings these and other musical worlds together beautifully and creatively. Dave is a genius of textural mastery and is the boat that carries this band through landscapes, styles and journeys.'

Irabagon's opening solo of The Man of Flesh and Bone is full of humane, spontaneous melody that is the sound of hope, shared bountifully with Miller's guitar underpinning, a presage to Cortinas' Drum Solo for the End of Time, in which he melodises the drums in a cosmic anthem of drumspeak and drumsong.

I asked him whether he saw his album as an echo of the 60s' and 70s' campaigning albums of Roach, Mingus and Archie Shepp. 'Jazz has a brave history of activism,' he replied, 'and as a social music has shown a power to reflect the grievances of our society. Schoenberg, on a different paradigm, also expressed the necessity for music to reflect the chaotic and dissonant nature of our world. I resonate deeply with the work and mission of these human beings whom I deeply admire, and at the same time - perhaps like them - I find it inevitable to not be disturbed/inspired by what's going on, and consider it an exercise of sanity, integrity and love to speak up and reflect this in my music.'

(The Crisis Knows No Borders is available on Desafio Canente Records)

Sylvie Courvoisier (Switzerland) - Pulsating cadences at the apex of jazz

Sylvie Courvoisier - Lonelyville, Sylvie Courvoisier
Mark Feldman Quartet - To Fly to Steal & Birdies for Lulu
(2017)

Born in Lausanne, Switzerland in 1968, the pianist Sylvie Courvoisier had a conventional enough classical music education in conducting, composition and piano at the Conservatoire de Lausanne before moving to Brooklyn in 1998, where she dived deeply into jazz, developing a number of musical formations, including two remarkable trios. Abaton included her husband, the Chicagoan violinist Mark Feldman and cellist Erik Friedlander, and the all-woman Mephista was created with the veteran French bassist Joelle Leandre and US-Filipina drummer Susie Ibarra.

One of her first of a series of albums for the Swiss label Intakt was Lonelyville, recorded in her home city in 2006. With Feldman and Courvoisier are the Detroit African-American drummer Gerald Cleaver, the Parisian cellist Vincent Courtois and the Tokyo-born Ikue Mori on electronics. Feldman's ice-hot strings are at the centre of the 22-minute opener, Texturologie. They cut through the harmonies above Courtois's more temperate cello and Courvoisier's grounding notes, while Cleaver's scattering drums keep the music earthen and solid. Courvoisier rides her keys, bucking their wild sounds in a sudden thumping solo with Mori's tinkling timbral currents seething around her.

Cosmorama reflects the four continents of the musicians but also the unity between the electric and the acoustic in Courvoisier and Mori's opening palaver. Cello and violin have their moments of colloquy and Feldman touches the stars in his solo beside Courtois's pizzicato artistry. If you wanted proof that these are so powerful contemporary jazz instruments, listen to Cosmorama. Mori's sounds, like dripping crystal water, enfold Courvoisier's notes in Contraste 2005 before Feldman's serene unaccompanied solo, and the final, title track, with Cleaver's rumbling drums and Courvoisier's strident chords, has the bleak aura of a Lausanne blues.

By 2009 Courvoisier and Feldman were co-leading a lasting quartet with the Californian bassist Thomas Morgan and the drummer from New Haven, Connecticut, Gerry Hemingway, a leader in his own right and collaborator with Anthony Braxton, Marilyn Crispell and Wadada Leo Smith. Their album To Fly to Steal was recorded in New York in July 2009. The bold drama of the opener, Messianenesque, is a sonic dance between the four instruments, with Feldman's spiky violin moving and sounding like the lone horn. The pictorial soundscape of Whispering Glades is of a saltwater marsh at sunset suddenly disturbed by human presence. Morgan's bass digs into the sodden earth.

Another audio-visual impression is Coastlines, with Feldman painting the margins of land and sea and Courvoisier's pounding notes stressing their jeopardy. Feldman's quicksilver bow and Courvoisier's frolicsome runs mark The Good Life, with Five Senses of Keen exposing the violinist's melodicism and intense lyricism beside Hemingway's quiescent booms and Morgan's empathetic throbs. Courvoisier's jerking, stop-start avenues of sound are at the worrisome heart of Fire, Fist and Bestial Wail.

By 2013, the quartet had two new members, with veteran New York drummer Billy Mintz replacing Hemingway and Angeleno bassist Scott Colley in for Morgan, and they came together to cut the album Birdies for Lulu in New York in November of that year. The opener and closer is Feldman's three-part Cards for Capitaine, dedicated to a late Swiss friend and written on index cards which were arbitrarily shuffled immediately before the recording. Nothing mournful and full of zany humour with Colley's breathless bass brilliantly setting the pace. Feldman's violin stomps and wails, Courvoisier's serpentine waves of sound roll and Mintz's drums shuffle, saunter and stroll.

From the heart of Europe to the apex of jazz she came, innovating all the way. Hear her all the way through, but especially on this album's heartsblood track, Shmear, where her pulsating cadences and sprints up the keyboard are joy to the ears. Jazz brings many human miracles, and Switzerland in Brooklyn on a rocking piano is one of them.

(Lonelyville, To Fly to Steal & Birdies for Lulu are released on Intakt)

Stanley Cowell (USA) - Determined and ancestral beats

Stanley Cowell - It's Time
(2014)

In a very special place in my vinyl collection sits Stanley Cowell's first album, Blues For The Vietcong, cut in 1969 on the Freedom label, with Andrea Klein's compelling sleeve design of the Vietnamese flag peppered by bullet holes but still defiantly unfurled and flying.

Cowell was born in Toledo, Ohio, in 1931 in the same city of earlier piano genius Art Tatum, who used to stop by at the Cowell household when

Stanley was a boy to practise at their family piano. 'He played so much piano,' Cowell remembered, 'that he scared everyone. One day when he played, my mother ran out of the house and refused to return until he stopped.' Cowell studied classical piano from four years old, before working with local R&B and dance bands as a teenager. He trained in music at Ohio's Oberlin College before spending a further year of study in Mozart's city, Salzburg.

While at the University of Michigan in 1966 he joined up with avant garde altoist Marion Brown, where he formed what was to become a long-lasting creative partnership with trumpeter Charles Tolliver, with whom he established the influential Strata East label in 1971, which issued a series of powerful albums including some by the Tolliver/Cowell band Music Inc and the redoubtable Gil Scott-Heron.

Cowell's most recent album It's Time (2011) has the same imperative title as two powerful predecessors. In 1962 Max Roach, an ardent supporter of the civil rights movement, cut his album It's Time as a vibrant successor to his epochal 1960 album We Insist! The Freedom Now Suite, with its referencing of the struggle against racism in both the southern US states and South Africa. Then in 1964 there was another It's Time, the Blue Note creation of a quintet led by the fiery New York alto saxophonist and Charlie Parker inheritor Jackie McLean. Tolliver, making his recording debut on the album, was McLean's front-line partner. So given this history, it is not surprising to discover that Cowell's retrospective Civil Rights Suite is an integral part of his own It's Time album more than four decades on, composed of a hornless trio session with bassist Tom Dicarlo and drummer Chris Brown, both of whom are Cowell's ex-students at Rutgers University.

Yet it is Cowell's musical reflections on the 1960s space exploration, happening simultaneously with the civil rights struggle, that begin the album with the two pieces Cosmology and El Space-O. White people in the US were going for rings around the moon and finally stepping on its surface as their black compatriots organised and campaigned for rights always denied their communities. Cowell's complex patterns of notes provoke long thoughts of such truths.

He expresses his internationalism towards Indian and Chinese realities with the three parts of his Asian Art Suite, inspired by his reactions to exhibits in the Philadelphia Museum of Art. Cowell's dramatic two-handed eloquence, Brown's flickering cymbals and Dicarlo's heart of earth combine to carry the jazz message to faraway terrains.

But it is a long way home for the Civil Rights Suite, beginning with Roach's own It's Time, as it always was for the momentous drummer born in New Land, North Carolina, in 1924. Cowell stomps along his keys full of energy, his eyes and hands still on the prize, while Brown lets fly on his skins and Dicarlo unleashes his deep soul beat. Next comes King, composed by Cowell's old tenorist confrere in the Roach band, Roland Alexander. A ballad and praisesong, its notes are noble and strong, and Dicarlo's long solo is full of muscled beauty.

Finally there is the wit and solidarity of We Shall 2 with its sonic connections to the great anthem We Shall Overcome. It is the African link for Long Vamp when Cowell, after starting on piano, shifts to his Kalimba, or thumb piano, with Dicarlo digging deep beside him. And it is back to 1969 for the album's final tune Abstrusions, written by Cowell for the Roach album Members Don't Get Weary, recorded shortly after the murder of King to help the movement hold on to its faith and stamina.

It is as if the long-campaigning and beautiful music of Cowell refuses to go away and is as determined as it is ancestral.

(It's Time is available on Steeplechase)

Stanley Cowell (USA) - Melodies and memories rendered into a most beautiful form

Stanley Cowell - Are You Real? & No Illusions (2018)

You can hear virtually the entire century of jazz glories in Stanley Cowell's piano. His lifetime doesn't quite stretch that far - only three-quarters of that history. He was born in the city of Toledo, Ohio, in 1941 and met the greatest jazz pianist Art Tatum, a regular visitor to his parents' house and player of their family piano, when he was six. But his years encompass an extraordinary richness of playing with, and being inspired by, some of the truly epic figures of the music.

The works of some of these are the themes of Cowell's very singular piano artistry on his 2014 album, Are You Real? in which sheer serendipity caused him to be accompanied by two other powerful confreres, bassist Jay Anderson from Upland, California, who began his career playing with the Woody Herman Orchestra and has played with almost everybody else since, and the 57-year-old drummer from Newport News, Virginia, Billy Drummond - leader of his own bands and accompanist of pianists from Andrew Hill, Carla Bley and his wife Renee Rosnes. Drummond and Anderson had been booked to be recorded alongside pianist Freddie Redd, but he fell ill and Cowell stepped in with the superb Are You Real? album as the result.

The trio begin with a Cowell tune which was featured on his first trio album of 1969, Blues for the Viet Cong, called Photon in a Paper World. You'd think these three musicians had played together all their lives, such is their immediate rapport. The instant empathy intensifies in McCoy Tyner's You Taught My Heart to Sing, where Cowell's unified power of melody and improvisation tell a whole narrative. Anderson's solo is beautiful in its depth of quietude.

Jaki Byard was another of Cowell's beloved pianists and his romping portrait of Charlie Parker's mother, Mrs Parker of KC, is played with swing and gusto and in I Remember Diz, the homage to Cuba-loving Dizzy Gillespie by

Cuban saxophonist Paquito D'Rivera, you can hear the Caribbean waves of rhythm from Drummond's irrepressible tapping drums and cymbalism. Tadd Dameron's classic bebop opus Hot House with its familiar theme played so often by Gillespie, Parker and their generation, moves with an enticing lightness and forward motion in Cowell's salute to his forebears. Then it is the album's title tune, written by Benny Golson, one-time tenor saxophonist of Art Blakey's Jazz Messengers who made the theme their own in the late '50s, a formidable hard-bop signature tune. Drummond's drums preface it, as Blakey's used to do, and Anderson plays a delving, dancing solo.

No better end piece for the album than Monk's Off Minor and the trio essay its sudden turnings and angular leanings with musical brilliance. So warmly and proficiently did this accidental trio perform together, and with such artistry, that they were back in the studio in December 2015 - this time by definite pre-arrangement - to record another album for the Steeplechase label, No Illusions, with a fourth member, the alto-saxophonist Bruce Williams, from Washington DC.

Apart from John Lewis's Milano, which opens the album, all the compositions are Cowell's and the apex track is his Nostalgia for Homelands from the piano suite Juneteenth, in which he imagines 'what would have been in the minds of the slaves of Texas who were denied their freedom for two years after the Emancipation Proclamation of New Year's Day 1863.' Williams' brief, abrupt phrases signal the sense of betrayal and broken promises made to native Americans too and Cowell's piano chorus, with its curt and brusque note clusters, compounds the narrative of historical and continuing treachery of Charlottesville, Ferguson and many other places.

Cowell plays thumb piano with Williams and his flute on Lesdoodis and Kyma, which he describes as 'a sound-design work station,' on the sonically descriptive Sunlight Shifting and Celestial Women, where electrical sounds flutter, quiver and make a new timbral undergrowth. But it is back to the traditional quartet format for the expressively melodic B Minor Folksong where Cowell's notes make evocative patterns and Williams's horn arouses their people's historical memories and melodies to render simplicity in its most beautiful jazz form.

(Are You Real? & No Illusions are available on Steeplechase)

Marilyn Crispell (USA) - Jazz as medicine for the soul

Prolific pianist Marilyn Crispell's softly chiming notes bring a 'beautiful quietude' to her records

(2017)

A compelling pianist whose sounds span the perceived gulfs between classical music and jazz, Marilyn Crispell was born in Philadelphia in 1947 and studied classical piano and composition and the New England Conservatory of Music as a young woman. She virtually abandoned music for medicine for six years, but began singing blues in a folk rock group after the breakdown of her marriage. She then discovered the free jazz beauties and profundities of John Coltrane's A Love Supreme and the pioneering free pianism of Cecil Taylor, and since the 1970s she has performed and recorded prolifically as a jazz artist and improviser with many of the US eminences of the avant-garde, from multiple reedman Anthony Braxton and arch-bassist Reggie Workman to European free masters like Evan Parker and Barry Guy.

Over the last decade she has become a regular artiste with the Munich-based ECM label, recording a series of fine albums as one third of a stellar trio, with two other US veteran virtuosi including bassist Gary Peacock, who goes back to some of the earliest startling albums cut by rasping tenorist Albert Ayler, and those of long-time confrere Keith Jarrett in the pianist's renowned Standards Trio. The subtle and feathery drummer is Paul Motian of Armenian heritage who played on some of Bill Evans' most brilliant trio albums between 1959-63 and, after a lifetime of powerful jazz achievement with some of the music's greatest originators from Lee Konitz and Charlie Haden to Jim Pepper and Don Cherry, died aged 80 in 2011.

Amaryllis, recorded in New York in 2000, is described by Crispell in her sleeve notes as 'very inner space,' containing several 'slow free pieces.' The tracks are mainly short and have a beautiful quietude, through which Crispell's softly chiming notes, Peacock's essential yet exploring heartbeat and Motian's serene brushes unify to create a peculiar hushed and tranquil peace, as in Motian's Voices, where Peacock's bass sounds like a giant and deep-cushioned hammer, Peacock's tuneful December Greenwings which sounds anything but the sheer improvisation that it is, and Crispell's Silence (for P) where the trio's interactions are sublime. The exception is the free-jumping Crispell piece called Rounds, which skips and kicks like a children's dance. Morpion too is fast, free, almost weightless as it glides through the ears.

Storyteller of 2004 brought in New Jersey-born Mark Helias for the ever-busy Peacock. Jazz is all about sonic narrative and the album's three musicians are also the writers of its stories. Crispell's opener, Wild Rose, is almost anthemic, a praise song to a flower alive with Motian's rustling brushes and Helias's mollifying bass. Motian's Flight of the Bluejay has such spring in his drums that these birds levitate over Crispell's caressed keys and Helias's soft melodism. Then Crispell's Alone, with its few enough notes of stark solitariness aches to tell more of its story. Helias's track Limbo is a complex improvisation, with Crispell's excursion belying any easy dancing which is saved up for the fleeting, lightweight movement of Motian's Play. If listeners bring their own events to this music's promptings, there are stories galore stemming from the trio's album.

Vignettes can be engraved illustrations with no definite borders - an ideal concept for jazz improviser or character portraits. It is also the title of Crispell's solo album recorded in 2007 in Lugano, Italy, and dedicated to her father. There are 17 short tracks on Vignettes and without stalwarts like Motian,

Peacock or Helias, Crispell's chiming sounds seem strangely naked (listen to Vignette II for example) but nonetheless beautiful. The slow accumulation of notes on Valse Triste bursts with emotive power, and within Cuida Tu Esperito it is as if every line of improvisation is an emergent melody. Notes of hope seem to pour from Gathering Light, and the concluding Little Song for My Father which very powerfully and tenderly exemplifies within its brief three minutes the words of Cecil Taylor, Crispell's great piano inspiration, who declared that her music was creating 'a new kind of lyricism' in jazz.

Finally there is One Dark Night I Left My Silent House, a 2010 album Crispell made with US clarinettist David Rothenberg, who is also a philosophical naturalist who has written influentially on music and the natural world in his books such as Why Birds Sing and his study of the sounds of whales, Thousand Mile Song. Tracks like Stay, Stray, Grosbeak, Owl Moon and Still Life with Woodpeckers pursue these studies into jazz and Rothenberg's own woodwind birdsong harmonises engagingly with Crispell's naturalism of sound, particularly in the Hawk and the Mouse, when she directly plucks the piano strings. Inside the house is silent, outside the night brings an orchestra of natural sound. Crispell is there to hear it and bring it to us.

(Vignettes, Storyteller, Amaryllis & One Dark Night I Left my Silent House are available on ECM)

Jacqui Dankworth (England) - I'm not a folk singer or jazz singer, I'm a singer of songs

Jacqui Dankworth - Windmills
(2025)

It's not easy for a talented daughter of two outstanding musicians to carve out a lifetime in music in her own right, but singer Jacqui Dankworth (born in 1963) has certainly done that with a beautiful excellence and originality.

As the daughter of John Dankworth (1927-2010) and Cleo Laine (born 1927), Jacqui is immensely proud of her parents, and not only because of their musical prowess. John was bandleader, alto saxophonist, orchestra maestro and composer much admired by the great Duke Ellington - Jacqui told me that her father was in awe of him and 'almost crumbled when he was in his presence' - and Cleo, of course is a vocalist lauded in Britain, as well as Europe and America.

But much more than this. In the early 1950s Dankworth was largely ignorant of Apartheid when he took a band to South Africa to play in Johannesburg. Jacqui takes up the story: 'As they were rehearsing in the theatre a black cleaner approached dad saying how much he loved his music and that he also played the saxophone. Dad said: 'Then come to the concert tonight, I'll get you a ticket.' 'They won't let me in. I'm black,' he replied.

'Dad never got over that and vowed never to play to segregated audiences again or return to South Africa while Apartheid reigned. It was an education for him. He became an active enemy of Apartheid wherever he went, publicising how evil it was all over the world. And he helped to get black musicians, like trumpeter Hugh Masekela, out of South Africa. After dad died I met him and he gave me a big hug. 'That's for you and your dad,' he said.'

Jacqui carries this pride in her voice, always remembering these events. Her mum and dad were also founders of the Stars Campaign for Inter-Racial Friendship in 1959, established to combat the fascist White Defence League.

Her new album is Windmills, another expression of her protean imagination. 'I'm not a folk singer or jazz singer, I'm a singer of songs,' she declares. 'I'll sing anything!'

I think the first time I heard her sing was Ben Webster's Mood on the 1996 Michael Garrick album, For Love Of Duke... And Ronnie. When I reminded her of that she sang it wordlessly down the phone to me; it still sounded beautiful.

But how has her voice changed since those days, singing in a multiplicity of styles - and acting too - including opera? 'I've a lot more confidence now. I bring all my life experiences into my songs, my sound and range is much broader.' With pianist Charlie Wood as arranger and accompanist, the Carducci String Quartet and saxophonist Julian Siegel as guest conductor of The BBC Big Band, the versatility of Jacqui's soft-focused and serpentine voice, the rises and falls of her notes and the way she lingers patiently over key words such as 'day...' in London By Night, all compound some memorable performances.

'We had already arranged the songs and performed them many times live, so we thought, why not make an album of them?'

What is her favourite track? 'I find listening to myself very difficult, but I like So Many Stars, the Sergio Mendes song, particularly, with Sammy Mayne's superb alto saxophone solo, and Stephen Sondheim's Send In The Clowns.'

For me, I find the sadness and pathos of If You Go Away very moving, a contrast to her voicing of Lucky To Be Me, where the string quartet comes to the fore in a sound of pure happiness and optimism. Jacqui's own song, Will You Wait For Me, and its invocation of seasonal change and the steadfastness of love which overcomes it, is expressively sung alongside Wood's tolling piano obligatos and Oli Hayhurst's plangent bass.

If you're anywhere near my age, her beautiful, swooping voice will remind you not only of her parents' lifetime achievement, but of a woman taking her own road through her own unique and very different musicianship, marking her words and the lyricism of her voice with a special passion and artistry.

(Windmills is available on Perdido Records)

Kris Davis (Canada) - Universal jazz kitchen
The Kris Davis Trio, The Vortex, Dalston, London
(2025)

Outside, Gillett Square was Saturday night Dalston-buzzing, and the cooking smells of Ethiopia, Nigeria, Mexico and Thailand were blowing like a universal kitchen all the way up Kingsland Road.

Here for one night were the Kris Davis Trio, with pianist Davis from Calgary, Alberta; Detroit bassist Robert Hurst and Philly drummer Johnathan Blake.

How they played in this curtained upstairs chamber, music that would blow away a thousand Trumps with their impassioned brilliance from their album Ride the Gauntlet, dedicated to six powerful female pianists: Carla Bley, Marilyn Crispell, Angelica Sanchez, Sylvie Courvoisier, Renee Rosnes and the late Geri Allen.

In Knotweed, a long duet between Davis and Hurst prefaced a sudden acceleration, with Blake's rattling snares and golden cymbals and Davis's flashing fingers making notes like raindrops. In Coda Queen, Hurst sounds as if he were on horseback, so rhythmically does he gallop alongside Blake's pummelling drums.

This is expertly manicured music, played with a warm, co-operative spirit, the trio siblings smiling and acknowledging mutual virtuosity, completely attuned to each other's artistry.

Across the square, Dalston life-energy and tumult still surged on. Was that Johnny Cash's Wheel of Fire I could hear as I walked back to catch the Overground at Dalston Kingsland station? A thousand musics, a cosmos of London's humanity all around me.

Elton Dean (England) - Brilliance in Brazil
The Elton Dean Quintet - Welcomet: Live in Brazil
(2015)

There are three incomparable horn heroes of British jazz on this marvellous album, recorded live in concert in Sao Paulo while they were touring Brazil in 1986.

The first is Barbados-born trumpeter Harry Beckett, who arrived in London as a teenager and never stopped amazing his listeners. The second is extraordinary reedman Elton Dean, playing alto saxophone and saxello on this album, who played with Long John Baldry's blues band and jazz rockers the Soft Machine before setting himself loose on the jazz scene.

The third is mercurial trombone genius Paul Rutherford, always seen with a Morning Star sticking out of his pocket. A pioneer free jazzman of the multisonics of the slide, he was a member of the Spontaneous Music Ensemble, Iskra, Mike Westbrook's Brass Band and the London Jazz

Composers' Orchestra. When he died in 2007 his horns were bequeathed to the young musicians of Cuba.

With them at this concert are Rio de Janeiro-born bassist Marcio Mattos and drummer Liam Genockey, a Dubliner who played with alto saxophonist Trevor Watts in his bands Amalgam and Moire Music. Both musicians are still very active, performing and recording, and Mattos's new album SOL(os), entirely comprised of cello and bass solos, with his own electronics accompaniments, has recently been released on the Emanem label.

The Welcomet album expresses the jubilation of a concert featuring Europe-based horn men playing in a nation famed for and permeated with its very own exultant and festive sound, and the 40-minute-plus opener Welcomet begins with a long solo from a euphoric and buoyant Rutherford, a south Londoner on fire in Brazil's largest city. His unique and astonishing slidework, inducing complex patterns and rhythms from his horn is urged on by Genockey's crashing drums. Accompanied by Mattos's pulsing bass, next to solo is Dean on saxello, with its quasi-Asiatic and carping tone leaping from note to note. On his heels comes a crackling Beckett, his lightning phrases sharp and incisive, with Mattos's bass playing a subterranean dance of a chorus warmly received by the audience, before Genockey's drums complete a first series of solos and the quintet moves into ensemble mode.

Dean's second solo is bristling with melody inside every moment of improvisation, as Rutherford returns beside Mattos in a colloquy of continents and Beckett's Caribbean ardour begins as a gentle flame before an extended ensemble eventually takes the theme home.

The second track Rio Rules, close on 35 minutes, starts with Genockey's effervescent drums before Beckett and Mattos come throbbing in, the sharp edges of the trumpeter's sound razoring the air. Rutherford's ascendant slides continue the momentum with Genockey's fiery cymbals until the Rio bassist takes a long and eloquent solo, almost as if he were offering a praise song to his birth city. After a long horn confabulation, drums and bass sit it out and the three kindred horn men exchange their own discourse of breath and sound.

As a listener you wonder what they are saying to each other within their sounds - for what expression there is of marvel and amazement, realising where they are and who is their audience, having grown accustomed to London pub venues where sometimes they played to only a score of avid listeners. This precious album shows just how far free music can take you and how it can reach out to people on the other side of the globe.

(Welcomet: Live in Brazil is available on Ogun)

Elton Dean (England) - Borne along in a Happy Daze
Elton Dean's Ninesense - Happy Daze/Oh For the Edge
Elton Dean's Unlimited Saxophone Company
(2013)

Elton Dean had unusual jazz provenances. Born in Nottingham in 1945, the son of two Salvation Army officers who ensured that he learned piano and violin as a boy, he turned to the saxophone at 18. At 21 he joined the R&B band Bluesology, with Long John Baldry and a pianist called Reg Dwight who created a stage name by taking Dean's Christian name for his first name and Long John's Christian name for his surname.

1968 was his key musical year, with a crucial meeting at the Barry Jazz School. With cornetist Marc Charig, trombonist Nick Evans and pianist Keith Tippett as leader, they formed a sextet. From 1969 to 1972 he played in Soft Machine and throughout the '70s in the Dutch jazz-rock band Supersister and South African Chris McGregor's seminal big band, the Brotherhood of Breath.

In 1975 he formed Ninesense and two of its albums, Happy Daze and Oh For the Edge, have been reissued as a single CD by the Ogun label. This was one of the most momentous bands of its era, grounded in rhythm by two South African stalwarts, drummer Louis Moholo-Moholo and bassist Harry Miller. The band had six horns - Dean, Charig and Evans, plus tenorist Alan Skidmore, Barbadian trumpeter Harry Beckett and, on Happy Daze, Innsbruck-born trombonist Radu Malfatti. Tippett returned as pianist. Eight of the 10 tunes are by Dean, while Friday Night Blues is a composition by his old South African trumpet confrere and one of the original members of Ninesense, Mongezi Feza (1945-75). The emphasis is upon ensemble arrangements and often long, narrative solos.

On Seven for Lee Dean tells his story on the saxello, an extended soprano saxophone-like horn, and Skidmore's hungry notes dominate Sweet F.A. together with a cascading solo by Tippett. On Nicrotto, Evans and Malfatti share a guttural slide colloquy, always with the unified rhythmic heartbeat of Moholo and Miller. Three For All brings the trumpets to the centre after the more rhapsodic Skidmore, Beckett's breathy solo soaring above Tippett's chuntering keys.

It was a live session in March 1976 at the 100 Club in Oxford Street that produced the final six tracks. Dance gets into immediate furore with Evans's trombone, full of passionate and inventive fire. Skidmore's tenor comes pounding in over Moholo's crashing drums and Tippett's baroque interpolations. The band jells and bounces in a way not common in British jazz, and with such unleashed energy that as a listener, you wish that you were there. Dean rides over the full ensemble in Fall in Free and is at the centre of proceedings too in Forsoothe before all horns blow in free splendour. Feza is celebrated in Friday Night Blues and Skidmore leads the way with some bursting choruses.

By 1989 Dean had formed the Unlimited Saxophone Company which brought together a saxophone quartet with bassist Paul Rogers and drummer Tony Levin. The other horns were Kentish tenorist and baritonist Paul Dunmall, Simon Picard on tenor and the veteran free altoist Trevor Watts, a pioneer of British free improvised music in the Spontaneous Music Ensemble and Amalgam. They were recorded in the same year at the Covent Garden Jazz Festival, which, as Dean tells in his sleeve notes, was their very first gig.

The opener, Unda, is leavened by Rogers's springing bass. Dean's saxello levitates over it before Dunmall's baritone comes growling in. Rising has more potent Dean all the way through leading the horn ensemble, poised, impassioned and incendiary. This is an album of saxophone contrasts and comradeship, four horns of England all within the saxophone family, mature voices in a burning reed dialogue. None more so than in the vibrant and modestly titled Small Steps and Seven for Lee one more time, where the saxophone conversation is intense and revealing of the lifetimes within the sounds.

And in the centre is Dean, born in sacred music in Robin Hood's city and right up to his death in 2006 struggling to encompass every note in his heart-songs' meanings, leaving us with his living sounds of a horn of solidarity with the world.

(Happy Daze/Oh For the Edge & Elton Dean's Unlimited Saxophone Company are available on Ogun)

Decoy (England) - East End promise

Decoy and Joe McPhee - OTO & Decoy Vol 1 Spirit (2012)

There was truly a time, a long era indeed, when the nucleus of British jazz was in London's West End when such venues as Soho's Ronnie Scott's, Oxford Street's 100 Club and the Flamingo lit up the London groove and jazz musicians from the east of the city all travelled west to perform. Not anymore. Now the heart of London jazz is in the east, and most particularly in the Hackney village of Dalston where performance spaces such as the Vortex and the Café Oto, so close to the London Overground, have made their neighbourhood seethe with new and breathtaking sounds. If you want real testimony of this, get hold of the vibrant 2009 album OTO, recorded live at the Café with the powerfully innovative Decoy trio playing with the Florida-born septuagenarian multi-instrumentalist Joe McPhee, who puts aside his pocket trumpet and flugelhorn to blow his tenor and soprano saxophones.

Decoy are a threesome of extraordinary virtuosity. The keyboard man who plays the Hammond B3 organ is Alexander Hawkins, born in Oxford in 1981, a young master pianist who seems to be everywhere on the British jazz scene. He co-leads the transatlantic Convergence Quartet and also plays in the co-operative band Barkingside and with veteran South African Louis Moholo-Moholo in the drummer's group alongside the prime British bassist John Edwards, who also plays in Decoy. The trio's drummer is another British quasi-veteran Steve Noble, a stalwart of the free jazz and improvisation movement with years of experience.

The Dalston groovers must have rocked with awe that December night when Noble's outrageous drumburst signalled the first number, the 39 minutes of Opening Might, with Hawkins's monstrous chords, Edwards's fierce undertow and McPhee's piping entrance on his red-hot soprano. This gallimaufry of boiling sounds is quite an annunciation, and even the remarkable McPhee, who has played everywhere and everything, would not have expected this in the heart of Hackney. Unperturbed and hugely stimulated, he plays like a fiery prophet in a new land with his three British confreres, before Hawkins steams in with an exuberant response. Edwards slams his bass and makes it whine with joy and Noble plays like you think Art Blakey would if he were ever exposed to such a startling free jazz setting. When McPhee changes to tenor and spits out his first notes it seems that what has just passed is an epochal-long moment in British jazz history.

The second track is the aptly named Breakout and all through its upsurge McPhee, who is the most democratic of hornmen, shows again that there must be no singular 'star' in any band that he plays within, that every head leads as part of a collective enterprise. And Decoy is just that - no member is a mere accompanist. Hear Edwards's scintillating and ever-surprising basswork next to McPhee's rampaging soprano and Noble's riveting cymbalism when McPhee switches to tenor above Hawkins's undercurrent of deep chords. And when he does 'break out' it is a huge sonic swell Sweeping across the Dalston rooftops.

I've yet to find the Wolf Road in the East End, but the album's third and final track is called Dancing On The Wolf Road. It is so full of heat you wonder about the dance it would provoke. Edwards's rasping bass growls out the opening notes, McPhee's tenor enters with a simple theme over Hawkins's organ bounce and then whirls into irrepressible motion with Hawkins's keyboard bubbling like a cauldron.

Away from Dalston, in a studio enclave, Decoy's 2009 album Vol 1 Spirit was cut. And if you think that this trio would be any the less remarkable in a non-live or hornless context minus the brilliant McPhee, just hear this record. It begins with Outside In, memorable in particular for Noble's cymbals, striking like frenetic gongs all through the track above Hawkins's galloping chords. The thickness, comradeship and quality of sounds these three men create make you think you are listening to a dozen or more musicians. There is a beautiful sequence on the track called Decoy when Hawkins strides out with an irresistibly swinging chorus set off by Edwards's walking bass and Noble's chomping drumbeat, and at the start of Episode No 69 Hawkins's notes sound like patters of rain; with Edwards's bowed bass a moaning wind.

The longest track is the 14 minutes of Native Origins where Hawkins's organ sounds almost churchlike in moments and Noble's crashing drums quasi-apocalyptic. As Hawkins stirs himself into a timbral frenzy, Edwards's grounding beat stirs the London earth and Noble's overarching drums and cymbals are everywhere, you realise what a unique trio this is, definitely made in England out of a universal jazz sound, and full to the brim of a sonic future.

(OTO & Decoy Vol 1 Spirit are available on by Bo'Weavil)

Jack DeJohnette (USA) - Lamentations passed down to brilliant sons

Jack DeJohnette / Ravi Coltrane / Matthew Garrison - In Movement (2016)

This is an album with powerful historical allusions spanning two jazz generations. It is a trio at work. The drummer and pianist is Jack DeJohnette, born in 1942 in Chicago and veteran of pioneering post-bop ensembles such as those of Charles Lloyd and Miles Davis (he played on Davis's iconoclastic Bitches Brew album of 1969) and longtime drummer of Keith Jarrett's Standards Trio. The saxophonist is Ravi, the son of Alice and John and the bassist Matthew Garrison, the son of Jimmy - the bassist of the greatest of Coltrane's quartets. DeJohnette and his family cared for both his bandmates when they were boys after they both lost their fathers. 'We are connected at a very high and extremely personal level that I believe comes through the music,' DeJohnette said.

The opening track signals the album's epochal echoes of half a century ago. It is the threnody Alabama, written and recorded by the Coltrane quartet in 1963, two months after the racist murder of four black girl choristers in a church in Birmingham, Alabama at the zenith of the civil rights movement. Now, as the Black Lives Matter campaign grows stronger and stronger across the US, Coltrane's horn, Garrison's bass and DeJohnette's drums take on a potent new salience as if this lamentation passed down to brilliant sons were for those shot dead by police across US cities all through 2016. 'Ravi and Matthew are aware of their heritage,' says DeJohnette, 'but part of the intention of their music is to be recognised for who they are.' And the times that they live in too, without nostalgia.

The title track follows, and it is Garrison's use of looping electronic timbres behind Coltrane's dancing soprano horn that creates a 21st- century soundscape from evocations of past decades. And then on to Two Jimmys, dedicated to Garrison and Hendrix and a fusion of their music. Coltrane's tenor pulsates alongside the looping electronica and DeJohnette's relentless rhythmic drumshots. More than a homage, it is a sonic exploration.

Blue in Green, originally a part of Davis's Kind of Blue album of 1959 in which Coltrane's father blew a featured role with Julian 'Cannonball' Adderley on alto saxophone, is given a contemporary airing. Piano and soprano begin a colloquy, with Coltrane's mellow sound never so pure and serene. Next is the trio's version of Serpentine Fire written by the leader of Earth, Wind and Fire Maurice White - an old musical compadre of DeJohnette - who gives a pounding backbeat alongside Garrison's sturdy bassline. Coltrane's soprano radiates a birdsong lyricism, as if its sound is swooping over open water before Garrison's electronic bass solo brings back the earth.

Lydia is a praise song to DeJohnette's wife: melodic, tender - its notes fleet and almost weightless in their beauty. Then with a DeJohnette roll and it is the trio's salute to John Coltrane's last great drumming partner Rashied Ali, with whom he made the duo album of 1967 the year of his death, Interstellar Space. For Ravi Coltrane, Ali held a special place in his life: 'Rashied Ali was an incredible drummer, and somebody who affected us personally in a very deep way,' he said. 'Rashied was like a second father to me, just like Jack has become a second father to me.'

In the midst of men like fathers, Coltrane picked up his soprano saxophone and played his and DeJohnette's tribute Rashied like a master with DeJohnette's enfolding drums around him. No ghosts here, only real musicians playing out the stories of their lives and the lives of beloved others.

The last track is Soulful Ballad, in which DeJohnette turns back to piano, his first instrument. Ravi's soprano tone carries a message of endearing lucidity which is absolutely his own. And for 73-year-old Jack, it is a new sound chiming: 'It's a moving of our music forward. I know I haven't heard any combination like this. There's the past and the present and the future in what we're doing.'

(In Movement is available on ECM)

Directions in Music (USA) - A jazz dalliance

Directions in Music, Massey Hall, Toronto
(2005)

Seven faces look out from the stage of the historic Massey Hall in Toronto for the final concert in a 25-venue tour made across US and Canadian cities by the Directions in Music band - those of five marvellous musicians and two computers.

But, in truth, the most powerful personage was the performance chamber itself. Erected in 1894, a gift to the city from the "wealthy industrialist" Hart Massey - according to the plaque on its front outside wall - it holds within its imperial bricks a powerful jazz narrative and culture. For, 52 years ago, it was the venue of "the greatest jazz concert ever," when a quintet including Charlie Parker, Dizzy Gillespie, Bud Powell, Charles Mingus and Max Roach performed to a half-empty hall. Mingus recorded the event with Parker playing a plastic alto saxophone and it has been a part of jazz mythology ever since. Steeple-terraced with circle and upper circle, proscenium-arched and graced with ringing acoustics, every note still echoes in the ear, as they did from Parker and his confreres in 1953. But what would they have made of Directions in Music, of Herbie Hancock's computerised keyboards or Michael Brecker's EWI - electronic wind instrument?

Of the five hugely accomplished players, perhaps trumpeter Roy Hargrove seemed the most constrained. A joyous, soaring, free-spirited hornman, it was bizarre to watch and hear him popping and spitting into his instrument while the computerised electronic sounds whirled all around him from Hancock's buttons and keyboards and Brecker pressed the valves of his EWI beside him. Not that he didn't have his own sublime moments - his breathy horn crackling fire on his own track Brown, or the much slower and ritual led Poet, with a swarm of notes touching all corners of this chamber bursting with ghosts, before drummer Terri Lyne Carrington's clicking rimshots. In such solo opportunities, his volcanic intensity, partly submerged, sounds akin to another Roy of a previous generation, surnamed Eldridge.

Brecker admits that there is fun for him in playing his EWI and, in the band's "severely deconstructed" version of Hancock's own Dolphin's Dance or Wayne Shorter's Pinocchio, he gives us both EWI and some burning tenor. On the former, he strikes up an incandescent duo with Carrington, who, throughout the entire performance, plays with an urgency which defies electronics and grounds all her colleagues with a spirit of the earth, linking directly with the hall's immanent history and what is enfolded within its architecture and heartbeat.

In 2002, Directions in Music recorded a live album here, dedicated to the 75th anniversary of the births of Miles Davis and John Coltrane. But there are no Davis or Coltrane reruns this time - the concert is dubbed Directions in Music - Our Times. Hancock is, of course, a jazzman of extraordinary accomplishments. Stretching back to his first Blue Note album in 1962 - Takin' Off - through his epochal period with Miles Davis (1963-69) and his first electronic jazz Mwandishi albums (1969-71), he has exerted huge influence within the music as well as being a virtuoso pianist throughout.

And so it was a loss not to hear more of his famed impressionistic solo piano brilliance, for through much of the concert, he is twiddling buttons and adjusting electrical devices. The few times he breaks out into acoustic solo glory, it is like a huge relief.

Speaking to the Toronto Star before the concert, Brecker said: "This time it's not a dedication. It will be more reflective of our own tunes with a little more electric content. Herbie will play some keyboards, I'll have a wind synthesiser and Roy will have some gadgetry as well. It won't get in the way, however, and it's essentially an acoustic concert." It isn't - and only Scott Colley's powerfully resounding bass and Carrington's irresistible drums seem to defy the electronics.

And Massey Hall itself, of course, is steeped in its millions of musical moments and the living spirits of Bird, Mingus, Diz, Bud and the survivor Roach imbibed into the beamed ceiling, naked wooden pillars, high absorbent walls and the stained glass windows under the roof. They have been there too long to be distracted.

Lou Donaldson (USA) and Lonnie Smith (USA) –
Playing under the influence
Jazz Café, London
(2001)

Charlie Parker inspired a whole generation of saxophonists and one of the most luminous of these was Lou Donaldson. Donaldson, born in North Carolina in 1926, made his reputation in the '50s, when his hard-edged, bluesy alto sound featured strongly in the heyday of be-bop. In one of the most vibrant and celebrated live recordings of the era, he was there at the Birdland club in 1954 playing alongside Art Blakey, Horace Silver and Clifford Brown in a prototypal version of the Jazz Messengers, his searing, razored alto sound piercing through numbers like his own Lou's Blues. He became one of Blue Note's regular recording heroes, with albums like Blues Walk, Sunny Side Up - or the recently reissued Man With A Horn.

He also pioneered the organ/sax combo, moving towards a species of blues-funk with organists like Jack McDuff and John Patton or the blues-soaked guitar of Grant Green. One of jazz's true non-stoppers, in his 75th year, Donaldson is on stage again at Jazz Café alongside his long-time organ partner Lonnie Smith and breathing the old fire and insouciance into his horn. The saxophone-organ combination is a jazz standby with a populist edge that has drawn many a fellow-traveller into the heart of the music. Donaldson and Smith inhabit the genre with a diehard brilliance and nothing of the zest and artistry of either stalwart has withered, backed by Randy Johnston on guitar and Vikoshi Tanaka on rattling drums.

Smith, resplendent in a white turban and even-whiter beard, cast a bizarre contrast with the nattily tied-and-suited Donaldson. As they burst into a blues variation of Summertime, the altoist's blues-bop lines were as sharp as ever, sounding as much like the wailing horn of Eddie 'Cleanhead' Vinson as Parker himself. The quartet went belting into The Best Things In Life Are Free at a frantic pace, Donaldson sprinting like a septuagenarian Linford Christie through the melody. It was joyous, springing music, with Johnston plucking his blues guitar with an astonishing speed, his cascade of notes falling all over Camden Town.

Donaldson's Laura wore the blues with a sad and beautiful abandon, while Smith's mellow, ruminative notes laid out the narrative of the melody with a grounding, evocative sense of lamentation. The spirit still shone out of Donaldson's Blue Note jazz-funk classic of the '60s, Alligator Boogaloo.

Lonnie Smith eating up the blues is one rare spectacle, his arms a-waving as he lifts them from the keyboards, his teeth a-baring and his turban a-gleaming. 'Blues is suffering music,' declares Donaldson as he introduced Vinson's Whisky Drinking Woman, but this was buoyant and uproarious too.

> *'She drinks whisky in her coffee,*
> *Whisky in her tea.*
> *She puts whisky in her whisky*
> *And puts the rest into me!'*

'I'm glad that you appreciate classical singing,' he guffawed.

Everybody did, but it was his soaring horn, filled with the life and breath of seven-and-a-half decades that defined his art and expressed his years of glorious music.

Pierre Dorge (Denmark) - Joy and promise of a band of the world

Pierre Dorge and the New Jungle Orchestra –
Live at Birdland, Zig Zag Zimfoni & Dancing Cheek to Cheek
(2013)

Why would a jazz guitarist born in frosty northern Europe, in Copenhagen, Denmark, in 1946, a long way away from the heat of the tropics, create a band called the New Jungle Orchestra? The answer to this is found in the extraordinary jazz life of Pierre Dorge. He never had a record player as a boy and 'there was only one hour a week of jazz on Danish radio,' he remembered. 'I had to write my own songs because I couldn't learn standards by hearing them once on the radio.'

He played in the Copenhagen Jazz Quintet and set his ambition to become a teacher, but in 1969, he met the Danish/Congolese saxophonist John Tchicai, who had played with John Coltrane on his album Ascension.

Dorge threw himself into jazz experiment and performance, seeking to create an amalgam between Ellington's early 'jungle' sound, African and Asian musical forms and free improvisation. In 1980 while in the US he met Ornette Coleman. 'I was able to go to his loft in the Bowery. We would talk and I would play. It wasn't really a lesson in the usual way, it was Ornette's way.' Then in 1982 he spent time in Brikama in Gambia, which gave him the final inspiration to create the New Jungle Orchestra and also solidified his powerful musical eclecticism. 'I try to connect cultures in jazz, which itself is basically a folk form,' he wrote, 'to create a global language.'

Between 1984–1987 Dorge made a series of rampaging albums for the Danish Steeplechase label with some surprising guest soloists. Tchicai plays on Brikama and Very Hot, Even the Moon is Dancing (1985) with the South African bassist Johnny Dyani, and Johnny Lives (1987) is a tribute to Dyani with Tchicai again, Barbadian trumpeter Harry Beckett and US free drummer Hamid Drake. The Orchestra has played on into the new millennium, touring the world and cutting new albums on the Danish Stunt label. One of the most vibrant of these is Live at Birdland, a record of immense spirit and immediacy which radiates a jazz cosmopolitanism that is huge and relentless.

There are several lively encounters with Ellington - the Mooche, Caravan and a bass-emphatic Black Beauty - a piece of spoof-Africa, Monkey Forest by Dorge's piano–playing wife Irene Becker with some storm-riding percussion by Ghanaian drummer Ayi Solomon, and a spiritedly Scandinavian version of the St Louis Blues with Dorge's fire-breathing guitar lines and some rasping trombone from Kenneth Agerholm. Lion of Shanghai is the closer, with a gushing solo from tenorist Morten Carlsen and the ensemble full of Chinese echoes.

The year 2000 brought the album Zig Zag Zimfoni, where another part of the planet and its people enter the stew with Arab–inspired melodies and rhythms. Hear the titles - Bahrain, In Aquis or Arab Klap, with a free flute outcry by Carlsen beside Bent Clausen's drums and a tempest of chanting. Jakob Mygind's keening soprano saxophone is at the kernel of Bahrain and the Danish/African pulse still drives tracks like the strutting Zig Zag Zalza and the swaying and celebratory rhythms of Kwanda Wedding. But hear the amalgam of Sun Ra and the Duke in Ellingtonian Space is the Pace, as the jungle blooms on Saturn - via Copenhagen of course.

And don't let the title of the 2004 NJO album fool you. Dancing Cheek to Cheek has really very little to do with Fred Astaire and Ginger Rogers. It is more about an unshackled musical universalism. Rosa Abe Dongola means in Mandinka speech 'Rosa is dancing.' Rosa is Dorge's granddaughter, and the singer is the Gambian kora player Dawda Jobarteh, whom Dorge first met in 1982 in Brikama when he was five. Two continents meet and their sounds harmonise. Kaper Tranberg's cornet shines.

Munzun Mun is Dorge's tune about a Hindu movie in an African cinema played by Danes plus a US trombonist, Ray Anderson, whose slides howl and growl like a polar wolf. Syncretism is alive and powerfully thriving in Dorge's sonic way, and in his arrangement of the 1958 anti-apartheid tune Something New for Africa, which the NJO played for Mandela in Pretoria's National Theatre in 1996, they were coming home to Johnny Dyani's earth as he had once come to theirs. Joy is the note and promise too.

Finally there is Xing Xang, as Dorge traversed Indonesia, Vietnam and China. The sheer musicianship of the soloists - Becker, the Norwegian trumpeter Gunnar Halle, Tranberg and flautist Anders Hagberg, and Dorge himself - makes you marvel. A band of the world, indeed.

(Live at Birdland, Zig Zag Zimfoni & Dancing Cheek to Cheek are available on Stunt)

Phillip Dornbusch' Projektor (Germany) - It's a white man's pandemic

Re/construct

(2023)

Oury Jalloh was a Guinean asylum-seeker who died by fire in a police cell in Dessau, Germany, in 2005. His hands and feet were tied to a mattress. The police ignored the cell's fire alarm, which was switched off.

Such is one racist crime remembered by Phillip Dornbusch's Projektor Band in their campaigning album, Re/Construct. Their engaging electric sounds combined with Dornbusch's powerful saxophone, Johannes Mann's seismic guitar and Johanna Summer's piano, create a riveting listening experience.

A defiant musical statement by young Germans, exposing racism in their own country: 'It's a white man's pandemic,' declares vocalist Juju Rogers.

Hear Mann's delving notes on Constant Vacillation, Dornbusch's fluid phrases on Demons and Roger Kintoph's plangent bass on Anthem. Quoting Martin Luther King, an 'inescapable network of mutuality' shines out with a declamatory vision of a new Germany. It is the improvisation of hope, crying out from a Berlin studio.

(Re/construct is available on Berthold Records)

Kit Downes (England) - The New Orleans pioneers would have loved it

Obsidian

(2025)

Jazz began its life amid the melodies and improvisation arising from hymnal tunes and street parades in New Orleans, Louisiana, more than a century ago. So perhaps Kit Downes' organ rhapsodies in the churches of Suffolk villages of Bromeswell or Snape, or in London's Union Chapel, are not so far from the source.

Downes, born in Norwich in 1986 and a graduate of the Royal Academy of Music, played piano in bands like Empirical, Troyka, Stan Sulzmann's Neon and with Clark Tracey before he turned again to the organ, which he had played in church in his youth. And what a glorious sound he makes with it, as I discovered when I heard his free concert on the Royal Festival Hall organ at the 2018 London Jazz Festival.

Several tunes he played at the RHF recital are featured on his ECM record, Obsidian, which is dedicated to the late Mancunian arch-pianist, John Taylor. All compositions are by Downes, except The Gift, which was written by his father, and the Appalachian folk song of Scottish provenance, Black is the Colour. For Downes, all the tracks are 'structured improvisations' and in this sense they have a jazz soundscape, while the three organs themselves, despite their antiquity, 'felt new' to him and powerfully 'liberating'. As he said of the organ sessions, 'they helped me to expand my musical language and feel less locked down to the piano. Since coming back to the organ, I find that when I return to the piano now, I feel freer.'

Jazz organ in the U.S. context has been organically a part of the blues - think of Jimmy Smith, Jack McDuff or Jimmy McGriff, for example. Yet Downes calls his organ album 'Obsidian', the colour of dark, vitreous lava or bottle-glass, a very different hue from the blues turned into sound. From the opening track, Kings, the long notes of the Union Chapel organ, elemental, extended and stretched, create a timbral effect powerfully pastoral, while Black is the Colour, despite its Americanness, resonates with a very rural British beauty.

What would have Sun Ra, who played no mean organ himself, made of Rings of Saturn, his own mythical birth planet, recorded on the smaller Snape organ? The repeated notes sound as if they have no end, just infinite sonic space, full of a boundless sublimity, as if Downes' space is also the place. Modern Gods is back to the huger, almost rampaging sound of the Union Chapel, then the more delicate and tender cry of the Snape organ for The Bone Gambler, with a steady, walking bass foundation. Flying Foxes is lighter, more buoyant, as if all its notes have been released from their leashes and are scrambling to be free from their sacred bonds. The melody of Ruth's Song for the Sea, serenely pipe-borne, is especially gentle, and the long, heavier notes of Last Leviathan are more menacing - are they ever going to stop?

Downes plays his father's tune on the miniature Bromeswell organ, which he describes as being 'a single manual instrument with no pedalboard, basically a converted harmonium .... it has a very personal voice.' The hymnal theme is full of an intimate, lyrical beauty. The New Orleans pioneers would have loved it, played it, and given it their own musical blessing.

(Obsidian is available on ECM)

Paul Dunmall Double Quartet - Impro at Oto

An evening of boiling improvised jazz

(2025)

A double quartet of roaring boys at the Café Oto, led by the hotwired, gushing and ever-inventive saxophone master from south London, Paul Dunmall. With him are two drummers, his evergreen confrere Mark Sanders and the younger Miles Levin, two basses; the Hounslow monster John Edwards and his delving sibling James Owston; guitarist Steve Saunders, storming trumpeter Alex Bonney and the protean pianist Liam Noble at the Café Oto grand.

At the outset Edwards's and Owston's bass duo seemed to come directly, Jules Verne-like from the centre of the Earth when Noble punctuated their deep tempest with his chiming, almost bell-like tolling phrases and the combined thrashing drums of Sanders and Levin essayed the entry of the furious Dunmall. Potency and turbulence, howling notes, snatches of familiar riffs and extracts – I thought I could hear, under it all, half-melodies of Peanut Vendor and Friendly Persuasion – blasting out sequences that threatened to implode the venue's Victorian ceiling.

After hearing so many Sanders performances, I have never heard him play with such cyclonic force as tonight, in communal sound with the pounding Levin – a maelstrom of drums. Then a sudden relative quietude, and Bonney's respiring horn, blowing until just naked breath came heaving from it, while Edwards's bow sawed at his lower strings and his bass brother earnestly plucked right beside him, then joined him in an intense arco colloquy as Saunders came to the fore with his muffled, chinking, low-down notes and Noble's keyboard runs, Don Pullen-like, scattered the piano's sonic cosmos.

The rest was Dunmall, his septuagenarian power blowing out a life story in huge creative measures until a sudden halt and the music turned to silence: once-played, never repeated, gone and applauded but never forgotten.

Johnny Dyani (South Africa) - Joyful rebel bass booms from the vault

Rejoice/Together

(2017)

The booming South African bass virtuoso Johnny Mbizo Dyani was born in the Duncan Village township on the edge of East London in 1945. By the early '60s he was a member of a forbidden multiracial band, The Blue Notes. 'We rebelled against this apartheid regime that whites and blacks couldn't play together,' he declared. 'We stood up!' In 1964 the Blue Notes left South Africa for a European exile. Dyani's fire was soon noticed by the soprano saxophonist Steve Lacy, who took him on a tour to Argentina and recorded the classic album The Forest and the Zoo with him in 1966.

By the early '70s Dyani was based in Copenhagen and, after a decade, he moved to Sweden. During these Scandinavian years he made a succession of fine albums - five of them on the Steeplechase label, and played with such jazz eminences as Leo Wadada Smith, Don Cherry and David Murray, taking his South African pulse to the very heart of jazz. He died, much mourned, in 1986.

This reissue of two of his finest albums on John Jack's precious Cadillac label is a rare gift of sound. In October 1972 Dyani made Rejoice in a trio ensemble called Xaba – a Xhosa name of God - with his confrere from the Blue Notes, Queenstown-born trumpeter Mongezi Feza, and Istanbul-born drummer Okay Temiz, a graduate of the Ankara Conservatory who found his way to Stockholm and played on Don Cherry's album Orient. The opener Mad High begins with a lightning burst from Feza with Temiz's Turkish drums and cymbals splattering over Dyani's uplifting and humming bass. Feza's excitation continues spurred by his confreres' relentless rhythmic undertow, before

Dyani's sonic trampoline of a solo and Temiz's percussive fury unites the Cape with the Bosphorus.

Feza's own Golden Horn is at the heart of Makaya Makaya, a reference to the Cape Town-born drummer Makaya Ntshoko, who made a similar journey to a European uprooting with Abdullah Ibrahim in 1962. Dyani's bass sounds huge and Feza almost funereal as he begins, but as he breaks into ecstatic phrases and bold cadences he seems to be expressing the cruel frustrations of exile. Dyani's solo springs mightily beside Temiz's fragile bells. Dyani's throbbing solo notes in Pukwana open the tribute to his old Blue Notes bandmate. Bass strings have never been plucked so hard, so beautifully or with so much drama, and when Feza enters the music morphs into melody and dance, almost miraculously, and Temiz's drums crash like giant waves next to his notes.

The simple tune of Imbongolo spills from Feza's horn before his inspired improvisation which retains its joyous air and soaring invention until Dyani's palpitating notes and a unified vocal chorus takes the music home, ready for the 20 very restless minutes of Mad High Revisited, showing Xaba in even more exalted splendour. Johnny's Kwela is sheer cavort, with Pukwana blowing the theme above a raucous communal vocal and Hassan Bah's restless congas. Marabi Soweto lets loose the spirit of dance with Dyani's musical muttering at one with the stamping beat. Kenny Hakansson's slashing guitar rakes through Kalahari and Dyani's tune for the infamous Cape township, Crossroads, evokes the ferment of anti-apartheid defiance that its people generated over decades of resistance.

Finally there is the last tune, Tula Tula, where Dyani's repeated emphatic cry of 'You Did it! You did it!' alongside the saxophones and Perrera's cutting-edge harp is a message to his people and also a message to the world.

(Rejoice/Together are available on Cadillac)

Bokani Dyer (Botswana/South Africa) - A unique piano voice

Bokani Dyer - Emancipate the Story (2017)

Bokani Dyer was born in Gaborone, Botswana in 1986, the son of a family living in exile from apartheid. His father is Steve Dyer, a South African saxophonist, so Bokani was steeped in music from his earliest years. He remembers hours of listening to his father's music as a boy, but it wasn't until he was 16 that he started playing the piano, provoked by hearing some Janet Jackson songs and then going on to take formal piano lessons.

When he left school after periods of living in both Gaborone and Johannesburg, he studied the jazz programme at the University of Cape Town - now free from the strictures of apartheid. He graduated in 2008 and in 2009 was awarded a three-week scholarship in New York, where he was tutored by the prime pianist Jason Moran.

By 2014 he had achieved recognition in South Africa as a major jazz force, had made two albums and was invited to perform at the London Jazz Festival, both at the Vortex in Dalston and the free stage at the Royal Festival Hall with British stalwarts like Soweto Kinch and Shabaka Hutchings.

Completely fortuitously for me, having just listened to a marvellous early evening set by a reincarnation of the South African Blue Notes (who arrived in London also as exiles from apartheid in 1964, setting the jazz scene ablaze) in which Dyer, Kinch and Hutchings had prime performing roles, I found myself sitting next to Dyer at the late evening concert of his country's greatest jazz pianist, Abdullah Ibrahim - born in Cape Town in 1934.

We were both very moved by the performance, and Bokani - as one of the great Ibrahim's true inheritors - was imbibing his every note, every sound. He very generously gave me one of his own Cape Town-produced albums, Emancipate the Story - and listening to it, it is clear that he has a unique piano voice, with a particularly close kinship to the late South African genius of the keys, Bheki Mseleku.

Bokani gathered a vibrant group of young South African musicians together for the Emancipate session, which has a very different timbre from recordings cut in Europe or the US. The opener is Fanfare, with an almost mordant tone to its ensemble before Bokani plays an expansive chorus, and trumpeter Marcus Wyatt's solo has considerable potency in his notes. Tenorist Buddy Wells holds the sense of suppressed menace. Bokani is the composer of all the album's pieces, and Meditation Suite is another slow burner with more breathy Wells and mellow Wyatt before Bokani drums his keys and heralds the conclusion. Kgalagadi has a pounding rhythmic foundation with Shane Cooper's emphatic bass and more scope for Mark Buchanan's whining guitar.

In the next track, Tales, it is as if the pianist is a griot who has travelled to a place where he begins to tell his stories, while the receptive ensemble listen and then join him. On Hoods, Bokani plays a Rhodes electric keyboard and Buchanan's guitar echoes his modernism, while, as through the whole album, drummer and percussionist Ayanda Sikade and Tony Paco stoke up the propulsion.

What is the message and testimony of Sermon? Again, its timbre seems to hold jeopardy and Wells's and Wyatt's lucid attestations perhaps hold warnings and cautions as well as messages. Cooper's plunging bass anticipates Bokani's sombre tidings of a solo. In 1973 Ibrahim called one of his earliest solo albums African Piano, but Bokani's tune with the same name has a very different sound. He plays his Rhodes with the percussion hedging all around him, with new narratives spurting from his keys. It is a very different South Africa now, although the final track Zim Zim echoes the 1970s days of Ibrahim's epochal Mannenberg. Wells's horn sometimes resounds like that of

Basil Coetzee, showing that Bokani and his compadres are as much about South African musical tradition as they are of its future.

(Emancipate the Story is available on Dyertribe Records)

Silke Eberhard (Germany) - Beauty is a rare thing

Silke Eberhard and Dave Burrell - Darlingtonia

Silke Eberhard and Aki Takase - The Ornette Coleman Anthology (2013)

It may seem like an unusual enough duo - a septuagenarian African-American pianist bred and flourishing in free and ever-roving jazz, Dave Burrell, and the much younger Silke Eberhard, a German alto saxophonist born in 1972 in Heidenheim an der Brenz, her inspirations the great US altoists Eric Dolphy and Ornette Coleman. They first met in 2009 at the Jazzwerkstatt Festival, when Eberhard was performing her Dolphy 'Potsa Lotsa' tribute, and the year after they combined at the Schlot Berlin jazz club for their very first live performance, which was recorded and became their album Darlingtonia. Nothing to do with the Durham town or its football club but named after a botanist whose name had been given to the cobra lily, with each track being allocated the Latinate title of a particular species of bug.

Burrell was born in Middleton, Ohio, in 1940 and educated at the University of Hawaii and subsequently at the Berklee College of Music in Boston, where he gained his degree in musical composition. The names of two of his earliest bands, the Untraditional Jazz Improvisational Team with Philadelphian tenorist Byard Lancaster and the 360 Degree Musical Experience with trombonist Grachan Moncur and drummer Beaver Harris, tell of Burrell's unconditionally original jazz pathways, including long stints with powerfully iconoclastic hornmen Archie Shepp and David Murray.

Eberhard had long admired Burrell's work with Shepp. Burrell had heard and been impressed by Eberhard's homage album to Ornette, the Ornette Coleman Anthology, with Japanese pianist Aki Takase. So their live Berlin meeting had all the promise of a truly creative and empathetic sonic rendezvous, with two burning jazz spirits set on a performance of mutual timbral discovery and co-operation from far distant origins.

Lytta Vesicatoria is the first species to be found in the duo's insectarium and as it flickers, leaps and pauses from Eberhard's European horn and runs apace along Burrell's ever-agile American keys, you, the listener, can but marvel that these two musicians, generations, ethnicities, oceans and continents apart, have never played together before - such is the instant bonding of their notes. The second track, called Meloidae, is an improvisation provoked by some gripping unaccompanied Eberhard, but as it develops it makes its own instantaneous tunefulness as Burrell works out a repetitive pattern of notes and Eberhard adds her responses, creating melody by sheer colloquy. Is that what the insects do?

Liloceris Lil II opens with some brilliantly pounding Burrell pursued by Eberhard's breathlessly buzzing and screeching alto response, while the 14 minutes of Rhyncoris Iracundus is built on Eberhard's plaintive blues-like cry before Burrell's astonishingly ubiquitous keyboard replies. Ensifera puts away the microscope with some rumbustious Eberhard romping above her partner's grounding chords, closing a scintillating album.

The Ornette Coleman Anthology is as good as Burrell averred, another duo effort, with this time Eberhard sharing the sounds with the amazingly eclectic Aki Takase, whose wildly diverse recordings run the gamut of jazz artistry, fusing her versions of the early blues with freely conceived tributes to jazz genius as far apart as Fats Waller and Eric Dolphy.

Embracing Ornette, the twosome immediately invoke his extraordinary melodism, from the very first notes of the opener Turnaround to the final sounds of Una Muy Bonita two hours and two CDs later. Eberhard said that the Texan Ornette Coleman's music provided her with 'a giant question mark,' and the tunes chosen by the duo are those he wrote and recorded during his first great challenge to the world of jazz, between 1959 and 1968, now recreated by two brilliant and faraway women.

Takase plays her stride-based phrases gleaned from an era three decades before that of Ornette and applies them to another, five decades after. For Eberhard it is as if she is discovering these tunes for the first time. Hear her bass clarinet, unaccompanied and seething in Cross Breeding, or her alto digging and dodging back through musical history in The Sphinx or Folk Tale.

The tracks are kept short and the tunes are rarely submerged under long improvisations as if Eberhard's birdlike choruses show how much Ornette's tunes were made to whistle and sing for all time, which is what this record's listeners will be doing after they hear Mr and Mrs People, Takase's pounding chords in Broadway Blues or Eberhard's sublime tone in Peace.

As Ornette said through one of his most memorable tune titles, 'beauty is a rare thing' - and you have it here for two gorgeous hours.

(Darlingtonia is available on Jazzwerkstatt & The Ornette Coleman Anthology on Intakt)

John Edwards (England) / Caroline Kraabel (USA) /
Khabat Abas (Kurdistan-Iraq)
Café Oto, Dalston, London
(2025)

This was the first session of the Café Oto residency of the groundbreaking London bassist, John Edwards. With him in a daunting trio were Californian alto saxophonist Caroline Kraabel and the cellist from Kurdistan-Iraq, Khabat

Abas, whose life in music includes playing with symphony orchestras as far apart as Iraq and Gothenburg.

On a sweating Dalston night the sounds began with the dark humming of bowed bass and bowed electro-cello as if coming from subterranean places deep below the Café Oto's stone floor, while over it Kraabel's reed and voice simultaneously made continuous soft and siren-sounding notes.

Soon, Edwards' bass became an uncanny, thumping drumset while Abas laid a wooden wedge over her cello bridge as her bow sawed on. Kraabel's sudden saxophone screeches and Abas' mallet blows on her strings in an instant took my mind to the agony of Gaza, as if horn and strings made harrowing empathy with its mothers and children. Edwards played with a bow in each hand, making powerful dark fire across the lowest regions of his bass.

There was no domination. Each virtuoso was in complete adventurous and inventive accord with their trio-mates, as Abas stroked her strings so gently with her torn and withered bow it was like a lullaby for Gazan infants, until Kraabel's saxophone made new, optimistic pace to create what sounded like a children's song.

What processes of music were here! The art of the musician is to make sounds which make meaning: the art of the listeners is to imagine and interpret that meaning in their own lives and the lives of others. Cellist and bassist were two drummers drumming, as strings became surfaces, skins, the bark of trees, while Kraabel's horn sang, harmonised and told her stories, on and on.

At the end of the performance I told Abas and Kraabel that I thought I had heard and seen Gaza in their sounds in this ex-paints factory in the heart of East London. 'I must play what I see in the way the world is,' replied Abas. 'You heard it too!'

Louis Armstrong (USA) and Duke Ellington (USA)
The Great Summit
(2017)

Two of the great pioneering geniuses of jazz are united on this epochal record, created from sessions cut in April 1961 when Duke Ellington sat in as pianist with Louis Armstrong's All-Stars, a touring band which Louis took with him all over the world. I was discussing a lifelong love of jazz with Pedro, a Chilean friend, a comrade who had been a militant during the Popular Unity years and later a socialist prisoner in Pinochet's prisons who had managed to find refuge in Britain with the support of Sheffield trade unionists in the mid '70s. Yes, he said, he had heard of Armstrong and his All-Stars in his home city of Valparaiso as a boy, and the vibrancy of his sound had never left him. That's what Louis did to his listeners, inspired them for life, all over the world.

On these 'summit' sessions the common factor for both musical giants is the New Orleans clarinet virtuoso Leon 'Barney' Bigard, a staunch member of early post-war versions of the often-changing All-Stars, while also a veteran of Ellington's greatest orchestral line-ups between 1927 and 1942.

Bigard's curlicuing, rococo clarinet licks were an essential part of many classic Ellington recordings. From Mood Indigo to Creole Love Call and Harlem Air Shaft, his waving reedsong was one of the Duke's great sound posts.

All the tracks are classic Ellington tunes, starting from a vibrant rendition of Duke's Place with the quasi-stride Ellington piano, Bigard's birdsong clarinet and the rumbling notes of the wonder trombonist from Savannah, Georgia, Trummy Young. Louis's regular rhythm men, bassist Mort Herbert and drummer Danny Barcelona, keep the beat succulent and on I'm Just a Lucky So-and-So the lyrics are absolutely born for the soulful and eternally optimistic Armstrong treatment.

Ellington is completely at ease, having at last found an equal jazz brother. He zooms into Cottontail: Bigard catches his old maestro up with his serpentine phrases and Louis digs into his notes in no fear at all of being left behind. Trummy growls a chorus and Louis joyfully scats his way towards the end. Bigard, who blew on the original 1930 recorded version of Mood Indigo, now hears Armstrong etch out its chorus before he enters, low and beautiful, prefacing the improvised Louis vocal while Duke noodles on his keys. It is the height of jazz insouciance, and these incomparable elders love it.

It seems strange to hear Black and Tan Fantasy, its muted and wailing 1927 trumpet solo a Bubber Miley creation, played with Armstrong's mighty and crystalline notes, but it works powerfully and the Duke's piano seems well in the mood too as a muted Trummy comes growling in and Bigard's clarinet seeks the skies. It's followed by Louis's amble through Drop Me Off In Harlem, the home of black genius as well as 'red beans and rice,' its savour pouring out of the horns of Bigard and Young.

Ellington's familiar prelude to The Mooche introduces Bigard's transcendent solo and Young's gruff slides above Herbert's jumping bass. Louis comes striding in, his notes like bugle calls of peace and Ellington chivvies up his keys in a summative ending. In a Mellow Tone follows with the Duke in fine fettle and Trummy in mellifluous form: all a prelude to the undeniable Ellington dictat voiced by Louis, It Don't Mean a Thing if it Ain't Got That Swing, and all six of them prove it, with the Armstrong horn as lucid as ice.

Solitude could have been written for Louis, so sharp and impassioned is its tone, and there is a defiance too in the two giants' version of the 1941 song from Duke's musical revue Jump for Joy, its title to become an anti-depression rallying cry: I Got It Bad and That Ain't Good. Louis plays its theme plain and truculent like the slogan for betterment that it was, then sings and scats its love-worn lyrics like a man somewhere near the end of his tether as Duke thumps his own tune all along the keyboard. As Louis exclaims his satisfaction at the very end of the track over Ellington's shoulder, you can sense his happiness that this summit meeting ever happened.

But it did and we can listen and wonder just like Pedro did, marvelling at Armstrong in Valparaiso, Chile, some five or more decades ago.

(The Great Summit is available on Essential Jazz Classics)

Duke Ellington (USA) - A galaxy of troubadours

Duke Ellington Orchestra - Ellington in Grona Lund 1963 (2017)

I first heard the Duke Ellington Orchestra live in 1963 on their umpteenth European tour, while at the Grand Theatre, Leeds. It was during my first year at university. It wasn't quite the same personnel as on the version of the orchestra that played at this concert recorded at the Grona Lund Dance Inn in Stockholm a few months earlier in June 1963, but very close - the stratospheric trumpeter Cat Anderson came in for Ray Nance, otherwise it was the same. So this double album brought back not only Ellington's singular genius but also the phenomenal musicianship of then bandsmen: trumpeters Nance, Cootie Williams, Swede Rolf Ericson, who joined the band at this concert and stayed, and Eddie Preston; trombonists Lawrence Brown, Chuck Connors and Buster Cooper; reedmen Johnny Hodges, Paul Gonsalves, Harry Carney, Jimmy Hamilton and Russell Procope; bassist Ernie Shepard, drummer Sam Woodyard and the Duke himself on piano. What a galaxy of troubadours! I've still got the Leeds programme sold to me on a cold December night, with photos of almost all of them.

There was very little that was predictable about an Ellington concert. You knew you were going to hear Take the A Train sometime in the evening, but everything else constantly changed. On the programme at Grona Lund, for example, the Orchestra played the 20 minutes of Suite Thursday, the Duke's musical adaptation of John Steinbeck's novel about the people of a southern Californian fishing village. The musicians weren't expecting to play it, and as they scuffle to find their music sheets, Ellington buys a little time for them in his announcement.

The concert begins with a tune by Ellington's collaborator and alter ego Billy Strayhorn, Boo-Dah, but soon moves into the ballad Laura with a beautifully serpentine tenor saxophone solo by Gonsalves. Main Stem features Nance, Hodges, Hamilton, Cooper, Gonsalves and Brown in majestic succession and Ellington plays a long and fluent preamble before the ever-recognisable theme of Take the A Train, with Nance's flag-waving solo. Then it is Suite Thursday and its first movement Misfit Blues. Ellington's keys rock through Schwiphti and Hamilton's levitating clarinet is fragilely serene in Zweet Zursday. Nance's bowed then plucked violin is featured on the Suite's last piece Lay-by. On to Hamilton's singing clarinet in Deep Purple and Silk Lace and the muted glory of Williams, who had recently come back to Ellington after a more than two-decade absence. He plays New Concerto for Cootie and Tootie for Cootie as if he had never left.

Grona Lund and its people seem transfixed as Hodges' alto blows beauty through The Star Crossed Lovers from Ellington's Such Sweet Thunder

Shakespeare suite and he stomps and swings along the familiar street of Things Ain't What They Used To Be, down a well-trodden path.

After the interval, Ellington comes back alone, doodling on the piano through Intermission Music before Shepard joins him, then as the musicians drift back, Woodyard and Hodges join him for the ballad I Didn't Know About You and the perennial hodges feature Jeep's Blues before Brown blows as only Brown could all through Rose of the Rio Grande.

As in most Ellington concerts, the classic tunes come one after another. A muted Nance, Procope and Brown revive Black and Tan Fantasy of 1927, the whole orchestra surges through Rockin' in Rhythm first waxed in 1930 after Duke has prefaced it with some boiling stride piano in Kinda Dukish, and Gonsalves makes his Scandinavian mark with a delicate, almost icicled version of 1935's In a Sentimental Mood. Each performance as with every Ellington performance, is anything but routine: it is sheer reinvention, no matter how vintage the tune, and when the huge, guttural sound of Carney's baritone saxophone makes its grounding contribution to Sophisticated Lady of 1933, you suddenly realise how many times he has played it, in how many theatres in the world - and each time different.

And then after Duke's long intro to Lullaby of Birdland, something very special happens. Out of the heart and heat of the orchestral fullness comes the solo Swedish trumpet voice of Ericson, there on the earth of his own northern zone, thousands of miles away from Ellington's land, yet utterly attuned, completely involved, signally beautiful. It is one of jazz's real moments, a defiance of borders, of race difference and nationality. But that was Ellington, every sound, every note.

(Ellington in Grona Lund 1963 is available on Storyville)

Duke Ellington (USA) - Meets Coleman Hawkins (USA)

(2025)

This is truly one of the great jazz encounters: the only recorded meeting of the first master of the tenor saxophone, the Missouri-born Coleman Hawkins (1904 - 1969) and the orchestral maestro of them all and also an understated brilliant pianist, Duke Ellington (1899 - 1974), with the duo playing nine Ellington compositions.

Recorded in 1962 when both musicians were in their full vintage, Ellington brought with him to the studio some of his most mature and veteran confreres: trumpeter and violinist Ray Nance, the peerless baritone saxophonist Harry Carney, trombonist Lawrence Brown and the most outstanding alto saxophonist of his generation and sublime melodist, Johnny Hodges. Other Ellington orchestra regulars, drummer Sam Woodyard and bassist Aaron Bell, were also in the groove.

'After 400 years, we made it!' quipped Hawkins - also known as Hawk or The Bean. 'You know I want you to make a record with me, and I'm going to write a number especially for you,' Ellington had said two decades before this studio tryst, and at last he was true to his every word.

When we hear this now-times reissue, we can still sense the ambiance of huge musical respect and love which radiates from the session, but also the spirit of fun and discovery from the very first track, Limbo Jazz, in which Woodyard, totally unguardedly, hums and chortles all through the piece, as one by one, his bandmates essay their solos while still laying down a springing Caribbean beat. Hodges blows a short aery solo, Nance's trumpet is pure and burnished, Brown's creamy slides take a chorus, Duke's ivories chime and then it is Hawk; soft, purring and melodic before his fellow horns re-enter with Woodyard's mesmeric chant.

Mood Indigo is a tune of simple Ellingtonian beauty which Paul Robeson loved to sing. Here it is all Hawk playing with all the sublime authority for which he was renowned. Jazz writer and commentator Stanley Dance was present at the session and wrote that as Hawk 'entered his second chorus, Duke turned away from the piano with his arms swinging, a characteristic gesture when he is moved.' You can understand why; one nonpareil musician responding to the essential sonic truth of another.

Woodyard's shuffling drums are the foundation of Ray Charles' Place, where the Hawk is very much at home alongside his fellow soloists Brown and Nance. It's a swinging house all right. Then it's on to Wanderlust, written with Hodges in mind in 1938. His saxophone almost levitates in his solo, before Nance blows in, muted and full of the blues. After a gruff Brown chorus it is all Hawk, the engine of his improvisation in full throttle, perhaps remembering his own five years in Europe (1934 - 39), and his time as featured soloist with Jack Hylton's Orchestra, and his freelancing days with Django Reinhardt and Stephane Grappelli.

Then it is on to You Dirty Dog, with Ellington's stride-based piano and Hawkins belting straight in before some luscious solo Hodges and growling Brown. But the real apex of the album is the rendition of the Duke's promised tune for Hawk, the beautifully sombre Self Portrait (of the Bean). As his compadre horns blow a harmonic obligato behind him, Hawkins' solo is supreme, expressing the fullness of his artistry in a mere four minutes.

Another Hodges favourite (named after his sobriquet) is The Jeep is Jumping. Its speedy riff takes off and Hodges races through his solo, followed by Nance's ascendant notes and the marvellous gravelly eloquence of Carney. Brown blows hard before Hawk storms in over Woodyard's rimshots and Bell's plunging heartbeat. It is as if Hawk has been with Duke all his life.

Ellington's witty piano begins The Ricitic with its Latin edge and Nance's leaping violin. Hawk's horn gushes with creative life and fire. And as he opens the final track, Duke's much-played blues melody, Solitude, it is as if he plays it as a tune composed especially for his saxophone brother, and so integrated are all members with the music, particularly Nance's violin, that the warm communality of sounds seems to contradict the very spirit of isolation marked by the tune's title.

There are five more Hawkins' performances of Ellington tunes on this reissue - including a moving version with pianist Randy Weston of his Romeo and Juliet theme, The Star-crossed Lovers, but without Ellington. But the Duke/Hawk recordings are indispensable, with two legendary musicians at their creative zenith.

(Meets Coleman Hawkins is available on Poll Winners Records)

Enji (Mongolia) at the Vortex and Tashi Dorji (Bhutan) at Café Oto (2025)

Mongolia and Bhutan came to Dalston, East London last night, in the extraordinary sonic personages of vocalist Enji and slashing guitarist Tashi Dorji.

At a packed house at the Vortex, Enji was in mouth-bending, circular breathing and vocally cyclonic orbit, alongside bassist River Adomeit and guitarist Paul Brandle. Born in Mongolia's capital, Ulaanbaatar in 1991, Erkhembayar Enkhjargal learned the skills of Urtin Duu, a form of throat-singing and free-form melodies from her childhood. She remembers: 'Every day after my parents came home from working in the local power factory, they would gather with a group of friends in our yurt to unwind, and someone would always begin to sing. Soon we would all join in, singing old folk songs to keep warm and to express ourselves long into the night.'

As she began to sing at the Vortex, the fragile beauty and precision of her voice, its growth in power and lyricism from almost a mollifying whisper to a gradual assertive boldness, singing her folk-inspired melodies made me remember Joan Baez's live recordings of the 1960s. Few people present literally understood her words, but all could find union in the feeling and delicacy of her voice.

There was a springing optimism to her melodies as she sang tracks from her new album, Sonor. The quiet accompaniment of Adomeit's beating bass and Brandle's blues-affected guitar added a piquancy to her words. She sang a song to her mother: 'I'm going to embrace the whole world with the love of my mother,' she said, adding that her father would sing it as he repaired his bicycle. Another song was about half-sleep, about being nearly awake and nearly asleep, urged on by some blues phrases from Chandler's empathetic guitar.

Her last choice of the set was a song of farewell, a message of 'no hard feelings or regrets', with some serene climbing passages falling away as they ended, leaving sensations of an infectious melodic quietude in the listeners' minds.

Then it was down the Vortex stairs, past the Palestine flag in its window, across a bubbling Gillett Square and a 200 yard saunter up the multi-food cosmos of Kingsland Road and I'm outside Café Oto. Coming around the corner at me from Ashwin Street was an electric storm of Bhutanese guitar strings, with Steve Noble's echoing giant gong and pounding toms, and John Edwards' brilliant bass underworld.

Once inside, I thought: 'Blimey! If Jimi Hendrix had been born in Bhutan, perhaps he would have played like this!' Dorji's clanging, crunching, whining guitar, the screams coming from his agonised strings - sometimes struck by a metal rod he took out of his back pocket, created an ambiance of many sharp edges, almost as if stalagmites were springing up from Café Oto's century-plus old stone floor. But whatever his sounds, Dorji had unquestionably met his London match with Edwards and Noble and the spirit of response and challenge that met his every surging note.

It was a night of sheer and extreme mid-Asian contrasts, right here, right now, in the teeming heart of East London.

Kahil El'Zabar (USA) & Billy Bang (USA) – A dynamic duo's songs of redemption

Kahil El'Zabar & Billy Bang – Spirits Entering (2012)

Billy Bang, born William Walker in Mobile, Alabama, in 1947 and who died in April last year, was one of the truly innovative violinists of jazz. Self-taught, his music profoundly self-imagined, he grew up poor in Harlem and the Bronx.

As a youth he played some violin but had put it away before he was drafted to Vietnam at the age of 18, just before the outset of the Tet offensive. He became a 'tunnel rat' in the brutal heat of the conflict and the violence of its memory never left him and marked his every note. 'For decades I've lived constantly with the pain of these experiences,' he wrote in the sleeve notes of his haunting 2001 album Vietnam: The Aftermath. 'At night I would experience severe nightmares of death and destruction, and during the day I lived a kind of undefined ambiguous daydream.'

On his return to the US, he seized the violin again, much influenced by its greatest swing virtuoso Stuff Smith, and through the mentoring of the avant garde violin pioneer Leroy Jenkins. He began recording in 1980, and having co-founded the String Trio of New York in 1977 and served a stint in Sun Ra's Arkestra with Jenkins, he became the defining artiste of the free jazz violin.

For the next three decades he made a host of pulsating recordings, climaxing with his two sonic reflections of the epochal war, Vietnam: The Aftermath and Vietnam Reflections (2004) where he sought reconciliation with the Vietnamese people by bringing together US jazzmen who were ex-combatants with Vietnamese musicians.

One of his prime recorded sessions prior to these records was the one which produced the duo album Spirits Entering in 1998 with the Chicago percussionist Kahil El'Zabar, whose musical experiences stretch between his home city's blues-baked South Side and its Conservatory of Music to Ghana.

Bang said of him: 'He has such command over so many colours, whether he's playing traps or hand drums or anything else, that it almost makes me feel cheated because I've got the same old girl - I mean, my instrument - in my hands. He makes me try even harder to find varieties of colours and flavours on the violin.'

Thus with this duo, communion and emulation are forged together, with simultaneous sonic beauty and discovery. The session begins with the title track, with Bang's swirling phrases recalling Stuff Smith's humour and lithe movement and El'Zabar's snares creating a crisp, earthen rhythm - although it's his hand drums that he calls his 'earth drums.' They are soon in powerful evidence on the lyrical Sweet Irene, where Bang's folksy melody moves sinuously all around El'Zabar's thudding rhythmic centre. 2 Was Now has a stop-time formation, with Bang's bow in lightning mode and El'Zabar's rolls and flourishes keeping pace in rustling movements. It contrasts with the mysterious opening of Love Outside Of Dreams, which catches speed and upward pitch as it hurries forward.

El'Zabar's Ghanaian tutelage sparks with his playing of the mbira or thumb piano on The Dream Merchant with Bang's serpentine choruses creating a sonic unity which sounds much fuller than that made by just two musicians. Song Of Myself is not Walt Whitman but profoundly Billy Bang and who knows what life memories are bursting from his solitary notes, urged on by his drum comrade's scuttling percussion? Continents switch as El' Zabar turns to the Brazilian berimbau all through The Ituri Fantasy. Here are two men moving through the musics of three great continents as if there were no seas. Perhaps Bang's corrosive Vietnam-ghosted notes make it four, as his bow-scraped strings wail somewhere between pain and joy.

As he asserted, playing with El'Zabar is like 'being on the same page but also getting as far from it, into creativity.' The duo achieve this by plunging deep into their own US tradition in their version of Old Time Religion, with El'Zabar's relentless hand drums and voice with the aching folk blues of Bang's violin. The closer is the endless sublime calm of the duo's Golden Sea, a dream perhaps of peace and an end to war and misery.

It's what Bang sought after the horrific jungle trauma of his late teens. With this music of serene discovery he may have found it.

(Spirits Entering is available on Delmarc)

Charles Eubanks (USA) - Love for life amid the ruins of Iraq

New Beginnings & Birds of Baghdad
(2013)

It is June 2003 and the echoes of the war in Iraq won't go away. In London, where a million have marched against war in February. In Washington, where George W Bush sits imperiously in the White House. In Detroit, where pianist Charles Eubanks was born in 1948. In Canton, New York state, where his solo piano album Birds in Baghdad is being recorded. And nowhere more so than in Baghdad itself, where the consequences of Bush and Blair's 'shock and awe' are still killing and maiming hosts of Iraqis every day.

Jazz has often been a carrier and campaigner for peace, and the album and specific track Birds of Baghdad express its ancestral message in every note. The birdsong chirrups from the opening notes but it is a worrisome song, repetitive and desolate, made even more so by deeper, power-driven strikes of the keys as if these birds face other beings and threats from skies hitherto theirs, but theirs no longer. Perhaps it is humans with their music and birds with their irrepressible song who long for the carefree movement of Eubanks's journey of his sleeve poem, across a land-scape below, a 'hazardous terrain' where there is 'back-sliding but skipping forward' and where beings can 'Run skip walk / Dance a lot / Rest listen / Tweedily Dee / Peace.'

But not in Iraq and its capital city.

The other tracks of the album show Eubanks's electric stylistic influences - from Monk, Miles and Irving Berlin to four of his own compositions. From the '60s onwards he plied his trade in Motown session work before he entered the sphere of radical horns like Archie Shepp, Dewey Redman and Oliver Lake and played with Coltrane's last drummer Rashied Ali.

The opener is the angular but brooding Landscape, and the listener guesses how the land lies - urban, rural, flat, undulating but troubled, yes. The 18 minutes of the singularly subjective Making Overtures is sequenced into My Motives, Pensiveness and Solace with blues overtones. The sheer inventiveness of his phrases rise out of repeated chords and riffs and wandering melodic snatches as if his consciousness is finding other kindred souls. Monk's opus Trinkle Tinkle has Eubanks striking the keys hard, reducing its humoresque quality but enhancing its drama and sense of perturbation, while just two-and-a-half minutes of Miles's Dig is powerful, full-noted and rampant. Eubanks plays How Deep is the Ocean? on the very cusp of its melody, as if its narrative were below the waves of its tidal notes.

Tom McIntosh's Cup Bearers is played as a tribute to another great Detroit pianist of the previous generation, the lyrical bopper Tommy Flanagan, whose light-fingered keyboard touch is not emulated by the strident and forceful sound of Eubanks but is resolutely moving all the same. Traditions are revealed in Roadmap to Swing, as Eubanks examines his instrument's own journey. It sounds complex and tough and full of diversion and allusion, but follows a hard, determined route all the way.

The album concludes with another take of Landscape, and such weight of blows to the keys. Eubanks is one of piano's drummers of situation, melody and beauty. This was already proven two years before in his first solo album, in the same hall at the same resonating piano, and called New Beginnings, for it was the first album under his own name at the age of 51. The notes tumble and splash all through his opener, Nocturnal Falls, with a potent sense of natural force, while in the longest track, Sand Prints, Eubanks leaves his marks with a more reflective seal, his imprint definitive and powerfully lucid. He turns to Thelonious again, this time for Ask Me How, the melody sauntering and bouncing through a fountain of notes. There's also a nod to one of his former maestros in the stop-time, quasi-honky-tonk performance of Rashied, and a condensed, concentrated passion in the innermost sounds of Heart Strong. He makes an astonishing piano adaptation of Coltrane's Count Down for four pulsating minutes before he embarks on Charlie Parker's Donna Lee and Sippin' at Bells for two surprising miniatures of bebop jewels.

But back to 2003's Birds of Baghdad and Kara Rusch's expressive sleeve painting of the Iraqi birds swarming over a bomb-blast cloud. Eubanks's keening notes tell us of a similar love for life at the very moment those who would only treat it with contempt and hatred reigned.

(New Beginnings & Birds of Baghdad are available on CIMP)

Maria Faust Sacrum Facere (Estonia) - Marches Rewound And Rewritten
(2025)

I read in this morning's papers that Putin's warplanes have been flying threateningly over the airspace of the Baltic Republic, Estonia. Almost simultaneously, I received a review copy through the post of the new album by the Estonian saxophonist Maria Faust, recorded in Denmark.

It's a record that stares the prospect of war in the face, by lampooning the tradition of the military march, and is a brilliant sonic satire. As a London suburban boy, growing up in the minds and artistry of New Orleans jazzmen, it was their stomping versions of Gettysburg March, Moose March and other regimental tunes turned to vibrant peace parade themes, that I loved and grooved to. One of the first records I ever bought was a 78 rpm vinyl single of the George Lewis Band playing Bugle Boy March, led by the vibrant trumpet of Elmer Talbert, Jim Robinson's gruff tailgate trombone and Lewis' soaring clarinet curlicues. How its joyous, postwar notes rang through our Romford house!

But Faust's Marches Rewound and Rewritten is a very different conception arising from a profoundly contrary era. It even has a sleeve note written by an ex-President of Estonia, Toomas Hendrik Ilves, in which he writes:

'For too many, war is something abstract, glorified and exalted... a source of national pride, true of many empires past and present. And for some, war, its effects, the suffering and horror and its consequences of occupation and reprisals, the march is a part of living memory, quite real and tragic. This is what Maria Faust makes us understand.'

The relentless pounding of Emanuele Maniscalco's snares, Peter Ole Jorgensen's percussion and the haunting Danish ensemble of militaristic riffs begin the album before Faust's weeping horn cries out her solo, telling stories of grief and torment that could be songs of Gaza, of Sudan, of Yemen, of Ukraine. The band shouts out 'left, right, left, right' as if they were on the parade ground before Mads Hyhne's trombone says his prayer for peace, followed by a free incantation of all the horns striving for earshot.

Maniscalco's rattling, incessant snares are the album's hallmark as the march goes on and on as if it were tramping across the breadth of Europe, with Kasper Tranberg's rasping trumpet forays seeming to express the threatened breath of life. In March No. 5, the timbre is mournful, almost elegiac, rising to a climax of horn chorus before the marching inevitably returns, faster and with more intent, before a final sound of quasi-birdsong dissipates its menace. The March No. O is almost a reincarnation of Joe 'King' Oliver's New Orleans rhapsody of Chimes Blues, with its bell-like horns before the pounding, marching percussive boots smother it with fear.

This is an elaborately-composed, dissident suite taking from the jazz tradition and pressing into the listener's consciousness of the imminence of war. Not easily forgotten, it is indeed, a cry of our times.

(Marches Rewound And Rewritten is available on Stunt Records)

Guitarist and singer Piers Fallini (England/Italy) - Shapes of the Fall (2020)

Piers Fallini talks about 'the daily round of news detailing our free-falling ransacking of the planet', and his new album 'Shapes of the Fall' is his lyrical, defiant and beautifully cosmopolitan response to 'a daily witnessing of the dismantling of the natural world around us.'

Fallini was born in Luton in 1970 to a dentist mother and a pathologist father, a mix of Italian, Irish and Ashkenazi. 'I carry immigrant songs in my blood,' he told me, 'like fragments of a lost homeland I'll never find.' He learned piano, guitar and wrote songs from his early teens. 'I discovered Malian songwriters like Ali Farka Toure and Boubacar Traore, and Mississippi bluesman Skip James. I swapped electric for acoustic guitar and went in a folk direction from then on. I've a passion for musical dialogues around the Mediterranean that became a cornerstone of European musical culture - places where Christians, Muslims and Jews cohabited and flourished from North Africa and Southern Europe. Places where people met via trade routes and returned with new ways of learning, musical modes and rhythms. Conversing, crossing and leading to new, more hybrid ways of writing, narrating and playing music.'

For Fallini, 'such musical dialogues are our common ancestry' and are a vital dimension of his album, with Moroccan singer and Gnawa griot Abdelkebir Merchane and Californian songwriter Ben Harper strongly featured, along with African instrumentalists playing guembri and bendir drums. Fallini's lyrics are powerfully lucid and moving, and full of paradox. 'I wanted to drown in the dust of a drought.' he sings. He says he was influenced by Sufi poets like Hafez or Rumi, and that he 'imagines early poets singing their words before the invention of printing presses.'

He describes his songs as both laments and searches for hope. 'The album dances towards hope via the exploration of ancient trance rhythms. The hope comes because I went looking for it in musical rhythms that have traditionally been used for healing. They exude a kind of light to offset the darkness.'

Fallini lives in the remote French mountainous region of Les Cevennes. He sees very closely on a daily basis the toxic climatic effects on trees, insect life or birds. 'Turn the tomorrow leaf over years/Page after page bled out tears', he sings in Foghorn Calling. Or in All Aboard he exclaims: 'All aboard, watch paradise burn/Douse the flame, will it ever return?' In Paradise Fell he could be referencing Australia, California or the Amazon, or calling anywhere to 'Bird on the branch with no say/Sing a little now for another way.' For Fallini sings about rebirth after the fall: 'You were the blood kissed by the thorn/I was the wind in the leaf/I wanted to fall or be reborn.' Or in Epilogue, as he reminds us, we are all birds 'dipping into skies, aching to know flight.'

What about his post-pandemic plans? 'I hope to tour with these songs. Playing live is my lifeblood. To tell these stories and share my music again. I miss it.'

(Shapes of the Fall is available on No Format Records)

Ricky Ford (USA) - They couldn't believe what they heard. Where'd this guy come from?

Veteran tenor saxophonist Ricky Ford
(2024)

He's truly one of the great, if also greatly underestimated, tenor saxophonists in the century of jazz. Ricky Ford, now a septuagenarian, has spent much of his musical life living outside the US in France. His huge achievement as a 20-year-old, of being invited to join the Duke Ellington Orchestra to fill the vacant chair of Duke's recently departed legendary tenorist Paul Gonsalves, happened shortly after the maestro's own death, when his trumpeter son Mercer Ellington inherited the leadership of the orchestra.

Born in Boston, Massachusetts, in 1954, Ford grew up in a professional household. 'My father was an attorney-at-law, my mother was a nuclear medicine specialist,' he told me. 'At 12 I studied drums and played melodica. I started to play saxophone in 1968 and I never looked back. After a few gigs at Wally's Paradise in Boston, I joined Mercer Ellington in late 1974.' He studied at the New England Conservatory, and after his second year Ellington tenure he continued a rich jazz life when he joined Charles Mingus, staying until 1977, when he began to play in a band led by Mingus's powerhouse drummer, Danny Richmond, followed by stints with Lionel Hampton and the South African pianist, Abdullah Ibrahim.

Among his albums are jewels like American-African Blues and Manhattan Blues, with the brilliantly protean piano of fellow Massachusetts virtuoso, Jackie Byard, and a luminous joint album with Yusef Lateef, where the two tenorists play tribute to their great saxophone compadres from Sonny Rollins and Joe Henderson to Stanley Turrentine and Wayne Shorter. 'I always loved Yusef,' he exclaimed: 'He came to hear me during a concert at Amherst. After the concert he asked me to record with him.'

For one night in February he crossed from Paris to play with a trio of London-based musicians at Soho's Pizza Express. You couldn't keep me away! 'The pianist, Emile Hinton, is my former student and bassist Larry Bartley and drummer Rod Youngs are two musicians I greatly admire,' he told me. It was a powerful session, coinciding with the release of his latest album, Paul's Scene, remembering the saxophonist he replaced in the Ellington Orchestra.

'Once an Ellingtonian, always an Ellingtonian!' he declares in the album's sleeve notes, remembering his first concert with the orchestra: 'The guys made me play on every tune. I'd stand up there and all these cats had their heads down, just listening. They couldn't believe what they heard. 'Where'd this guy come from? He knows the whole book!' they said to each other.'

In Soho, Ford's horn gushed with life-force, with his power of improvisation in the strongest, most muscular fettle. Beginning with the Kenny Graham opus Mabulala (Graham, an Ealing-born composer, arranger and saxophonist, is a musician whom Ford particularly admires), and moving on to Fer, inspired by a Turkish maqam melody (Ford taught for several years at Istanbul's Bilgi University). He also blew hard and breathily through Reggae 7, illustrating another aspect of his jazz cosmopolitanism, well appreciated by his London bandmates. There was a beautifully serene rendition too of McCoy Tyner's Search for Peace.

As for the Paul's Scene album, Ford has some powerful confreres, with fellow veteran drummer Barry Altschul, bassist Jerome Harris and pianist Mark Soskin, and they play with a rousing energy and musicality, empathetically tuned in to Ford's sinewy sound - hear Altschul's accompanying drums explosion to Ford's onslaught in Fer, showing that neither the hornman's vigour nor the drummer's might have diminished an iota over the years.

Seven of the compositions are Ford's, but there is a remembrance to the father of the tenor saxophone, Coleman Hawkins in The Stockholm Stomp, and the pianist Hank Jones in Paris Fringe. Ellington is represented by his enigmatic tune Frustration. Ford shows his ballad excellence on I Can't Wait to See You and Angel Face, and the title track takes you back to the serpentine flow and Cape Verdean life-beauty of Gonsalves's unique and unforgettable sound.

What is it about the ever-changing timbre yet eternal heartsblood of the tenor saxophone? 'Everything is always evolving in terms of music and playing the saxophone. When I was younger the general idea was to be your own voice. Years later, as a result of teaching, you start to appreciate what you stayed away from, in the search to find your own sound.'

Ford has certainly found it: a unique and unmistakable combustion of sonic brawn and tender, creative beauty.

(Paul's Scene: The Wailing Sounds Of Ricky Ford is available on Whaling City Sound)

Freedom of the City - Annual mayhem sets creative spirits free

Conway Hall, London
(2010)

There could hardly have been a more appropriate message than the inscription 'To thine own self be true' above the Conway Hall stage where the annual Freedom of the City: A London Dream, took place on Mayday.

The sound of scores of improvising musicians revelling in notes of freedom was their response to that exhortation, from the immense horn power of Evan Parker's tenor saxophone and Peter Evans's astonishing cosmic trumpet to Okkyung Lee's grunting cello. Earlier in the day her strings had coughed and rasped as her bow sawed next to Paul Lytton's tapping, quivering drumsticks.

Eddie Prevost, the 68-year-old drummer, played with the youth, swing and verve of a percussionist with the whole of jazz drumming behind him from Baby Dodds to Jo Jones, Max Roach and Sunny Murray. What an amalgam he made in his SUM trio with Ross Lambert's crunching guitar and Seymour Wright's wailing alto horn.

The London Improvisers' Orchestra - all 34 of them - included three sets of drums, three basses, three bass clarinets, vibes, piano, a cybernetic whistle and four soprano saxophones just for starters. Playing freely yet with uncanny unison, there were break-outs from howling ensembles like the two trombonists and the blasting parade power of their New Orleans tailgate slides.

The cawing song of Lol Coxhill's wild soprano horn next lo the scraping boom of Dominic Lash's delving bass in notes of unpredictable joy and invention, made one reflect that if Londoner William Blake had played music, it would probably have sounded like this.

But the stand-out was a trio of two drum sets with the unleashed trumpet power of Ishmael Wadada Leo Smith from Mississippi with Englishman Steve Noble's ringing drums and cymbals.

They were aided and abetted by the percussive comradeship of the Cape Town maestro Louis Moholo-Moholo, who listened assiduously lo every sound bleeding and howling from Wadada's horn and added his own drum testimony with restraint, reserve and empathy.

All in all, it was a stirring annunciation of May and musical hope expressed in the unambiguous sound of humanity reaffirming the enduring creative energy of jazz improvisation.

Chico Freeman (USA) and Von Freeman (USA) – Unity across the jazz generations

Lord Riff and Me

(2013)

Fathers and sons blowing saxophones together; John Coltrane never lived to groove with his son Ravi, but there were Jackie and Rene McLean in New York City, Dewey and Joshua Redman making their album African Venus together in the same city or, in London, Jimmy and Alan Skidmore crossing generations and genres together. Or fusing in Chicago, the huge impact of two giant saxophonists - Von and Chico Freeman - each a virtuoso, both of them masters of their horns in different epochs, different contexts.

Lord Riff and Me was issued as the son Chico's album, with the Lord Riff of the title being his father Von (short for Lavon). By 1987 when the album first appeared Chico, born in Chicago in 1949, had become a prime tenor saxophone contender and an international jazz traveller while Von, also born in Chicago in 1922 and who died in the same city in August last year, preferred to spend his time and artistry in his home city, becoming a local horn legend with his own unmistakeable caustic, gurgling and bluesbaked Shytown sound resonating from local clubs and bars.

Chico's playing had taken a different direction to that of his father. Much influenced by both the R&B bands he played with as a young hornman and the avant-garde ideas of the Chicago-based Association for the Advancement of Creative Musicians, he developed his own powerfully eclectic sound, making a series of acclaimed albums on the India Navigation, Contemporary and Black Saint labels.

The hour of hornpower on the Lord Riff and Me includes the contributions of three more master musicians. On Piano is George Cables, New York-born gripping soloist and attuned accompanist to potent reedmen like Dexter Gordon, Art Pepper and Joe Henderson. The bassist is the post-bop supremo Cecil McBee from Tulsa, Oklahoma, and the arch-drummer is: Billy

Hart, a Washingtonian veteran of the bands of Miles Davis, Herbie Hancock and Wes Montgomery. So all in all, quite a quintet.

They open up with Von's Blue Baby Do, which begins with some jaunty Cables before Von stomps in with a characteristically leaping chorus. Son and father play the melody of McCoy Tyner's Ballad for Aisha in unison, above Hart's fluttering drums and Cable's splashing notes before Chico's soprano slides into a haunting solo above McBee's springing bass. Nearly 11 minutes of Coltrane's familiar Moment's Notice begins with Chico's tenor dancing off Von's blown bass chords. Von's pugnacious solo pushes all before it - fast, breathless and relentless, and as Chico takes over, lighter, almost weightless compared to his father's sound, the melody and its variants begin to fly and soar, propelling Cables into a pulsating chorus of rapid motion and airy intervention.

Back to history's impact upon the present and the enfolding of tradition with the aching notes of the spiritual Motherless Child. The theme is played with the pain of the elders and two succeeding generations bursting through in the horns and in Cable's chorus, with McBee seeming to measure out the long years of struggle through the wood of his calibrating bass. The past vibrates in every note.

Sneakin' Peakin' is McBee's playful tune in which his bass is on heat and the two tenors romp through their pacy solos with a joyous sense of freedom followed by an inspired Cables. Chico nourishes the ballad I Fall In Love Too Easily with a beautiful but earnest melodism, with McBee's eternal twang shimmering below him, and Von's South Express picks up fire and speed as it travels with Hart's drum energy providing the steam for the elder horn's powerful engine.

Vonce is another of Von's themes, a languorous blues with one of the confreres howling behind the horns, The apparently valedictory message of the album's final track Bye Bye Blackbird also radiates hope and the promise of renewal and further meetings. It's son before father on the solos, with Von in blustering fettle followed by McBee with a huge buzz in every deep, deep note.

Von and Chico were to record again together in 1989 on the India Navigation album Freeman and Freeman, but I love the verve and informality of Lord Riff and Me, carrying a marvellous jazz message of the unity of generations and telling its constant story of continuity and permanent motion.

(Lord Riff and Me is available on Why not)

Paolo Fresu (Italy) - Drenched in creative beauty and meaning

Paolo Fresu and Daniele di Bonaventura - In Maggiore (2016)

Many years ago I stopped worrying about what is or isn't jazz, my ears having sensed many times over the wisdom of Duke Ellington's words that the best in music and musicianship is quite simply 'beyond category.' And this album is a lucid case in point, made by two Italians who are humans of the world and whose sounds are drenched in creative beauty and meaning. Masters of their instruments, the music that they make is beyond borders, beyond boundaries, improvised beyond predictability with sounds anew and memories bursting from their notes. That's jazz for me, for the world and its fullness comes out in their every sound.

Recorded on the shores of Lake Lugano in 2014, the album brings together the Sardinian trumpeter and flugelhornist Paolo Fresu (born in Berchidda in 1961) and the bandoneonist Daniele di Bonaventura (born in Fermo, in Italy's Marche region in 1966). Fresu's early musical life was nurtured in his island's marching bands, while di Bonaventura began to learn classical piano at eight, played cello too and studied composition and orchestration before concentrating upon the small accordion-like bandoneon.

Strange that the album begins with what is conventionally a closing movement, the Da Capo Cadenza by di Bonaventura, a slow, mournful melody blown with transcendant beauty by Fresu and di Bonaventura's bandoneon sounding close to a miniature church organ. Fresu's Ton Kozh has its origins in a Breton lullaby and his horn sounds distant, dreamlike, as if there were a sea between his breath and your ears. Chico Buarque's Brazilian melody, O Que Sera is played with a restraint and quietude which is deeply affecting as the duo weave between each other's notes, improvising their phrases and delicate accretions to the tune.

Then suddenly, in an instant, out of one sonic world there comes another as the bandoneon moves into the Chilean freedom anthem that we heard and chanted ourselves a thousand times on solidarity marches in the 1970s: El Pueblo Unido Jamas Sera Vencido, and out of a few very familiar notes the words come back to us, memory and now-times find unison and it is a sublime musical moment.

Non ti Scordar di me is a Neapolitan song by Domenico Furno and Ernesto de Curtis famously performed by Gigli and Pavarotti.

Fresu plays the melody with an agile lightfootedness as if he were bouncing off his partner's chords. The trumpeter's tune Apnea was born in his reading of a novel by Lorenzo Amurri about a musician waking from a long coma after a near-fatal ski accident. He reaches some high-pitched vertiginous passages, brilliantly realised, a precipice of sound.

The Chilean singer-guitarist Victor Jara's revolutionary song Te Recuerdo Amanda, written before Allende's electoral victory with Unidad Popular, tells the story of two lovers (the names of Victor's parents) Amanda and Manuel. She runs to the factory 'splashing in the puddles, raindrops in your hair' to meet Manuel who will soon 'vanish to the mountains' to fight. The impending tragedy of Chile and Victor's murder are movingly expressed in the story told by these two Italians' beautifully wrought sounds.

The burnished and bell-like clarity of Fresu's horns is riveting: hear him on his own concluding title tune or through Se va la Murga by the Montevideoborn songsmith Jaime Roos, where di Bonaventura comps and strikes his bandoneon before he sets himself free with a snatch of melodic invention. Or there is Fresu's own brief and sky-reaching Calmo which makes you imagine the echoes of his sound over the lake, grounded by di Bonaventura's earthen chords.

Who would have conceived of two jazz musicians performing a waltz from their compatriot Puccini's opera La Boheme? Yet Quando m'en vo Soletta per la Via becomes prime jazz territory as first trumpeter and then bandoneonist play the theme and interweave unique harmonies and colloquies between their sounds.

It's a pity that Duke never heard this twosome, for they are another living and sonic truth of his universal assertion. For delving into while going beyond categories is what they do on this record, so readily, so meaningfully and so beautifully.

(In Maggiore is available on ECM)

Natsuki Tamura (Japan) / Satoko Fujii (Japan) / Ramon Lopez (Spain)
Yama Kawa Umi
(2025)

The Japanese words 'yama, kawa, umi' mean 'river, mountain, sea', and are the title of an album by a superfine trio, Japanese pianist and trumpeter Satoko Fujii from Tokyo and Natsuki Tamura from Otsu, and Spanish drummer Ramon Lopez, born in Alicante in 1961. The title is a listener's metaphor for the life of a river, from source to sea. Which river? All rivers. Which life? All our lives, everywhere, stretching as far as the musicians' breadth of humanity and beyond, recorded in Paris, released by Not Two - a Polish label, with excellent liner notes by John Sax, a writer from Belgium.

The sudden volley of notes in the opener, Headwaters, from all three troubadours suggests a dramatic birth, a free spring of waters, before Fujii's echoing solo piano gives suggestions of volume to come, and Tamura's horn intensity the power to come. In Signpost, it is Lopez's erratic drums that show that this river's life will be complex and unpredictable, like the sounds and collective harmonies of all three musicians, especially Tamura's breath-laden pointillistic notes.

Sparkling Water pictures a youthful river - Tamura makes his trumpet talk while Fujii ploughs her keys, and One Day Later Tamura's horn respires while Lopez's drums are everywhere. Fujii's piano is pensive, almost immobile at the outset of Cold Water.

Lopez's drums salvo opens the title piece while Tamura blows like a man on fire and Fujii's solo turns and meanders like a stream in maturity, before Tamura's muted horn echoes its complexities, its ox-bows and the jeopardy of its flood plains. His oxymoron of muted lyricism passes into the very heart of Dusk Sky, as Lopez's skins and cymbals scuttle and throb beside him.

It's an album, which like the best of recorded sound, cries out to its listeners' imaginations to visualise and sensualise its soundscape. The soul of all rivers, great and small, rural or like the small, polluted brook of the 'River' Ching which runs inexorably through my urban neighbourhood, all flow through this record: streams of life, kept alive by music like this.

(Yama Kawa Umi is available on Not Two Records)

Tia Fuller (USA) - Beyonce's saxophonist dazzles with her own jazz band

Decisive Steps and Angelic Warrior

(2017)

For the seething alto-saxophonist Tia Fuller, who plays in the all-woman band which accompanies Beyonce, as well as in regular jazz formations, 'playing in front of 16,000 people or 60 people it's the same, because it's all about people, transferring energy, uplifting and encouraging spirits and sharing the love of music.'

Born in Aurora, Colorado in 1976, the daughter of teachers in the Denver school system who were also musicians, her girlhood was full of the sounds of Charlie Parker and John Coltrane, as well as the piano of her sister, Shamie. Starting from the flute, she grew into the saxophone and by 1998 she had graduated in Music from Spelman College in Atlanta.

In 2001 she moved into the jazz scene in New York, playing in stellar company with Jimmy Heath, Ralph Peterson, Don Byron and Jon Faddis, among many others, but it was in 2006 that another way beckoned when she became a featured horn in Beyonce's band, and thus began a strange coupling of jazz and superstar pop, while she also established a high reputation for teaching, both in Aurora state schools and at prestigious college level.

Her 201 album Decisive Steps has sister Shamie on piano and her drum mate in Beyonce's band, Kim Thompson, with bassist Miriam Sullivan forming a central quartet, and male guests in Christian McBride (bass), Sean Jones (trumpet), vibesman Warren Wolf and tap dancer Maurice Chestnut.

Tia says that the fist altoist that she ever transcribed was Cannonball Adderley, and there is something of his fleeting brilliance in the album's title tune opener, with Shamie's pacy solo following her notes. These four women fly, their sonic union levitates, as it does on Windsoar, where Jones's soft-toned trumpet joins the swooping, swallow-like sound.

Thompson's emphatic drumbeat and McBride's electric bass ground Tia's dug-in notes in Ebb and Flow, where she sounds full of the earth before Jones's soaring chorus. The old standard I Can't Get Started gets a soulful unaccompanied intro by Tia before McBride's acoustic bass throbs out into its heart and Wolf's mallets put it into a new age. Kissed by the Sun has some groovy Shamie and a beautifully filigreeing soprano saxophone chorus from her sister, while Night Glow, written by Shamie's husband Rudy Royston, gives Sullivan her moment, her bass sound ancestral but still palpitating.

Wolf's lucid vibes match Tia's luminous clarity and McBride's cavernous notes in Clear Mind, and in My Shining Hour it is the quartet pulsating out with a vibrant sisterly swing, Tia's saxophone song full of verve.

In 2012 she released the album Angelic Warrior with Royston on drums. On the opener, Royston Rumble, Shamie and she set up a rapid pace before Tia's alto comes leaping in and guest John Patitucci's piccolo bass is also sprinting. The more sultry Ralphie's Groove (dedicated to Peterson) features Tia's lithe soprano and another virtuoso drummer, Terri Lyne Carrington, guests on the title tune, her complex drum patterns scattering under Tia's melodic lead. The saxophone test-piece ballad, Body and Soul, is given a bass-emphatic performance in honour of Tia's bass-playing father, while Dianne Reeves's expressive vocal is a tribute to her singing mother. Tia's horn bleeds with feeling, and in Descend to Barbados, a tribute to her bass player Mimi Jones and her Barbadian parents, her cadences fall like Caribbean rain.

Back to urban reality in Simpli-City, her horn, full of the streets, struts over Jones's walking bass, and she ends with her salute to Beyonce, Ode to B, showing that her artistry finds no barriers between the very different genres that she plays within - 'beyond category,' as Ellington used to say. And as Tia herself declares: 'I think musicians are taking a step forward on both sides; we're moving forward with combining all forms, and more people are accepting that concept, because it's all interconnected. We, as people, are taking decisive steps.'

(Decisive Steps and Angelic Warrior is available on Mack Avenue Records)

Korhan Futaci (Turkey) / Mark Sanders (England) / Charlotte Keeffe (England) / Esat Ekincioglu (Turkey)
Live at the Vortex, London
(2025)

Two English, two Turkish - but they weren't competing against each other last night at Dalston's Vortex - just finding a hot, cooperative and far-flung groove. Saxophonist Korhan Futaci and bassist Esat Ekincioglu, trumpeter Charlotte Keeffe and drummer Mark Sanders had never played together before, but that didn't worry them. Their conflagration of boiling sounds fused in an amalgam of Istanbul and London, bringing rhythmic excitation and fiery hornplay to a venue where, in music certainly, all nations meet.

Futaci began with a wooden recorder-like pipe, Keeffe joining in by blowing down a cardboard tube, plastic toys and a rasping mouthpiece, while bass and drums gave a strong rhythmic undercurrent. Then Futaci turned to his alto sax, blowing like fire and unleashing strangulated phrase after phrase before Keeffe took her first trumpet solo. Volleys of blistering, belching vibrato brass she made with superb control and invention - as much breath as sound, while Ekincioglu's bass bow sawed on beside her and Sanders pummelled out with his superfine groundings and pounding solo, ending with his ringing strikes of small cymbals lying on the skins of his snares.

In their interplay, the horns of Anatolia and Lincolnshire searched out together new modes of union in a searing colloquy, so close in their scorching fury as if the Bosphorus didn't exist. When Ekincioglu took his final plucking solo it seemed like a coda of virtual relief, although you wished too that it would all go on and on.

Such are the brilliant contradictions of this music as it blazes live and real into the listeners' ears.

Red Garland (USA) - A Red unity of sound to get the Korner buzzing

Red Garland Trio - Swingin' on the Korner
(2015)

William 'Red' Garland was a Texan, born in Dallas in 1923, whose father was a lift operator at the First National Bank. 'William, we're not musical,' father told son, 'it must be something you were meant to do.' Red followed two very contrary arts with his hands, being both a boxer in his youth and, after a stint on the clarinet, a prime pianist. 'Discovered' by Hot Lips Page in his home town, by the early 1950s he was playing in New York with some of jazz's greatest saxophonists, from Coleman Hawkins to Charlie Parker and Lester Young.

By 1955 he became part of Miles Davis's first great quintet, with John Coltrane, bassist Paul Chambers and the jewel among the drummers Philly Joe Jones, before he began to cut a series of rampant trio albums for the Prestige, Jazzland and Moodsville labels. By 1965 the first Davis quintet had disbanded and Red's mother died in Dallas. He returned to his family and, apart from a few rare forays to New York and Los Angeles for club dates, he stayed in his home town, out of the jazz spotlight.

Swingin' on the Korner was recorded at San Francisco's Keystone Korner during five nights of performing in December 1977, just seven years before Garland's death. He is playing with two old and intimate confreres - the ebullient Philly Joe and the rampaging 'walking' bassist Leroy Vinnegar, born in Indianapolis in 1928. It is almost incredulous to learn that they never played as a trio before as they perform superbly through two hours of live rapture, with Red manifesting in his every note what another great Texan pianist, Cedar Walton, said of him: 'No practitioner of the art of jazz piano swung any harder or with any more soulful lyricism than did the great Red Garland. He paved the way for so many of us.' From the blazing opener Love for Sale, the trio blare into a succession of ballads and bop standbys, with Red playing on the cusp of each melody, Vinnegar pulsing within their very innards and Philly Joe's speed of percussive reaction and depth of empathy creating three swinging souls in each one. Each performance has a narrative, as if these so-often-played tunes like I Wish I Knew, The Christmas Song, Autumn Leaves or Never Let Me Go are telling entirely new stories which the listener is prompted to create by the trio's sheer freshness of delivery.

The sudden quietude of It's Impossible is sublime in its suddenness, with Vinnegar's deep effervescence and Red's notes so carefully chosen, chiming like keyboard bells. After folk tune Billy Boy, three bop classics follow - firstly the very un-American Dear Old Stockholm and its evocation of another faraway harbour city, a trio palaver of close musical comradeship. Then there is Kenny Dorham's Blues in Bebop, where Red brings together his epoch and his heart's blood, and where you bless the now-times exuberance of live recording. The third is a very singular, almost tender, version of Green Dolphin Street.

The second CD begins with Red playing Monk and Straight No Chaser with Philly Joe's astonishing foreground drums. Lucky were the listeners at the Keystone Korner that night to be so close to it all as Philly tears up the leather and Vinnegar's bass throbs so relentlessly alongside Red's boiling pianism. Some more reflective minutes pass with On a Clear Day You Can See Forever before the trio go gently into a climatic rendition of The Best Things in Life Are Free before transforming it into the naked poetry of swing.

This session has never been released before. If you want to hear unity of sound and creativity of conception to an nth degree - here are your moments with Red, Philly and Leroy.

(Swingin' on the Korner is available on Elemental)

Matyas Gayer (Hungary) / Dave Green (England) / Steve Brown (England) Trio

Pizza Express, Soho, London
(2025)

An unusual tryst this. Here on the edge of Soho, in a basement of Dean Street where Blake, Shelley and Marx had walked, were a superfine jazz trio. Matyas Gayer, a young pianist from Nagykanizsa, Hungary, near the frontiers of Croatia, Slovenia and Austria: Steve Brown, a Mancunian drummer who as a young jazz recruit in 1990s London, had accompanied American jazz eminences like Harry Edison, Benny Golson and Junior Mance; and veteran bass virtuoso Dave Green, born in 1942, who had grown up in Edgware, London with Rolling Stones drummer Charlie Watts and in his youth had played and toured with such U.S. legendary jazz horns as Coleman Hawkins, Ben Webster and Rahsaan Roland Kirk. Here was a trio defying all years, geography and genre.

I was sitting at a table a yard and a half from Gayer's keys, looking over his pulsating shoulders, my mind throbbing with the effortless swing of his opener, Monk's Eronel, before Green took his dancing solo and Brown his aery breaks. Then on to Hungarian classical composer Zoltan Kodaly's adaptation of a folk tune, Evening Song, with Gayer's beautifully simple solo piano opening and Green's elegiac bass lyricism, which all those years ago had been part of the mighty Hawkins' rendition of Body and Soul, in full accord with Brown's tenderly supportive brush strokes along his cymbals. The looks and smiles of brotherhood between these trio-mates were as close and endearing as the notes they made together: pure happiness in music!

Then Blue Mitchell's The Cup Bearers. The speed and lucidity of Gayer's phrases matching Brown's superbly empathetic drumming and Green's resonating strings. Next was the Billy Strayhorn tune, Ballad for Very Tired and Very Sad Lotus Eaters, with Gayer's bell-like notes tolling over Green's almost subterranean bass springing up from the Soho earth like the clearest of springs.

Finale of the set was a strident tune from the Wolverhampton bassist Dave Holland: Jumping In. How joyfully Gayer attacked his keys with skill, zest and freedom! I had a sudden vision of Blake, Shelley and Marx bent over on the street outside, their ears to the pavement, listening to the music below and loving it!

Mike Gibbs (Zimbabwe) - Wild sublimated emotion

Mike Gibbs Band - Just Ahead
(2015)

In the '60s and '70s exiled African jazz musicians had a powerful and profound effect on the progress of British jazz. While the refugee Blue Notes from South Africa - Dudu Pukwana, Mongezi Feza, Johnny Dyani, Chris McGregor and Louis Moholo - spread their sounds among London-based progressive jazz artistes with an incendiary influence, another brilliant musical head, a white African, born in colonial Rhodesia in 1937, Mike Gibbs, also brought his own original jazz genius, immersed in both African and US traditions, to stir into the mix.

Gibbs took a circuitous route to London. He came via the Berklee School of Music in Boston, Massachusetts, where he prospered under the tutelage of mentor Herb Pomeroy between 1959 and '63, and the Lenox School of Jazz run by John Lewis, pianist of the Modern Jazz Quartet, where he studied alongside fellow trombonist and great bop pioneer JJ Johnson.

Gibbs returned to Rhodesia, but left when the draft threatened, to South Africa. He found himself 'so against the scene there' that he moved on again. So he arrived in London already with a host of musical influences and, as trumpeter Ian Carr once wrote of him, he was ever open to more. 'Mike

Gibbs listens to and learns from 'straight' music, pop, rock, jazz and anything else that, as he puts it, catches his ear.'

By the late '60s his compositional and band-leading prowess had come well to the fore, and the ebullient album Just Ahead, recorded from four consecutive nights at Ronnie Scott's in May 1972, shows his big band alive and thriving with some of Britain's finest horns, including trumpeters Kenny Wheeler, Henry Lowther and Harry Beckett, trombonists Chris Pyne and Malcolm Griffiths, and saxophonists Stan Sulzmann, Ray Warleigh and Alan Skidmore. Roy Babbington is on bass, John Marshall on drums, Chris Spedding on guitar and electric sitar and Frank Ricotti plays vibes. All of them were definitely up for it, and Ronnie's was throbbing and bouncing all that week.

The opener, Grow Your Own, has some Africa-fermented motifs, surging rhythms and roaring ensembles, not unlike some of those themes from McGregor's Brotherhood of Breath rampaging big band, before Spedding flies out of the horns, his strings palpitating. Three is almost all Warleigh, fecund and lyrical over the blues-inspired colorations of the other combined horns and Marshall's presiding drums. Country Roads, described by Gibbs as 'country and western blues,' has an astonishing rock-oriented solo by Spedding and Dave MacRae's electric piano spitting out its notes. Trumpeters Lowther and Wheeler step up for Carla Bley's Mother of the Dead Man, encircling its slow, serpentine theme with beauty and watchfulness as it grows louder and stronger.

Skidmore is the protagonist of Just A Head, with Babbington's plunging bass and Marshall's crashing drums urging him on as he plays faster and faster, unleashing chorus after chorus of raw and passionate sound for 10 tempestuous minutes. Nowhere was written for the US civil rights activist and co-ordinator of the voter registration campaign in Mississippi, Bob Moses, now being played in the heart of Soho. A gently percussive beginning breaks into a series of solemn, collective horn chords before Marshall's drums and pounding, booming and splashing cymbals carry the band in huge and wild fanfares to its denouement.

Another Carla Bley piece, Sing Me Softly of the Blues, opens the road for Stan Sulzmann's muscular and deep-throated tenor, followed by a long and discovering vibes solo by Ricotti, echoing through Ronnie's rafters, its phrases supported and prompted by the band's ensemble arms. Griffiths's growling bass trombone introduces the 21 minutes of So Long Gone with Spedding's twanging electric sitar chords closely following, before Pyne's mournful slides hold the centre.

It is an astonishing big band performance of both time and place - disciplined yet wild with sublimated emotion, its ensembles tightly woven, its soloists, like Pyne and MacRae with his razored electric piano choruses rise almost like nature itself from its fertile soil in the midst of a great European city's hard and tarmacked streets.

Then as the African rhythms come bursting out, the singular cosmos of the musical mind of their maestro, steeped in the sonic traditions of three continents, is marvellously manifest.

(Just Ahead is available on Beat Goes On Records)

Frode Gjerstad (Norway) - Starkly original sounds
Frode Gjerstad and Derek Bailey - Nearly a D &
Frode Gjerstad, John Stevens and Derek Bailey - Hello Goodbye
(2013)

Born in Stavanger, Norway, in 1948, the saxophonist Frode Gjerstad spent his youth in the teeth of bitter coastal winds and I often wonder how deep they still blow through his horns, even within the midst of the hottest improvised music. Gjerstad recalls: 'There were only about 50,000 people living in Stavanger and the cultural life was mostly the theatre and the orchestra, plus the occasional concert. If you wanted to get into something, you really had to search for it.'

After discovering jazz on the family radio, in particular the 'incredible' flute-playing - 'it sounded like a bird' - of Eric Dolphy, he had found that something. He heard the saxophones of Ornette Coleman, Albert Ayler and Jimmy Lyons across the airwaves, and was transfixed by a photograph of Ayler on the front cover of the first Downbeat magazine that he ever bought. In 1968 he bought a saxophone and began to make up for lost music while working as a social science teacher. In 1979 he met the British free drummer John Stevens on a visit to London, and two years later telephoned him from Norway, inviting him for a joint gig. Stevens came and Gjerstad's life changed.

The drummer contacted the South African ex-Blue Note bassist Johnny Dyani and they formed the trio Detail, which soon gained international exposure - including a British tour with US trumpeter Bobby Bradford and the cutting of a series of fine albums. Gjerstad and Stevens remained close confreres and collaborators right up to the drummer's death in 1994.

Gjerstad vividly remembers one particular session at Stevens's regular haunt The Plough pub in Stockwell, with Dyani and Bradford. 'We played very well that night,' he remembers. 'It was the last gig with Dyani and the last time I saw him. The place was completely packed and we had a good audience. And it was very damp - my jeans were wet after we ended.' That's what it was like - The Plough in a nutshell.

Memories of the wonderfully magnetic and formidable Stevens are certainly stirred on the 1992 Emanem album Hello Goodbye when he and Gjerstad formed a trio with the Sheffield guitarist Derek Bailey at a Stavanger date. An unlikely enough threesome - London, Sheffield and Stavanger, and a long, long way from New Orleans.

But jazz is the sound of surprise from the most unusual and bizarre combinations and unities. And how they play, this trio on the watery edge of

Norway. Free, united, musically brave and starkly original. 'It was one long workshop lasting 13 years,' Gjerstad said of his time with Stevens.

And Hello Goodbye has that immediate and completely spontaneous ambiance from the very first sounds of the opener Hello. There is Gjerstad's own alto saxophone birdsong, angular and piercing, sometimes terse, other times mollifying, Stevens's scuttling, rebellious drums and Bailey's raking, plucking strings, full of echo and vibrato, his city's steelworks epitomised in every harrowing note. Listen to their amalgam of sounds on the astonishing Three Two Three Two One - such a fusion of blatant differences for 21 naked minutes, completed by what must be the longest recorded note in jazz, only to be overtaken by the 24 minutes of Three By Three, where Gjerstad warbles extravagantly and sometimes hurriedly, Bailey itches and scratches his strings beside Stevens's relentless cymbalism.

With Stevens gone eight years before, Gjerstad and Bailey met again as a duo in Bailey's Hackney flat in 2002, and Nearly a D was the recorded result. The opener Bells has some chinking rhapsody from Bailey while Gjerstad blows a piercing clarinet at its topmost reaches. At one point Bailey's string cadences sound as if he is falling down a long staircase, so urgent are his notes. 'We do not have solos in our music, only two or three people playing,' declared Gjerstad. It's just a few unaccompanied guitar notes at the outset of A Cup Of Tea and then it's an intense, empathetic unceasing drink of togetherness all the way through until Bailey exclaims: 'Let's have a cup of tea then!' Well, they deserved it.

Since Nearly a D Gjerstad has made a succession of fine albums with US musicians, in a trio with arch-bassist William Parker and drummer Hamid Drake, and with the Brooklyn vibes and drums of Kevin Norton.

And as for the free jazz improvisation they all play, he says: 'The fact that more and more of the commercial music is created in such a way that all spontaneity is lost and the end product is very often extremely boring and slick, will maybe lead to more interest in this music because it is the opposite.' Amen to that.

(Nearly a D & Hello Goodbye are available on Emanem)

Will Glaser (England) - Music of the Terrazoku (2025)

When you first listen to drummer Will Glaser's Music of the Terrazoku, two tapes of 'ethnographic recordings from an imagined future', you may ask of these genre-defiant sounds; 'how far out can you go?', but then you begin to think, almost immediately, 'how far in can you go, how far inside the world we live in is this, and its future in the present?'

The Terrazoku are a many cultured, multi-ethnic, planet-loving community of survivors of environmental catastrophe. It is their fictional narrative, devised by Glaser, which holds this extraordinary sonic experience together, and Glaser has assembled a rendezvous of powerful musicians to express it with consciousness and brilliance.

Glaser was born in 1991 in Worksop, where his father managed a Halford's cycle shop before qualifying as a building control surveyor, and his clarinet-playing mother combined piano teaching with working nights in Tesco. 'I wanted to play clarinet like her, but the teacher told me my teeth were too crooked to play, so Mum directed me towards the drums',- after he had been fascinated by a West African djembe drum his parents had bought at a car boot sale.

He played in the Nottinghamshire Youth Orchestra, was gripped by rock bands like Led Zeppelin and Pink Floyd and eventually became drawn into jazz by his Grandad's love of the music, and began to buy a succession of jazz albums marked by four stars in the Penguin Guide to Jazz Records: by Max Roach, Wayne Shorter, Sonny Rollins, Herbie Hancock and 'decisively' - Ornette Coleman's At the Golden Circle. When he left school, he studied at the Guildhall School of Music, where he met and was deeply affected by drums tutors Trevor Tomkins and Paul Clarvis. He swiftly became one of Britain's most creative improvisational drummers. When I interviewed him, he had just finished a tour through Poland with the great protean violinist, Nigel Kennedy.

From his early years his love of music fused with his love of nature. As a boy, his father would take him to the Pennines, which drew out his wonderment: 'I really loved nature. Even now, if I'm having a bad time, I sit by trees. I find them inspirational.'

Perhaps these experiences prompted Terrazoku, for it is musical storytelling at its most intense. As soon as you hear Ruth Goller's quasi-subterranean bass on Sunshower or James Allsopp's haunting bass clarinet and the incessant electronic wind of the planet's desperation through Howl, with Glaser's drums as the first, ever-continuous and last sounds of the spoliation of nature and Earth, you witness in music its agony and collapse.

Glaser uses a deft trio of electric drums, field recordings of hives and bass on Bees; electronic birdsong on When the Clouds Pass, and on Theft the slight and vulnerable sound of Alex Bonney's recorder matched with the pummelling artistry of two drummers - Glaser and Jem Doulton, creates gripping timbral drama before the screaming imprecations of Ed Dudley warns of the reality of a thousand now-times waterways in There's Shit in the Rivers.

Yet the hope and struggle of the Terrazoku strive to return the world from disaster to new life, their determination finding the words of Chinese poet Yang Licai, sung with crucial meaning by Lauren Kinsella beside the sawing cello of Estonian Kirke Gross: 'Rain is another name for heaven and earth,/All in the end is water' as Glaser creates rainsound by a field recording of water slashing against a metal staircase. Everywhere is sound, brought into art: 'I was allowing sounds to shape themselves into something,' he says.

'It's about loving nature and a lamentation about what is being lost by a relentless urge for profit, but it's also a celebration of what must be reclaimed and rebuilt. We have to say something in our music. I get frustrated with the merely theoretical aspect of music and just seeing performers embroiled in their own individualism.'

'There is genocide in Gaza and millions more will die if we don't do something about it. Like Max Roach in his album of Civil Rights, 'We Insist!', we have to say all this in our times too. The only way I can make sense of the world is through my music: to process my feelings of planetary grief but also to imagine, compose and play for a better future for all of us - or any future at all. For me, as a musician, there's no other option.'

(Music of the Terrazoku is available on Not Applicable Recordings)

Robert Glasper (USA) - In memory of those misrepresented and abused by the laws of their land

Robert Glasper – Covered
(2017)

The dedicatees of the Houston-born pianist Robert Glasper's new album Covered will never hear its power and beauty. They are those who have been killed by police and their cohorts in the US, all those whose names have been kept alive by the incessant resistance and love of their families, friends and millions of other US citizens demonstrating and marching through the streets of their cities, outside courthouses and police stations in the very faces of those who have misrepresented and abused the laws of their land.

It is not until the final track of Glasper's album, called I'm Dying of Thirst, that his dedication becomes fully explicit, when a group of children recite the names of the victims, many of them, from Trayvon Martin of Florida to Michael Brown of Ferguson to Eric Garner of New York beside Glasper's softly comping piano, Damion Reid's clipping drums and Vicente Archer's delving bass, and one boy delivers the communal message of pride and happiness in selfhood beyond colour. The words resonate alongside the music, and cross an ocean too.

Covered was recorded live in December 2014 in a Hollywood studio with a warm and receptive audience. Reid and Archer make up the same longtime trio on Glasper's first two Blue Note albums (Canvas 2005 and In My Element 2006) and the threesome play with an intimate understanding of, and empathy with, the subtleties and unique ways of each other's music.

As soon as Glasper moves into I Don't Even Care, what immediately impresses, unusually from a pianist with strong hip-hop connections, is the compelling lightness of his touch on the keys, as if his piano ancestry goes back to Teddy Wilson or Tommy Flanagan, although the repeated rhythmic and percussive sound of his notes also remind you of the pianism of Mal Waldron - an attachment which becomes more and more apparent as he plays Reckoner. His notes in Barangrill pulsate and tingle beside Reid's cymbalism and Archer's dancing beat, and during the 13 minutes of In Case You Forgot his sound gains force and sharpness as he begins to address the song's melody between pounding interpolations supported by Reid's ever-inventive drums. When Archer comes pulsing in, his relentless throb only thickens the heartsound.

So Beautiful is a melodic love song, softly and wistfully played, Glasper's notes finding kindship with the quietude of Musiq Soulchild's chanted vocal. Through The Worst he strikes his keys harder, making communion with Reid's drums and chiming almost bell-like in his long, searching chorus. On to the only standard in the album, the familiar theme of Stella by Starlight recorded by a host of jazz pianists. Glasper plays it like no other, with short, jerking phrases of improvisation on the very cusp of the melody, which comes and goes like a sonic ghost almost between the bristles of Reid's flickering brushes.

As the album moves towards its close, there is one astonishing track simply called Got Over, albeit a bare two minutes long. Glasper joins with 88-year-old Harry Belafonte, who talks softly and huskily about his life in Harlem, in Jamaica, in Harlem again - always in discovery and struggle, while the trio, nearly six decades younger, listen and play softly with him. 'I am one of the ones of colour who got over,' he declares, 'one of the ones the bullets missed. I'm dyslexic, the son of immigrants from an island of slaves who endured.' So when immediately after the children, 80 years his juniors, read out the names of those who the bullets didn't miss, it is especially moving and becomes a stark, chilling commentary of now times.

For people such as I, who remember Belafonte offering us in 1956 our first inkling of Caribbean working lives in The Banana Boat Song, and also remember his activism all through the civil rights era, his campaigning against apartheid and his excoriation of the warmonger Bush and those he named as the president's house slaves - Condoleeza Rice and Colin Powell, who, he said, 'are serving those who continue to design our oppression,' we have the feeling that his life has been with us all our lives.

Three generations of resistance come together on this record, a remarkable young Texan pianist generating truth in the present and hope in the future.

(Covered is available on Blue Note)

Sound Miracles Galore: London Jazz Festival 2009

The best possible start for a jazz festival: as I walked into the lobby of the Albany Centre in Deptford, to hear the New Orleans trumpeter now resident in London, Abram Wilson, there he was blowing with a group of primary-aged jazzmen and jazzwomen, African-Caribbean, Asian and white, being with his jazz where jazz should be. Wilson's gig was but one of scores all over the capital throughout the week, and it seethed with life and artistry. Playing with a trio of young English contenders, Wilson's notes danced and scintillated as he played tunes from his new album, Sound Portraits.

Pianist Peter Edwards opened up his upright to show the chiming legs of his keys all through From Dusk to Dawn, while Karl Rasheed-Abel's delving bass moved the riverside earth under Deptford's tar and concrete. Wilson's melodic skill, both with mutes and a burnished open horn as in the ballad Even Though You're Bad for Me, pushed upward by Graham Godfrey's empathetic drums, created a little neighbourhood of the Crescent City not next to the Mississippi but just south of the Thames.

Still on the South Bank the next night, but in the much more exclusive surrounds of the Queen Elizabeth Hall - and that certainly didn't put off the largest proportion of black listeners I have ever seen at such a venue. The reason was the presence of the hip-hop inspired pianist Robert Glasper and his trio, plus the vocalist Bilal, who are all featured on Glasper's new album Double Booked.

Glasper is a percussionist of the piano, and bassman Vicente Archer stands in the middle of two drummers, sounding a deep earthy twang between Glasper himself and Chris Dave with his formal drumset. Archer digs a ghostly shaft with his notes all through the gripping Downtime, inspired by falling rain seen through a window, and when Bilal delivers his startling, wailing vocals, his bass manages to tether them to the Thameside mud. But Glasper can play with a beautiful quietude too, and as he softens out his notes with a soothing confessional blues, he plays the taped voice of Martin Luther King and the sudden phrase of 'music we need... when our words fail us.' Many heads all around me nodded.

Another day onward and another Southern pianist. Glasper is a young Houstonian but Marcus Roberts is 46 and from Jacksonville, Florida, playing in the classical acoustic confines of Wigmore Hall with drummer Jason Marsalis, the youngest of the New Orleans brothers, and the Memphis-born bassist Rodney Jordan. A blind man, like Art Tatum, and a weaver of sound miracles too, his touch on the keys is as light and buoyant as a flying Autumn leaf, and as he works through his neoclassical programme of tunes by Cole Porter, Ellington, Fats Waller and Monk, he redefines their themes, finding his own narrative.

Take Waller's Jitterbug Waltz. His opening cadence tinkles like the stony downflow of a pellucid Pennine stream over Marsalis' skipping brushes and Jordan's bass so soft like a newborn infant's heartbeat. As in Waller's original creation, his version invokes nature and the human like something real, even under the Victorian romantic ceiling splurge over his head. The music breathes life as the beat of the trio levitates.

Next night at the QEH and another pianist, Carla Bley, full of humour, mischief and surprise, starts off her concert with her quartet, The Lost Chords, with Three Blind Mice. The composer of many a big band performance and joint founder with Charlie Haden of the Liberation Music Orchestra, Bley, born in Oakland in 1938, wears her jazz with both madcap and revolutionary scarf. Her

Lost Chords are true jazz creators, like bass guitarist Steve Swallow, entirely in tune with her perturbations. Or brilliant drummer Billy Drummond, whose concentrated grimace as he plays resembles the focus of a gargoyle. Or Wiltshire-born tenorist Andy Sheppard, whose flowing notes, each eliding seamlessly into the next, are like sounds leaking from an echoing cavern.

Her tunes are replete with Monkian starts, stops, pauses, sudden bursts of notes, quizzical interludes and lingering codas, each performance a rhapsody of the unexpected hinged with the defiant, exactly replicating her long jazz life. Elegiac and wistful too, as in the duet she played with the ever-effervescent Swallow from her album of Christmas carols - stemming from her early years as a child of a church musician. O Holy Night it was, its sheer beauty expressed by two jazz septuagenarians.

The final foray was at the same venue; a concert celebration of Devonian John Surman's sixty fifth birthday. Baritone and soprano saxophonist, bass clarinettist, electronics musical wizard and composer of countless pieces, the first half of his concert had him accompanying electronic motifs, then partnering the Norwegian singer born in 1937, Karin Krog. Their partnership goes back four decades, and as Surman's bass clarinet punctuated and improvised around her succession of Norwegian folk songs, the old empathy was still radiant. But it was when she began to sing Billie Holiday's God Bless the Child with Surman at the piano, and the American nightmare of individualism and self-seeking emerged from the lyrics, I remembered how Krog's life itself had suddenly changed when as a girl she truanted school to hear Holiday sing in Oslo, and jazz had kidnapped her from a routine Scandinavian life.

The concert's second half featured the ripe quartet of Surman with Chicagoan drummer Jack DeJohnette, veteran guitarist John Abercrombie and arch-bassist Drew Gress, playing tunes from their rampaging album on ECM, Brewster's Rooster. It is difficult to transmit the unleashed power of this quartet's sound. In Slanted Sky, DeJohnette's crashing drums uplift Abercrombie's throbbing strings and Surman's surging baritone, while in Hilltop Dancer, the amalgam of ecstatic notes, grounded by Gress' pounding bass was sublime in its union, a trans-Atlantic alliance of jazz genius made in London and not easily forgotten.

Harry Gold (England) - Socialism and jazz Gold

Harry Gold and his Pieces of Eight – Bouncing Back (2010)

'I was amazed at the verve with which, at 91 years of age, he soloed on bass saxophone, directed the band, led the ensembles, and berated the audience when it was slow getting up to dance, and led everyone in a rousing rendition of The Red Flag. This in itself suggested a political zeal as undiminished as the zeal that drives his music.' So wrote the jazz writer Roger Cotterrell of the one and only Harry Gold, leader of The Pieces Of Eight, jazzman all his working life during eight decades, and ever-active trade unionist and socialist on the London music scene. His maternal grandparents ran an east London tobacconist shop, his father was a Stepney tailor and Harry was born near Dublin in 1907 when his parents were on a short stay in Ireland.

They soon returned to live in Leytonstone. In his autobiography Gold, Doubloons And Pieces Of Eight (Northway Publications, 2009), Gold recounts a first memory -in the same way as my own father told it - of 'a huge cigarette-shaped airship caught in a blaze of searchlights, one moment seemingly perfectly motionless and the next a blazing inferno' as Lieutenant Leefe Robinson shot down a zeppelin over Essex in 1916. The incident somehow reflected the fiery passion of Gold's life in music, caught with a stomping power and energy in the album Bouncing Back, recorded at two live dates in Lancashire - one at Preston in 1988 and the other from Oldham in 1991.

Gold told how in 1919 his father took him to hear the Original Dixieland Jazz Band on tour from the US at the Hammersmith Palais, and how it changed his life. 'Then and there I resolved to be a musician. To this day the sound of the band has never left me.' The ODJB were a five-piece band, and although their echoes may be heard in Gold's eight-piecer, the latter always raised the sparks and spirit as if they were a mission.

The Lake label has also issued another vibrant session from the 1984 Pieces Of Eight tour of the German Democratic Republic, called Live In Leipzig, but the Lancashire performances show the octogenarian Gold in full and remarkable throttle with a swinging band of earnest Englishmen for 75 pulsating minutes. The opener and title tune is Gold's own, a swinging vehicle which gives solo opportunities to clarinettist Ron Findon, trombonist Derek Wadsworth and Gold's belching bass saxophone, a rare enough instrument on British bandstands. Then it's straight on to ODJB's standby Ostrich Walk - also a Bix · Beiderbecke favourite. Findon is in juicy form and trumpeter Nick Stevenson emulates the mighty Bix.

Gold's arrangements, neat, brief and well-defined, give plenty of space for short solo work. Little Rock Getaway offers a stomping start to pianist Austin Malcolm and Findon's clarinet takes more fire, and in King Oliver's Temptation Blues, Wadsworth blows a little Kid Ory-inspired tailgate trombone. It's back to New Orleans for Panama, and the band sound as if they would get the street followers jiving through the Crescent City or even up Gray's Inn Road outside the pub where they used to play so regularly. Even the novelty number, I Wanna Be Like You from The Jungle Book, is full of good spirits, with Gold's solo squelching out life. Another tune with Beiderbecke associations, Since My Best Gal Turned Me Down, has Gold belying his years and some fine moments from Stevenson and Meade Lux Lewis's Honky Tonk Train Blues shows Malcolm revelling in some stirring stride piano.

When Gold played There'll Be Some Changes Made, there's no doubt that he believed it. You can feel more than a little of his socialist fire in the notes that blaze from the huge horn that dwarfed him, but that he controlled so dexterously. Long live his joyous sound and the lifetime of commitment that poured from it!

(Bouncing Back is available on Lake)

Benny Golson (USA) - Sublime sound of the sax

Roots, Ronnie Scott's, London

(2000)

'This is a saxophone band!' announced tenorist Benny Golson, introducing Roots at Ronnie Scott's this week. And he's right. Four sublime veteran saxophonists displaying the glory of their horns and providing a chronicle of post-war jazz in the beauty and power of their sound.

Golson himself - boyhood friend of John Coltrane in Philadelphia, ex-member of Art Blakey's Jazz Messengers during some of the most explosive years with Lee Morgan and Bobby Timmons is remembered, too, for his co-leadership of the Jazztet with Art Farmer. He is also the writer and arranger of classic hard-bop tunes like Moanin', Along Came Betty and Blues March. Now he plays hot and mellow, as he and the spirit of jazz chooses.

Nathan Davis - soaring with his soprano sax on Coltrane's Impressions, bludgeoning with his gutteral tenor on Rollins's Doxy or the Pres's Lester Leaps In. A collaborator and friend of Eric Dolphy during his final years and an artist of superb versatility and strength of sound. Odean Pope - ex-Max Roach sideman and leader of the Saxophone Choir - is a profoundly original player, close to a baritone sound, but on tunes like the Harlem celebration Uptown Afterburn is by turns breathlessly mobile or honking and changing pitch like a downhome bluesman. And finally, the British contribution Peter King - playing, like he'd been in the same auspicious company all his jazz life, brilliantly lithe and inventive, sending his alto sound in six different directions at once in great showers of notes. Something of a saxophone pantheon indeed, giving a marvellous and many-faceted meaning to the complexities and ambiguities of the reed.

And backing them up, the loping pianist Kirk Lightsey - offering his own tunes like Heaven Dance, but much more too in his romping solos and relentless subliminal foundation for the horns. US drummer Greg Humphries banged and whipped his drums around as if he was drumming for a big band - which, in truth, he was, grounding the saxophones in the percussive earth of deep power. And as for the other European in the band, bassist Bob Magnusson. His speed over the strings, bowed dexterity and stunning range made him a potent solo voice as well as providing a surging undertow of beat.

In short, a group of musicians who carry the story and message of jazz like a banner and, in particular, the primal, sublime sound of the saxophone that has been at its core ever since Coleman Hawkins first blew his heart and brain through its shimmering body many years ago.

Paul Gonsalves (USA) - Saviour of the Duke

Paul Gonsalves - Ellingtonia Moods and Blues (2012)

The names and lives in music of Duke Ellington and Paul Gonsalves will always be unified, and not only because Gonsalves played tenor saxophone in the Duke's orchestra for more than two decades between 1951 and 1973.

By 1956 Ellington had reached a nadir in his popularity and prestige. The rise of bebop had provoked a growing neglect of the great jazz tradition of the big bands, and Ellington's genius had become strangely unfashionable. Then, at the Newport Jazz Festival that year, the Ellington Orchestra played the Duke's Diminuendo and Crescendo In Blue. Gonsalves stood up unexpectedly and uproariously played a 27chorus solo which set the festival alight and caused such attention and admiration for Ellington and his music that it was frequently claimed that Gonsalves's roaring notes that day were responsible for a huge revival in Ellington's popularity and fortunes for the rest of his life. He became Ellington's inseparable lead saxophone soloist until they both died, within days of each other, in 1974.

Gonsalves was born in Boston in 1920, the son of an immigrant from the Cape Verde islands off Senegal, notoriously one of the driest clusters of islands ·on Earth. Yet his saxophone sound was positively riverine, his solos full of great serpentine curves of notes which no other horn player has ever emulated. As a boy he played the music of his ancestors, learning guitar in the Cape Verde style and singing the Creole folk songs from the islands. After wartime service he plunged into big band jazz as a tenor saxophonist, first with Count Basie and Dizzy Gillespie before pledging his horn to Ellington.

Gonsalves cut relatively few small group albums compared with the scores that he made with the full Ellington Orchestra, but two, both from 1960, are brought together on the CD reissue Ellingtonia. Ellingtonia Moods and Blues was a session with some of his stellar Ellington Orchestra confreres, including Johnny Hodges on alto, trumpeter and violinist Ray Nance and trombonist Booty Wood. A springing rhythm section of pianist Jimmy Jones, drummer Oliver Jackson and bassist All Hall, plus a menu of tunes by Hodges, Billy Strayhorn, Gonsalves and the Duke himself give a typical Ellingtonian small group ambience, Gonsalves is utterly in his element, playing beautifully wavering solos in It's Something You Ought To Know, as well as Chocataw.

Hodges, his perfect alto foil for more than two decades, slips into his blues soaked, melodic self and Nance's vulnerable and searching timbre is very much a part of the same Ellingtonian geography. Gonsalves, closer to his Newport sound, grooves and digs into his choruses in The Lineup, and Hodges flies, rises and swoops through Way, Way Back before a croaking, muted solo by Wood and Gonsalves's breathy chorus. Strayhorn wrote the tranquilly tuneful Daydream specifically for Hodges, but this version is all Gonsalves, playing as if pure melody is sheer sonic smoke from his horn. All members are on well-trodden ground on I'm Beginning To See the Light and Hodges is matchless in his solo before Gonsalves equals him throughout the final opus DA Blues, blowing with such composure and invention that his notes seem to hold the same naturalness as breathing.

The other session, which created the 1960 album Gettin' Together, is a very different jazz preposition with Gonsalves uniting with a group of second generation boppers led by trumpeter Nat Adderley on cornet, with drummer Jimmy Cobb fresh from the 1959 epochal Miles Davis Kind of Blue date, Jamaica-born pianist Wynton Kelly and archbassist Sam Jones. Gonsalves squeezes huge emotions inside the four minutes of I Surrender Dear beside the lyrical Kelly, builds up an earthy groove on J And B Blues, and takes a smoking chorus on the downhome opus of Low Gravy next to Adderley's blues-laden comet.

Every time that the Tube rumbles through Finsbury Park, I think of the brilliant Gonsalves playing at Ellington's last London concert in 1973 at the Rainbow Theatre and imagine the happiest of reunions listening to him live again, with the giant musical will and brain of Ellington at his elbow, urging him on.

(Ellingtonia Moods and Blues is available on Gambit)

Grand Union Orchestra
Oxford House, Bethnal Green, London
(2025)

If music is the true food of diversity, as a certain Elizabethan groover might have said, he would have loved the marvellous cosmopolitan sounds of the Grand Union Orchestra, who are playing at a concert to mark International Migrants' Day in Bethnal Green's Oxford House in their East London heartland on December 19 - a venue once the base of Tower Hamlets Movement Against Racism and Fascism during the anti-National Front activism of the 1970s.

The Grand Union are a musical microcosm of how we would want England to be, bonded together in one London borough, with fine musicians from England, Bangladesh and India, the Caribbean, Chile, Russia and Brazil, South Africa, China, Australia and Germany. They are a creative riposte to Farage and his minions, showing how music is a catalyst of unity beyond genre, beyond category bringing a diverse nation together in real time, in a real place that lives it every day.

Every successive Grand Union concert is a tribute to the internationalism of its creation, and to its instigator too, Tony Haynes (1941 - 1924), who founded the orchestra in 1984. As its powerhouse South African trumpeter, Claude Deppa, another of its pioneers, said: 'Tony had an irreplaceable talent for imaginative music that allows every musician to tell a story. His influence and spirit remain strong, as we aim to continue his work and break new ground.'

The stories from our neighbours from everywhere will tell of their talents in this concert expressively called 'Songs from Our Beautiful Island', in a part of London where over the centuries, Huguenot and Flemish weavers, Jewish tailors, Irish dockers, Somali seamen and Bangladeshi garment workers all worked to live and make music.

Come and hear the sounds of their jazz narratives and now-times lives: you'll love it!

What a mesh of rhythms and sounds was here! Drums everywhere - almost every orchestra member, whatever other instrument they were playing, sat with a hand drum in front of them. Grinning primary school children playing bright blue violins and cellos next to grey-haired veterans, Zhu Xiao Meng's beautifully melodic Chinese guzheng next to Amisha Karsan's rolling Indian tablas, with Chilean percussionist Carlos Fuentes' drum set and Siemy Di's Cameroonian guembri. Australian Louise Elliot's tenor saxophone suddenly transformed to a flute and Deppa exchanging fiery trumpet phrases with East London boy Freddie Abel Parish. The world in an orchestra, and as they played Haynes' musical adaptation of the U.S. children's poem, I Live in the City, the summative words rang out emblematically from Russian vocalist Anna Opochinskaya and Bangladeshi troubadour, Sultan Akash:

I live in the city, yes I do,
Made by human hands.
Black hands, brown hands, yellow and white
Built the buildings tall and bright,
Black hands, brown hands, yellow and white
Filling everyone with shining light.
Black hands, white hands, yellow and tan,
The working woman and the working man.
I live in the city, yes I do,
Made by human hands.

And outside, all up and down Bethnal Green Road as the market sellers folded up their stalls in the evening hubbub, its people walked and talked in a stew of words and tongues, constant expressions for all of us living in this 'beautiful island', inside and out.

Devin Gray (USA) - In a world ever more consumed with social media and AI, this music is truly handmade

Melt All The Guns Trio - Melt All the Guns 2 (2024)

Melt All the Guns are a revolutionary jazz trio formed by drummer Devin Gray, trumpeter Ralph Alessi and Haiti-rooted pianist Myslaure Augustin. Their music radiates now-times in the US and Berlin, where Gray spends much of his time. I ask him about his life in music and the themes of the trio's new album, Melt All the Guns 2.

Born in Portland, Maine in 1983, his father a businessman, his mother a health worker, it was his grandfather who set him on the road to jazz. 'He knew and really loved tons of classical music and jazz - Ellington, Coltrane, Monk and Max Roach - and gave me my first LPs by drummers Gene Krupa and Buddy Rich. He helped me know bebop through the history of the civil rights movement. At middle school I started on piano and drums and around 16 I spent a summer school with some New York musicians, which truly brought history in line with real jazz happenings.'

In 2006 he moved to New York for a master's at Manhattan School of Music. 'I'd started playing professionally at high school because I wanted to play and work at music all day, rather than at some boring job that took me away from music. My drum heroes were Max, Elvin Jones and Tony Williams, with Terry Lyne Carrington and Cindy Blackman. Many others too, wow!'

I ask whether he felt the trio inherited the strong political alignment of Roach and Charles Mingus. He seizes on Mingus's name: 'Mingus is amazing all around for me - as composer, songwriter, bassist and just a bad-ass person and truth spreader - alongside Max and his freedom suites. I'm absolutely inspired by them because they made me realise that you can actually speak the truth through music, that they go hand in hand and actually make a difference in the world, waking people up to the things that matter by their brilliant historical groundwork.'

Why Berlin? 'I first went to Berlin on tour in 2006, and went back every year until the pandemic. I knew it was the place for me, a wonderful city with a rich history and brilliant cultural traditions, a city of endless artistic dreams. It's a more sincere place to focus on my musical work.'

And in the midst of 'Trumpery,' had the trio been targeted by hostile media and forces of political backwardness? 'Trump is nothing to care about, look up to or listen to. A trash-can ego psychologically ill! Yes there have been some strong backlashes against our music from gun lovers and NRA lobbyists and supporters. I'm happy about that - that's the point. What people need to hear is opposition against such stupidity, the sounds of real change and progress for the people.'

What about his two trio-mates? 'Ralph is a brilliant musical interpreter. He just burns when it comes to melodic improvisation, what a quick musical thinker! I love Myslaure's musical touch and sound and her sense of groove. She grew up listening to Mozart, Beethoven and the rhythms of Haitian music and gospel in her family church.'

In the album's opener, East Berlin 2024, the threesome, Alessi in particular, don't just approach sound, they attack it, and in Swing States Myslaure's swinging sonic undercurrents and Gray's thrashing drums are the pulsating bedrock of Alessi's bursting notes. In Administration Rulez Alessi's high notes and Myslaure's sure-fingered, rampaging solo break through bureaucracy, while the album title tune gives a trumpet voice of sorrow over Myslaure's ivories of lamentation, gradually turning to tenderness and fading birdsong.

No More Walls is a riposte to Trumpery, with Alessi's horn, Myslaure's lyricism and Gray's defiant drums speaking openness, friendship and warm welcome: no slogans, only human sounds. Gray sounds like a William Morris of jazz when he says of his trio's music: 'In a world ever more consumed with social media and AI, this music is truly handmade, an artisanal, human creation. We need these things to wake us up, aesthetically and culturally, heart and mind.'

(Melt All the Guns 2 is available on Rataplan Records)

Al Grey (USA) - Borne by a jazz balloon

Al Grey, Featuring Harry Edison & Junior Mance – Centerpiece: Live at the Blue Note
Ray Brown Trio - Seven Steps to Heaven
(2010)

By the time Centerpiece was recorded in 1995 the two ex-Basie-ite horns who were its protagonists had a century and a half of experience between them. Both of their sounds were entirely recognisable - Al Grey's gruff, often plunger-muted trombone and Harry 'Sweets' Edison's minimalist trumpet powerful enough when it was warranted.

Sweets, born in 1915 in Columbus, Ohio, was with the Count Basie Orchestra through his greatest years - from 1938 to its first break-up in 1950. His subsequent career as a studio musician found him playing solo trumpet on many a Sinatra session. And when he returned to jazz he re-joined Basie several times and played on countless small-group swing recordings. Grey played in big bands led by Jimmy Lunceford, Lionel Hampton and Dizzy Gillespie before he joined Basie as a featured trombonist in 1957, finally leaving in 1977 to lead his own smaller groups.

There is plenty of space on the album for the Chicago blues-to-bop pianist Junior Mance and the Texas multiple reedman Jerome Richardson, with the support of veteran drummer Bobby Durham and Ben Brown on bass. Grey is well qualified for the opener Diz Related, as is Mance, as he toured with Gillespie from 1958 to 1960. The latter begins with a rolling blues chorus before the horns storm in and Grey growls out a typical fierce and snarling solo followed by some boppish Richardson alto and some unusually multi-note Edison. These spirited beginnings are continued through Mance's own salutation to his Chicago provenance, South Side. Richardson wails out the blues on his alto and Sweets enters with deft economy of sound, yet still telling a never-ending story, continued by the southern-blues-brought-north of Mance's throbbing keys. Edison's feature I Wish I Knew is picked out above

Brown's springing bass while Homage To Norman gives solo opportunities to all brethren in a tribute to Norman Granz, the founder of Jazz at the Philharmonic.

Richardson's ample dexterity on flute is showcased on Nascimento, a bossa nova by the Detroit pianist Barry Harris, dedicated to the Brazilian composer-guitarist Milton Nascimento. But it is back to Basie for the Count's orchestral anthem for Lester Young with the band at full pelt, Lester Leaps In. This brings back Sweets's fire and he begins his solo with a scramble of notes in passionate excitation. Bewitched is all Grey, complete with plunger mute. His sound is like a rasping human voice telling a story of love and marvel, his notes curling around Durham's brushes and inside and outside Mance's founding chords - pure trombone narrative. And as the band exit with Edison's swinging opus Centerpiece, the spirit and quality of the sound belie the ages of the central characters still blowing out their verve and passion.

Also reissued on the Telarc label is the 1995 album by the Pittsburgh-born virtuoso bassist Ray Brown, Seven Steps To Heaven, playing with his trio plus the guest guitarist, the Swede Ulf Wakenius. This is unfettered small-group swing, with the veteran Brown's artistry casting the music with his extraordinary buoyancy and supported by the two young confreres of drummer Gregory Hutchinson and the Oscar Peterson-protege of a pianist Benny Green. Just listen to the second track, for example. The Thumb/Blues For Wes, a Wes Montgomery tune that moves so lightly it seems to be levitating, or Brown's own Dejection Blues, where you feel that the blues has rarely been filled with such uplift and elation. As for Brown, his solo bass sound has so much spring and bounce it is as if he is trampolining. And on the title tune it is as if all four musicians are vaulting the staircase three steps at a time - their notes are like leaps.

Even the ballads like My Romance or No Greater Love seem weightless, filled with jazz air. And after an hour of the album it is as if you have been borne by a balloon.

(Centerpiece: Live at the Blue Note & Seven Steps to Heaven are available on Telarc)

Sonny Grey (Jamaica) - Spirited sounds from a fine Jamaica hornman

Sonny Grey and his Orchestra in Concert, 1967 (2017)

The little-known trumpeter Orell Delroy Grey (known as Sonny Grey) was born in Jamaica and learnt how to play cornet in his school band. By 1943 he had become a professional musician, and part of a generation of future Caribbean virtuosi, from Jamaican saxophonists Joe Harriott and Wilton 'Bogey' Gaynair, to fellow trumpeters Jamaican Alphonso Son 'Dizzy' Reece, Vincentian Ellsworth McGranahan 'Shake' Keane and Barbadian Harry Beckett.

Grey travelled the Caribbean playing in several bands, nourishing his admiration for US trumpet aces Clifford Brown and Dizzy Gillespie. Then in 1951 he visited London with Harriott as a member of the Jamaican All Stars, before taking a more decisive plunge in 1953 and like many of his contemporaries, emigrating to Europe. For Sonny it was Paris, where for the next 10 years he found work as a hornman in a succession of French bands and orchestras.

By 1963 he had decided to form his own 17-piece big band, not easy for a foreign black musician in a virtually white musical world and where most of his sidemen almost certainly would be white. But he achieved it with great courage and distinction, as this powerful reissued album proves, featuring Grey's orchestra performing live in Spain and France in concerts in 1967 in Barcelona and a year later in Aix-en-Provence.

This is marvellously accomplished swinging music, full of solos from powerful bandsmen almost lost in time whose choruses leap from the surging ensemble with a fiery and often tender zest. This album is a real sonic find. As for the remarkable Grey, he leads from the front with successions of exuberant and potent solos. Listen to him on the opener, Nat Adderley's Work Song, soaring over the ensemble with confidence, verve and eloquence before Bill Tamper's trombone adds his message and pianist Michel Sardaby adds to the narrative. Drummer Hans-Peter Giger and bassist Jack Sewing work up the band for Herb Geller's Scotch Squatch with its echoes of Scotland the Brave, before altoist Jean Aldegon swings out with a quirky solo. Sonny's gentle side is beautifully manifest through Spring Can Really Hang You Up the Most and in Blue Jones he follows the trombone with a crackling blues chorus.

The great Paris-based bop pianist Bud Powell wrote Budo, Sonny shares his romping spirit in his solo and in his version of Roy Eldridge's classic, Little Jazz, his Jamaican chops are as vibrant as those of the Pittsburgh ace. Sardaby plays a soulful solo after Sonny's poised thematic narrative to tenorist Benny Golson's Cry a Blue Tear and the orchestra's version of Charles Mingus's Nostalgia in Times Square fired up by Ginger's rampant drums shows how fine European musicians can reinvent a very American piece of music. Aldegon's alto solo is buoyantly beautiful in Come Rain or Come Shine and Sonny is at his most balladic. The last tune, No Sleep, shows the orchestra's power of ensemble - an achievement forged by its leader, who also takes a swift-paced solo.

The Aix-en-Provence tracks continue the orchestra's abiding unity, huge enthusiasm and musicianship. Sonny's tune Antony gives him a sustained, inventive solo and the 11 minutes of Sonny Rollins's Tenor Madness gives full vent to Sonny's boppish urges and those of his two altoists Dominique Chanson and Philippe Mate. Scorpion offers more ensemble impetus before Sonny's solo and Sewing's pumping bass chorus accompanied by the members' shouts of joy, and the final piece, Head Under Legs, is a humorous jogging tune with the orchestra's brass section in sure fettle and Luis Fuentes's trombone taking a confident solo.

This is the only recording of Sonny Grey's big band, and more's the pity because it truly resonates. Its leader never found the limelight and the years that followed were hard for large-scale jazz orchestras. So we're lucky to have this spirited and dynamic album and the memories it gives us of such a fine Caribbean hornman.

(Sonny Grey and his Orchestra in Concert, 1967 is available on Fresh Sound)

Lars Gullin (Sweden) - The heart is the seat of my musical thoughts and the brain is their rhythmic laboratory

Portrait Of The Legendary Baritone Saxophonist Lars Gullin: Complete 1956-69 Studio Performances (2015)

You couldn't get much further from jazz's birthplace in New Orleans, Louisiana, than the Swedish island of Gotland in the Baltic Sea, but it was there in the town of Visby in 1928 that one of the music's greatest exponents of the baritone saxophone was born.

Lars Gullin astonished all those around him as a child accordionist, but when he moved from his home island to Stockholm in 1947 his reputation grew first as a pianist and then as a baritonist after 1949 when he first heard Gerry Mulligan on the Birth of the Cool sessions. He played baritone horn with altoist Arne Domnerus and trumpeter Rolf Ericson in Stockholm from 1951, also working and recording with visiting US musicians like Clifford Brown, Zoot Sims, James Moody and the very influential saxophonist Lee Konitz. By 1953 he was leading his own group and by '54 his Swedish recordings had achieved such popularity in the US among jazz listeners that, despite being based in Stockholm and having never been Stateside, he won the Best Newcomer award from the prestigious Downbeat magazine and had Swedish-made records released across the US on renowned labels like Atlantic and Contemporary.

His subsequent career was much despoiled by narcotics, although his 1954 visit to England included a rapturous response from London audiences at the Royal Festival Hall - 'More Gullin! More Gullin!' they shouted after his performance - and the inspiration to write two of his most memorable tunes, Soho Blues and the beautifully soulful Manchester Fog.

He spent time in Copenhagen - he recorded a fine album with Archie Shepp there in 1963 - settled in a forest home in southern Sweden and devoted himself to composing, sometimes for jazz musicians and symphony orchestra, and died in 1976 having just typed: 'The heart is the seat of my musical thoughts and the brain is their rhythmic laboratory.'

The four CDs of this compelling Fresh Sounds Records compendium of Gullin tracks brings together his complete studio recordings of the late '50s, when his artistry was at its apex and he was recording regularly with other outstanding Swedish virtuosi like altoist Rolf Billberg and Domnerus, trombonist Ake Persson and trumpeter Jan Allan. The selection is peppered by US songbook standards, but by far the most engaging performances are those of Gullin compositions that reach deeply into Swedish folk traditions.

Listen to Gullin's serenely buoyant and meandering solo on his original Fedja followed by Domnerus's similar light-touched chorus. You almost forget who is the baritonist and who is the altoist, so twin-like are both reedmen's featherweight sounds and conceptions. Or the beautifully and sadly melodic Ma, deeply un-American in its timbre and including a softly tranquil solo by Gullin. Or there is the vibrant Perntz, full of life and unsuppressible optimism, the tune Gullin dedicated to his Stockholm psychiatrist.

On the third and fourth CDs there are more powerful Gullin themes. Allan and Billberg shine on the March and April dates, in particular on The Flight made with a nine-piece band, where Gullin takes off supremely and fizzes aerially alongside his baritone sax confrere Rune Falk and Billberg in Scandinavian splendour. Or there is Icarus on the Moon in a quintet with Allan, who plays with an appealing lyricism in a gently-poised chorus before Gullin enters for a beautifully fluid solo which seems to levitate in the Stockholm air.

Gullin and Billberg came together again in the octet sessions of 1959 for four more Gullin tunes. The aptly titled Fine Together includes some fine work by tenorist Harry Backlund and pianist Lars Bagge, Gullin's baritone sings amiably through The Black Rose and his Merlin is also affable and warm-noted.

In 1960 the octet reassembled for the February sessions that produced Gullin's The Yellow Leaves' Love to the Earth and the poetry wasn't only in the title. The horns' harmonies and Gullin's finely honed solo beside Bagge's comping piano are powerfully evocative. The jaunty Blue Mail has some striking choruses from trumpeter Bengt-Arne Wallin and Billberg, and Baritonome has some more impressive Billberg and Backlund. The Swedes had their own rich pool of jazz musicianship, that was for sure.

The penultimate Gullin tune is the potently full and busy Stockholm Street with Gullin in confident and unique gait striding down its centre with his ever-talented compatriots, creating their very own sounds in their very own way, to which Lars Gullin undoubtedly gave his own excellence.

(Portrait Of The Legendary Baritone Saxophonist Lars Gullin: Complete 1956-69 Studio Performances is available on Fresh Sound Records)

Iro Haarla (Finland) - A marvel of musical transmigration

Iro Haarla – Northbound
(2018)

Iro Haarla was born in 1956 in Tampere, Finland, 70 miles north of Helsinki. After school she studied classical piano and composition at Helsinki's Sibelius

Academy, where she also discovered an empathy with great jazz pianists like Thelonious Monk, Bill Evans and the Canadian Paul Bley. She identified strongly with Bley's 'silence and dissonance.'

Haarla met the Finnish jazz drummer, later her husband, Edward Vesala, in 1978 and put aside her classical ambitions, joining his ensemble Sound and Fury as arranger and self-taught harpist, bringing a new architecture to his music. They made several albums for the Munich-based ECM label, the last being Nordic Gallery in 1994, five years before Vesala's death.

The tracks are sonically sculptured by Haarla with unusual jazz instruments like accordions, harp, cello and bass flute. Tracks like Bird in the High Room have a mournful beauty with Versala's powerful, almost funereal drums and Fulflandia has a quasi-Indian sound. The Quay of Meditative Future has some evocatively Nordic harp sequences from Haarla. It is as if the European north is reflecting both south and north in surprising union.

In 2005, Haarla led a new quintet on the album Northbound. It was a Finnish-Norwegian band with compatriot Uffe Krokfors on bass and Norwegian trumpeter Mathias Eick, saxophonist Trygve Seim and veteran drummer Jon Christensen. It was recorded in Oslo. I remember, after hearing this ensemble at the London Jazz Festival nearly a decade ago, how the radiance of the horns resonated with Haarla's harp strings. Hear Eick's neo-Arctic trumpet in the opener Avian Kingdom or the deeply soft tone of Seim's tenor saxophone alongside Haarla's piano in Barcarole and Krokfors's tunnelling bass notes.

Haarla's tenderly ruminative keys introduce With Thanksgiving and the horns harmonize with affecting beauty after Krokfors's deep prologue to Time for Recollection. Thought is sacrosanct along with sound all through this album, as if the pondering mind can hear too. Then the music takes in Finnish land and sea. On the Crest of A Wave has Eick's trumpet in angry waters, Christensen's drums beat down on the Waterworn Rocks and Veil of Mist has a haunted fanfare by Seim with Light in the Darkness an anthem of nature with Seim's tenor exalted. There is nothing fast in Northbound, as if speed were an irrelevance. Slow is sublime in this album and never a message of dejection. Haarla's harpstrings are of both snow and sun in Yarra, Yarra ... - you can hear them quivering in your ears.

The same five musicians were back in the same Oslo studio again in 2011, recording the album Verspers, and, as soon as you hear the harp/horn colloquy of Haarla, Eick and Seim on the opening A Port on a Distant Shore, you realise how complete their union has grown.

The title tune is a song of evening dedicated by Haarla to her father. Her piano strikes are like bells beside Krokfors's earthen bass and Seim blows with a pulsating beauty, still slower than slow, as are The Warm Currents of the Sea below the warm ice of Eick's notes. In Doxa the pace suddenly quickens, with a sense of menace in the timbre and Seim turns to his soprano saxophone in Satoyama and plays it as if the studio walls could break with his sound and open on to the Scandinavian lands.

The senses are fused and crossed over all through this album. In The Shimmer of the Stars you see the serenity of the Arctic night sky with sounds which cast a beguiling night on your ears, then your eyes. As you listen to Vespers you wonder how the New Orleans pioneers marching down Canal Street or Basin Street 100 years ago could ever have anticipated this music and musicianship in a faraway country of dreams and snow - a marvel of jazz transmigration, indeed, in forever formation.

(Northbound is available on ECM)

Charlie Haden (USA) - Music bridges troubled waters

Festival where musicians from around the world defied dark times with a sense of musical unity

(2016)

The menace of the impending Trump presidency was reflected in the anxious soundscape created by many of the musicians at this year's London Jazz Festival.

Tenor saxophonist Trish Clowes asked everyone at her free-stage Barbican performance to shake hands and hug each other in anti-Trump solidarity before she played her tune Blue Calm, while young pianist Elliot Galvin said it was 'now very pertinent' to play Kurt Weill's Mack the Knife, conjuring an aura of murderous dark forces at work as he did so. And the diaphanous blues cadences of Are You Glad to Be in America? rang out from the slashing guitar of James Blood Ulmer at Rich Mix.

So much great music within a week, where to start? How about the great tenor saxophonist Chico Freeman blowing his own looping and mellow melody To Hear a Teardrop in the Rain or the veteran Cecil McBee with his lithe, plunging bass playing The Peacemaker at The Cookers concert in Cadogan Hall, preceded by Eddie Henderson's visceral trumpet choruses and Billy Harper's surging saxophone solo in Call of the Wild and Peaceful Heart?

There was more tenor sax eloquence from Andy Sheppard at the Laurent Cugny big band gig at Rich Mix, where he played a long, lustrous solo in Goodbye, Pork Pie Hat, Charles Mingus's tribute to Lester Young. At the Foyles Jazz Salon, Denys Baptiste paid homage to John Coltrane in his renditions of Ascent and After the Rain. He finished with a moving tenor duet with one of his own early saxophone heroes, Steve Williamson, on Vigil, which was underscored by the lucidly beautiful piano notes of Nikki Yeoh, Gary Crosby's delving bass and Rod Youngs' empathetic drums.

Gambian kora virtuoso Sona Jobarteh conducted a brilliant call-and-response with her band's hand drummer at Rich Mix while at the Barbican Afghan-German singer Simin Tander 'looked for the divine among ourselves' with her Norwegian pianist Tord Gustavson and drummer Jarle Vespestad as she sang Norwegian hymns and folksongs in Pushto, creating a sensuous and transcendent soundscape. The sonic intercourse of the acoustic and electronic was at the heart of Black Top's astonishing performance at the same venue with Pat Thomas's keyboards and Orphy Robinson's marimbas and computers, conjuring the future in the present in every note.

At King's Place, the interactions of the three scintillating jazzwomen of Les Diaboliques - Swiss pianist Irene Schweizer, French bassist Joelle Leandre and Scottish vocalist Maggie Nichols – set the venue on fire with their joy, humour, tenderness and powerful musicianship. On the final night of this festival of jazz cosmopolitanism, there was a profound tribute to one of the music's great internationalists, the late Shenandoah-born bassist Charlie Haden. Haden's Liberation Music Orchestra, led by that Rosa Luxemburg of improvisation Carla Bley, confronted a troubled world with their living commitment to a better and more just life.

Long live their indomitable and revolutionary jazz spirit!

Charlie Haden (USA) - Solid roots of a sound bass man

Quartet West, Barbican, London
(2001)

There are three dominant strains within the extraordinary musical achievement of bass virtuoso Charlie Haden from Shenandoah, Iowa. Haden played country music with his family band as a boy. In the mid-'50s, he found his way to Los Angeles and eventually teamed up with Texan altoist Ornette Coleman, becoming the sole white member of the iconoclastic quartet which turned conventional jazz on its head.

On albums such as The Shape of Jazz to Come or This is Our Music, with its sleeve photo of Coleman, trumpeter Don Cherry and drummer Ed Blackwell, Haden's neat collar and tie, short well-groomed hair and poppish pose make him seem more like a member or The Crickets than the most innovative jazz ensemble since Charlie Parker's outbreaks 15 years before. Yet when you listen to those albums, you can hear a jazz revolutionary at the bass.

For Haden played his instrument not as a timekeeper or a foundation for others, but as a musical equal, weaving inside and outside his confreres' voices, sometimes pounding above them and taking his solos with the same rights as the horns. In this sense, Haden played as a true original, emancipating the voice of a stereotyped and downpressed instrument. But more than this, just as he sought to liberate the sound of the bass, the same energy moved through his politics.

In November 1971, at a concert with Coleman's quartet in Cascais, near Lisbon, Haden dedicated his Song for Che to the liberation movements of Angola, Mozambique and Guinea-Bissau, while other members of the quartet raised their fists in salute. The next day, Haden was arrested by PIDE, the Portuguese secret police, and the second Lisbon concert was cancelled. Mass public protest caused the decision to he reversed and the concert took place amid an atmosphere of a cultural struggle of solidarity well won.

Haden formed the Liberation Music Orchestra in 1970, recording republican songs from the Spanish Civil War, such as The Fifth Regiment, The Four Generals, which Paul Robeson used to sing, Song of the United Front as well as his Song for Che and We Shall Overcome on the path-breaking Impulse album during the same year. He played alongside musicians such as altoist Dewey Redman, drummer Paul Motian, the Argentinian tenor saxophonist Gato Barbieri and Canadian pianist Carla Bley.

The orchestra's subsequent repertoire included other international pieces, like Haden's song to Sandino, his tribute to Dolores Iburruri – La Pasionaria, Grandola, Villa Morena which signalled the beginning of the Portuguese revolution in 1974, Quilapayun's Chilean anthem El Pueblo Unido Jamas Sera Vencido and a people's song from the war in El Salvador, The Ballad of the Fallen. This is how Haden continued and developed the revolutionary and insurgent tradition at the very core of jazz.

Yet, besides this musical militancy, a third dimension of Haden's sound is his romanticism, a popular based nostalgia that is profoundly American and Angelino, and which centres around his performances and recordings with his Quartet West - who are playing for us at the Barbican.

Haden now suffers from hearing ailments, including tinnitus, and plays his bass 20 foot behind the other members of the quartet, separated from them by a screen of glass baffle boards and a raised platform at the rear of the stage.

As the quartet moves into the evocative Farewell My Lovely, which is imbued with a uniquely LA and Californian mystique, the fluid tenor saxophone sound of the estimable but very under-estimated Ernie Watts fills the auditorium. while the drums of bebop veteran and ex-Charlie Parker and Dexter Gordon sideman Laurence Marable undertones the rhythm. Marable, according to need, plays either with a soft and buoyant brush-work or with a Roy Haynes-like crisp, uplifting rattle on his snare with the be-bop-bass-drum bombs exploding in some surprising places.

As for Haden, as he plays a solo on First Song and Child's Play, it is that immense wooden sound that still booms from his bass, as if he is plucking the branches of a giant hollow tree of the redwood forests and the reverberating sounds are thundering from its trunk. His bass massiveness enters your blood like the voice of Robeson and he physically swings the body of his bass companion, a partner of similar height and substance, as if he is rocking her to sleep in a gentle and trance-like dance.

Pianist Alan Broadbent's chordal comping and lyrical flourishes are both kin and foil to Watt's soloing. The latter plays mostly in the tenor's higher register, but, when he pushes out cascades of notes from screeching highs to rasping lows, he kicks his leg backwards as if the power of the sound is energising his entire body, as he does several times in his long and passionate coda that ended Child's Play.

In the quartet's records, Haden frequently samples sounds from the '40s, from Django Reinhardt's guitar in Where Are You, My Love? to Jo Stafford singing Alone Together, creating an even more highly charged romantic nostalgia.

At the Barbican, the samples are replaced by the soft and velvet voice of Ruth Cameron, who sings My Old Flame and Body and Soul with a quiet and moving tenderness, with Watts adding obligatos and solos between the lines and verses, making a sense of unity between voice and tenor sax that creates the echoes of Billie Holiday and Lester Young. Perhaps there is a sense of romantic lyricism in the breast of every revolutionary - it is there in abundance within the musical heart of Charlie Haden.

But not at the expense of humour. In the middle of Marable's fertile drum solo that dominates a quartet calypso selection, Haden climbs down from his plinth, leaving his beloved bass on its side, and approaches a window in the dividing screen. Taking a cloth, he begins to clean it, applauding Marable's virtuoso drumwork as he peers through.

A warm and loving moment of a concert brimful with artistry and the re-conception of an era when racist thuggery, the cold war and the hearings of an un-American activities committee also struck a less than blessed meaning within the Californian consciousness.

Charlie Haden (USA) - The Ballad of the Fallen
Charlie Haden and the Liberation Music Orchestra
The music and life of a fallen jazz legend
(2017)

'Don't ask me who I am/ Or if you knew me/The dreams that I had/Will grow even though I'm no longer here.' These words are from a poem found in the clothes of a student who was killed when the US-backed national guard of El Salvador attacked a demonstration against their country's tyrannical government at the University of San Salvador in 1982. They are set down in the sleeve notes of an album by the Liberation Music Orchestra led by bassist Charlie Haden and pianist Carla Bley, The Ballad of the Fallen, released in 1983.

Haden died in July 2014 after literally a lifetime in music.

On his album Rambling Boy there is a recording of the Haden Family country band of Shenandoah, Iowa, made in 1939 during their weekly radio show, with two-year-old Charlie as a featured singer. For the first decade-and-a-half of his life he played constantly with his parents and siblings. 'Then,' he wrote, 'when I went to a concert of jazz at the Philharmonic in Omaha, Nebraska, and heard Charlie Parker play, my life changed forever and I knew I had to play jazz.'

After he left school, he moved to Los Angeles, where in 1957 he met an alto saxophonist from Fort Worth, Texas - Ornette Coleman - and became the bassist in his quartet, which sparked huge perturbations across the jazz world. Always a political radical, at the Cascais Jazz Festival of 1971 just outside Lisbon while on tour with Coleman, he dedicated his tune Song For Che to the liberation fighters of the then Portuguese colonies of Mozambique, Angola and Guinea-Bissau, in the very face of the Portuguese fascist government and to huge applause, and was later arrested at Lisbon airport.

In 1969 with the brilliant arranging skills of Carla Bley, he convened the Liberation Music Orchestra for their first album, playing music from all over the struggling world in support of freedom movements. Haden was a committed internationalist who made dozens of albums with many powerful musicians from all over the world. His devotion to freedom for all peoples was characterised in the hugely resonating sound of his booming acoustic bass, sounding as if he had attached strings inside the hollowed trunk of a giant redwood tree. He was also an unashamed romantic with a love of the American Songbook tradition, attested by the deeply beautiful records that he made with his Los Angeles-based Quartet West.

But back to The Ballad of the Fallen, one of his and Bley's prime achievements. It begins with a Catalan anthem from the Spanish civil war, Els Segadors, with the dramatic vibrato of Haden's bass, then segues into the Salvadorian folk song and album title tune and the elegiac guitar of Mick Goodrick. A scintillating pocket trumpet solo from Don Cherry, Ornette's brass partner in the original quartet, rings out from another Spanish civil war song, Si Me Quieres Escribir, and Gary Valente's gruff trombone peals form Grandola Vila Morena, the song played over the radio as a signal to revolt in the 1974 Portuguese revolution. The Chilean resistance song The People United Will Never be Defeated follows, then comes Silence, with Haden's eloquent sleeve note: 'This song was written with the thought that there are infinite possibilities for humankind contained within the brilliance of the universe.' Bley's stark piano and Haden's naked bass exchange a compelling commotion all through Carla's tune, Too Late.

Haden wrote powerful tributes to liberation heroes like Che, Sandino or, as here, La Pasionaria, dedicated to Dolores Ibarruri, who as Haden wrote, 'inspired the Spanish Republic against fascism with the slogan No Pasaran!' It includes stirring sounds by tenorists Dewey Redman and the native American Jim Pepper, and a palpitating solo by Haden's bass.

Robert Wyatt, who last played with Haden at the Royal Festival Hall in June 2009 and sang Song for Che alongside him in the Liberation Music Orchestra, said of him: 'He has been an enormous influence on me. He expressed the true feeling of the people's heart beating through his bass in a string of perfect notes for 50 years. He was a real folk musician. He picked up the people's anthems of hope with Carla, and conveyed as a witness their love of freedom, using his jazz knowledge to make their songs new again and organic as if they were the most natural sound in the world.'

Long live Charlie Haden's deep sound of the Earth and its people!

(The Ballad of the Fallen is available on Emanem)

Herbie Hancock (USA) - Feast of great music

Bobby Hutcherson, Herbie Hancock & Terri Lyne Carrington,
The Barbican, London
(2003)

Those jazz lovers lucky enough to have heard the McCoy Tyner and Bobby Hutcherson Quartet at their Barbican concert in July last year enjoyed a feast of great music.

A pianist and a vibist of epochal dimensions, with vibrant young drummer Eric Harland and Charnett Moffett, an extraordinary bassman who is the son of palpitating drummer Charles Moffett - both Ornette Coleman alumni. Now a year later, a CD by the quartet is released and, when you listen to it, it is as if the year between has passed in an instant.

Moffett's unmatched bass sound is as good a place to start as any. On If I Were a Bell, it is as if his instrument is splitting with vertiginous force at every beat, as if every strike of the strings is making splinters, while Tyner's unremitting attack on the keys and Hutcherson's ringing chords build layer upon layer around the melody. And then there is Moffett's deep and huge singing bowed solo in Tyner's own composition Manalyuca, which follows Hutcherson's exploring choruses and Tyner's grandiose solo, teeming with notes. If a passage of music could be said to be hypnotic to the ears, it is these unique bass phrases. And hear the rampant Tyner on Back Bay Blues as he pummels and sprints in turns through his solo with bullish energy, then to leave the airways first to. Harland's rattling, busy drums and then to Hutcherson's concluding vibes charge.

For All We Know is one of the great US ballads, but Tyner makes it sound like a symphony on one instrument, unaccompanied, alone and audaciously gestured.

The Search begins with a dramatic Harland drumroll and Moffett racing up and down the scales with Tyner in hot pursuit and Hutcherson only entering when a full steam has already been achieved. Moffett's solo resembles the vibrating wings of some giant insect, compelling pianist and vibesman to enter the chase, as Harland finishes the track as it began, with drums resplendent.

Seven out of the 10 album tracks are Tyner compositions and Contemplation is perhaps the most familiar, with its simple dignified melody, a platform for a strong, melodic solo by Hutcherson. The quartet exits on an Ellington note, with a vibeless trio and In a Mellow Tone, showing, again, how the Duke's tunemaking is there to be creatively applied to every jazz juncture. You remember Tyner's stomping piano and Harland's energising skins. but it is the vibrating bass notes of Moffett that come booming through with an immense sound that leaves you with the real sense that. in this 'land of giants' (the name of the album) it is his step that is the most sonorous and holds the most weight.

Now a year later, it is the Barbican again, and Hutcherson too, but this time alongside him are Los Angeles-born Scott Colley on bass and drumwoman Terri Lyne Carrington from Boston. And the pianist? Another jazz giant, ex-Miles Davis man, watermelonman, electronic jazz fusion and jazz-rocker who played with the Chicago Symphony Orchestra at a concert when he was 10 and has never stopped advancing musically - Herbie Hancock. 'This band is a brand new collaboration,' announced a jovial Hancock before the quartet started into the first unannounced selection, dominated largely by Hutcherson's coruscating runs of notes.

What soon becomes evident is that the Hancock/Hutcherson partnership, solidified by some memorable Blue Note Hutcherson albums of the 1960s like Components and Happenings, is a very different one to that forged by Hutcherson and Tyner. Davis once compared Hancock's playing to the motion and sound of a waterfall, but Hutcherson is very much a cascading player too. emitting showers of notes spraying from his restless mallets to all corners of the Barbican.

Sometimes you think that these two veterans have parallel musical consciousnesses that stem from the same creative jazz imagination, so similar - yet on different instruments with totally different techniques and ranges - are the scattering, impressionist sound-shapes of their solo-choruses. Whereas, last year, Hutcherson often contended with and became as another within Tyner's orchestral piano and hugely enfolding sound, Hancock's dissonances are more dispersed and pointillistic, his technique more mannered with much more space for Hutcherson's picked-out notes.

Yet what surprises the listener and is freely acknowledged by Hancock in his rambling commentary between selections is that it is the firmer lines of Colley' s bass and, finally, the crisp and frequently melodic drumming of Carrington that seem to be leading the quartet. 'I usually get lost,' quips Hancock 'and it's Terri Lyne who finds me the way out!' And this percussion-pathfinding soon becomes apparent during a long, long - I timed it at 35 minutes plus - arrangement of Hancock's much-played tune from his 1965 Maiden Voyage album, Dolphin Dance.

This suite-like extended version begins with several varieties of quietude, with a tender dispersal of piano notes, only accompanied by Carrington's very gentle drum tapping. Then, Hutcherson enters with some soft colourations, followed by Colley's soulful plucking, provoking Carrington's whole palette of besotting percussive sounds as she stares aloft, her braided hair falling back over her shoulders. Hancock's rapidfire re-entry suddenly transforms the sound, speed and rhythm - led again by Carrington, cymballing hard and Colley holding steerage from the guiding hull of his bass.

Several times, Hancock's huge jazz imagination becalms this sea of sound, with only the tranquil notes of each musician revealing the hidden life below the surface and Carrington's tinkling cymballic waves concealing while revealing the ceaseless undersea speech of dolphins. Yet it is as if every becalming movement leads on towards the next storm and the succeeding phase of another stillness into which the ending finally flows, almost as if the very wind in the music itself has made it do so. Almost a symphony for four is this millennial version of Dolphin Dance, prompting a return to the Maiden Voyage of four decades past to reflect upon how much Hancock's music has changed yet still remaining true to itself and its origins.

Also particularly fine was Hutcherson's superb playing on November, his flying mallets producing a scintillating sound, this time contrasted with Hancock's pounding, virtually monosonic choruses. Another engrossing piano/vibes encounter in the centre of London and, as with Moffett for the Hutcherson and Tyner performance, perhaps the true credit for the Hutcherson/Hancock artistry should go to the conceptual clarity and roadmaking of the compelling woman at the drums.

(The Land of Giants by McCoy Tyner and Bobby Hutcherson is available on Telarc)

Rita Hargrave (USA) - What more can music do?
Salsa De La Bahia: Vol. 3 Renegade Queens
(2025)

Renegade Queens is a powerful double album from San Francisco which bears surging sonic witness to the fecundity of women's Latin and Afro-Cuban music in the Bay Area. From Venezuela, Cuba, Colombia and Brazil the insurgent music erupts with rhythmic fire from some superb instrumentalists and vocalists in all-women and mixed ensembles, creating a synthesis of tempestuous rhythmic freedom.

'We were born to drum,/We were conceived in rhythm/Whether we knew it or not./It was the beauty and sanctity/Of the rhythm that created us,/The rhythm of mothers' birth pains.' So sings Christelle Durandy, her heritage in Reunion Island and the French-speaking Caribbean, in the opening track, and these are the key words by poet Avotcja of the entire double album, produced by trombonist Wayne Wallace and film-maker Rita Hargrave.

I asked Hargrave about the album's conception and subliminal messages, shining out from the American disaster of Trumpery, MAGA, ICE and racist and sexist oppression. 'The Bay Area arts community has attracted women musicians from across the country and around the world for decades.' she told me. 'Cultural centres, music schools and summer music camps bring together women of all ages and skill levels to join what Carolyn Brandy (master percussionist and founder of the annual music camp for women, called 'Born to Drum') calls 'the global movement for women playing drums'.'

'Our musicians come from the internationally-known halls of SF jazz to Bay Area community organisations like La Pena or Mission Cultural Centre, which have a long history in dedicating themselves to education, preservation and innovation of local artists from around the world. We've seen the success of regional artists of all ethnicities and their collaboration with performers from all over the African diasporan world.'

And how are they achieving this now, in Trump's version of America? 'The social, political and economic challenges we face are daily struggles for all women. What do we do? We work, teach, get the job done and problem-solve together. We also cherish our allies, male and female.'

Hargrave is proud that Renegade Queens represents the work and artistry of over fifty women musicians who have performed in Cuba, Mexico, Brazil, Barbados and across the USA in New York, Illinois, Washington D.C., Philadelphia and Florida. 'The album has received stunning reviews and climbed to the top of the playlist of many Latin and jazz radio stations across the country.'

And you won't be surprised at that as you listen. Hear the expressive, soulful vocals of Xiomarra Torres from Cali, Colombia on Me Quedo Contigo or Venezuelan Maria Marques on the blues-like La Lagrima. They lucidly and movingly tell the stories of the beautiful multilingual syncretism and unity of the now-times Bay Area.

Voices are matched with deeply affecting instrumental virtuosity. There is the stomping beat of La Mensajera and its succession of inspired solos finishing with the rampaging trumpet-song of Marina Garza. The familiar strains of Ellington and Puerto Rican Juan Tizol's classic theme, Caravan, played by the Montclair Women's Big Band, features warm, inventive solos by Sonja Jason's alto saxophone and Sarah Cline's trombone, and the concluding Samba Nova has some bird-like flute from Robin Nzingah.

I asked Hargrave, what were her favourite tracks, and she answered: 'I love every selection of both CDs because they reflect the artistry, courage and adventurous creativity of this diverse community of women. The first selection, We are Born to Drum, says it all. We've been here since the first day and we're here to stay - making music, lifting spirits and shaping hearts and minds in our own special way.'

(Salsa De La Bahia: Vol. 3 Renegade Queens is available on Patois Records)

Northumbrian Blues: The Lost World Of
Big Pete Deuchar by Colin Harper (England)
(2025)

When this book arrived, I first of all flicked through the photographs of the protagonist and his cohorts from the early 1960s. There he was, snapped in 1961, playing banjo with Dick Charlesworth's City Gents, a band I often used to hear at the St. Louis Jazz Club, Elm Park Hotel, East London, as I worked in the cloakroom, hanging up the groovers' donkey jackets and duffle coats. My friend Spud's dad ran the club, and I would get free entry for my cloakroom labours and handing out pass-outs to those who wanted interval drinks in the pub next door.

The early life of this banjoist is what holds this book together. 'Big Pete' Deuchar was the grandson of a Newcastle brewery magnate who turned his back on his origins and dedicated his life to stimulating a thriving culture of New Orleans jazz in the city during the 1950s, when the imitated sound of the Crescent City could be heard in urban venues right across Britain.

Colin Harper's book is more than a sparky musical biography: it is an invaluable piece of social and cultural history of a post-war era when live 'traditional jazz' crowded into teenage hearts and consciousnesses in its own very British way, led by the music of the 'Guv'nor' Ken Colyer, recently returned from a sojourn in New Orleans, who transplanted its jazz in pub rooms and often dingy venues from Glasgow to Bristol, from Nottingham to Elm Park.

Deuchar was an early Colyer disciple who was determined to make Newcastle swing with the music of Bourbon Street, and established his Vieux Carre Jazzmen in what the Newcastle Evening Chronicle described as the 'dark, dirty, dangerous' fully-licensed ex-Labour club in Melbourne Street, Newcastle 1.

But although Deuchar's early life in music is the book's narrative thread, it is much more a chronicle of a time of youth discovery and insubordination. Colyer and his band led the hugely-supported protest marches to the Atomic Weapons Research installation at Aldermaston, Berkshire, and the music he fervently embraced was that of an oppressed black and creole community still living under racist Jim Crow laws in Louisiana. In England, to love the music was to hate racism, and the visits of the veteran ex-docker New Orleans clarinetist George Lewis to play with the Colyer band, and those of blues musicians like Big Bill Broonzy, Sonny Terry, Brownie McGhee, Little Brother Montgomery, Memphis Slim, Howlin' Wolf, Muddy Waters and Jesse Fuller (who I remember well singing the blues in Elm Park) were evidence of a younger generation moving away from the Teddy Boy licks of Bill Haley to a black American music which carried a vital message of anti-racism and struggle. The records they made with British musicians are still there to bear witness and are well worth searching out.

There's an excellent chapter of Deuchar's 1957 stay in New Orleans, where he played (but not on public platforms - still disallowed by quasi-Apartheid laws) with virtuosi like clarinetist Alphonse Picou and trumpeter Kid Thomas Valentine, and another on the Lewis band's 1959 Britain visit, where the veterans were welcomed by enthusiastic crowds at Liverpool Docks and Kenny Ball's Band (who were stopped in mid-chorus by an aggressive police presence), and given momentous plaudits in concert venues across the nation, including Manchester, Southampton, Leicester, Bristol, Glasgow, Birmingham, London and of course Newcastle City Hall. As the Melody Maker reporter put it: 'George Lewis received the most fantastic jazz welcome ever when he arrived at London's Euston Station on Sunday: and then he retired to bed!' All this was jazz against racism at its most dedicated and explicit..

Such was the ambiance of 70 years ago, powerfully described in Harper's book, which in its own way is an inspiration for now-times. But play the music while you're reading it!

(Northumbrian Blues is published by Jazz in Britain Publications)

Tom Harrell (USA) - Memorable moving pictures show in Soho

Tom Harrell Moving Picture Quartet, Ronnie Scott's, London (2021)

There's something modestly heroic about trumpeter Tom Harrell. His physical frailty as he walks onstage is manifest - his wild, white hair and beard, his unsteady and shaking gait, his bent back, his languid demeanour, his frustration with the microphones.

Yet, as he blows either trumpet or flugelhorn, his sound is one of beauty, power and ascendant lucidity, shaking the rafters and startling every listener into sudden moments of acute surprise.

Harrell, born in 1946, spent his early musical years in the big bands of Stan Kenton, Woody Herman and George Russell and made his debut at Ronnie Scott's with Horace Silver in 1974.

With him now are three remarkable and much younger confreres - German-Nigerian bassist born Ugonna Okegwo, Latino-based drummer Adam Cruz, veteran of the Mingus Big Band and David Sanchez Quartet and pianist Danny Grissett, Harrell's piano partner for more than a decade.

Harrell's compositions are strongly melodic. He finds his high notes almost without stretching for them and the sculpted clarity of his choruses is sublime and, in his duo with the ever-inventive Grissett, his sky-pitched flugelhorn sound seems to stream from the past, with everything that is human expressed.

Ukegwo's delving, dancing bass and the Latin subtlety and tempestuousness of Cruz's drums create surging rhythms. This is a quartet born and forged in cosmopolitan fire and their sonic unity blows up Frith Street and out into the heart of Soho.

Joe Harriott (Jamaica) - An array of unified Caribbean talent

Joe Harriott Quintet - Southern Horizons, Free Form and Abstract (2016)

The cover photograph on the 1960 Joe Harriott album Southern Horizons of a posing Christine Keeler lookalike under a Union Jack certainly belies the

Caribbean musical genius, hidden under the alienated sleeve, which comes bursting out of the grooves.

Alto saxophonist Harriott, born in Kingston, Jamaica, in 1928, who arrived in London in 1951 playing licks like no other in Britain, is joined by bassist Coleridge Goode, born in St Andrew on the south-eastern side of the island in 1914. On the last five tracks of the album, trumpeter Hank Shaw is replaced by the startling hornman from St Vincent, Shake Keane (1927-97), who had moved to London in 1952 to study literature, and who was a very sharp poet himself (hence 'Shake' for 'Shakespeare'). On two of the album's tracks the Latin-tinged, resonating bongo skills of Frank Holder (born in Georgetown, Guyana, in 1925 and still playing in London) are heard. Holder had served in the RAF during the war, played in Jamaican Jiver Hutchinson's band then in the post-war John Dankworth Seven, before forming his Latin American band Paz and playing with almost everyone of note on the British scene from bop stalwarts like Tubby Hayes and Ronnie Scott to the Ethio-jazz of the Mulato Astatke from Jimma, Ethiopia.

So, an array of unified Caribbean talent here, plus two Englishmen - pianist Harry South and drummer Bobby Orr - all exercise their bop credentials on the opener Still Goofin' with Harriott's effervescence in a cosmos of its own. Goode's bass booms out through Horace Silver's Senor Blues and Jumpin' with Joe is exactly that with a turbulent chorus from Harriott. But as Keane and Holder come into the reckoning on the title tune, it is back to the islands. Harriott is more relaxed, Keane skips to Holder's skins and the latter's bongos fly from shore to shore. On the Ellington/Tizol standard Caravan, this is definitely a Caribbean travelling company, pulsed by Holder's South American drums which find union with Orr's London battery. The balladic beauty of Keane's Vincentian horn and his Jamaican partner's tonal serenity are revealed again on You Go to My Head and an unlikely time for a groove, Tuesday Morning Swing has all members in the mood, with Keane and Harriott particularly lively and Goode's thudding brilliance inside the skins of everyone.

As soon as the opening track of the November 1960 album Free Form begins, you know this is very different music. The bop orthodoxies have gone and two more startlingly innovative musicians have come in: the Edinburgh-born Pat Smythe as pianist and the drums dynamo from Burton-on-Trent, Phil Seamen. All the compositions are Harriott's with much arrangement to the fore, but space too for some powerful solos - hear Keane's delicacy, played with the keenest of empathies with Goode and Seaman in Coda and Harriott's cascading cadences on the same track. Keane's high-note flurry on Abstract is brilliant and Harriott is terse and enigmatic on Impressions, where Smythe's piano takes a surprising ramble.

The album Abstract was cut in two sessions during 1961-62 with Orr on the final four tracks and Seaman returning for the first four. Holder also comes steaming back with his bongos full of Guyana's earth on Compound in a duo with a goaded Seamen, until the horns step in for a last chorus. Subject has Goode digging some deep foundations and in Shadows Harriott and Keane create a colloquy of excitation and in a call and answer palaver above Goode's bowed and plucked bass. The only non-Harriott turn is Sonny Rollins's Oleo, whose Virgin Islands roots hold a special compulsion for the two hornmen. Keane's brass rhapsody is superb and Harriott and Goode both give out Caribbean echoes before the quintet unite for a final chorus of Rollins's memorable theme.

Well met, like thousands of their post-Windrush compatriots, in a London fervently changing.

(Southern Horizons, Free Form and Abstract are available on Fresh Sound)

George Haslam (England) - Joys of spring in the south of the world

George Haslam and Friends-Cuban - Meltdown & September Spring (2013)

George Haslam, the Preston-born baritone saxophonist, is proud to tell that he led the first British jazz band - a quintet - to perform in revolutionary Cuba in 1986. And with the Greenwich trombonist Paul Rutherford he brought free improvisation to Havana in1988. He remembers that playing at the same venue in 1988 was a 13-piece salsa band. He and Rutherford persuaded them, at first reluctantly, to join them in a free jazz rendition on the bandstand. They had never encountered the music before but nervously agreed. Eventually, the two Englishmen stepped unobtrusively down, leaving the 13 Cubans improvising with their own Caribbean freedom and invention. Thus was free jazz brought to Cuba!

Perhaps there are echoes of that night in the marvellous album Cuban Meltdown. The first five tracks were recorded in Abingdon, Oxfordshire, in 2004 with two Cubans reliving those pioneering days, flugelhornist and percussionist Bobby Carcasses and vocalist Maria Cecilia Colon, who joined Haslam and Rutherford in a binational octet playing this time like Cubans. Hear the astonishing Rutherford playing in the way of a true Habanero on Villancico's Blues or Haslam's throaty, sucking undertow on A Perfect Love. Carcasses sings appealingly on his unity opus, Havanabingdon, and plays some rich and mellow flugelhorn followed by some moving choruses from Haslam and Rutherford, creating a praise-song to internationalism.

The last four tracks are Cuban-born and recorded in Havana, two of them with Carcasses's outstanding home-based octet. Bobby's son Roberto is featured on piano to compelling effect. Haslam and Carcasses renew old friendship on the final two tracks, recorded in 2007, with Blues for Benny More a particular jewel. Carcasses sings and plays a nimble, blues-laden piano before switching to flugelhorn, and Haslam finds his Caribbean element, completing a unique and powerfully engaging album.

Haslam has also been a courageous cultural ambassador to Argentina since the decade following the war in the Malvinas. He was the first

British jazz musician to play in the country and began to record in Buenos Aires during his first visit in 1991. He has cut three albums of his Argentine Adventures, playing: with some truly impressive local musicians including pianist Ruben Ferrero and tenorist Daniel Harari. On a more recent visit in September 2006 he recorded the sessions which comprise the inspiring album September Spring, and by sheer coincidence this sojourn coincided with the visit of the eminent New York bassist Hilliard Greene who has been a pivotal presence on recordings by some of the prime US free spirits, from trumpeter Roy Campbell and violinist Leroy Jenkins to tenorist Charles Gayle. Argentinian bassist Mono Hurtado begins the opening track Bajo Profundo with a deep, deep volley like a fogbound ship on the River Plate estuary and Haslam's low entry is like a fellow lost craft - a low-down rhapsody indeed, beautifully played.

Percussionist Horacio Straijer splashes between Haslam's bass clarinet and Hurtado on Baile con las Pulgas, and Harari's second horn gives Cumbre Coghlan and 4x1=1x4 an extra weight and fluidity, implanted by Hurtado's relentless and earthen bass power. Straijer bangs on a can among other surfaces in the latter piece, Hurtado saws with his bow before Haslam's solo baritone exhales a lyrical song of intense and complex beauty.

The trio session with Greene and Ferrero took place the following day. Haslam plays bass clarinet on Amigos Nuevos and Ferrero moves to kalimba and sings beside Haslam's long and breathy notes in Tranquilo. Greene plucks the locomotive power on Early Morning Train, which is almost Ellingtonian in its sonic train depiction, with Haslam's baritone playing the Harry Carney role.

North in the Americas comes further than the deep south in the trio's version of the spiritual Wade in the Water. This is Greene's history in particular and it is his visceral bow which grinds out the theme, with Ferrero's crashing notes and Haslam's transatlantic empathy in close engagement. The threesome's raw and mutual solidarity binds together a memorable performance, as deep as the past.

As for the Ferrero/Haslam duo, Vidala y Vidala, essayed by an Englishman and an Argentinian in combined artistry and jazz comradeship, it explodes all the militarism and Thatcherism that ever came between these two faraway peoples. Springtime it was in the south of the world where men had fought and killed each other in competing authoritarianisms two decades before. And the music budded with peace, jazz and promise.

(Meltdown & September Spring are available on Slam)

Vaughan Hawthorne-Nelson (England/Jamaica/St Kitts) – An unlikely venue hosts a memorable concert

Vaughan Hawthorne-Nelson, The Eastside Jazz Club, Leytonstone, London (2025)

Here's an unlikely venue for some hot jazz: the Leytonstone Ex-Serviceman's Club, East London.

Up the stairs and it's a large, comfortable chamber with a lively bar and excellent acoustics. And who were playing tonight? A quartet of Caribbean-rooted luminaries with powerful, liberating sounds, led by saxophonist Vaughan Hawthorne-Nelson, with Stepney-born drummer Mark Mondesir, master pianist Robert Mitchell from just up the Central Line in Gants Hill, and veteran bassist Larry Bartley.

Hawthorne-Nelson's prowess on alto and soprano saxophones is outstanding. As he opened with his alto's fleeting, lightning runs on his own tune, Cereal Killer, with Mitchell swinging his keys like a sonic athlete, Bartley walking his bass expertly and Mondesir chomping on his drums, it was soon clear that this was to be a luminous night of music.

The mood changed as Hawthorne-Nelson picked up his soprano and played his passionately provocative Pain, with a beautiful almost weeping melodism as if every note were a tear. The ambiance was sustained by the equally moving Peace for Palestine, which even in a venue radiating an ex-military ethos, created a strange but poignant anti-war aura.

Throughout, Hawthorne-Nelson retained his affecting, emotive tone, never overblowing, always restrained in his artistry, and as he moved into a most evocative coda for the final notes of his reading of the songbook ballad, My Ideal, hearts stopped all through the venue.

His tribute to Coltrane showed where his true signature lay, as this English Caribbean quartet clarified to everyone listening that for that night at least, Leytonstone belonged to them, and the people of Palestine too.

Vaughan Hawthorne-Nelson (England/Jamaica/St Kitts)

Redemption (2025)

He's an outstanding saxophonist whose artistry and emotional power stagger the ears. Vaughan Hawthorne-Nelson was born in 1968 in Finchley, North London, his Jamaica-born mother was a teacher and his St. Kitts-born father a journalist. He started on classical clarinet and piano at eleven, began on saxophone at 14 and discovered jazz at sixteen. 'I fell in love with Charlie Parker's playing first, but it was the Marsalis brothers who really inspired me, and British trumpeter Digby Fairweather who put on a jazz workshop at school when I was fifteen.'

A prodigious young musician, he went to Berklee jazz college in Boston, USA. when he was just seventeen. 'It opened up a whole new world. London pianist Julian Joseph was my room-mate, trombonist Delfeayo Marsalis was across the hallway and saxophonists Antonio Hart and Mark Turner, and trumpeter Roy Hargrove were also my peers. We jammed, shared ideas, performed and recorded together. It was a wonderful, creative time when anything seemed possible musically. The great alto saxophonist Bobby Watson was a mentor to me - mentors are so important!'

'When I returned to London, I jammed and performed at the 100 Club, Jazz Café and the Bull's Head, and made my first album, Emanem, at 19.' A powerful inspiration was the South African pianist Bheki Mseluku, with whom Vaughan made two albums in 1999. 'He had such a spiritual grounding. His music was highly accomplished technically but had a depth I've not experienced since. He instilled in me the need to connect emotionally with the audience. The technical aspects of music should service this aim, but they are not in themselves the aim. I want to connect emotionally with those listening.'

Vaughan is a profoundly serious and committed musician but not a headliner, and there have been long spaces between his recordings. 'There have been times in my life when music has not been at the forefront. I knew from my early twenties that I didn't want to make music to the exclusion of other pursuits. I also teach primary age children. I find the interplay between different endeavours allows me to create music in the way I like.'

His new album is the luminous and beautifully-played Redemption. He says he composed its music to showcase 'the incredible playing' of his quartet-mates. Pianist Robert Mitchell is 'a technical master of all aspects of the piano, particularly the percussive range of the instrument.' Bassist Larry Bartley is 'a master with a deep sense of time and melody. He swings hard and drives the music beautifully.' As for dummer Mark Mondesir, he is 'a virtuoso of rhythm and musical structure. He's one of the great drummers.'

Among the album's original compositions are two which reflect the struggles of Palestinians, Intifada and Peace in Palestine. 'My aim, with the gift I have been given, is to use it in a small way to bring light to this injustice. Our world is out of balance. Music can help to re-set this and help people tune into a vibration that gives us the strength to hope, heal and help others, but also to stand up as a collective against the injustice around us.'

Another compelling and serenely echoing track is Song of the Ancestors, where Vaughan plays solo alto and soprano saxophones. 'One of my mentors was Malidoma Some, a shaman from the Dagara people of Burkina Faso. He taught me this song and its significance in initiating young people into the adult world. Music, especially drumming, has an important role in this tradition. I try to identify with this, and when this happens I feel connected to all my ancestors from the great continent of Africa.'

He plays alto and soprano through the album, 'depending on an intuitive process of what sound I think works best on a particular piece. I like the mood we created on Peace for Palestine - it was just what I was hoping for, and on the title track Mark's playing is out of the world.'

Vaughan is a sincere and superfine jazz virtuoso who shuns the bogus false glow of superficial artifice. Go and hear him and his superb troubadouring brothers. You'll love them!

(Redemption is available on TML Records)

Roy Haynes (USA) - This beauty is drum-skin deep

The Roy Haynes Quartet, Pizza Express, London (2000)

Before going to hear the Roy Haynes Quartet at the Pizza Express, I played some tracks from the 1954 recording of Clifford Brown and Sarah Vaughan's memorable voice and trumpet coupling, particularly on the hauntingly beautiful September Song and I'm Glad There Is You. The empathetic and tender drummer was one Roy Haynes. And Haynes goes back further. In the '40s, playing with the Charlie Parker Quintet, with Bud Powell, Thelonious Monk and Miles Davis. And further still for this brilliant percussionist born in Massachusetts in 1926, whose earliest work was with swing geniuses like Frankie Newton and post-New Orleans orchestras like that of Luis Russell and whose first recordings were made with Lester Young. Then forward to the '60s and stints with Eric Dolphy and Roland Kirk, with key albums like Out Of The Afternoon with Kirk or Cracklin' with Booker Ervin.

Haynes is still playing red-hot drums on his 75th-birthday tour, radiating a phenomenal emission of youth with a luminous quartet. His septuagenarian energy is still at a full intensity. Rising up and down from his seat to acknowledge his fellow musicians, his modesty allied with a titanic professional skill and drum explosiveness, he is a percussive survivor still creating and transforming with the music after six decades of ever-changing jazz. And here is a quartet of real heat. Pianist David Kikoski stridently pumps the brand new grand, making every string scintillate. Dwayne Burno is a placid pillar of a bass, reticent to come forward, his foundation always huge and cavernous. But the brilliance of tenorist Don Braden matched even that of his leader. As he sat listening to his confreres before his own solos, which came out as hut flooding springs of sound poetry, he some-times had a tinge of the tone and sound of a youthful Don Byas.

A bluesy intro from Kikoski led into a ruminative I Thought About You, with Braden's sublime solo and Haynes's subdued, communal support. Haynes plays like no other drummer that I have ever heard. Of the great bop drummers, with Art Blakey, the weight and fury was ever-present. With Max Roach, the orchestration of power and subtlety could break out at every moment. With Elvin Jones, a combustive cohesion of multiple forces underlays every note. But, with Haynes, it is the element of sudden, audacious explosions combined with an incessant grounding of clipped almost alarming lucidity that makes his sound so unique - plus cadences that fade away to the soft clicking of wood and the disappearance of all sound, making it invisible too as his drum-sticks missed striking each other and the drum becomes a dance.

As Braden moved into a soulful opening coda for Body And Soul, you began to wonder whether, after Coleman Hawkins and every subsequent tenor saxophone player, is if still possible to find renewal and creative originality from that nonpareil or ever-deep and astonishing melody? Braden proved it so with inventive, aching phrases bluesing through the familiar framework of notes of the most jazz-worn sequence of them all.

And then to Monk, one of the veteran drummer's old guvnors and Trinkle Tinkle played at a high speed and galvanising spirit by this stomping quartet. Rumbustious piano and tenor exchanges, interacting in a frantic dialogue while Haynes, mannish boy and boyish man, playing under and over the dialogue as he has done for over half a century.

Miho Hazama (Japan) - An epochal album pushing jazz forward

Miho Hazama - Time River

(2016)

A young Japanese woman comes to New York, the epicentre of global jazz activity and in a handful of months becomes the maestro of a predominantly male, 14-piece orchestra recording a brace of remarkable albums and establishing a formidable reputation. 'It was definitely a great experience in finding myself in a lot of ways,' she explained, 'not only as a composer but also as a person from a classical musical background and as a Japanese woman.'

Miho Hazama was born in Tokyo, began to play piano and organ at the ages of five, studied classical music at the Kunitachi College of Music and worked with the Tokyo Philharmonic Orchestra, then moved stateside to the Manhattan School of Music in 2012, making her first album Journey to Journey. 'Since I used to study classical music, I love writing for symphony orchestras,' she declared. 'I couldn't help but hear strings in my mind when I was composing those tunes.'

When asked about her extraordinary switch from orchestral classical music to big band jazz she replied: 'To be honest, I don't really like categorising music. I just need some kind of concept, plan or structure in my mind.' Her new album Time River certainly manifests this. She is leading and co-operating with musicians with whom she has formed a close working bond: 'I really want to work with musicians that I have trusted for a long time, hopefully, forever. I want to keep working for them, working with them and having a fun time with them.'

The opening track The Urban Legend fades in surreptitiously, before the ensemble builds and pianists Alex Brown solos over Sam Anning's pounding bass and Jake Goldbas's clipping drums. The harmonies are complex before Ryoji Ihara's tenor and soprano saxophones mark out their choruses over the quartet of strings. The amalgam of Tokyo/New York metropoli continues to be invoked in Cityscape with Sam Harris's piano and James Shipp's vibes lighting up the streets. Matthew Jodrell's trumpet blows a muted chorus as if the dawn is rising. The solo keys of Gil Goldstein's accordion break the silence before Under the Same Moon, as if people are awakening to commute, work and converse, telling each other of their lives. Ihara's soprano stirs the orchestral sound, as if it were a human voice. Then it is the enigmatically titled Dizzy, Dizzy Wildflower, where Cam Collins's alto takes a long pulsating chorus before Jodrell's crackling trumpet solo, showing how much Hazama knows, trusts and empathises with her soloists - these musicians she wants to make sounds with 'forever' - with a similar belief, love and conviction that Ellington had for his.

It is in the two tracks, Introduction and Fugue that Hazama's classical roots shoot out into the bloodstream of her jazz, when she plays piano with the female string quartet integrated within her orchestra. In Introduction, her repeated strikes of her keys and melodic theme create a colloquy with the strings, making an amalgam of music which is, in Ellington's phrase: 'beyond category.' Goldbas's solo drums begin her Fugue, defined as a polyphonic composition in which a short melodic theme is introduced by one of the parts and successively taken up by the others. This is exactly what happens between piano, violins, viola and cello, as classical forms grow new sonic pathways at the very heart of a jazz album.

The prime saxophonists Joshua Redman, son of the great Ornette Coleman confrere Dewey Redman, opens the title track with his softly-focused soprano saxophone. Jordrell's vulnerable-sounding flugelhorn continues, before Redman returns with his vigorous yet tender tenor to take a long and compellingly-wrought solo.

Time River is an epochal album which shows again that there is something new in the world of jazz. Whether it is Maria Schneider in the US Midwest, Laura Jurd in London with her Chaos Orchestra or Hazama in New York, remarkable female musicians are leading orchestras, composing for them and making powerful and beautiful music.

(Time River is available on Sunnyside)

Jimmy Heath (USA), Frank Foster (USA) & Pharoah Sanders (USA) – Rendezvous of jazz brothers

London Jazz Week
(1999)

Three veteran tenor saxophonists, collectively exemplifying huge and crucial movements in the history of jazz, powered out their notes in London last week.

First there was Jimmy Heath at Ronnie Scott's, playing with his two brothers, bassist Percy and drummer Tootie - plus a stomping young pianist called Jeheb Patton. This brotherly rendezvous began with a galloping version of All The Things You Are, and it made me reflect on all the things they are. These three Philadelphia brothers have nothing to prove. They have 216 years between them, with each taking his own route through the fertile landscape of post-war jazz.

Percy Heath alone spent a mere 45 years as the foundation of the Modern Jazz Quartet, and Jimmy had played at the very birth of bebop. Little Bird they called him through his emulation of Charlie Parker and his minute stature and boyish exuberance on a tenor that rivalled his own height. Tootie, kid brother at 65, has drummed behind almost every bop horn and had only to touch his drums to make them swing, even with his fingers pounding the skins like his brother percussionists in Africa - as he did at the outset of Jimmy's classic composition, Gingerbread Boy. This was musical genius born of jazz survival against the odds and a whole epoch of creative stamina stemming from one black American family.

Jimmy's tenor was finely fluid. He spoke in a cluster of perfectly hewn notes what other less judicious musicians would take a whole evening's blowing to say. As he glided into Mal Waldron's haunting Soul Eyes, there were the bop hallmarks - the sudden changes, the Birdlike accelerations, the melodic line playing host to interpolations of other tunes, from Softly As A Morning Sunrise to You'll Never Walk Alone, accompanied by Tootie's humming grunts and Percy's relentless bass empathy. As he introduced the ballad I'm Glad There Is You, he remembered how he 'turned left' when he first heard Parker. Then nothing else mattered. Percy too invoked CP in his version of Yardbird Suite played on cello accompanied by Tootie's jumping brushwork and flashing, clicking sticks. Sibling legends, and, when Jimmy called the lucky listeners to acclaim 'my brethren there' and the brothers went into a zooped-up waltz rendition of Billy Strayhorn's Daydream, I thought only how fortunate I was, just to be there and to hear such jazz lifetimes of sounds.

The later part of Ronnie Scott's week was devoted to 72-year-old Frank Foster – Cincinnati tenorist, composer, and arranger for the 'atomic' Count Basie band from 1953 onwards. Foster was another early Blue Note bopper, but one who threw in his lot with one of the great swing orchestras though never losing his bop roots.

Playing within a typical hard-bop framework, with Fats Navarro look-alike and note-bending trumpeter Derrick Gardner, Earl May on bass, David Gibson on drums and Daniel Mixon's Red Garland like piano, Foster revealed a fluidity and lightness of sound that occasionally seemed to touch the beauty of Basie's greatest tenorist Lester Young as well as ranging toward Coltrane.

His own compositions like Shiny Stockings and Grey Thursday showed him playing with an improvisational artistry of both sound and phrase that struck a fine balance of inventiveness and direction that all those Basie years have forged. In Lee Morgan's Ceora, while Gardner took powerful flight in a solo that brought reminders of its composer, Foster's controlled surge belied his age and spoke only of his massive musical experience. As he played his own You're Only As Old As You Look, there was irony, too, in the absolute youth of his notes.

All week at the Jazz Café as part of the London Jazz Festival, Pharoah Sanders was blowing his tempestuous tenor with the multi-talents of pianist William Henderson, drummer Yoron Israel and phenomenal bassist Alex Blake, who struck and punished his bass while embracing it so tightly that you'd think after an hour of his music his hands would then be bleeding flesh-ends. I have never seen such furious and percussive bass-playing, comparing so extraordinarily with Percy Heath's septuagenarian caresses of the night before. As for Sanders, there was the never-lost deep, meditative surge of saxophone sound, at once ancestral and futuristic; ruminative, tender and rasping, a great salutation of notes

The opening selection lasted for an hour. At its end, Blake was shaking with the physical frenzy of his art and Israel had performed a universal anthem with the drums - from the tender to the celebratory and the ferocious, ending in softness, a long depletion of sound, a cadence until silence. Between 1963 and 1965, Sanders made the John Coltrane Quartet a quintet. The Little Rock-born tenorist has always played up to and beyond the limits of his instrument.

When the frontier of saxophone sound is reached and there is only the voice left with which to howl, the beseeching, the prayer and the glory of the instrumental sound turns to the vocal explosion, screaming back down the bell as if in communion with the gigantic sounds he had just created, while the solemnity of Henderson's piano was as if a jazz church was airing hymns in the heart of Camden Town.

A breathless week of music, made by the human breath and African-American genius plunged into three saxophones and the strings and skins pounded and stroked behind them.

Duncan Heining (England) - Jazz pastures: a landmark study of six jazz masters of Britain

And Did Those Feet: Six British Jazz Composers by Duncan Heining (2023)

There are some rare books where the artistry of the cover design truly matches the excellence of what is written inside. Such is this book where an adaptation of William Blake's 1794 painting The Ancient of Days, with the crouching Urizen playing a keyboard, complements the insights and critical essays of the works of Michael Garrick, Mike Gibbs, Barry Guy, John Mayer, Keith Tippett and Mike Westbrook, all of whom are the Tyger's sonic progeny. They were all musicians who came to fire during the 1960s, postwar troubadours whose self-belief and confidence in their own creativity sounded in an era when US shackles were unloosed and British jazz musicians began to believe they could achieve without imitation.

Heining writes from a wide knowledge of the music and its inseparable connections with social and political reality. He writes in depth about each composer, discussing not only their orchestral works but also their small group musicianship - Garrick, Tippett and Westbrook with their pianism, Guy with his bass virtuosity and Mayer with his violin in the series of Indo-jazz fusions that he created. Like a literary critic of old, Heining knows his timbral texts intimately, frequently writing about them with a poetic eloquence.

He illuminates the work and lives of six brilliant musicians whose artistic labours have never been fully appreciated. Take Garrick (1933-2011), who for me personified the struggle of musical brilliance within the ambiance of a disinterested arts establishment. Whenever I reviewed his records in the Morning Star, he would write or telephone me, thanking me for my words, saying how little attention the commercialised media gave to his work. Tippett did the same, reinforcing his adage 'may music never become just another way of making money,' as it wasn't for any of these six maestros.

Heining details Garrick's attempts to bring jazz and poetry together and the prolific content of his composing in many small group and orchestral contexts; Gibbs's meanderings between Boston's Berklee jazz conservatory in the US and his BBC projects in London; Guy's love for his bass and how 'improvised music was pushing us into new areas of expression... and to do that you had to extend your technique on the instrument to embrace all these new ideas.'

He describes Mayer's lifelong self-commission to integrate jazz and Indian classical music with Caribbean masters, the saxophonist Joe Harriott and trumpeter Shake Keane, and Tippett's polymath ability to compose and play as soloist for small groups like the Mujician quartet and vast ensembles like the 50-piece Centipede for the unique album Septober Energy. His superb chapter on Mike and Kate Westbrook, detailing the content of all their albums over 60 years of music, is a precious compendium of critical illumination.

But it is in his book's final short chapter, like a Coltrane coda, that Heining realises its most expressive moments. He writes of jazz not as 'a musical genre or style but rather as a way of making music based on its manipulation of the relationship between improvisation and form. In this sense it is always unfinished. It is always imperfect. It is always in dialogue with itself, its history and tradition, never fully realised but rather waits to be realised again by those creating it anew.'

I doubt if any previous writer has said it better, and just to emphasise his words and the music, there is an attached double CD of the six musicians at their best in previously unreleased recordings. A true gift for brain, ear and imagination combined. Blake would have loved it!

(And Did Those Feet: Six British Jazz Composers is published by Jazz in Britain)

Julius Hemphill (USA) - Starkly adventurous sounds of the city

Roi Boyé and the Gotham Minstrels
(2017)

Julius Hemphill's extraordinary multitracked 'audiodrama' was recorded in Toronto in March 1977, but its imaginative setting is a Gothic sonic vision of New York City, full of what Hemphill called 'phantasmagorical associations' which provoke 'anguish and other human emotions within that range.'

So what was an alto saxophonist born in Fort Worth, Texas, in 1938 and tutored by his great clarinet-playing townsman John Carter, doing, writing and recording such a fiercely original work about a huge cosmopolis so far from his home city? Hemphill played in R&B bands, did his stint in the US army and blew saxophone in Ike Turner's band before moving to St Louis, where he helped form the Black Artists Group, started a working band and a record label Mbari on which he cut his first album, Dogon, in 1972. He settled in New York from 1974 and became a key figure in the avant-garde jazz loft scene. In 1976 Hemphill became a founding member and the leading writer/arranger of the World Saxophone Quartet. Always an innovator and the protagonist of a host of revolutionary musical projects, his final years involved a constant struggle against a chronic heart condition. His work often had a keen political edge, such as his Chile/New York album of 1980. He died in 1995 after a life of pushing many a jazz boundary.

The Roi Boyé and the Gotham Minstrels double album is starkly adventurous. It is a solo work of jazz theatre, but one in which prepared tapes are as essential as the palette of sounds of the alto and soprano saxophones and flute that Hemphill plays throughout the recording. In his sleeve notes he writes that 'the environmental sounds and verbal images are peculiar to various landmarks and locales within the New York area.' And he goes on to particularise the New York Subway, where 'the sounds merge to form a specific cacophony; the larger stations amount to urban caverns that, during the pre-dawn hours when there is hardly any passenger traffic, allow the most minute sound to swell to awesome proportions; footsteps become the voice of a whip barking.'

And this was 1977, still not very long after some of the worst racist violence of the civil rights struggle and three years after the massacre at Attica prison in New York State, ordered by Governor Nelson Rockefeller, one of the richest men in the world. Sounds that are echoes of these events, as well as those in Latin America and south-east Asia, where the US government's brutal interventions and atrocities were still ripe and murderous, burst from the gut of Hemphill's horns. It is not the pseudo-heroics of Batman but the ghosts of Vietnam that hover over this Gotham City. This 'audiodrama' has no subtitles or demarcation of separate tracks. From its first notes and the double-tracked duo between alto saxophone and flute, it is an evocation of New York's propensity for the blues, which seem to be seeping from its very brick and asphalt in one man's troubled palaver between two levels of consciousness.

Yet the extraordinary dialogue of sounds is much more than a colloquy within the self. For the living city is the prime protagonist, the vast city itself and its swathe of peoples, overground and underground, on concrete and in the air, in the multiplicity of people who live within, of all origins, of many histories, of a plethora of struggles. Or those, who like the urban butterflies that Hemphill watches, 'that don't flutter, that don't fly.' After a pause, he blows a sweltering alto solo, almost Parkeresque, accompanied by the gradually increasing sound of the subway and a shout of '42nd Street: Watch the closing doors' before the discourse of horns continues.

It could be London, it could be Paris, it could be Toronto - it is the cosmopolis speaking. Or it could be Manchester, or Liverpool, for the only comparable album which I know was recorded in Liverpool and the voices are the saxophones of Phil Hargreaves and Caroline Kraabel. Where We Were: Shadows of Liverpool, the album's called, and the city's sounds are everywhere.

But Hemphill's solo album is that of a pioneer, an urban explorer from black Texas who found macabre and beautiful sounds in a faraway city that had become a new home for thousands of his people. As such, it is a work of prophetic and perturbing truth.

(Roi Boyé and the Gotham Minstrels is available on Sackville)

Paul Hession (England), Simon H Fell (England)
& Alan Wilkinson (England) –
Formidable free jazz: three great British jazzmen
Hession/Wilkinson/Fell - Two Falls & A Submission,
Alan Wilkinson – Practice & Simon H Fell - Frank and Max
(2017)

A formidable trio here - two Yorkshiremen and a Londoner who first began playing as a threesome in 1989. 'White heat improvisation; full throttle free jazz' is how The Wire described their music, while The Guardian's John Fordham wrote of their 'unquenchable energy... spontaneous music of a scorching and unrelenting intensity.'

Drummer Paul Hession was born in Leeds in 1956 and found his first live music singing in his church choir as a seven-year-old. He was a self-taught teenage drum enthusiast who played rock 'n' roll in working men's clubs before hearing Elvin Jones at Ronnie Scott's in 1975 switched his life around. He turned to free jazz, helped to form the Termite Club in Leeds and has since played with some of the music's great horns from Joe McPhee and Marshall Allen to Evan Parker and Peter Brotzmann.

Simon Fell is a Dewsbury bassist, born in 1959. He studied English literature at Cambridge and has led a full musical life as both instrumentalist and composer, establishing his own record label (Bruce's Fingers) and a number of free improvising groups from Badland to the 'electro acoustic improvisation' of IST, which in contrast to Hession/Wilkinson/Fell pursued a much more quiet and serene sonic approach.

The reedman is the London-born (in 1954) soprano, alto and baritone saxophonist Alan Wilkinson, who studied fine arts at Leeds University before working with Hession to create the Termite Club and developing his powerfully abrasive and gutteral saxophone voice in Leeds, and London after 1990, and also in New York where he made a trio with the duo Talibam!

Two Falls & A Submission celebrates 21 years as a trio by remembering childhood delights watching televised wrestling - and the real thing too, as Hession's evocation of live matches over Leeds's Roundhay Park as a boy in his sleeve notes testify. Musical 'grappling' is a metaphor he uses to apply to the trio's interactions. 'We can throw each other around and pin each other to the canvas,' he analogises. And from the first notes of the opener First Fall you know exactly what he means. Wilkinson's alto is sizzling, Hession's burning drums are everywhere and Fell is somewhere beneath it all, delving, tunnelling. The horn is angry, irascible, full of bite and when it becomes a baritone it sounds even more implacable, with Hession's skins answering blow by blow for almost 33 minutes.

You wonder what the listeners in the Queen's Head, Monmouth, made of it all, particularly when Fell emerges from the undersounds to create a series of rasping and agonised bow motifs which set the nerve endings crackling. Wilkinson's solo baritone fusillade which sets off The Submission seems like a provocation to his two confreres and wrestling begins to seem the mildest of conceits for the uproar which follows. Second Fall has a more bluesy timbre, with Wilkinson's woesome horn stoking more and more fury from Hession's thunderous pulses, and seeming to almost crack open the highest part of its register. At two sessions in January 2010 and July 2011 Wilkinson cut the tracks of his new solo album Practice in Stoke Newington, north-east London, following the years he spent in a 'practice space' in a disused hospital in Dalston, also north-east London. It all expands the truth that Dalston, with its vibrant performing venues like The Vortex and Café Oto, is now the leading and throbbing jazz 'hood of the capital, emphasised by Wilkinson's two long outings, Flush Dalston No 2 and Dalston No 1 which, as with the rest of the tracks, burn with artistry and sonic intensity.

In the former he starts off by snoring though his horn as well as kissing the stars. Wilkinson is a saxophone and multiphonics originator, audacious and musically brilliant to the core - listen to his haunting version of Ornette Coleman's Lonely Woman. It stays with you relentlessly. Fell has his own solo album in Frank And Max: Bass Solos 2001-2011, half recorded in the Old School at Bracon Ash in Norfolk, the other tracks cut in St Dizier-Leyrenne in Creuse, France.

His pieces are mostly dedicated to great bass men from the US (Mingus and Barre Phillips); Britain (Barry Guy and John Edwards) and South Africa (Harry Miller) plus one to his wife Jo (who made his five-string bass) and Patrick Charton, the French bassmaker who tuned it and set it up for playing. So the album becomes a praisesong to the bass, to its beauty, complexity and, in a host of skilled hands, to its humanity. Fell's bow-stroked strings seem to be weeping through the compelling For John Edwards, while the essay to Phillips is made of fingers as strong as the earth. The piece to Guy creaks and scurries eerily from the urban canyons of the imagination.

But Fell's rendition of Bill Evans's Turn Out The Stars is his apex, freeborn yet carrying and carried by Evans's tune, and superbly climaxing an astonishing record.

(Two Falls & A Submission, Practice & Frank and Max are available on Bo'Weavil)

Hiromi (Japan) - We know how to make each other shine

Hiromi and the Trio Project - Move and Alive
(2016)

When I first heard the Japanese pianist Hiromi live, in the Royal Festival Hall at the London Jazz Festival in November, it was as if a hurricane had hit the keys, with her hands traversing them with so much speed that her arms were a blur like some dazzling impressionist image. And out of this came so much sound, with her contrabass guitarist, the New Yorker Anthony Jackson, laying down such a pulsating, succulent beat and her London drummer Simon Phillips within the mental compound of his steelworks of cymbals crashing and booming his message through the air of that most formal of venues.

Hiromi Uehara was born in Hamamatsu, Shizuoka in 1979 and began the piano when she was six, which was when she also enrolled in the Yamaha School of Music. When she was 20 she went to the US and began at Boston's Berklee College of Music. One of her tutors took a tape of her playing to the veteran jazz pianist Ahmad Jamal, who judged it 'nothing short of amazing,' and she made her first album, Another Mind, in 2003 - the first of nine so far. In 2009 she recorded with Chick Corea in a piano duo concert, and with Stanley Clarke's band on his Jazz in the Garden album, and in 2011 she cut her first record with Jackson and Phillips, called Voice.

Move, released in 2013, was the trio's second album, in which Hiromi sought to create 'a sound track for a day.' So devoted had she become to Jackson and Phillips, that she 'really wanted to extract the unique beauty of their playing.' Perhaps it is the bounty of extra jazz influences that her two bandmates embrace that create such powerful rhythmic eclecticism. Jackson has played with Steeleye Dan and Paul Simon as well as Corea, and Phillips's rock pedigree includes The Who, Judas Priest, David Gilmour and Jack Bruce.

'We know how to make each other shine,' declares Hiromi, and that is soon more than apparent in the pounding beat and pulsating tempo of the opening title track. Brand New Day is lyrical and melodic, but Jackson's divergent, inventive pulse never wavers and Phillips's drums are huge without being domineering. Three continents find a kindred fire within this trio, and despite Hiromi's pyrotechnics, a trio culture it certainly is, a musicianship of powerful unity. Endeavour features Hiromi's piano and synthesizer in palaver with Phillips's universe of drums and Rainmaker has Hiromi's notes like drops of showers, but this is not a gentle fall. Reality is the first part of her Suite Escapism and she rampages along her keyboard with Jackson with her at every step: his notes will neither be lost nor smothered. 'What great chemistry!' Jamal declared about the empathy of this trio, and in the surging kindred sound of In between and 11.49pm, you begin to know exactly what he means.

In 2014 the trio returned to the New York Avatar Studios to record Alive, with Hiromi rhapsodising about the talents of her two partners - Jackson's 'incredible counter-lines when I solo' and Phillips's drumsound: 'He's like an orchestra.' Together, she declared, 'they understand so many different genres of music.' Each track deals with one of life's key moments, challenges or strategies, from the first, Here I Am, Born and Alive, to the finality of Life Goes On. For me the ace track is Wanderer, where Hiromi suddenly quickens pace with Jackson's sonic shadow beside her and Phillips's London drums urge her onwards. And she goes, with such dynamism, taking her two companions alongside her, surging together.

As I listen to this artistry on tracks like the ruminative Dreamer or the sparkling Firefly, the vivid memory of her tiny frame and dancing hands bringing miracles of musicianship from the Royal Festival Hall concert piano, cannot leave me.

(Move and Alive are available on Telarc)

Fred Ho (China/USA) - A dream and plan in harmony

Fred Ho and the Saxophone Liberation Front's Snake-eaters (2017)

As I was sitting in the Barbican Concert Hall at last year's London Jazz Festival, waiting for the start of Archie Shepp's revival of his incendiary suite of 1972, Attica Blues, a fellow listener sitting next to me saw that I was writing notes and we began talking about the politics of jazz. 'If you do reviews, then make sure you review these!' he exclaimed. And he listed on his programme some of the albums of the Chinese-American baritone saxophone revolutionary, Fred Ho. Some of the records on his list I'd already reviewed here in the Star, but I'm grateful to him because our encounter reminded me that I'd recently been sent from the US a Ho album which I hadn't tackled yet with the evocative title Snake-eaters, by Fred Ho and the Saxophone Liberation Front.

So thank you, unknown fellow groover! The Saxophone Liberation Front is clearly inspired by the World Saxophone Quartet, and has a similar instrumentation. Ho plays his baritone, the Iranian-American Hafez Modirzadeh, born in Durham, North Carolina, in 1962, plays soprano, Bobby Zankel, born in Brooklyn in 1949, plays alto saxophone and Salim Washington, an African-American born in Memphis, raised in Detroit and educated at Harvard, where he wrote a PhD on John Coltrane, is the tenorist.

Snake-eaters is composed of two suites - the first is Yellow Power, Yellow Soul Suite, the second is Beyond Columbus and Capitalism, with some other more ruminative tracks, beginning with the opener inspired by Curtis Mayfield's song We are the People who are Darker than Blue, and called Darker Than Blue. The crunching horn ensemble of the foursome, grounded by Ho's earthen baritone and raised up by Modirzadeh's exultant soprano is full of the breath of struggle and unity. The first movement of the Yellow Power suite, Fishing Song of the East China Sea, is almost bird-like as it begins, but as the combined pitch of the saxophones dives and then morphs into the dancing second movement, Tanko Bushi, it moves from air to sea to land with waves of gasping energy.

Baeng Nori is more like a pacy march and Hero Among Heroes a reed salutation by four diverse Americans to Chinese warriors of freedom with powerful melodic lines and ensemble flourishes. A more recent dragonic figure is celebrated in Jeet Kune D: The Way of the Intercepting Fist - Bruce Lee, a personification of the street-fighting spirit. There are snatches of melody, stomping harmonies and Modirzadeh's flying solo soprano in this sonic portrait. Tuneful adaptations of themes by two great African-American pianists follow. The first is an airy reading of Monk's Reflections with Washington's tenor then Zankel's alto leaping out of the ensemble. The second is another pianoless version of Erroll Garner's Misty (Misty ification). It is all the tune, lucidly set down before the saxophones rise to a crescendo, and a last falling moment.

The punning titles of the four movements of Beyond Columbus and Capitalism point to the irony of many of its sounds and sequences. The first is My God, My Gold: The European Invasion and a strangely vaunting sound emerges as the tenor seems to arrogantly push its way over the other horns before the soprano has the final word. In Civilisation or Syphillisation the sudden changes of pace and agonised reed testimonies of soprano and tenor before Ho's pumping message are telling a brutal imperialist story, and The New World Odor, with Ho's gurgling solo and the squeezed, whining message of the other horns, essays the truth. Ghost Dance on the Grave of Capitalism is the last movement and seems to swerve into Native American forms, with a call and response structure between Ho and his confreres, with the baritonist blowing the riff and the other horns springing around him, dancing and improvising in joy and creation.

A dream and plan in harmony - and not one that will fade away.

(Fred Ho and the Saxophone Liberation Front Snake-eaters is available on Mutable/Big Red Media)

Fred Ho (China/USA) - Gung Ho sax

Fred Ho and the Afro Asian Music Ensemble - Big Red! (2012)

The reprieve in December of Mumia Abu-Jamal, one of the most high-profile US political prisoners, was only a partial victory for an innocent man and his supporters. But his final removal from death row after so many years of mass campaigning, litigation and struggle was recognition of the huge international support for the former Black Panther and radio journalist, who was wrongfully convicted on trumped-up charges of murdering a Philadelphia police officer in 1981.

Support for Mumia came from a host of quarters, not least the world of jazz, through the music and benefits of Fred Ho and his Afro Asian Music Ensemble. Ho, who died in August 2006 of bowel cancer, wrote the Free Mumia Suite in Italy in 2002 when the campaign to save Mumia was at its apex. It has now been issued posthumously along with other powerful Ho compositions as part of the Big Red! album.

Ho, a Chinese Californian born in 1957, was a thunderous yet subtle baritone saxophonist who led a band of committed musicians and whose albums for the Soul Note and Innova labels like Tomorrow Is Now, The Underground Railway To My Heart, The Black Panther Suite and the anti-rape suite Yes Means Yes, No Means No, Whatever She Wears, Wherever She Goes underlined jazz as a music of defiance and resistance. The ensemble is a Mingus-like band of long-serving confreres, including pioneer members like tenorist David Bindman and drummer Royal Hartigan. Indeed, the longest track on Big Red! - some 17 minutes - is the Suite Sam Furnace, dedicated to the altoist who died in 2004 and who was a member of the Afro Asian Music Ensemble since 1982.

The album opens with Ho's huge solo baritone sound on Kayasong, a version of the Korean folk opera form of pansori, in which Hartigan employs a modified drum set with a Korean hourglass drum while Rami Seo sings in the Korean language. Deep, deep is Ho's horn on the Furnace Suite with Masaru Koga's contrasting alto skyward soar, Art Hirahara's rocking piano and the pulsating bass heartbeat of Wesley Brown. In the sleeve notes poet Magdalene Gomez celebrates Furnace's life of burning notes - 'No! I am here! I am alive! This song will never be over!'

The five short movements of the Mumia Suite carry explicit titles like Voice Of The Voiceless, Political Power Growing and Stop The Execution, Start A Revolution! Hirahara moves to organ on the final section and throughout the sextet stomps and declaims, with the three united and solo horns eloquent with their own reed oratory, Bindman's tenor saxophone building a virtual speech of sublime insubordination coming to the fore again with his two horn comrades riffing behind him as the suite concludes.

Brown's jumping bass and Hartigan's African percussion ground Gadzo, based on a Ghanaian Ewe song. At the centre is Bindman's rousing solo, breaking into an unaccompanied burst and preceding a breathy, incandescent chorus from Ho's inspired baritone. The Un...! And Ir...! Suite is Ho's indignant riposte to the widely screened Ken Burns TV documentary on the history of jazz and its ignorant commentary on the free movement of the 1960s, which centred on the crucial contribution of tenorist Archie Shepp and his Afro-centric and socialist perspectives. The horns play in harmony, the pace successively quickens and slows down, Ho takes a quivering solo and a long ominous break beside Hartigan's crashing cymbals.

The final track is charged by Shepp's early musical-poetical fusions. It is the album's title track, dedicated to Malcolm X and Mao Zedong, telling the story of Chinese immigrants in America and ending with the imagined poetical narration of Kwan Gung, a young Chinese-American murdered by racist violence in 1982. Bindman delivers a profound and history-laden tenor rhapsody and Ho affirms that 'Justice can't be stopped by syncopated baseball bats' and that 'the souls of our ancestors never die, not while the living must get organised.'

It has a hindsight that makes it an epitaph for a brilliant jazz musician who never left the people and whose music reflects and roars like their testimony.

(Big Red! is available on Innova)

Fred Ho (China/USA) - Tells it straight

Fred Ho and the Afro-Asian Ensemble - Yes Means Yes, No Means No, Whatever She Wears, Wherever She Goes (2011)

The establishment press often tells us that Minister of Justice Ken Clarke is a lover of jazz. If that's the case, and in light of his recent pronouncements on the gradations of rape, I wonder if he has ever listened to the powerful 1992 album by the Chinese-American baritone saxophonist Fred Ho (born 1957) and this resonating band, which is aptly called Yes Means Yes, No Means No, Whatever She Wears, Wherever She Goes. It might give him some scope for thought and action, or maybe not. It is a reflective and campaigning musical statement against the all-times criminal horror of rape, cut with empathy and intense musical skill by a group of committed men and women of Asian-American and African-American provenances.

Ho is a jazzman and composer with a brave and distinct political agenda who has made a series of fine albums which fuse a sonic and socialist vision, including the superb Underground Railway To My Heart (1993), the quasi-folk ballet narrative of Once Upon a Time in Chinese America (1999) and his rampaging 2009 album Celestial Green Monster. In all contexts he blows his horn with a fierce engagement and a full, pugnacious beauty. Throughout this album his sound is inspired and booming in brotherly struggle. With him are his musical comrades of the Afro-Asian Ensemble. Two more saxophonists, Sam Furnace on alto and tenorist David Bindman, bassist Kiyoto Fujiwara and drummer Royal Hartigan, with Diana Herold on marimba and vibes plus guests Robert Levin on trombone, Peter Madsen on keyboards and vocalist Valecia Phillips.

Ho's founding principles of life, music and struggle are set out in his sleeve note to the 11 resonating minutes of his tune The Last Shall Be First, The First Last, which he describes as 'an allegorical description of socialism, which is blues. The blues is not about sorrow, but about hope. Hope is the face of oppression, suffering, pain, misery and misfortune. Not a religious hope, a hope that one day, the last shall be first, the first last.' It is within this context that his album was born and flourishes with advocacy for women's (or preferably womyn's) freedom and a campaigning hatred of rape. 'I have the political view that violence against womyn will only end when womyn defend themselves by any means necessary and over-throw patriarchy,' he writes.

So what about the music? The 22 minutes of the title suite are a powerful polemic with Phillips's burning vocal of the condition of American women, where 'we are night prisoners in our homes almost without fail/under house and mental arrest for being female.' Bindman's empathetic obligatos create a call and answer pattern and Hartigan's ubiquitous drums crack a resolute undertow to Choose Coke and a grounding determination for Furnace's rampant alto.

John Coltrane's praise song to his first wife, Naima, is given lyrics by Nadrea Lockett and becomes a homage to all African women, ending with 'Throughout history/she is fear-less and free/she will take the lead to build a world of peace.' Just 45 seconds of the insurrectionary African-American anthem S(w)ingin' With a Sword in my Hand preface The Last Shall Be First, where all members thrive. Furnace's alto seethes out of the rousing ensemble, Herold's vibes rock, Levin's keys pulsate with joy above Hartigan's thrashing drums, Fujiwara's twanging bass bounces into a solo and Ho's earthen baritone grounds it all.

African percussion is the soil in which the tune Nana grows, named after Ashanti queen Yaa Asante-waa who led resistance against British colonialism in Ghana and Kakuya Shakur, the daughter of African-American revolutionary Assata Shakur. Taken from Ho's opera Warrior Sisters: The new adventures of African and Asian Womyn Warriors, the drums throb and Ho's diving groundswell to Phillips's vocal is formidable, a rumbling fanfare of struggle. There is more of Ghana in Dagomba, birthed by the music of the Dagomba people and played as a long solo by the inspired tenor of Bindman.

Finally Ho performs his Absolute Solo!, taken from a Chinese farewell song and dedicated to the release of all US political prisoners. A potent message against rape and oppression and for human freedom bursts from every note of this momentous album and to all of us, including you, Mr Clarke.

What do you think, how does it make you groove?

(Yes Means Yes, No Means No, Whatever She Wears, Wherever She Goes is available on Koch Jazz)

Julia Hulsmann (Germany) - Pulsating strings that tell their formidable stories

Julia Hulsmann Trio and Quartet - The End of a Summer, Imprint, In Full View & A Clear Midnight (2016)

'My music is about melody' is a principle which the German pianist Julia Hulsmann holds very dear. Born in the turbulent year 1968 in Bonn, she started a life's piano odyssey at 11 years old, forming her first band at 16. After she moved to Berlin in 1991 she became a part of the Bundesjugendjazzorchestra, before joining with bassist Marc Muellbauer in 1996 and drummer Heinrich Kobberling in 2001. They have been her trio stalwarts ever since.

In 2008 the threesome cut their first album for the Munich-based ECM label, The End of a Summer, in an Oslo studio. The valedictory title is actually an introduction to a very different trio sound: the lucid, almost bell-like notes of Hulsmann in the title tune above the rustling Kobberling, Muellbauer's booming, dancing bass in the drummer's Konbawa, or the quiescent beauty of Seal's song Kiss from a Rose.

'Something simple that grooved' is how Hulsmann described Gelb and Hulsmann's tune Senza which has a string of elegy, with Muellbauer's pulsating strings telling a formidable story. Not the End of the World begins to swing almost wistfully through its cadences and Sepia is a brown-tinted and very European blues.

By 2011, when the album Imprint was recorded, the trio was even more deeply unified. The opener Rond Point has an almost intoxicating rhythmic base lifted by Kobberling's faintly swishing drums, and the sudden drama of Grand Canyon transports to another sonic plane. The sense of the solidarity in A Light Left On is, in parts, darkly yet luminously realised. Juni has a haunting theme, enigmatically concluded, while the imperative (Go and Open) The Door has folk echoes, a call and answer within three instrumental voices. After the worrisome dream of Hulsmann's Lulu's Paradise and the reflective strains of Muellbauer's Ulmenwall comes the trio's unexpected tribute to Thelonious Monk, Who's Next, full of jaunty Monkish corners, alleys and byways and showing new dimensions of their tradition.

In 2013 the trio became a quartet with the addition of, in Hulsmann's words, 'another melody player,' the son of Northamptonshire and Berlin-based trumpeter Tom Arthurs, for the album In Full View, and from his flickering notes Muellbauer's Quicksilver to his mournful tones in Hulsmann's Dunkel you begin to understand Kobberling's assertion that 'Tom adds hundreds of new colours to our band sound.' Arthurs's sure-edged timbre cuts through the drummer's mulling Forever Old where Hulsmann's notes ripple below his horn, and in Spiel his skyward sound cavorts joyously. His own composition Forgotten Poetry shows how much the trio has been reinvented as a quartet, with so much sonic empathy between the musicians.

After the quartet performed at the Kurt Weill Festival in Dessau in 2013, the album A Clear Midnight was born with vocalist Theo Bleckmann (born in Dortmund in 1966) singing lyrics of Weill, Langston Hughes, Walt Whitman, Ira Gershwin and Ogden Nash. An unusually slow and ruefully menacing version of Mack the Knife opens the album, with the Muellbauer's bass to the fore in Alabama Song. It's Hulsmann's music that accompanies Whitman's words in three pieces as he poses the question: 'No brokers or speculators - would they continue?' in Beat! Beat! Drums! with Hulsmann's throbbing keys in unison with him. Arthurs blows a translucent chorus in Gershwin's This is New and in Weill's River Chanty his fanfarish narrative carries the melody. What a duo! Langston Hughes's words and Weill's music in Great Big Sky, which is the album's finale: 'It's a great big sky/ And there's room enough for all? I know the night will pass!/ I know the dark will go!/ I know the dawn will come alright!'

Four Germans and an Englishman make the words and music theirs too, in a riposte to all the new racisms of Europe 'before the big sun rises in the sky.' It's a fine and inspiring album, a union of two continents and its powerful and committed artistry.

(The End of a Summer, Imprint, In Full View & A Clear Midnight are available on ECM)

Ineza (Rwanda) - I enjoy the company of women musicians
Women's Words, Sisters' Stories
(2025)

The Rwanda-born singer Ineza, says of her striking and beautifully sung first album Women's Words, Sisters' Stories: 'Its unifying theme is championing the works of female composers, singers and songwriters in the jazz world.' Her accompanying band are all women, with the exception of pianist Alex Webb: bassist Charlie Pyne, Katie Patterson on drums, trombonist Rosie Turton and tenor saxophonist Maddy Coombs. There is also an all-women string quartet

of violinists Johanna Burnheart and Annalise Lam, with Julia dos Reis on viola and cellist Miranda Lewis-Brown.

Adopted by a Belgian family, Ineza tells me: 'For the majority of my youth I knew nothing of my biological family. My adopted parents enjoyed listening to classical music but weren't musical themselves. I visited Rwanda for the first time when I was 18, before then I knew little of Rwandan culture.'

At 17, during her final year of secondary school in Bruges, she would dream of becoming a musical theatre actor. Then she discovered Amy Winehouse, then Ella Fitzgerald and other jazz vocalists like Sarah Vaughan and Betty Carter. 'I fell totally in love with the genre,' she says. She arrived in London in 2015 to study Jazz Vocals at Trinity Laban Conservatoire in Greenwich, and lived in Charlton, Lewisham and Hither Green. 'I found Britain had such a rich and diverse pool of musicians.' Singers like Brigitte Beraha, Pete Churchill and Liane Carroll gave her powerful encouragement.

Her album Women's Words, Sisters' Stories is a paean to some of the great women jazz vocalists. 'My favourite tracks are Billie Holiday's Who Needs You? which she wrote, but never had the chance to record; Betty Carter's I Can't Help It - I love the boldness of the lyrics - and Abbey Lincoln's Throw it Away. The lyrics are beautiful, introspective and sensitive. Over the years I've spent a lot of time analysing and learning about vocal phrasing. Listening to the freedom exhibited in their singing has greatly influenced my approach to any tune in any genre.'

What about her band? 'I mostly perform with male bands. There's nothing wrong with that, but I do wish there were more women in jazz. I enjoy the company of women musicians. It creates a different, supportive atmosphere on stage. The album is Alex Webb's brainchild. He pitched the idea to me and created the arrangements. The band is called The Copasetics, reflecting the highest compliment to the hep world, mostly associated with Duke Ellington's close collaborator, Billy Strayhorn.'

There are some intense ensemble sequences throughout the album, and stirring solos. Ineza's conversational vocal stylings radiate artistry. Hear her message on Don't Waste Your Time, her thoughtful, lyrical rendition of Good Morning, Heartache with Coombs's brief, soulful solo, or her floating defiance on Free Your Mind. Tell Me More pours out Billie's poignant heartsong with Pyne's plunging bass and Webb's empathetic keys.

How does she think Billie, Abbey or Betty would have reacted to these young women singing and playing with such verve and assuredness? 'I can imagine how pleased they would be to see so many of us taking up jazz. There was a time when jazz saw women in only a small and insignificant niche. Today's cohort is certainly changing that narrative. We can thank the great women jazz pioneers of the past for all that progress.'

(Women's Words, Sisters' Stories is available on Copasetic Records)

Jon Irabagon (Philippines/USA)
Server Farm
(2025)

The outer sleeve illustration of Jon Irabagon's new album, Server Farm, has microscopic humans walking down a huge and forbidding avenue of gross technology. The poem called Spy in the inner sleeve is about a bee, its 'kaleidoscopic partitions' holding the menace and 'lens of a tiny camera'. The sounds of the record and the pictures on its sleeve are dimensions of a now-times AI nightmare.

Irabagon was born in Chicago in 1978. 'I'm first generation Filipino-American; my Father was an electrician and mother a chemist. Neither my parents nor my siblings play music, but there was always plenty of music in the house: pop, country, smooth jazz, rock - even elevator music! I took piano lessons from my Aunt then started on saxophone in the fifth grade. I didn't take it seriously until high school, until school band director Tom Beckwith nurtured my love for jazz and introduced me to Sonny Rollins, Cannonball Adderley and Sonny Stitt, my first saxophone influences. I grew up in Chicago, falling in love with jazz, an American art form. My Filipino culture makes itself present in the open sections of my music - our family parties were always fun; loud and rumbustious. I love all that, and my music loves it as well.'

What about the meanings of Server Farm and the fable poem of the bee? 'I hope it brings awareness and action to the growing threat of AI. I definitely had a story in mind when I was going through its compositional process, and hopefully listeners can create their own as they listen. Each track is special to me. They all convey ideas and philosophies on the topic. I'm especially happy with the final 'Spy' track as it's the first time I've featured my own lyrics (as well as sax effects pedals) on my own albums.'

With the outrageous political dominion now held by AI billionaires like Musk, how can musicians resist such power? 'The first part of resisting this form of control is to be aware of it and start discussions. The album has already had an effect by getting people talking about the next steps. There's a lot of research and outreach to be done. I actually attempted to recreate AI processes when I composed the music. I listened incessantly to as much of the recorded history of each band member as I could for several months, often for hours each day, looking for repeated patterns, ideas or gestures from each musician, and then incorporated them into the compositional process. In this way I was able to gain as much pertinent information as possible and then re-purpose it all for my own use.'

'These nine musicians are some of my favourite people and players in the world, so I wanted to make sure they had plenty of freedom throughout the album, with many textural and improvisational choices. It was a delicate balance between composing just enough material to get my ideas across, and to encourage these musicians to shine and be themselves.'

And I thought as he spoke, isn't this what in earlier eras what Ellington, Basie, Gil Evans and other great maestros have sought to do, to write their compositions or arrangements to give scope to fully express the genius of their members, whether it was for Johnny Hodges, Cootie Williams, Harry Carney or Ben Webster for Ellington or Lester Young, Buck Clayton or Dickie Wells for Basie or Miles Davis for Evans? Certainly the full artistry of Irabagon's colleagues like pianist Matt Mitchell, guitarists Miles Okazaki and Wendy Eisenberg, galactic trumpeter Peter Evans, violinist Mazz Swift and Irabagon himself on tenor and soprano saxophones is fully delivered, but this time with the active help of AI.

Server Farm puts jazz once more fully in the centre of new ideas and action. Remember Irabagon's enslaved bee, 'its wings a frantic blur, its body majestic and pure', its nature now corrupted, made servile by dragons like Musk and Trump. It mustn't become a metaphor for any of us.

(Server Farm is available on Irrabagast Records)

Abdullah Ibrahim (South Africa) - Heart of Africa

Fats, Duke and The Monk & Ancient Africa

(2017)

A million ancestral drums pound in these two albums made in 1973 by the shamanic South African pianist Abdullah Ibrahim, expressing his devotion to the continent of his birth and three great musicians of an adopted nation and an adopted music. And yet they are both solo piano performances recorded in the Thunder Sound studios of Toronto in the depth of a Canadian winter, the sounds of a genius of the oppressed and disfigured south struggling against apartheid deformity, created during a few blissful hours in a receptive and admiring north on a far continent of exile.

Ibrahim had left South Africa as Adolf Johannes 'Dollar' Brand in 1962. Found by Duke Ellington in a Zurich nightclub, he first found landfall in the Americas in 1965, where the Duke organised his first US recording session. He played at the Newport Jazz Festival and within a few months he was working with Coltrane's great drummer Elvin Jones and living in New York. By the time of his 1973 Toronto sessions he had turned to Islam and had returned from his first hajj.

The long, compelling tracks of these albums segue into each other in a seamless unity. They are a huge shout of art and life as one, telling the story of a musical griot's influences and inspirations from two continents, while never leaving the sounds and blood of home, with Ancient Africa stirring through every note and phrase in a frozen, faraway land. No performances more passionately and with such powerful virtuosity express the musical unity of Africa and the US than those which are given to us on these two records.

Fats, Duke and the Monk is the middle track of the first album and the sonic shadows of Waller, Ellington and Monk are cast clearly in Ibrahim's sounds. The Duke's Harlem melodism, so closely mirrored in many of Ibrahim's tunes, emerges with a singular beauty in the South African's version of Ellington's The Single Petal of a Rose while Ibrahim's own urban patterns romp through his Ode to Duke. Waller's Honeysuckle Rose is a tribute to Fats' mastery of the New York 'stride' piano style which he learned from his own mentor James P Johnson, and which found its way to Cape Town to be picked up by Ibrahim and given his own township timbre. Then comes Thelonious and his Think of One and Ibrahim's tribute, Monk from Harlem, to complete the trinity. The opening suite 'Salam Peace' is brimful of Ibrahim's own numbers, including Hamba Kahle, Blues for a Hip King and Gwidza all streaming in and out of each other, his drumming piano causing Africa to rise irrepressibly through the lakeside Ontario snow.

The 24 minutes of the long concluding track - African Portraits - are a homage to the South African musicians either left in South Africa or fellow exiles escaping apartheid. There are salutes to trumpeter Hugh Masekela (also in the US), trombonist Jonas Gwangwa and the essential alto-saxophonist Kippie Moeketsi, who was Ibrahim's bandmate in the pioneering Johannesburg band the Jazz Epistles. Ancient Africa is a jewel of an album, an epic praise-song to Ibrahim's true continent, its earth, its people, its rivers and mountains, its relentless drums.

The engrossing notes of Water's Edge and its repeated chorus flow into Bertha in Turquoise and the mesmeric Krotoa. It is as if Ibrahim has never left the eternity which is Africa and that it must go with him wherever he travels. All the time and beyond the sound of the chiming keys is Ibrahim's wailing, wordless, chanting voice as if he is calling upon history, his home and the ever-close people that he loves.

Released in 1973, all the tracks are Ibrahim's compositions and, as he moves into The Aloe and the Wild Rose, Cherry or Bra Joe from Kilimanjaro, he carries his transoceanic African-American inspirations - Fats, Duke and the Monk - back to Africa with him as a conductor of their own astonishing creations.

(Fats, Duke and The Monk & Ancient Africa are available on Sackville)

Abdullah Ibrahim (South Africa) - Melody fired in the furnace of racist terror

Abdullah Ibrahim and the NDR Big Band, Barbican, London (2001)

It was a wonderful evening - and not only because of the music. Here was a jazz orchestra, made up predominantly of white Germans. whose lives and many of those of the generation before them had their provenances in the racist hell of nazism. They rose from their seats, one by one, to come to the microphone at the front of the stage to play brilliantly textured and passionate solos within the composition of the one black man among them, the Cape Town-born South African Abdullah Ibrahim, who, for most of his life, struggled physically and through his creative genius against the devilish system of apartheid.

For Ibrahim, the idea of playing his Africa-founded music in such a context would once have been a forbidden dream. For some of the grey-haired and ageing members of the NDR Big Band, what historical memories would be lodged within their brains? What recollections, now so strongly revoked within their own superb musicianship, of the vicious claims of the degeneracy of black music and the racial impurities of jazz? So, as those whose own origins knew of fascism and race terror on two continents made African music together, no wonder the pianist concluded a soaring performance of his own African Market Place with the words: 'Where ancient dreams are traded for hopeful tomorrows.' And, if ever the human being wanted confirmation that neither he nor she were a prisoner of history, it was here, in London at the Barbican, that such could be found.

Like Duke Ellington, whose music was constantly evoked throughout the evening, Ibrahim is a profound and lucid melodist. Each selection that the orchestra played gave testimony to this, none more so than the tribute piece, Duke 88, dominated by the Johnny Hodges-like alto of Fiete Felsch. Ibrahim's tunes, with their spacious, deceptively simple, folk-like and sometimes church-like themes owe much to the cosmopolitanism of the Cape Town of his boyhood and the fusion of African tribal music with carnival sounds, Chinese, Malay and Indian influences and the importation of the jazz adventure from the US - the discoveries of Monk, Parker and Gillespie that blew into the youthful artistic mind of the pianist like an ocean storm.

The amalgam of all this heterogeneity is there in the CD that the concert launched. Ekapa Lodumo. All the selections from the performance are included and what emerges is a serene and beautiful record - testimony to Ibrahim's memorable compositions and the NDR capacity to transmute them into big-band performances through the arranging skills of Steve Gray and Fritz Pauer.

One of the most powerful selections is Pule (Rain), dedicated to Namibia - which was. of course, invaded and colonised by l9th-century German imperialism. 'Namibia. Namibia, daybreak rains are tears.' lamented Ibrahim in a poetic preface to the performance. which included a gentle flute solo by Felsch, followed by a scaring trumpet chorus by Reiner Winterschladen.

But perhaps Ibrahim's African glory came through with most power in his Mindif, named after a mountain in the Cameroons. Here is an anthem for flute, clarinets and the reed section of the NDR, which exposed the heart of Ibrahim's genius - and all those "hopeful tomorrows" of human solidarity and the defeat of the crimes of history that every note of his music so hopefully expresses.

Jabula (South Africa) - A South African praisesong
Thunder And Happiness: The Complete Albums (2013)

Between anti-apartheid activism, demonstrations and educational work during the '70s, there was also the generation of powerful South African musicians-in-exile, alive and grooving in Britain, adding their defiant sounds to the protest and affirmation. Chris McGregor's Brotherhood Of Breath with fellow ex-Blue Notes Mongezi Feza, Dudu Pukwana, Louis Moholo-Moholo and arch-bassist Harry Miller, playing with local confreres like Evan Parker and Harry Beckett, were blasting London with Pukwana's bands like Zila and Spear and Miller's Isipingo. But another prime South African band who I used to hear regularly in Oxford Street's 100 Club was Jabula (the Zulu word for 'happiness'), formed in 1974 by drummer Julian Bahula from the Pretoria township of Mamelodi, which spawned the Malombo Jazzmen with Bahula playing the tall, booming Malombo drums with his flying mallets. 'We sought to marry jazz with the music of our ancestors,' declared Bahula.

When he found himself playing illegally with the white musicians of South Africa's leading rock band, Jo'burg Hawk in 1972, he decided that he could not continue to live and work in the apartheid state, so he moved to Britain in 1973 and continued his cultural activism for the ANC in London. In 1975 Jabula recorded their first eponymous album, followed in 1976 by their second, Thunder In Our Hearts. The reissue, Thunder And Happiness, contains all the tracks from both albums, with Bahula, guitarist Lucky Ranku and bassist Mogotsi Mothle playing throughout, and there are some notable other personnel too. Hearing the opening tracks again, nearly 40 years after, with the joyous vocals of Maureen Koto Lembede and Vicki Busiswe Mhlongo, the chorus of saxophones and Bahula's pounding drums I remember how that smoky, subterranean chamber of the 100 Club used to shake and tremble and how much it used to make you think and reflect about the struggling millions at the tip of the continent.

Badishi-Herdboys is carried on Mothle's throbbing bass. Pukwana plays a wailing chorus and the vocals pulsate with life. Our Fathers is an invocation to the ancestors to awaken and inspire, with Ranku's guitar at its centre. It is Pukwana's alto and Nick Evans's fierce trombone that emerge from the ensemble of Baleka - Run Away, while George Larnyoh's soaring flute precedes another clanking and blues-baked Ranku solo in Naledi.

Bahula transports the band homewards on his tune Ithumelang Ba Mamelodi and its township sounds crowd above Mothle's incessant heartbeat, and the ensemble of horns and percussion on Baile - They Are Gone make almost a big band compared with the quintet that used to comprise Jabula in their club performances. Mothle uses a bow at the beginning of Journey Of Afrika, Evans's slides howl and at its end many horns are blowing. Tears of Afrika follows, and they are still falling as Mothle cries out under the ensemble: 'Africa, why did we leave?'

Thandi is full of speed with Ranku at the wheel and a stinging chorus from Pukwana, and it is followed by Thunder Into Our Hearts, full of Ranku's tricky guitar runs and Mothle's echoing bass. Soweto My Love follows, a praisesong to the people of the giant Johannesburg black suburb, whose children were mown down by apartheid guns seven months after the song was recorded in Chalk Farm, London, in November 1975. The final track is Ranku and Bahula's Let Us Be Free, with some stratospheric trumpet be Eddi Quansah and Bahula's drums in full glory before Ranku's long and fading chorus.

As for Bahula, he remained active in London until the fall of apartheid, among much else, organising the concert to celebrate Mandela's 65th birthday at Alexandra Palace in 1983. In 1997 he was badly injured in a car accident in South Africa, but he recovered and was honoured in his homeland for his contribution to the musical and political struggle.

He remembers Jabula with pride and says of this combined album: 'Listening to my first UK recordings I have a good feeling. The music we made back then is great and hadn't been heard by many people, except those who supported our struggle. Now that our country is free, let the music come out for everyone to hear!'

(Thunder And Happiness: The Complete Albums is available on Retro)

Naissam Jalal (France/Syria) – Souffles
(2025)

We may know souffles as egg-based dishes from France, but the verb 'souffler' means to blow, breathe, inflate or puff. That's what happens on the beautiful album Souffles, a series of duets between the Paris-based flautist of Syrian heritage, Naissam Jalal, and eight separate partners playing saxophones, clarinets and trombone.

Naissam was born in Paris in 1984 and grew up there, but later returned to her roots and studied at the Institute of Arab Music in Damascus, and subsequently in Cairo. She plays a fusion of Western chamber music, Arab classical music and jazz, and in Souffles has created a succession of serene and lyrical harmonies with eight other wind virtuosi from France, Cuba and the USA.

The opener features Thomas de Pourquery's alto sax, which enters after Naissam's poised solo beginning, her lines layered on de Pourqury's breath as the twosome move into intense sonic unity. Then comes the Klezmer clarinet of YOM (Guillaume Humery), whose rhapsodic and rhythmic notes become a bed for Naissam's wordless voice, followed by Sylvain Rifflet's tenor saxophone obligatos, which become part of a spontaneous melody created by Naissam's flute.

On all these duets the partners create the closest of musical empathies, none more so than the Naissam/Louis Sclavis coalescence. Sclavis' weathered bass clarinet begins from the deep unknown, before Naissam's flute rescues the theme and brings it to the surface, meshing in a harmony of extremes. This duet contrasts with that with the Cuban soprano saxophonist Irving Acao, finding unity from the very first note, as Acao brings a rhythmic underpinning while Naissam launches into a skyward solo.

Robinson Khoury's agile trombone slides seem to emulate Naissam's opening solo notes before they find unity, with Khoury's short, almost snorting phrases creating the rhythmic ground for Naissam's ascents, while Emile Parisien's soprano and Naissam's flute find instant harmony, her sounds roving and wandering as his notes remain on the rhythmic earth.

But the climax of these unique pairings is with octogenarian tenor saxophonist, Archie Shepp, born in faraway Fort Lauderdale, Florida in 1937. His husky hornsound is immediately recognisable and elides seamlessly with Naissam's vocal and flutesong. Neither musician is fazed by the other despite the half-century-plus between them. Naissam's still youthful breath and Shepp's griot-like sound and aged but ageless voice become as one in what seems like a plea for world peace in a beautiful summation of sound.

(Souffles is available on Les Couleurs de Son Records)

Ahmad Jamal (USA) - Veteran proves he can still ignite the jazz fires

Ahmad Jamal, Barbican Centre, London
(2013)

'I live until he makes another record - all my inspiration today comes from Ahmad Jamal,' Miles Davis wrote of the Pittsburgh-born pianist in the 1950s.

The octogenarian genius lives up to Davis's words at this Barbican concert, where he is accompanied by the strident bassist Reginal Veal and two Caribbean drummers. Herlin Riley, steeped in the carnivals and parades of New Orleans, is joined by the Puerto Rican Manuel Badrena who employs a range of the percussive and vocal effects which feed his restless musical spirit.

As they play the brilliant balladic miniature Laura, all the qualities which enraptured Davis are present in a number which lasts a mere three minutes. The stop-start tension, drama, cadences and crescendos are strongly present and the same qualities come into play as the quartet tackle Blue Moon, Ain't Misbehavin' and This Is The Life. There is a zest and playfulness, as if the tunes are toys full of the veterans' wise old humour.

All these numbers plus some Jamal originals are on his compelling 2012 album Blue Moon which, apart from its possible attraction to Manchester

City fans, is for the rest of us a thing of beauty, fire, surprise and intense melodism. Davis was right - Jamal is an inspiration. And at the age of 83 he's still memorably defying the years, the space between them, and the conventional unity of sound.

(Blue Moon is available on Jazz Village)

Eddie Jefferson (USA) - Ebullient songs of boppish swing
The Jazz Singer & The Main Man
(2017)

Eddie Jefferson, born in Pittsburgh in 1918, was a true jazz original. He began working as a tap dancer in the '30s, but by the late '40s he had developed a singing approach called 'vocalese,' in which he took the recorded solos of jazz horn players, wrote lyrics to them and sang them as tributes to their creators.

One of the first of these was James Moody's tenor saxophone solo in a recording of I'm in the Mood for Love. Jefferson recreated it as Moody's Mood for Love, which became a big hit when recorded by the rhythm and blues man King Pleasure in 1952. But Jefferson was not to be outdone, and in succeeding years recorded a string of humorous and moving lyrics to saxophone solos by Charlie Parker (Now's the Time), Lester Young (I've Got the Blues) and Jimmy Forrest (Night Train). He took Miles Davis's trumpet solo from So What and devised words to that.

Jefferson never achieved the recognition that his innovative contribution deserved - that was taken by his many imitators. He was ultimately shot and killed outside a club in Detroit in 1979 - another tragically curtailed jazz life. His album The Jazz Singer includes songs recorded in three sessions in 1959 and 1961, when he was performing with Moody and trumpeters Howard McGhee and Johnny Coles. Jefferson is in ebullient and boppish mood, and the wit and lucidity of his singing radiates his customary joy of giving back thanks to the musicians who inspired him to write words to their improvisations.

So What begins the album, a praise song to Davis and Coltrane, with tremendous zest and verve before Moody swings in for a brief solo, a preface to Moody's Mood for Love in which the sax man himself shadows Jefferson's words attuned to his own chorus. The version of It's Only a Paper Moon lyricises a Lester Young solo. As Yuri Gagarin and the space dog Laika were circling the Earth in real time, Jefferson's words take his listeners up there in vocalese. 'Goodbye world! put your suit on and we'll soon be off,' he sings before a breezy scat interval.

Jefferson's version of Now's the Time is a tribute to Charlie 'Bird' Parker's sheer brilliance just four years after his death. 'Come reminisce with me, and think about the Birds,' he sings, bursting into ultra-rapid phrases recalling Parker's own supersonic alto saxophone bursts. 'I never thought he'd be, so awfully close to me, until I heard his message, and he set me free.' Coleman Hawkins's famous solo from his 1939 recording of Body and Soul is given vibrant new life by Jefferson, and the Hawk's gigantic jazz stature and recognition all over the world is set down in Jefferson's lyrics. In Baby Girl he sets words to Young's 1947 recording of These Foolish Things, imagining the hospitalised horn man writing a letter to his wife. Very touching it is too as its empathy moves right inside the great tenorist's mind.

The Main Man was cut nearly 20 years later in 1977, two years before Jefferson's death, and he has a stellar band to accompany him, with a rhythm section of drummer Billy Hart, bassist George Duvivier and Harold Mabern of Memphis on piano. They all move off grooving with Jeannie with a zooming Richie Cole alto solo and Forrest's big hit Night Train is made into vocalese with Jefferson waiting at the station for his girlfriend, singing of his anticipation before the gravelly baritone saxophone solo by Hamiet Bluiett.

There are new versions of Moody's Mood for Love and Body and Soul, while Bird's Confirmation has rapid-fire scatting and lyrics and Cole and trombonist Slide Hampton swinging out.

But the classic track, rocking with humour, is Benny's from Heaven, with the familiar tune telling the story of a US soldier returning from three years fighting the war in Europe, finding his wife with a new-born child, whose arrival, she tells him, must be by immaculate conception, hence the title. Charles Sullivan's crackling trumpet and Mabern's piano add their solo commentary.

Jefferson sings George Gershwin's Summertime straight, with a powerful upsurge of rhythm and oral energy and a gusty solo by Junior Cook's tenor. He sang of Bird that he 'left a lot of swing in the air.' So did the unique Jefferson, and it streams and gushes from both these albums.

(The Jazz Singer & The Main Man are available on Inner City)

Ron Jefferson and Tricky Lofton (USA) - A Fine Musical Amalgam

Love Lifted Me & Brass Bag

(2016)

On the sleeve photograph he lights a long filtered cigarette in a cigarette holder and smiles ruefully downwards. He seems to be contemplating the making of the single album under his own name in September 1961 that brought him some limited recognition - the frequently groovy and sometimes haunting Love Lifted Me. He was the drummer Ron Jefferson, born in New York in 1926 where he started as a tap dancer before turning to the drums, playing with some of the great tenor saxophonists like Coleman Hawkins and Lester Young, and forming a part of the powerfully innovative Jazz Modes with Charlie Rouse and French horn virtuoso Julius Watkins in 1957.

When Love Lifted Me was cut in the Pacific Jazz studios of Los Angeles he was part of the highly successful West Coast blues-driven trio led by pianist

Les McCann with 'walking' bassist Leroy Vinnegar. Jefferson's studio band included Vinnegar, pianist Frank Strazzeri and two fine but little-known hornmen, tenorist Wilbur Brown and the startling trombonist, Tricky Lofton, born in Houston in 1930, whose eclectic skills had been honed by tutoring with trombonists at two ends of the then-times jazz spectrum: the New Orleans pioneer of Louis Armstrong's Hot Five, Kid Ory, and the bebop trombone innovator J.J. Johnson.

To add to the stylistic mix there was the young vibes master Bobby Hutcherson, a twenty year old local Los Angeles prodigy, who was to be one of the key musicians of the New Wave, including Coltrane, Shepp and Dolphy, shortly to rise. So quite a musical amalgam here. The opener, Ivy League Blues, has a relaxed, sonorous sound with an exquisitely-wrought solo from Brown, and Lofton - muted for his first few bars then playing free and low-down, taking the piece onwards. Jefferson's scuttling drum sticks begin the title tune and Tricky ambles in for a solo before Hutcherson swings out and Brown saunters in for a chorus. Vinnegar takes a bouncing interval before the band comes home.

The bassist's tribute to the Indianapolis pianist Carl Perkins, who had died in Los Angeles in 1958, exudes feeling. Brown's solo is a swinging threnody, Hutcherson taps out blithe tears, the composer lends his heartbeat and the sad cadences of the theme fade into memories. Little One begins with a sublimely lucid Hutcherson solo, Tricky enters full of verve and Brown's tenor makes a mellow groove. The familiar strains of Flamingo give balladic cues for Hutcherson and the two horns. George's Dilemma gives Jefferson his long drums moment after solos from Hutcherson and Brown, a drummer's true tom-tom feast.

In April 1963 Lofton led Strazzeri, Vinnegar and Jefferson back to the same L.A. studio for an album of mainly big band themes to be called Brass Bag, with four more trombones and the ringing Kansas City trumpeter, Carmell Jones. Off they stomp with the classic Basie theme Moten Swing, with Tricky's solo slides in full and joyous fettle and Jones springing out of the blend with a piercing chorus. On to Ellington and Mood Indigo, and the five trombone ensemble makes an almost hymnal sound before Tricky's mute moans out his message. He plays with creamy splendour all through Angel Eyes, and the strangely named Celery Sticks at Midnight is a brass banquet. Arranger Gerald Wilson's title tune has a blistering Jones chorus. Dizzy Gillespie's bop theme Ow! has a more rumbustious Lofton and a Kansas peach of a solo from the fired-up Jones, and Wilson's Bluer than That has more skilful slidework from Tricky and high-pitched eloquence from the under-rated Jones.

Jefferson died in New York in 2007, and the whereabouts of Tricky is unknown. Perhaps, somehow, he'll read this review in the Morning Star and get in touch. Then I can at least thank him for these glorious sounds that he and his inspired bandmates made in a Los Angeles studio more than half a century ago, now happily reissued so we can hear them many times more.

(Love Lifted Me & Brass Bag are available on Fresh Sound Records)

Sofia Jernberg (Ethiopia) and Alexander Hawkins (England) – Powerful and audacious musical internationalist

Sofia Jernberg - Alexander Hawkins: Musho (2025)

Perhaps it was her childhood experiences that has made the Ethiopian singer Sofia Jernberg such a powerful and audacious musical internationalist. Her new album, Musho, with the Oxford-born pianist Alexander Hawkins, has songs from Ethiopia, Armenia, medieval Sweden and Shakespearian England. And she states with pride that her artistry 'stems from having grown up in two countries that defeated the West: Ethiopia and Vietnam.'

'I was born in Addis Ababa in 1983 and grew up with a single mother who adopted me while she was working as a diplomat in the Swedish Embassy. She worked in Ethiopia and Vietnam before we arrived in Sweden when I was ten, when she started work at the Swedish International Development Agency. We had an electric piano and record player at home and I listened to music from all over the world. The LP player became my best friend. I was constantly singing, but I never thought it could be a profession until I was in my mid-teens.'

' I speak four European languages well, but understand many more. My mother spoke Amharic and loved Ethiopia, so it has always been part of my life, but its culture for me was always connected to a deep sorrow and involuntary separation. It still is. I didn't know what jazz was until my teenage years. Before that my interest was Western classical music. But I was always curious about all kinds of music, and as I looked at jazz shelves in record libraries and stores, that curiosity deepened. I struggled to understand it, did all the listening by myself and never talked to anyone about it. I went to jazz concerts and avant-garde performances by myself. I never studied Music at a higher level, but I learned what I needed - how to read and write music. I learned by doing, listening to and playing records of musicians I admired. I didn't become a full professional singer until I was thirty, but had stood on a stage and sung regularly since I was ten, since I went to choir school.'

She developed a love of many art forms, including dance and visual performance. 'I chose music because it's a language in itself. It brings people together, uniting us in a unique way. I sing with people who often have opposite views to myself, who are twice my age and who I would never have met otherwise. All the ugly social structures go away when we make music. I'm a musician rather than a singer, and I sing without words for a whole concert to achieve that. Words can sometimes get in the way and singing without them means that everyone, regardless of language, can access what I sing.'

What about her partnership with the remarkable Hawkins? 'We met when the musical director of Bimhuis, the Amsterdam jazz club, put us together. I love his ambition, dedication and creativity in his life of music and piano, constantly pushing himself, always evolving and surprising me with the most magical moments. His musical knowledge is very rich and we share a love for all kinds of music, which is why I so often learn something new or hear something different because of something he said.'

Why was the album called 'Musho'? 'It means 'sad song' in Amharic, and it was clear from the start that we would play melancholic music. My favourite track on the album is Willow, Willow. I was so pleased that Alex wanted to play something English, even Shakespearian, for the English music tradition connects us and has given me so much.'

Musho exemplifies the gloriously syncretic power of jazz, and Hawkins' protean pianism unites with Sofia's voice in a brotherly musical companionship to her surging, saddening and always deeply moving voice. When she sings the traditional Ethiopian song Adwa, remembering the victory of Ethiopian forces over the invading Italian army in 1896, there is both a defiance and soulfulness in her voice that eclipses all genres. In that sense her voice embodies the cosmopolitan spirit of Robeson, Makeba, Peggy and Pete Seeger, Ewan McColl, Woody Guthrie and Nina Simone, and has a global reach which sings for all humanity.

(Musho is available on Intakt Records)

John Jenkins (USA) - A fiery musical talent
Young Jenkins: 1957 Quartet Sessions
(2018)

A strange life was that of the alto saxophonist John Jenkins. Born in Chicago in 1931 he went to Du Sable High School, which had an extraordinary music teacher called Captain Walter Dyett, who tutored some of the most powerful saxophonists of the pot-bop epoch, including Johnny Griffin, Sun Ra's great tenor horn John Gilmore and Clifford Jordan. Much influenced by the Charlie Parker sound and Parker's disciples Jackie McLean and Sonny Stitt, Jenkins gigged for several years around Chicago before moving to New York in March 1957, where he very soon found himself playing in the Mingus band.

Within a few months he had been picked up by major jazz record producers at Prestige, Savoy and Blue Note labels and two of the albums that he made are featured on this Fresh Sound reissue: Young Jenkins. His virtual disappearance from the New York jazz scene was almost as sudden as his ascent and by 1962 he had bade the life farewell, working as a messenger in Manhattan and a stallholder in street markets, only reappearing as a busker in the late '80s and briefly reconnecting with Jordan before his death in 1993. And yet these 1957 albums give ample testimony of his fiery talent and musical skill.

The first was a Prestige New Jazz album in July with Jordan, pianist Bobby Timmons - who played on some of Art Blakey's greatest Jazz Messenger albums, the booming Chicago bassist Wilbur Ware and Mingus' favourite drummer, Dannie Richmond. Off they go with a Jordan composition, Cliff Edge, with the two horns in unison before Jordan's terse-toned chorus grips the quintet and Ware's earthy bass holds it all together. Jenkins' keen alto shapes more pliable phrases until Timmons' soulful notes come loping in. The ballad Tenderly shows Jordan's more tranquil side before Ware digs deep in his solo and Jenkins' alto almost sings as you hear the words in his soft tones. Princess is a cheerful Jenkins tune and the composer takes the first solo, imbued with sunshine and optimism which seems to affect Jordan as he comes sauntering in, full of fluency and a sense of hope. Timmons skips into his chorus.

It was trombonist Julian Priester who wrote the very lively Soft Talk, heralded by a Richmond roll. Jenkins' effusive solo almost leaves the studio floor and levitates as he spins out his patterns of sound and a much gruffer Jordan keeps up the hectic pace until Jenkins comes back for more. Blue Jay, another Jenkins opus, is the final track, begun by a succession of deep, deep notes from Ware before Jenkins lays bare the lyricism and offers citations from English Country Garden, there in Rudy van Gelder's famed studio in Hackensack, New Jersey. Jordan is beautifully eloquent and Timmons adds his gospelly notes while Ware's bass walks beside him. It's the end of a fine session and doubtlessly Captain Dyett would have been more than proud of his two boys.

A month later and Jenkins was back in the same studio recording for Blue Note. This time there was still Richmond but Sonny Clark was the pianist, the bassist was Paul Chambers of Pittsburgh and the featured guitarist was young Kenny Burrell of Detroit. They swing niftily into Cole Porter's From this Moment On with Jenkins in full radiant fettle and Burrell strumming an interval. Clark plays a punchy chorus and Burrell's fleet fingers peck out a very rapid solo. Jenkins' first composition is Motif, which his horn explores with a full assurance, Burrell follows, ever inventive, sparking Clark to formulate a bluesy theme before Chambers' dancing bass marks out its way.

Everything I Have is Yours is blown with full balladic beauty by Jenkins, as if it were the night's last dance and Burrell's incisive yet gentle notes add to the serenity. Sharon is another Jenkins tune and its open, groovy theme gives Burrell in particular a foundation for some keen lines of invention. The album's finale is Burrell's Blues for Two, a pacy theme with all members excelling. As it ends and you hear again the sound of his blues-baked timbre, you wonder again about the life and talent of the young and enigmatic Jenkins and why that one single year of exposure in the jazz centre of the world didn't launch him into a life of his own new and expressive music.

Who knows? At least we have this brief but brilliant recorded legacy to remember and celebrate him.

(Young Jenkins: 1957 Quartet Sessions is available on Fresh Sound Records)

Darius Jones (USA) - The sound of surprise, even more unexpected

Little Women - Throat & Lung

(2016)

Four men make up Little Women, as American as Louisa M Alcott's children's novel, although what she would have thought about this quartet's sounds is best left to historic conjecture. Travis Laplante plays tenor saxophone, Darius Jones is on alto, Andrew Smiley the guitarist and Jason Nazary is the drummer. This is what Kevin Williams, writing in the Chicago Tribune, said of them: 'These guys are ripping their guts out, you think. And so they are. It has structure and elegance in the tornado of noise and beauty which cuts through the maelstrom like a ray of light.'

They are known as a 'Brooklyn punk-jazz' band, but Jones is from Richmond, Virginia and burst onto the New York jazz scene in 2008. His trilogy of AUM albums, Man'ish Boy, Big Girl and Book of Mae'bul showed his blues chops to the full, but Little Women is a different entity. Their press release to their second album Lung declares that the quartet 'creates music whose aim is transcendence via brutally precise sonic assault and ascendant melodies.' Some oxymoron here. And Jones is even more 'precise.' He asserts that 'we do not filter, we don't pull back at all. We just go in and blast your brain out.' And he continues: 'We're not afraid to make the saxophones be ugly, but we're also not afraid to make it sweet, 'cos those two things go together. And we're not afraid to make people dance.'

So how does this 'badass' music fare on the two Little Women albums? The first is Throat, cut in 2009 and made up of seven different parts. The quartet say that their music is 'very structured compositionally,' but as Nazary's drums crash into frenzy and the two horns lock together in a riff of fury, structure seems strangely irrelevant and the sheer sound becomes all. In part 2 the horns vibrate in atonal disharmony making a duet of agony which is weirdly beautiful before Smiley's slashing guitar and the pounding Nazary add more colours of deformity, out of which arise conflicting messages of form and shape, and yet you wonder how it happens, how it is possible.

Yet out of this sonic melee in part 4 there comes an aching blues theme from Jones's alto, almost like a testimony of relief, like a southern air coming north to Brooklyn and making its space in an urban nightmare, affecting the musicians with its soul, sending Smiley to phrases of heartfelt tenderness - the contrary sensations to all that has come before. Such must be the 'ascendant melodies,' soon to revert to the angry and unified peals of sound as if such gentleness can only ever be transient in this urban soundscape.

In part 5 Smiley chinks his strings as if he were forging a Brooklyn lullaby before the combined horns create a universal wakefulness. Smiley is some mean guitarist to break through these horns and make his presence understood. And as the record ends with an ensemble of gruff wordless voices, its title reminds us the 'throat' is all.

2013 brings the successor to Throat, and it is Lung, with a theme of the seasons, beginning with spring. 'Capture a ray of emerging light through a piece of broken glass,' says the sleeve note; 'Consider the image as it is refracted.' That is Spring, and such words seem a long way from 'blasting your brains out' - as do the opening 102 seconds of the record before Nazary's clatter of cymbals, for the only sound is one of deep breathing and the lungs fully at work. When the saxophones and guitar enter, they are soft and benign, as unlike a 'tornado of noise' as you could imagine.

As the sound morphs into a long single-note vocal chant, it presages a change of season too. The horns blow with a mutual, empathetic lyricism and Nazary's drum rolls import powers more dangerous, affirmed by the roaring reed chords that follow in a tumultuous ensemble and the lungs breathe on, ever alive, provoking consciousness.

In Autumn, the listener is enjoined to 'find a flower that is dying, but is not yet dead/ Hold it in both hands/Gaze at its beauty until you cry.' Not a punk message, hardly a badass one either. But Little Women make the sound of surprise even more unexpected and incredulous and frequently beautiful too, and they make music from the very sound which gives life to us all, as if the lung itself were the essential bellows of culture.

(Throat & Lung are available on AUM Fidelity)

Darius Jones (USA) - Blown away at Café Oto

Darius Jones, John Edwards and Steve Noble, Café Oto, London (2024)

A hot, hot Sunday night in downtown Dalston, made even hotter at the Café Oto with the boiling sound of Darius Jones's alto saxophone, straight from the heat of the USA.

Jones, born in Norfolk, Virginia in 1978 and now a Professor of Music at Wesleyan College, Connecticut, was playing in a superfine trio with two British nonpareils, bassist John Edwards and drummer Steve Noble. And how they coalesced! Their notes bestrode the ocean, as a certain Elizabethan groover might have written, as if no geographical gulf or barrier can stop the free passage of hot music.

I was sitting some two yards away from the blistering Darius, whose belligerent horn belched and guffawed sizzling notes into my ears. He began with ear-splitting shrieks, almost like a nightmare before bedtime, but one calibrated by its own ferocious beauty, and nothing, even this, could take aback the co-operative artistry of the response and challenge of Edwards and Noble.

Noble thrashed his drums with a careworn yet carefully chosen array of sound with his powerful sticks and mallets while Edwards, his bow at the lowest ebb of his strings, plucked with his dauntless fingers and drummed on his faithful bass' enduring frame as if there were two drummers drumming to add more furious sound to Jones's scalding horn.

Sometimes his saxophone, as if exhausted by its own sounds, seemed to become another woodwind being, as its soundmaker made it sound like an oboe, a soothing bassoon or an overblown clarinet, and interspersed its simmering sound with precious and gentle moments of tenderness.

Certainly, nothing could have sounded less like a professorial encounter than Jones's dog-days of August educational tryst, and I found myself wishing that my own tutorial days some 60 years ago in the book-filled studies of Leeds, could have sounded so fulminating!

Elvin Jones (USA) - The man machine

The Elvin Jones Jazz Machine, Ronnie Scott's, London (2000)

Having experienced the piano wonders of McCoy Tyner just two weeks ago. London now has inside it the other surviving half of the legendary 1960-65 John Coltrane Quartet. Elvin Jones is in town again and it is as if you can hear his drums pounding and his cymbals crashing and whispering in turns down every street in Soho. Jones's Jazz Machine is the closest we have to the hard bop 40 year phenomenon that was Art Blakey's Jazz Messengers.

Like Blakey, Jones frequently changes his sidemen. bringing on the young and exposing again the power of the reviving veteran. His latest version retains the heartbeat of Steve Kirby on bass, but includes Monk inspired pianist Eric Lewis, trombone-playing member of the renowned New Orleans jazz family Delfeayo Marsalis (of which the venerable Jones declared: 'every one of them is either a musician or a preacher') and the Italian altoist Stefano di Batista. 'He's a fellow I met just a few months ago,' exclaimed the septuagenarian drummer, as if the encounter had been on a Turin bus or in a Rome street. Jones surrounded by his drums is a mythical sight and one not to be missed by any lover of jazz. Resplendent in a T-shirt with a central image of the Sphinx, he reminds you how much of Africa and its joy and power is in his art.

The youngest of the three musical brothers from Pontiac, Michigan – Hank, Thad and Elvin - belies his age still with an astonishing energy and sharpness of sound. You can hear the whole history of jazz drumming in the fullness and huge complexity of his sound. It has the authority of its entire century-old history in his military rolls, his Baby Dodds-like rapping on his rims and the Coltrane-foundation in the thunder that rises from his polyrhythmic skins.

Beginning with Monk, composed by the disciple Lewis, Thelonious's chords and angled notes, played with a moving skill were succeeded by Marsalis' solo. Sounding like a fusion of J J Johnson and the tailgate tradition of his native city, the trombonist entered a fascinating dialogue with Jones' drums, followed by di Batista's soaring alto and the deep caves of Kirby's notes in a lucid solo. In Sajitso, one of Elvin's regular tributes to his Japanese wife, the Italian's spellbinding soprano saxophone solo made a labyrinth of upward spirals and diving cadences in his notes, preceding some dazzling inter-play between piano and drums. There was more than an echo of Johnny Hodges in Johnny's Time, di Batista's alto feature and you began to marvel again at the heralded Italian meeting between veteran drummer and saxophone man.

It began an interlude with Ellington, but a route to the master via Monk as these musicians proved that It Don't Mean A Thing If It Aint Got That Swing, starting with a piano improvisation of crystalline clarity which carried Monkish chords and patterns, a stepping back further almost into the age of the celeste and an explosion of stride power which made you think that James P. Johnson had suddenly walked onto Ronnie's stage.

As the Jazz Machine swung into the chorus with anything but a mechanistic sound and Marsalis's enigmas and di Batista's furies emerged in more fine soloing, you could only thank Jones, a great jazz force and one of its authentic tribunes, for being here again.

Here's to the next time - and make sure you go.

George Khan (England/Pakistan) - Ah!
(2025)

There's quite a span of years on the double CD called Ah!, featuring the revolutionary horns of flute, soprano, tenor and baritone saxophones of the freest of free improvisers, George Khan, born Nisar Ahmad Khan in 1938 to a father from the Punjab and a mother of English, Italian and Swiss heritage who had a stall in Petticoat Lane. They begin in the insurgent year of 1968, where Khan's quintet, including percussionist Terry Day, were performing in solidarity with students protesting against funding cuts at Hornsey College of Art, and the final tracks were recorded in 2005 during a Mopomoso performance at the Red Rose, London's true home of free improvisation, now demolished.

The Khan family emigrated to Pakistan in 1951, and listening to this record now, you can only wonder what sounds dominated his years as a secondary school student there. His parents both played piano and George learned alto saxophone, and hearing Charlie Parker for the first time there in the Punjab 'was the most exciting sound I had ever heard'. He returned to London in 1956, went to art school, decided to become a professional musician prompted by lessons in New York (where he stayed for four months) from prime hornmen, Booker Ervin and Sam Rivers. Back in England he played and recorded with Mike Westbrook and was also a member of The People Band, whose members were regulars at the Starting Gate pub in Wood Green, north London, where he met and befriended Terry Day.

The opening 33 minute track is Battling the Sound, a duet with Day recorded at the London Musicians Collective space, an ex-railway storeroom near Euston Station 'around 1980'. Both musicians really go for it, with Khan's blasting signature tenor like a runaway locomotive, and his soprano and flute holding nothing back, with Day's thrashing drums, gongs and alto in full railwayana accord in breathless and relentlessly fierce volleys of improvised fury.

The next two tracks are the soundscape of the 1968 Hornsey sit-in, with Khan and Day joined by Albert Kovitz on clarinet, Peter Lemer on piano and bassist Frank Flowers. The build-up is quieter and more gradual, but you can still hear the eagerness in Khan's notes to let loose at any juncture, particularly at Lemer's prompting.

The Unity Theatre has a long tradition of rebellious art activity, back to the days of Paul Robeson and the Workers Theatre Movement of the Thirties, but in May 1975 it was Khan's Unity moment, along with Day's scuttling drums and Charlie Hart playing bowed electric bass and violin. The threesome's two tracks, called Trio in Unity 1 and 2, have Khan off-limits, his horns gurgling, guffawing, belching, roaring and declaiming on stage with a Falstaffian, stuttering, voice-like turbulence, as if the venue's conscious history were urging its thespian and agitprop spirit all over the music.

The final two tracks are 2005 Khan solos, the Mopomoso Flute Suite and the Mopomoso Baritone Suite. Both performances express Khan's sheer virtuosity on both instruments, with the baritone valediction somehow unconsciously acknowledging that this double album, righteously titled, was to become one of the final records released by that great human gift to improvised music and pioneering founder of Emanem records, Martin Davidson (1942 - 2023). Much missed and through records like this, never forgotten!

(Ah! is available on Emanem Records)

Soweto Kinch (England/Barbados) - Pertinent politics in consummate jazz outing

Soweto Kinch Trio - Ronnie Scott's, London (2021)

Soweto Kinch is in prime fettle during this Ronnie Scott's gig, with the searing narratives of his alto saxophone enhanced by the intensity of the sound - matured since I last saw him a few years ago - here underpinned by Will Glaser's crackling drums and the earthen vibrato of Nick Jurd's pulsating bass.

He begins with a scintillating unaccompanied horn passage, full of gradual ascents and audacious tumbling cadences, playing themes from his album Nonagram, which he has described as a succession of abstracts, shapes and 'sacred geometry.' Melodic lines burst from his tune Crossroads, as if garrulous conversation were breaking from his gut-wrenching, improvised patterns of sound and engaging with Jurd's fiercely plucked strings.

He raps and seeks audience support through What's It All For? which he describes as a message of 'post-austerity angst,' a warning about those who seek to rule our lives. 'Remember when the deaf lead the blind/They cut off your legs and leave you all behind.'

But his tune The Engine Drivers carries a truly impassioned message, with his introduction to it reminding the audience of the millions who really drive the economy and those who have suffered the mounting blows of recession. As he blows with the resolute storytelling power of a griot of old, it's the sense of his powerful flow of sound and the raw energy of his river of notes that is most moving.

It's as if on the same small stage where for half a century the great saxophone artisans who have built the foundation of his sound - masters like Coleman Hawkins, Ben Webster, Sonny Rollins, Archie Shepp and Rahsaan Roland Kirk - are all answering the testimony of his now-times breath.

(Nonagram is available on Musicglue)

Soweto Kinch (England), Barry Guy (England) & Cassie Kinoshi and Chelsea Carmichael (England) - Best of 2019

Barry Guy – The Blue Shroud, Purcell Room, London Jazz Festival
Soweto Kinch – The Black Peril, EarTH, Hackney, London
Cassie Kinoshi and Chelsea Carmichael – She Is Jazz, Royal Festival Hall, London
(2021)

The three most powerful gigs of 2019 were all at this year's London Jazz Festival, beginning with veteran British bassist Barry Guy's Purcell Room concert The Blue Shroud, a musical reflection on Picasso's great anti-fascist mural Guernica.

At the UN in 2003, a blue curtain was hung over the tapestry reproduction of the painting while US Secretary of State Colin Powell outlined the US and British invasion of Iraq. Guy's 71-minute contemplation was marked by his 14-piece orchestra radiating a hymnal melodic beauty and moments of rapture, horror and defiance.

Percy Pursglove's haunting, breathy opening trumpet chorus, Maya Homberger's rhapsodic violin, the truculent drums of Lucas Niggli and Ramon Lopez and Agusti Fernandez's resonant piano all gave sonic reality to Picasso's warscape so that sound and image held the same urgent truth.

At EarTH in Hackney, Soweto Kinch's The Black Peril was a musical narrative of the waves of black resistance in Britain a year after the end of the 1914-18 War, from Cardiff to Glasgow and from Liverpool to South Shields.

The amalgam of sound from 20-plus musicians included bassist and drummer Junius Paul and Makaya McCraven and members of Tomorrow's

Warriors, with dancers, newsreels, screen images, drama and mime combining with Kinch's rapping words and visceral alto saxophone. The themes of "black peril, red terror, fever time," in an era when the scourge of eugenics and slogans like "Britishers First!" abounded were met by oppositional cries of "We Deserve Better!"

All created a hyper-vibrant and multi-faceted approach to knowing and learning from living history.

She Is Jazz at the Royal Festival Hall featured a prodigious ensemble of 40-odd women musicians and chorus, most in their teens and younger, led by saxophonists Cassie Kinoshi and Chelsea Carmichael. Full of youthful fire and precocious musicianship, their wonderful London cosmopolitanism challenged the institutional staidness of the venue

A seven-year-old girl played a poised trumpet solo on the opening tune, East of the River Nile, and the ensemble was marvellous as they as rocked into Kinoshi's tune Interplanetary Migration. Sun Ra would have loved it.

I have been going to jazz performances for 60 years and no other has filled me with such a sense of hope and belief in the future of truly creative music.

Soweto Kinch (England) With The London Symphony Orchestra - Soundtrack Of The Apocalypse

The Barbican, London

(2025)

Talking to Soweto Kinch, a burning saxophonist, composer and rapper, an outstanding musician who I've been hearing regularly over the last 25 years, I had to pinch myself to realise that he is almost a jazz veteran. Born in 1978 in Ladbroke Grove, West London two years after the heroic South African young people's resistance that bears his name, he spent his childhood in Wandsworth, south London with his parents - the Barbadian dramatist Don Kinch and his English/Jamaican Shakespearian actress mother, Yvette Harris. As a youth he moved to Birmingham, the setting of his superbly narrative early album, A Life in the Day of B19: Tales of the Tower Block.

He remembers well when his father took him with his theatre company to the Edinburgh Festival to perform his play, Foxtrot in the Sand. With him were formidable veteran jazz griots, the Guyanese percussionist Frank Holder and the Detroit tap dancer, Will Gaines. 'They were like uncles to me. They helped demystify jazz, which until then, seemed a little remote.'

He studied History at Hertford College, Oxford, but it was meeting U.S. jazzmen like Wynton Marsalis in 1991 ('He was a sage, and treated me warmly, like an elder cousin') and the pathfinding drummer Max Roach, whose music had emblazoned the U.S. Civil Rights struggle, that brought the young Soweto fully into jazz. 'I played some very basic saxophone with Max, and he asked me about my heritage. I said it was Barbados, and he said he could recognise it in my speech, because many Barbadian slaves had been brought to the Southern U.S. to work on the plantations. 'I'm from North Carolina, you're from Barbados,' he said. 'Listen! We did it, you can do it too!'

He certainly has done, and continues to do so. On November 14 at the Barbican, along with the London Symphony Orchestra, he will be performing the third part of his history-telling trilogy following The Black Peril (2020) and White Juju (2021), called Soundtrack of the Apocalypse. I asked him about its themes.

'I'm using the word 'apocalypse' in its true meaning - revelation, uncovering, unveiling. I'm trying not to make the stitching of its narrative too obvious, but to give listeners the space to reflect and understand. The disjunct between what we are conditioned to hear by Musk and Trump and their corporate power, and the reality we see around us is profound. Mass demonstrations in support of Palestine are derisively dismissed as hate marches when hundreds and thousands are marching to expose that Gazan babies and children are being slaughtered.' When I said that as an old man, I believed that the multitudes on those marches were the real England of the future - multiracial, multi-religious, Asian, African, African-Caribbean, white, Jewish - all of us, the many not the few, he agreed with me.

'But the opposing interconnectedness between genocide, weapons manufacture, environmental disaster, Netanyahu's settler colonial violence, Musk's empire of lies and Trump's white supremacist expansion of corporate power is also the truth for us all to see. Yet many people stare at this truth, internalise it, retreat into themselves and blame those who are suffering the most. The billionaire class nexus has never been more powerful and rampant.'

In the sleeve notes of White Juju Soweto writes about the upsurge of anti-racist activism across the world following the racist police murder of George Floyd in Minneapolis. Prophetically, he wrote that this 'may only be momentary' and that 'toxic nationalism' would soon re-exert its reactionary power. He was right - Trump's militarisation of American cities, Musk's alliances with European neo-nazis, 'Tommy Robinson in his Maccabi Tel Aviv shirt.'

But Soweto is a prime historian and a unique musical chronicler which he demonstrated with great multisonic and multi-media dexterity in The Black Peril, the story of the 1919 - 21 black resistance throughout postwar Britain. He wants an 'inter-cultural, inter-generational dialogue between all of us' to emerge from his Soundtrack. 'It shouldn't leave us in despair. I want us to realise what it feels like, viscerally, to be in receipt of the truth. I want it to inspire listeners to write their own stories. Stories are malleable, they give us a million ways of delivering the truth.'

He used a new word for me, although as a teacher I realised that I had been doing it all my working life. I called it 'The Pedagogy of Story', he declared:

'We need to narratavise, to put our specifics, our stories, into a world framework so that we can share them, learn from them, empathise with them.'

What about his choice of musical ensemble, why a symphony orchestra rather than a more common jazz unit like a quartet, a sextet, a tentet or a big band? 'It's such a beautiful opportunity to play with the London Symphony Orchestra. I started out small-scale with Soundtrack of the Apocalypse with the beat of a drum machine. Then it was recorded in a studio setting with a septet. Now the Barbican concert completes the cycle with a symphony orchestra. Every note was conceived from my imagination. For centuries the implications of class and race have told black people that such orchestras are not for them, and that has held the music back. If they don't see race, why do we keep being erased? There's still a huge amount of work to be done, but now we have a symphony orchestra!'

The marvellous Max Roach would have shared his thoughts immediately and instinctively. Soweto is 'doing it' and nothing will stop him. As he told me. 'it's time to rip the chains off!'

Peter King (England) - This West Ham boy's book is a moving and powerful read

Flying High: A Jazz Life And Beyond (2011)

Hear him play his burning alto saxophone. He soars, he flows, he dives, he jets, he leaps, he crawls in the blues, he powers in sonic glory - a master of unique musicianship and rhapsodic beauty.

This is Peter King from a West Ham family who emigrated to the US - the birthing land of jazz - in the years before the first world war, where his grandfather worked on the railways in Pennsylvania before he was killed in a points accident. His grandmother brought the family home and they settled in Kingston where the boy Peter was born in 1940, and where he had his first musical experiences through his uncle Alf, who taught him to play God Save The King on the piano with his nose.

He tells his own riveting life story in his autobiography, Flying High: A Jazz Life And Beyond, with the beyond being a narration of the gradual defeat of any number of phobias through his dedication to music, the worst and most destructive being an addiction to cocaine and heroin, which threatened to completely despoil his life and musical brilliance for far too many years.

King still plays his alto like a dream, and his musical skill has led him to write Zyklon, an opera about the life of Fritz Haber, the Jewish-born nazi scientist who developed the killer gas of the concentration camps. But Flying High shows that he is also a very fine and expressive writer whose storytelling power causes many incidents in his life and the people who provoked them to remain indelible in the minds of his readers.

Firstly there are the memories of the great and epochal jazz giants with whom he played. First among those is the archetypal bop pianist Bud Powell. King writes: 'We all hear music through the prism of our own emotions. I hear in Powell's music a strangely disturbing but beautiful world, tinged with elements of his courageous struggle against insanity.' King was hardly into his twenties when he was invited to sit in with Powell at the Blue Note in Paris. He writes about the life-blasting experience with both insight and emotional rawness which makes you want to return again and again to Powell's records.

Or there are his memories of the prime US horn men who performed throughout the sixties at Ronnie Scott's, where he had played at the club's opening night of October 30 1959, and the unpredictable tenorist Lucky Thompson, who gave him an invaluable lesson in always keeping his fingers touching his horn's keys, never lifting them off. Or Ben Webster, whose all-powerful and serene tenor saxophone voice filled the empty club as he rehearsed for an evening session, 'an indescribably beautiful sound coming from a dimly lit room.'

Or his meeting with Ray Charles and how he declined his invitation to become part of his touring band because of his impending marriage, a union which saved his life and eventually lifted him out of addiction. Or there is the deeply moving passage describing the night his mother died, when he found himself pouring his heart out to one of the truly great jazz drummers, Elvin Jones, as they sat in a car waiting for another drumming legend, Philly Joe Jones, to score in a nearby house. It is a set of circumstances told so wrenchingly that it makes your nerves tremble.

For Peter King is a survivor of a jazz generation much affected and much afflicted by addiction. He tells much about the British drums genius Phil Seamen of whom Elvin Jones said: 'That's the way we'd all play if we could.' Yet Seamen too was an addict whose habit put terrible chains on his achievement. As King concludes, for himself and many confreres of his era: 'Confronting and then trying to haul yourself out of such total destruction of your self-esteem can take many years and you never shake off the mental scars completely. Things reached rock bottom and the only thing left was to try to climb out of the hole I had dug for myself.'

Yet climb out he did, after many years, and his book is eloquent testimony of a struggle that we can all learn from: 'I've had to confront some half-forgotten nightmares along the way," he admits in his coda, "but have revisited some wonderful experiences too.' Perhaps that is the story of jazz itself. But catch him at a jazz venue near you as he tours with his own quartet or as a featured altoist of John Donaldson's Unity, playing their tribute to the late South African pianist Bheki Mseleku.

You'll fly too with the surge of his horn.

(Flying High: A Jazz Life And Beyond is published by Northway Publications)

Tony Kofi (England/Ghana) - Protean saxophonist delivers another winner

Point Blank by Tony Kofi and the Organisation

(2019)

On Point Blank Tony Kofi is joined by The Organisation, specialists in soul, jazz and funk. His pulsating baritone saxophone rocks the grooves of the album, with organist Pete Whittaker, guitarist Simon Fernsby and drummer Peter Cater contributing to the rhythmic impetus.

On opener Minor League, an opus from Duke Pearson, Cater strikes his skins and is joined by Kofi's baritone, deep and guffawing through a signature solo. His horn maintains a serene lyricism and Whittaker's organ phrases are subtle, unforced and often gentle in a moving version of McCoy Tyner's Search for Peace. It's very different from the down-home sound of organist Lonnie Smith's LS Blues, with a groovy Whittaker and a gritty southern-sounding Fernsby chorus.

Kofi lives up to the earthy brilliance of the great baritonist Pepper Adams's-penned Boss Allegro and on Wes Montgomery's romp Full House Fernsby shines, with Kofi following him on a guttural solo from a deep, deep place in his horn. Fernsby is quick off the blocks during his solo on trumpeter Woody Shaw's Moontrane, full of reminders of the blues of the great Grant Green. Then it is Horace Silver's Summer in Central Park, with Kofi's notes placid and relaxed.

Organist Jimmy Smith devised and popularised the organ quartet in his Blue Note and Verve albums of the 1950s and 1960s and his tune Ready and Able makes for an apt and swinging finale, with all members in prime fettle. Not that Point Blank is any bland imitation of great records from the past. It a vibrantly contemporary album, full of freshness and vitality. And it's an open invitation to go and hear the ever-active Kofi and his bandmates in the many venues across the country where they carve out their sound.

(Point Blank is available on Last Music)

Dudu Kouate (Senegal) and Asumana Soso (Gambia) at Café Oto

(2025)

Laid out on the new raised stage of Café Oto are a multiplicity of objects and would-be musical instruments. An upturned half of a calabash gourd at their centre is surrounded by upcycled wooden, ceramic, metal and plastic tubes, whistles, toys, dishes and plates and a large metal cooking pot filled with water, tambourine, cymbals and shoulder drum.

First onto this seemingly cluttered stage was the smiling, personable kora virtuoso, Asumana Soso, born in Sukuta, The Gambia in 1995, his father a legendary balafon player, his mother a celebrated singer. 'I learned to play the instrument like I learned to talk,' he says, as he fits the cowskin covered, metal-studded, calabash body of his 21-stringed instrument between his knees. His left thumb created a rich bassline while his right plucked out beautiful, sometimes lullaby-like melodies with their Mandinka lyrics. The speed of his artistry and power of his improvisation on tunes like Simba were wondrous to hear, born out of a family skill and love - with his last song which was 'played by my Grandad', full of emotive upsurge.

A short break and suddenly sitting down low in silence on the stage on a single brick tied to a towel, was Dudu Kouate, born in Dakar, Senegal in 1963 in another griot household 'where my father listened to jazz and my grandmother told stories. I discovered jazz at an early age. I didn't go to a conservatoire, I memorised many of the standards by heart.' Yet everything he plays, from casserole pot to plastic piping and mini-washboard on this East London stage is born out of the sanctity of African tradition: 'we evolve, progress, change and improve,' he declares.

He begins with a metal pipe whistle, his haunting breath amplified as he swings whooshing red plastic pipes over his head, blows wooden flutes, breathes through a long dark rubber tube into the pan of water, pouring Tupperware containers of more water into the pan as he drums on metal plates and crashes cymbals. His semi-gourd becomes a bass drum. It is an orchestra of commonplace, hackneyed sounds, as layer upon layer, they are recorded and sound together. He calls it 'elemental: water, fire, wind, earth, all connecting,' with such connections an aural metaphor of a 'deep listening of each other.'

The Café Oto full house is entranced, swept away, making us more and more aware as we step outside into the Dalston streets that music is everywhere, made from anything: people - and everything they do and use, birds, cars, buses, trains every step we take up Kingsland Road, told to us again by this African virtuoso of the mundane.

Caroline Kraabel (USA) and Phil Hargreaves (England) – The echoing sound of Liverpool's soul

Caroline Kraabel & Phil Hargreaves - Where We Were: Shadows of Liverpool (2013)

There have been a succession of recordings over the century of jazz that have sought to describe cities and their stories with their sounds. There is Yusuf Lateef's Detroit: Latitude 42 Degrees 30, Longitude 83, Malachi Thompson's 47th St Suite of Chicago or George Russell's New York NY with Coltrane blowing a metropolitan storm. Much further back there were Ellington's sound essays of Harlem, New Orleans street songs and marches or Fats Waller's London Suite from Soho to Limehouse, from Chelsea to Whitechapel - all evocative of the ripe humanity of city life. But few musicians have used the actual acoustics of real urban locations in one particular city to contribute to the sound textures of their recording.

Here is one that does just that, with deep sonic understanding of a city and a unique timbral beauty. From ordinary urban sounds, of Liverpudlian voices and echoes of pubs, performances, roads and tunnels, sirens and voices, engines, rivers and boat horns, applause and crowds, sheer solitude and warm company, light and darkness.

An insight of saxophones into the living soul of Liverpool is the album Where We Were, by a woman and a man, a Californian and a Yorkshireman born in other cities - San Francisco and Leeds - and their horns alone, with not a rhythm instrument in sight or hearing. It's an astonishing record, nothing trite, a unique sound conception, love song, and a praise song indeed to Liverpool and its people.

Caroline Kraabel grew up in Seattle and came to London as a teenager 'just too late to realise my punk dreams.' Instead she directed her alto saxophone towards free improvisation, has recorded with bassist John Edwards and pianist Veryan Weston, and the large-scale London Improvisers Orchestra, always conscious of 'the implications of electricity related to recording, synthesis and amplification.'

Phil Hargreaves - the sole horn of the amere3 trio - is the multi-instrumentalist of Where We Were, playing tenor and soprano saxophones and flute. He lives in Liverpool, whereas Kraabel describes in her sleeve notes, he 'was tireless in finding extraordinary acoustic locations' for the recording, which include The Grapes public house on Mount Street, the Jump Ship Rat on Parr Street, the Wallasey Tunnel and Picton Library, a street and alleyway near Penny Lane, a greenhouse on Sefton Park Allotments to the Anechoic Chamber of Liverpool University and St George's Hall in Lime Street. Such are, as Kraabel puts it, 'the diversity and beauty of the sonic spaces' explored through this album. I'm a Londoner, so I'd need to know the city of Liverpool better than I do to recognise these spaces, intimate to Liverpudlians.

As the record opens, the pub atmosphere, warmth and company changes to the rhapsody of the two horns burning out of the distant whine of sirens before the riverine and subriverine silences, sounds and menace - and the vehicles which hum and groan across and under the Mersey, every second, every day, every night. Hargreaves blows a chorus of spitting notes while Kraabel's long, almost agonised howls give out the host of voices of a struggling city and the music ripe in Liverpool's soundshapes and the Scouse incantation of all the moments of human life and hope.

There are sudden and sometimes startling 'crossfades of one space blossoming into another during the same musical material,' as Kraabel describes it, so much so that the desolation of one sound picture, perhaps in a bleak tunnel gallery, can change to another, perhaps in a green allotment smallholding, filled and chiming with a blessed birdsong. For this recording is full of changes, rapid like nature, yet of human growth and fullness too, as in all our cities.

Kraabel wrote that this record embraces 'the specificity of spaces and sounds that only live acoustic music can completely celebrate,' and it takes audacious musicians to attempt and achieve it. It radiates the spirit and sound of Liverpool yet it speaks, sings, whispers, howls and narrates to city-dwellers everywhere, in every country.

A man and a woman, two horns and a city - with machines to eternalise their sound and their humanity. That's what it takes.

(Where We Were: Shadows of Liverpool is available on Leo)

Caroline Kraabel (USA)/John Edwards (England)
Sparrow Dance
(2025)

Here's an extraordinary record. It comes in a home-made, gingham cloth sleeve and a cardboard envelope with an inken, avian design.

The unity of John Edwards' bouncing, stepping, singing, plunging, sawing, percussive acoustic bass and Caroline Kraabel's sad, singing, somnolent saxophone somehow expresses the pathos yet resilience of London bird life. Sparrows can't sing, the songline goes, yet these two musicians give them a multilayered, reveried, throbbing voice which cries, observes and reflects, but never dies.

"The sparrow interaction was a dream I had," says Kraabel. "We placed our music's sheets of notes in the garden, on the ground. The sparrows walked over them - in doing so they chose the best music, showing us which parts to discard."

You don't hear many albums like this, so close to life and nature. Be quick though, there aren't many copies.

(Sparrow Dance is released on Crosshatch Records)

Joachim Kuhn (Germany)/ Majid Bekkas (Morocco)/ Ramon Lopez (Spain) - A cacophony in unity
Kalimba, Out of the Desert and Chalaba
(2017)

'A Moroccan in between a Spaniard and an East German - that's far out!' This is the way in which the Leipzig-born (in 1944) pianist Joachim Kuhn describes the trio which made its first album Kalimba in 2007. The Moroccan is Majid Bekkas, virtuoso of the guembri - a bass-like lute. He was born in 1957 and grew up in Zagora in the south of the country, close to desert rhythms and sub-Saharan cultures. He studied at Rabat's National Conservatoire from 1957 and became one of his nation's great musical performers. In 1996, after an encounter with the French saxophonist Louis Sclavis, he turned increasingly towards jazz.

The Spanish drummer is Alicante born (in 1961) Ramon Lopez, whose percussive spirit combines his own national folk tradition with his devotion to Indian classical music and the tabla, an essential part of his teaching at the Paris Conservatory. In 2000 he recorded a momentous album of anti-fascist songs from the Spanish civil war with a group of French musicians. As for Kuhn, he studied as a classical pianist from his boyhood, and during his long life in jazz has played with free spirits from Archie Shepp to Ornette Coleman. As for the trio with Bekkas and Lopez, he says: 'We demonstrate that people from different cultures who hold different beliefs are approaching each other. Dissonance does not exist; if it does, then it is an intentional, positive one.'

Bekkas's powerful voice strikes out on A Live Experience, the opener of Kalimba alongside the strident guembri bass undertow and Lopez's splattering drums. 'One day they asked me: 'Where do you come from?' sings Bekkas. He answers himself: 'I'm a citizen of the world!' His guembri bounces through Hamdouchi, and Kuhn's ringing keys echo as if in a vast, empty place. On Kalimba Call, Bekkas plays kalimba or thumb piano with a tingling lyrical beauty beside Kuhn's empathetic piano: master musicians of different worlds of sound, two versions of piano radiance together, inseparable.

Rabih's Delight is Kuhn's tune which the trio make theirs: its sudden changes of pace transports them. The longest track is Sabbatique, in which Lopez's rustling sounds, his tapping, booming heterogeneous drums seem to coalesce from all over the world, embracing Bekkas's guembri pulse and Kuhn's relentless travelling up and down his keys and a compelling alto saxophone chorus.

The trio recorded Out of the Desert, their second album, in a Rabat studio with guest musicians from the Saharan regions Morocco and Benin. It was March 2008 and Kuhn's 64th birthday, and, in his own words, 'an amazing musical inspiration.' The fuller hinterland of percussion immediately diversifies Africa's huge story in Bekkas's opener, Foulani, creating the cosmos of an amalgam with Kuhn's post-bop piano. And in One, Two, Free, Bekkas turns to kalimba, Kuhn plays his alto saxophone, Kouassi Bessan Joseph from Benin pounds his talking drums and Lopez his tabla in an astonishing palaver of three continents, three musics. Joseph is central too in Chadiye, Bekkas plays his molo (a stringed guitar-like instrument of northern Ghana) and Kuhn's piano rides through the African rhythmic upsurge as if he were born within it.

'Blues was not discovered in America but comes from Morocco and Mali,' asserts Kuhn in the sleeve notes to the trio's third album, Chalaba, recorded this time in Zerkatt in Kuhn's home country in 2011. The second track, Asmaa, was composed by Bekkas but is a powerful acknowledgement to Lopez's roots. Bekkas's oud takes on a flamenco sound in the midst of Lopez's skipping tablas while Kuhn's deep chordings earth the music in Iberian soil. The album's title tune is a traditional Moroccan lament, Bekkas's deeply elegiac guembri from the outset prefaces the sadness of his voice while Lopez's mournful bass drum underlines the mood.

When Kuhn's mollifying piano chorus quickens the music's pace the tone changes as if a new life is springing from the old. Kuhn's alto replies to Bekkas's almost spoken words in Soon in June before his guembri throbs in, and Mimoun Saadiyamou, a Saharan desert song, is transformed into a jazz opus in the most unlikely and surprising of syncretisms.

But in truth these three albums, with all their contradictions, have a strange but wondrous dissonance of unity.

(Kalimba, Out of the Desert and Chalaba are available on ACT)

Steve Lacy (USA) - Notes big and small, and imagination huge

Steve Lacy The Sun, Saxophone Special, Avignon and After & Hooky (2016)

When he was playing alongside the great Thelonious Monk in 1960, the soprano saxophonist Steve Lacy would write down some of the pianist's most pregnant dictums. One he transcribed was: 'A note can be small as a pin or as big as the world, it depends upon your imagination.' Powerful words these, as relevant to Lacy's work as they were to that of Monk.

Notes big and small, and imagination huge; such was certainly the message of Lacy, born Steven Norman Lackritz in New York City in 1934, who began his musical life in the 1950s as a Dixielander, inspired by playing with some of the music's most brilliant virtuosi like the New Orleans trumpeter Henry 'Red' Allen and the rasping Chicago clarinettist Pee Wee Russell, before moving through genres and eventually finding the avant garde with his participation on the debut album of pianist Cecil Taylor in 1965 Jazz Advance.

Lacy's discography is enormous: over 130 Lacy-led albums, many of them solo soprano saxophone, 16 as part of the duo with his longtime piano confrere Mal Waldron and dozens of others as a sideman with small groups and big bands like the Globe Unity Orchestra. But some of his most original and divergently brilliant albums within his canon were cut with the London label Emanem during his long tenure in Europe between 1965 and 2002, with producer and sound engineer Martin Davidson at the helm, and sometimes featuring pathbreaking British improvisers.

Take Saxophone Special for example, recorded in 1973-4 with members of the pioneering free improvising Spontaneous Music Ensemble, including London drummer John Stevens, Sheffield guitarist Derek Bailey, Bristolian tenorist Evan Parker and York-born altoist Trevor Watts. Two Americans, Lacy's soprano sax player Steve Potts and the New Hampshire bassist Kent Carter, were also present, with synthesiser man Michel Waisvisz. In nearly 80 minutes of eclectic delights, Stevens is all over his drums on the first four tracks recorded at Oxford Street's 100 Club with Lacy and Potts blowing a minor tempest.

Bailey's unique chirruping guitar is at the centre of Flakes while the sopranos soar again on the track dedicated to Black Panther Huey Newton, Revolutionary Suicide. The last six tracks are gifted with the superb acoustics of the Wigmore Hall plus Watts and Parker and Waisvizs's ghostly electronics. The four saxophones intertwine their notes like joyous birdsong, particularly in Dreams, and Parker plays a rare baritone horn in the swirling Swishes. There are four soprano saxophones in colloquy all throughout the exquisite Sops, and within the improvising of the two tracks of Snaps there are some compelling moments of sheer melody and the rasping undertow of Parker's tenor.

Davidson described Lacy's 1967-8 album The Sun as his 'most polemical' work, radiating a passionate opposition to war, born out of the mass protests against the US war in Vietnam. Lacy and his cellist and vocalist wife Irene Aebi were inspired by 2,500-year-old words of the Chinese poet Lao Tzu and these were meshed with free improvisation and the electronics of synthesiser pioneer Richard Teitelbaum, a wild amalgam of the ancient and the modern telling the ages-old story of war's oppression and absurdity.

War's horror blasts through the 12 minutes of Chinese Food where Lacy's winding notes and Lao Tzu's lines like 'Even the finest arms are an instrument of evil, spread like a plague' tell the story of the US food of hatred in Vietnam - a story continued in the 1973 Zurich recording of The Woe, where Lacy is joined by Potts and US drummer Oliver Johnson.

Avignon and After (recorded in Avignon in 1972 and Berlin in 1974) and Hooky (recorded in a Montreal church in 1976) are both albums of solo soprano saxophone, although the astonishing track Stations on the first CD was dedicated to Monk and was recorded with a woman singing indistinctly on the radio in the background as Lacy breaks suddenly into the theme of I Feel Pretty from West Side Story. Lacy wrote Original New Duck for the great Ellington tenorist Ben Webster and The Dumps was inspired by the early jazz achievement of Jelly Roll Morton, which tells his listeners how deeply Lacy delved into the tradition to find his music. These solo albums are testimony to both Lacy's sheer artistic inventiveness and the same jazz audacity that provoked Anthony Braxton to record the first solo saxophone album For Alto in 1968.

As you listen to Lacy alone you are hearing a birdman with his individual sounds like a pin or like an entire world, and as you take them in as he blew them in France, Germany or Canada it makes you realise (thanks to Monk) that there really is no difference, and all is expressed and blown out of mind and body by peace and beauty.

Thanks again, Steve Lacy, gone from us since 2004.

(The Sun, Saxophone Special, Avignon and After & Hooky are available on Emanem)

Byard Lancaster (USA) - Stories, sounds and palavers

The Byard Lancaster Quartet – Pam Africa & Ancestral Link Hotel

'My message is aimed at awakening our community. When others enjoy my music I am extremely pleased and invite all to visit Philly, birthplace of America, the spiritual capital of the world. Our city has learned to use great black music as the tool of progressive enlightenment. Newest Africa sounds... dictate that we rise to the responsibility of rebuilding America.'

Some commitment here, within the words of a record sleeve of 72-year-old Philadelphian, the saxophonist Byard Lancaster, whose two albums Pam Africa and Ancestral Link Hotel were cut on successive days in April 2005 and who declares his path has been guided by 'angels' from John Coltrane to Shirley Scott, from Lee Morgan to Paul Robeson. Lancaster made his first records on the ESP-DISK label in 1966. A much-travelled jazz musician, for long his desire has been 'to return home to develop my community,' and after stints with wandering geniuses like Sun Ra and McCoy Tyner, Philly has stayed his home, its people his primary listeners and inspiration.

The title track of Pam Africa begins quietly and almost out of time, like an old English military fife and drum duet, with Lancaster's afro flute and Harold E Smith's throbbing skins making a compelling duo. The two basses of Ed Crockett and Bert Harris make their entrance on Softly, As In A Morning Sunrise, with the sublimely sensitive acoustics of The Spirit Room in rural Rossie, New York state, picking out every petal of sound from Lancaster's alto and the delving bass undertow. The quartet crosses an ocean for Harris's Capetown and the solidarity with Africa pours from Lancaster's soprano horn and 'his confreres' rhythmic power. It's a simple tune played with a beautiful clarity.

Sonny Rollins recorded I'm An Old Cowhand for his early Way Out West album of 1957 and Lancaster's reprise, nearly half a century later, has a certain ironic fire, with many a chomp and gurgle. After Rollins it is two from Coltrane, one of Philly's 'angels.' First Blue Train from 'Trane's 1957 Blue Note album with the same title, full of Smith's rumbling drums and Lancaster's rolling, repetitive phrases, reanimates a classic theme. The bass on that 1957 session was played by the pioneering Paul Chambers, and with two basses with Lancaster, perhaps Mr P.C. had to be played. The blistering pace and roaring language of Lancaster's tenor is an amalgam of artistry and passion well worthy of the tune's great creator, and to have two pulsating basses, bells, whistles and pounding drums all superbly alive is to give new life to one of Coltrane's eternal themes.

Another Coltrane favourite, Bye Bye Blackbird, is given a rousing outing by the quartet, with the two basses pinging and Smith's bouncing drums resounding off Lancaster's familiar choruses. The final track is the hornman's own Justified Sacrifice, where his lone saxophone sings out a dream of beauty and longing.

The next day the foursome were back in the Spirit Room and the 21 opening minutes of the title track begin with wordless vocals, bells, whistles and Smith's didgeridoo while the bowed basses underpin Lancaster's piercing soprano horn. It's a hotel of many stories, sounds and palavers built on a passage to Africa.

Smith's snares rattle through Holy Buddy while Lancaster blows free and the powerfully dawdling Slow Blues In G launches his alto on a long liberation walk. Two bop classics unexpectedly follow. First is Miles's Milestones of 1958 with 'Trane and another Philly boy, drummer Philly Joe Jones. Byard hurtles into the theme, the basses twang and Smith's drums rap and clatter. Then there is Killer Joe, by Philly-born tenorist Benny Golson, whose tribute album to his city-mate Coltrane, This Is For You John, was issued in 1983.

Lancaster's twin albums start and end in Philly, but cover enormous expansions of land, sea and sound in between. Great music and enduring music makers remembered.

(Pam Africa & Ancestral Link Hotel are available on CIMP)

Ingrid Laubrock (Germany) - Transmuting Dreams

Ingrid Laubrock – Sleepthief, Anti-House & Ingrid Laubrock Octet - Zurich Concert
(2016)

The German saxophonist Ingrid Laubrock was born in Stadtlohn in 1970 and went against the grain by listening intently to free jazz from an early age. She moved to Berlin after leaving school and then crossed to London, busking with her alto horn on the underground, where she found her first audiences. She took her first formal lessons from the ex-Jazz Messengers tenorist, Jean Toussaint, before returning to Germany and finding another teacher in the Brooklyn-born ex-Miles Davis sideman Dave Liebman.

Then, with such inspired tutelage behind her, she came back to London and studied music at the Guildhall School of Music and Drama, where she was strongly influenced by Brazilian musicians. In 1997 she cut her first album, Who Is It on the Candid label, and also joined the F-IRE Collective which caused her to broaden her sonic palette and embrace west African music.

By 2007 he had changed to the Swiss-based Intakt label and had recorded the album 'Sleepthief' with the English pianist Liam Noble and Californian drummer Tom Rainey, after first meeting him at the Cheltenham Jazz Festival. The bass in the trio is Rainey's bass drum which is prominent, for example, in the opener Zugunruhe, but as a counterpoint to the chomping keys and Laubrock's filigreed and wondering horn. She is breathy, almost adenoidal at the beginning of the title tune and Rainey's drums, from the quietly menacing, morph to a ghostly rustle. As for the track called Oofy Twerp, Laubrock's saxophone chirps like a nesting bird. The powerful dissonance of

Noble's piano is at the centre of Environmental Stud, where Laubrock's terse notes sometimes have the sound of Steve Lacy, and Noble's bell-like intro to The Ears Have It provokes a quasi-choking solo by the reedwoman. Amelie, all Noble with Rainey's distant bass drum, closes an album brim-full of keen-edged timbral exploration.

Laubrock goes from three to five in her 2010 New York album, 'Anti-House.' Rainey is with her again plus bassist John Hebert - of Cajun ancestry from Louisiana, the Boston guitarist Mary Halvorson and as a guest, the Vancouver-born pianist Kris Davis of whom her fellow keyboard virtuoso Jason Moran said: 'She lives in every note that she plays.' And this diverse group of men and women play like a dream. In fact, Laubrock says in the sleeve notes: 'I wanted the album to be almost like a dream, where anything can happen, but instead of waking up it just keeps going.'

Hear Laubrock's searing soprano saxophone and Halvorson's piercing guitar on Slowfish Glowfish, Halvorson's clanking strings on the brief Flowery Prison Cell or Hebert's pulsing drive on Messy Minimum. Laubrock's tenor snarls through Quick Draw yet pours out a lyrical sadness on Tex and Clementine, with Rainey's scuttling drums.

Davis's stop-time piano becomes an essential asset to the amalgam on the title tune, and chimes eerily through Big Crunch. Rainey plays glockenspiel on Tom Can't Sleep and Laubrock's solo is full of expressive beauty, sidling into his drums while Halvorson reverberates and Hebert casts his southern twang. Altogether, this is an album of many creative delights.

The reverie-like qualities are intensified even more in the Laubrock Octet's 2011 concert in Zurich. Perhaps her days and nights in the London Underground are recalled in the hallucinatory sound of the album opener Glasses, or in the spectral accordion of Ted Reichman in Novemberdoodle. Halverson's agitated guitar is a tour de force in Chant and Laubrock's gasping tenor makes a worrying palaver in Matrix with Tom Arthur's chuntering trumpet.

But dream constantly transmutes to reality, as in Nightbus where a city's loneliness and sense of desolation is given a disturbing soundscape in Laubrock's perturbed solo, and the disquieting ensembles into which her saxophone meshes.

These are now times, in which sonic commentaries from musicians use and mould dreams to recreate the world around us.

(Sleepthief, Anti-House & Zurich Concert are available on Intakt)

Ingrid Laubrock with Andy Milne, Angelica Sanchez, The Jazz Doctors & Julie Tippets - Best of 2023: Jazz albums

The Jazz Doctors – Intensive Care
Julie Tippets – Sound on Stone
Ingrid Laubrock and Andy Milne – Fragile
Angelica Sanchez - Nighttime Creatures
(2023)

For me, the record of the year is the re-release of a precious vinyl disc on CD of the Jazz Doctors, who toured the UK in in 1983-84, and recorded their first session as Intensive Care on John Jack's Cadillac label in a Hoxton studio in November 1983.

Val Wilmer's expressive sleeve photograph shows squatting tenor saxophonist Frank Lowe, drummer Dennis Charles with a cymbal under his arm, violinist Billy Bang and bassist Rafael Garrett fresh from the US, posing in an East End park. As they romp into Jackie McLean's Little Melanae, they play with prescriptive fire in the heart of London.

The record includes an unreleased session of November 1984, with bassist Wilbur Morris and drummer Thurman Baker, with the Doctors still offering a full dose of groove. My favourite track is the 12 minutes of Ornette Coleman's Lonely Woman from the 1983 date, its haunting melody set on edge by Garret's throbbing bass, Lowe's moaning horn and Bang's palpitating strings: marvellous!

(Intensive Care is available on Cadillac Records)

In 2020 jazz lost the great Bristolian pianist Keith Tippett. The album Sound on Stone, was created by his vocalist wife Julie (formerly Julie Driscoll) in 2022, using extracts from recordings of Keith from his tour of Holland which sparked the making of his 1979 album The Unlonely Raindancer, and other unreleased waxings made in Bologna (1991) and the Welsh College of Music and Drama (1995-96). This final album of the Couple in Spirit duo is a brilliant amalgam of Keith's pianism and Julie's effervescent voice, including a memorable version of Michel Legrand's ballad, Windows of Your Mind.

Elaborately reinvented, beautifully harmonised, extraordinarily fused, this landmark album fully expresses one of jazz's blessed unities. An outstanding track is the title song, Stone on Stone, and as Julie sings "Who stood enraptured?/ How many echoes call/Sharp on the breeze?" we know it is us, the listeners, spellbound by their sound.

(Sound on Stone is available on Discus Records)

Another powerful duo album is Fragile, full of co-operative beauty by Stadtlon, Germany-born saxophonist Ingrid Laubrock and the pianist from Hamilton, Ontario, Andy Milne.

Both musicians explore their sonic vulnerability on tracks like Fragment or Shard but the power of their inventiveness seems boundless, with Laubrock giving full scope to her soprano horn and Milne playing with a potent empathy and, as a student of a master, Oscar Peterson, with a deeply affective lyricism.

Although there are but two musicians at work, as a listener you feel that their sounds are coming from a much larger collective ensemble, giving them their strength and innovation, and making Fragile a profoundly memorable album.

(Fragile is available on Intakt Records)

The Arizonan pianist now living in New York City, Angelica Sanchez, a lover of big band music, moved to a secluded cabin while teaching upstate. She would walk in the woods at night and "realised that it was only my ears that were activated. I became fascinated by what I couldn't see."

Her album Nighttime Creatures recreates those moments where 'coyotes and other animals make noise in the dark.' It's where living nature stews up into ensemble music and the human imagination joins with the animate external world, with Sanchez tunes plus Ellington's Lady of the Lavender Mist and Carla Bley's huge influence with CB the Time Traveller and Wrong Door for Rocket Fuel.

Alongside eight other virtuosi like saxophonists Michael Attias, Chris Speed and John Goldberg, Thomas Heberer's trumpet and bassist John Hebert, Sanchez opens up the night and makes beautiful light out of darkness in a profoundly original and revelatory album.

(Nighttime Creatures is available on Pyroclastic Records)

John Law (England) - A truly evocative salutation

The John Law Quartet - Exploded on Impact, The John Law Cornucopia Ensemble - Out of Darkness & John Law's Congregation - Three Leaps of the Gazelle
(2016)

When I first heard John Law playing a very free and brilliant piano alongside the veteran South African drummer Louis Moholo-Moholo on the 1995 album The Boat is Sinking, Apartheid is Sinking, I'd no idea that he'd been a classical piano prodigy in his youth. He'd begun learning piano at four, given his first public performance at six and later won a scholarship to London's Royal Academy of Music and followed that by gaining another scholarship, awarded by the Austrian government to continue his classical studies in Vienna.

Then something happened in 1986. With this powerful classical background integral to his art, he turned to jazz and a profoundly free and experimental form of the music.

With bassist Paul Rogers and drummer Mark Sanders, he formed Atlas and by 1992 he had recorded his first Slam album, Exploded on Impact, with Sanders, Roberto Bellatalla on bass and the startling, but largely unsung, saxophonist Alan Wilkinson playing alto and baritone horns. There are five Law compositions on this album full of drama and surprise and none more so than his elegy for a dismembered Yugoslavia, Mother's Lament. Wilkinson's baritone is at its centre, growling and singing out its melody of a dying nation beside Law's chiming notes.

Bellatalla's mournful bowed solo preludes an astonishing passage from Wilkinson, his sound breathing agony and loss at the heart of his horn with the violence of Sanders's exploding drums enclosing him. It is deep and moving music of its times played with brilliance and humanity.

A Pissed-off-Tree (with reference to the felonious monk), which the listener assumes is a punning aside to Monk's Epistrophy, would probably have amused the great pianist, what with four adventurous musicians delivering jazz irony on his musical inventions in faraway London. Kaleidoscope is almost a whisper after what has gone before and the album ends with Joy Ride, begun with a volley from Sanders, a rampaging Law solo with Bellatalla plucking his route beside him before Wilkinson enters for a caustic alto chorus.

Jon Lloyd's sleeve notes to Law's 2004 Birmingham concert recording Out of the Darkness declares that 'his aim is to incorporate and integrate a jazz quartet within an ensemble of eight classical musicians.' Law's classical education in musical composition as well as his jazz impulse to improvise are key to his Cornucopia Ensemble, centred by the foursome of Law, saxophonist Andy Sheppard, veteran bassist Chris Laurence and drummer Paul Clarvis. Sheppard's tenor bursts out of the ominous and sonorous brass, woodwind and strings of the very composed and arranged title suite, with Law expressing his classical roots in a strange but often hauntingly beautiful amalgam of genres.

Sheppard's exquisitely poised soprano runs through the blood of the folk-inspired Talitha Cumi, and Nocturne creates a serene harmony of horns and strings within which Sheppard's wafting soprano rises like the dawn, before Laurence's delving bass and the entire ensemble see in the morning. The morning also sings in Law's new album Three Leaps of the Gazelle with his 2012 trio (which he calls his 'Congregation') including the Israeli drummer, late of Gilad Atzmon's Orient House Ensemble, Asaf Sirkis and the Russian bassist Yuri Goloubev. I heard the trio play live at the 2012 London Jazz Festival and for me the special moment of their performance was Law's tribute to the miners (played in 'minor' key) of the 1984-85 British miners' strike and the colliery bands, The Quiet Dignity of the Minor. This is a truly evocative salutation, the tranquility of its melody, of Sirkis's tender Levantine brushes, Law's lucid notes and Goloubev's heart wrenching bass solo make it an internationalist tribute to brave and defiant British communities, radiantly performed, and for all time too.

Law's story about the origins of his tune Finger on the Pulse tells much about his music and about the jazz which, both by design and circumstance, crosses categories and genres. Prompted by hearing pop music as he passed the open door of his teenage daughter's room, he was filled by an idea for a tune. As he played it in live performance, he found himself subconsciously interpolating a section of Schumann's Traumerei.

The result crosses boundaries and makes beauty as it passes - something of a parable of the progress of John Law and his music.

(Exploded on Impact & Out of Darkness are available on Slam, Three Leaps of the Gazelle is available on 33 Records)

Azar Lawrence (USA) - The master-seeker returns to the fore

Azar Lawrence - The Seeker
(2017)

Azar Lawrence was born in Los Angeles in 1952 and his life as a burning tenor saxophonist has taken him into the heartlands of jazz, as well as deep into the world of soul, accompanying pioneering talents such as Ike and Tina Turner, Roberta Flack and Earth, Wind and Fire. His impassioned sound, first inspired by that of Coltrane, was recognised by the community activist and piano maestro of Watts, Horace Tapscott, when he joined his Arkestra as a teenager. Then he met the great drummer of the John Coltrane Quartet, Elvin Jones, who took him to New York in 1973 as a crucial member of his own band, the Jazz Machine. He played with pianist McCoy Tyner (another Coltrane Quartet alumnus) on his burning 1974 album Atlantis, and with Miles Davis on his epochal live recording from New York's Carnegie Hall in the same year, Dark Magus.

Since those ardent days Lawrence has had a much quieter jazz profile, but he comes powerfully to the fore again on his new album on the Sunnyside label, The Seeker, in the midst of a band of unmitigated talents. The trumpeter is the New Orleans-born Nicholas Payton, veteran of a succession of key Verve albums of the '90s, born in the same year that Lawrence made his cross-continental migration to New York, and the drummer is Jeff 'Tain' Watts, born in Pittsburgh in 1960, who took fire in the early Wynton Marsalis bands. The bassist is the Omaha, Nebraska-born (in 1959) Essiet Okon Essiet, ex-pulseman of Bobby Watson's Horizon band and the pianist is the Venezuelan prodigy Benito Gonzalez.

The band's album The Seeker burst out of its New York City studio in December 2011. Lawrence's vehement timbre is immediately apparent from those 1973-4 sessions, as if it were the next day, the next impassioned cause, the next sonic earthquake. When you look at the title's opener it is simply called Gandhi, and rarely has he been depicted with so much fire. Gonzalez rocks his keys and Payton's solo is fraught with tension, agitation, beauty and excitation.

Lost Tribes of Lemuria has a march-like, almost anthemic theme with its narrative of a lost continent. Watts's drums pound and throb behind Lawrence's waywardly searching chorus and the brass defiance of Payton's urgent solo, a horn pealing through the mist of loss, as a huge landmass and its people aching to be found and vindicated. Lawrence blows out his album title tune on soprano saxophone with a Coltranish intensity as if his musical quest is in mid-journey and nowhere near completion. Payton begins reflectively, and as the rhythmic pace quickens he climbs, falls, soars, flies and plummets, with Essiet's earthen pulse reminding him that his journey too is both real and mundane. Gonzalez's solo offers shared discovery and communality within this search of life.

One More Time is the Venezuelan's composition; its Latin groove rousing the horns to new sonic areas. Azar's creative gusto and ascendant inventiveness and Payton plays low then on a soar of blistering notes, all-confident and full of poise. Gonzalez changes the rhythm to a more relaxed, sauntering stride as the fivesome come home together.

Apart from One More Time, all the tunes are Lawrence's, and Rain Ballad is the most evocative. Its strong, elegiac melody gives full vent to the wondrous and incendiary beauty of his tenor sound and eloquence rarely heard since the days of Coltrane. The slow, almost statuesque beginning to Spirit Night gradually quickens its pace until Gonzalez's tender, skittering solo, with Essiet's bass gently pulsing beneath him.

The album's finale is Venus Rising. Payton's lyrical chorus, full of light, flying high with lingering, translucent flames of sound is followed by a dashing Gonzalez solo before the sound fades. Although there are five master-seekers here on this record, it is Azar who rises from the past now in his sixties and blowing like he blew 40 years ago with Tyner, Miles and Freddie Hubbard.

Where is he going next? What will this relentless searcher find and create?

(The Seeker is available on Sunnyside)

Nguyen Le (France/Vietnam) - Nations absorbed in the oneness of sound

Ha Noi Duo by Nguyen Le and Ngo Hong Quang (2017)

'At any moment, this music will raise numerous questions. Is it Vietnamese? Or jazz? Or traditional music, blues, African, Indian... is it written - or is it improvised?' These questions are asked by the guitarist Nguyen Le within the sleeve notes of his extraordinary album with the 'traditional' musician also from Vietnam, Ngo Hong Quang.

Le was born in Paris in 1959 of Vietnamese parents and has spent a jazz life within two often powerfully contesting traditions. An inheritor of Vietnam's enduringly beautiful musical conventions and forms, yet he has lived within an entirely contrary musical culture too, among the European and US sounds and songs that have defined 'pop' culture.

In his album Songs of Freedom he brings together some of these songs, from Bob Marley, Stevie Wonder and Lennon and McCartney, and proclaims in his sleeve notes: 'Yet the music is like a bird: once released, it flies to every sky. The Earth becomes rounder and rounder, inviting cultures to mingle and soak up one another. Let's sing the flow of our crossed-over world!' This 'cross-over world' is at the heart of Le's jazz and his Ha Noi Duo album with Ngo Hong Quang and his Vietnamese fiddle, lute and Jew's harp also brings in a number of brilliant guests including the Sardinian trumpeter Paolo Fresu, the Indian tabla virtuoso Prabhu Edouard and Mieko Miyazaki of Japan on koto. It is sounds of the world, fused in one, with Le's own acoustic and electric guitars.

The opener is Cloud Chamber. The Indian tablas roll and the Vietnamese strings are plucked against the Parisian skies before Fresu's beautiful Mediterranean horn blows out its chorus. Nations and their separate musics are absorbed into the oneness of this sound, and Five Senses - a tune written by Le the jazzman - as he puts it in his notes, becomes 'transformed by the timbres and accents of traditional Asian instruments.' What a sonic mix is here!

In Like Mountain Birds, Quang's vocal has wings to carry it skywards after Le's almost forlorn guitar opening, as if his notes are the waiting earth below, pleading for this bird to return. The acoustic lucidity of Le's guitar picks its way through the love song, A Night With You, Gone. As Fresu enters, distantly, like a lamentation, you know this must be the lovers' last meeting.

Quang's Jew's harp quivers behind his voice at the beginning of The Graceful Seal and Le's quasi-blues like guitar cries out, grounded by percussion and set on fire by Fresu's solo. Then on to Quang's tune dedicated to the Tay mountain people of Vietnam, Heaven's Gourd, in which Le plays his 'north African-sounding acoustic guitar,' thus invoking the sound of yet another continent and Le's 1998 album Maghreb and Friends.

Chiec Khan Pieu, a song from the '70s, with Prabhu's pounding tablas, then Le's rocking guitar chorus and Fresu's far-sounding horn creating an amalgam of civilisations and continents, and Monkey Queen, written by Le for the Monkey festival, gives full precedence to Quang's virtuoso performance with the single-stringed Vietnamese instrument, the Dan Bau. How can such melodic beauty and complexity ring with such power from a single string?

In the 14th century in the north of Vietnam, nomadic blind beggars established the Xam style of performance, which Le links to the southern Mississippi blues. Ironic that the musical forms of two such erstwhile bitter 20th-century enemies could have found such harmony in their music, but such is the marvel of jazz, expressed with such poignancy in Beggar's Love Song.

The record ends in the serenity of the northern Vietnamese sound picture of Silently Grows the Rice. I thought of Ho Chi Minh's prison poem Pastoral Scene, but also reflected on Le's final sleeve sentences: 'Like threads of silk, cultures from yesterday and today weave a complex and diverse beauty... a part of the essence of Vietnam with its millennial roots, its tormented past and its future full of hope. They also take us to the heart of life itself.'

(Ha Noi Duo is available on Act)

Jihye Lee (Korea) - Moving elegy marking Korean ferry disaster

Jihye Lee Orchestra – April
(2018)

Young Korean musician and composer Jihye Lee wrote this work in response to the sinking of the ferry the MV Sewol in April 2014 off the coast of South Korea, when 304 passengers, most of them secondary school students, perished and both the Seoul government and the ship's owners drew sharp criticism for their handling of the disaster.

April is a six-song suite, performed by a 20-piece orchestra, drawn from the Berklee College of Music in the US city of Boston where Lee was studying and other local musicians. It reflects a searching and defiant musical response similar to that following the 2005 Hurricane Katrina destruction in New Orleans in albums by Terence Blanchard and James Blood Ulmer, in which the Bush government's neglect and inaction provoked similar outrage.

It is an album of the unexpected and the impressive, particularly when one learns that Lee had never led an orchestra before and had but a slight exposure to jazz. In Korea she was much more attuned to folk and rhythm-and-blues idioms as a pop singer and songwriter.

Opener April Wind, in which Mark Walker's strident and ominous drums punctuate an apparently calm and melodious surface, has solos from pianist Alain Mallet and saxophonists Shannon LeClaire (alto) and Allan Chase (soprano), who build a growing sense of dark, impending events within the fullness of the ensemble. Sewol Ho follows, marked by John Lockwood's submarine bass work and menacing stop-time phrases from trumpeter Greg Hopkins and trombonist Jeff Galindo before Ben Whiting's bass clarinet and LeClaire's clarinet exchange a palaver above the orchestral waves.

Original and well scored, it's followed by Deep Blue Sea, which includes Lee's wordless, almost spectral voice within the full orchestral sound. Rick DiMuzio's long tenor saxophone solo is powerfully serene and mournful, full of the tragic narrative of lost youth and their scarcely lived lives. On Whirlwind, in a surging and sudden change of rhythm, the ferment provoked by the catastrophe, private and public, is evoked. Throughout the track Guilty, the tones are accusative and wide-reaching, held in focus by the bass and drums of Lockwood and Walker and a penetrating guitar solo by Bruce Bartlett under DiMuzio's hovering soprano saxophone.

Finale You Are Here (Every Time I Think of You), part lamentation, part elegy, has a moving chorus by renowned trumpeter Sean Jones. His solo has an anthemic quality, as he blows an oratorio to the sacrifice of the young all over our world, provoked by the musicianship of a young woman from Korea.

(April is available on jihyemusic.com)

Viktoria Leleka (Ukraine)
Sonce u Serci (Sun in Heart)
(2022)

The Ukrainian singer resident in Berlin, Viktoria Leleka, calls her music Ukrainian Folk Jazz, or 'improvised folklore.'

Taking traditional songs from her native land and singing them with a soft and lilting lyricism with the accompaniment of an outstanding trio: pianist Povel Widestrand, bassist Thomas Kolarczyk and drummer Jacob Hegner, she has created a memorable album which she calls Sonce u Serci, or Sun in Your Heart.

There is more than a touch of jazz/soul in her instrumental mates. Hegner's drumming is brilliant throughout and hear Kolarczyk's dancing plucked strings in Sleep or Widestand's sharp-edged pianism in Rose.

This is a pre-invasion album made in 2021, yet the lyrics carry ominous presages as well as a sustaining optimism.

'The sun hides everything in the storm clouds,' sings Leleka. 'But we have our own suns in our hearts / And the whole world is illuminated by this.'

(Sonce u Serci is available on Initiative Musik)

Liberation Music Collective (USA) - Portraits of rebellion against injustice in tune with the times
The Liberation Music Collective - Rebel Portraiture
(2021)

In the heart of Trump's cruel and buffoonish US, the troubadours of freedom are still making music, as evidenced by The Liberation Music Collective - two young scientists from Indiana who are also jazz musicians. Bassist Hannah Fidler is a neuroscientist and trumpeter Matt Riggen a biologist and, in 2015, they gathered together a group of comrade musicians to give testimony to 'a better, safer and freer world for us all,' using the messages and humanism of jazz. They were present in Ferguson for the Black Lives Matter protests and played their music on the Women's March on Washington and at the demonstrations against the Dakota Access Pipeline. They go where the people and their protests go, their instruments sounding out for rebellion and justice.

Their new album Rebel Portraiture celebrates the lives, sacrifices and heroism of today and throughout history in the US and the struggling world. It is a profoundly educative record, as well as one of powerful musicianship with stories stretches from Salem and Ohio to Honduras, Syria and South Africa, using the musical genres of African, Asian, European classical, Latin American and US traditions.

Its first narrative of resistance is based on the hymn Passing Away and dedicated to Giles Corey, who was crushed to death for refusing to plead guilty at the Salem witch trials in 1692. Ana Nelson's luminous soprano saxophone tells his story, accompanied by Fidler's earthen bass and Matt Waterman's expressive trombone. Riggen's crackling chorus adds edge to Corey's courage. The deaths of the four students of Kent State University in Ohio, shot down by the National Guard in 1970 as they protested against the war in Vietnam, is marked in An Afterlife for Jeffrey Miller, which includes a poem written by one of the four and a note to his room-mate, followed by a movingly picked-out guitar solo by Kyle Schardt.

Fidler's bass introduces An Afterlife for Berta Caceres, a Honduran activist murdered for opposing the Agua Zarca Dam construction which threatened her people's water resources. Yael Litwin plays the gyil, a Ghanaian traditional stringed funeral instrument, while the French horn of Brennan Johns and Fidler's recorder add unusual orchestral voices.

In 2015, Syrian journalist Ruqia Hassan was killed by Isis and An Afterlife for Ruqia Hassan is dedicated to her and other Syrian and Iraqi journalists whose words led to their murders. Schardt's guitar artistry excels, playing tribute to journalists all over the world dedicated to the 'investigation of abomination.'

Two pieces remember the tenacity and resistance of South African LGBTQ campaigner Noxolo Nogwaza who was raped and murdered in 2011. Her body was abandoned by a roadside and Ditchside Monument and An Afterlife for Noxolo Nogwaza commemorates the aftermath of her death when 170,000 South Africans petitioned their government to provide protection for LGBTQ citizens but, as yet, there have been neither arrests nor convictions for Nogwaza's murder. In a succession of moving solos, Riggen's horn weeps, while Miro Sobrer's trombone mourns yet is filled with hope. Sean Imbroden's tenor saxophone soars with pride for Nogwaza's courage and Fidler's bass solo provokes memories of the great bassist Charlie Haden's evocations of heroes such as Che and La Pasionaria on his Liberation Music Orchestra recordings. At the climax, the activist's struggle becomes a universal symbol.

This bold and often beautiful record needs to be broadcast and learned from everywhere. Its jazz testimony and human consciousness is absolutely in tune with our times.

(Rebel Portraiture is available on Ad Astrum)

Abbey Lincoln (USA) - Live set from one of the world's greatest jazz artists

Abbey Lincoln - Sophisticated Abbey
(2016)

Abbey Lincoln was born Anna Marie Wooldridge in Chicago in 1930. She began her career in song as a supper-club singer and later as a film performer (singing in the 1957 Hollywood film The Girl Can't Help It). Then in the same year she met and later married the great bop drummer Max Roach, and together they were swept into the civil rights campaign and together recorded two highly conscious albums: We Insist! The Freedom Now Suite (1960) and Percussion Bitter Sweet (1961), and she spent the rest of her life as a brilliantly radical singer proving through her singular artistry that the woman could certainly help it.

After long periods away from recording, her series of Verve albums during the '90s like You Gotta Pay the Band (1991), A Turtle's Dream (1994) and Wholly Earth (1998) found her leading bands, including luminaries like bassist Charlie Haden, trumpeter Roy Hargrove, altoist Oliver Lake and vibraphonist Bobby Hutcherson, and were characterised by carefully chosen songs - often with deeply meaningful lyrics and always marked by her devotion to the singing of Billie Holiday.

The previously unissued High Note album Sophisticated Abbey keeps all those principles alive, despite being cut in a San Francisco nightclub, The Keystone Korner, in 1980. Towards its denouement and in the middle of singing We May Never Meet Again, she dedicates the song to Holiday, and we see again the mark of her true provenance as a singer.

She has a fine trio too to accompany her. On piano is Phil Wright, with whom she recorded in the late '50s and who knew her music intimately. The bassist is James Leary, who as an ex-Basie rhythm man was just as used to playing with a big band as a trio, and the drummer is Doug Sides, who also played on the renowned 1967 John Handy albums New View and At the Monterey Jazz Festival.

Scattered through the album are songs of three 'ladies.' The opener is Abbey's own Painted Lady, her profoundly now-times observation of celebrity culture giving young women 'a vision of another world, I can take you there.' Ellington's Sophisticated Lady and Leary's earthen bass lend her a critique of a life of 'smoking, drinking, never thinking of tomorrow,' and Stevie Wonder's Golden Lady is a blind man's astonishing visual declaration of beauty, sung with Abbey's very own beautiful lucidity and passion.

Her utterly life-affirming rendition of Long as You're Living, composed by three jazz contemporaries, trumpeter Tommy Turrentine, vocalist Oscar Brown Jnr and trombonist Julian Priester, contains the lines that were Abbey's watchwords: 'Brother, sister, this is your time!' She declares: 'While you are sleeping/lifetime is creeping/Wake up and taste it!/Foolish to waste it!/Live every minute!/Put yourself in it!/Long as you're living!' An accurate enough summary of her own life, also expressed in the optimism of her chosen love songs like Somos Novios, There Are Such Things and Whistling in the Dark, all in their own ways calls to action.

But the real jewel of the album is her own anthem People in Me, a song inspired by her mother and 'the nation' within her own family history, 'where the whole world is turning in me.' She sings a song of huge human empathy: of 'the Indian in me, the Chinese in me, the Japanese, the Vietnamese, the Jewish, the Arab, the Mexican, the Algerian, the Watusi, the Zimbabwean - the whole of Africa turning in me.' And, unbounded human knowledge: 'Lessons, learning, whatever people know/Inside of me!' It's a song of wisdom and huge humanity.

To finish her performance it must be Billie, and it is a version of God Bless the Child and Holiday's chilling commentary on the effects of US capitalism: 'Them that's got shall get/Them that's not will lose/The strong get more/While the weak ones fade/Empty pockets don't/Ever make the grade.'

1980 and 2016, still ripe, still true, still naked and Abbey Lincoln, no longer with us since 2010, still turns, sings and speaks through our turntables, her sense of melody, diction and clarity of insight as strong as ever. And if you want proof of what singing of, for and about people really means, this record is a prime place to start.

(Sophisticated Abbey is available on High Note)

Erica Lindsay (USA) - Powerful sense of music and artist unity

Erica Lindsay and the Alchemy Sound Project - Further Explorations (2017)

Some decade or so ago in a second-hand record shop in Toronto, I came across an album led by the San Francisco-born (in 1955) saxophonist Erica Lindsay. Dreamer, It was called, cut in March 1989 in New York City, and it was full of fire and artistry, led by a hornwoman who was described in the album's sleeve notes by Nat Hentoff in these terms: 'Erica is protean. That is she composes, she arranges, and she plays tenor, soprano, flute and clarinet. She has a distinctive clarity and fullness of sound as well as an acute sense of dynamics.' He was right too, that's for sure.

So when I saw that the makers of the 2016 album Further Explorations was a co-operative ensemble called the Alchemy Sound Project including Erica, I cottoned on to it immediately. Her band mates are brother saxophonist Salim Washington, with Samantha Boshnack on trumpet and flugelhorn, trombonist Willem de Koch, Sumi Tonooka playing piano with David Arend on bass and drummer Max Wood.

Lindsay's early years were spent in Europe where her parents were teachers, and when she was 15, she studied with another brilliant US musician in Europe, the percussive pianist Mal Waldron. 'He's a very strong influence,' she said. 'He showed me a whole way of approaching composition. From Mal,

I got a sense of freedom, so that composition becomes a feeling process, not thought process.' As she grew older, John Coltrane had a huge impact upon her music. 'What impressed me,' she declared, 'was that every player was equal' when Coltrane blew, and now 25 years after the recording of Dreamer, that same sense of equality and unity radiates from the Alchemy Sound Project.

The opener is Charcoal, Clear, Beautiful All Over, prefaced by Tonooka's crystalline piano and Washington's delving bass clarinet. It's Washington's tune and his solo is lucidly beautiful before Erica's tenor adds another dimension. On Lindsay's album title tune, Washington plays alto flute and Arend's deep, quasi-subterranean bass pulsates below the reeds. Erica's tenor sounds lonesome, almost ominous. Alchemical is a Boshnack composition but it is Tonooka's chiming keys and Wood's resonant drums that mark its beginning, before Lindsay's vibrant tenor chorus. Then comes Waiting and it is Tonooka's turn for tune-making. Either Washington's or Lindsay's burning tenor is at the track's centre, before Washington's flying flute sees it out.

Lindsay's second album piece is the promenading Beta with Arend's sauntering bassline and Tonooka's bustling piano dynamics that carry the tune forward. Arend is the Sound Project's fifth member to show his composition skills on the album, taking his Her Name is Love from a work by Leos Janacek, and creating repeated cadences which fall away repeatedly with a transient beauty. His second piece, Archetype, follows directly after with Boshnack's soft-focussed horn leading the solos before Lindsay's rolling saxophone and Tonooka's scurrying piano.

This is an album with a powerful sense of musical unity-in-artistry with no dominating figure, a feature emphasised during the ensemble that begins Boshnack's Divergency. Her horn sings out all the way to Tonooka's Joie de Vivre, where there is a subliminal sense of concord. Wood's drums crash behind Tonooka's keys, there is a Lindsay saxophone surge and Arend's pounding bass jumps behind Washington's flickering oboe, and all the way through there is the musicality of sheer elation of being able and privileged to be making such sound together.

The finale is Washington's tune The Call, which very strangely reminded me of the old second world war song that Vera Lynn used to sing, Now is the Hour. Boshnack and Tonooka have fiery solos, but it is the total effect of the band that carries the power, its unremitting sonic solidarity: a memorable record.

(Further Explorations is available on ARC)

Charles Lloyd (USA) and Maria Farantouri (Greece) –
The voice of a defiant Greece

Charles Lloyd and Maria Farantouri - Athens Concert (2012)

I sit looking at the one o'clock news. There is a 24-hour strike in Athens and mass protests against severe austerity policies, a record unemployment rate of 24 per cent and spending cuts in welfare, education, health and pensions of €11.5 billion. The message of the streets pours from the lips of one interviewed protester. 'We strike against the measures that will destroy our lives,' she declares. 'We cannot sink any deeper, or the Greek people will die. It is like we are at war.'

Words of September 2012 which echo the sounds of a concert held in Athens in June 2010, at the very foot of the Acropolis, the living result of a deep friendship between the veteran Memphis-born tenor saxophonist Charles Lloyd and the Greek singer Maria Farantouri, of whose voice Lloyd wrote: 'It can soothe, excite, inspire and lift us to the Hyperions.'

Precious verbs indeed for the Greek people in their defiant struggle against the hugely powerful forces of the combined European Central Bank; the EU Commission, the IMF and their own compliant government - with the growing menace too of the fascism of Golden Dawn and its connections with the Greek police.

With Lloyd are his trio, three youthful veterans of international music, and here deeply imbibing Greek song, musical poetry. The drummer is Eric Harland who has played with an array of prime horns from altoists Kenny Garrett and Greg Osby, trumpeter Terence Blanchard, tenorist Joshua Redman, plus vibesman Stefon Harris and the epochal pianist McCoy Tyner. Bassist Reuben Rogers also knows his way round the circuits and also spent time with Redman and New Orleans trumpeter Nicholas Payton. Houston pianist Jason Moran is an experienced leader in his own right, with a batch of luminous Blue Note albums.

As for Lloyd, who the singer calls 'a shaman of jazz,' the mass appeal of his performances goes back to his huge popularity at the 1966 Monterey Jazz Festival, his 60s concerts at San Francisco's rock venue the Fillmore or his tour of the Soviet Union. He virtually retired from performing in the '70s, becoming a teacher of transcendental meditation, but he returned in the 80s with a new quartet, relentless touring and a series of powerful albums.

The tunes of the Athens Concert are mostly Greek traditional songs, but with two by Lloyd. Some of them have a truly transplanted taste of the Aegean Blues like Lina Nikolakopoulou's lyric, Oh Eyelid!, where Farantouri gently demands, 'My closed eyelid, /ah, my lucky one! / Don't come out, dawn star, / don't be afraid!'

The new imperatives of the Greek people are just as urgent, and they sound out with a potent intensity in Farantouri's sublime voice and Lloyd's floating, mystical horn. Farantouri has been a consistently insightful interpreter of the songs of the Greek people since, as a young woman of 20, she went into exile after the 1967 fascist coup. Her voice has also coaxed the meaning and beauty from the words of Lorca, Brecht, Yannis Ritsos and Brecht. But listen to her sing the Seferis poem I Kept Hold Of My Life, with Lloyd's buoyant obligatos and Moran's gentle phrasing. Or Agathi Dimitrouva's Requiem of bleak times when 'silent shadows / lean over the earth / like trees hanging in midair / with no roots in life.' Is this how the Greek people feel, now? Yet Moran plays with such optimistic fluency it is as if his empathy is total.

Lloyd blows lyrically and not without mystery on his own Dream Weaver, where Rogers's bass rings, Harland's drums clip with Moran's chiming chorus, but it is with the traditional Greek tunes where his internationalism is invoked like a Robeson of the saxophone. On-the folk tune from the Dodecanese Islands, My Little Sea, his flute dances in the waves with the lyre of Socratis Sinopoulos. Through the love song from the Epirus region, Little Lemon Tree, Harland's drums crash and Lloyd's notes warble powerfully over the roofs of the ancient city. In the Black Sea song The Castle Of The Sun the fierce pace of the Greek lyrics are matched by Lloyd's own very American chorus, with the ancestral sounds of Lester Young burning in his notes.

The closing track is the Epirus lament My Yanni about the pain of leaving your home for 'lonely foreign lands,' a feeling shared by the many migrant peoples in Greece. The universal, common theme is understood intuitively through Lloyd's airy solo, and the two pianos of Moran and his Greek confrere Takis Farazis share in combined understanding and solidarity. Athens Concert is a resonating double album and you will hear its melodies, improvisation, poetry and artistry whenever you see the defiance and resistance of the brave people of Greece.

(Athens Concert is available on ECM)

Charles Lloyd (USA) - Glorious records full of defiance and optimism

Charles Lloyd - Wild Man Dance & Charles Lloyd and the Marvels - I Long to See You (2017)

Half a century ago in the centre of Haight-Ashbury's San Francisco hippie blossoming, the tenor saxophonist Charles Lloyd brought jazz as close to a new age heart as it ever came. Lloyd's quartet, including pianist Keith Jarrett, bassist Cecil McBee and drummer Jack DeJohnette performed to huge audiences at rock venues more used to Jefferson Airplane and Big Brother and the Holding Company, (hear their 1967 album Love-in: The Charles Lloyd Quartet Recorded at Fillmore Auditorium in San Francisco). And they broke other barriers in their tours of eastern Europe and the albums that followed, like Charles Lloyd in the Soviet Union of 1970.

Lloyd, born in Memphis, Tennessee in 1938, had played in blues bands with BB King and Bobby Bland, and much influenced by Coltrane, with jazz groups led by Chico Hamilton and Cannonball Adderley, before his iconic performance at the 1966 Monterey Jazz Festival. Then by the mid-'70s he had virtually vanished from the jazz scene as swiftly as he had arrived, becoming a teacher of transcendental meditation. A decade later, by the late '80s, he reappeared with a series of powerful albums with European musicians on the Munich-based ECM label, his recording home for the ensuing two decades.

His 2015 return to Blue Note records, Wild Man Dance, has him playing at the Polish Wroclaw Jazztopad Festival with compatriots Joe Sanders (bass), Gerald Clayton (piano) and Gerald Cleaver (drums), plus the Greek Sokratis Sinopoulos, virtuoso of the stringed lyra and the Hungarian Miklos Lukacs, playing the mallets and strings of the cimbalom. Lloyd's Wild Man Dance Suite was written for the countryside around Wroclaw: 'What birds fly there? Do rivers run through it?' he asked himself. The answers rise from the music, lucid but still mysterious as cimbalom and lyra begin the suite's first movement, Flying Over the Odra Valley.

As Lloyd's tenor joins them, it could be the Mississippi and Memphis that he is flying over: 'I'm a blues man on a spiritual journey,' he says. 'The blues comes out of a quest for freedom.' And it is there in his serpentine notes, in Clayton's flowing phrases, Sanders's depth and Cleaver's ringing Detroit cymbals.

The track simply called Lark has a particular beauty. Clayton's naked piano begins, Sinopoulos's bowed strings sing sadly, Sanders's arco bass joins him before Lloyd's musical wings fly in. Ever a citizen and working troubadour of the world, he makes a musical unity of all his roots and influences. Here in Poland too, in the most cosmopolitan setting with internationalist bandmates, the quest continues.

In 2015 he was in Santa Barbara, California, recording his most elegiac of albums, I Long to See You with two guitarists - Bill Frisell and the pedal steel specialist Greg Leisz, drummer Eric Harland and bassist Reuben Rogers. It is as if the '60s have reprised with memories of Vietnam with Bob Dylan's Masters of War, Joan Baez's luminous voice with All My Trials and Joe Cocker's soulful tones with You are So Beautiful.

Masters of War begins the album and as you consider the huge arms sales to Saudi Arabia and the slaughter of thousands of Yemenis you wonder what has changed. Of Course Of Course goes back to Lloyd's 1964 album of the same name. Sombrero Sam is from his 1966 album Dream Weaver and Frisell's guitar bursts with creative zest.

Shenandoah is heartfelt and soulfelt; its beautiful melody flowing from Lloyd's horn like its subject's waters, free and undammed. Harland's drums enhance its sheer natural power. All My Trials brings back a whole era, and guest Willie Nelson's querulous vocal on Last Night I Had the Strangest Dream recalls decades of draft resistance: 'And the people in the streets below were dancing round and round. / And guns and swords and uniforms were scattered on the ground.'

I Long to See You is a glorious record, full of hope, reflection, defiance and optimism shining through the agency of music. 'The deeper I drive into the ocean of sound, I find there is still deeper and further to go,' declares Lloyd after 78 years. Keep on diving!

(Wild Man Dance & I Long to See You are available on Blue Note)

Harold Lopez Nussa (Cuba) - Infused with the sounds of Cuba

Harold Lopez Nussa Trio - El Pais Maravillas (2013)

When Duke Ellington spoke about 'the West Indian influence' in African-American music way back in 1943 when he introduced his revolutionary suite Black, Brown and Beige at New York's Carnegie Hall, I wonder if the prospect of this Cuban trio was somewhere in his huge musical mind.

Its spark is the young pianist Harold Lopez Nussa, Havana-born into a family of musicians, and educated in both Cuba and France. He was a student of classical music at the Havana Conservatoire, but from his early twenties he became a devotee of jazz and a perennial performer in Havana clubs and jazz venues.

He toured Europe in 2005, playing in London, Verona and Paris, and won the piano award at the Montreux Jazz Festival, then recorded his debut solo album Sobre el Atelier, which was followed by Herencia in 2009. Now comes El Pais Maravillas, a trio album with his younger brother and drummer Ruy Adrian Lopez Nussa and Felipe Cabrera on bass. The Puerto Rican tenor saxophonist David Sanchez joins them on four tracks, giving a wider Caribbean dimension to the soundscape. Eight of the 12 tunes are Harold's creations, with Ruy Adrian and Cabrera contributing one each. This trio, and the 'country of wonders' of their record's title, is definitely all-Cuban.

The opener is Guajira and immediately the Latin influence permeates, with the handclapping, Cabrera's basswork and Harold's edgy and scintillating Cuban rhythms. Caminos introduces Sanchez. Born in Guanaybo, Puerto Rico, in 1968, he began on the tenor saxophone at the age of 12 and moved to New York City in 1988, having decided to become a musician after a year studying psychology. He studied at Rutgers University, joined Dizzy Gillespie's United Nation Orchestra in 1990, and made a powerful series of albums on the Columbia label, like Obsession (1998) Melaza (2000) and Travesia (2002) in which his powerful Puerto Rican nationalism, Caribbean loyalty and love for peace were all committedly manifest.

In Caminos Sanchez blows the theme in unison with Harold, who plays a spiky chorus. Sanchez returns for a jerking serpentine solo next to Ruy Adrian's thrashing percussion. The title tune begins with meditative solo piano before the bass and drum entry as the particular marvels of the trio's interplay begin to unify, with Harold leaping into rhythmic motion next to Ruy Adrian's clicking snares and a hummed riff sounding out behind them. Sanchez returns for La Fiesta Va with its jaunty theme and Ruy Adrian's crackling drums. Sanchez and Harold spiritedly converse, with the former's horn making belligerent arguments and Harold's talking keys giving powerful and defining answers - call and response, the centuries old, Africa-founded sonic structure.

The serene quietude of Perla Marina is a stark contrast. Harold's piano sways, with Cabrera's steadying undertow and Ruy Adrian's mollifying cymbals. It could be a lullaby, conceived next to the gentle Caribbean surf. Not so the stomping Pa' Gozar... y No Parar, which seems to be dancing down the Havana streets, full of joy and shouts of exuberance.

The strongly melodic A Camilin features Cabrera's twanging bass, full of vibrato and deep earth soundings, before Sanchez returns for the rhythmic outing of Bailando Suiza where his bold Puerto Rican horn is totally attuned to his Cuban compadres, his cadences plunging into their unified one-Caribbean sonic unity.

E'cha has Brazilian echoes even though Harold wrote it, and its melodic centre flows southwards through the Caribbean basin. Ruy Adrian's prodigious percussive energy is everywhere. In Volver there is an unaccompanied piano passage which precedes Cabrera's solo, flowing with riverine beauty, and Sanchez plays an upper-pitched chorus with notes that shower down in cadences upon his confreres.

The final track, Amanecer, which has all dawn's sense of daily discovery, with Cabrera's bass heartbeat ever-present and Harold's melodism simple and profound, concluding a precious album with Cuba at the centre of jazz creation and beauty.

(El Pais Maravillas is available on World Village)

Joe Lovano (USA) and Dave Douglas (USA) – Blistering riposte to Trumpery from jazz legends

Joe Lovano and Dave Douglas Sound Prints Quintet, Ronnie Scott's, London (2021)

It's not often that a US band will begin their gig at a world-renowned jazz venue like Ronnie Scott's with one of its co-leaders declaring about their nation's president: 'We're not the Americans who voted for the guy. We're part of the resistance!'

Such were the words of the New Jersey-born trumpeter Dave Douglas at the outset of the performance of the Sound Prints Quintet and they drew applause from almost all those present. The other co-leader, Italian-American tenor saxophonist Joe Lovano, nodded in agreement and, with the quintet playing with such vibrant unity, the sentiments were clearly commonly held.

On drums was Joey Baron, the bassist was Malaysia-born, Western Australia-bred Linda Oh and the young pianist was St Louis prodigy Lawrence Fields.

Lovano's long, rasping solo on the opener Full Sun was followed by Douglas's hard-blown and blistering chorus in a colloquy with Baron's drums, while Oh's bass work discovered a sonic mine of scintillating invention, tracing out deep, fast-changing patterns.

In Dream State, dedicated to the great tenorist Wayne Shorter, Baron - the most sociable and communal of drummers - palavered with Fields who, in Douglas's tune Ups and Downs and the Shorter classic Juju from 1964, created a piano sound of his own. Rolling yet reflective, each note-cluster of his improvisation was a timbral thought-shape.

Douglas and Lovano have created thousands of performances worldwide and dozens of albums between them over the passing decades and, hearing the beauty and power of the trumpeter's searing horn and the plunging cadences of Lovano's saxophone, you could catch the cultural resistance seething from their every breath, withering Trumpery with each note.

Humphrey Lyttelton (England) - Humph breaks the mould

Humphrey Lyttelton - Humph Experiments (2012)

Humphrey Lyttelton was always a jazz innovator and understood well how the music needed to relate to the real lives of its players and its listeners.

During the early '50s, while playing benefits for the Daily Worker and other progressive causes, he was also gradually moving away from the conventional New Orleans jazz line-up that had marked his immediate post-war music. In 1951, while sharing the same London house with the visiting Australian band leader and pianist Graeme Bell, Humph arranged some recording sessions with members of the Aussie band, including - horror of horrors to the New Orleans purists - 'Lazy' Ade Monsbrough playing alto saxophone. Even the word 'saxophone' was virtually a swear word to the jazz puritans of the time, and the presence of Monsbrough - the predecessor .of the much more adventurous altoist Bruce Turner caused Humph to be viewed by these elements as a musical apostate.

But fortunately his record producers at Parlophone included fellow innovators like a young George Martin - later of Beatles fame - and Denis Preston, who was to produce a string of classic British jazz albums from the late '50s onwards for Columbia under his Record Supervision company.

The sessions with Bell and Monsbrough are now available again on the reissue on the Lake label Humph Experiments. The Bell-Lyttelton tracks are full of grit and energy. Humph's brass lead is strong throughout with Wally Fawkes's swirling clarinet ever-present, particularly in Open House, with Monsbrough's husky alto timbre occasionally sounding a little like Pete Brown.

The two additional trumpets and trombones on Apples Be Ripe give the band a much fuller sound and Small Hour Fantasy, with Fawkes and trombonist Keith Christie soloing powerfully, creates the illusion of an early Ellingtonian small group.

But the truly historic tracks on Humph Experiments are those featuring the Grant/Lyttelton Paseo Jazz Band. By the 1950s the Windrush generation of Caribbean newcomers to Britain were establishing their own music in their adopted nation. Lord Beginner's joyous calypso celebrating the 1950 West Indies cricket triumph at Lord's, Victory Test Match, had established calypso as a familiar genre, and Caribbean musicians had been an integral part of British cultural life for centuries. Humph recognised this and joined with the Guyanese reedman Freddie Grant to form an occasional band. When he played New Orleans tunes to Grant, the Guyanese recognised them from his own tradition, confirming again New Orleans as a Caribbean city.

The union of two bands of black and white musicians playing New Orleans jazz in London became natural and organic. Lyttelton and Fawkes joined the Grant rhythm section, including bongos, cuatro, claves and maracas and Fitzroy Coleman's springing guitar, for a recreation of some Crescent City standards by Jelly Roll Morton, Kid Ory and WC Handy. The paseo is a dance in Trinidad but this band stretched from Guyana to Louisiana. Handy's Friendless Blues starts off the April 1952 session with pianist Mike McKenzie's blues-laden chords and Grant's clarinet blowing alongside Fawkes's bass clarinet and Humph playing third clarinet.

The two versions of Original Jelly Roll Blues feature Humph's dancing trumpet and the clarinets duetting in familiar unity. Grant is very much at home with the creole sounds of Mam'selle Josephine and the music soars away in Caribbean joy. Fat Tuesday has George Roberts on cowbell with Donaldo's bongos and the rhythm goes straight back to the islands in a carnival mood. In Morton's King Porter Stomp the band could be marching down Bourbon Street with Fitzroy Coleman's guitar ablaze, but the real classic of the session is London Blues, with the presence of the veteran Jamaican altoist Bertie King blowing alongside an inspired Fawkes. King's solo is rhapsodic and streaming with beauty, and he features again on McKenzie's Mike's Tangana.

These are not only superb jazz moments but also proud recognitions and assertions some 60 years ago of London as a burgeoning cosmopolis and a throbbing city of the extended African and Caribbean diaspora. Music as prophecy, a jazz message indeed.

(Humph Experiments is available on Lake)

Humphrey Lyttelton (England): 1921-2008

(2008)

I remember coming home from school one late afternoon in the mid-1950s, switching on the wireless and hearing a dancing, searing muted trumpet flying across the sitting room. 'What was this?' I thought, transfixed by its beauty and the cry of its sound, playing over a stomping blues piano. The announcer soon told me, as the swinging choruses faded into the flowery wallpaper - Bad Penny Blues played by Humphrey Lyttelton with Johnny Parker's piano. It was British jazz uncharacteristically in the British hit parade and Humph's waxed performance had impressed, inspired and snared me for life.

So, who was this man who died at the weekend but whose music always blew a message of life indestructible? Morning Star readers have frequently reminded me that this was the same musician who, from the most unlikely of backgrounds, had played at many a Daily Worker benefit in the postwar years and identified with a class that certainly wasn't the one that he was born into.

Humph was the son of an Eton housemaster, born within the walls of the most elitist private school in Britain. As a teenager, he was sent to a south Wales steelworks to do his penance among the workers and to be able to more fully understand the great gift to them of the British ruling class. The experience transformed his consciousness. He identified and empathised with the steelworking families, repudiated the steel owners and became a socialist.

He had been playing the trumpet since his boyhood and, having joined the Grenadier Guards in 1941, the story goes that he landed on the Salerno beaches in Italy in 1943, a young man armed with both gun and horn to scatter the fascist enemy.

Directly after the war, he signed up for Camberwell School of Art, met clarinettist and cartoonist Wally Fawkes - known as 'Trog' - and they both joined one of Britain's first New Orleans-inspired jazz bands, George Webb's Dixielanders.

When the Camberwell two set up their own band, Webb joined them. By the end of 1949, they had achieved jazz fame by recording with the visiting Crescent City jazz genius, clarinettist Sidney Bechet. Listen to Humph's lucid lead on Some of these Days and how he paves the way for Bechet's visceral solo. Louis Armstrong himself was later to praise Humph's trumpet talent as he became Britain's most highly regarded and leading jazz brassman.

Humph's alto saxophonist confrere, the Saltburn-born Bruce Turner, another jazz socialist who joined Humph's band in 1953 and helped to give it a transformed Kansas City sound, once told me that, put simply, there were two sorts of jazz musicians. There were those who conceived and played their music out of respect and love for the ordinary, mostly poor and black people who invented and played it from their hearts and heads, and those who played it merely as a sonic artefact with no connection to the lives or struggles of humanity. I remember that he put Humph squarely in the first category.

If you listen to the 11 minute long Blues Excursion on the prime Lake double CD Bad Penny Blues 1955 - 56, you can hear both Bruce and Humph playing with intense beauty, artistry and the deepest of feeling with Fawkes, Parker and trombonist John Picard in a way which fully illustrates Bruce's words.

Humph also became celebrated as a writer, raconteur, a broadcaster and wit, but it is his music which made him and his recorded canon will always sound out his brilliance. In 1964 and 1966, he made what I think were his greatest recordings, with one of his horn heroes, the pitch perfect Kansas trumpeter and veteran of the late 1930s Count Basie Orchestra Buck Clayton, to be heard on the Lake album Le Vrai Buck Clayton.

They played like virtual twins, so much so that, even when you listen very, very closely, it is sometimes impossible to tell the black Basieite and his white emulator apart, so profoundly do they share a mutual praise song of music and life.

That record, among hundreds, is Humph's living legacy as well as his epitaph. Hear its notes and mark them well, for they tell his story more than any words.

Harold Mabern (USA) - Tasty fare from blues-baked piano maestro

The Harold Mabern Trio - Ronnie Scott's, London (2016)

Soho was bristling this week with the piano sounds of Memphis, Tennessee, a city which has given birth to great jazz pianists - think Phineas Newborn and James Williams for a start.

But one of its finest is Harold Mabern, born there in 1936. During the late 1950s, Mabern took his keyboard brilliance to Chicago and then New York, where he played with some of the towering figures of the music, from Lionel Hampton and Sarah Vaughan to Lee Morgan, Sonny Rollins, Miles Davis and Wes Montgomery.

Between 1968 and 1970 he cut four powerful albums for the Prestige label and has never looked back. Even now, he's an integral part of the saxophonist Eric Alexander's quartet and is still making vibrant records for the High Note and Smoke labels.

At Ronnie Scott's he was accompanied by regular Massachusetts-born drummer Joe Farnsworth and London bassist Larry Bartley and the threesome went romping away with 'something from Antonio Carlos Jobim but I think he got it from Chopin.'

Mabern's hard-struck, improvisatory piano playing, Farnsworth's rhythmic undertow and Bartley, in his first outing with Mabern and playing with jumping artistry, set Ronnie Scott's alight.

As Mabern wove into a blues for Art Blakey's Jazz Messengers, you could hear his southern roots sounding, earthy yet transcendent, with

Farnsworth's drum solo tracing out a blues melody. Then the trio broke into My Favourite Things - a John Coltrane perennial - and huge Mississippi power burst from Mabern's octogenarian hands as he played it.

This was a blues-baked pianist, ageless and consummate.

Sound artist Bint Mbareh (Palestine) with Joe Namy (Lebanon)

Café Oto, London

(2025)

'I want to hit where it hits Israel the hardest. What I do doesn't change anything. I can sing my lungs out and there will still be a genocide going on right now.' Bint Mbareh's words are not those of resignation though. At the Café Oto, sitting on a low stool, her laptop making music between her and her Lebanese compadre Joe Namy, who pounded his hand drum, her voice and recorded sounds rang out the cry of Palestinian resistance. They were playing together in public for the first time.

Born in Nablus, West Bank, Bint now lives in Catford, south-east London. Her architect mother was from a village called Beit Iba, near Nablus, her civil engineer father's Palestinian family lived in Jordan. She grew up during a rare era when there was 'a semblance of peace after the Oslo Accords,' before 'all those veils were dropped.' She studied Music at the Edward Said National Conservatory with its slogan 'Today an orchestra, tomorrow a state', and in The Netherlands and Amman before she embraced Anthropology of Music at Goldsmiths' College, University of London, where she 'focussed on rain-summoning practices in the parts of Palestine I could reach.'

Namy is from Deir Mimas, in the olive groves of southern Lebanon, where Israeli drones and white phosphorus have savaged family farms: 'Their survival is a testimony to resilience. Our olive trees connect us to our land. They are rooted, enduring, a symbol of belonging.' And he adds, 'as an artist, it is difficult to create without responding to what is happening around us.'

As Namy drummed with his fingers, brushes and mallets, Mbareh strummed her lute-like buzuq and her hands slid across her laptop as she sang with a walling timbre, pulling at her long hair as she sang. I could hear the sound of water running from her keys and a voice speaking in distant Arabic. It seemed like a sound-artistry of grieving, of the sound of drones, of lamentation, while on the same night the appalling Trump announced his so-called 'peace plan' with a total ignoring of any semblance of Palestinian self-determination while he drooled for a Nobel Peace Prize.

As a sound researcher and singer Mbareh has said that she wanted to produce 'anonymised music. I wanted to avoid music as a category, so that it takes away 'I am here and I am making the music.' What does she mean by that? I asked.

'I think we live in an era where every aspect of our being - our faces, voices, languages and all our specificities, are being mined for money. So one way I've found we can resist this theft is by being anonymous, or being unintelligible to those models. One way we can do this is by joining voices such that we're not as easily identifiable as ourselves. This gives us respite from being constantly searched and identified by our devices which we surely can't live without.'

'When I talk about avoiding music as a category, I generally mean there's a musical tradition now of people entertaining other people for money and that tends to overshadow every other type of sound in music-making, like music for health, music for togetherness, music to bring the rain and music as a warning of war. I want to belong to the latter categories rather than being an entertainer.'

'I partially think that the music we or I make falls rather flat in its attempt to end the genocide. because the results are clear: the genocide is ongoing. I would rather know this failure than pretend I am starting a revolution with my music. Instead I've been recently moving towards thinking that the economic structures that the music serves and lives in are impactful, and that I can move my efforts towards more seriously changing them. For example, If I make a song that becomes successful without the aid of Spotify distribution, it is a bigger success for me than a song that I aesthetically love, but needs Spotify to survive.'

'The only option I'm confronted with is to be present with the genocide in Gaza. This happens because I'm usually curated as a result of being a Palestinian - sometimes in tokenising ways, and sometimes not. Our worlds are so tangled economically that it is quite difficult to avoid hypocrisy when I say I'm making music for Palestine. I'm still implicit in the suffering of my loved ones over there when I distribute through Spotify, when I play in venues funded by Zionists or I buy certain items from complicit companies. I find myself searching for liberatory alternatives and potentials that the world can learn from in Palestinian tradition and culture.'

'When I began making music a while ago, I was concerned with rain summoning as an alternative means of governing water bodies and sharing them amongst ourselves and our animal kin, in such ways that were challenging to hostile cultures. I think this project still lives, seeing water as a method and medium to sing with grief and memory, to point at the contradictions of trying to draw fascist borders around both the water bodies and the sounds of this world. Thinking through rain summoning helps me to demonstrate the advancement of a Palestinian culture that is using means to negotiate the seasons, time and garnering complicity and collective decision-making technologies through song.'

'In the performance you heard at Café Oto and in many others, I play an interview with a martyred political prisoner, Walid Daqqa, to indicate that the dead can still use our living bodies as mediums for their echoes and voices. It turns all those present to people who are echoing, or being the physical mediums through which his voice moves, even after his death. We can be mediums for haunting, and the haunting is a necessary political decision when so many are being vengefully killed or silenced.'

'In the interview, Daqqa talks about his closeness to the sea and that he wants to be reunited with the sea more than anything else. So I made recordings of the Mediterranean from Tunisia, and every time I play his voice, I play them together. Additionally my use of drone sounds is a choice I make to make Palestinian drones, to counter the constant, faceless, omnipresent drone warfare that Israel commits against Palestinians. I try to make drones out of human voices to give us our anonymity back for a few moments, but these drones, homemade by my Palestinian hands, are a good stand-in. I call them counterdrones. They may sound like suffering but in the expansion of suffering I try to infuse some defiance to constant settler surveillance, violence and colonialism.'

A listener like me can only write about what I hear with an imaginative understanding of what the musicians create in my ears and brain. At Café Oto I gave Mbareh some poems on Palestinian Intifada resistance written by my Sheffield school students 30 years ago. She would have been a small child then. I thought they carried the same notes of determination and defiance: words and sounds, sisters and brothers in struggle and across time and geography, here and now in East London. In her poem called 'Lifeland', Yemeni steelworker's daughter, fourteen year old Nadia's lines rang out with the dreams of Palestinians now, whether in the West Bank or in Gaza. 'To be free and to live like everyone else in the world/To be with our families/To sleep in our homes in peace/And to hope for a glorious morning!' Bint wrote to me: 'The poem by Nadia stays with me very dearly. I'm so grateful you shared it.' Words too for Bint and Joe and for Gaza now, the West Bank now, Lebanon now, Palestine now.

Chris McGregor (South Africa) - The brilliance behind a relentless upsurge

Chris McGregor's Brotherhood of Breath - Procession: Live at Toulouse (2017)

The most accomplished and farthest out of the cream of British free jazz virtuosi were ever-eager to be a part of the Brotherhood of Breath, so they too could be a confrere of this astonishing and so often rampaging music direct from the deformity of apartheid-accursed South Africa.

This was the '70s, when exiled South African horn-men like trumpeter Mongezi 'Mongs' Feza and altoist Dudu Pukwana, pianist Chris McGregor, the bass pulse-makers Johnny Dyani and Harry Miller and the thunderous subtlety of drummer Louis Moholo-Moholo found creative comradeship with English jazz rebels like tenorists Alan Skidmore, Gary Windo and Evan Parker, altoists Mike Osborne and Elton Dean, trumpeters Mark Charig and the Barbadian ace Harry Beckett in a seething amalgam of sound.

It was a decade when this London-based band proved with every note that it sprung the lies and brutal folly of the apartheid state and everything that it stood for. London-based, yes, but constantly travelling throughout Europe, sounding their living example everywhere they played. Hear their albums like Bremen to Bridgwater, Live at Willisau (Switzerland), Eclipse at Dawn (Berlin) or this uproarious concert recorded live in Toulouse, France, in May 1977 less than a year after the massacre of schoolchildren in Soweto. Procession, the album was called.

The seemingly indestructible Feza had died in December 1975, and Charig continued with the Austrian trombonist Radu Malfatti, Moholo-Moholo, Miller and Dyani, with Osborne, Pukwana, Parker and Bruce Grant on saxophones and McGregor somehow holding all this collective brilliance together. The magical pocket trumpet and irrepressible spirit of Feza is brought to life again in this opening tune You Ain't Gonna Know Me 'cos You Think You Know Me. McGregor's sonorous opening chords and Beckett's fanfare of notes introduce Mongs's familiar theme. And then it is the Brotherhood's customary sonic complexity: a continuing ensemble and bursts of solo fire over all souls playing free and a startling rhythmic base as if all the rest were drums as one theme segues into another - into McGregor's Sunrise on the Sun, Feza's Sonia or Pukwana's Kwhalo.

You hear Skidmore's Coltranish notes over the mass of sound or Parker's gurgling tenor and nothing is disconnected from the brotherly timbre, every sound is a part of the whole, an essential moment of their urgent unity. Malfatti's adenoidal solo belches its way out of the ensemble of Sunrise on the Sun above Moholo-Moholo's whistles, before Grant, playing flute, blows its antithesis with a beautiful bird-like chorus above McGregor's fraternal comping.

Sonia is a call and response theme between McGregor and the horns with the two basses plunging and vibrating while the pianist's almost church-like introduction of Kwhalo preludes nearly 19 minutes of ensemble endeavour, with individual soloists in turn emerging from the common sound but never leaving or appropriating it but staying within a constant amalgam, like the hopes of the struggle for liberation in Africa that their sound so resonantly represented. A wondrous track this, full to its brim with the promise of freedom.

Two tunes by McGregor complete the album. The first is TBS - slow, almost mournful and processional. It is Skidmore's tenor that speaks out, its narrative one of a beautiful solidarity by an English musician to this South African bandmates.

Andromeda is the final track, a tune with a powerful infusion of joy. The Caribbean man Beckett takes a solo, then the wailing Osborne and behind them the rhythm and Moholo-Moholo's everlasting African drums continue their relentless upsurge, for nothing will stop them.

(Procession: Live at Toulouse is available on Ogun)

Chris McGregor (South Africa) - Defying apartheid via piano

Chris McGregor Septet - Up To Earth
Chris McGregor Trio - Our Prayer
(2010)

Every sound he forged on his piano was a defiant riposte to apartheid - every tune he conceived for the Blue Notes, every performance blast of the Brotherhood of Breath. The son of a preacher man and born in Umtata, South Africa, in 1936, Chris McGregor's life in music was formed when, week after week as a boy, he listened to the Xhosa congregations sing hymns in his father's Church of Scotland mission. Their sound echoed in his notes all through his life.

In 1964, disgusted by the apartheid restrictions on their making music together and the deformity visited upon their nation, the Blue Notes left South Africa for Europe. After some sporadic work on the Cote D'Azur and Switzerland they arrived in London for a fortnight's gig at Ronnie Scott's - McGregor, drummer Louis Moholo-Moholo, Bassist Johnny Dyani, altoist Dudu Pukwana and trumpeter Mongezi Feza.

Life for the Blue Notes belied London's liberal reputation. Gigs were rare, money was scarce, accommodation was heartbreakingly expensive and rehearsal and practice venues were limited to Ronnie's original club venue and the Little Theatre Club in Garrick Yard. The Blue Notes soon split and followed their individual fortunes in Denmark and South America, while McGregor pursued his dream of an internationalist big band of free music, the Brotherhood of Breath. In 1969 four of the Blue Notes re-assembled in London and out of the recorded sessions came these two albums now released for the first time after four decades.

The septet session Up To Earth includes McGregor, Feza, Pukwana and Moholo-Moholo with British stalwarts John Surman on baritone and bass clarinet, tenorist Evan Parker, bassist Danny Thompson and as second bassist the San Franciscan Barre Philips. The sense of unrestrainable energy released from the first to last note of the five McGregor tunes of Up To Earth is astonishing. The session begins with the incendiary Moonlight Aloe, in which the horns, inspired by Feza's liberation fanfares, tear everything out of the theme.

The freedom of the music is irrepressibly infectious and British reedmen Parker and Surman are swept into its sheer verve and the message of its notes as if South Africa were their country too, bursting for an end to the deformity that had engulfed its people. The track ends with the becalmed fury of McGregor's coda, with only Moholo-Moholo's clicking percussion sounding him forward. Thompson's sure-walking bass founds Yickytickee, with all horns rampant like impassioned town criers proclaiming their freedom message, and Pukwana in particular in strident voice. And as the tune morphs into Union Special the performance becomes a spontaneous street march. McGregor's piano is wildly beautifully on the title tune. By the time that the final track Years

Ago Now has finished its long blast, the listener knows that this unequalled music is exactly that, born of a time when its musicians and their northern comrades yearned for South African liberation with their every proud utterance and breath.

The trio tracks of the Our Prayer album resonate just as much, with Philips's bowed intro to Church Mouse and the tinkling frenzy of McGregor's keyboard perturbations stirring the listeners' spirits. African earth and flesh radiate from another version of Moonlight Aloe, while Philips's Spike Nard has Moholo-Moholo in tempestuous tempo and McGregor matching Cecil Taylor's piano pyrotechnics.

Finally there are the 26 rousing minutes of the title tune. Called a prayer, it is also praise song for a beloved land, an anthem of its people's resistance and a chorus of hope - a story of his continent by a proud white man of Africa.

Now we have it after four decades and McGregor, who died still in exile in 1990, never had the chance to play it on his own earth. At least we can hear it now and marvel at its makers' fire, love and artistry.

(Up To Earth & Our Prayer are available on Fledg'ling)

Benet McLean (England) - Searing sound in touch with the world

Benet McLean - In the Land of Oo-Bla-Dee,
Live at the 606 & The Bopped and the Bopless
(2016)

His life in music started when he was three, when he pestered his music-loving mum to buy him a violin. Then, a few years on, a schoolmate played him his Charlie Parker and Dizzy Gillespie bop albums, and that was that - Benet McLean began his journey in jazz.

Violin, viola, guitar, cello, sharp lyrics and a stomping piano all became his fortes and by the time that he cut his second album In the Land of Oo-Bla-Dee in 2008, he had found some powerful bandmates, including saxophonist Jason Yarde, drummers Shane Forbes, Steve Washington and Troy Miller, and bassist Chris Dodd.

The album is all of a piece, with each track segueing into the next. Charlie Parker's Klact-oveeseds-tene is the opener, setting out McLean's bop loyalties with rapid and riotous skill, with Miller and Dodd keeping apace and they move on to Coltrane's Giant Steps with swinging aplomb. It moves into the slow and beautiful duo piece Rakhi, with Yarde's soprano sax birdsong hovering over McLean's earthen keys. Yarde blows a powerful alto chorus in God Be With You, where McLean's pianism began to remind me of the surging Mississippi bop rhythms of the '50s. There's much musical hokum and laughter unleashed in the album's title tune, with Yarde refusing to stop blowing an endless note at its end, and Tears Back in Time has more intense

Yarde, this time on soprano, with the inventive energies of McLean, Dodd and Washington's urgent drums bringing the album to its close.

In 2012, McLean recorded a live album at Chelsea's 606 Club as part of a fiery quartet with saxophonist Duncan Eagles, drummer Saleem Raman and bassist Jonathan 'The Wolf' Harvey.

Eagles's spiky soprano is at the centre of In the Night and McLean gives a yearning quality to Sam Cooke's A Change Gonna Come. He reveals a subliminal piano inspiration in his breakneck notes of Tatum Meets the Rap Pack and plays with a compelling assurance soloing, then comping behind a flying Eagles and a delving Harvey through Tubby Hayes's A Pint of Bitter. He's back with Coltrane in a potent reprise of Giant Steps, then steps up to Monk for a finale with a reflectively beautiful and instantaneous solo rendition of Round Midnight.

At the heart of McLean's 2016 album The Bopped and the Bopless is the huge gulf in Britain between the rich and the poor, expressed through jazz's own figurative terms, as he sings: 'This goes out to the bopped and the bopless/ A metaphor for the hoped and the have-nots/ And the homeless souls just searching for the light.'

That's how the memorable opening song makes its message with Harvey, Raman and Eagles plus Gareth Lockrane's shimmering piccolo, Noel Langley's trumpet, Donald Gamble's percussion and Ashley Slater's trombone - a big sound, with Eagles's solo stirring the mix and McLean remembering Monk again with phrases from Straight, No Chaser. Harvey's mysterious bass lines create a deep, deep vision of The Planets before the full band is crackling again on Babylon's Burning and McLean pounds his keys like a latter-day Jerry Lee Lewis with new great balls of fire burning through his notes.

Isabella-Maria Asbjornsen's scintillating harp strings introduce the love song Polly, with McLean reassuring that Tomorrow's Fear Belongs to Yesterday. Yarde's baritone comes back to Electric Bopland and the full band pulsates.

The closing track Shizannah is based on a Gabriel Faure pavane and shows another side of McLean's extraordinary musical eclecticism. His piano, violin, viola are all a part of his sonic concoction and inseparable strands of his musical oneness. The Bopped and the Bopless stews up its music with the world we live in and all its inequities as well as its joys and is a very original and potent album indeed.

(In the Land of Oo-Bla-Dee is available on BCLN, Live at the 606 on 33 Records & The Bopped and the Bopless on 33Xtreme)

Joe McPhee (USA) and Chris Corsano (USA)
Trio triumph at Café Oto
(2016)

Miami-born saxophonist and trumpeter Joe McPhee, whose father came from the Bahamas, and the phenomenal drummer Chris Corsano from New Jersey played in two separate groups with English musicians at Café Oto. On the first night they accompanied arch-bassist John Edwards and, as he settled in with McPhee and Corsano's scintillating free sounds, indulging in some fascinating call-and-response palaver, his bass was like another horn.

As McPhee blew a cawing phrase, Edwards's strings boomed their answer. McPhee's tenor saxophone was like a locomotive, reminiscent of the tone and power of the pioneer Coleman Hawkins, with Whitmanesque yelps shooting through Corsano's eternal percussive rattle-song. Here was an Anglo-US trio of joyous unity.

The next night a quartet, who'd never played together before, took the stage. McPhee and Corsano were joined by London drummer Eddie Prevost and the Caribbean-based Orphy Robinson, with his marimbas and the box-like kalimba played by fellow percussionists in Jamaica. When McPhee began to blow his tenor, there were three sets of mallets suddenly striking fire behind his horn and, as he rasped into gasping, shrieking notes, the concord of percussion behind him made storms in a furious yet still subtle sonic context.

Orphy's light yet deep kalimba strikes rendered McPhee's horn a special poignancy, while Prevost's deft cymbals gave him warm company and Corsano's flickering drum sound, suddenly turning to thunder, never left him.

Cross-Atlantic, black and white, this was a confluence of generations in a blessed East London house of sound.

Joe McPhee (USA) And Monster at Café Oto
(2025)

Of all the musicians that I love to hear live, the nonpareil of saxophone freedom and commitment to creative sound must be Joe McPhee. 86 now, Florida-born, New York State-domiciled and beloved by listeners Stateside and Europe-wide, hearing him again at Café Oto with his deepest bass heartbeat, John Edwards of Hounslow, London, is always an experience of real sonic moment. 'Protect our cultural quarter! Wake up and start to dream!' declared a large canvas placard in Ashwin Street, outside the Dalston venue, and that's what McPhee does to my consciousness, and that of thousands, although we must add the verbs 'resist' and 'organise', for all of us in Trump-and-Starmer times, both sides of the Atlantic.

Tonight McPhee and Edwards are playing in a quartet dubbed 'Monster', with two virtuosi women, Austrian bass clarinettist Susanna Gartmeyer and drummer Maria Portugal from Sao Paulo, Brazil. I was lucky enough to be sitting two yards from Portugal with her myriad of sticks, mallets, rods, gold and silver metal brushes and bars, a handsaw-like bow, tambourine and two boomerang-shaped organic shakers, all ready on a small table next to her drums.

She began with Edwards, making a symphony of scraping and sawing on her rims, with the horns of McPhee and Gartmeyer playing in a visceral unison. Gartmeyer's subterranean notes sounded mournful while McPhee blew as low as low gets on his tenor saxophone. It was like a New Orleans funeral function on a Dalston night, going home to the very provenances of jazz, before Edwards' bass began to twang with excitation and Portugal's sticks rebounded off all her nearby surfaces.

I don't know how many years and generations separate McPhee from Gartmeyer and Portugal, but the four played like close family, siblings of improvisation all, with Edwards' deeply growling arco bringing together the closest unity of sound. Portugal sang softly in Portuguese, with beautiful and inspired breath while the two horns all but sang beside her, before Gartmeyer's fleet and runaway solo suddenly radiated a burst of musical athleticism. The sounds Edwards made from his instrument were like those of another human voice: humming, throbbing, lamenting, plucking, lyricising - all from the strings and mellowed wood of his aged, companion bass.

Their third piece began with an astonishing drum solo by the Brazilian right next to me: polyrhythmic, full of volcanic fire and earth, switching from sticks to fingers with her drumsticks clenched between her teeth, she swirled the tambourine and small cymbals on the skins of her snares, becoming a drum orchestra in herself, before the octogenarian griot McPhee blew a solo like his hero Paul Robeson's voice, full of story, history and hope for now-times, truly the future in the present, for those lucky listeners here, and those passing humans in the seething London streets outside.

Rudresh Mahanthappa (USA/India) - A warm March night, with a special magnetism

Rudresh Mahanthappa, Pizza Express, Soho (2022)

After many records expressing the depth and complexity of his own unique musical essence, alto saxophonist Rudresh Mahanthappa's new eponymous album with his Hero Trio - bassist Francois Moutin and drummer Rudy Royston, he counts it as 'an immense pleasure to record music that is not my own.'

At Soho's Pizza Express he performed a selection of these tunes with astonishing fluidity, breakneck speed and warm empathy with his confreres. Moutin's deeply twanging artistry and Royston's command of every percussive surface created a threesome unity of rampaging and moving sound.

The coda of the sprinting opener, Charlie Parker's Red Cross, pealed out like some joyous birdsong. Mahanthappa told his listeners how at the age of five, he heard Stevie Wonder's Overjoyed while watching Sesame Street and how much it affected him. He played its theme with a lovingly emotive remembrance.

A life's journey carried on singing from his horn as he played Keith Jarrett's The Windup, which as a teenager he learned from an album he borrowed from a Boulder, Colorado, public library. Full of the fire of discovery and youth, you could believe it when he confessed how much the tune had changed his life.

The album includes tracks remembering Ornette Coleman, Gershwin and Johnny Cash, and as he played such a diversity of themes succoured by his own Indian heritage, you could hear first-hand a musical life relived with love and gratitude.

Hear the trio live or buy the record, its invocation of an age of music savoured and fully lived is powerful and memorable, and provokes our own lives of loved sounds. Here, in the midst of Soho on a warm March night, it had a special magnetism.

(Hero Trio is available on Whirlwind Records)

Nduduzo Makhatini (South Africa) - We are looking at spiritual affinities and how these liberate and at the same time transcend the political

South African pianist Nduduzo Makhatini
(2024)

Nduduzo Makhatini is an extraordinary pianist. Born in Umgungundlovu, Pietermaritzburg, South Africa in 1982, his musical universe carries the spirits of his Zulu ancestry, engendered through his piano studies at Durban University of Technology and his doctoral research at the University of Stellenbosch. His new album, Unomkhubalwane, delves into his people's spiritual history. Its title is the name of the rain goddess and symbol of creation and fertility.

With him are bassist Zwelakhe-Duma Bell Le Pere, born and raised in the US, whose father and grandfather (an ex-secretary of the African National Congress) were steeped in the liberation movement, and the veteran Cuban drummer Francisco Mela, born in Bayamo in 1968 and a virtuoso who has played with such US jazz luminaries as pianists McCoy Tyner and Kenny Barron, and saxophonist Joe Lovano.

What are his musical roots? 'I was born into a musical family and village,' says Makhatini. 'Growing up, I was introduced to various styles of Zulu indigenous music, mostly within the context of ritual ceremonies. My mother Nomajerusalema was my first piano teacher and my greatest musical inspiration, period. Then I started playing professionally in 2001, when I studied music at the University of KwaZulu, Natal.'

How has his music sought to overcome the scars of Apartheid? 'My music responds to all forms of dehumanisation,' he explains, 'by focusing on transcendent strategies that allow for the break with the metaphysical, as a way to rise above the normative oppressions that engulf humanity.'

'Unomkhubalwane stands as a symbol to remind us that Africa is the mother of creation and all ancient civilisations. Using the language of water, she reminds us of our own freedoms.' A sad reflection on our own polluted and sewage-filled rivers. 'Essentially,' he says, 'the album's music seeks to enunciate from a place of text, myth and discourse, to bring our attention to creation principles that can save the humanity project that has gone so wrong. This album is an invitation to a kind of rebirth.'

Some commission this, from the classic Blue Note label that seven decades ago gave us the beginnings of Miles, Coltrane, Blakey and Rollins. For the trio of Unomkhubulwane irrigate the now-times soundscape with their balmy, liberating notes and there is no timbral aridity about their music. Le Pere's bass dances and flows, and Mela's drums gush with Caribbean springs and streams. Nduduzo's piano - sometimes like Abdullah Ibrahim in libation tracks like Uxolo or the water spirits of Izinkonjama, and at other times splashing down their very own cataracts and cascades of sound - waters the soul with their freshness.

I ask him about Mela's Cuban drumming, a Cuito Cuanavale of revolutionary sound, reminding listeners of Cuba's contribution to finally defeating the South African Apartheid army in Angola in 1987/88. 'Those connections are definitely there,' he asserts. 'But more than anything we are looking at spiritual affinities and how these liberate and at the same time transcend the political. We are concerned with modalities of healing black lives and moving towards collective memory.'

And such memory embraces the great generation of hugely influential South African musicians who came to Europe to escape from and continually defy Apartheid from the 1960s onwards: Ibrahim, the Blue Notes, Harry Miller, Claude Deppa, Nchuks Bonga. 'I feel grateful to be part of such an important history and lineage of South African jazz, both in our country and in 'exile' discourses that emerged in London and elsewhere in Europe during Apartheid.'

'And there is definitely a generation of musicians now in South Africa that shares with the earlier musicians in building consciousness which would help to liberate the nation from postcolonialism. This is expressed in current jazz music through musical memories and connections with the past.'

Unomkhubulwane as an album is a progenitor of this musical discourse. It's a beautiful listen to a new Africa in fluid sound, and a statement of a defiant past in the present too.

(Unomkhubulwane is available on Blue Note Records)

Ron Miles (USA) - I Am A Man & Old Main Chapel (2025)

In February 1968 a strike of 1,300 sanitation workers in Memphis, Tennessee for improved pay and conditions was called, following the deaths of two workers, Echol Cole and Robert Walker, crushed by the compactor of their garbage truck after segregation laws prevented them finding shelter from the torrential rain in a nearby building. Their widows were refused insurance benefits, and were granted just $500 funeral expenses from the city authorities.

The strike provoked widespread attention and support, and amongst those who joined the defiant march of March 18 was civil rights leader Martin Luther King. After police sought to repress the march another was called. On the eve of the rearranged march of April 4, King was assassinated while standing on his Memphis motel balcony.

The epochal slogan of black working class assertion was 'I am a man', the message on a thousand placards on their marches. These words were revived by the late trumpeter, Ron Miles, as the title of his 2017 album, one of his last and finest before his death from lung cancer in 2022.

Miles had been born in Indianapolis in 1963, where his parents were federal civil servants. The family moved to Denver, Colorado in 1974, where his parents thought the cooler climate would give relief to Ron's asthma. He started on trumpet at high school, studied Music at the University of Colorado and earned a scholarship to the Manhattan School of Music. During a 35 year career, mostly spent in Denver, and twelve albums, he became Professor of Music at the Metropolitan State University of Denver.

The album 'I am a man' has Miles playing in an all-star quintet with Houston pianist Jason Moran, Shreveport, Louisiana drummer Brian Blade, guitarist from Baltimore Bill Frisell and Californian bassist Thomas Morgan. It's a memorable album with virtuoso playing by all members, bringing back historical memories of courage and struggle.

The title tune has a powerful melody made stronger by Miles' lyrical horn and Frisell's chinking notes. As Miles' ascendant phrases reach skywards, all the history comes singing for justice. Moran's Texan piano echoes the blues in Darken My Door as he opens the track with Morgan's delving bass and Blade's rattling snares. Miles blows his ardent and insurgent Christian message in Revolutionary Congregation, and his belief that 'standing up and fighting for others.... the idea of social change and fighting for social injustice is a holy cause'. A free improvising ensemble sequence underlines his assertion.

Miles' salute to his mother, Mother Juggler, is upbeat with all compadres in positive spirits. His horn sings with love and Frisell and Moran play like empathetic brothers. All the album's compositions are by Miles, and the closer, Is There Room in Your Heart for a Man Like Me? appeals with a beautiful gentleness and delicacy from Miles' trumpet.

Miles' superb musicianship has been well-remembered since his passing, no more so than in the live posthumous Blue Note album Old Main Chapel, where he joined his old confreres Frisell and Blade in a finely recorded 2011 concert in Colorado University's Boulder campus. 'If I could play any place in the world,' he declared, 'it would be in this room.'

The album's first notes from the opener Mr. Kevin, are played with Miles' customary subdued fragility and amplified perfectly by the Chapel's acoustics, signalling the sensitivities of all three musicians for the entire concert. Miles has an understated pastel sound, never overblowing, and all through the concert it is as if he is quietly talking through his horn.

When I interviewed the Oregon-born trumpeter Nate Wooley in 2024, he told me what a profound influence Miles had upon him when he was a young musician. 'I found Ron's music when I was still at high school and met him when I was at college in Oregon. He was always practising and thinking about music, and I felt a kinship with that. He kept me going at a time of personal crisis when I was ready to quit. He helped me move to Denver, where I was able to get things together, just working on trumpet. I don't go a day without thinking of him when I practise. Beyond all the music, Ron was a perfect model of an empathetic and ethical human being. Our playing diverged after a time, as it should be, but I've never lost my love and respect for who he was as a searching musician and a human being living a strong but gentle life in the world.'

Just listen to his hornsong, and the trio brilliance on the Old Chapel album - on tracks like There Aint no Sweet Man that's Worth the Salt of My Tears, or the thematic, quietly assertive I Will Be Free. They say everything that those Memphis sanitation workers declared and demanded about their humanity in 1968: 'I am a man'.

(I Am A Man is available on Yellowbird Records and Old Main Chapel on Blue Note Records)

Harry Miller (South Africa) - A flaring spirit of jazz

Harry Miller - Different Times, Different Places (2014)

I remember him as the bulwark bassist of a monster trio that used to play most weeks in a public bar, smoke-filled and cramped, where beyond what you paid for a pint of bitter there was no cost to hear some of the finest avant-garde musicians in Britain like drummer John Stevens, pianist Stan Tracey and the archbassist born in Johannesburg, South Africa, in 1941 Harry Miller.

This was an unremarkable pub called The Plough in Stockwell, south London, during the early '70s. Miller lived in a council flat with his wife Hazel - the co-founder of Ogun Records - just up the road, near Stockwell Tube station. He came to London as an exile from apartheid in 1961, in the wake of other epochal South African musicians like drummer Louis Moholo-Moholo, altoist Dudu Pukwana, bassist Johnny Dyani and pianist Chris McGregor - all members of the Blue Notes who blew such storms within the relatively placid British jazz scene of the time. Like then he was a torch within British jazz, flaring for a little more than two decades, before dying in the Netherlands in 1983, when a huge wind caused the van that he, other band mates and his bass were riding in, to leave the road. It was a tragic loss to all music and the difficult but glorious art of the bass. Miller was one of its prime exponents, and if you want to know how he did it listen to this record. It is made up of two sessions, one in London in 1973 with Moholo-Moholo, McGregor, Nick Evans on trombone and the miraculous British altoist Mike Osborne. The other, from 1976, was recorded at the Chateauvallon Festival in France, with Moholo-Moholo and Osborne, but with three other Englishmen - trombonist Malcolm Griffiths, trumpeter Mark Charig and the Bristol pianist Keith Tippett.

The opening London track is the beautifully balladic Bloomfield, in which Miller's pulsating strings ground Osborne's singing alto as McGregor's notes gradually take strength. This rhapsodic soon changes for the fleeting pace of Quandary with Evans's quicksilver slides racing through the first section before Osborne comes rampaging in, fronting Moholo-Moholo's crashing drums. Evans comes blustering in, with passages which sometimes sound as if he is in the midst of a New Orleans street parade. McGregor's fiery fingers rediscover all his keys, and behind everything is Miller's eternal pulse, adding a universal life to all his confreres. The horns blow out a familiar riff on Touch Hungry, then Evans's long, growling chorus gives sound to the needy stomach before Osborne breaks in alongside Miller's phenomenal bounce. McGregor hurtles through his notes, as free as a bird above the veldtlands before Miller's bass has a jumping, springing interlude and the quintet reunites for a final ensemble.

The opus Mofolo is the first Chateauvallon track and the extra horn creates a much fuller sound, another layer of brass with Charig's edge-filled trumpet sound responding to Tippett's combustive piano phrases and Harry's throbbing heartbeat. Osborne comes in racing, his notes splattering everywhere. Griffiths's tuba-like solo explores the lower depths.

The almost churchlike beginning to Something Like This gives the sensation of Miller's vibrating notes sounding like a huge insect buzzing in and out of the pews. Moholo-Moholo rattles behind him and Tippett charges up the keys. Griffiths enters growling and distressed, like a lost tailgate trombonist in an unknown Crescent City back alley, before Tippett strides out on a familiar riff and Charig enters on a higher plane, leading the ensemble.
Osborne's alto comes singing through the harmonies for an impassioned Ornette Coleman-like chorus, as the theme segues into a French version of Touch Hungry, with Charig testing his chops with an outstanding opening chorus.

The final track is the 17 minutes of Eli's Song, and Miller's bass is in the lead, superbly recorded, with all his confreres' solos stemming from his audacious, elemental bass at the centre of the sound.

And thanks be to the pioneering spirit too of Ogun Records which keeps him there as an example to anyone, anywhere who ever picks up their bass.

(Different Times, Different Places is available on Ogun Records)

Charles Mingus (USA) - Forceful political engagement

The continued importance of Charles Mingus who infused contemporary jazz's with uncompromising political comment (2022)

April marked the centenary of the birth of the great jazz bass virtuoso, Charles Mingus. Born in Nogales, Arizona, on the US frontier with Mexico with a father who was a sergeant in the US army and a cosmopolitan lineage of African-American, Chinese and Native American, he grew up in Watts, Los Angeles, a tough and conflicted black neighbourhood.

His innovative music fused with the political realities of the times he lived through - compositions like Fables of Faubus, lampooning the racist buffoonery of the state governor of Arkansas, who in 1957 blocked the entry of black students into the high school of Little Rock with state troopers, or in 1964 his Meditation on a Pair of Wire Cutters, gave full support to the Civil Rights movement. While his Oh Lord! Don't Let them Drop that Atomic Bomb on Me of 1961 anticipated the Cuban Missile Crisis, his 1965 recording, They Trespass the Land of the Sacred Sioux put his huge cultural weight behind the US Native American movement. Later titles on his two Changes albums of 1975 exposed the racist prison violence of Lockdown America with his Remember Rockefeller at Attica and the rampaging Free Cell Block F, 'tis Nazi USA.

Always a mentor of huge youthful talent, his bands developed the jazz genius of saxophonists Eric Dolphy, George Adams, Clifford Jordan and Rahsaan Roland Kirk and pianists like Jackie Byard, Horace Parlan and Don Pullen. Even decades after his death in 1979, the Mingus Big Band still tours the world, keeping his music alive.

And 2022 brings other Mingus delights. Mingus: The Lost Album (Resonance Records) is the first-ever pressing of a jewel of a discovery, its superb sound quality reviving Mingus's final London performances at Ronnie Scott's, Soho, in August 1972 with some brilliant confreres: 19-year-old trumpeter Jon Faddis, alto saxophonist Charles McPherson, drummer Roy Brooks and two virtually unknown but super-charged sidemen - pianist John Foster and tenor saxophonist Bobby Jones.

It's a throbbing album, fully redolent of its era - 35 minutes of Fables of Faubus has some superb, flying McPherson with Mingus's earthy, grounding bass in full accord, a high-note, incisive Faddis, some stop-time rollicking Foster piano and Jones's audacious horn reinventions before Mingus extraordinarily allusive, witty bass recalls all Americana: When Johnny Comes Marching Home, Over the Rainbow, My Old Kentucky Home, Down by the Riverside and more and more.

Mingus 2022 has been given to us at another Soho venue, round the corner from Ronnie's at Pizza Express, Dean Street, where seasoned British bassman and outstanding jazz mentor Gary Crosby of Jazz Jamaica, Jazz Warriors and Nu Troop, leads a sextet recalling the tunes of the late-life Mingus album, Mingus Moves of 1973. With him are youthful and powerful jazz talents: trumpeter Mark Kavuma, altoist Aleksandra Topczewska, pianist Alex Ho, tenorist David Kayode and drummer Daniel Smithson, their musical souls deep in the jazz tradition.

Feeding from Crosby's plunging bass, Ho's swinging notes and Smithson's crackling beat, Topczewska's melodic flair, volleys of succulent notes and piercing flutesong flew through Soho, while Uganda-born Kavuma's red-hot, sharp-edged sound cut through the air like a re-born Howard McGhee. Kayode's warm-toned horn on his debut outing with the band blew a more soothing message. It was a fitting and diverse way to celebrate the music of a great jazz innovator and militant.

Mancunians, jazz lovers all! Don't miss them when they play at Band on the Wall! You're in for another grooving session. Mingus's music lives on across England too, north and south, with all its heat, subtlety and rebellion.

The Mingus Big Band (USA/Russia) - Stirring Fusion of Jazz and Politics

Live at Ronnie Scott's & Blues and Politics
(1999)

The musical genius of the late Charles Mingus found vibrant expression during a recent week of performances by the 14-piece Mingus Big Band at Ronnie Scott's, which also heralded the release of the band's new album Blues and Politics, featuring some of the great bassman's most committed and passionate compositions.

The Mingus Big Band has a fluctuating personnel and the Ronnie's line-up was as superb as it gets. Altoist Bobby Watson gave a soaring performance, while the cavernous tenor saxophone sound of John Stubblefield - who every year looks more and more like his late tenor hero Ben Webster - filled every square inch of the venue with his own huge and beautiful tone. Fellow tenorist, the Vancouver-born Seamus Blake, offered a yearning rendition of Mingus' tribute to Lester Young, Goodbye Pork Pie Hat. In the trombone chairs, the young Jamal Haynes - his locks as long as his horn - sat next to Ellington veteran Britt Woodman, who was a youthful friend of Mingus in Los Angeles and persuaded him to change his main instrument from cello to double bass in their teens.

In a memorable Oh Lord! Don't let them Drop that Atomic Bomb on Me, Haynes sang a bluesy chorus. 'Don't drop it! Stop it! Be-bop it!' he shouted, then growled a solo and left it to the brilliant slides of the older trombonist to add a solo from another era. To see these two generations juxtaposed in this way, with the younger showing such friendship and respect for his veteran bandmate, helping him with his mike and making him comfortable in that small space, was a deeply moving expression of jazz comradeship.

Among the trumpets, the driving high notes of Philip Harper made a startling contrast to the more picked-out and muted artistry of Eddie Henderson, as the band soared through Tijuana Gift Shop, Nostalgia in Times Square and the ruefully melodic Diane. Haitian Fight Song, Mingus' tribute to Toussaint L'Ouverture and the revolutionary tradition of Haiti, was played with passion and joy. Russian bassist Boris Kozlov reinvented Mingus' original opening cadenza and the performance included a rocking solo from the band's powerful and prestigious pianist, John Hicks.

The new album Blues and Politics contains a number of these tunes, plus others, performed in the same driving and utterly authentic way. It Was a Lonely Day in Selma, Alabama opens the album, with Mingus' original vocal chorus from a 1965 concert, which was re-discovered by his widow Sue (the band's instigator), spliced into the track. The writer's voice invokes 'the people gathering there to march and walk for freedom', and the Civil Rights struggle is brought into the heart of the present. As the now-times thunder of the band formed in his name sounds out in his words, Mingus speaks to all of us:

'So stand fast young/old mules,
Soothe in contemplation,
Thy burning whole and aching thigh,
Your stubbornness is of the living
And cruel anxiety is about to die.'

Don't Let it Happen Here employs Pastor Niemoller's anti-fascist lyrics ('One day they came and they took the communists/And I said nothing because I was not a communist...') in a new context, with a narration by Mingus' son Eric and forceful solos from trumpeter Randy Brecker and baritone saxophonist Ronnie Cuber. Memories of the repression suffered by Civil Rights activists inspired Mingus to write Meditations for a Pair of Wire Cutters, when one of his bandmates at the time, altoist Eric Dolphy, told him that he had seen prison camps in the South where militants were being kept behind electric barbed wire fences. Alex Foster, playing alto saxophone and flute, bassist Kozlov and altoist Vincent Herring relive the historical moment through a succession of searing solos.

For those who doubt that the jazz idiom can forge the most highly-charged and inspiring political music - full of beauty, movement and intense power - they should hear this selection from the Mingus Big Band. It combines extraordinary artistry with a profound sense of commitment to recreate an era when the United States was on the edge, fascist forces loomed large and real - and brave men and women used and gave their lives to push freedom forward.

Alongside Mingus, they also thought that 'no matter what kind of work people did, they should involve themselves totally with all the discrimination they ran into.' And not 'just the black ghettos. but the white ghettos and the Japanese ghettos, the Chinese ghettos, all the ghettos of the world.' Mingus lives again in the musicianship of the Mingus Big Band in performance and on disc. Make sure you make the trip to Ronnie Scott's for their next tempestuous visit.

(Blues and Politics is available on Dreyfus Records)

Robert Mitchell (England/Grenada) & Omar Puente (Cuba) – Across the Caribbean

Robert Mitchell and Omar Puente – Bridges (2009)

'One Caribbean!' was Maurice Bishop's eternal cry and his words were manifested with no greater depth and vitality than what Cuba gave to the 'Revo' in Grenada's four years of revolutionary upsurge. Bishop's defiant slogan came roaring back to me as I listened to the beautiful duo album Bridges and the unity between London-born pianist of Grenadian roots Robert Mitchell and Omar Puente, a violinist from Santiago de Cuba, also living in London.

Puente dedicates the album to his homeland. 'For my education and health, for the chance to play with and learn from some of the greatest talents in music and for the culture and environment that made me want to.' That included studying classical music at the Escuela Nacional de Arte in Havana, alongside jazz masters such as Chucho Valdez and Cuban traditional music maestros Ruben Gonzales and Guillermo Rubalcaba - an apprenticeship like no other for a London-based jazz musician. The Ilford-born Mitchell had his dose of serious tuition too at the Guildhall School of Music and Drama, before stints with Tomorrow's Warriors and Gary Crosby's Nutroop, as well as his own sextet Panacea.

Mitchell and Puente are two genuine originals and their union throbs with invention and artistry. Puente plays electric violin, which amplifies his resonating vibrato effects astonishingly, as if he is a string quartet in one. Mitchell's notes are full, magisterial and thunder with sound and energy, but he can also play with a quiet and moving delicacy. Between them they share six of the album's eight compositions.

The opener Somebody Backstage is Puente's tribute to all those who have helped him. 'Every performance needs more than a performer,' he asserts in the sleeve notes. He plucks his strings like a bass virtuoso, while Mitchell chimes out his chords like defiant bells. The melody is almost anthemic, Puente's bow sawing with immense power.

Almendra is all-Cuban. Puente describes it as his parents' favourite and plays with a joy and brilliance, which clearly affects his partner's eastern Caribbean lineage and vibrancy as Mitchell pounds into a solo of life-loving rapture. The 13 minutes of Reflection Of A Bee-Hummingbird is a tribute to the zumzum, the world's smallest bird and native to Cuba - 'a testament to the will to survive,' affirms Puente. It is a track of dazzling contrasts, gentle melodies from Mitchell's keys and rhapsodic episodes from Puente. Power, tenderness and beauty, a commentary on the Cuban revolution's brave survival too, during half a century of assault and contempt from its most powerful neighbour.

Why is it that, when I hear these two musicians at work, I remember the Cuban doctors, agronomists, dentists and airport construction workers who I met during the 'Revo' in Grenada, which was made by Caribbean people 30 years ago this week. It is because Bridges is a proud sonic poem to Caribbean oneness and nationhood - made in London.

(Bridges is available on F-1RE)

Anmol Mohara (Nepal) - Across The Sea
(2025)

I never thought I'd ever be reviewing a jazz album birthed in the foothills of the Himalayas, but the Nepali percussionist Anmol Mohara's Across the Sea is certainly that, and plenty more too. 'My music is deeply rooted in Nepali culture and tradition, but I blend these roots with my love for the improvisational element of jazz and the wide range of musical influences that have shaped me,' he asserts.

Born in Dharan, Nepal in 2000, he grew up in an urban setting. 'I started playing congas at five with my uncles in cultural festivals,' he told me, but in 2009 he began to study at the Nepal Music Centre in Kathmandu, taking lessons on tabla and madal - a two-headed cylindrical hand drum. 'As a teenager I liked many different styles, particularly rock, fusion and funk.'

'I arrived in England in 2015 because of my family's Gurkha background. There's a strong British Nepali community here in places in London like Woolwich and Plumstead, and Colchester, Reading, Bracknell and Aldershot. The older generations who grew up in Nepal love the traditional music, but the younger ones aren't so exposed to it. I was always curious about jazz. There's a small jazz scene in Nepal, which is getting stronger.'

His studies at the Royal Academy of Music (2016 - 2018) took him further into the music. 'Early inspiration albums for me were Miles Davis' Nefertiti, Joe Henderson's Page One and Michael Brecker's Tales from the Hudson.' But it was his later studies at the Guildhall School of Music and

Drama that inspired Across the Sea.. In a cosmopolitan musical setting with young Guildhall musical friends from Nepal, Romania, Brazil and Britain, its songs' lyrics are in both English and Nepal's Tharu language. Sakhiye Ho, for example, celebrates Naghi, a major Nepali festival, and Silu is a traditional song about a pilgrimage to Lake Gosaikunda, with a beautifully delicate tenor saxophone solo by Simeon May.

Mohara sees his song Migrant as 'the album's heartbeat, with a bitter-sweet feeling.' It's the closest sound to a Nepali blues. With a tone of lamentation he sings: 'Where do I fit?/I ask myself/Where do I fit?/It's so hard to breathe/With a smile outside there's so much to hide.'

Yet this doleful tone is not typical of the more exuberant air of most of the album. 'It's a joyful record that explores themes of tradition, culture, identity, migration and belonging,' he affirms. 'I started composing my own music a few years back while I was studying at Guildhall, so the music on the album is the first I've ever composed or arranged. My time there helped boost my confidence as composer and performer.'

It is the evolving multi-rhythmic virtuosity of Mohara's percussive skills that creates the very different ambiance of the album's rhythmic bloodstream.. Just listen to the track called A Rhythmic Guy for evidence of this. 'I'm stimulated by traditional Nepali rhythms and those from other cultures,' he declares, 'so it's quite varied. I enjoy putting traditional rhythms on the drum kit.'

As an ever-expansive musician he is looking forward to creating 'more musical collaborations and in-depth musical stories', and has already played them at venues like Ronnie Scott's and the Vortex. So look out for him and hear the rootsy sound of Nepal across the heart of Britain.

(Across The Sea is available on Lomna Records)

Louis Moholo-Moholo (South Africa) - Sheer sonic adventure

The Dedication Orchestra - Ixesha (Time)
(2012)

It's too simplistic to say that jazz came from the United States. For a whole generation of the finest and most original British jazz musicians now reaching their vintage years, it came rampant with inspiration and defiant dreams of freedom from the apartheid-cursed and humanity-blessed earth of South Africa.

It came with the bitter exile of the horns of the Queensborough trumpeter Mongezi Feza and the Port Elizabeth alto saxophonist Dudu Pukwana, with the strident piano keys of Abdullah Ibrahim of Cape Town and Chris McGregor of Umtata, with the thundering drums of Louis Moholo-Moholo, another Cape Towner and the last surviving member of the epochal band the Blue Notes, and the plunging, pulsating bass strings of Johnny Dyani of East London and Harry Miller of Johannesburg, all exiles from horrific and demeaning state racism, all seekers of musical and political liberation, all artistes of astonishing craft and sheer sonic adventure.

Ixesha is an eloquent and joyous expression of this South African influence. Take its players - tenorist Evan Parker, pianist Keith Tippett, trombonist Paul Rutherford, Harry Beckett and Kenny Wheeler, London-based faraway trumpeters born in Barbados and Toronto respectively, Lol Coxhill the busking soprano saxophonist of Charing Cross and the Embankment, baritonist Chris Biscoe and bassist Paul Rogers. All were indelibly marked and fired by this sudden pantheon of phenomenal Africans making music across the smoky cellars and bustling pub venues of the London jazz scene of the 1960s.

Powerful jazz comrades too these South African and British musicians became and by 1992, when the Dedication Orchestra was formed to record its first album for the Ogun label, Spirits Rejoice, Feza, Dyani, Pukwana, McGregor and Miller had all died. The Blue Notes Memorial Trust was formed to help the continued development of jazz in South Africa and the proceeds from the record helped the work of the MAPP (Musical Action for People's Progress) school in Cape Town as well as fund memorial stones at the burial places of Dyani, Feza and Pukwana. Ixesha followed in 1994 and tenorist Sean Bergin, Moholo-Moholo and trumpeter Claude Deppa were also on hand to add the South African notes.

From the off, with Coxhill's soprano piercingly resplendent, McGregor's jaunty Travelling Somewhere, which also has a wondrous blast from Rutherford's slides, the Dedication Orchestra is definitely on the move. Moholo-Moholo's drums and brushes keep Feza's Sondela beautifully buoyant and Deppa has a poised chorus, while on Blues For Nick, dedicated to the original Blue Notes tenorist Nick Moyake, Biscoe's baritone is blistering, gushing out burning up notes.

Miller wrote Mofolo in 1971 after a momentous trio performance at Soweto's Mofolo dance hall. Tenorist Sean Bergin and ex-Soft Machine altoist Elton Dean blow their horns with a jubilant power, while Biscoe's still fiery baritone growls and Marc Charig's trumpet wails and soars through the mysterious journey of McGregor's tune The Serpent's Kindly Eye.

A marvellously long Beckett moment heralds Pukwana's Mra (Mate). Fleeting, gifted with breath-wings he flies above Pukwana's rumbustious theme of friendship and love. Angel-Nomali was Pukwana's tune for his daughter, arranged by Wheeler. Tippett's opening unaccompanied solo sounds like a song for a child and the trumpet ensemble blow their own lullaby before altoist Mike Williams plays a soothing refrain, Neil Metcalfe's flute flies around the cot, Deppa is the dream-maker and Rogers's bass footsteps walk into slumber - a track of profound tenderness.

Rogers and Moholo-Moholo create an astonishing duet at the start of Dyani's With You Sunshine, a blessing-song of health and prosperity. Deppa's chirping brass is almost like birdsong. Pukwana wrote Bird Lives for his great

Kansas City predecessor Charlie Parker, one of his prime inspirations. Tippett begins with some untypical bop piano before the ensemble saunters in and Williams blows a dancing alto solo. The final track is also the title track, celebrating the fall of apartheid by Moholo-Moholo, the only Blue Note who lived through to its end. Part chant, part anthem, part praise-song for the South African future, it takes hope and power from Bristolian Parker's huge tenor chorus at the heart of the orchestra.

It fades into the present, leaving its listeners suspended in now-times, perhaps remembering the serene and exultant music of a generation who found both joy and resistance in the very heart of the unique and freedom-forming sounds that they made, living in banishment but also living in the midst of the absolute liberation of their music. Ixesha (Time) told and will certainly tell again.

(Ixesha (Time) is available on Ogun)

Louis Moholo-Moholo (South Africa) - Cymbals and sonic fire

The passion and urgency of the Blue Notes' music
during the apartheid era is powerful, political jazz at its best
Louis Moholo-Moholo, Dudu Pukwana, Johnny Dyani
with Rev Frank Wright - Spiritual Knowledge And Grace
Blue Notes - Before The Wind Changes
(2013)

From June to July 1979 while anti-apartheid resistance within their home nation South Africa was raging, the four surviving Blue Notes, altoist Dudu Pukwana, bassist Johnny Dyani, Pianist Chris McGregor and drummer Louis Moholo-Moholo toured Holland and Belgium, bringing powerful jazz as their political message to thousands of dedicated listeners. Their fifth confrere trumpeter Mongezi Feza had died in British exile four years before.

On June 22 the series of live appearances was due to begin at the Jazzclub De Markt in Eindhoven but McGregor had been detained by transport problems and only three of the band members were there. News got around that pioneering free tenor saxophonist the, Rev Frank Wright, born in 1935 in Grenada, Mississippi, was in town and keen to play, and so for the night the Blue Notes took on a totally new instrumentation. Moholo-Moholo had played with Wright before as a part of Peter Brotzmann's band Alarm, but for Dyani and Pukwana this would be a completely novel encounter. The 69 minutes of music on the album Spiritual Knowledge And Grace consists of two long tracks the first of which, Ancient Spirit, begins with bells, Moholo-Moholo's rattling drums and the two horns in free colloquy.

Wright began his musical career as an electric bassist in R&B bands before a life-changing meeting with Albert Ayler in Cleveland in 1963 showed him how a tenor saxophone could howl, rhapsodise and preach. By the early

'70s he was in Europe, where his avant-garde sounds found appreciation and many kindred spirits, and Pukwana in particular with his rampaging lines and whistling birdsong is a powerfully empathetic partner. Dyani's bass throbs with deep fire and Moholo-Moholo's drums are everywhere. Dyani and Pukwana both have chordal stints on the piano. When Wright returns to solo on the 25th minute, his is a testifying to the joy of being with African musical griots there in Europe, and the pain of knowing well the reason why they are there. And it is as if Dudu finishes the story that he begins, with grace, speed, blues and witness.

The other track is Contemporary Fire, and perhaps all four are thinking of fellow South Africans close to the Cape as they play. Dyani plays piano alongside Dudu's skittering alto, Wright bursts into a storm of cymbals and the sonic fire blazes across the Veldt, there in the Netherlands. When Dyani returns to his vibrating bass strings and the voices begin to leap out through the restless notes, the return to Africa sounds almost complete.

Nine days later and a different, if more accustomed, foursome were set to play at the Jazzclub de Hoop in Waregem, Belgium. McGregor was there with his three old Blue Note companions, and some of the material was more familiar too as the quartet start the night's proceedings with Dyani's Ithi Gui. The quasi-folk melody is jaunty and joyous and Pukwana's breezy assurance is as if he is blowing at a family wedding feast. McGregor's keyboard lines reach out to Moholo-Moholo's complex rhythms - these are brother-artistes who know each other's music intimately, a truth also illustrated all the way through McGregor's composition Mange, where Pukwana plays with a more blues-drenched sound and Moholo-Moholo's cymbals clash with mounting relish.

Lonta Uyagula is a traditional tune translated as 'the poor child is sick' and the grim news is shouted and blown to all ears. Pukwana's horn is the crier with the news and the message is direct and momentous and grows in passion and urgency, even picking up Ellingtonian echoes of In A Mellotone as it calls out its warning. Pukwana's piece, The Bride, combines free choruses from the composer and McGregor, taken at a flying pace while the 23 minutes of Dyani's Funk Dern Dudu gives all members powerful release. The session ends with Dyani's Wish You Sunshine, prophetic enough of the end of apartheid after more than a long decade hence.

The wind was always changing for the Blue Notes, and how they missed Mongezi's ever-ebullient horn after 1975. As the years passed after this recording, first Dyani died in Berlin in 1986, then 1990 brought the farewells to McGregor in Ager, France and Pukwana in London - all in exile. The survivor is Moholo- Moholo, still hugely active at 72, both in his homeland and during his frequent performing and recording visits to Europe.

As they all shout for freedom at the end of Funk Dern Dudu, 'Amandla!

(Spiritual Knowledge And Grace & Before The Wind Changes are available on Ogun)

Louis Moholo-Moholo (South Africa) - Good vibrations from the capital

A great week at the London Jazz Festival
(2010)

My week began at the South Bank's Purcell Room to catch trumpeter Bobby Bradford blowing with three improvising Norwegians - saxophonist Frode Gjerstad, bassist Ingebright Haker Flaten and drummer Paal Nilssen-Love.

Bradford's breathy fanfares, meaningful quietudes and horn narratives wove into Gjerstad's flickering sopranino saxophone to create an astonishing amalgam.

Next up was the saxophone glory of two outstanding British veterans at an evening session in Soho's Pizza Express. Peter King swung and soared through Jobim's Brazilian opus Wave and with pianist Steve Melling, bassist Geoff Gascoyne and drummer Alex Riel he urged on tenorist Art Themen. As the latter blew through Dexter Gordon's Cheesecake and he and King took care of Coltrane's Impressions, you realised again what fine and powerful reedmen they are - and have been for nigh on five decades.

The next night I was at the Baltic Café in Southwark at a table a mere three yards from a pair of the true greats of contemporary jazz, Bronx bassist William Parker and Louisiana drummer Hamid Drake. Both attacked their instruments with artistry and power, the origins of their musicianship deep in the African and American earth. I could only marvel at the sound, so close and between them the young Russian Igor Strihalev, assured and unfazed, played his rasping alto as if it were an appendage to his larynx.

I followed that up in the salubrious environs of the Barbican. First up was Norma Winstone, the long underestimated singer from Bow, East London. She was backed by a brilliant combo, including Klaus Gesing, the bass clarinettist and saxophonist from Dusseldorf and the Italian pianist Glauco Venier. Winstone has a uniquely hyper-melodic voice exemplified by the song Among The Clouds yet she also transforms her delivery into something solid and concrete in a startling rendition of Everybody's Talking from the film Midnight Cowboy.

A very hard act to follow, yet the Charles Lloyd Quartet did just that. Lloyd's sound carries a mysticism all of its own, grounded by drummer Eric Harland, Reuben Roger's delving bass and pianist Jason Moran's musical hybridity. A foursome to dream of.

Dalston Junction and the Vortex, the friendliest and warmest of jazz venues, was the next port of call to catch Chicagoan alto saxophonist. Matana Roberts accompanied by youthful British trio Robert Mitchell, drummer Seb Rochford and bassist Tom Mason. Roberts played like a storyteller, her horn as full of ardour as the human voice - guttural, vituperative, reflective, full of humour and passion from her very first blasting note. Her expressive utterance, connected to real life and packed with experiences, memories and truly free speech cracked open her bandmates' shells with Mitchell in particular finding a new and free articulation of the seething Hackney streets right outside the venue.

Ending the week back at the South Bank was the great drummer from Cape Town, Louis Moholo-Moholo. 'I like stories! I play stories!' he told us before the set began as he spoke about resisting the 'heavy manners' of apartheid against black and multiracial musicians. As Moholo-Moholo steamed into his duet with old Bristolian confrere pianist Keith Tippett, more than 40 years of mutual jazz achievement surged out. Tippett's explosive keyboard runs, interspersed by folkloric passages and sequences of plucked piano strings, were joined by Moholo-Moholo's relentless clicking pulse and thudding skins, sudden stops and thunderous silences.

This was only a prelude to the drummer's 7 For 70 band which included three Englishmen - pianist Alex Hawkins, arch-bassist John Edwards and long-blowing trumpeter Henry Lowther plus fellow South African tenorist Ntshuts Bonga and the Caribbean power of vocalist Francine Luce of Martinique and alto and baritone saxophonist Jason Yarde.

The horns blew anthemic riffs and roaring improvisations, while Luce sang with Creole lyricism as Hawkins charged up and down the keys and Edwards showed a fleet artistry.

Septuagenarian drummer Moholo-Moholo relentlessly pounded out the story of Africa and the world in the universal language of jazz. It was a percussive message which was ceaselessly optimistic. Every strike of his drums reverberated down the Thames to the open sea, telling the story of a better future.

An unforgettable end to a week that blew by.

Louis Moholo-Moholo (South Africa) - Freedom was everything to him!

Remembering Louis Moholo-Moholo
(2025)

It was June 1976, a week after the massacre of schoolchildren in Soweto, South Africa, murdered by the Apartheid police as they were demonstrating for their language rights, to learn the international language of English rather than the compulsory word-fetters of Afrikaans.

At our school in Poplar, East London, the Bishop of Stepney and founding father of the Anti-Apartheid Movement, Trevor Huddleston, had just given a moving assembly, lamenting the deaths and praising the resistance of so many young children, some of whom had been the sons and daughters of his ex-parishioners. Immediately after this, our 14 year old students sat at their desks and wrote poems and stories extending themselves to the young protesters, words of imaginative empathy and solidarity across thousands of miles.

To accompany their writing I played on our classroom stereo the Dudu Pukwana and Spear album 'In the Townships' (Caroline Records, 1974) a rampaging session of township jazz featuring Pukwana's alto saxophone, Mongezi Feza's trumpet and Louis Moholo-Moholo's drums - all three musicians of the Blue Notes plus bassist Harry Miller, rebels and refugees from Apartheid who had arrived in London in 1964 and turned British jazz inside out with their insurgent artistry.

The students grooved to their sounds and their words gave witness. I remember Ghana-born Andrew's verse:

'Children fell to the ground
Like leaves from a tree,
The sight was unbelievable,
You should have been there to see ...'

And his white friend Philip wrote:

'The Afrikaans language we'll not stand,
They call us slaves, they work us to the ground.
We'll go on that march and tell the whites,
'No Afrikaans! We have our rights!'

And later in his poem, as the protesters marched:

'One's been shot, he's dead , he's dead!'
There's something coming out of him,
its colour is red ...'

These lines came cascading back to me after half a century when I learned last week of the passing in his home city of Cape Town of the great drummer Moholo-Moholo, called by his last powerful bassist, Londoner John Edwards, 'our beautiful Louis.'

I'll leave it to the musicians who loved him to describe his incomparable influence. Fellow drummer Mark Sanders, his roots in Belize and London, told me: 'Louis' tremendous skills as a musician with power, subtlety, nuance, groove and freedom were a mind-blowing joy to behold for me as a young drummer starting out in London, and a gift for all his fellow-musicians and audiences alike.'

His final pianist-compadre in his last band, (they also made a riveting duo Ogun album together. 'Keep Your Heart Straight' in 2011), Alexander Hawkins, said this of Louis' compelling brilliance, modesty and humour: ' If I had never met him, Louis would have had a profound influence on me from his recorded legacy and for what he represented, but the truth is I had the privilege of hearing him from one of the best seats in the house for well over a decade (and even then was the baby of the band). That was an education and joy which it's hard to describe. He was at the same time among the most supportive drummers in the world as well as constantly stoking the fires, driving everyone on the bandstand to levels which they didn't necessarily know were there. Freedom was everything to him, but it was a celebratory 'freedom to ...' rather than a 'freedom from...' as defined by someone else's rules. Where the music was really happening, he'd often come off stage after the gig, exhausted and with a grin turn to us and break out his best Oliver Hardy: 'Another fine mess...'

So much of Africa's genius is born in the drum. Louis embodied that, and lives on in the many recordings he made for Hazel Miller's marvellous Ogun label. His throbbing pulse will live forever, just like it did on 'In the Townships' fifty years ago, as our East London children, now in their mid-Sixties, wrote their poems of love and solidarity to the children of South Africa. Long live his drumming and message of freedom!

Little Brother Montgomery/Memphis Slim/Jimmy Cotton/Speckled Red (USA/England)

- The Devil's Tracks

Dealing with the Devil's Music: Bluesmen in Britain (2017)

During the early 1960s at the height of the so-called 'Trad Fad', when white British bands playing a very Anglicised version of New Orleans and Dixieland jazz were filling up jazz clubs, upstairs or side rooms in pubs and provincial cinemas and concert halls, US blues singers were frequent guests to Britain. An appetite for their music had been fuelled by the skiffle craze across the country - which found its inspiration from great blues artistes like Big Bill Broonzy, Leadbelly and Sonny Terry - and many of the prime British bands like those of Ken Colyer, Chris Barber or the Avon Cities had skiffle interludes in their performances. There were also gigs when the visiting US bluesmen played with members of the host bands, usually guitarists, bassists and drummers, and a fascinating U.S./Anglo blues unity developed.

There is some very fine and moving music here in the Lake album Dealing With the Devil's Music: Bluesmen in Britain. Little Brother Montgomery was born close to New Orleans in 1906 and grew up playing piano when Jelly Roll Morton was a regular music to the Montgomery household. He absorbed the blues as well as ragtime, boogie-woogie and the myriad of styles that found their amalgam in the Crescent City. Here he is accompanied by British blues pioneer Alexis Korner on guitar, Bob Guthrie on drums and bassist Jack Fallon for the hard-driven Farish Street Jive and his own signature New Vicksburg Blues.

Pinetop's Boogie Woogie is borrowed from Pinetop Smith with a new commentary. Chinee Man Blues is more evidence of New Orleans' cosmopolitanism and Old Maid Blues is about old age and loneliness, told with a touching humour. Little Brother's final track is the standard Canadian Sunset, played straight but with a moving blues underbelly.

It was Barber who brought the prime harmonica man Jimmy Cotton to these shores in 1961 to perform at the Beaulieu Jazz Festival. Born in 1935 in Tunica, Mississippi and tutored by the great Sonny Boy Williamson, he migrated to Chicago to play with Howling Wolf and Muddy Waters. On these tracks Barber plays bass, Korner guitar and Keith Scott piano. Cotton wails his way through Dealing With the Devil. Korner plays some sharp guitar on Waters' Standing Around Crying, and Slow and Easy has a howl which is as bluesy as a London studio ever heard. Scott thumps his keys with a quasi-delta authenticity in Broonzy's Rock Me Mama and Barber picks up his trombone. In Curtis Jones' Decoration Day Blues (Jones too was to visit London in 1963 and record a stirring album with Korner and Fallon), Cotton laments another lost love with a yowling eloquence.

The next seven tracks are all Memphis Slim, recorded in 1962 when he was touring Europe with Willie Dixon. As a young man Slim went upriver to Chicago and played with Broonzy before becoming a piano force in his own right, and is immediately recognisable in his own Rock and Roll Boogie and his classic Everyday I Have the Blues which became a staple of Joe Williams and the Count Basie Orchestra. He laments with urgency all through I Can't Get No Mail and his prolific sense of swing rocks him through Walkin' the Boogie. There's a cautionary tale in Beer Drinkin' Woman and 'the tears are fallin' like rain' through his hard-hitting pianism in Misery. His superb rolling artistry, fast, passionate and full life of the blues pours from his keys all through Pee Wee's Blues.

The last bluesman of the four is the gruffly articulate Speckled Red. He is also the veteran, born in Monroe, Louisiana in 1892. He recorded in spurts between 1930 and the 1950s and was rediscovered in 1970 for the soundtrack of the film Blues Like Showers of Rain. He sings the album's final three tracks, the most full of life being the marvellously assertive Oh, Red, where his piano clinks and stomps below his adenoidal voice, accompanied by Lennie Hastings on drums and bassist Bill Reid.

It was Korner who concluded about these legends from across an ocean: 'There just weren't any better teachers and that's all there was to it.' They came, they told their blues stories, and they left more than something of their lives and brilliance which has never been forgotten.

(Dealing with the Devil's Music: Bluesmen in Britain is available on Lake Records)

James Moody (USA) - Rare jazzman and humourist

Ronnie Scott's, London
(1999)

Bebop virtuoso on at least three instruments - alto and tenor saxophones and flute - pioneer soloist in Dizzy Gilespie bands from 1946, comedian, jazz traveller of the world and, now at 75, playing like a man half a century younger, James Moody is back in London, fronting a British rhythm section. Listening to the youthfulness of his notes, the allusions, inflections, Parkerisms and Dizzyisms as he rang the changes with his lightning phrases and sudden accelerations during the romp through Secret Love at the beginning of his first set, it seemed uncanny, almost impossible to conceive, that bop is now over five decades old - and here was a man who made it happen.

Moody is small, portly, bespectacled, stubble-faced and beaming. His jokes are almost as bad as those of Ronnie Scott himself. As he introduces I Can't Get Started, affecting an Etonian accent, he declares to his listeners that 'I just wanted you to know that I'm bilingual' and then bursts into his alto sounds with cries, howls, laughter and squeaks, soaring into a caressing final coda as if years were nothing.

Strongly backed by ex-Scott accompanist John Critchinson, Mark Fletcher on drums and the exceptional bass talent of Tim Wells, memories of those performances with Gillespie in the 1950s and 1960s come pounding back - what other bop veterans are still playing with such musical wit?

As he flew into a fluted version of Antonio Carlos Jobim's Wave, out came all the melodic digressions into Grofe's On the Trail, then English Country Garden and an ironic dig at Dixie, perhaps remembering his own birth place in Savannah, Georgia. Moody's great talent is his ability to juxtapose, as if it is merely natural, the hilarious with sounds of great sensitivity and elegiac lyricism to stand the affable next to the beautiful.

In achieving this, he keeps the two contradictory sides of his old partner Gillespie alive and blowing. Vibrant, ageless sounds - sometimes tender, sometimes uproarious, always with the soul of the blues and the blood of a long jazz life. Go and hear this rare musician.

Jemeel Moondoc (USA) - Rhythmic hornscapes blowing over the world

Active Ingredients – Titration
(2016)

Titration was a new word for me before I saw the sleeve of this album. According to my dictionary, it means 'observing the quantity of a solution necessary to convert a constituent into another form.'

So as I heard the music, I asked myself: 'Does this solution of sounds titrate? Do they convert into soulful, grooving music?' Oh yes. Not half! And all within the diverse thunder of leader Chad Taylor's drums. His band, Active Ingredients, are a Chicago outfit, although Taylor, born in Tempe, Arizona, in 1973,moved with his family to the Windy City when he was 11 years old, gaining a jazz apprenticeship listening to free players like Muhal Richard Abrams, the Art Ensemble of Chicago and Henry Threadgill.

Seven years in New York followed, including studies with powerful drummers like Joe Chambers and Pheeroan Aklaff before he returned to

Chicago to play with a succession of mighty horns like Fred Anderson, Joe McPhee, Roscoe Mitchell and Ernest Dawkins.

With him on Titration is the trombonist from Newark, New Jersey, Steve Swell, his bassist friend from New York, Tom Abbs, and the astonishing alto saxophonist, too seldom recorded, Jemeel Moondoc. Born in Chicago in 1951, Moondoc played in blues bands in Boston, followed free pianist Cecil Taylor from college to college for two years for the privilege of playing in his rehearsal bands, before becoming a regular of New York's loft scene, with other innovative souls like violinist Billy Bang, trumpeter Roy Campbell and vibes virtuoso Khan Jamal.

The opener is dedicated to the pathfinding South African bassman Johnny Dyani, and Song for Dyani bounds like veldt land antelopes, with Abbs and Taylor making the ground surge.

Moondoc's alto is like no other, prancing, levitating and leaping through its notes, titrating madly, full of primal life. As Swell joins him like a lost tailgate slide-man from New Orleans, the music seems to vault from city to city.

Velocity begins funereally, its harmonies parade-like, before Moondoc howls out of the ensemble and Swell's gruff cadences ring ruefully. Slate brings in guests to augment the quartet: David Boykin's wild tenor, Rob Mazurek's cornet and Avreeal Ra's comradeship of drums. Visual Industries has a rubbery undertow, with Abbs ever active and Moondoc's worried solo brimful of the blues, as Taylor's drums palpitate. Modern Mythology is played by the full septet, the double drumsets creating a pulsating rhythmic groundswell and Moondoc's notes hold ancient messages before the other insurgent horns come in with their own freedom colloquy. Absence is haunted by Mazurek's strained and mournful cornet in a sad horn song of solitude.

Dependent Origination is Taylor's track, an almost five-minute drum solo, potently original yet growing from a love of drummers from Ed Blackwell of New Orleans, Dennis Charles of the Virgin Islands and Steve McCall from Chicago. All their lives, timbres and brilliance have been ingested, but it is Taylor's drumsound which emerges, a throbbing of his own life and art.

The closing track is the quartet again - a foursome of very active sound masters - all through the 14 minutes of Other People's Problems titrated into their own musical solutions. Abbs' singeing bowed bass, Swell's growling slide-work, Taylor's almost subterranean drums and the marvel that is Moondoc, his unique hornscapes blowing over Lake Michigan and over the world: a record to nourish and savour is this one.

(Titration is available on Delmark)

Jason Moran (USA) - New star in the jazz firmament

Jason Moran at the Pizza Express, Dean Street, Soho, London

Jason Moran – Modernistic

(2003)

Towards the end of the '90s, young New York-based pianist Jason Moran emerged as an essential member of a group of brilliant young musicians. Led by the St Louis-born altoist Greg Osby, the group included other prodigious talents like tenorist Mark Shim, drummer Nasheet Waits and reinventor of the vibes Stefan Harris. You can hear them together on the astonishing album, New Directions.

On his first Blue Note release, Soundtrack to Human Motion (1998), Moran sought to create the sounds echoing through his daily life. On one track, he took a piece from one of his sources of emulation, the pianist Andrew Hill, played it backwards and used it for his starting point. 'You never know where you'll find inspiration!' he declared.

Another album, Black Stars (2001), is a wide-ranging sounds essay, played alongside veteran reedman and permanent contender Sam Rivers, but, in Modernistic, his new release, he is performing entirely alone. The first track shatters any mould in which the listener may be tempted to enclose Moran. You've Got to be Modernistic was written and recorded in the late 1920s by the father of 'stride' piano James P Johnson. Moran's torrential embrace of it is entirely unexpected. But then the hallmark of all Moran's jazz enterprises embodies musical surprise.

In the album's concluding selection, Cane River South, he remembers the location of his Louisiana family roots and immediately preceding this is his version of Schumann's Auf Einer Burg - having passed through a reflective and virtually unrecognisable exploration of the evergreen Body and Soul, avant garde pianist Muhal Richard Abrams's Time into Space into Time and Afrika Bambaataa's rap anthem of 1982, Planet Rock as well as his own Moran Tonk Circa 1935. Clearly, his reference is piano history and not only jazz piano history. This is why, for example, he can move from Schumann's Europe to his own Southern provenances with such unforced sophistication and sense of truth.

At the Pizza Express, Moran sidles between the tables and walks onto the low stage in a grey suit, red shirt and homburg hat. As he explains after the first selection, 'That tune was dedicated to James P Johnson. Hence my hat, Harlem-style!' Before he begins to play, he turns on a tape of some spirited New York neighbourhood talk, which becomes the only accompaniment to his own piano vocalese. And it is this integrally oral quality that streams through his performance, even when he turns the tape off, his piano is still talking.

His keys speak of ragtime, stride, blues, honky tonk, Bud Powell and Monk, all the variegated piano voices of his city. Hard voices, shouting notes and those played like drums, force-struck phrases, making the house piano roar like a shining wooden lion. As his head makes circles above the ivories while he plays, his reflection and that of the taut strings are painted on the glossy underside of the raised piano lid. To the onlooker, it is as if two musicians are playing as one, each striking and reflecting upon the other's sounds while their notes peal around the underground room.

As Moran passes from one profound and melodic passage to another - anything but a 'light touch' player - he jousts with his keys as Erroll Garner did, as McCoy Tyner does. Sometimes his sound is more jagged, sometimes more percussively tender and serene. He reminds me of pianist Don Pullen, who carried similar contradictions to the ears of his listeners.

With sudden thunderous phrasing, vaunting runs, unpredictable keyboard bombshells with every crashing note clearly picked out and calibrated, followed by long moments of intense emotive beauty, almost calmness. 'I am a man of many tributes!' he confesses, having dedicated and played tunes to pianists Muhal Richard Abrams (Time into Space into Time) and Jackie Byard (Out Front). And it is Byard that you recognise in Moran's encyclopaedic jazz piano knowledge. He also plays too Brahms's Intermezzo No 2, with a Harlem accent and a jazz artist's true care.

He turns on his tape again and we hear the voices of elders, which the musician respectfully accompanies in a message of piano love. It is a sound of roots, a rural sound, a southern sound that senses history. As he explains, 'This is my grandparents speaking about their grandparents. I carry them on the road with me. I might meet another person who knows them, perhaps in Ireland.'

As he plays, the piano shakes, the walls of Dean Street rumble, Soho shakes too with the undertow of Moran's charged solo music that contains centuries of the African, Mississippi and Irish past with it. Agonies and dreams and hopes. And, as you walk back up a late-night Oxford Street to catch the Tube, you reflect that, for the last hour or more, your ears have picked up an emergent jazz piano genius and that you have learned some crucial history too.

As Art Blakey used to say, 'Truly, a new star is in the firmament.'

(Modernistic is available on Blue Note)

Best Jazz Records of the Year
Mujician – In Concerts
Charlie Rouse – Cinnamon Flower
Wadada Leo Smith – Angel Falls
Tony Coe's Axel – What Say We Play Today?
(2025)

Many jazz listeners have affirmed, that in the long wake of the John Coltrane Quartet, the foursome that has since most touched its brilliance is the English quartet, Mujician. Composed of the Bristolian pianist Keith Tippett, the south London tenor and soprano saxophonist Paul Dunmall, Luton-born 7-string bassist Paul Rogers and the Shropshire drummer, Tony Levin.

Between 1990 and 2005 they waxed six memorable albums on the US Cuneiform label, but now a triple CD has been created by Jazz in Britain, recorded from concerts in Cheltenham (1993), Vienna (2003) and Birmingham (2010). It is a beautiful sonic triptych called Mujician in Concerts, with the four members playing at their unified peak.

Sometimes haunting and hymnal as if coming from ancestral spirits - as in the opening message of Dunmall and Tippett in Cheltenham, other times rhapsodic and joyous: 'We never spoke about the music beforehand,' declared Dunmall, 'we just walked on stage and trusted in the music and each other.'

Rogers is a virtuoso bassist like no other, playing an instrument like no other, and Levin's sense of time and moment is deeply empathetic, knowing instinctively the musical minds of his quartet-mates. Tippett and Levin are gone, but thanks to devoted and skilled travelling recordists, Andy Isham and Steve Trent, these long and precious musical instants are still with us, throbbing with life and artistry.

Between 1959 and 1970, Washingtonian tenor saxophonist Charlie Rouse (1924 - 1988) was the featured horn of Thelonious Monk's Quartet, and his husky, quasi-adenoidal tone became the companion sound to Monk's genius melodies and 'brilliant corners'. But he showed another sphere when he recorded Cinnamon Flower in 1977, an album full of sounds of Brazil. The new reissue on Resonance Records includes this release with some overdubbing, plus the tracks in their undubbed, original form.

So we have a Latin feast of Rouse with Brazilian compadres trumpeter Claudio Roditi, pianist Dom Salvador and drummer Portinho, plus the great Michigan-born bassist Ron Carter, late of the Miles Davis Quintet. Rouse is joyous, in another element, on Cinnamon Flower, buoyed up by a relentless rhythmic upsurge and melodic beauty, for example on Desencontro (Disenchantment), and his notes leap up blissfully on Alvorada. It's a powerful reissue, racked with elation and flair.

The great Mississippi-born trumpeter Wadada Leo Smith is 84 this year, but it hasn't curtailed his mighty breath. His new album is Angel Falls (Intakt Records), partnered with the Swiss pianist Sylvie Courvoisier, whose pianism he describes as 'advancing as if she's going there to save creation.' In a destructive era of Trump and Musk that is certainly what they are both doing, with power and beauty too. Wadada's horn talks fire and Courvoisier's keyboard words make a palaver of freedom. No wonder one track is called Sonic Utterance, for that is what the entire album is.

Finally there is the burning saxophonist of Canterbury, the late Tony Coe. In 1977 his quintet, Axel, recorded the tracks of What Say We Play Today? (Jazz in Britain Records) at the Camden Jazz Festival. It's taken 48 years, but now it's there for us.

Pianist Gordon Beck, guitarist Phil Lee, bassist Chris Laurence and drummer Bryan Spring join Coe for a gripping performance, with the final title track reaching 28 minutes. Throughout, sheer musicianship excels, with the luminous, underrated Lee taking on the prominence of a second horn, and Coe playing clarinet, bass clarinet, soprano and tenor saxophones as if he were born to each. The fivesome create their own inventive sound, driven by uniqueness.

(In Concerts & What Say We Play Today? are both available on Jazz In Britain, Cinnamon Flower on Resonance Records and Angel Falls on Intakt Records)

Jim Mullen (Scotland) - Jim Thumb

Glaswegian guitarist Jim Mullen

(2024)

He's one of the truly great guitarists of a century of jazz, with a sound all of his own rooted in his love of the songs of Robert Burns. Jim Mullen tells me that he 'grew up with his songs and their soulful timelessness.' Just listen to his beautiful millennial album Burns and you'll hear what he means.

He was born in Glasgow in 1945: 'It was the post-war baby boom. My dad was a carpenter, my mum worked in a department store. She would sing along to Bing Crosby and Frank Sinatra on the radio, and when I began playing I half-knew these songs. As a toddler she would offer to read me a story at night, but I would ask her to sing me a song instead. After begging my dad for a guitar, he tried to make me one but the fingerboard proved too difficult. He allowed me to buy one on the never-never, paid for by my after-school paper-round - with dire warnings it would go back to the store if I missed a payment.'

'I joined a neighbourhood skiffle group aged nine or 10, until an older friend introduced me to jazz. I was hooked. Hearing records of great guitarists like Tal Farlow, Barney Kessel and Mundell Lowe, I began the long process of trying to figure out what they were doing. After leaving school I worked as a journalist in Glasgow, first on the Daily Record then the Evening Times, before moving to London to try to survive playing music for a living.'

He found a living all right, playing and recording with Pete Brown's Piblokto and Brian Auger's Oblivion Express, developing his distinctive Wes Montgomery-style technique of picking his strings with his thumb. While touring with the Average White Band in the US he met the Surrey-born tenor saxophonist Dick Morrissey, and back in England they united to form the Morrissey-Mullen Band, straddling jazz and rock and making a series of acclaimed albums together.

I ask him who were the musicians he most remembered playing alongside. 'The great Glaswegian saxophonist Bobby Wellins was a local hero who I played a few gigs with and we recorded an album but it was never released. Then I began a 15-year association with Dick Morrissey, who took me under his wing and was a good example to follow. I've been fortunate to play with many great musicians, but most memorable are Dick, of course, and US pianist Gene Harris.'

His most recent album is Volunteers, of 2018. 'It came about after I survived serious illness in 2015, and all the musicians involved played for free and helped my recovery. Flautist/arranger Gareth Lockrane arranged some of my tunes and encouraged me back playing again after my illness. It's one of my proudest moments.'

It's a beautiful album, full of a spirit of musical union and friendship, beginning with a Mullen tune Medication, and fine solos from Lockrane's flute, Mullen and Mark Nightingale's trombone, Tristan Maillot's drums and Mick Hutton's bass giving a pumping rhythm. Mullen's ear for picked-out balladry is serenely expressed on When I Fall in Love, with Steve Fishwick's soaring trumpet ascents and Mullen's old Burns confrere, pianist Gareth Williams, adding a riveting chorus.

Saxophonists Alan Barnes and Julian Seigel have their moments on Spare Change, and Seigel's bass clarinet rumbles and rises on Back in the Day. Mullen's thumb picks like lightning on his own composition Speed of Sound, and on the album finale, Rule of Thumb, that's exactly what it is, with Mullen leading with his miraculous digit and all his musical brothers in the finest fettle.

I asked him, what most compelled him towards a long jazz life? 'What I love about jazz is it's a democratic art form and I enjoy being an equal member of a team. Jazz for me is the most challenging music because you have to reinvent it every time you play.'

Like our old friend Robert Wyatt would say: 'Different every time!' And so it is with the marvellous Mullen.

(Volunteers is available on Diving Duck Recordings)

Jim Mullen (Scotland) – A local groove

Some serendipitous jazz goings-on with Jim Mullen
(2024)

In the upstairs room in my local pub just up the road - The County Arms in Highams Park, East London - Sunday evenings are jazz feasts. There is always a guest musician of renown, a local accompanying trio of bass, drums and keyboards, followed by a chance for local musicians, young and old, to share the stage with the guest, and gain invaluable confidence from the encounter.

Last week it was the great veteran Glaswegian guitarist, Jim Mullen, who played an opening set including beautifully sharp ballads like I'll Close My Eyes, I Can't Get Started and Angel Eyes, with bop classics like Clifford Brown's Sandu and Wes Montgomery's Road Song.

As he picked out his notes with such melodic power, tenderness and verve, suddenly it was as if the peeling wallpaper, chipped paint, the cardboard patches on the stained ceiling and the 1950s carpet were all transformed into a local palace of soaring and moving sound. And the democratic imperative was always at hand. After the opening set it was the turn of local musicians who had brought their instruments to join in. A young woman with a tenor sax played There'll Never Be Another You, four different young drummers took their turns, an elderly fellow guitarist strummed and chipped out Softly, As a Morning Sunrise, and another saxophonist played a rousing version of What a Wonderful World. Singers too: a greying woman scatted her way through Ellington's Take the 'A' Train, and a man shaking with either glee or nerves sang out I Remember You.

It was a collective expression of William Morris's words on the pub sign outside: Fellowship is Life. As I walked the couple of hundred yards home, I thought to myself, how wonderful is the jazz impulse - the chance to hear a master like Mullen in the midst of aspiring musicians of all ages, adding their sounds to the unifying mix. And all in an upstairs session of a local pub full of joyous spirit. It's what people's music is all about.

Matthew Muneses (Philippines) & Riza Printup (Philippines)
PAG-IBIG KO Vol.1
(2025)

The beautiful sleeve painting of a Filipino woman picking flowers, is only one dimension of the album PAG-IBIG KO VOL.1, by the harp/saxophone duo of Riza Printup and Matthew Muneses. It's a surprising combination giving added impetus and creative tension to the genre of Filipino love serenades known as 'kundiman.'

Muneses, who arranged them, sees the songs as a riposte to 'an era when anti-Asian sentiment has been on the rise in the United States. I've felt torn between being grateful to live here and angry at the injustices perpetrated.'

Printup's soothing harpsong unifies with the melodism of Muneses' horn to create serene sounds as a complete contrary to the maniacal voice of Trumpery.

Jazz was born from melody, from New Orleans creole songs, hymns and marches. Who would have thought it would come too, a century later in notes blown and plucked from the far Philippines?

(PAG-IBIG KO Vol.1 is available on Irabbagast Records)

David Murray (USA) - Give me a poem and I'll write a song with it

Renowned US tenor saxophonist David Murray
(2024)

No other saxophonist has so mastered the jazz tradition, while simultaneously playing out of it with such musical freedom, as David Murray. Born in Oakland, California, in 1955 he became a nonpareil of jazz saxophone within the post-John Coltrane, post-Sonny Rollins generation and, as he approaches his 70th year, he is still making wondrous sounds of fire, compassion and verve, as his newest album Francesca testifies.

Murray's mother Catherine was pianist and musical director of the Missionary Church of God in neighbouring Berkeley. His father Walter was head deacon and played guitar. Murray became president of the Junior High School in Telegraph Avenue, Berkeley, in 1969 when the police used tear gas to disperse the mass demonstrations supporting the People's Park in which he took part. Later, he became a Black Panther and campaigned for Bobby Seale to become Mayor of Oakland.

All this activism was central to his education as a young musician, 'but the church and my mother's brilliant music inspired me more than any politics,' he says. 'I was inspired too by the great trumpeter and Ornette Coleman alumnus Bobby Bradford. When I went to Pomona College near Los Angeles my English teacher was the jazz critic Stanley Crouch. At that time I wanted more than anything to be a writer - the new Ishmael Reed! I had learned piano from my mother at nine. Then I learned alto sax, but when I heard Sonny Rollins at the Berkeley Jazz Festival in 1967, I changed to tenor. I loved the saxophone playing of older players like Coleman Hawkins, Ben Webster and Paul Gonsalves, but to me Rollins was the most complete saxophonist. I liked Coltrane too but I didn't study him too much because every young saxman was trying to be Coltrane No 2.' When he was 20 he went to New York. 'Some great musicians took me under their wing and inspired me - pianist Don Pullen and John Hicks and drummers Billy Higgins and Ed Blackwell.'

I ask him about his love of melody, so powerfully and movingly expressed on the new album's title tune to his wife, Francesca. 'I love melody. I always wanted to be known as a songwriter. Give me a poem and I'll write a song with it. The song form is at the heart of my love of structure in music, the structure that brings freedom. Yet I want to construct and de-construct through my improvisations at the same time.' Inside and outside musical structure simultaneously - the true Murray musical power.

What about his use of the bass clarinet, such as on the track Richard's Tune, composed by Don Pullen? 'My bass clarinet gives my listeners a chance to breathe. The constant sound of the tenor saxophone can be overwhelming, exhausting. With the bass clarinet, particularly on slower numbers, you can really hear the wood of the instrument. And the great oceanographer, Jacques Cousteau, once telephoned me after hearing, he said, just 30 seconds of one of my bass clarinet solos. He told me the sound was like the song of the whales and it was if they were talking to him.'

The track Free Mingus, dedicated to his son and released following the great bassman's centenary, remembers how he and his music would have been at the centre of all the protest and resistance following the Minneapolis death of George Floyd. 'That kind of thing goes on every day in America,' he explains: 'Thank God for those kids who witnessed it, and their phones.'

What about his young quartet-mates from a new generation of young virtuosi? 'Marta Sanchez is a very powerful pianist, one of the finest of her generation. And I've played with so many great bass players - Art Davis, Wilber Morris, Fred Hopkins. Luke Stewart is in their tradition and reminds me very much of the wonderful Hopkins. Drummer Russell Carter plays like all the drummers I really like - Max Roach, Billy Higgins, Ed Blackwell. I hear bits of all of them in him.'

Who would he pick out among British musicians? 'There are a lot of great ones. If I was to name them all, we'd be here a while! There's saxophonists - Denys Baptiste, Tony Kofi - he was a student of mine, I'm so proud of him. And Soweto Kinch, I love him! And looking back there were Ronnie Scott, Trevor Watts and drummer John Stevens. They're great, and a part of jazz history itself.'

And what is it about the qualities of the greatest jazz music? 'To me it's undefinable. It inspires its listeners and players to wonder, but it's a science too, you can do so much with it. It excites me that I can reflect human life and emotions - some moments in our lives, sometimes tragedy, sometimes happiness!'

It's all in Murray's beautifully creative and relentlessly energetic sound. Give Francesca a spin and you will know.

(Francesca is available on Intakt Records)

David Murray (USA) - Notes that crack the sky

David Murray - Live At The Lower Manhattan Ocean Club
Jamaaladeen Tacuma - Coltrane Configurations
(2010)

Jazzwerkstatt is a Berlin-based label with a very congenial address at Walter-Benjamin-Platz 2. It specialises in live recordings, old and new - many of them made in Berlin itself and some from the archives of the East German broad-caster Rundfunk der DDR. The Lower Manhattan Ocean Club live album of 1977 bursts with life and artistry, featuring a youthful David Murray - born in Oakland, California, in 1955 - on tenor and soprano saxophones, and trumpeter Lester Bowie.

Bowie, one of the great brass wits and humorous innovators of jazz, was born in 1941 and raised in Little Rock and St Louis. He was the grandson of a trombonist and son of a music teacher who began learning trumpet at the age of five. By 1977 he had already established himself as the brass lead of the avant-garde Art Ensemble of Chicago and in 1981 was to cut The Great Pretender, the first of his albums as leader of Brass Fantasy.

On drums was Phillip Wilson and completing the quartet was the booming Chicago bassist Fred Hopkins. The recording quality is exceptionally fine and as you listen you feel you're sitting at the club's front table, right beside the musicians. You feel too that the 22-year-old Murray is just burgeoning, truly discovering his massive range and talent. But it is Bowie's cutting and caustic phrases that throb through the opener Murray's Nevada's Theme, full of a breathy resilience and twirling, audacious utterances earthed by Hopkins's resounding twang and Wilson's rattling snares - prefacing Murray's prodigious reed explorations of every part of his tenor.

With Murray on soprano and emulating a past master on Bechet's Bounce, the quartet play in the spirit and freedom of a New Orleans parade, with Bowie's notes cracking the sky. Eighteen minutes of Butch Morris's Obe offers full scope to the many dimensions of Bowie's horn - rampaging, tender, supplicating, fully assertive and declamatory, suspiring, groaning and laughing. It adds up to an astonishing performance.

The tribute For Walter Norris, offered to the Little Rock-born and Berlin-based pianist, shows the ever-evolving Murray's early brilliance, digging deep and soaring high. His sound is multitudinous and indicative of all he was to achieve through the oncoming three decades. And as the quartet play the short ensemble piece Let The Music Take You with a potent sense of union, you realise that Bowie, Hopkins and Wilson are all gone and only the mighty sound of Murray still remains.

Back to 2009 and a live session in Dortmund with a quartet led by the bass guitar of one of Ornette Coleman's old confreres who joined the master's Prime Time band at the age of 19 in 1975. This is Jamaaladeen Tacuma, a Philly-raised innovator who became a session player with such figures as Stevie Wonder and Joe Cocker, while never leaving the jazz heartland.

In Dortmund he has the brilliant New Jersey-born pianist Orrin Evans with him, plus drummer Tim Hutson and the Nottingham-born saxophonist of Ghanaian roots, Tony Kofi. Called Coltrane Configurations, the album includes five of Trane's most beloved compositions and begins with a tape of Coltrane saying how he tries to play the multitude of sounds in his head, but in a spirit of unity.

Then straight into the opener India, with Kofi putting aside his more usual baritone in favour of his soprano horn and Evans playing electric keyboard. The echoing, cavernous current-filled phrases that Tacuma squeezes from his bass guitar provide an altogether novel grounding for Coltrane's familiar themes, particularly through Dahomey Dance in which Kofi 's alto horn finds a west African homeland with a poised and passionate solo.

The mesmeric theme of Impressions provokes ecstatic choruses from Kofi, an acoustic piano surge from Evans and some pounding Tacuma, while the sublime melody of Naima flows with a singular loveliness from Evans and Kofi. An unusual and eloquent tribute this, some 42 years after Coltrane's death, still creating life and beauty.

(Live At The Lower Manhattan Ocean Club & Coltrane Configurations are available on Jazzwerkstatt)

David Murray (USA), Paal Nilssen-Love (Norway) &
Ingbrigt Haker Flaten (Norway)
Café Oto, London
(2025)

From San Francisco's Bay Area to the more quasi-Arctic locations of Molde and Oppdal in Norway is a long journey, particularly if you stopover in Hackney, East London. But such was the traversing of the free intercontinental trio of Oakland, California-born tenor saxophonist David Murray and Norwegian drummer and bassist Paal Nilssen-Love and Ingebrigt Haker Flaten.

Septuagenarian hornman Murray is the prime U.S. saxophonist of his generation, while Nilssen-Love and Flaten are free virtuosi who over the last decade have become renowned for their rebellious Nordic artistry. As Murray began temperately, Nilssen-Love and Flaten gradually built up improvising steam and created a boiler-house of sound, like two super-animated Peer Gynts moving towards climaxes of life journeys, as Murray's galvanising breath searched for and found every conceivable sound of his rampaging horn.

Some way into their third selection, there was a loud ruckus at the Café Oto door, as someone shouted splenetically into the venue. 'Come and sing with us!' shouted Murray and Nilssen-Love with collective camaradie that crossed mountains, deserts and oceans. The world outside in an instant became the world inside.

Murray is a uniquely melodising improviser. As his notes move away from melodies they re-create their own, so if you were to try to separate out his improvising phrases, you would hear snatches of old and new tunes as new timbral patterns are born and multiplied. His trio-mates know that very well, and sensed every fresh melody tumbling from his saxophone with their very own rhythmic and harmonic brotherhood.

For all its century-plus existence, jazz has been a music of syncretism and unity. Both were expressed in earfulls on this Hackney night, with the western Pacific and the northern Atlantic flowing together as one down the Balls Pond Road, as these three troubadours of free sound set East London alight with their invention, passion and beauty.

Sunny Murray (USA) - Free drummer on a roll

Boom Boom Cat by Sunny Murray, John Edwards and Tony Bevan (2017)

Before he became a percussion pioneer of the avant-garde, the Oklahoma-born drummer Sunny Murray had played with jazz musicians from almost every tradition of the music. With the New Orleans horn of Red Allen, the New York stride piano of Willie 'The Lion' Smith and the bebop alto saxophone of Jackie McLean, he had kept approved time and rhythm. But when he began playing with the 'new' musicians such as pianist Cecil Taylor (from 1959) and rasping tenorist Albert Ayler (from 1964) as well as Ornette Coleman and Don Cherry, he began to create a new drum architecture, dispensing with the erstwhile rhythmic regularity and being the accompanist, to forging the drums as a free, surging, improvising force in their own right, liberating the concepts of time and flow and helping to create new musical freedom for the new horn innovators including David Murray and Charles Gayle.

When the music of the album Boom Boom Cat was recorded at the Vortex in east London, in September 2009, Murray was already 72 but striking his drums with an undimmed artistic skill and energy. And with him too were two highly accomplished Englishmen, powerful enough jazz virtuosi in their own right but when inspired by the explosive presence of the mighty Murray, their music ventures to places previously unknown and unexplored. Tony Bevan is a Buckinghamshire boy, born in Aylesbury in 1956. He studied classical flute at secondary school, earned a philosophy degree at Southampton University and was given his first soprano saxophone by Aylesbury's most renowned jazz son, the veteran reedman and legendary Thameside busker Lol Coxhill. On Boom Boom Cat he plays soprano, tenor and bass saxophones, the latter a rare enough jazz instrument, its only prior British master (for six decades and more) the impish Dixielander Harry Gold. The third trio member is the ubiquitous British bassist of improvising albums and among the music's prime plunging stringmen, the brilliant John Edwards, one of the jewels of the British avant-garde tradition and a consummate musician.

As the trio sets off on the 56 minutes of the title number, images of the jazz past assailed me. Right through the history of recorded jazz the impact of US jazz giants playing with their British confreres has always brought out the most inspired and vibrant sounds of the Brits. Think of alto saxophonist Benny Carter's Maida Vale sessions of 1936 and Fats Waller's London Rhythm of 1938, or play Humphrey Lyttleton's 1949 sessions with Sidney Bechet or the marvellous 1966 recordings with Buck Clayton where the two trumpeters play like brass twins. Or Stan Tracey's partnerships with Sonny Rollins, JJ Johnson and Johnny Griffin as '60s house pianist at Ronnie Scott's, right up to Hamid Drake drumming with Paul Dunmall's quartet in Bristol in 2004 - an extra dimension always erupted from the hugely fired up and driven British musicians hosting US jazz genius on their own soil. They play with something extra, some added dimension; a febrile cross-cultural spark ignites their imagination and musicianship.

For on Boom Boom Cat, Bevan and Edwards play as equals with their great septuagenarian drums partner, who starts the performance with some free drum flourishes before Edwards's bouncing beats and Bevan's gruff tenor come pounding in. It's a relentless trio and right through the performance none of the threesome tire or slacken. Bevan's phrases rise, fall, are repeated with minimal differences, soar, rasp and plunge, contort then march straight ahead, twist and reverse, thrust forward by Murray's listening drums and Edwards's pulsating beat.

When Edwards and Murray play as a duo it is as if the bassist is striking another drum, stygian and deep under the concrete and Dalston earth. Then Edwards sounds like a giant buzzing insect with Murray's perennial drum and cymbal blows waving him away. Bevan returns for more forays, with a caustic soprano onslaught, and then, following a surge with his bass sax, at first almost tender and pacific, then bursting into rumbling fire and ferocity, urged on by the combustive Murray.

The only other track, the 12-and-a-half minutes of Ballad for G, seems like brevity itself after its predecessor. Murray begins on solo brushes before Edwards's bass creeps in and Bevan's bass sax melodises deeply and serenely. Slow, sensuous and beautiful is this ballad, showing another aspect of this profoundly powerful Anglo-American trio. The first day of September it was in Hackney, and right across east London it was Sunny's night all right.

(Boom Boom Cat is available on Foghorn)

Allexa Nava (Peru) - No Language
(2025)

It's a long, long way from Lima, Peru, where she was born, to Dalston, East London, but the young saxophonist Allexa Nava was on hot form at the Vortex, when she played to a young and appreciative audience one cold March night.

'At home my Mom was always listening to music,' she told me, 'and when I was a teenager i went through different phases, listening to pop music and hardcore bands while at the same time I was at school and studying classical music at a conservatoire.'

What about Peruvian folk music, is it at the heart of her sound? 'I think my articulation and the phrases I play are influenced by it. When I started gigging I was learning the classics and also playing Afro-Peruvian music. That had an influence, but I'm currently very much inspired and always listening to Latin music.'

Certainly the Vortex listeners loved her sound, which she calls 'a fusion of styles', characterised by an often harsh and terse horn-power, which lifts a more gently intense emotive lyricism when she plays slower melodies with a raw passion, like her tune For Those not Here. 'I wrote it after the pandemic. It's dedicated to all those we lost during that time.'

'I became interested in jazz when I came to England in 2018. I started going to sessions with Tomorrow's Warriors and the National Youth Jazz Orchestra to learn more. When I first got into jazz it was mainly through jazz fusion records like those of Chris Potter, Michael Brecker and Brad Mehldau. Then when I went to Trinity Laban Conservatoire in South London I got into learning the roots of jazz. I used to listen loads to the records of the Chilean saxophonist Melissa Aldana. I love her playing so much!'

She was taught by Gary Crosby of Tomorrow's Warriors and saxophonists Denys Baptiste, Tom Challenger and Tony Kofi. 'But I remember hearing someone telling me about Music Education. They said, 'We may learn jazz/classical theory, but in the end we play what inspired us in our teenage years.' That's what I hear, they are the ideas in my head when I play, and this is what comes out.'

At the Vortex her first set was in trio formation. 'I've been playing with drummer Cassius Cobbson for a number of years. I love his fearlessness when he plays, and he is super-versatile, truly an artist. I began playing with pianist Emile Hinton last year. He was able to understand my vision so quickly and his playing is insane! He's also very versatile and super-interested in many different musical styles.'

Hinton's rhapsodic unaccompanied solo opened Good Job, Philip, and Cobbson's opening drum solo on No Time introduced the unusually rampant tone of Allexa's tenor saxophone, almost like an accordion sound, seeming to come from some hidden bellows inside her lungs. When Hinton switches to electric keyboard, she kneels, almost invisibly, at the front of the stage.

During the second set, her full band, with trombonist Jai Patel and electric bassist Matt May storm into Copycat, another of her compositions. It's a piece of powerful rhythmic velocity, with Allexa playing at a Johnny Griffin-like speed and Hinton's quicksilver keyboard solo dancing off swiftly into the Dalston night. As the listeners were swept into her band's universal timbre, it made me wonder why she called her first record 'No Language'. 'I decided to express myself in my own way, regardless of genre,' she replied.

I'm certainly looking forward to her first full album. 'I'd love to make a longer record,' she confided, 'I have the music composed and ready to record.' For all her listeners from London to Lima, I hope we don't have to wait too long.

(No Language is available on Newtone Records)

Steve Noble (England) - I hope I can keep on keeping on until the last drum roll and tattoo rolls out of my being
(2025)

The four CDs of HEMP are a drummer's sonic autobiography, played through the brilliance of master-percussionist Steve Noble's love for the four drummers who changed his life. 'I came across them the day I bought my first drum kit aged 12, and they've been a constant source of inspiration ever since,' he told me. Each of the discs is a homage to one of the four: Dutchman Han Bennink, New Orleans-born Ed Blackwell, New Yorker Milford Graves and Burton-on-Trent-born Phil Seamen. 'I never heard Phil live, but I would go to hear the others whenever they were in England. Even now, my early morning practice is accompanied by listening to Jamaican Joe Harriott's Free Form, with Mr Seamen's utterly fantastic drumming.'

Noble was born in 1960 in Streatley, Berkshire. 'It was a wonderful time and place. My dad was an NHS dentist and my mum did secretarial work. He was Scottish and we went to Edinburgh every year. I loved to hear the pipe bands march down Princes Street - definitely an early influence! I was into rock and pop and saw The Who in 1972 - I even met their drummer, Keith Moon, the same year as I got my first drum set. I was introduced to jazz and improvised music through the magazine Drums and Percussion, as well as Melody Maker weekly. I'm self-taught, but had a few lessons when I was 15.'

In 1977 he moved to London, worked as an auctioneer's porter, 'and then went all-in on the drums, practising for hours, going to gigs and trying to meet like-minded musicians. In 1979 I met Nigerian drum master Elkan Ogunde and we played many concerts [and] workshops together - a great learning experience. By the mid-80s I was organising concerts and festivals and performing with Sheffield guitarist Derek Bailey, another huge influence, which continued until his passing in 2005.'

'Thirty-one years ago I toured east Africa from Dar es Salaam to Cape Town with accordionist Dean Broderick and Oren Marshall on tuba. Our repertoire was wide but the Kwela-style tunes got the folk up and dancing and for me that was a blast!'

What about the drummers saluted on HEMP?

'The width of Han Bennink's sound-world was so mind-blowing when I first saw him. I probably copied him for a short time. He helped me so much to find myself as a drummer. Ed Blackwell had such great swing, amazing rhythms and a truly individual drum voice. Ornette's quartet records with him on are still so inspiring. 'Milford Graves was so unique and powerful. His concept so strong and his sound a delight. And Oh Boy, Phil Seamen! Fantastic drum sound and an amazing take on African drumming - one of the greatest English drummers ever!'

In a drumming life Noble has played with 'so many inspiring heavyweights, but playing with Derek in my 20s was a dream come true. I've developed so much since he passed that it would be a joy to play with him as I am now - maybe I'll have to wait until I pass on!'

He also venerates the times he played with the viscerally beautiful German saxophonist Peter Brotzman in a trio with London arch-bassist John Edwards. 'We played with him from 2010 until his passing in 2023. Whether it was in duo, trio or quartet he would want you to push and make the music as vibrant and honest as possible - no bullshit! I played with him on his last Café Oto gig in February 2022. It'll be released soon on the Oto label.'

On much of HEMP he drums alone, but other tracks also feature clarinettist Alex Ward, trumpeter Gabriel Wonck, Alan Wilkinson on bass clarinet and James Allsop on tenor sax. 'I'm always searching for new sounds,' he declares. 'It doesn't stop! For each group I put together a drums and cymbals set that will best suit the group's particular sound. I'm fascinated by music and drumming from all over the world. Korean court music, for example, is so close to free jazz. I'm always listening to it.'

And how does he see the present state of free improvisation in Britain? 'I'm fortunate to play with so many world-class UK players, and it's very encouraging to see many younger musicians coming through. I hope I can keep on keeping on until the last drum roll and tattoo rolls out of my being.'

All his listeners do too, for in giving tribute to his beloved drum legends, he very modestly becomes one too.

(HEMP is available on Ping Pong Productions)

Aine O'Dwyer (Ireland) & Han Bennink (Netherlands) - A rare musical tryst

Aine O'Dwyer and Han Bennink, Café Oto, London (2024)

A brilliantly unlikely musical encounter took place in Dalston, East London last week. Standing on the stone floor of the Café Oto before a packed house was the sculpted form of a beautiful wooden harp, next to an unremarkable set of drums. These were the instruments of the Limerick-born harpist Aine O' Dwyer, and the octogenarian Dutch free drummer, Han Bennink, who as a young man in the 60s had played and recorded with legendary U. S. saxophonists Dexter Gordon and Ben Webster, and had been the drummer on Eric Dolphy's last date in 1964, in Hilversum, Holland.

Bennink introduced the session by saying that he had never played with a harpist before, while O' Dwyer smiled, her head leaning warmly against the upright of her harp.

What followed was a unique sequence of improvised chamber jazz pieces, with Bennink's toms and rattling snares making undercurrents of forthright rhythms. He drummed his knees and struck a drumstick clenched between his teeth with another, while O' Dwyer played softly, sometimes singing wordlessly above Bennink's percussive perturbations, sometimes stroking her strings so wistfully, you thought it was a lullaby she was making for those mothers and children outside pushing their prams in the seething Hackney streets.

There was a parallel empathy to her astonishing April 2016 album, Music for Church Cleaners, recorded at St. Mark's Church, Islington, which included the sounds of women hoovering and sweeping around the pews, accompanying her playing of the church organ.

As she strummed and plucked the multiple strings of her harp, I was reminded of the song Minstrel Boy, written by Irishman Thomas Moore (1779 - 1852) which Paul Robeson used to sing, telling the story of the rebel harpist whose 'songs were made for the pure and free, they will never sound in slavery'. With the insurgent drums of the veteran Bennink rumbling and crackling beside her, it was a musical tryst of astonishing free timbral spirits.

Leila Olivesi (France/Mauritius) - Radiant record's sunlit orbit

Leila Olivesi Quartet (featuring David Binney) – Utopia
(2017)

It's not customary for a jazz musician to record an album directly inspired by a 17th-century philosopher, free-thinking author and polemicist, but Leila Olivesi's Utopia is just that.

Cyrano de Bergerac (1619-1655) the philosopher, was not the character created in the late 19th century play by Edmond Rostand, but the writer of the posthumously published The States and Empires of the Moon and The States and Empires of the Sun, jointly titled The Other World. I don't know whether Sun Ra of Birmingham, Alabama, the first iconic jazz space traveller and man of Saturn, ever read de Bergerac's works, but with his Arkestra he imagined a soundscape in the stars, a universe which Olivesi forms and creates in an entirely contrary way with this album.

Olivesi, of French and Mauritanian roots, is a pianist with the lightest and most tender of keyboard touches, and her record radiates an unusual and quiescent beauty. The benign lyrics of her song Sunland (she sings on two of the eight tracks of Utopia) hint at the creative sources of her music: 'Dew drops fall/Flowers blossom looking at the sun,/In the morning daze/I hear the din of something.' And it is the kindly echoes of that 'din' that inhabit and personalise that outcry, uproar and silence of the stars mediated through her gently powerful piano voice.

With her on Utopia are guitarist Manu Codjia, bassist Yoni Zelnik with Donald Kontomanou on drums. On four of the tracks the Miami-born alto saxophonist David Binney makes up a quintet. Olivesi likens her wish for a utopia of sound to 'the freedom to talk to trees, to flowers, to birds' and she has four confreres here who do that too with a sense of love and prime artistry.

The opener is Le Monde de Cyrano, a sauntering melody with Binney's skipping alto making the melody and palavering with the comping Olivesi.

There is nothing sombre about this world and when Olivesi dives into her dancing solo alongside Kontomanou's flickering drums, she expresses a place of joy and exuberance. In Sunland there is intimacy of musicianship between her piano and Codjia's softly-talking guitar: 'Sit my friend close to me,' she sings, 'I'll tell you the great story of Sunland.'

Her Utopia still has Night and Day and Cole Porter's beautiful tune, Darkness and Light Among the Planets, illuminated by Codjia's brilliant guitar and Olivesi's journeys up and down the keys of space. The time suddenly turns march-like as the journey's end approaches, and straight into the electronic sonic world of Revolutions and the orbits of change. Zelnik's delving bass, the heart of the quartet, leads the changes, and Kontomanou's restless drums drive the engine of insurgence.

Con Calma is the story of a lonely bird growing to strength and power. 'In the woods, strong as a tree,' sings Olivesi, 'Tiny bird can fly and sing.' And he burgeons and thrives with the music: 'In the blue, light as the wind/Shining bird has lit his wings.' Binney's alto sings a lyrical narrative, exchanging storytelling with Codjia's guitar in a colloquy of nature before Olivesi's lucid summative piano chorus. The tones of Binney's horn sound centuries old, like Cyrano's words during his theme statements of Symphonic Circle, and as his pitch climbs he walks into modernity side by side with Olivesi's crystalline notes. Lune is a direct allusion to Cyrano's States and Empires and is heralded by Kontomanou's scattering drums. Binney's notes fly everywhere and Codjia follows, picking up his patterns.

The final track, Summer Wings, won the Ellington composer award, and she is back to birdflight and birdsong. Codjia plays the melody, serene and temperate, Zelnik's solo bass pecks into the earth, and Olivesi is grounding it all with her pianism, never dominating, never grandstanding, the least egocentric of musicians but one whose portion of sound is absolutely essential and formative.

Four centuries ago Cyrano asserted freedom of thought, of expression and of life. Olivesi does the same in her own sonic world.

(Utopia is available on Jazz and People)

Roella Oloro (England/Nigeria) - When it comes to Britain's colonial past, music can be part of that reckoning

Roella Oloro, Vortex, London
(2025)

It was an especially groovy session at the Vortex, with Roella Oloro's sparkling piano, the plummeting, dancing bass of Rio Kai and the deft, everywhere drums of Andee Liu. Roella plays in and out of the tradition with such pride and skill, that if you shut your eyes you could be hearing moments of Geri Allen,

Mary Lou Williams, Tommy Flanagan or her earliest inspiration, Oscar Peterson. How they would have loved her!

As she began, listeners knew the unambiguous sources and springs of her artistry, dedicating her first piece to all those who marched for George Floyd, with her trio-mates adding a depth of insurgent undertow to Roella's passionate power. As her wordless vocals stretched skywards, Kai's bass stayed close to the earth like the soil of the soul, and his exchanges with Liu's restless drums were like the palaver of brothers. The three of them: so young, with so much precious talent, as they strode into The Saints as you have never heard it played before, or the tenderness of Coltrane's Naima, the beauty of its love-melody passing gently over Dalston's rooftops.

Roella was born in Gloucester in 1998, with an IT prison teacher mum of Jamaican heritage and a Tesco delivery driver Dad of Nigerian roots. They both played piano 'as a passion rather than a profession,' and her mum was her first piano teacher before she began on clarinet at 7 and saxophone at 13. As a child she would jam on piano and bass guitar with her younger drummer brother.

'Growing up in rural England as a young black musician, my friends liked pop and there was an emphasis on classical music if I was to be seen as a proficient pianist. I now recognise this as some internalised racial stigma, because I would think I was pre-disposed not to have a good classical technique because I was a black musician, there being no examples of black classical musicians available to me. So thank God for Nottingham's Kenneh-Mason family in our current age! The rise of that family sent me on a learning journey!'

'As a teenager I loved jazz, listening to Oscar Peterson and Tommy Flanagan, then bebop via Charlie Parker and Cannonball Adderley. It took me a while to get used to the angularities of bebop as my ears hadn't yet learned to recognise all the implied harmonies. I heard a lot of reggae growing up, mainly from hymns in the local Pentecostal church. When I left school I took a gap year to mentor a student with functioning autism in my old secondary school. Then, in 2017 I went to Laban music school in south London. I was much encouraged by BBC's Young Jazz Musician of the Year, pianist Deschanel Gordon, young saxophonist Sylvan Biscoe, drummer Simon Lamb and the other young peers I met through the Tomorrow's Warriors project. It was at Laban that I became attuned to my Nigerian culture, as I lived in Woolwich with its strong Nigerian community.'

What about Rio and Andee, her present trio-mates? 'I perform with many configurations, but Andee I met at Berklee College, Boston, USA where I studied from 2019-2023. He's an incredibly talented Welsh-Chinese drummer. Rio's bass playing captivates me. Equally good on upright and electric bass, he has a great sound and incredible ears, with beautifully constructed linear ideas. At Berklee, my tutors, drummer Terri Lyne Carrington and Panamanian pianist Danilo Perez are developing the next generation of socially conscious musicians. They both played in the great saxophonist Wayne Shorter's last quartet. The kind-hearted and passionate concern for the world around him which infused his music formed part of Terri and Danilo's social justice inspiration for equity and equality through music. She is director of the Jazz and Gender Justice Institute, calling out the music's patriarchal nature and combatting the erasure of women's contributions to jazz history, and he is artistic director of the Global Jazz Institute.'

'I'm grateful I studied with both at Berklee, and now recognise how their teachings relate to Britain. When it comes to its colonial past and how this still feeds into its complex societal issues, there's still a lot of reckoning and unearthing to do for forward movement to be attained. Music can be a part of that reckoning.'

'It can help to forge better relations between the current state of our multicultural population and the interconnections with their future offspring. The London jazz scene is already a strong catalyst for inciting this change, with bands like the Ezra Collective, Koko-Roko and artists like saxophonist Nubya Garcia gaining international reach as strong sonic voices for British youths of minority ethnic backgrounds.'

Mike Osborne (England) - Osborne to be wild

A session captured in 1976 is hot and alive - and it only just exists

Mike Osborne Trio – The Birmingham Jazz Concert (2012)

You wouldn't instantly recognise the cathedral city of Hereford and the quiet rural habitat of Much Wenlock in Shropshire as venues of hot jazz, but they produced two of Britain's stormiest jazz musicians - alto saxophonist Mike Osborne and drummer Tony Levin. And add to them the plunging bass heartbeat of the exiled Cape Towner Harry Miller, who arrived in London in the early '60s as bass guitarist of the Manfred Mann group and grew into one of the prime bassists of free jazz, then you have a trio of boiling sound.

When Levin died in February 2011, he was the last survivor of this threesome. Miller had died in a car crash in Holland in 1983, and Osborne - whose musical life had been set aside by illness since 1982 - was taken by lung cancer in 2007. Now a recording has come to light which shows what a powerful trio they were when they were performing at their triple apex. It stems from 1976 when they appeared on a series of sessions organised by Birmingham Jazz at the city's Grand Hotel. We owe a huge debt not only to John Jack of Cadillac Records, who put out the performance on a double CD, but also to George West, who has kept his tape of this sonic adventure pristine and exceedingly groovy for all of these 35 years.

He recorded the performance as a souvenir on a Maxwell C180 tape and it 'remained unplayed in my files until unearthed in 2009,' as another example of the huge debt that jazz owes to all the amateur sound engineers who have preserved so many marvellous and spontaneous sessions over many decades.

There were no announcements of tune titles, leaving educated guesses for most of them by the trio's followers and contemporaries. As soon as the first track Ossie's Opener begins, as a listener you are right there standing next to the musicians and sucking up the sheer excitement of their sound. Osborne is fleet, lucid and blowing fire through his horn, while Miller's vibrating beat never leaves him and Levin crackles ceaselessly. As the ensemble slows down at the end, it is as if an express train has at last found its buffers.

But there is no halt as the trio moves immediately into the nine-minute improvisation of More Mike, in which Miller takes a chorus as his deep strings sing and oscillate as if they are subterranean. The lack of pause or interval between tunes means that Osborne leaps directly into Coltrane's Cousin Mary, with Levin's drums and cymbals thrashing all around him. Ossie's pace is so fast and relentless that the walls of the Grand hotel must have levitated.

Suddenly, unheralded, there is calm and grandeur with Miller's tune Awakening Spirit, but its intensity leaves it no respite - only a preface for Levin's tempestuous drums. Then, with hardly with a gasp in between, the trio launches into the familiar chops of Sonny Rollins's Alfie, which Osborne essays with an astonishing fluency and tonal beauty. Only at its end is the first momentary break for applause, before the trio bursts into Osborne's tune Journey's End, segueing into All Night Long and finally into a song which sounds more than a little like I'll Take You Home Again, Kathleen, but is marked down as Almost Home Kathy. It brings to an end the unremitting sonic propulsion of the first disc.

Monk's Nutty is immediately recognisable as the first tune of disc 2, and so fresh and audacious is it, with Osborne projecting his shapes and ideas with such clarity and humour that you wish that this trio had cut a whole album of Monk themes, earthed by the marvellous Miller's universal twang. Osborne makes his horn chime like an outrageous clock at the beginning of One For George, presumably dedicated to the precious work of West. Its successor Ken's Tune is a prodigious swinger, and Osborne sounds like a rampaging birdsong.

By the time that the 10 minutes of Don't Stop the Carnival have transpired after another longer, arco version of the hymnal Awakening Spirit, you know well that this was a brilliant, riveting and often breathless live session, typical of its era. It makes you realise again not only what a timbral miracle this trio was during that night nearly four decades ago in the very gut of Britain, but how much these superb and unique three musicians are missed and longed for.

(The Birmingham Jazz Concert is available on Cadillac)

Raphael Pannier Quartet (France)
with Khadim Niang's Sabar Group (Senegal)
Live in St. Louis
(2025)

'Live in St. Louis' was not recorded in St. Louis, Missouri - a nursery of jazz, but an ocean away in St. Louis, Senegal, in a startling fusion of African, Caribbean and European musicianship.

The root of it all is the Sabar tradition of group drumming, a percussive form of eight drums speaking a devotional language of the ancestors passed between villages and communities across Senegal. Yet into this complex musical discourse led by the veteran Sabar drummer Khadim Niang - an ex-bandmate of the late Senegalese master, N'Diaye Rose, came three Frenchmen, bassist Francois Moutin, pianist Thomas Enhco and Parisian jazz drummer Thomas Pannier, alongside the alto saxophonist from Matanzas, Cuba, Yosvany Terry, and a new sonic union was born in the heart of the St. Louis International Jazz Festival in May, 2024.

It's a palpitating tryst, Yoruba melodies such as Sine Saloum, African hymnal themes with an Albert Ayler groove such as Xalat Bou Set (The Holy Spirit) and a tribute to a great drummer, Hommage to Doudou N'Diaye Rose, are all grounded by the pulsating Senegalese percussion, while the session begins with a haunting version of Ornette Coleman's Lonely Woman, with Terry's quivering alto dancing a solitary blues over the pounding drums. I'm sure Ornette would have loved it. Then another surprise: the cool 1960 melody of the Dave Brubeck Quartet's chart-topping Take Five, given the Sabah undercurrent. Terry's liquid, swinging alto is very different to that of its composer, Paul Desmond, yet the Atlantic makes no difference as the 64 years between the two versions melt away like the genres they are supposed to represent.

The Europeans come powerfully to the fore in Kalat Bou Set, with Enhco's electric piano creating cross-continental vibes with the rhythmic African drum-soil of the Sabar drummers. Then it is Coltrane, who has to be there too. His Naima is played with restrained lyricism by Terry, with Enhco's tender acoustic keys and a gentle solo by Moutin before the errant choruses of a soaring Terry.

The homage to the great African drummer has the eight Sabar drums in eloquent unison over Moutin's bass, and by the time of the final track, Djolokanete, Terry has made Sabar drums his own, as if they had sprung from his own Cuban earth. This is an unforgettable session with the everlasting truth that all musicians, from everywhere in the world, are one.

(Live in St. Louis, Senegal is available on Miel Music)

Charlie Parker (USA) - The greatest jazz concert ever?

Charlie Parker & the Quintet of the Year - Jazz at Massey Hall (2013)

Forty years ago I bought a 'two-fer' double LP of what was billed as 'the greatest jazz concert ever.' The sleeve showed the roof levitating above a blazing Victorian concert hall. It was the recording of the concert at Massey Hall, Toronto, of May 15 1953 that featured 'the quintet of the year' - possibly the most august line-up of jazz musicians ever to perform together in the same venue.

Five musical giants indeed. Charlie 'Bird' Parker on a plastic alto saxophone he had borrowed for the evening, trumpeter Dizzy Gillespie, bop master pianist Bud Powell, Max Roach on drums and archbassist Charles Mingus setting up his own recording equipment. Together in Toronto, though some bad date-setting meant that it was the same night as the world heavyweight championship fight in New York between Rocky Marciano and Jersey Joe Walcott.

That meant the historic theatre was only about a quarter full and Gillespie, a big boxing fan and admirer of Walcott, was using every pretext he could to retreat towards the radio in the wings to check the progress of the bout. So the context was hardly ripe for a momentous concert. But listen to it again, as you can now on a single CD some 60 years later. It was amongst the essential moments of bop, a form of jazz that one of the originators of the music, Louis Armstrong, had called 'Chinese music' - and not as a compliment either.

Here were five of bop's inventors, loose and at ease, and on neutral Canadian territory. All the concert's performances are here, including the six trio tracks of Powell, Mingus and Roach in their original order, and as Roach's ever ready snares roll and the five-some break into the opener Wee, Parker weaves magic and Gillespie pursues him with his own burning notes. Powell races up and down his keys in frantic motion and Roach, in rampant fettle from the off, hurtles into a bespoke solo, rattling the old theatre's rafters.

Next up is Tadd Dameron's Hot House, its melodic cadences pouring out of the horns and Bird's solo melting the plastic of his saxophone. The rhythmic pulse is held back and Gillespie sways on it, his phrases cutting through the lakeside air, all down Yonge Street. Powell makes complex patters through his courses as if it were his fired brain striking the keys. Mingus comes forward for his twanging solo and the floor bounces to another level.

A Night in Tunisia follows in this night in Ontario and Parker's first miraculous break opens the listeners' imagination to any part of the cosmos.

Dizzy takes the solo on his own tune as if he is conceiving it for the first time as he blows. Powell is restrained and you feel the intensity of his concentration in every cluster of notes that he spins out. The next track is solo Roach, Drum Conversation - nearly five minutes of drum reinvention before the trio's performance.

Five tunes they play, beginning with I've Got You Under My Skin and Embraceable You, two ballads which show that bop can be soulful, slow and sumptuous - opposite qualities to the rumbustious power of the trio's Cherokee, a storm of notes with Roach's brushes full of furious strokes. Hallelujah swings relentlessly and Englishman George Shearing's Lullaby of Birdland becomes Powell's romp of joy.

Back to the quintet with Perdido, its Caribbean lilt from its composer, Puerto Rican Juan Tizol, finding flavour with Parker's blues-baked sound and Gillespie's intense love of the Afro-Cuban as he hovers on its ascendant notes. Parker introduces the next tune, something of a novelty number written by 'my worthy constituent,' Dizzy Gillespie - Salt Peanuts. Its astonishing pace, which the two horns essay with unstinting nerve and puckish humour, made it a huge crowd-pleaser and even the depleted Canadian audience on this spring night caught the wide-open groove.

The closer is another ballad, Kern and Hammerstein's All the Things You Are. Strange that it became something of a bop anthem, and the quintet treats its transcendent melody with respect and love despite Parker's sudden allusion to the Kerry Dance.

Who wouldn't have been in Toronto that evening to take one of those unsold seats? And as a tail-piece and much to Dizzy's chagrin, Marciano beat Jersey Joe by a knockout.

(Jazz at Massey Hall is available on Essential Jazz Classics)

Evan Parker (England) - Music For David Mossman

Evan Parker, Barry Guy and Paul Lytton: The Vortex, London (2017)

It's an uncanny experience as well as a privilege to sit in an intimate venue like the Vortex in Dalston, East London, listen to and watch carefully three brilliantly innovative musicians at the closest possible quarters, then a full two years later, play a recording of that very same session on your own stereo in your own front room.

Bristolian saxophonist and Londoners drummer Paul Lytton and bassist Barry Guy, all pioneers of British free jazz stretching back to the Sixties, are a septuagenarian trio who defy all musical norms. In July 2016 they performed at the Vortex as a tribute t its founder, David Mossman, and as a recognition of its significance in the history of jazz in Britain. 'It is my haven from the demands of the road,' declared Parker. 'I cannot imagine life without it.' And there are many other musicians and music-lovers who would say something very similar.

I reviewed the session for the Morning Star and was sitting so close to the remarkable Lytton that I could have shared my drink with him. To watch so closely his every strike, rustle and brush caress as if his arms were mine was the most blatant of fantasies, but his huge collection of percussive surfaces - skin, metal, wood and plastic, his assortment of sticks, mallets, brushes and rods reminded me of the time that I sat at the same proximity to Art Blakey's thunderous rolling drums at Ronnie Scott's four and a half decades before.

But down to the music and the record, for it is full of the discovering and the unique, as you would expect from three alchemists of sound. The first track begins with Guy's pulsating, leaping strings and the scuttling, diverse fury of Lytton's percussion. Parker's tenor saxophone seems to emerge rising from below the tarmacked Dalston earth, and grows more muscular and belligerent as his confreres' sounds become more relentless and intense. Parker always sounds like Parker, but there are times when the motor within his lungs and the sheer power of his plunging cadences crosses sounds with the entire history of his horn, from Hawkins and Webster to Rollins, Coltrane and McPhee.

Guy's springing, delving bass sound, exuberant and inflamingly beautiful, exhilarates the opening of the second movement and leads to the unleashed excitation of Parker's sawing sound, a passionate horn oration which subsides to a musician telling secrets with his notes, while others are still yet to be told. As for Lytton, although his drums and cymbals are continually in motion and in colloquy with his trio-mates, they are also perpetually listening to any new step or fresh direction that they take, for it is the ears of his drums that provoke every sound or perturbation that they make.

The third movement is the longest and most climactic. Parker's ascending riffs and quivering vibrato give way to an astonishing palaver between Guy and Lytton. Guy seems to have twenty hands, so many notes does he play, and Lytton is never far from him, his rattling snares and showers of cymbals in absolute concord with the bassist's throbbing strings.

Three men here whose life is music and its creations and freedoms, and the truth that this blessed venue gives them and their transfixed listeners the chance to unite in artistry, is what the music celebrates and honours: long live the Vortex!

(Music For David Mossman is available on Intakt Records)

Evan Parker (England) - All Knavery And Collusion
(2025)

As a boy, some seven decades ago, I used to go with my family for annual holidays to the Isle of Sheppey. My father would hire two bikes in Leysdown - a cosmos of holiday camps - and we would ride them southwards over the low pasturelands and marshes to Harty, opening and shutting all the iron gates over the road to stop the sheep from roaming. There, on the edge of the Swale, the channel which separates Sheppey from the mainland of Kent, my father would buy a pint and orange juice at the Ferry Boat Inn, and we would sit on a bench and look towards Sittingbourne, the other side of the Swale.

There are two reasons why I recall this as I listen to the Evan Parker Quartet's record, All Knavery and Collusion. Firstly, it was at the nearby Warden Bay Hotel that the great pioneer of the tenor saxophone, Coleman Hawkins of St. Joseph, Missouri, played one of his final English gigs in 1968, the engine of his horn echoing over the Harty marshes. Secondly, this 2019 recording was made in the Rimshot Studios of Sittingbourne. You can hear Hawkins and the whole history of the jazz tenor saxophone in Evan's volleys of notes, and his sounds on this record make an uncanny amalgam with those of the great Hawk.

Yet it is a quartet playing, and what a quartet! I have listened to, watched, written about and marvelled at John Edwards' bass playing many, many times. He holds his bass as if it were another person with whom he is dancing, for in his arms his bass is human, speaks and sounds like a man or woman, making living twangs of human joy, contradiction, sorrow, love and hope. Watching Paul Lytton close up, seeing his array of drums and percussion surfaces is as much a spectator pleasure as a sonic one, yet the complexities of his sounds and his ability to both follow and lead his confreres so intuitively makes him a very special musician who strikes, brushes, raps, caresses and nuzzles a universe of drums.

Then there is the youngest soul of this quartet, pianist Alexander Hawkins, who strikes out his powerhouse riffs and repeated use of suspense and space as if all the bells of Kent are ringing. Yet his flights into improvisation are somehow formed by self-created, one-time melodies that having been invented once and now, will never be struck again. I can always hear Africa in his notes even though he is an Oxford man: perhaps it is the infectious energy of playing so often with the Cape Town drum griot Louis Moholo-Moholo. Some sonic gift has been given and powerfully received in Hawkins' pianism, for it is one talent to make such rampant runs along the keys back and forth, but another compounded artistic skill to create pristine themes and snatches of instant beauty as you do it.

In All Knavery and Collusion Lytton's drums mutter and roll as Parker's horn meanders and expostulates. This title, and three others, are taken from Daniel Defoe's account of the 1665 London epidemic, 'Journal of the Plague Year'. Not so The Alchemy of John Edwards, which is not to turn base metal into gold but to turn bass sound into subterranean symphony. Edwards creates a union of founding strings and embroiled percussion, slapping, plucking and pounding out a new, transformed musical element. In A Well Staring at the Sky, the parched earth longs for liquid sounds as Parker's circling breath draws them to the surface. Edwards' almost menacing beginning to The Influence of the Dog Star is drawn into Hawkins' clinking notes as if by an impulse to be unified. A Blazing Star or Comet Appeared begins with Hawkins' angular, pointillistic pressing towards some galactic moment in the skies above the bleak and muddy Swale.

I write this just beyond what we are told is the peak of the coronavirus epidemic, in Britain anyway, of 2020. Listening to this music has both revived me and urged me to reconstitute hope. Perhaps it would have emboldened Defoe too 'and scum off all the Gall of our tempers, remove the Animosities among us, and bring us to see with differing Eyes, than those which we looked on Things before.'

(All Knavery And Collusion is available on Cadillac Records)

Evan Parker (England), John Edwards (England) & Robert Jarvis (England) – Unity is the brilliant strength

Vortex London

(2019)

The improvising tenor saxophone of Evan Parker, joined by that Godzilla of bassists John Edwards and the sometimes ferocious, sometimes tender slides of arch-trombonist and sound-installation artist Robert Jarvis are a free-playing playing and virtuoso trio, as they demonstrate at this gig.

As they open, Edwards's bow seemed to mow his strings with long, lingering notes, while Jarvis's moaning slides seem to go back to New Orleans and Kid Ory's Savoy Blues and his curling, luxuriant multisonic speechifying suddenly interrupts Edwards's quickfire plucking and the percussive embrace of his bass.

Through it all, Parker's tenor blows out circles of sound - snatches of Coleman Hawkins, echoes of Sonny Rollins and sound-spectres of John Coltrane - in notes showering out of his horn. It's as if a century of jazz is coalescing, earthed by a bassist whose pounding brilliance makes a drum for this percussion-free trio.

None of the three are present for mere accompaniment or for the horns to fly as mere individual embellishment or the setting loose of egos. This is ensemble music, collectively inspired and co-operatively played, with each musician as much a simultaneous listener as a simultaneous sound-maker.

In its own unique way, it's a parable of democracy, with a surprising edge of drama and history and a solid, ever-moving body of sonic beauty.

Evan Parker (England), Tony Coe (England) & Julian Arguelles (England) – Frank and fearless foursome in fulsome form

Vortex Jazz Club, London

(2017)

Miraculous are the changes within jazz lifetimes. The last time that I heard the sublime Canterbury-born saxophonist Tony Coe play, he was in the Humphrey Lyttelton Band of the early '60s, blowing Humph's version of mainstream. Now 81, he's playing at the Vortex alongside two master tenor saxophonists of different generations. Also in the line-up are septuagenarian Evan Parker and the 20-years-younger Julian Arguelles, with pianist Frank Campbell as the only man without a horn.

I always thought that Coe's serpentine reedsong was just about as close to that of the great Ellingtonian Paul Gonsalves as any other saxophonist has ever got. But to hear him in a much freer improvising context shows the immensely wide dimensions of his music.

Co-veteran Campbell is the unifying presence all evening and his duet with Parker, mysteriously blues-like, has him plucking the piano's strings while Parker's deep beauty rumbles beside him. Campbell then leads Arguelles into the ballad Nancy With the Laughing Face, played with a muscled yet fragile power. His subsequent duo with Coe's soprano saxophone is a skyward dance, with the pianist's earthen chords as its shining floor.

The quartet move on with a set of Campbell's structured compositions, ensemble pieces in which their free impulses are ploughed into some astonishing harmonies, with Coe's soprano filigreeing in and out of his confreres' pungent tenors.

A Dalston chamber foursome indeed, blending with the half-muffled sounds of crashing dominoes, reggae and Caribbean-London voices in the square outside.

William Parker (USA) - The fires of flowers and revolution

William Parker and the Little Huey Creative Music Orchestra - Sunrise in the Tone World, William Parker - Neptune & William Parker/Raining on the Moon - Corn Meal Dance

(2013)

This is what the Bronx-born bassist William Parker writes about the inspiration of his big band, The Little Huey Creative Music Orchestra: 'Huey Jackson was an aspiring poet who grew up in the housing projects of the south Bronx. Huey envisioned a world where anything was possible. Talking flowers, bright blue trees, green snowflakes against a yellow sky. Every-one around Huey discouraged him from being a poet. To Huey the word 'poet' was synonymous with the words 'human being.' Huey continued to write until he passed away shortly before his 18th birthday.' Parker tells us that Huey's orchestra began in 1944 and 'is committed to all those who are told not to dream. 'We exist,' he declares, 'for those who have had the flame of hope put out in their lives. All those torn apart by war, poverty, madness, loneliness and hate.'

Quite a commission here, and the orchestra's first album, a double CD called Sunrise in the Tone World, was dedicated to 'restoring life, with keeping the fire of human compassion burning. The fire of flowers as well as the fire of revolution.' The title could be that of a Sun Ra album. Yet Parker does not travel the spaceways and behold the planets, neither does he claim to be a sojourner from Saturn. Instead, he walks the streets of the Bronx and like Huey or Blake walking the chartered London streets, he sees and feels the humanity all around him, who feed 'the ideas of my imagination,' as they struggle to make sense and hope of this world where the waters of the Styx pour into the Hudson River.

Hear the stupendous ensemble of the title tune and Rob Brown's vertiginous alto sax, or Steve Swell's huge trombone slides in The Bluest, blown out of the midst of the orchestra's surge of unified sound. Huey wrote in his diary in 1968: 'Today I was lying under a tree just about to die and I noticed light coming through a green leaf. This instantly saved my life so I could go on another day.' The 40 minutes of Huey Sees Light Through a Leaf tells this story sonically, with, in Parker's words, the 'whole band playing a form of collective solo,' all 25 of them, with a whirlwind of reeds like giant insects in a marsh, furious drums by Susie Ibarra and belligerent brass. Roy Campbell's note-splitting trumpet crackles through Mayan Space Station. Then there is Sunship for Dexter, dedicated to the great tenor saxophonist Dexter Gordon who 'inspired us to create from creation' and for whom Huey's tenorist Ben Koen blows through the spheres.

By 2007 Parker was developing his concept of 'universal tonality, which is based on the idea that all sounds like human beings come from the same place.' This idea found expression in his album Double Sunrise Over Neptune, recorded with a 16-piece orchestra at the Orensanz Arts Centre in New York.

It's a unique strings-emphatic ensemble including two violins, two violas, a cello, banjo, guitar and oud, giving a powerfully multisonic and rhythmic underlay to four reeds, two sets of drums and Sangeeta Bandyopadhyay's high-pitched, keening vocals - as in Morning Mantra and the 27 minutes of Lights of Lake George, where she sings in the Persian improvised devotional form of the Tarana. A long journey for jazz, but one taken with an astonishing naturalness and spontaneity by Parker's musicians, with memorable passages by Lewis Barnes's trumpet, Rob Brown's alto, Sabir Mateen's clarinet and the relentlessly uplifting drumming of Hamid Drake and Gerald Cleaver.

In the same year Parker recorded Corn Meal Dance with his sextet called Raining on the Moon, comprising Drake, Barnes and Brown with pianist Eri Yamamoto and vocalist Leena Conquest, who sings the accomplished lyrics by Parker and herself. The album is a potent amalgam of sound and word, and the most powerful alliance of poetry and jazz since Langston Hughes combined with Mingus's Jazz Workshop in another New York studio in March 1958.

Barnes, Brown and Yamamoto all play with fiery eloquence on Doctor Yesterday. Tutsi Orphans, where Parker sees a 'black angel standing by / writing poems in the sky' is tethered to the earth by the pumping rhythm of Parker and Drake.

The life of a militant black socialist writer is celebrated in the duo by two jazz women, African-American and Japanese, Conquest and Yamamoto in Poem for June Jordan, and memories of Sun Ra's great tenorist John Gilmore ride out the album as the musicians doff their own hats in the heaving Gilmore's Hat.

A marvel of an album this, by a jazz artiste for all seasons, all moments.

(Sunrise in the Tone World, Neptune & Corn Meal Dance are available on AUM)

Joe Pass (USA) - Synanon songs: music that healed its makers

Sounds of Synanon

(2015)

The post-war years of jazz were set alight by the explosion of bop: the astonishing new sounds of Charlie Parker, Dizzy Gillespie, Bud Powell, Thelonious Monk, Max Roach and a host of disciples and imitators. But with this joyous sonic revolution came its curse in the rise of drug culture and the misery of addiction, depression and self-harm. This was often provoked by a blind emulation of afflicted heroes like Parker and the frequently fostered myth that substances like heroin were catalysts for musical originality and brilliance.

This collapse into narcotics addiction was all too common in southern California and several prominent jazz musicians fell under its curse. One of these was the phenomenal guitarist Joe Pass, born Joseph Passalacqua in New Brunswick, New Jersey, in 1929. Pass became a professional musician while at high school, played in swing bands, spent two years in the US marines before settling in Los Angeles where the early promise of a life in music was derailed by narcotics addiction.

He spent time in prison and nearly four years at the public health service hospital at Fort Worth before joining the therapeutic community in Synanon, a residential treatment centre on the ocean shore at Santa Monica, where his constant positive exposure to music and fellow musicians eventually cured his addiction.

It also led to the unique album Sounds of Synanon, cut at the Pacific Jazz studios in Los Angeles in July 1962, where Pass on his recording debut joined other musician residents of Synanon as a celebration of the clinic's healing powers. Pianist Arnold Ross had attempted suicide before his stay in Synanon, trumpeter David Allan had been an Ornette Coleman accompanist before addiction, drummer Bill Crawford was a reformed addict who had joined Synanon's board of directors and conga man Candy Latson had, like Crawford, learned how to drum in the clinic from volunteer teachers.

The album's opening track C.E.D. is dedicated to Synanon's founder and co-ordinator Charles E. Dederich, an ex-alcoholic. Pass's guitar leads the way with some lightening chops above the restless beat of the drummers and bassist Ronald Clark, while on the bluesy Allan tune Aaron's Song, both the trumpeter and Ross play poised and eloquent choruses. Pass is relaxed and inventive on Stay Loose and Projections gives an opportunity for Greg Dykes to show his powerful mettle on baritone horn with more fluent lines from Pass.

The ramifications of the title of the track Self-image were crucial for its players and within its nine minutes Allan's tune becomes a burner for them all. Allan's tone is soft and tender while still reaching the heights, Dykes plays with emotive creation, Pass's chorus is sheer beauty and invention and Ross's solo, quietly and thoughtfully wrought, seems to exemplify the self-examined life and behaviour freely encouraged at Synanon.

This reissue on the Fresh Sound label is a diamond, for not only does it contain the rare Synanon tracks but also those on another singular album of 1962, with Pass in a trio context with his New Jersey confrere on organ, Richard 'Groove' Holmes and local drummer Lawrence Marable. This is not the conventional Jimmy Smith-model rumbustious organ trio, but more complex, intricate and subtle in its soundscape.

Hear the serenely balladic It Might As Well Be Spring with Holmes's coolly caressed melodism over Pass's chords, or Parker's bop classic Moose the Mooche where the guitar-organ interaction is superb and Pass launches himself on a soaring flight of notes before Holmes returns with a flying solo. Groove's Bag is a deceptively simple opus with Holmes unstoppable in his relentless swing and Pass well abreast of him.

Sweatin' is an apt title for the album opener, with so much excitation do the trio announce themselves. Pass's solo on Duke Pearson's Jeannine is short and sublime and Holmes's own composition Minor Surgery is a trio colloquy of rare brilliance, on a session once forgotten but now found again after more than half a century.

(Sounds of Synanon is available on American Jazz Classics)

Danilo Perez (Panama) Wayne, Brian, John and I

Celebration Vol 1 by the Wayne Shorter Quartet (2024)

In October 2014, the giant Newark, New Jersey-born tenor and soprano saxophonist Wayne Shorter (1933-2023) played one of his final concerts in Stockholm Concert Hall. This has now been released as Celebration: Volume 1. His longstanding superfine quartet-mates, bassist John Patitucci, drummer Brian Blade and the insurgent Panamanian pianist, Danilo Perez, were with him.

I ask Perez about his own life in music, and the impact upon it by the great Wayne. 'I was born in Monte Oscuro, Panama City in 1965,' says Perez. 'My father, Danilo Perez Sr, was a professional singer and educator whose teachings profoundly influenced me. His approach to interconnected music and using music as a tool for social change laid the groundwork for my later work as founder and director of the Berklee Global Jazz Institute in Boston.'

'My Panamanian roots have been instrumental in shaping my artistic vision, prompting me to blend diverse cultural elements into my music, particularly the guidance of remarkable mentors early in my life: my first piano teacher Cecilia Nunez from Chile, and Professor Edgardo Quintero. My family supported me to study music - as long as I was able to study another career. I chose electronics for a while.'

I ask him about his deep feelings for Panama. 'My love for my country,' he says, 'its rich history, cultural diversity and geographical position profoundly influences my music. In my upcoming record with the Bohusian Big Band there's a title called Galactic Panama. I envision Panama's future as a place that embraces the challenges of globalisation with wisdom and innovation. Galactic Panama blends jazz with tamborito, a folk music style known for its drumming and call-and-response vocals, reflecting African influences in Panama. The rhymes and traditions from my early years continue to inspire, blending seamlessly with global styles in my work. They are at the heart of my creative soul.'

In 1985 Perez won a Fulbright Scholarship to study in the US, followed by a Quincy Jones scholarship for Berklee, America's most prestigious jazz college. But it wasn't easy for a young Latin American jazz musician who believed fervently in the cultural sovereignty of his own people to build a musical career in the epicentre of imperialism. After playing and recording with many prime jazz musicians, in 1989 he became the youngest member of the great bebop pioneer Dizzy Gillespie's United Nation Orchestra.

Gillespie became another paramount mentor: 'From Dizzy I learned the transformative power of music, how it can bridge and unite cultures, connect peoples and foster understanding across boundaries. We call it global jazz. He showed me that we can create a cultural passport through music to bring people together.'

In December 1989, two days before he was to play his first major concert in Panama, the US invaded his country and he decided to express his cultural defiance at this imperial aggression. 'Even with the unrest, we decided to go ahead with the concert, which became an example of how music can heal during troubled times. Afterwards, I made albums like The Journey and Motherland to process the upheaval and celebrate our rich Panamanian identity. I wanted to share our nation's varied sounds and resilience with the world.'

His partnership with Shorter, Blade and Patitucci, which began in 2000, has deeply affected the pianist's musical life and growth. 'Wayne's mentorship pushed us out of our comfort zones and made us be fully present, leading us to develop concepts like 'comprovising for spontaneous composition', and Zero Gravity, which explores new musical frontiers. I also developed a harmonic system founded on an innovative approach that uses tetrachords and the blues to generate new sonorities. All this has been polished on the bandstand with John and Brian, under Wayne's guidance. His brilliance as a composer and player, combined with his profound love of life has magnified our vision of the world. He taught us that when music is intertwined with daily life and used as a transformational tool, it reveals the potential of a far greater society.'

You can hear the timbre of Perez's words all through the Celebration album. 'In Wayne's later years he was fully devoted to performing with complete musical freedom. The record captures our passion for exploring the unknown and communicating music in its most unrestricted form. For nearly 20 years, before each concert, we gathered in a circle with our heads together and felt aligned, making a sound. This ritual symbolises our deep familial connection and collective commitment for entering the unknown. Wayne's emphasis on artistic freedom enabled a truly open and creative partnership, reflecting his unwavering quest for musical discovery.'

And what about his other bandmates? 'John's artistry is defined by innovative bass technique, blending grooves with rich melodic lines, creating very personal statements. Brian is a painter on the drums: his adaptable drumming style combines complex rhythms with soulful and powerful performances. They are my galactic, telepathic brothers.'

For the past half-century I have listened to Wayne Shorter as Musical Director of Art Blakey's Jazz Messengers, through his explosive years with Miles Davis, his deeply innovative Blue Note albums of the '60s, his fusion masterpieces with Weather Report and his succession of albums with his final quartet. But I've never heard him play so freely and uninhibitedly as on this Celebration album, which is the fullest soundscape of Perez's final words to me.

'Wayne will be remembered as one of the visionaries and geniuses of our time, whose deep desire to express the importance of life and unite people through music has inspired us to view life through a creative lens and embrace the unknown with courage and joy.'

(Celebration Vol 1 by the Wayne Shorter Quartet is available on Blue Note Records)

Ivo Perelman (Brazil) - Cosmic force of jazz and improvised music

Armageddon Flower (with Matthew Shipp, William Parker and Mat Maneri) (2025)

The Sao Paulo-born saxophonist Ivo Perelman is truly one of the cosmic forces of jazz and improvised music. 'When I am playing saxophone I am actually singing,' he says, and adds this about his bandmates on their album, Armageddon Flower: 'Matthew, Mat and William all know that what we are trying to represent as musicians is the vocal quality of the human body, of the human species.'

Born in 1961 to a piano teaching mother and a businessman father, Perelman was a musical child prodigy, learning classical guitar, piano, cello, trombone and mandolin before he was sixteen. He played Scarlatti, Italian baroque and Villa Lobos on the guitar, but then turned first to clarinet then saxophone, and embraced jazz. 'It was difficult to find records, but I found some by Sonny Rollins while at the same time being deeply affected by Brazilian folk music and children's songs. African-Brazilian chants helped to free my musical thought, getting away from preconceived structures.'

'But still, 1960s Brazilian popular music also stimulated me a lot, the tone and intimacy of Jobim and bossa nova, which I played in bars and other gigs, still influences me. It was the era of severe military dictatorship in Brazil, when musicians were discouraged to meet and were not free to express whatever they wanted. Recordings were released, then suddenly taken off the market. There were strict restrictions of what could be said artistically. For me, my singing was through my saxophone. In Brazil, if you say you're a musician, people will assume you're a singer - instrumentalists are seen as inferior and only there to accompany singers.'

After dozens of albums - many with pianist Matthew Shipp, bassist William Parker and viola virtuoso Mat Maneri - comes Armageddon Flower. 'It's a unique album in my discography,' says Perelman, 'and sums up all the aesthetic questions that I have been probing for all these decades.' As for his bandmates: 'they're all magical, brilliant musicians in their own unique ways, and we share the conceptual ideas of what sound is. Not music, it is sound that comes first, music is made of sound. We seek deep, molecular responses, deeper than reflecting on the results that melodies and harmonies have. We go deep, and from that depth, we take off.'

'We try to instil hope in the hysteria of the times. This is one of the most critical times we have ever experienced as humans, just look at the desperate political instability of the events around us, we are at a turning point. My own journey has been tracked by art to shape one's life, amplified at a social level. Our intention is that our music brings the message of hope, that in time we can sort it all out and get back to our positive nature as human creatures.'

What about his bond with British musicians? 'I admire and was influenced and stimulated by them, and their discipline, sense of history and structure. They have a different type of perspective which often reflects a classical background.' Having recently recorded a duo album with the Brighton-born saxophonist John Butcher, Perelman was full of praise for his musicianship and considers their album a high point in his canon. 'I was mesmerised by John's creativity, originality and deep research into multisonics.'

As for Armageddon Flower, its artistry is a summation of four extraordinary musicians at the apex of their powers, a work where individual brilliance and cooperative union find an epitome, where a saving grace of improvised beauty is created at the brink of Trumpian disaster. 'Art can promote a positive, cathartic perspective in a troubled world,' Perelman told me; 'through the abstract language of sound, music can say things that would otherwise be kept inside us and remain silent. We need worldly, cosmic love that only pure sound can propagate.'

Get hold of Armageddon Flower, and amidst its luminous contradictions, contrasts and dissenting beauty of divergence, hear what you think.

(Armageddon Flower is available on Tao Forms Records)

Oscar Peterson (Canada) - Rightful king of the keys

The Oscar Peterson Quartet - Oscar Peterson Plays Count Basie (2009)

The loss of the marvellous Montreal-born veteran pianist Oscar Peterson in 2007 has made millions of jazz lovers worldwide consider his half-century of luminous achievement. His father was a railway passenger attendant on the Canadian Pacific Railway who had been born in St Croix in the Virgin Islands, while his mother was a cook and housekeeper from St Kitts. Peterson's prodigious piano skills were nurtured by his sister Daisy and developed in his teenage years as the featured artiste on a Montreal radio programme.

In 1949, jazz impresario Norman Granz heard of his excellence and invited him to New York to play at a Carnegie Hall Jazz at the Philharmonic concert. Peterson never looked back, becoming house pianist for Granz's emergent Verve jazz label and forming a celebrated trio on the Nat King Cole model with piano, guitar and bass.

So outstanding was Peterson's technique - the two-handed flood of notes, his speed, phrasing, harmonic knowledge and relentless swing, that he became one of the prime jazzmen of his epoch and accompanist of the jazz pantheon from Louis Armstrong to Billie Holiday, from Coleman Hawkins and Lester Young to Roy Eldridge and Milt Jackson.

There have been plenty of reissues of Peterson's early albums since his death, but none better than the 1955 Los Angeles studio session Oscar Peterson Plays Count Basie. Now, Basie and Peterson were opposites in many aspects. The minimalist Basie played about one note to maximalist Peterson's every 10. Yet they were kindred spirits and both swung mightily.

In the 1970s, Granz put them together for a series of key albums on the Pablo label, naming them Satch and Josh after two contrary baseball legends Satchel Paige and Josh Gibson, a deadly pitcher and big hitter respectively. Who was who in terms of Peterson and Basie is up to the listener to surmise.

The 1955 session has the very dextrous Herb Ellis on guitar playing as if he had a horn, the arch-bassist Ray Brown and spectacular swing drummer Buddy Rich. The quartet bounds into motion with Young's opus Lester Leaps In, which he played with the entire Basie orchestra behind him. But it is Peterson and Ellis leaping wildly here, after some introductory thrashing of the drums from Rich. Played at a breakneck speed of I-don't-know-how-many notes a minute, the musicians hurtle through the familiar theme as if a thousand cops were chasing them.

After this sprint, the sauntering pace of Easy Does It and 9.20 Special seems like relief, although the rapidity picks up again on the Basie standby Jumping at the Woodside, with Ellis's strings vibrating in glee and Rich's brushes swatting feverishly.

Not celebrated as a great blues player, Peterson certainly does well enough on his own Blues for Basie. In an exercise of creative self-restraint, he limits himself in a very Basie-ite way to a modicum of notes. Brown adds a twanging solo. In Blue and Sentimental, the quartet slows right down and Basie's sublime melody is crystalline. On Broadway, Brown's bass is like an urban heart-beat, while Ellis soars away through the metropolitan mist in his solo and Peterson swings between the high rises. Topsy oscillates too, with Peterson especially frenzied in a dialogue with Rich's buoyant drums.

One O'clock Jump was Basie's signature tune and Peterson gives it particular respect, offering Ellis plenty of improvising space before he takes his solo, gradually moving towards the Count's economy of notes - almost as if by playing his tunes he is also transforming his style.

A great album, this. Follow it up by getting hold of the Satch and Josh sessions - simply, two of the great masters of jazz sparking off each other's dissident genius.

(Oscar Peterson Plays Count Basie is available on Verve)

Courtney Pine (England) - Sound steeped in Caribbean soul

Courtney Pine - House of Legends
(2012)

'I've never done an album like this. Every track is driving!' said Courtney Pine of his 13th album House Of Legends. It's a recording dedicated to his own Caribbean history and the people who made it, from Samuel Sharpe, the educated slave who organised the Christmas 1831 rebellion in Jamaica, to Trinidadian communist and maker of the Notting Hill Carnival Claudia Jones, to the young black Londoner and martyr Stephen Lawrence. The breath of Caribbean verve, music power and imagination, it is Pine's apex, full of the islands' beauty and brilliance. Courtney's band is its usual pan-Caribbean in body and spirit.

Cameron Pierre's Dominican guitar and Mario Canonge's Martinican piano sound out everywhere and the notes of esteemed guests are continually chiming at the door. Hear Annise Hadeed's Trinidadian pan on Claudia's tune or The Song Of The Maroons, the South African earth of Lucky Ranku's guitar and Claude Deppa's flugelhorn on the anthem to Mandela, Ma-Di-Ba - or the trombone of Rico Rodriguez, whose slides I first heard on his Trojan album Blow Your Horn, which I bought for 14 and six in a Brixton record shop 40 years

ago, still blowing strong on Pine's celebration of half a century of Jamaican independence, Kingstonian Swing.

House of Legends is a praise-song to Caribbean musical achievement and burns like a wild beach fire of history. Pine puts aside his tenor sax and bass clarinet throughout this album for his soprano saxophone. 'To me the sound of the soprano fitted, and was easier to sing through,' he said, 'on the types of grooves I was dealing with from the Caribbean.' And the opening track is The Tale Of Stephen Lawrence, a duo lament between Pine's surging soprano and Mervyn Africa's piano.

There is pathos, beauty and resistance in their timbre. Next up is Kingstonian Swing, where the first soprano notes sound like Peer Gynt in Jamaica. Rico follows, full of rampage and ska memories. 'Liamuiga' is the word used by St Kitts' Caribs for 'fertile land,' also used to denote a cook-up. It's a swinging feast indeed, nicely spiced by Hadeed's pan. There's an anthemic theme at the centre of Samuel Sharpe and the courage and brainpower of the great rebel rings through Hadeed's solo and Pine's stinging chorus, reminding us once again of the title of Richard Hart's great books of slavery and resistance, the seminal Slaves Who Abolished Slavery. Think of this tune while you read them. Ca C'est Bon Ca, written by Pine for his wife, and based on the Zouk Love musical style from Dominica and St Lucia, brings in a string quartet and an exquisite melodic strain. The tribute to Claudia is full of dance and headed up by her homeland's steel pan. Pierre's solo flickers and skips before Pine's soprano sings out in love, joy and remembrance. The society of runaway slaves in Jamaica's Cockpit Country is soundpainted in Song Of The Maroons. Pine plays banjo and Michael Bammi Rose plays solo flute in an ensemble of respect and an evocation of the people's defiance of slavery.

One of my first memories of television in the mid-'50s was watching the Grenadian bandleader and dancer Leslie 'Jiver' Hutchinson, also known as 'Hutch.' House Of Hutch is Pine's salute to this musical pioneer. Pine's horn and the trombone of Trevor Edwards lead the way. Canonge plays a jivey piano solo above Rod Youngs' drums and Miles Dango's plunging bassline. The sheer velocity of Pine's notes and their boiling sound express the power of Hutch's inspiration.

From The Father To The Son acknowledges Pine's life-array of teachers and exemplars. He soars through a colloquy with trumpeter Eddie Tan Tan Thompson before Hadeed's splashing pan enters to make a declamatory threesome. Five minutes of Caribbean sonic heaven here.

Ma-Di-Ba unites South Africa and the Caribbean in a darkening London studio. Lucky Ranku and Pierre make an amalgam of hot, improvising guitars and Deppa's on-the-edge flugelhorn creates a special transcontinental excitation calling into recognition Mandela's 94 years. The familiar Latin sounds of the Brazilian Choro opus Tico Tico, one of Canonge's indelible tunes of boyhood in Martinique, close the album. Canonge lets himself loose all along his keys after a springing solo from Pierre before Pine springs home as fast as his three Jamaican 'brothers who came one, two and three in the 2012 Stratford Olympic 200 metres' - full of zest and Caribbean glory, like this entire album.

(House of Legends is available on Destin-e World Records)

Terry Pollard (USA) - Marvels from a pioneering Motown woman pioneer (2021)

In 1955, when pianist Terry Pollard recorded her only album as leader on the Bethlehem label, English jazz critic Leonard Feather commented on the grotesque attitudes towards women in jazz. 'The role of the feminine performer has taken on a slightly offside significance in jazz. Presumably because of the unwritten social law decreeing that a charming young damsel looks less alluring with a trombone ruining her lipstick, or a tuba spoiling her smile ...'

Pollard became one of the prime resisters to such backwardness during the postwar years. Born in Detroit in 1931, she launched an unlikely career, first in Motown bands and then with vibraphonist Terry Gibbs, with whose band she toured the country and began her time from 1953 to 1956 as a recording artist. She recorded her eponymous album with bassist Herman Wright, guitarist Howard Roberts, drummer Frank DeVito and trumpeter Don Fagerquist, who features on three tracks.

Pollard plays with a beautiful swinging fluency through a series of familiar songbook ballads, savouring their melodies - particularly in her slowly drifting version of The More I See You with Roberts, Wright and DeVito beside her in a gently pulsating empathy, and her inventiveness on Where or When has more than a flavour of the great Bud Powell. And she romps away with Fagerquist's horn on Almost Like Being in Love, as Roberts picks out a fleet solo.

Pollard seizes on Charlie Parker's bop classic Scrapple from the Apple with gusto, her speed of attack almost leaving her confreres behind. Wright catches up with her and plays a throbbing solo, DeVito has a few moments and Pollard chases away again. She strikes her keys forcefully all through Emaline and Fagerquist delivers a muted high-note chorus. Autumn Serenade plays on the cusp of familiar themes like Summertime and I'll Remember April and there are sparking solos from Roberts, Pollard and Fagerquist, while on Fedj Pollard stomps forward on her own composition and Roberts plucks out a lively solo.

In 1956 Pollard joined forces with Gibbs, drummer Jerry Segal and Wright again to make two albums, Terry Gibbs and Mallets-a-Plenty. Lonely Dreams finds her in truly balladic mood, playing the theme with a gentle beauty before Gibbs enters to embellish his own tune. Pollard spins lyricism too on Mean to Me, but it is on Dickie's Dream, written by Count Basie and his tenorist Lester Young, that she really lets go. As she swings through her opening solo. Gibbs is full of verve as the quartet surges through the joyous track.

Nutty Notes shows that there was nothing fragile about Pollard's artistry, as she scatters her sound through the studio in harmony with Gibbs's vibes. Then it Happens is slow and easy, with Pollard making melody out of improvisation and Wright's earthen Motown bass delving deep.

Despite the relative brevity of her recording years, Pollard was very much a Detroit jazz woman pioneer. She made the fine album Soft Winds with groundbreaking jazz harpist Dorothy Ashby and cut a path too for the powerful Detroit pianist Geri Allen and car worker's daughter and virtuoso violinist, Regina Carter. The elder sister of many a Motown artist, she died in 2009, but her brilliance lives on in this reissue.

(A Detroit Jazz Legend is available on Fresh Sound)

Dudu Pukwana (South Africa) - Sounds of liberation

Bob Stuckey and Dudu Pukwana - Night Time Is The Right Time: '60s Soho Sounds
(2010)

The volcanic alto saxophonist Dudu Pukwana was born in Port Elizabeth, South Africa, in 1938. His father gave him his first music lessons on the piano when he was 10, before the family moved to Cape Town. While he was a teenager he joined a band called Tete Mbambisa's Four Yanks. He learned to play the saxophone directly from the rare, imported US jazz records he managed to get hold of and from Nick Moyake, with whom he was later to play as a member of the Blue Notes when pianist Chris McGregor asked him to join in the early '60s.

The band achieved legendary success with their township performances, but composed as they were of black and white musicians there was neither cultural nor legal space for the Blue Notes under apartheid. In 1964 they left for Europe, staying first in Switzerland and later settling in London.

In 1969 Pukwana moved to the US to be a part of fellow exile Hugh Masekela's Union of South Africa and in 1970 he returned to London to form his own band Spear, which also featured ex-Blue Note drummer Louis Moholo-Moholo and trumpeter Mongezi Feza, together with South African bassist Harry Miller and tenor saxophonist Bixo Mngqikana. Pukwana's records were full of blazing sounds of liberation. I remember in 1976, after the young people's protest and massacre in Soweto, playing the Spear album In The Townships in my east London classroom while the students wrote poems of solidarity with their South African counterparts. The insurgent music provoked huge imaginative leaps from Limehouse to Soweto among the young East Enders and had a powerful impact.

These 1967-8 records were made at Ronnie Scott's Old Place, the first venue of the famous club in Gerrard Street, Soho, where Pukwana found himself playing with three groovy and talented young Englishmen - Hammond organist Bob Stuckey, drummer John Marshall and guitarist Phil Lee. They come from the precious archive of the Cadillac label's record producer John Jack and they are as much invaluable social and cultural history as they are marvellous musical testimony.

The opener Kicks For Sale introduces a blast of Pukwana's searing notes before Stuckey swings away on some vibrant choruses and Lee grooves in with his fiery guitar. Jauana's Dream, another Dudu tune, reminds us how unique the Pukwana alto sound was. Rich yet terse like no other, it tears at your ears and your heart and the notes in Lee's solo are like drops of tropical rain. Dudu's horn sings a love song in his tune B My Dear and the listener finds the words to match the expressive notes. Messengers is another Pukwana melody which Lee embraces with a scorching solo. Kippie is Abdullah Ibrahim's tribute to Dudu's pioneering Johannesburg-born alto predecessor Kippie Moeketsi, who played with Ibrahim and trumpeter Masekela in the legendary Jazz Epistles before they both left South Africa in disgust at the apartheid system. There is something deeply moving about this London performance in recognition of a great South African jazz artist and his everyday struggle against racist tyranny.

Moonshine is Stuckey's composition and his Hammond bounces through it in sheer abandon before Lee comes sauntering in and Dudu gurgles his notes in joy and assurance. Marshall's sharp drums give Like We Did Yesterday a Latin edge there in London's Chinatown, and all four members are up for it, with Lee in particular picking at his notes with precision and surprise. Blessing Light is another Pukwana tune, radiantly happy and played with zest and verve by the quartet.

I never thought I would ever hear a jazz composition about Brentwood, an Essex suburban town where as a boy I used to go and watch Essex play cricket and swim in the open-air baths. But Night in Brentwood is a real swinger with the composer Lee burning some hot licks, Marshall jubilantly setting free his drums and Dudu letting rip with some wild sound patterns that I must have missed in the placid and sober Brentwood I knew.

The last five tracks are recordings of a trio composed of the formidable Stuckey, Terry Smith on guitar and drummer Martin Hart. Full of life and sonic fire, particularly Stuckey on I Feel Pretty from West Side Story, a very lively When I Grow Too Old To Dream where he strikes echoes of Milt Buckner and his own Bob's Hop, which leaps up and down Gerrard Street in exuberance.

Thanks to John Jack for this hour of long-gone jazz joy and artistry, full of the era's sense of hope and renewal, and Pukwana's cry of African defiance and beauty.

(Night Time Is The Right Time: '60s Soho Sounds is available on Cadillac Records)

Don Pullen (USA) - Notes never to be sidelined or forgotten

Don Pullen featuring Sam Rivers - Capricorn Rising (2018)

Of all the array of great pianists who have been at the centre of a century of jazz, I have to say that my nonpareil of the keys was a man from Roanoke, Virginia, called Don Pullen.

Pullen was born in 1944 of mixed African-American and Cherokee heritage. He arrived in Chicago in 1964 to become part of the experimental and community-rooted Association for the Advancement of Creative Musicians while finding his living playing in many a rhythm and blues context.

His outrageously progressive talent was recognised by Charles Mingus, who in 1973 made him a member of his band and he played on Mingus's two brilliantly subversive Changes albums, on pieces like Remember Rockefeller at Attica and the prophecy of Charlottesville, August 2017, Free Cell Block F 'Tis Nazi USA. He made a succession of luminous albums with tenor saxophonist George Adams (find them on YouTube playing What a Wonderful World together at a Japanese festival) and sadly, his trio and Afro-Brazilian Connection albums on Blue Note are now all deleted. But try to get hold of his uniquely moving salute to his Native American roots, Sacred Common Ground, and the trio album Random Thoughts on which he plays his piercingly critical opus, Endangered Species: African-American Youth.

Fortunately, the Italian label Black Saint recorded him on a succession of fine albums and one of these has been reissued - an extraordinary pairing of 1975 with saxophonist Sam Rivers, called Capricorn Rising. Rivers, born in El Reno, Oklahoma, in 1930, made pioneering albums for Blue Note in the 1960s like Fuchsia Swing Song and Contours, played with Miles Davis on his Live in Japan album and became one of the creators of the experimental New York 'loft scene' of the 1980s. The other two quartet members are drummer Bobby Battle, born in Detroit in 1944, with a Black Panther past and a vital, propulsive presence, and Alex Blake on bass, whom I once saw playing and attacking his instrument with a phenomenal multisonic power, accompanying tenorist Pharoah Sanders at the Jazz Café in Camden Town.

The opening track is aptly named Break Out and the foursome tear into the piece with a torrential energy. Rivers' horn is furious, Pullen's keyboard strides are struck with a shuddering force and Blake and Battle summon up a fierce rhythmic undertow. Perhaps Pullen is still in the mindset and soundset of Free Cell Block F as he breaks out of the strictures of structured pianism in the vigour and momentum of his notes. Blake plummets and then rises up his strings to find ardent crescendos, and Rivers returns on soprano saxophone, fiery and free, as if this breakout will never be contained.

Next is the album title tune and it begins with some adenoidal Rivers on tenor alongside Pullen's leaping chords before he switches to flute and begins to dance and fly, his lightweight notes buoyed up by Blake's running basslines. Pullen's brief interval becomes a palaver with the insurgent Rivers, now come back on tenor. It is a long colloquy with questions and answers by both masters posed and retorted simultaneously. Then Pullen's piano strikes out percussively with an incendiary brilliance, before Battle's urgent toms signal an importunate freedom. We don't know who the protagonist of Joycie Girl, the next track is, but she has a jaunty gait, and Rivers' soprano paints her as a woman of energy and defiance. His sonic lines spark many sides of her humanity, and when Pullen's solo amplifies the fullness of his own tune with rampant keyboard runs and reflections, we feel that we know something of the complexity of this woman.

The final track is the longest: 15 minutes of Fall Out begun by Blake's irresistible twanging bass, Rivers' gurgling tenor and Pullen's combustible keys. His solo has elements of Monk's sharp corners, Cecil Taylor's charging runs and evocations of stride piano going back to the origins of James P Johnson and Fats Waller. Yet it is uniquely and absolutely Pullen, his notes bold, truculent and ever-rebellious at the very heart and future of his music, never to be sidelined or forgotten.

(Capricorn Rising is available on Black Saint)

Qotob Trio (Syria) - Crossing continents, from Damascus to Brussels

Qotob Trio – Entity
(2018)

The heartsblood of jazz is syncretism - a crucible of musical forms, cultures and peoples. In the amalgam of sounds from the Caribbean, Europe, the Americas and the Mississippi Delta, jazz was forged a century ago in the Louisiana port city of New Orleans and immediately began to spread relentlessly outwards throughout the world.

It keeps happening today in the most unexpected of locations. In 2016, young cellist Bassel Abou Fakher, from a war-ravaged neighbourhood of Damascus, found refuge in Brussels. In his home city he had been part of a quartet of young musicians including a trumpeter, percussionist and zither player who had struggled to keep music alive in a context of barbarism and deathly conflict. They called their band Qotob - the Arabic word for axis or pivot - and, using music, they sought to keep their people in accord. They combined Syrian traditional themes and classical genres with contemporary jazz forms and managed to release an album which they promoted as a message of unity.

In Brussels, Abou Fakher found his way into musical meetings and jamming sessions and met the pianist and trumpeter Jean-Baptiste Delneuville, who had a deep interest in jazz and classical music as well as Balkan, Gypsy and Middle Eastern forms. They joined with Piet Maris, the Belgian accordion and guitar virtuoso from Meerbeke, who is also a committed campaigner for the rights of refugees, to form a Brussels-based reincarnation of Qotob. It became 'a platform, a pole, a point of reference for musicians to meet and communicate through music.' The trio played at benefit events for refugee action, including at a large-scale celebration of the UN Human Rights Day in Brussels in December 2016.

Uncannily, the three make melodies and improvise as if they have been musical confreres all through their very different lives. On the album's opener Yara, they create and invent notes with their phrases rising, falling, pausing and increasing and decreasing pace apparently instinctively and with a powerful spontaneity. At the start of that title track - all the tunes are his compositions - Abou Fakher's cello begins the narrative before Delneuville enters beside him. There's a slight pause and a sudden much weightier and faster sound and a tripartite harmony which expresses the power of their extraordinary sonic unity, as if there were many more instruments being played.

Cone has a mournful opening, with Abou Fakher's full and mellow notes pealing from their wooden womb and you wonder if this is the same cello that he played in the war-torn buildings of his neighbourhood in Damascus? Delneuville's strongly struck solo follows, slowing almost to stillness in exchanges with Abou Fakher's bowed beauty.

Maris's accordion begins Epidemic with an ironic, tuneful levity before Delneuville builds up the intensity with a stream of fast-paced notes. As the speed slackens, Abou Fakher's cello is sombre and a similar mood opens the longest track, the 11 minutes of Demonstration, where he plucks his strings while Maris's notes sing out with a tender serenity. Delneuville's playing is sometimes reminiscent of Bill Evans, at others of the muscular sound of Errol Garner. The steps seem to be heavier, more forced and determined, as Delneuville's keyboard passion moves to a climax of excitation. His notes carry a resolute timbre at the outset of Resisters before the reflective piano and cello duo guides you to think of Syrians in their own land or as refugees in an unwelcoming Europe. This music embraces them all with a powerful empathy.

Al Ruba begins with an echoing solo cello before Delneuville and Maris add their wordless voices to their keyboards. On the final track is Onec, the three instrumental sounds seem to coalesce across continents to become one. As Delneuville says of their Brussels encounter, prompted by sheer serendipity and chance: 'The values of sincerity and the search for beauty are universal, far outweighing differences of origin, culture and life journey.

'The balance between us speaks of these values, which are indispensable in today's complex and constantly changing world. Certainly Entity is a record to savour, as well as one to provoke similarly deep reflection.

(Entity is available on Choux de Bruxelles)

Ernest Ranglin (Jamaica)- His true heart was in jazz

Queen Elizabeth Hall, London

(2001)

The promoters of this concert call themselves 'Joyful Noise' and no duo of words could be more apt to describe the music of the evening. Ernest Ranglin was born in Manchester, Jamaica in 1932, and like many in his family, picked up a guitar at home and played it. From church music, through his island's own Mento rhythms, he went on to play in several Jamaican big bands. Taken on by Island Records' founder, Chris Blackwell, his arrangements became instrumental in the production of a host of pioneering ska, rock steady and reggae hits.

But Ranglin's true heart was in jazz. He emulated the great swing guitarist Charlie Christian and propelled himself into bebop. But it was a form of Caribbean bop, which was unique with waves of Jamaican sound, the echo of the sea and the Blue Mountains deep within the contours of his strings. Like other West Indies rooted jazz virtuosi from Shake Keane to Sonny Rollins, Dizzy Reece to Joe Harriott, Wynton Kelly to Monty Alexander, Ranglin's Blue Note is a Caribbean Note. In a powerful album with Alexander, he called his music Jamento and dug deep into his own Jamaican earth to uncover its extraordinary vibrancy. If Charlie Christian had survived to become a grandfather or had been born in Jamaica, he may have played like Ranglin.

Dressed conservatively and quietly in sports jacket, flannelled trousers and brogue shoes and surrounded by African and Caribbean musicians who could have been his grandchildren, he held the middle of the Queen Elizabeth Hall stage with a huge authority that is born of modesty and phenomenal instrumental skills. Grounded by two sets of drums, a West African talking drum and electric bass, he built his solos on this African-Caribbean foundation. He strums what seems, at first, like a pedestrian phrase, then takes flight into licks which sound like combinations of Christian, Django Reinhardt and Kenny Burrell, his stream of notes pealing from his guitar like lightning as his fingers make a blur, running up and down its neck. He exchanged choruses with Denys Baptiste's muscular and rasping St. Lucian tenor, making his guitar a musical equal - and his dialogues with the piano had a sense of a familiar and intimate conversation.

The hall was packed, and a large proportion of the audience was from the London African diaspora. They loved Ranglin's original conception of a music of African roots, Caribbean reinvention and the influences of jazz patterns and styles born in the USA There are few musicians who manifest this degree of trans-Atlantic unity with such artistry as this brilliant Jamaican.

Iiro Rantala (Finland) - Forged in the sonic smithy

My History of Jazz and My Working Class Hero

(2017)

With hardly a conventional route for a jazz pianist, Iiro Rantala was born in Helsinki in 1970, had a powerful musical upbringing as a member of Cantored Minores, a renowned Finnish boys' choir, an education as a classical pianist and then a course in jazz studies at the Manhattan School of Music. He performed for 18 years as part of the iconoclastic jazz group the Trio Toykeat ('The Rotten Trio') while continuing to play classical piano and writing for films, television and theatre.

His 2012 album My History of Jazz is a musical narrative of his life and how he embraced a polyglot of jazz influences. 'Bach's music became my life already when I was six,' he writes. 'At the age of 13 I heard jazz and it suckered me into its fascinating world. I wanted to become an improvisator, composer, performer and band leader.'

And it is Rantala's brilliance as an 'improvisator' that radiates through his story, which begins and ends where he began, with Bach. He has bandmates Lars Danielsson on bass and cello, drummer Morten Lund and violinist Adam Baldych to spin his chronicle with, and from the outset of Bach's aria they play with a compelling unity. They romp through Gershwin's Liza straight after, followed by the Ellingtonian standby Caravan written by trombonist Juan Tizol and Monk's Eronel - and you realise again how boundaries between genres of music are entirely artificial. Baldych's violin sizzles in Caravan and Rantala is joyously inventive all through Eronel as Danielsson's bass bounces beside him.

He plays Kurt Weill's September Song in a quasi-stride style, and while he openly says that he's never played the blues, his expression of what he calls 'Scandinavian melancholiness' wafts from the quartet's rendition of Danny's Dream written by the virtuoso Swedish baritone saxophonist Lars Gullin, with a dextrously plucked cello solo by Danielsson.

'I just don't know why I love John Lennon's songs so much,' confessed Rantala in the sleeve notes of his 2015 album My Working Class Hero. 'Maybe because I really am from a working-class family. My mother and father used to run a bicycle store in Helsinki, and that's where I grew up. I heard Lennon before I knew any jazz. Happy Xmas was the first encounter with his music when I sang it in our music class choir in 1983. Even back then it took my breath away. How can this guy write something so simple yet so powerful at the same time? Same effect with Imagine.'

Lennon and McCartney's Norwegian Wood begins with a repeated percussive chord like nature's beating heart, before Rantala's melodic sense embroiders the familiar tune with chiming keyboard runs. The title tune begins as a laborious toll of life, as if the tune is being forged at a sonic smithy as it rises to a climax which is the tune itself, repeated and carved into sound. In

Just Like Starting Over the tune takes a long time to arrive but when it comes it is lucid and transparent.

Rantala plays Woman without concealment, before the pace changes and pianist becomes 'improvisator' striking the keys hard and true on the cusp of the tune. Then it is Imagine played as if the melody were being discovered all over again and each note carrying fast its indelible word and inseparable meaning.

I had always thought Help an ephemeral song and unremarkable tune, but Rantala gives it a new depth. He pounds out its theme, then suddenly its chorus becomes gentle, almost pleading its message before it reverts to a rushing foray of notes until the chorus next time. After this, you feel you'll never hear it in the same way again. Lennon and Yoko Ono's Oh My Love is taken swiftly as a running tune, almost as a preface to Lennon and McCartney's In My Life, played as if the theme were leaning sideways, away from itself, but still with an emphatic power. And when the melody finally comes it's as if it is suddenly standing upright to cast its message out into the world with a forthright beauty.

The listener can imagine how the schoolboy Rantala was so impressed and affected by Happy Xmas (War is Over) and the strength of Lennon's tunemaking. He introduces All You Need is Love by a half-chorus of God Save the Queen, and how you wish that the former were the national anthem, or Imagine, or snatches of both. One day maybe, but in the meantime play Rantala's immensely fine and moving album. It makes you wish that the Liverpool boy could hear it too, all the way from Finland and his dad's bike shop.

(My History of Jazz and My Working Class Hero are available on Act)

Emma Rawicz (England) and Gwilym Simcock (Wales) – Big Visit
(2025)

Here's an intensely inventive collaboration between a young Devonian woman of Polish heritage, Emma Rawicz, and the ever-inventive Welsh pianist of Bangor, Gwynedd, Gwilym Simcock, playing in duo formation a series of compositions by each one, with final outings on a Stevie Wonder evergreen and Carl Fischer's You've Changed, a favourite performance-piece of the great tenor saxophonist, Dexter Gordon.

How they both 'go' at Simcock's opener, His Great Adventure, which is for certain 'hers' too, as Rawicz sets herself free, inspired by the chasing keyboard runs of her partner. But it's all change on its successor, Rawicz's tune The Shape of a New Sun, where her soprano saxophone attacks her own melody, twisting and turning it in a host of directions, but never letting herself completely loose from its lyrical beauty.

In their joint sleeve note, these two well-met troubadours describe their musical tryst as one of 'freewheeling abandon', and their improvisations soar with joy and freedom, but also with a sorrowful perplexity in You've Changed, but they never lose touch with the sense of melody that glues all the tracks together.

The special beauty of Simcock's piano artistry is how he makes his piano sing, rising above its inherent percussiveness to give it a sound very close to a voice. as if he with his keys and Rawicz with her horn are stretching for words together. This quality is especially effective when they play both Stevie Wonder's Visions and You've Changed, as when Rawicz falls slowly and sadly into her cadences and Simcock's piano voice both joins yet somehow restrains her. It is a deeply moving wordless rendition where, if you know the words, their power takes on a new imaginative meaning, not an easy achievement by a magical duo.

(Big Visit is available on Act Records)

Dewey Redman (USA) - Radical revival

Dewey Redman Quartet, Pizza Express, London (2001)

Born in 1931, in Texas, Dewey Redman played in the same high school band that included Ornette Coleman and Charles Moffett. During the '50s, after qualifying with a master's degree from North Texas State University, he became a teacher. Heading for California, he then decided to make a living from the saxophone. He freelanced in San Francisco and, eventually, picked up his association with Coleman again.

As Coleman became the leading edge alto of Free Jazz. Dewey took on the role with his tenor, particularly in the band Old and New Dreams, where he played with the rest of Coleman's quartet. He played with Charlie Haden's Liberation Music Orchestra and he made a series of powerful albums as a leader in the '70s and '80s. including The Ear of the Behearer, The Struggle Continues and Living on the Edge. The titles themselves signalled both his musical and political commitment.

Now, in his 70th year, there is still that same elusive quality of restlessness about his playing, as if nothing must he routine or formulaic, even in a West End club date like this performance at the Pizza Express. The leading edge can still cut sharp and new avenues, open up from almost every phrase of his improvisation.

The avant garde radicalism of his sound has moved towards a more eclectic and inclusive genre. He began with a fluid and buoyant selection - there were no announcements or titles of numbers - steaming into fleeting passages of notes, before changing to a ballad that included one particular beautiful trickle of a phrase, which splashed tranquilly from his horn and out of the main narrative of his melody.

Redman frequently offered grunts of approval at the work of his fellow musicians. The sonorous and tree-like sound of bassman John Menegan was converted into sharp solo virtuosity, along with the by turns nuanced and power-housing undercurrents of the young drummer Mark McLean. The dissonant beauty of pianist Rita Marcotulli's piano makes an amalgam with Redman's tenor that seems to revive old radical days.

From a reflective Everything Happens to Me with an exploring final coda to a spectacular selection, when he plays a small, almost bagpipe-like sounding African horn that sets him dancing and posturing defiantly. Redman moves back to the Rhythm and Blues mode of his youth, blowing and honking his tenor in true Texas style. He steps off the low stage and meanders between the tables of pizza, wine and garlic bread, like an old-timer revivalist.

Here is a musician whose every sound makes offshoots and even in a finale that used Ellington's Take the 'A' Train as its theme, you could hear echoes of music that, nearly four decades ago, shook the jazz world out of its periodic lethargy with brave and novel invention.

Eric Reed (USA) - Echoes of Robeson with creative fire

Eric Reed – Groovewise

(2018)

In May1952 and again in August 1958, the great singer, actor and cultural militant Paul Robeson, having been denied a passport by his own US government and confined within the boundaries of the world's most powerful imperial nation, gave historic concerts on the back of a flat-bed truck in Blaine, Washington state, under the Peace Arch, a few feet from the Canadian border.

He sang across the US/British Columbia frontier which he was forbidden to cross, to 40,000 US and Canadian citizens in a unique and defiant performance of international solidarity. I thought of these momentous events and Robeson singing Joe Hill, No More Auction Block or Ol' Man River as I listened to the first very evocative track, Powerful Paul Robeson on the live album by the Philadelphia-born (in 1970) pianist Eric Reed and his quartet, recorded at New York's Smoke Jazz Club in 2014, and called Groovewise.

Fittingly, the Reed Quartet's tenor saxophonist Seamus Blake is a Canadian from Vancouver, British Columbia, very close to the location of the Peace Arch. He is a very powerful hornman too and, with the rhythmic undertow of Reed's long-time flatmate Greg Hutchinson on the drums and plummeting bassman Ben Williams, here is a quartet that does Robeson proud indeed.

Powerful Paul Robeson was written by the Chicago tenor saxophonist Clifford Jordan and was the opening track of the marvellous Strata East album Glass Bead Games of 1973. Reed's quartet relives those days with their 2014 version, with Blake's magnetic opening solo alongside Hutchinson's booming drums. The quartet generates almost a big band feeling. Reed played for years in the Wynton Marsalis Orchestra while Blake is still a regular in the Mingus Big Band and they create the illusion that they are both playing in a much larger unit. Perhaps it is the huge spirit of Robeson that makes this happen for they both play like inspired men, full of creative fire.

Then it is on to the Reed compositions, beginning with the ominous theme of Until the Last Cat Has Swung. Reed's solo has a strange, inventively hypnotic quality and Blake makes melodies out of his improvised lines, again spurred by Hutchinson's leaping drums. Reed tears into Manhattan Melodies with speed and freedom, Blake slows things down a little with a solo bursting with innovation before Reed and Williams enjoy a brief palaver.

Groovewise is an album of memorials. Reed's The Gentle Giant is dedicated to his friend and brother pianist, the late Mulgrew Miller, from Greenwood, Mississippi. This is a piano trio track, with Reed's emotions spilling from his keys, remembering a giant pianist as well as 'a big guy and a sweet person.'

He salutes another southern pianist, the Dallas-born Cedar Walton who died in 2013, by playing the tune written by bassist Christian McBride, The Shade of the Cedar Tree, with Blake's grasp of both melodic and improvising beauty strongly to the fore and the rhythmic artistry of Williams and Hutchinson fully supportive. Between these homages to two pianists is Reed's tribute to Ornette Coleman, Ornate, a tune which continually turns corners and grasps new avenues. Brief and surprising, it precedes the Reed tune on more familiar and common ground, Bopward, which the quartet embrace with a particular relish.

Reed posits that the tune could be 'something that I think Charlie Parker would have composed, had Bird lived.' Hutchinson has a novel solo, Blake plays alto and there is more than a glimpse of an earlier jazz age sprinkling through the notes. There's yet another tribute to a dead pianist in Una Mujer Elegante - this time, it's Marian McPartland, born in Windsor, England, in 1920. Williams is particularly strong, and gentle, and Blake plays with a profound freshness and beauty.

A fine album this, full of live sensation and remembering diverse musical heroes. Yet it is Robeson you hear in every note, still and always inspiring us.

(Groovewise is available on Smoke)

Django Reinhardt (Belgium) - Miracle guitarist
Complete Solo Guitar and Duet Recordings
(2012)

If you're used to hearing - as I have through most of my listening years - the gypsy brilliance of Django Reinhardt's guitar in the midst of a small group setting, plucking fire with the Quintette du Hot Club de France along with violinist Stephane Grappelli, his brother Joseph on rhythm guitar, another guitar and Louis Vola's bass, then this double CD will give you an experience of the sheer unexpected.

Reinhardt, who was born in Liverchies, Belgium, in 1910 and died in Fontainebleau, France, in 1953, made a number of solo and duo recordings scattered throughout his musical life. They have been collected on Complete Solo Guitar and Duet Recordings.

As you listen to Django alone, exposed and vulnerable, or with but one confrere, you realise even more the miracle of a guitarist who at the age of 18 lost the use of two of his fingers on his fret hand in a caravan fire and yet whose music continuously touched the stars, whoever he was playing with - even if it was just himself. Many of the solo recordings made between 1937 and 1953 at various locations from Paris, Rome, London and Chicago are numbered as 'improvisations,' on the spot spontaneous gushings of notes that spring so rapturously from his strings.

Reinhardt learned to read neither music nor letters and it was Grappelli who eventually became his first literacy teacher when they were performing together as a nightly routine. It's only on the solo memorised readings of tunes like his own Nuages or Belleville, or standards like Tea for Two or To Each His Own, that there is a skeletal theme from which to launch his staggering sonic patterns. Sometimes, as in the rippling Improvisation No 1, Perfum or the two takes of Improvisation No 2, he momentarily sounds almost close to a Louisiana bluesman of astonishing technique like Lonnie Johnson who also played with Louis Armstrong's Hot Five and the Ellington Orchestra, while all through Echoes of Spain he expresses the European genius of the quasi-flamenco tradition straddling the two faraway continents.

Naguine is a short solo rhapsody to his wife, his notes bubbling with love, while Improvisation No 7 - recorded live at Chicago's Civic Opera House - has Django playing electric guitar and striking crescendo ladders to the delight of his US audience.

The duet sessions begin stompingly with Grappelli and I've Found A New Baby. The mutual empathy, as ever, is almost tangible and Django hurtles through his rhythm guitar chords while Grappelli saws his violin in-blithe artistry. Another pioneering jazz fiddler, nicknamed the 'dark angel,' was Eddie South, who accompanies Django with raw emotion on Eddie's Blues of 1937 and returns for an expressive version of Somebody Loves Me, his improvising full of bursting invention. Django's regular bassist Louis Vola steps in for You

Rascal You, booming and bouncing while the guitarist picks and strums out his notes with joy and pace.

Django cut some powerful tracks in Rome in 1949-50 with the Hungaro-Armenian altoist Andre Ekyan, but their two 1937 duo recordings, Pennies From Heaven and Tiger Rag, are full of Ekyan's smoky alto sound and a breathless rhythmic movement. Over just two-and-a-half minutes of Tiger Rag pick up a lightning zest and speed.

The only other horn on these tracks is the trumpeter from Paris, Kentucky, Bill Coleman - resident in the other Paris in November 1937 he cut Bill Coleman Blues with Django, blowing with a quiet and beautiful lyricism, entirely attuned to his partner. The other duo selections are mostly with Grappelli playing either violin or piano, the pair of compadres making sound as if they emerged from the same womb of jazz.

The finest is perhaps another 1937 Paris track, the remarkable Stephan's Blues, where in a mere three minutes seven decades ago the life stories of two musical geniuses are told with astonishing beauty and intense longing.

The album ends with Django back in Belgium, playing both violin and guitar in a 1942 Brussels session on Vous Et Moi and Blues en Mineur, his gypsy spirit ever alive and creatively defiant. Get this one - it will hot you up on the coldest days.

(Complete Solo Guitar and Duet Recordings is available on Essential Jazz Classics)

Howard Riley (England) - Huddersfield's finest

Howard Riley and Elton Dean - One To One

Howard Riley, Art Themen, Mario Castronari and Trevor Tomkins – Classics Live

Howard Riley and Lol Coxhill – Duology

(2013)

The Huddersfield-born pianist Howard Riley is a celebrated solo artist - hear him alone on Air Play or Making Notes - but he has made a number of other powerful albums with eminent British horn improvisers, which have been issued on the marvellously vibrant Slam label. Each record is a rich expression of the hornman's distinctive artistry when working in creative unison with a brilliant piano compatriot, and the sadness is that two of these saxophonists have now left the stage after lifetimes of jazz achievement.

The first is Elton Dean (1945-2006), the son of Nottingham Salvation Army parents brought up in the heart of sacred sound, who turned to jazz-rock with the Soft Machine and the huge and liberatory message and anti-apartheid anthems of the Brotherhood of Breath in the campaigning years of the '70s and '80s. The album One To One, a succession of Riley/Dean duets recorded at the

1993 London Jazz Festival, with the final two in January 1999 in the sublime acoustic setting of Oxford's Holywell Music Room, is a very powerful record indeed, full of life, fire and artistry, with a tune each by Bill Evans and John Coltrane, a lone standard and five Riley/Dean improvisations.

Evans's Turn Out The Stars gets a truly Blues-laden rendition by Dean's alto, with Riley's comping notes jumping beside him. It's a wild and free-sounding track and a virtuoso performance by the duo, and when the familiar theme of Darn That Dream arrives it suddenly peals like a place of safety. When Riley grasps his solo, the pace quickens and intensifies as if he has instantly seen another destination. The pair move into their own improvisation, Shared Confidences, which morphs into Coltrane's anthem Crescent, into which Dean pours the testimony of his sacred apprenticeship, and Riley finds gospel echoes and sounds of his own wayward spirit.

The two Holywell performances have a different and wholly engaging timbre. One To One is exactly that - two artists' colloquy superbly realised, the notes vibrating, scintillating, while the album's closing improvisation, Spires, must have Chesterfield Church spire as one of its inspirations, so twisting and gyrating are the two musicians' sounds, so full of diminishing sonic circles and unique accents and cadences. And so together too, in extraordinary empathy.

In March 2002 Riley returned to the Holywell Room to record Duology, another album of duets, but this time with the singular and brilliant soprano saxophone genius Lol Coxhill (1932-2012) much more attuned to blowing his straight horn on London's streets and bridges than in the sanctified surroundings in the City of Spires. So not for nothing is the first improvisation called Breaking The Habit, where Lol's breathy exhalations have the sound of a lost ship's forlorn horn blasting through the hallowed venue as Riley's keys chime out a unifying message.

Solo For Lol is all Riley, dedicated to his partner with love and complexity, and Exemplary is an Oxford conversation, a lively palaver full of juice and bounce. Blankets is full of Lol's long, straining notes and its end is more like a vanishing, while Eat My Hat has Riley plucking his piano's innards as Lol wails his message.

Two Timing is an 18-minute improvisation, at times almost ghostly with Lol's spectral warblings and Riley's solidly grounded chordal patterns - an amalgamation of two divergent musical geniuses.

A different dimension of Riley's artistry emerges in a 1994 session recorded at the Bull's Head in Chislehurst, with the saxophonist and orthopaedic surgeon Art Themen, bassist Mario Castronari and Trevor Tomkins on drums. In the sleeve notes Riley asserts that the quartet's objective 'is to be as spontaneous and free as possible within the context of a standard repertoire' which stretches from Body And Soul to Rombert, Monk and Miles. From the opening onrush of notes of Riley's rampaging solo in Monk's Straight No Chaser with Castronari's throbbing pulse beside him, this is another Riley entirely attuned to Themen's bop-inspired tenor.

So much so, that through Davis's All Blues with Themen on a restless soprano saxophone, it is as if the foursome are exploring a vast empty building, so eerily do their notes resound.

The pure melodic beauty of Round Midnight is rediscovered by Themen's tenor, Riley's flourishing keys and a delving Castronari, and the final tune Softly As A Morning Sunrise is like surprisingly meeting an old friend on an unexpected road. Lucky listeners were the Chislehurst drinkers that night.

(One To One, Classics Live & Duology are available on Slam)

Max Roach (USA) – Militant of the drums

Max Roach's Beijing Trio, Royal Festival Hall, London (2001)

The stage is in virtual darkness, although you can trace the veteran drummer's silver hair in the streaks of dull light. A young Chinese woman crosses the stage and a spotlight encircles her. She sits down and begins to play a thin, dazzling-stringed instrument which balances upright on her knee. The bow shimmers, scintillates with a violin-like melodic sound.

Other spotlights illuminate a Chinese man at the piano and an old black man behind a set of silver drums. This drummer is one of the extraordinary men who made bebop, one of the geniuses of jazz, along with his musical comrades, Charlie Parker, Dizzy Gillespie and Thelonious Monk. Here is the nonpareil of jazz and percussion, Max Roach. He was born in New Land, North Carolina, in 1924.

Roach's life in jazz has always been a deeply political one. The titles of his albums tell the story - Deeds Not Words, Speak Brother Speak , Lift Every Voice, which was dedicated to Robeson, Lumumba, Martin Luther King, Malcolm X and Garvey, and Birth and Rebirth. Perhaps, his most celebrated record was We Insist! The Freedom Now Suite of 1960, with its sleeve photograph of a group of black men desegregating a restaurant in the US south. On this record, you find Roach in the heart of the civil rights struggle, with his own selections of Freedom Day, Tears for Johannesburg or his triptych Prayer/Protest/Peace.

For Roach has always been a jazz rebel, a militant of the drums - a musical adventurer who is perennially at the edge, looking over to see the burgeoning new vistas of jazz. Of course, it takes a drummer to truly know a drummer, so Roach was an obvious choice of Robert Wyatt for his Meltdown South Bank Festival.

And here was the master playing in new and discovering company. The drum is often seen as a martial instrument - proclaiming war, charges of armed men, agony and death. But Max Roach drums for justice, internationalism and peace. In the strident and beautiful sounds of Jon Jang's piano, Jie Bing Chen's two-stringed erhu and Roach's drums, there were exchanges of musical gifts and an amalgam of peace from Africa, the Americas and China. The empathy between these three musicians was intense and deeply moving. Jang's, by turns, gentleness and fury, Chen's lyricism and Roach's still astonishing virtuosity found their apogee in a memorable playing of Duke Ellington's Come Sunday, from his epochal celebration of African-American history Black, Brown and Beige.

The Beijing Trio appeared hard on the heels of the avant-garde US piano-bass duo of Matthew Shipp and William Parker, who played a long searching and finding version of another classic Ellington tune, Take the 'A' Train. While Shipp pulverised the Royal Festival Hall keyboard with astonishing runs, startling percussive chords and cathedral-like chimes, Parker sawed the strings of his bass, using his bow as far down the bridge as is possible, emitting sounds which fused pain and ecstasy, joy and frenzy. The sounds were beyond surprise, the spectacle a powerful combination of the fierce and the serene that made the Beijing Trio's later featuring of Chen' s erhu feel like rubbing of balm.

Max Roach is in his 76th year and is still a relentless innovator and insurgent of music. And I was reminded just how much so about an hour after the end of his concert, I arrived back home after a short Tube journey, sat down and turned on the television. It was an episode of Ken Burn's series on the history of jazz. On November 26, 1945 at the Savoy record studios, a defining moment in the long birth of be-bop occurred. The Charlie Parker Quintet was playing Koko. There, behind Parker and Gillespie, are the drumbeat s and ringing cymbals of a black-haired young Max Roach, playing with that same brilliance and poise that I had just heard in the flesh, some 55 years later. Listen to his tight and burning solo.

And Robert, thanks for getting him here.

Matana Roberts (USA) - Pursuing greatness

Matana Roberts Quartet - The Chicago Project
(2008)

There have been precious few women saxophonists who have made it through US jazz's thick masculinist undergrowth. Tenorist Erica Lindsay is one. Listen to the beauty that she blows on her Candid label album Dreamer.

Altoist Vi Redd of Los Angeles is another and it was not for nothing that she declared that women 'are taking up instruments. You see more of it now, but there is ... the glass ceiling. But, like all injustices, we're going to have to pursue, pursue, pursue.'

Well, in hot pursuit is altoist Matana Roberts of Chicago, who grew in her artistry alongside some of the powerful and veteran brethren of the Chicago-based Association for the Advancement of Creative Musicians (AACM), pioneers of free jazz improvisation, who were determined to reach out to and take inspiration from the Windy City's black community. Roberts's new album The Chicago Project is a tribute to her home city and features three bandmates strongly active in Chicago's progressive musical life. Josh Adams is the bassist, the guitarist is Jeff Parker and Frank Rosaly of Ken Vandermark's Crisis Ensemble plays the drums. The guest saxophonist is a local legend and co-founder of the AACM, tenorist Fred Anderson, who was making ground-breaking albums 40 years ago and rarely left Chicago, opening live venues and helping to build up a thriving free jazz tradition. His most famous club was The Birdhouse, where no alcohol was served, much to the perplexity and chagrin of the Chicago police, who so frequently raided it.

Opening track Exchange begins with a fierce, vibrating cadence before Abrams's striding bass leads the quartet forward, Parker plays an enigmatic break and Matana winds slowly back, her alto blowing through unexpected pathways beside Rosaly's crashing drums. In Thrills, she and Parker prompt each other through an urgent improvised dialogue, while, in the much milder and more lyrical sounds of Norma, the conversation continues, mollified and gentle, from both alto and guitar.

Anderson's contribution to the album is in three unaccompanied duets with Matana. Fittingly, they are called Birdhouse 1, 2 and 3, three saxophone colloquies that make fascinating listening. They blow with the closest of empathies, calling and responding to each other, alternately leading, following and chiming out in unison. Anderson is 78 and a jazzman of huge experience. Matana is a young woman. They are several generations apart, yet they play as siblings, discovering new dimensions of jazz language and artistic connection in every breath. So intense and capacious is their duo that its fullness dominates the entire album and, when the quartet returns, despite its excellence, you miss Anderson's huge authority and you realise again the power of his sound through its absence. Yet this is not to deny the power of the quartet tracks. In Love Call, Matana coaxes all kinds of sounds from her horn.

During the first part of the performance, it is as if she is playing a restrained, almost courtly and detached love theme. Then, suddenly, the mood changes, charged by Rosaly's ebullient drums. She strains for a terser, wilder timbre and finds it, her notes becoming more raw and abrasive, racked with emotion. In South By West, she accepts the challenge of melodism, blowing out the lucid theme before returning to another duet with Parker after Adams's twanging solo.

An engrossing album, this, and a new breath, a new saxophone voice sparking new areas of sound and creation and growing in power through association with a seasoned and acknowledged master. A new mistress of the reed, her sound full of strength and beauty.

(The Chicago Project is available on Central Control)

Perry Robinson (USA) - Tear up the old world and turn it into something new

Funk Dumpling by Perry Robinson 4
From A to Z by Perry Robinson Trio
(2025)

The clarinetist Perry Robinson (1938 - 2018) grew up in a committed musical and political environment. His father Earl was a film composer in Thirties' Hollywood and a powerful figure of left culture, deeply embroiled in political struggles. In 1936, two years before Perry was born, his father wrote the great American labour anthem about the revolutionary Swedish immigrant singer and troubadour, Joe Hill, made famous as Paul Robeson sang it at rallies and concerts all over the world.

Perry though, was in every way his own boy, as Woody Guthrie reminded him when he was seven: 'You have always created everything in your whole world by yourself. You love to play, you love to fight and most of all you love to tear up the old world and turn it into something new.' He chose the clarinet as his instrument, which in the late Fifties, when he began to play with advanced musicians like Paul Bley, Archie Shepp (who talked of Perry's 'immeasurable ability') and Bill Dixon, was seen as a conservative instrument, associated with the white big band sound of Benny Goodman and Artie Shaw. Perry was determined to transform its identity, and in an era defined by Charlie Parker's brilliant bop alto saxophone, to re-invent it as a messenger of a revolutionary jazz sound. His long musical education included a period at the Lenox School of Jazz, where Ornette Coleman was a co-student.

The first record made under his own leadership was the 1962 album Funk Dumpling, now reissued on the Fresh Sound label. With him were three innovative Philadelphia musicians: the prime bassist Henry Grimes who had already recorded with Sonny Rollins and Thelonious Monk, pianist Kenny Barron who began to play with arch-trumpeter Dizzy Gillespie in 1962, and Paul Motian, drummer of the most renowned Bill Evans trio.

The quartet begin with a beautifully lithe rendition of Midnight in Moscow, a tune which the Kenny Ball 'trad' band were making a big hit in England. Robinson's agile sound leaps over the 'iron curtain', urged on by Barron's fluid piano and the dancing beat of Grimes and Motian. The bassist's tune Sprites Delight is a gift for Robinson's nimble clarinet, and its pure lightness of tone is almost featherweight.

Robinson's reflective and dreamlike Wahayla is a reverie, as Grimes' plummeting strings search for musical truth, and in the bassist's opus Farmer Alfalfa, Robinson's clarinet shows another timbre - flickering, soaring and constantly palavering with the rhythmic dexterity of his bandmates. Margareta is melodic, with a quasi-New Orleans incandescence, and the album's title tune, composed by Grimes, is full of life, a joyous track, as if the four musicians were levitating on their own notes. The closer, Robinson's Home is Where the

Hearth Is, evocatively simple in its theme and ringing with a lingering sonic purity, is a moving end to an album of true rediscovery.

All his life a musical adventurer, Robinson always pursued an avant-garde direction, and among his last albums was A to Z, cut in Germany in 2008 in his seventieth year with bassist Ed Schuller and drummer Ernest Bier, and there amongst all the new tunes and improvising passages is his father's masterpiece, Joe Hill. Play it after listening to one of many Robeson versions and you will sense its Twenty-First Century re-imagining of Joe's struggle, with the 'copper bosses' embodied as Trump's cohorts of Wall Street and the death ranks of U.S. militarism. Schuller's phantasmagoric sawing bass sounds contrast with the beauty and purity of Robinson's clarinet and Bier's marching beat.

It's an outstanding trio album. Schuller's pounding bassline is to the fore on Switchbacks, while A.K.A. Snake is an outing for Bier's percussive artistry and Robinson's stop-time clarinet mastery, and Mountain Soup brims over with his solo and accompanied notes. Sooner than Before has a Caribbean lilt and the trio interaction and empathy at the heart of Unisphere creates one world of music.

Recorded jazz began with the Crescent City clarinet mastery of Johnny Dodds and Jimmie Noone in the Twenties, and Perry Robinson was their true son, discovering his newfoundland of woodwind sounds, inspired by Joe Hill's mass popular response to the eternal mobiliser of the oppressed and exploited, which is music.

(Funk Dumpling is available on Fresh Sound Records and From A to Z on jazzwerkstatt Records)

Sonny Rollins (USA) - Conjuring Sonny's spirit of jazz
Sonny Rollins Quintet, Barbican, London
(2001)

Here is a jazz musician who, truly, is what jazz is. Looking through his recording career is to consider half a century of jazz history - that part of the music's story when it exploded into ideas of unrestrained freedom, fearlessness and innovatory genius. And a time when it told itself that its true way forward was to revolutionise the act of musical improvisation carried by a black and insurgent cry for racial justice. And the artist who has achieved that, with an energy of imaginative longevity and stamina, has been the monumental Sonny Rollins with his tenor saxophone.

In 1958, from the smithy of the Civil Rights movement, Rollins reflected in the sleeve notes of his epochal Freedom Suite, using the Robesonian language of the time. He stated: 'America is deeply rooted in negro culture - its colloquialisms, its humour, its music. How ironic that the negro, who. more than any other people, can claim America's culture as his own, is being persecuted and repressed, that the negro, who has exemplified the humanities in its very existence, is being rewarded with inhumanity.'

Over 40 years on and Rollins is at the Barbican in London, now playing like a septuagenarian titan. The same clipped notes, adenoidal sounds - notes which seem to project high and low simultaneously, a subterranean rasping and skywards soaring in one, notes which gurgle and fly at the same moment. Idea upon idea, phrase upon phrase, inchoate melody upon inchoate melody straining from his horn from an aural imagination of unbelievable marvel.

He starts off with his own Salvador, played with calypso rhythms, lifting his instrument as if it were weightless - the last adjective that you would use to describe his playing, which is of such weight and authority. While trombonist Clifton Anderson sails away in his Caribbean schooner of a solo and Stephen Scott rollicks his piano, it is obvious that Rollins is a Caribbean man as well as pure New Yorker. His Virgin Islands origins come soaring from his notes as they did decades ago in the astonishing cadences and rushing seas of notes from St Thomas on his Saxophone Colossus album.

On to Ellington's In A Sentimental Mood and a solo from Bob Cranshaw. who also holds a firm place in the history of bebop bass virtuosity. Then it's Rollins, loping and prowling across the Barbican stage, waving his instrument like a flag of jazz, stooping down then thrusting his whole body upward, swinging his saxophone as a young mother would rock her baby toward sleep.

He introduces Sweet Leilani as a children's song - 'one I learnt when I was a little boy, a long, long time ago.' And he plays it as a groovy lullaby. How does he convert a winsome love song like Irving Berlin's They Say That Falling In Love Is Wonderful into a virtual saxophone anthem? By conjuring the spirit of jazz and transmuting every note with such life and humanity.

Then there is Global Warming, which Rollins describes as his Freedom Suite for modem times. And Tenor Madness, on which he duetted with John Coltrane in the album of the same name in 1956. This time, his prime partner is the rumbustious Scott, who does him proud in conversational exchanges between tenor and piano.

As he introduces one for London, A Nightingale Sang In Berkeley Square. Rollins flies away in an unaccompanied opening chorus, but, just as much as any bird life, the power of his sound makes you think of that square's giant plane trees, with their mottled trunks and huge branches, just arriving to bud and leaf.

Rollins's blasts of seemingly endless improvisation, his astonishing rhythmic freedom and disturbing yet endearing tonal distortions still carry his music into his eighth decade, still making new with unquenchable sound.

Wallace Roney (USA) – Inspired prodigy

The Wallace Roney Quintet, Pizza Express, London (2001)

During the early days of June, any jazz lover who was night-cruising the streets of Soho might have thought that he was hearing the sounds of musical ghosts rising up from a particular basement in Dean Street. No, it wasn't Miles, but it was a serene trumpet voice that had absorbed the solitariness and beauty of his notes. It was a horn which has moved onward to find the complexity and uniqueness of its own jazz utterance.

It is the sound of Wallace Roney. 'He is the only trumpet player who understands how Miles did what he did,' said bass virtuoso Ron Carter, who is himself an ex-Miles Davis sideman, of the man to whom the great trumpeter bequeathed his instrument. Perhaps Wallace Roney, in a deterministic way, has little choice.

He was born in Philadelphia in 1960 and he began studying and playing the trumpet at the age of five, prompted by a father whose favourite musician was Davis and by a mother who adored Thelonius Monk. When Davis died in 1991, Roney was chosen by his ex-colleagues - Wayne Shorter (tenor), Herbie Hancock (piano), Tony Williams (drums) and Carter to play trumpet in the Tribute to Miles band.

Yet, as soon as he begins to play in Dean Street, an unaccompanied, crystalline and beautifully poised succession of notes, which are full of the spirit of Miles, yet reach beyond, the listener knows that Roney is not a copyist of neo-classicist past inspirations, but a jazz discoverer of immense power. His pellucid-toned introduction provokes the birth of a mighty drumstorm from Lenny White and sustains the booming bass of Clarence Seay. This rhythmic undergrowth prompts an open horn solo of swift runs and enormous brass from Roney, which makes you remember Clifford Brown and Lee Morgan as much as Miles, with keyboard man Adam Holzman setting loose simultaneously on electric piano and synthesizer.

Roney's quintet is made complete by another burning hot horn played by bop and fusion veteran altoist Gary Bartz, who was born in Baltimore in 1940. He is also a veteran of the Davis band from 1970-71. His extraordinary 1990 album There Goes The Neighbourhood, with its searing Racism Blues, is one of the classics of the last decade and, as he begins to play alongside Roney, the passion of his intense, leaping alto sound was almost solid, fronting the thunder of White's drums that carried a sound, the like of which, I have rarely heard since being knocked awry by Art Blakey's tempests with his Jazz Messengers some 30 years ago. White doesn't merely accompany soloists, whoever they may be, he sets up equal duets with them, dialogues and answers them, with bass, both horns and keyboards - whether acoustic or electric.

Roney's talent as a composer is also formidable. The quintet are mostly playing his tunes, although their performance of the soft and expansive ballad Christina by Buster Williams, who is another of Roney's regular bassists, is perhaps the evening's most memorable selection. On the foundation of Seay's twanging, repeated single bass note and some lyrical piano from Holzman, first, Roney and then Bartz pour out their skill and emotion, with Bartz, now on soprano saxophone, hunching over the microphone and weeping his sound across this small, precious underground cavern of jazz.

It is not often that you get the opportunity to hear such close, vibrant jazz played by artistes of such huge commitment to and authority over the sounds that they create. And, as for Roney, he is an approaching jazz giant in all his mid-life power, having assimilated the genius of the past, such as the Davis legacy. Yet, he has turned it towards new pathfinding directions in a music which never rests, but risks new and untamed terrain every day.

Renee Rosnes (Canada) - A musical exposition of the evolutionary process

Renee Rosnes - Written in the Rocks (2016)

Tiktaalik is an Inuit word given to the fossilised body of an amphibian prehistoric creature that first made the move from ocean to land, discovered among the rocks of the Canadian Arctic. Raised along the same Pacific coastline, hundreds of miles south in British Columbia was the phenomenal pianist Renee Rosnes.

Her new album Written in the Rocks celebrates Tiktaalik as a part of her Galapagos Suite, a musical exposition of the evolutionary process and the transition of life from sea to land. The record's sleeve notes remind us that Darwin loved music, which, as he wrote: 'Arouses in us various emotions', and 'awakens the gentler feelings of tenderness and love.' Rosnes's pianism certainly does that, but also awakens deep grooves and sensations of invention, swing and improvisation. They are all on fire in Written in the Rocks.

Born in 1962 with an Indian mother and adopted by Canadian foster parents, Rosnes studied classical piano in Toronto, moved to New York in the mid-'80s and played alongside a host of jazz virtuosi from Wayne Shorter and Joe Henderson to JJ Johnson, married the drummer Billy Drummond, forming the quartet Native Colours and making a succession of brilliant Blue Note albums, particularly Ancestors (1996), which explored her roots, and As We Are Now (1997).

For Written in the Rocks she assembled a powerful quintet. Peter Washington is the bassist and Bill Stewart the drummer. On flute, soprano and alto saxophones is the Virginian Steve Wilson, presently featured in the Maria Schneider Orchestra, with the hugely experienced Pittsburgh-born Steve Nelson on vibes. The suite opens with The KT Boundary reminding listeners of the titanic rock missile which crashed into the Earth during the dinosaur age, destroying much of life on the planet. Rosnes's deep chords, Stewart's booming drums and Wilson's soprano and flute tell the story. The next track Galapagos she describes as 'a sonic painting of the surf and the exotic birds and wildlife' of the islands that Darwin knew so intimately. Wilson's flutesong, Renee's flickering notes and Nelson's restless mallets paint that land and seascape.

Darwin wrote in On the Origin of Species of the march of evolution 'from so simple a beginning endless forms most beautiful and most wonderful have been, and are being, evolved.' In So Simple a Beginning this history of life is told. Wilson's keening flute is at the centre of the narrative, Rosnes's lyrical solo marvels at its fruition, Nelson's chimes resonate and Washington's bass delves into the earth of us all.

The discovery of the bones of the skeleton named as Lucy in the Awash valley of Ethiopia in 1974 finds music in Lucy from Afar with Nelson's vibes breathing a grooving life into her bones, 3.2 million years old, the earliest woman or man as yet found. Rosnes's galloping solo tells us how fast she could run; and the beauty of the album's title track, its melodic harmonies and swinging lilt makes this essential history indelible to our ears.

Tiktaalik's crucial moment is dramatised in Deep in the Blue, a swinging piece showing that this creature certainly had a share of jazz in her soul, with Rosnes's piano making landfall too with Stewart's deft drumming pushing her forward and Wilson's flying alto striking skywards. Nelson's notes are as if Tiktaalik's progress up this Arctic Canadian beach was at least a stomping one.

I have rarely listened to a jazz record that is so educative while being full of so much artistry and beauty as Written in the Rocks, and it makes you wish that all our ancestors, no matter how far back, along with Lucy, Darwin and the Inuit neighbours of Tiktaalik could have heard it with all its soulpower and brainpower. As for Rosnes, she declared that 'to compose music about our planet's evolution was a stimulating concept and one brimming with musical possibilities.' Right again - listen and discover!

(Written in the Rocks is available on Smoke)

Charlie Haden (USA) & Gonzalo Rubalcaba (Cuba) –
Weaving empathy that cuts across US's cultural isolation

Charlie Haden and Gonzalo Rubalcaba - Tokyo Adagio (2017)

When the Shenandoah-born bassist Charlie Haden was in Cuba with the Liberation Music Orchestra in 1986, performing at the Havana Jazz Festival, he found himself playing at the same concert as a young, classically trained Havana-born pianist called Gonzalo Rubalcaba, who had just returned from touring the Soviet Union.

Haden introduced himself to the young prodigy, and they began a friendship which lasted until the great bassist's death in July 2014. The US ban on Cuban musicians meant that any performances on recordings with Rubalcaba had to be made outside the US frontiers, and Haden overcame this obstacle by inviting the Cuban to 1989 Montreal Jazz Festival as his guest, and in 1990 he recorded his first studio album outside Cuba, Discovery, in Montreal for Blue Note Records, followed by The Blessing in 1991 with Hayden and the drummer Paul Motian.

'For me, just beginning my career, the way Charlie went about opening the path for me made all the difference,' Rubalcaba later explained. 'Despite the gap in our ages, he never treated me as an inferior in any sense. We had each other's confidence. We could talk about politics, life, family, business. Spending so much time with him, I learned not only about music but also about being. Our connection was about love for the music and for our families, for each other.'

The empathy and brilliance that cuts across cultural isolation and political embargo is also beautifully expressed in the album that the duo made in Japan at a live performance in 2005, Tokyo Adagio. The title suggests slow movement (Haden often called himself 'an adagio guy'), and throughout his powerful and profound throb moves below Rubalcaba's keys with a slow grace, a heartsblood of human hope and passion which also runs through into his companero's notes - hear the pianist's Transparence for a sublime expression of this.

The album's opening track is the Cuban guitarist and songwriter Rojas Martin's tune En la Orilla del Mundo (The Edge of the World). Slowly wrought and ponderous, Haden's heartbeat thickens Rubalcaba's sharply etched notes and gives them a deeper message of love's vulnerability. The weaving between Cuban and US songs and their essential musical unity marks the comradeship of two musicians overcoming division and forced discord. In Johnny Mercer and David Raksin's US ballad My Love and I, it is Haden's deep and reverberating notes which mark out the melodic theme. Rubalcaba replies with ringing phrases as if the colloquy means everything.

Haden first came to jazz prominence as bassist of the Ornette Coleman Quartet on the 1959 revolutionary albums The Shape of Jazz to Come, Change of the Century and This is Our Music. So Ornette's tune When Will the Blues Leave, first recorded with a quintet without Haden on the 1958 album Something Else, and then with him on the Live at the Hillcrest Club session in Los Angeles in the same year, is apt and full of memory. Haden and Rubalcaba move out of the adagio mood with a sudden zest and pace, and Haden's solo bounces trampoline-like along the Tokyo streets.

Haden first recorded his tribute to the Nicaraguan revolutionary Sandino on the 1989 Liberation Music Orchestra album recorded at the Montreal Jazz Festival. He had written it as part of the soundtrack to the film about the Sandinista revolution, Fire from the Mountain, during an era when US forces were directly collaborating with the Nicaraguan 'contras.' It is an open-hearted, forward-thrusting melody, not 'adagio' at all, and Rubalcaba picks out its phrases with an inspired sense of communal movement, above Haden's volcanic and quasi-subterranean beat.

Solamente una Vez (You Belong to My Heart) is a love song by the Mexican singer and songwriter Agustin Lara Agustin which the duo had recorded as part of a larger band on the 2004 album of Mexican tunes Land of the Sun. It has been sung and recorded over the years by people as diverse as Frank Sinatra and Elvis Presley, but Rubalcaba and Hayden express the simple truth and beauty of its message of love and union as it applies to musicians and their peoples across partitions and frontiers as, of course, it did for them.

(Tokyo Adagio is available on Impulse!)

Gonzalo Rubalcaba (Cuba) & Chucho Valdes (Cuba) – Pianists strike a memorable chord at London Jazz Festival

(2020)

This year's London Jazz Festival was something of a praise song to cosmopolitan jazz piano and it begins with Cuba. When two keyboard stalwarts, Chucho Valdes from Quivican and Gonzalo Rubalcaba from Havana, play opposite each other at two pianos on the Barbican stage, the musical genius of the revolutionary island swings and surges.

Valdes's rippling runs up the keys and Rubalcaba's emphatic, hard-struck and crystalline notes chime the shared bells of piano joy, melody and rampaging improvisation.

It's as if each of their magical instruments has many more keys than they actually have and they evidently enjoy their London meeting as much as their enraptured audience.

At the Cadogan Hall, veteran Polish trumpeter Tomasz Stanko is joined by the much younger members of his New York quartet - Detroit drummer Gerald Cleaver, bassist Reuben Rogers from the Virgin Islands and another Cuban pianist, the brilliant David Virelles.

Stanko's terse, rasping and nerve-cutting horn, starkly blown, provides generous solo opportunities for his bandmates. And, as Rogers's bass dances, Cleaver's drums mix subtlety and power and Virelles fuses waves of Caribbean rhythm and New York stride, the quartet swing like fury.

It's a long time since Abdullah Ibrahim, then Dollar Brand, exiled himself from apartheid South Africa and met a marvelling Duke Ellington in a Zurich night club. His US band Ekaya play proudly as they reinvent some of his old tunes at the Royal Festival Hall, including a spirited version of Scullery Department, written by his old bebop jazz friend from The Jazz Epistles, alto saxophonist Kippie Moeketsi.

Ibrahim reminds his listeners of the time when black musicians waited for their gigs to begin in segregated Johannesburg hotels and you can feel that his bandmates, in particular drummer Will Terrell, bassist Noah Jackson, altoist Cleave Guyton and trumpeter Andrae Murchison, are reliving similar times from their own civil rights history.

The wonderful pianist Zoe Rahman plays a memorable lunchtime set at Soho's Pizza Express, with her Anglo-Bengali roots to the fore. She strikes the keys with her characteristic power and beauty on Ibrahim's Sunset in Blue, Ellington's Single Petal of a Rose, her own Dantastic - dedicated to her son - and a scintillating These Foolish Things.

Like Ibrahim, Virelles, Rubalcaba and Valdes, Rahman makes you thank the Earth for the piano and all those musicians globally who have loved and mastered it.

John Russell (England) – Improvisational greatness from a free spirit of the guitar

John Russell and Roger Turner – Birthdays
John Russell – Analekta
John Russell – Hyste
(2018)

Free improvising guitarist John Russell taught himself the instrument at the age of 11 while listening to the blues and rock of John Mayall, Frank Zappa, Muddy Waters and King Crimson, and the London Jazz Composers' Orchestra led by Barry Guy was also an influence.

He was a regular at John Stevens's Little Theatre Club where he met epochal saxophonist Evan Parker and free guitarist Derek Bailey, with whom he studied for a year, and all these experiences helped to form his music, forged too at free sessions at the Unity Theatre and the Red Rose club. There in the mid-'80s he formed the Mopomoso Club, a co-operative venture that brought committed free musicians together and enabled them to tour across Britain and Europe.

The experimental percussionism of his long-time drum compadre Roger Turner is truly empathetic on Birthdays, recorded at the Red Rose, and such is the intensity of the sonic unity on opener Absinthe, that deciding who is playing is all but impossible. The same is true on Ghosts of a Chance and The Monthly House, where the striking, strumming and caressing of skins, strings, metal and wood become all-inclusive, a music permanently in the making. The timbre is all but quiescent on What Feeling and, as you listen to the brief three minutes of Romney Marsh, you wonder what boyhood dreams inspire its evocations of nature.

Russell returned to the Red Rose to record Analekta, whose four tracks have three duos and a large improvising collective of nine musicians, Quaqua, including two Belgians, a German and a Spaniard. Russell's partner for The Bite is saxophonist Garry Todd whose horn guffaws, glides and rumbles beside Russell's ever-acoustic plucking and strumming. On Blart, veteran trumpeter Henry Lowther blows lyrically and high-edged and Russell's guitar is like a provocative playmate who leads his companion to ever more audacious sounds. On nonet piece So it Goes, the gathering of diverse improvisers plays together with such ardent connection as to forge an alliance of acoustics and electronics, combining breath, percussion, voices, strings, keys and reeds that make estrangement and division lost concepts.

Russell returns to his native Kent for solo album Hyste ('signal' or 'call'), with each track having a title in Kentish dialect. Russell is such a gregarious and company-loving musician that to hear him alone is almost disconcerting, but Hyste is a compelling record that enables the listener to recognise his truly unique artistry.

Lend an ear to Alleycumfree, an imaginary Kentish nowhere-land which Russell finds on his lone guitar journey of 31 minutes. There is no other comparable guitar sound in music - snatches of the blues and sheer melodism arriving at the heart of improvisation, that produces strange and uncanny beauty of daring and boldness.

(Birthdays & Analekta are available on Emanem & Hyste on psi)

Ray Russell (England) - The Complete Spontaneous Event
(2025)

'I think it comes down to this. You can develop a sonic signature, so that if anyone's listening, they know it's you.. This is the only criterion that matters. You play from the song. You influence it, without altering its essence.' Thus declared a true English polymath of the guitar, Ray Russell, born in Islington. London in 1947, an outstanding jazzman, yes, but also a multi-faceted musician who played with such legendary stars from Tina Turner ('a lovely person'), The Supremes, Art Garfunkel, Phil Spector and many more as a studio session regular. 'They all taught me something.' he declared, 'but not always about music!'

His father was an ex-Desert Rat turned worker in a timber company, his mother formerly in the Women's Royal Army Corps. The family were involved in theatre, with an uncle a stage manager at Collins Music Hall, Islington Green. 'My Dad was a pianist, mostly self-taught, who showed me the rudiments of music when I was twelve. Mum and Dad helped me buy a guitar and get to grips with playing. I'll always be grateful for that, it altered my life.'

'In the Fifties, jazz guitar's sound was semi-acoustic with little or no string-bending. Wes Montgomery and Jimi Hendrix were influences whom I translated into my own sound. They showed me more sophisticated paths and rock guitar showed me how blues had come through and how one bend can make the energy of every solo rise and connect. I went pro at nineteen and joined the John Barry Seven. The guys in the band were older and very gracious towards me. I blagged my way as I couldn't read music very well, but could read the name of the James Bond Theme better! We did many shows with the early rockers, so there was a lot of listening. They also taught me how to live on tour which was a big step in growing up, and I was asked to do the occasional recording session.'

'I was on one at Lansdowne Studios with two other guitarists, John McLaughlin and Jimmy Page. As we talked in a break, John said, 'I'm going to the States to join Miles Davis', and Jimmy said: 'Well, I'm off to start a rock band next week', (Led Zep, of course!)'

'John said to Georgie Fame that I might be a suitable replacement for him, so I jumped at the chance as R and B had so many elements that I loved about music, all good for guitar. I'd also got into Coltrane with Kind of Blue after playing at Ronnie Scott's Old Place with Bob Stuckey on organ, and tried to bring that into my playing. And on tour with Georgie I jammed with the Paul Butterfield Blues Band and other guys who were there, like The Four Tops.'

'One day I got a call from CBS Records, who wanted to start a British jazz label: 'CBS Realm Jazz'. Things were changing in my jazz head and this was a great opportunity to try my ideas out with a new quartet; with the late Roy Fry on piano, Daryl Runswick on bass and drummer Alan Rushton. We recorded three albums, with all our heads travelling in the same direction.'

By 1967 the bassist had become the Wolverhampton ace, Dave Holland, who was also shortly to join Davis, but not before playing a live broadcast for BBC Jazz Club. This is now released on a double CD release together with another live BBC session in 1969, by Jazz in Britain, with another of British jazz's great bassists, Shetlander Ron Mathewson. The opener, Coltrane's Mr. P.C. shows Russell's ultra-speed and the sheer dexterity of his improvising, alongside Holland's prodigious technique, Fry's swinging piano and Rishton's empathetic drums. Then on to the pure balladry of Rogers' and Hart's Falling in Love with Love and a succession of Russell originals played with his lightning fingers, which take up most of both sessions, with the special lyricism of tracks like Ballad and We Lie Naked in White Snow.

The albums made me wonder, what would have happened to Russell if he too had made the epochal trans-Atlantic crossing of Holland and McLaughlin, both of whom made classic recordings with the Miles Davis Band and created lifetimes of jazz brilliance and recognition. But 'what if' can never define life, particularly a life in music. As it is, Russell's musical lifespan has been invaluable and precious, marked by a protean inventiveness. As he told me: 'We were much involved in the politics of the era and also the feelings of what music can bring to people, what feelings it can stir.'

Listen to 'The Complete Spontaneous Event' and prepare to be stirred!

(The Complete Spontaneous Event is available on Jazz in Britain Records)

Paul Rutherford (England) - The continents mesh with fire and sound

Paul Rutherford - Neuph, Paul Rutherford, Julie Tippetts, Keith Tippett and Paul Rogers - Rottor: The First Full Turn & Lol Coxhill, Torsten Muller and Paul Rutherford - Milwaukee 2002

(2017)

A New York record waxed by the great Greenwich-born trombonist Paul Rutherford (1940-2007) is going to inspire a review (and not only because he was an inveterate Morning Star reader) because everything he played shone with originality and passionate musicianship as well as virtuosity. So here are three albums he made for the Emanem label between 1978 and 2002 which radiate all these qualities.

The first is the astonishing Neuph, made in studios in Rome, Pisa, and mid-Wales, which features a solo Rutherford over-dubbing on both trombone and euphonium - except on Paunch and Judies which also involved the howling of the studio dog Judy, who was run over shortly after the Rutherford session and left her canine memorial on the album. Paul's trombone is speeded up to double time as Judy wails her vocal to create a duet like no other in all music. With the overdubbing in Phase 2/2, for example, which sets afoot two trombones and two euphoniums, it is as if horns are coming from everywhere in a sonic maze of brass and on the title track the colloquy between the two instruments is intense and full of wit in a palaver of uncanny unity.

But Rutherford's true and unique artistry is in fullest and most extraordinary fettle in his solo trombone pieces Roman Tick and Pisa Ear, where his glides, snarls, snorts and all the rainbow sounds of his multi-phonics genius are set loose with preposterous abandon. In 1998 Rutherford was part of a quartet formation called Rottor with Bristolian pianist Keith Tippett, vocalist and thumb pianist Julie Tippetts and Paul Rogers on bass. They cut an album called The First Full Turn, comprising a 53-minute title track recorded at Le Mas theatre, with the dividend of playing solo trombone in St Giles Church in the City of London's Cripplegate for another 12 minutes of Another Solo Turn.

The long track is an amalgam or perennial surprise, with Julie's voice making a world of timbral diversity beside Rutherford's ever-talking horn. Tippett strikes his piano strings as well as his keys as he reveals a multiplicity of sounds from the very innards of his piano and Rogers's bass digs many a sonic tunnel beneath his bandmates' sounds, at one point providing a deeply echoing subterranean foundation to a blues-sound of one brief Tippett passage, with Julie's wordless and spectral voice hovering over all, and when Rutherford returns for an almost operatic duet with Julie above Tippetts's clattering keys, Rogers makes the stage floor pulsate and Paul's trombone sings with a guffawing beauty.

As for the solo Cripplegate performance, Rutherford, back on the other side of the river of his home city and its square mile of unmeasured wealth and profit, plays with a lonely eloquence, the church's quivering acoustics giving his untrammelled horn virtual quasi-angelic serenity.

In April 2002 Rutherford joined soprano saxophonist Lol Coxhill (more used to busking and troubadouring on the shores of the Thames) and the Hamburg-born bassist Torsten Muller for a concert by the side of Lake Michigan in Milwaukee, Wisconsin. The album, Milwaukee 2002 opens with three long solo performances by the three virtuosi, Rutherford's lasting for 22 minutes, taking his instrument back to the land of its provenance as a jazz voice with a prime rendition. The shimmering Coxhill isn't so bad either both on his own and with the slapping strings of the vibrant Muller, two European siblings of the blues who forge the closest of unions on the track Sax and Bass.

But when Lol and Paul coalesce on the all too brief Sax and Bone and the trio reach their summation on All Three, two continents mesh with fire and sound, and Rutherford's London horn rocks, invents and makes glory in the heart of the United States.

(Neuph, Rottor: The First Full Turn & Milwaukee 2002 are available on Emanem)

Paul Rutherford (England) - A multiphonic master

Paul Rutherford – Tetralogy
(2012)

'Paul read the Morning Star every day. There was always a copy stuffed in his pocket as he made his way around. My oldest brother Len worked on the Daily Worker when Bill Rust was editor, so the family connection goes back a long way. After Paul's death in 2007 we gave his trombones and euphonium to the Central School for Music and the Arts in Havana. We received a letter of thanks for this at the time. We have now heard that there is a seat dedicated to Paul's memory in the newly renovated Miramar Theatre in Havana. Perhaps I will manage to get there eventually to see it.' These words, about her brother Paul Rutherford, one of the genuinely great jazz trombonists, born in Woolwich in 1940, were sent to me by Chris Callaghan after the Star published my review of Raahe 99, recorded in Raahe, Finland, and featuring Paul with baritone saxophonist George Haslam.

I was deeply moved to read Chris's letter, and it sent me directly to another Rutherford album which I'd yet to review. And as I listened to it, I could only hear Paul's slides being played by some young Cuban on the shores of the Caribbean, and all the legacy of his brilliant notes and the immense creative power of his improvisation sounding out across the waves of Toussaint, Che, Fidel, Marley, Claudia, Fanon and Maurice.

The record I turned to is a double album on the precious Emanem label called Tetralogy, featuring Rutherford in four very varied musical contexts between 1978 and 1982. And if you want to know why he was such a distinctive and unparalleled brass genius, you will find many an answer in these extraordinary recordings. The first two sets go back to 1981 with Rutherford playing at the Actual 81 festival in his home city. The three Ele Ol tracks feature solo trombone and euphonium plus electronics, voice and tambourine with Rutherford creating an ocean of extraordinary improvisation through his mastery of multiphonics, when voice is so deep within the horn that it speaks and creates out from its very innards. No other hornman has ever made such sounds, such an amalgam of agony, joy and sheer artistry.

In the second Actual-81 set Rutherford blows with the Chicagoan free trombonist George Lewis, with Martin Mayes on tuba and French hornman Melvyn Poore. The 24 minutes of Braqua 1A begins the session and it is the empathy and instinctive ensemble understanding between the musicians which impresses, as if they were quadruplets of brass. Solos frequently break out of the union of sound, but the listener can only marvel at such spontaneity of invention born from within such sonic concord.

The three tracks named The Great Leaning were recorded at the open-air Pisa Jazz Festival in July 1978 and the solo Rutherford has only the birds to play with. His acoustic glory is fully demonstrated here - his squalls, mutterings, blasts, crescendos, tears, rumblings, voiceprints, shouts, murmurings, cascades, flights, cadences and laughter all forming an astonishing oratory of sound. You have to hear to believe that this Londoner is taking the jazz trombone to places the New Orleans veterans would never have dreamed.

As for the 12 minutes of The Great Leaning 2, Rutherford makes equally compelling timbral soundscapes on his euphonium. Tetralogy's final three tracks were cut in a London studio in 1982 and Rutherford is playing with the English archbassist Paul Rogers - he and Paul were to combine on the unique album Rogues in a 1988 - and drummer Nigel Morris. This three-man colloquy is powerfully realised. Nobody dominates and each's dexterity empowers the others to forge a session of powerful and virtuoso unity.

Christine wrote of her brother that he didn't only wield his trombone. The Morning Star would be wielded in the face of his adversaries whenever he engaged in political discourse - which was a frequent occurrence. 'I remember him standing on the stage at the Queen Elizabeth Hall, berating Mrs Thatcher. The bemused and slightly drunken audience couldn't quite fit this into the improvisational evening for which they had come prepared. Thinking about this, it seems that the musical form and political radicalism belong together, but that's a personal view.'

I agree with her - see what you think and get hold of the marvellous Tetralogy. It will set your mind and spirit racing.

(Tetralogy is available on Emanem)

Julie Sassoon (England) - Land of Shadows
(2025)

From the very first quizzical and unnerving notes of Just So, the opening track of pianist Julie Sassoon's album of 2012, Land of Shadows, you can hear that there is a powerful narrative struggling to escape.

Sassoon is a Mancunian who studied both Classical Music and Art at the University of Lancaster before continuing her studies at Leeds College of Art, specialising in jazz piano and Indian violin. She moved to London, was part of the trio 'Azilut!', and in 2009, to Berlin. This relocation was a move which had a tense and stubborn history. Her Jewish forebears had lived in a small Black Forest village and fled to England in 1939 to escape the Nazi pogroms and death camps. Her grandfather had been imprisoned in Dachau and her grandmother's parents had died in Auschwitz. As a child, Julie lived in a virtual silence about her own family's oppressed history, but it was there, redolent, in her very blood and pianism - as other infernally cruel Jim Crow narratives had been imbued within those musicians who had pioneered jazz in the streets of New Orleans over a century before. Perhaps it is no surprise that Sassoon chose jazz as her music.

Land of Shadows was recorded in the land of her ancestors and the city that was the base of their murderers, at the 'Neue Synagoge', Oranienburgerstrasse, Berlin. Hearing its starkly beautiful solo notes and evocative, hovering wordless vocals is an experience of deep ancestral immanence and empathy. The more you listen to Just So, the more its emotion sinks into and out of you, telling you that the past is in the present, in every newsreel of human suffering that you see, as if Sassoon's keyboard is an instrument into the human soul: a preface of a real and extreme narrative. Perhaps that is in the following track, What the Church Bells Saw...(Part2). What did they see? Was it Sassoon's ancestors? Was it Nazi helmets? Was it a populace turning their backs and giving their salutes while brave anti-fascists were killed beside Jews, Slavs and Romanies? For as you listen you can hear it all, and you know it was but eight decades ago, but is memory of history, as Gabriele Gunther's haunting sleeve-poem attests, as 'fine as ash' and so easily blown away, discarded and forgotten in now-times? It all emerges in Sassoon's notes, for as she confides, her grandmother was in her mind as she played them.

Within the twelve and a half minutes of the next track, Forty Four, there is a melodic lightness, a sense of hope. It is beautifully played and manifest, a testimony that not all memory is shadowland, and Sassoon's gently echoing wordless voice radiates from the piano notes like the sound of solace.

She picks out her slow, haunting notes on the title track as if her every step were unknowingly yet definitively tracing out a path in the crepuscular light, an excursion into a concealed and forbidding historical story. It is a sound that is solitary, yet also revelatory and beautiful. It moves onto the sonic maze of Shifting, and the sense of an urge to break free from a jail of unknowing, a state which Guenther in her poem describes as 'stones of smoke chained like dogs.'

Sassoon wrote New Life when she was pregnant with her daughter and its sound and tone change the ambiance of her album. She strikes the keys with a transforming boldness and the track picks up pace and joy with the confidence of healing. It is nineteen minutes long, as if there is a whole new story of the future to tell, as being in any way a prisoner of history will forever hold you confined in the territory of shadows.

Land of Shadows is a unique achievement, the tracing of a pianist's odyssey, a delving into a family's history to excavate and uncover the future in the present. It is dedicated to Omo, Sassoon's grandmother, yet the universality of its story and the vividness of its musical telling takes it far beyond ethnic or personal circumstance to become an Everywoman's narrative recounted with a jazz groove. As such it is a remarkable record, full of all our lives.

(Land of Shadows is available on jazzwerkstatt Records)

Alexander Von Schlippenbach (Germany), Evan Parker (England), Axel Dormer (Germany), John Edwards (England) and Paul Lytton (England) Live at Café OTO
(2025)

The aging building that houses Café Oto, with its iron pillars and stone floors, was once the factory of the famous Reeves' artists' paints and paint boxes, which many children of my generation were given for Christmas or their birthdays. Now it holds a paintbox of new and avant-garde revolutionary sounds, a palette of sonic freedom to all who listen.

It was a cold, cold Dalston night and here was a golden Anglo-German quintet giving us their much-wanted sonic heat. Their opening sound-song lasted fifty raptured minutes.. Bristolian Evan Parker blew his timbral circles of delving depth, pulling his listeners' ears into his maelstrom, while Cologne-born slide trumpeter Axel Dormer created a fragile, wind strewn sound as if he were blowing through the upper limits of a brass straw.

86 year old Berliner Alexander von Schlippenbach coaxed the Café Oto's grand with a rampaging lucidity, suddenly turning to surprising notes of a raw tenderness, as his improvisations turned around Monkish corners and found gentle avenues of sound.

Bassist John Edwards' fingers danced sublimely up and down his strings with an immense plucking power as the quintet's throbbing hub, and fellow Londoner Paul Lytton's empathetic and eternal drums gave time and foundation to a host of surfaces, as clear as the blue-inked letters OTO, which was stamped on all the listeners hands as we passed through the door.

What they played with such unique musicianship, like all true improvisations will never be heard in exactly the same way again. For these troubadours are one-time creators who tomorrow or the next time will find fresh sounds and harmonies new, the true and untrammelled mission of their artistry. As our old friend Robert Wyatt would say, 'it's different every time,' as it always is at Café Oto.

Maria Schneider (USA) - Big band sound evokes country childhood

Maria Schneider - The Thompson Fields (2017)

In her album The Thompson Fields band leader Maria Schneider contemplates and expresses her deep love for the countryside of south-west Minnesota and its people, and the farms and prairies of her childhood, in a most moving and unusual jazz achievement. 'When we see land as a community to which we belong, we may begin to use it with love and respect,' wrote Schneider's friend Aldo Leopold, and The Thompson Fields - remembering her neighbour's farm where she spent so much time in her early years - expresses the truth of humanity as an integral part of the natural world, with a profound beauty and wisdom and with a sonic reach as wide as the globe.

Schneider, born in Windom, Minnesota, in 1960, studied music theory and composition at the University of Minnesota, made early contact with big band specialists trombonist Bob Brookmeyer and drummer Mel Lewis, and spent three precious years with Gil Evans, one of Miles Davis's inspirational collaborators and supremo of orchestral composing and arranging. In 1989 she formed her own big band and signalled her allegiance to Evans's accomplishments by the title of her first album, Evanescence, of 1994.

In the opening track of The Thompson Fields, Walking by Flashlight, Schneider remembers her early morning girlhood walks along untarred country roads, and she evokes the poem of Ted Kooser and 'my circle of light on the gravel/swinging side to side/coyote, raccoon, fieldmouse, sparrow/each watching from darkness.' Scott Robinson's alto clarinet blows the dawn life with an intense and delicate beauty.

In Monarch and the Milkweed is explained by Schneider in the album's unique hardback sleeve booklet as an illustration 'of mystifyingly complex relationships in nature.' The young of the monarch butterfly, its habitat the native prairie, can only survive if the female lays its eggs on the milkweed plant, their only sustenance. Nature's story is told sonically by orchestral soundscape and two serene brass soloists, trombonist Marshall Gilkes and flugelhornist Greg Gisbert.

From Minnesota to New Guinea, from monarch butterflies to birds of paradise, the protagonists of Arbiters of Evolution, this is Schneider's reach, and here it is reedsong and the tenor and baritone saxophones of Donny

McCaslin and Robinson that express in their note the mating rituals of birds on islands that are oceans away.

It is in the title composition that I could find Schneider's kinship with the great US poet Walt Whitman, who wrote more than a century before, lines that are forerunners to her orchestral vision - 'O slender leaves! O blossoms of my blood!/I bequeath myself to the dirt I grow from the grass I love/If you want me again, look for me under your bootsoles!' For her music is as essentially American as Whitman's Leaves of Grass in the ways it humanises nature.

In The Thompson Fields she remembers the view from the top of the silo of her neighbours' farm, over the fields of beans being blown in the wind. 'From the vantage point of the silo, I felt the wind carrying all the intersecting stories of my youth, along with the stories of a whole community.' The orchestra's mollifying tones, and the solos of pianist Frank Kimbrough and guitarist Lage Lund create a natural world in harmony with all those, including humans, who live within it and tell their stories of it. In Home, Rich Perry's lush tenor saxophone rises from the midst of a timbral picture of how waving grass fields would look, and in Nimbus Schneider gives an aural portrait of a cloud-covered sky, with some rivetingly expressive alto saxophone choruses by Steve Wilson.

Other soloists resonate from this 18-piece band. Accordionist Gary Versace is the virtuoso of A Potter's Song, dedicated to long-time orchestral trumpeter Laurie Frink, and in Lembranca, a tribute to Brazilian saxophonist and samba composer Paulo Moura. Jay Anderson's plunging bass and Ryan Keberle's trombone add to the orchestra's passage to the streets of Rio.

The Thompson Fields is a unique album. Far from falling into childhood nostalgia, it builds on childhood to encompass the world with its sounds of its Americas, and makes music the commentary of nature and humanity as one.

(The Thompson Fields is available on ArtistShare)

Ronnie Scott (England) - Spirit of co-operation

Ronnie Scott - Fast And Loose: Live in 1954 (2017)

'Syncopated Marxism' was how the band's baritone saxophonist and jazz writer Benny Green described the music played by Ronnie Scott's nine-piece band in the mid-'50s. Almost permanently on the road, the band played their hot music in dance halls throughout the land, but still managed a wildly innovative sound.

It was made up of some prime British jazzmen of the era. Alongside Ronnie was the Dundee-born trumpeter Jimmy Deuchar, trombonist Ken Wray and the altoist Derek Humble, who was to become one of the leading horns of the Kenny Clarke/Francy Boland Big Band during the next decade. Also on hand was tenorist Pete King, who was Ronnie's business partner for years at their Soho jazz club.

The pounding drummer was Tony Crombie, the bassist Lennie Bush and the featured pianist and vibes player was the prodigious Victor Feldman, who in 1957 crossed the Atlantic, eventually becoming the pianist in Cannonball Adderley's band and recording with Miles Davis on his Seven Steps To Heaven album in 1963.

Although they played under Scott's name, they were very much a co-operative band, and Simon Spillett's vibrant sleeve notes tell how the band members 'drew equally' on their performance earnings. As Ronnie remembered: 'We encountered much petty jealousy from bandleaders and none at all from the musicians. The inference is clear. A thriving co-op band is a dangerous thing so far as bandleaders are concerned. They see communism round the corner and start worrying about how far they may go in exploiting their own musicians.'

Perhaps this sense of unity and equal respect within the band caused its sense of jubilant sound and Ronnie remembered that 'I've never laughed so much in my life as I did with that band.' The boisterousness, goodwill and joyously fine musical artistry comes boiling out of the new compilation Fast And Loose: Live 1954. It's there from the very first title track where Ronnie hurtles into full tempo in his solo and brother horn Humble is right with him. Crombie's drums are in full combustion and the band is bursting with fire.

Crombie's Body Beautiful shows what a fine bassist Bush was, before Humble and Deuchar take poised choruses. Then into Charlie Parkers's bebop classic, the Yardbird Suite, with Deuchar's pure tone ascendant with Humble's sheer fluidity preluding Feldman's rampaging piano runs. There were nine balladeers in the studio that March 1954 day too, with Wray's slides leading the way on a poignant version of If I Should Lose You and Ronnie digging deep for a beautifully mellow reading of Laura, abetted by Feldman's lyrical keys and Bush's ever-present bass heartbeat. The versatile Feldman brings out his vibes for This Can't Be Love and runs up the pace Lionel Hampton-style while the horns watch on.

From the Thames to the Mississippi for Dear Old Southland and the brassmen are shining as Deuchar comes down from the north for a lucid solo and Wray engages the trumpeter in a free colloquy. Leo Parker's El Sino gives the stage to the grace of Humble's alto and Wray's guffawing trombone before Green's rumbling baritone takes its moment. Billie Holiday gave her heart to I Wished On The Moon, and Humble's horn sings too with a disarming tenderness.

The album ends with seven tracks recorded for single 78s on the Esquire label in April 1954, by a quartet made up of Scott, Feldman, Bush and Crombie. The two takes of Sunshine On A Dull Day could be the last waltz at any of the dance hall venues from Stockport to Margate where Ronnie's bands played, and Fools Rush In and Poor Butterfly must have delighted many a romancing couple. But as you listen you still can't get the performances of the marvellously animated nine-piece outfit out of your head. The co-operative sound, the absence of egoism, the unity of musicianship, the comradeship of jazz going from city to city in a battered bus.

Music of its time and place, but now with this marvellous record, a gift for always.

(Fast And Loose: Live in 1954 is available on Acrobat)

Woody Shaw (USA) – I got my college degree from Art Blakey's university of jazz and life

Woody Plays Woody by Woody Shaw (2015)

The moving sleeve notes of Woody Plays Woody were written by Woody Louis Armstrong Shaw III, the son of the luminous trumpeter Woody Shaw, born in Laurinbug, North Carolina, in 1944 and who died on the New York subway in May 1989. All compositions on the album were recorded in live performance at San Francisco's Keystone Korner jazz club in 1977 (with Opec recorded at the same venue in 1981), and with Woody were some of the prime musicians of his generation, including drummer Victor Lewis, bassist Stafford James, pianists Larry Willis and Mulgrew Miller, trombonist Steve Turre and Carter Jefferson playing soprano saxophone.

Barely in his twenties, Woody was invited by alto saxophonist Eric Dolphy to work with him in Europe. Dolphy died in Berlin shortly after Shaw's arrival, but he stayed in Paris and played with Bud Powell and Kenny Clarke. When he returned to the US he joined the Horace Silver Quintet, played with Jackie McLean, Hank Mobley and McCoy Tyner and became a regular horn on Blue Note records before becoming a Jazz Messenger with Art Blakey. In 1973 he began leading his own groups, while also playing with Dexter Gordon, also home from Europe and as a part of the Junior Cook/Louis Hayes Quintet.

Admired for his fiery and audacious hornwork, he was plagued by failing eyesight in his latter years, but always remembered by the words of introduction given to him by fellow trumpet ace Dizzy Gillespie: 'Hey look out, look out! Here he comes!' Shaw composed all the tunes of Woody Plays Woody, and the first Little Red's Fantasy was written for his wife Maxine. His solo reveals many of his horn qualities - the piercing tone, the adventurousness of pitch, the potent improvising, the melodic sense, the intensity of sound. All are manifested before Stafford James's plunging solo.

The racing pace of Rahsaan's Run was Woody's tribute to one of his beloved confreres, the miraculous Rahsaan Roland Kirk, the blind saxophonist (he played three reed instruments simultaneously). Rahsaan supported Woody when he needed to deal with his own hereditary retinitis pigmentosa: 'If I can get on stage with Roland Kirk,' he declared, 'Rahsaan man is like a wizard. When I see people like that, it doesn't bother me.' Lewis is explosive on this one and Woody's opening solo sprints and crackles until the ever-nimble Turre's slides take the baton above Willis's powerful comping. A great track that Rahsaan would have relished.

'Once the inherent difficulties of the tune are solved, there are no limits to where you can go with it,' said Woody, and Stepping Stone illustrates this to dynamic effect. Jefferson's seething soprano boils up the stew and Woody's exchanges with him only compound the heat until Willis's galloping chorus gives but a modicum of relief as James furiously slaps his strings.

The Organ Grinder of the next tune's title was Woody's close friend of a Newark, New Jersey, youth, Larry Young, with whom he recorded the epochal Blue Note album Unity in 1965. Shaw was hugely influenced by the organist, who introduced him to African and oriental musics and when he died in 1978 Woody and jazz lost a true genius. He plays with poise and restraint and great beauty on this one, and Willis's solo emulates him with invention and respect.

Woody's solo on Opec burns, as his son puts in in his sleeve notes, with 'sheer vitriol' in a tune he wrote as a critique of the policies of the global energy conglomerate. Lewis is torrential too as Woody blows a storm of visceral notes into the Frisco skies and Turre carries on the damage, relenting not a wit, all the way to Saudi Arabia and the Gulf millionaires.

'I got my college degree from Art Blakey's university of jazz and life,' affirmed Woody; 'I'm very proud that I was a Jazz Messenger.' And Ginseng People was his tune to Blakey, named after the efficacy of the herb and the drummer's love for Japan and its people. Turre, another ex-Messenger, blows knots of sound in his solo above James's stamping bass before Woody comes surging in, his phrases flickering like agitated leaves of sound, his long, defiant solo urged on by thoughts of the mighty drummer and the reality of one of his true inheritors, the superb Victor Lewis, pounding right next to him.

Woody lives again.

Get out and get it.

(Woody Plays Woody is available on High Note)

Woody Shaw (USA) - Quintet reflect on troubled times

The Woody Shaw Quintet - Tokyo 1981

(2018)

The beautiful tumbling cadence towards the end of trumpeter Woody Shaw's rendition of Thelonius Monk's Around Midnight is a sequence of pure horn artistry and this album of Shaw's stellar quintet, recorded live in Tokyo in December 1981, resounds with such moments. For this session he combined with trombonist Steve Turre, pianist Mulgrew Miller, drummer Tony Reedus and bassist Stafford James.

Opener Rosewood has Miller introducing the simple, stomping theme before the two brassmen join for a powerful ensemble narrative. Miller takes a fast, bluesy chorus, Turre follows and builds the excitation before Shaw enters, blowing on the edge with an ear-splitting fervour. James uses his bow to saw out a long solo as the theme returns, set off by Reedus's clashing cymbals.

The melodic finesse of Around Midnight is given a breathy and precarious fluency in Woody's solo. It is as if he is cutting sound in half, so brittle and crackling is his timbre. Its 15 minutes includes a stridently reflective Miller solo, some eloquent Turre slides infused with the blues and a passionate and wondrous Shaw, who finishes his final chorus with an allusion to There's a Boat that's Leaving Soon for New York from Gershwin's Porgy and Bess. Miller's opus Apex follows, with a Jazz Messengers sound and some Art Blakey-like drumming from Reedus with a searing Shaw solo and Turre playing with real pace. The speed slackens for Shaw's ballad From Moment to Moment. Turre sounds deep, as if he is playing bass trombone and Miller's melodic solo is full of tenderness. Song of Songs is the album's climax. Recorded during the last phase of what he called the 'ridiculous' US war against the Vietnamese people, it is dedicated to them.

The Tokyo concert was six years after the liberation of occupied Saigon and Woody's horn remembers the conflict imposed upon his generation too with an intense, emotive sound. The undercurrents of a brutal, expansionist war resonate in the notes of these five musicians. Miller begins, scuttling his echoing keys, before James's mournful bowed bass and Shaw's last post-like chorus confronts his nation's militarism in 1981, spurred by Ronald Reagan. Then the rhythm ensemble mounts behind him as his notes dazzle and his chorus rises to a high-pitch climax.

Turre's solo stokes up a rumbling undergrowth of reflection as his phrases conjure a forest of sound, there on the eastern island edge of a continent that US forces had blasted and poisoned a decade before. It is as if these musicians are breaking out of their nation's own history.

Shaw died in May 1989, after being hit by a train on the New York subway, a horrendous loss to music and the brilliance of its truth.

(Tokyo 1981 is available on Elemental)

Archie Shepp (USA) - Never fade from memory

Archie Shepp - Attica Blues

(2003)

Who remembers the Attica prison rebellion in New York State of 1971? When 1,300 inmates, most of them black, took control of the prison yard and the 'liberal' Republican state governor and multimillionaire Nelson Rockefeller declared that the revolt was 'a step in an ominous world trend' and ordered its putting down with a bloody massacre and feast of death, with 39 prisoners and nine hostages killed by prison guards. This insurgency was partly provoked by the murder of another black man and prisoner on the other side of the US, when the brilliant essayist and revolutionary George Jackson - author of the epochal Soledad Brother - was shot down in San Quentin, California, in August 1971.

'I have been in rebellion all my life, I just didn't know it,' Jackson declared. The same could be said about the saxophonist and lyricist Archie Shepp, born in Fort Lauderdale, Florida, in 1937, whose 1972 album Attica Blues has been reissued along with all the memories of heroism and resistance that it evokes. The Attica events caused a musical rage among some of the greatest jazz musicians of the age. Charles Mingus recorded Remember Rockefeller at Attica and Free Cell Block F 'Tis Nazi USA on his Changes albums of 1975, but Shepp, characteristically, was first to make the strongest of jazz statements.

Hearing Attica Blues again after all these years only magnifies its profound sense of elegy. It is a celebratory and defiant lament for the heroes, lauded and ordinary, of black America, created within a context heralded in the lyrics of its title composition, as a chorus of voices sings out above the ensemble: 'If I could have had the chance to make one decision, Everyone would walk the earth on equal conditions.' Two of its tracks commemorate the two most titanic figures of jazz music. Goodbye Sweet Pops is a musical love poem to Louis Armstrong, who died in July 1971, with Shepp's soaring soprano backed by an ensemble of trombones, violins and cellos, marking out the life of the music's first genius.

Invocation to Mr Parker remembers the transformer of jazz, the reinventor, with Jimmy Garrison's hugely vibrating bass, Marion Brown's warbling flute remembering 'that driving music man' whose short life blazed incredible new pathways. Blues for Brother George Jackson creates a surging orchestral sound, with Shepp's angry, raging tenor springing out alongside Roy Burrowes's keening trumpet emerging from a forest of horns and percussion.

But, for me, the climax of the album are Shepp's two versions of his own tune Steam, as fine and moving as to be a true Lycidas of jazz. Steam was the nickname of a young cousin of Shepp, killed by gang violence. The lyrics are almost Miltonic. The dead young man is described as a 'comely' youth, 'a star gleaming bright as fire,' snuffed out by senseless internecine conflict, his humanity 'sweet as the end of pain.' now finished. Steam becomes one with the martyrs of Attica, with Jackson, with the glory of Armstrong's trumpet and Parker's alto, all stories of black America, its struggle, its unity, its beauty and achievement.

To underline this are two more tracks, Ballad for a Child, with Shepp playing a soft and tender Ben Webster-like tenor solo which, as adulthood approaches, changes to a growing harshness. And the concluding Quiet Dawn, sung by a child named Waheeda Masseyk and accompanied by rasping notes of menace from Shepp's tenor horn.

Attica Blues needs to be listened to many times before all its themes merge to cohere into one. It embraces music which tells of a whole era of US history and – resistance, which will never fade away into quietude.

(Attica Blues is available on Impulse)

Wayne Shorter (USA) - Jazz heartlands

Wayne Shorter Quartet, Barbican, London & the album Alegria (2003)

Wayne Shorter, who was born in Newark, New Jersey in 1933, is one of the greatest living jazz saxophonists and composers. Since his first Vee-Jay albums in 1959, through his four years as a Jazz Messenger with Art Blakey (1959-63), his period as tenorist in Miles Davis's second great quintet with Herbie Hancock (piano), Ron Carter (bass) and drummer Tony Williams (1963-70) and his leadership of Weather Report and his embrace of electronic sounds beginning from 1970, to his current return to fronting an acoustic quartet, Shorter has always been a jazz vanguardist.

Looking at him on stage and sensing the vibrant youthfulness of his mien and his musicianship, it doesn't seem possible that he is in his 70th year. Yet he is and it is also the year of Alegria, a new album which crystallises not only Shorter's instrumental brilliance with tenor and soprano saxophones but also his arranging and composing skills.

It also explores his musical internationalism, including a Spanish popular song, a traditional Celtic air, a piece by the Brazilian composer Villa-Lobos, a 12th-century carol and his own dedication to Angola - first recorded on his album The Soothsayer in 1965. The album begins with his new composition, Sacajawea, remembering the native American who guided those who claimed to 'discover' the North West Passage with Shorter playing both saxophones alongside his regular quartet colleagues, the Panamanian pianist Danilo Perez, John Patitucci on bass and Brian Blade on drums.

Shorter begins with a soprano burst, before a compact ensemble and the riff-theme takes over, followed by more Shorter and Perez's rippling piano solo - and a climax forged by recording technology which allows Shorter's two reeds to weave between each other. An orchestral setting with strings, English horn and bassoon delivers the melody of Leroy Anderson's Serenata, reprised by Shorter's pure soprano.

Those of us with musical memories of the 1960s may remember Joan Baez singing Villa-Lobos's beautiful Brazilian melody inspired by Bach, Bachianas Brasileiras No 5. Shorter's wavering tenor preludes, Charles Curtis's pristine solo cello then re-enters playing in that singular serpentine sound ,that has always characterised his tenor solos. The quartet setting of the traditional She Moves Through the Fair shows Shorter switching between the two saxophones, playing with a lyrical and reflective precision beside Perez's gentle notes.

His own composition Orbits and the Twelfth Century Carol are Shorter arrangements and played with larger ensembles. The former has a mysterious, worrisome sound. dominated by the leader's quivering, rasping tenor, while the latter is soprano-led and less enigmatic, with Shorter and Perez glorified, playing empathetically off each other. In the concluding Capricorn II, Shorter reverts to quartet, in quiescent mode with a breathy beauty that, in the final short coda, is an exhalation to be continued. Alegria, despite the message of its title, is certainly not all happiness but infused with that note of beguilement and perplexity that has always been at the heart of Shorter's sound.

At the Barbican. the quartet walks briskly onto the stage, take up their instruments and begin to play, without introductions or announcements of tunes. Perez's strident chords, Patitucci's surging bowed bass and Blade's muffled mallets make their sound next to Shorter's vibratoless tenor noodling. It is as if chamber music of another planet has descended into the heart of London. But this cosmos is the Americas and the myriad of its people and 70 years of a winding jazz saxophone journey. 'Life is a work in progress,' concludes Shorter in the programme notes. 'It's also eternal and different at every juncture.'

At the outset of the first selection, which lasts for 40 minutes. Blade is only lightly touching his drums. seeming to pull back his sticks millimetres before he strikes them. Yet, after 15 minutes. he is pounding in upon them, Shorter is exploding into a complexity of veering, twisting notes, Perez is beating hard on his keys and Patitucci's plucked notes become current and undercurrent in deep patterns of dramatic turns. The listener knows now that this is a quartet, an entity of players who know each others' capacities intimately yet who can never totally predict the next gyre or detour that any of them might take. Co-operation and solidarity in unforeseen sound - the essence of jazz. There is no grandstanding with Shorter and his confreres, no spectacular solos. It is as if each musician never wants or needs to depart from this ensemble of musical humanity. Brilliance is collectively welded, not individualistically garlanded and glorified. As Patitucci plays a solo of throbbing power, Perez reaches into the innards of the shining Barbican piano to join him by plucking its naked strings.

Shorter finishes on soprano saxophone, its first long notes sounding like a shepherd's call, before careering into piercing contours of sounds. Blade's drumming gathers volume. balanced by Perez's percussive comping. At one strange and ebullient moment, the drummer's sheer force meets the protest of his own drums and his tom-tom keels over onto its side, as if it can take no more. You wonder where each quarter of this quartet will go, but, wherever it is, you know that they will arrive there wholly together.

In the second, much briefer selection. Shorter's riverine flow of notes reminded me again of Ellingtonian tenor saxophonist Paul Gonsalves more than any other reedman. Blade is the most reflective and listening of drummers, hearkening closely to his companions. playing for them rather than for himself, following their music-steps while simultaneously pondering and stepping them out himself.

There. is nothing familiar nostalgically about this programme, considering Shorter's enormous range of experience in many distinct expressions of jazz, only discovery and new explorations. In the final selection, Perez's Latin piano wit, Patitucci's 's earnest virtuosity, Blade's tempestuous drumming and Shorter's soprano exclamations - redolent with the 'weird' meandering patterns that his first critics said that they heard breathing out of him in the late 1950s and early '60s in those albums like Wayning Moments, Speak No Evil or The Soothsayer - are concluded only by Blade's final thunderous bolt.

Irresistible, astonishing music from the heartlands of jazz.

(Alegria is available on Verve)

Alan Skidmore (England) - Supreme love of Coltrane

Alan Skidmore - Tribute to Trane, After the Rain & 50 Journeys (2010)

'As the son of a jazz musician I had listened to jazz all my life. Then I heard John Coltrane and my world changed for ever. His music touched my very being.' Those are the words of British tenor saxophonist Alan Skidmore, born in 1942 to the formidable Jimmy who had played sax for decades in the bands of George Shearing, Vic Lewis and Humphrey Lyttelton.

Alan turned professional at 16 and played in the bands of Eric Delaney and bluesman Alexis Korner before discovering Coltrane. In 1988 he recorded his Tribute to Trane, a powerful salute to his strongest influence, including seven of Coltrane's tunes. But this album is far more than just a tribute and Skidmore's muscular sound comes through, particularly in Lonnie's Lament where his rumbling choruses provoke a reflective solo from pianist Jason Rebello.

The rock-like resonance of bassist Dave Green and Stephen Keogh's always inventive drumming give the album a peculiarly English character, but one full of Coltrane's spirit. Listen to the fast-flowing Bessie's Blues and you will hear a superb quartet unflustered by the huge challenge they are daring to take on. It is as if Trane came back to England and played his heart out.

Coltrane also wrote After the Rain and this tune became the title of Skidmore's 1998 album, subtitled 'a collection of ballads,' including three by Coltrane. 'Skid' is accompanied by two large ensembles, the Radio-Philharmonic Hannover des NDR and Colin Towns' Mask Symphonic. Some of the tunes were born from jazz, like those of Coltrane, Benny Golson's I Remember Clifford or Ellington's In a Sentimental Mood. Others come directly from the huge canon of the American popular song - like Skidmore's beautifully melodic version of the Rodgers and Heart classic It's Easy to Remember.

In After the Rain itself, Towns' orchestral comradeship is compelling but unobtrusive as Skidmore blows the mighty theme. In Nature Boy the shimmering violins preface Skidmore's solo journey. Too Young to Go Steady is also on Coltrane's 1962 Ballads album. Skidmore meshes the rhapsody of his horn with the soothing strings of Towns' arrangement.

Coltrane's tune to his first wife, Naima, seems entirely attuned to this ballad-feast and is followed by Frank Sinatra's Nancy. The extraordinary grace and elegance of My One and Only Love is more evidence of Skidmore's mastery of the balladeer's art. His final coda is breathtaking, as is his narrative of Every Time We Say Goodbye. The album ends with Coltrane's Central Park West. Skidmore's breath steps out its notes with authority, love and beauty, completing an album close to being a masterpiece.

A very different Skidmore sound characterises his 2008 album, 50 Journeys. In 1991 he recorded the first of three albums, The Call, with South African ensemble Ubizo, which was followed by Ubizo in 2002. These are rampaging albums, full of life and hope, radiating African energy, militancy and wisdom, with Skidmore blowing hard, leading and learning.

Now comes the powerful 50 Journeys, with Saidi Kanda playing African violin, talk pipe, congas and kalimba and Musa Mboob is on sabarr drum and talking drum. Ingolf Burkhardt plays trumpet with pianists Steve Melling and Colin Towns, Neville Malcolm is on bass with Mike Paxton on kit drums. Coltrane's Blues Minor is the opener, with Melling's stomping intro before Skidmore comes pounding in, bringing Trane to Africa. There are 17 tracks, each one urgent and thick with percussive artistry and fury.

Mboob's Jamangam seethes with life, Sacred Places is nearly all slow and serene Skidmore. He digs out a deep chorus in the title tune and in Two Brothers Melling's piano phrases sound a little like those of the father of South African piano Abdullah Ibrahim. Skidmore blows movingly through Coltrane's Africa, his breath aflame. Maputo Moonrise is a Mozambican episode with a delving bassline and Skidmore aggressive and fiery, a potent musical essay of unity between Europe and Africa.

(Tribute to Trane & After the Rain are available on Miles Music; 50 Journeys on Provocateur)

Jimmy Smith (USA) - All hail the original Hammond man

Jimmy Smith Trio, Jazz Café, London
(2000)

All the bluesy clucking in the world was coming, last week, from a trans-Atlantic chicken shack in Camden Town. For installed there, behind his

Hammond B3 organ, was the maestro Jimmy Smith, the blues dripping like southern gravy from his agile finger-tips.

Smith - now a very youthful 75 - is a genuine jazz pioneer. His famous Blue Note albums of the late I 950s and early 1960s - including the hugely popular Back At The Chicken Shack - turned the organ into a fusion of bebop, rhythm and blues, gospel and funk which made him an orchestra unto himself.

His trios with guitarists like Kenny Burrell and Grant Green, and larger ensembles with saxophonists such as Stanley Turrentine and soloists like Lee Morgan, produced scores of imitators. Yet Jimmy Smith's sound stays unique. The walking bass lines of his feet, the left handed chords and the solo virtuosity of his right hand stomping across the keys are still working in gutsy harmony.

At the Jazz Café he was joined by two fine British musicians. On drums - although so smothered by huge cymbals that it was difficult to see his face - was Martin Drew, the ex-percussionist of Ronnie Scott, providing by turns crashing and humming support for Smith's booming chords. On guitar was Phil Lee who produced some down-home solos that could have come throbbing out of the organist's own Pennsylvania.

And there was quite a degree of hokum to the veteran's act. In between scintillating versions of his own tunes, like The Cat, or standards such as Summertime, Smith joked and played with a more than willing audience, getting one half of them to measure the beats, one to eight, in his breaks and the other half to count downwards, eight to one. Complaining of flu as be spluttered and sneezed into the microphone between rocking snatches and phrases of pure organ blues, he defied his years and expressed the essence of all the jazz he has hammered out for over half a century.

To hear a musician who practically invented a significant jazz instrument is a rare privilege and an increasingly rare experience. So, Jimmy Smith is a musical phenomenon definitely not to be missed.

Rudy Smith (Trinidad) - Steel drums make for a glorious sound

Glass World by the Rudy Smith Quartet
(2017)

A true jazz pioneer is the Port of Spain-born (in 1943) Rudy 'Two left' Smith who in the mid-'60s, when he arrived in Europe like thousands of other immigrant ships from the Caribbean, brought the vibrancy of his culture with him. Smith's surprising and unique contribution was to make the steel pan a true and innovative jazz instrument.

The steel drum, which Trinidadian percussive love created from oil barrels discarded across the island by US-owned multinationals like Texaco, has its origins in west African musical artistry and the virtuosi of the kora, sansa (thumb piano) and balafon. The beauty and excitation of its sounds would visit my ears every night in Tobago in the '60s as I marked my students' English essays. The steel band tent of Our Boys Steel Orchestra was 50 yards along from the flat I rented, and I would never tire of hearing the balladic and rhythmic artistry of the panbeaters' notes.

Smith grew up listening to some of his nation's finest steel band musicians, carnivallers and calypsonians. He played his first pan when he was six and, as he grew, he heard records of US vibes artists like Milt Jackson and Bobby Hutcherson and was much influenced by Oscar Peterson's piano and John Coltrane's saxophones, all helping to form his direction in jazz. As a teenager, he was part of a Trinidadian band called the Merrymakers. When calypso became popular in Europe in the 1950s he grasped his opportunity and, finding a base in Sweden and Denmark, he became an arranger, pan-maker and tuner as well as a powerful jazz soloist and improviser.

Since 1983 Smith has led his own quartet in Denmark, playing alto pan with veteran pianist and composer Ole Matthiessen, drummer Ole Streenberg and bassist Hendrik Dhyrbye. On his new album, Glass World, Danish saxophonist Jesper Lovdal and Swedish guitarist Bjarne Roupe guest on several tracks. Mathiesson is the writer of six of the album's nine tunes, and as soon as his opener Stand By begins and Smith beats his pan, you hear his ringing vibrato relishing the melody as if this were Maracas Bay rather than Scandinavia.

The foursome are utterly attuned to each other's musical ways, with Dhyrbye and Streenborg swinging relaxedly and Matthiesson's solo assured and in perfect empathy with Smith's mallets.

Blues for Rasta Prasta is an affectionate portrait and Smith's tumbling cadences are a delight. Dhyrbye plays a delving solo before Smith returns, and you can hear the spirit if Milt Jackson's blues-drenched vibes in his notes. One for Bent quickly picks up a jaunty chorus before Smith's agile notes skim off the caressed metal with a joyous aplomb.

Since the epochal 1939 recording of Body and Soul by the tenor saxophone nonpareil Coleman Hawkins, the tune has always been heard as a test piece for horn players. Smith's rendition makes it a feast for pan virtuosi too as the notes roll serenely across the studio and Mathiesson follows with a solo of effusive tenderness. Back to Trinidad for the Lord Kitchener calypso Old Lady Walk a Mile and a Half. There is a famous Pathe newsreel sequence of Kitch singing London is the Place for Me as he stepped off the Empire Windrush at Tilbury in June 1948, but on this record's evidence, it is Copenhagen that is the place for Rudy Smith. He plays the tune with a true verve, pride and swing, his roots bursting out of every note. Dhyrbye jumps in for a bouncing solo and Streenberg's drums are lent a springing Caribbean spirit.

It's very different from the Iberian rhapsody of Matthiesson's Spanish Sparrow, pecked by Roupe's guitar and the melodic lyricism of the pianist's Coming Home, where Smith's sheer buoyancy of sound seems to send his pans floating across the Baltic or the Caribbean for it is all one musical sea.

The title tune is gentle and beautiful and Smith's pans sound so sonically pure. It seems incongruous to think they were born from Trinidad's life of oil, and the constant resistance of the island's oil workers, who turned base and rusted metal canisters into glorious sound. This is one of the jazz year's most marvellous records: certainly one to buy and savour with a bottle of Trinidad rum and a roti.

(Glass World is available on Stunt)

Stuff Smith (USA) - A sultan of violin swing
Stuff Smith and Oscar Peterson
(2017)

The violin has often struggled in a jazz context but no musician had a greater impact in establishing it as a jazz instrument than Hezekiah Leroy Gordon 'Stuff' Smith, who was born in Portsmouth, Ohio, in 1909. His father, who was both a barber and a violinist, and his pianist mother taught him music as a child and put him in the family band. It was hearing Louis Armstrong play Savoy Blues while he was on a music scholarship at university in Charlotte, North Carolina, that signalled a lifetime in jazz, and at the age of 15 he became a professional musician.

He lived in Buffalo as a young man, eventually played with Jelly Roll Morton, and after moving to New York in 1936 he pioneered the amplified violin and led a quintet at the renowned Onyx Club with drummer Cozy Cole and trumpeter Jonah Jones. During the post-war years he made some stunning records with Nat King Cole, Dizzy Gillespie and Sun Ra and spent the last two years of a hectic touring and recording life in Copenhagen from 1965-7, where he made a series of fine albums with Danish musicians and fellow US expatriates like pianist Kenny Drew and drummer Wallace Bishop.

The joint session he made with Oscar Peterson in Los Angeles in March 1957 has been unavailable for many years, so its reissue on the Poll Winners label is a real gift from more than half a century ago. 'Play in tune. And play from the heart always,' declared Stuff, and both principles are exemplified all through this album, which in addition to Smith and the great Montreal-born Peterson has Barney Kessel on guitar, drummer Alvin Stoller and the virtuoso bassist of the bop age, Ray Brown, born in 1926 in Pittsburgh.

Stuff's husky, hoarse, hugely allusive and relentlessly swinging strings throb through the album from its very first notes. Desert Sands is the violinist's tune and he is soon making his tracks, forging a union immediately with Peterson, his kindred spirit of swing, whose solo verve soon follows Stuff's choruses with the undisguised quotations, this time from Pretty Baby and Joshua. Fletcher Henderson's Soft Winds, associated with Benny Goodman, follows and Stuff makes it his own, with a flickering guitar chorus from Kessel and a softly twanging, bouncing solo from Brown.

The first of three Ellington tunes, Things Ain't What They Used To Be, follows, with a bluesy chorus from Peterson before Stuff gets to do business, his grating, rasping beauty finding its crescendo. On to It Don't Mean A Thing If

I Ain't Got That Swing, and no-one was more qualified to play it than Stuff Smith. Peterson was a contender too and his chorus rocks the studio before Stuff comes frolicking in with huge zest and rhythm. The much slower Stuff tune Time and Again calms the confreres down a little but not for long as they sally into I Know That You Know with all strings blazing and Stuff in stop-time daring all through his chorus.

There were only six tracks on the original album, but this reissue includes those there was no room for plus two extra with the crawling-hands pianist from Indianapolis, Carl Perkins, recorded in Los Angeles in the same year. More Ellington and the Ben Webster tenor sax feature, In a Mellow Tone, is swinging meat and drink to Stuff, with Ray Brown shadowing his exposition of the familiar theme and Kessel cutting a neatly picked solo. Heatwave gives a rampaging Peterson his true swinging head and 10-and-a-half minutes of Body and Soul explores the finesse of Stuff's string artistry as well as Peterson's exquisite lyricism.

The two tracks with Perkins are both Stuff originals. Calypso doesn't have much of a Trinidad feel, but Stuff peels off his notes with fire and force and Perkins's solo is full of invention. I Wrote My Song is waltz-like and Stuff's violin is almost weeping, its tune uncovering what seems to be an uncharacteristic sadness, for who knows the flesh and blood of real life beating inside that extraordinary and infectious veneer of unmitigated swing?

(Stuff Smith and Oscar Peterson is available on Poll Winners Records)

Wadada Leo Smith (USA) - Liberation opus

Wadada Leo Smith - Ten Freedom Summers (2012)

If you want to learn about the long history of the US civil rights movement you could read about it in, for example, Taylor Branch's Parting The Waters or Henry Hampton and Steve Feyer's Voices Of Freedom, both fine and inspiring narratives. Or you could play the four radiant records of Wadada Leo Smith's Ten Freedom Summers, for here is sonic history and struggle vibrant and-telling in every note.

Smith is a 73-year-old free jazz trumpet pioneer born in Leland, Mississippi, who lived through the hard and brave decade from 1954-1964 that his music describes with such power, truth and emotive depth. There are some four hours of music to Smith's history and the brass griot has assembled two ensembles to perform it.

One is the Southwest Chamber Music, a ten-piece group conducted by Jeff van der Schmidt and containing harp, two violins, viola, cello, bass, flute, clarinet and percussion. The other is the Golden Quartet, composed of one or two drummers - Pheeroan Aklaff and/or Susie Ibarra, bassist John Lindberg and the Yale graduate and remarkable pianist/composer Anthony

Davis born in Paterson, New Jersey in 1951 - the son of professor of African-American literature, Charles T Davis. Smith and Davis were long-time collaborators and Davis' links with the Chicago free jazz movement as well as his saturation in historical narrative music - he wrote an acclaimed opera on the life of Malcolm X in the early '80s.

The musicians scoop up the chronology of the resistance and some of the key figures who provoked and led it, but it is the bold and determined mass of southern thousands who are Wadada's real heroes. His surging, breathy horn has the same naked power as when I heard him cracking the rafters at the Conway Hall right under the words 'To your own self be true' at the Freedom Of The City concert in 2010, but it is the truth of his people and their history that radiates here.

Hear the opening seconds of Emmett Till Defiant, Fearless where Davis's angry chords, Lindberg's heartbeat bass, Ibarra's flickering drums and Smith's mournful trumpet remember the teenage martyr murdered by racists in Money, Mississippi. The story is here, plunging through in Lindberg's earthen solo notes before the Southwest Chamber strings arise and Peter Jacobsen's cello invokes the long, long memories of a huge struggle for freedom.

A Dream Of Education, 1954, remembers the Brown vs Board of Education of Topeka case and the endless campaigns for equal schools free of discrimination. The two drummers pound out a relentless undertow to this endless campaigning narrative, and Wadada's soaring horn reaches for racial justice.

Disc two begins with a long remembrance of Rosa Parks and the 381 days of the Montgomery bus boycott. The Quartet drummer is Aklaff whose cymbals splatter under Wadada's anthemic horn and Davis' rolling keys. The voter registration offensives are celebrated by the Quintet in a slow and blues-sodden sonic story of relentless community agitation in the South's poorest heartlands. The Wadada/Davis timbral comradeship is especially close and deep in these moments of historical memory.

The Freedom Riders Ride begins disc three and the solidarity of other Americans and their coach-loads of support and human union blows in pride from Wadada's horn and Davis's hurtling up and down his keys.

The courage and sacrifice of the NAACP field secretary in Mississippi, the murdered Medgar Evers, is honoured in A Love Voice Of A Thousand Years' Journey For Liberty And Justice, performed by the Southwest Chamber Music as if the harmony of strings, harp and clarinet expressed the concord of Evers's essential humanity. There is also a recognition of The Little Rock Nine whose youthful boldness at the doors of their rightful university showed the entire world that this struggle could not be assuaged. Both ensembles unify. The strings are emphatic and shimmer for justice.

The fourth disc has a long tribute to Martin Luther King but the most moving sequence is that devoted to the ordeal and struggle of the militant campaigner Fannie Lou Hamer, who at Winona, Mississippi, in May 1963 was savagely attacked by local police after walking into a segregated waiting room at the local bus station with her literacy teacher Annell Ponder. Branch wrote that 'Hamer was beaten until the fingers protecting her head were blue and the skin of her back swelled up hard as a bone.' Such moments in the US's hidden story are made starkly manifest in Wadada's ringing, searching horn blown over Lindberg's bowed bass, the complex lines of Davis's piano and the drums, ofttimes subtle, oft-times thunderous, of Ibarra and Aklaff. This is how the truth of the US will be remembered.

Ten Freedom Summers - some 34 years in the making - sounds out beside Max Roach's We Insist! and Sonny Rollins' Freedom Suite as history told in epochal music, with jazz as its urgent chronicler.

(Ten Freedom Summers is available on Cuneiform Records)

Wadada Leo Smith (USA) - World trip with jazz legends

The global tracks followed in this year's London Jazz Festival made for a memorable 10-day extravaganza

(2012)

The jazz world was literally centred in London over the last few weeks. with the London Jazz Festival featuring some of the global greats.

Septuagenarian Yorkshire guitarist and Miles Davis alumnus John McLaughlin played the Barbican with fellow Tyke keyboardist Gary Husband. Cameroonian bassist Etienne Mbappe and Indian drummer Ranjit Barot. They were prefaced by the Lancashire Bengali Arun Ghosh with the youthful 'twin tenors' Idris Rahman and the Caribbean-rooted Wayne Francis, while at Ronnie Scott's there was a pulsating band led by Azerbaijani pianist Amina Figerova followed by John and Alice Coltrane's son Ravi and, at the Royal Festival Hall, Norwegian saxophonist Jan Garbarek was accompanied by Mumbai-born percussionist Trilok Gurtu.

Café Oto in Dalston provided a peak moment in this carnival of improvisers. There the Chicago Tentet, led by the rasping, adenoidal saxophone of Peter Brotzmann gargling out his unfettered sound, included a band of Norwegians, Danes and US veterans with their mighty multi-instrumentalist Joe McPhee blowing tempests from his pocket trumpet.

At Ronnie Scott's Ravi Coltrane's quartet memorably delivered Charlie Haden's Song For Turiya. Dedicated to the saxophonist's mother, it was a slow-burning tribute in which Coltrane's horn resonated movingly with intimate memories, followed by a blazing rendition of his father's stomping opus Countdown.

A stand-out too was the 82-year-old Sonny Rollins, the blood of his Virgin Islands forebears coursing through his veins, who hobbled onto the Barbican stage blasting out Sly Mongoose on his tenor horn. It was an astonishing performance. Rollins's improvisatory powers and huge sound are still intact and when he moved on to Once In A While, his saxophone complementing his longtime bass companion Bob Cranshaw, their jazz comradeship radiated through to the final coda. At that point, the horn slipped inadvertently from Rollins's mouth - even the legends are human - and as he surged on to a brave and beautiful conclusion we heard the murmur 'Oh Sonny, Sonny!' muffled into his reed.

Over at the Southbank, Egberto Gismonti told some arresting sonic stories of Amazonia and its aboriginal inhabitants. 'All my music comes from the people,' he declared and his long sojourns with the Xingu people of central Brazil chimed out with every note. Samba, the blues, classical guitar, Hendrix and Reinhardt were all present as if the flowing waters of the Thames outside the hall were moving back to the Americas, taking us on an auditory odyssey.

Another 82-year-old, Toronto-born trumpeter and composer Kenny Wheeler, led a 19-piece big band for his suite A Long Waiting, at the Queen Elizabeth Hall. Here were stalwarts of British jazz - veteran masters Evan Parker and Stan Sulzmann, vocalist Norma Winstone and young pretender Gwilym Silcock - who have played with Wheeler during his 60-year residency in Britain. Wheeler's flugelhorn solos were stunning, racked with power, beauty and narrative. The final tune, Upwards, with Wheeler's notes striking the sky, crystallised the meaning of a brilliant and ever-creative jazz life.

At the Bishopgate Institute, where Marx's inspirational words informing us that the point is not only to interpret the world but change it adorn the walls, Mississippi trumpeter Wadada Leo Smith was accompanied by his English pianist partner John Tilbury.

With his long locks shaking and his horn seething Smith blasted the nearby City banks, well within earshot, with rampaging notes and timbral patterns. He dedicated his last piece to the beat of the human heart - and how it rang out across the soulless City blocks and towers, telling every listening soul of the sound that really matters.

Paul G. Smyth (Ireland) - John Edwards (England) – Mark Sanders (England) – A monster trio

The Vortex, London
(2025)

This is one monster of a trio. I say 'one monster' for here are not three separate improvising virtuosi, but a trio unified. three-in-one, brilliance in amalgam: one Dubliner, two Londoners, every performance one musical birthing - truly triplets of creative sound.

As Edwards begins the Vortex session, it is tempting to think that his bass is this trio's nadir, its substructure. But he is just as much at the summit of his instrument, the siren-sounds of the highest limit of his strings pinging with altitude, not only attitude as he stretches them sideways, plunging his muscled fingers into them making them both groan and rejoice. As for Sanders, it is as if every sound he makes, every surface struck, stroked, brushed or rubbed with sticks, mallets or hands is ringing and singing with his multisonic drumsong, so tuneful that you could catch unknown, instant melodies of living skins and metallic mutation. As I listened I heard a triangle clang with a sound I hadn't heard since I was a primary schoolboy, nervously striking a metal equilateral in a music lesson in the school hall more than seven decades ago.

From the set's beginning there were three drummers drumming. Smyth was standing, leaning across the open innards of the Vortex grand, by-passing its ivories as if they were a temporary irrelevance, and strumming and pummelling its inner strings. Then it was as if he suddenly discovered that the piano had keys too, that it had an outside as well as an intestinal core within a gleaming wooden body-box. His timbral message came pounding off his keys, his pure, lucidly struck notes like the clearest Galway stream falling over endless ledges, sometimes changing to moments of quietude and calm as the waters and their notes meander towards the ocean.

Piano, bass, drums - all the sonic contrasts of discord in accord were in these common percussive sounds, in the geography of their ferment here in the cosmos of East London and the sheer dissimilitude of their unity in artistry: wondrous music!

Gunter Baby Sommer (Germany) - Beyond the horror of Kommeno

Gunter Baby Sommer, Savina Yannatou, Floros Floridis, Spilios Kastanis and Evgenios Voulgaris - Songs for Kommeno (2012)

'We shall make Kommeno a village of music, a grove of peace and culture.' So declared Christos Kosmas, the mayor of Kommeno - the Greek village where in August 1943 soldiers of the occupying German Wehrmacht massacred 317 villagers including 97 children and 13 babies-in-arms.

The album Songs for Kommeno emerged from a project led by the German free jazz drummer Gunter Baby Sommer, born in Dresden also in 1943, whose long experience began as a pioneer improviser in the days of the German Democratic Republic and who has subsequently played with some of the great free jazz giants, like Cecil Taylor and Wadada Leo Smith from the US and fellow Europeans such as Irene Schweizer, Evan Parker and Peter Brotzmann.

He affirms: 'What I can give is music. This is why I decided to develop a music project which puts the focus on the name of the village Kommeno and the memory of the suffering of the victims. What I have taken in from my ties with jazz since its beginnings is that we have to position ourselves in regards to the events taking place in our world.'

In the album Sommer joins with four Greek musicians to create a brilliant and moving sequence of evocations of the 1943 events. Savina Yannatou is an Athens-born singer of theatre and dance who has sung with free improvisers like bassists Peter Kowald and Barry Guy for two decades. The oud virtuoso is Evgenios Voulgaris from Patras and the soprano saxophone and clarinet master is Floros Floridis from Thessaloniki. Spilios Kastanis, who plays in a trio with Sommer and Floridis, is the bassist from a village in Arcadia near Patras.

In 2008, Sommer played a concert in Kommeno, beginning with a piece struck entirely on tubular bells 'without realising what kind of associations this would trigger... people rose from their seats, some of them started to cry, some of them clasped their necklaces with the cross. That moment was the starting point of a close relationship between the people of the village and me.'

'I postponed my departure for a few days and I was asked to go to visit them in their houses. They talked about their experiences, spoke about the massacre, of their families, fathers, grandmothers. They gave me food and drink and I didn't leave a single house without receiving a small gift.'

All this gave birth to Songs for Kommeno and the opening track, Tears, where the Greek strings of Kastanis and Voulgaris make sounds close to the blues which their German confrere said 'describes the love and suffering in life... the resignation, and awakening grief and joy.' It is all there certainly and stroked with beauty and memory with Sommer's rustling percussion.

As Floridis's clarinet enters over Kastinis's pulsating bowed bass these sonic tears could be shed in Louisiana, Cape Town, Gaza or Dhaka, so cosmic is their resonance. Of the track called Andartes Sommer writes: 'The Greek partisans called themselves Andartes. The introductory drum solo could stand for the situation of the hard-pressed Greek people.' Then and now, perhaps, as Sommer booms, crackles and crashes and Yannatou's wordless voice wails over the strings. The 18 minutes of Mirias Miroloi includes the voice of Maria Labri, one of the survivors of the massacre, and is begun by Kastanis's howling bowed bass and Floridis's mournful clarinet.

Sommer's drumming is astonishing. He resorts to gong chimes as Maria's chanting begins, along with Tibetan cymbals, metal sheets and bass drum until the free improvisation explodes from all musicians and Maria tells the story of the brave priest who was cut down by nazi guns as he tried to prevent the slaughter.

Arachthos has Sommer striking what sounds like a steel pan, and suddenly the sound of Trinidad travels to Greece, while Lullaby has Yannatou's voice like that of a child falling towards sleep. It prefaces Children's Song, where Yannatou and Floridis's clarinet find a floating amalgam of sound over Kastanis's plucked infant heartbeats.

The final track is Kommeno Today where the past is a springboard to now-times youth, dancing, grooving, setting their village beyond the horror of history. 'Jazz is also liberation from everything which unnaturally restricts and limits us' is Sommer's dictum and it applies here in earfuls as it does all through this extraordinary album.

Full of the past and full of the future. And how many more people will remember Kommeno and its people?

(Songs for Kommeno is available on Intakt}

Peter Somuah (Ghana) - Living the highlife

Peter Somuah – Highlife

(2025)

'I want to help educate Ghanaians, not to see themselves or their music as inferior compared to the Western world, but to embrace themselves and achieve whatever they worked towards in their own music.' So declares Ghanaian trumpeter and composer Peter Somuah, born in Accra, Ghana, where his mother was a clothes trader and his father worked for the Ghana Poultry Farms Association. He had an uncle in England who was a guitarist and named Peter on a visit to Ghana.

He began on trumpet at school, also playing drums, saxophones, atenteban (traditional bamboo flute), djembe and xylophone. 'As a teenager I really enjoyed brass band and highlife music,' he says. 'I played with brass bands in the street and listened to highlife all day on the radio.' A friend introduced him to jazz when he was 16. 'I went to his house and he showed me videos of Miles, Charlie Parker and Dizzy Gillespie. I was in awe as I watched them and said to myself, 'I want to play like that!' I started imitating them even though I had no idea what they were playing. I transcribed with my ears, without sheet music, inspired by Miles's Birth of the Cool and Bitches Brew, Parker's Now's the Time and Dizzy's Groovin' High'. When he left school he found a side-job in a cycle repair shop, 'while I earned money too in highlife bands in bars, at weddings and funerals.' His partner had moved back to the Netherlands, so he went to Rotterdam. 'I met some people there who were passionate about music. We jammed and they invited me to their gigs, playing jazz standards and original music.'

His new album, Highlife, is full of African fire, audacity, joy and critical consciousness. 'Ghana's musicians created highlife music during colonial times. The British had military bands which played styles from outside Ghana - waltz, bolero, samba etc, and Ghanaian musicians continued those influences with traditional drumming patterns, creating this new genre called Highlife.'

'Initially it was the colonial elite who got to enjoy the music in their fancy dance halls, (hence the name from 'high life'). But over time many sub-genres emerged that were played in the villages. Then 'Burger Highlife' came in the '80s when many musicians emigrated to Hamburg because of the military regime's evening curfew, which stopped them performing and earning an income. In the Netherlands, I found musicians very open to explore music outside of their regular circle. We rehearsed many Ghanaian rhythms, then in 2022 our band made a trip to Ghana to connect with local musicians.'

Thus, the album has deeply educative qualities which along with some hot playing from all members, includes snatches of vocals and interviews with highlife veterans like Pat Thomas, 93 year-old griot Koo Nimo and Gyedu-Blay Ambolley, while the track Mental Slavery recalls the album by US multi-saxophonist Rahsaan Roland Kirk - Volunteered Slavery - in which Rahsaan satirised the way in which mentalities are so easily bludgeoned, and dominated unconsciously by continuous hostile alien culture.

'My music is full of influences from many genres,' asserts Somuah: 'jazz, funk, highlife, Afrobeat, Latin, soul, Hip hop, gospel. I call it 'Global Sounds'. Hopefully we'll soon be playing it all in Britain.' After Hearing this album, I'll be first in the queue. And what about the prospect of playing alongside another virtuoso of Ghanaian roots who has taken jazz to his heartsblood, Nottingham saxophonist Tony Kofi? 'Yes, I'd love to play with Tony,' he exclaims. And I'd love to hear his searing trumpet with Kofi's rampaging Africa-rooted horn: that's something certainly to hope for!

(Highlife is available on Act Records)

Tyshawn Sorey (USA) - Trio of musical scholars
Café Oto, London
(2025)

Here are a trio of musical scholars, not only jazz virtuosi, led by a polymath from Newark, New Jersey, Tyshawn Sorey, who not only plays drums, trombone and piano but is also Professor of Contemporary Music at the University of Pennsylvania. He writes operas and other classical works, won a Pulitzer Prize in 2024 for his Adagio for veteran trumpeter Wadada Leo Smith, and in 2019 composed a song cycle called Perle Noir in memory of dancer and anti-fascist hero of wartime France, Josephine Baker.

Tonight he's playing drums in a trio, and never overplaying, he created a fertile percussive earth for his trio-mates, as they began with an extended, improvised version of McCoy Tyner's Peresina, the opening track of the threesome's new album with the engrossing name, The Susceptible Now.

Almost like students at the feet of their master-scholars, you could feel the concentration of the Café Oto audience as they listened intently to the bell-like notes of pianist Aaron Diehl from Columbus, Ohio on the very night that the trio's Head of State announced his ethnic cleansing and annexation plan for Gaza. It seemed as if the bells were tolling not only for the 'susceptible' and struggling people of Palestine but for all of us. The album's second track was next, Mingus' A Chair in the Sky, and it made you wonder what the great insurgent bassman would have made of it all.

Harish Raghavan, from Northbrook, Illinois, whose music combines Indian classical forms with jazz, played his bass with a plunging artistry, his fingers rising and falling across his strings with a plummeting power of improvised invention that built a foundation for everything his trio siblings expressed. He made the ground shake in Dalston, somewhere beneath the Café Oto's stone floor.

Long, deeply reflective and brilliantly played and sustained pieces from this trio of wise notes, in the very heart of London's cosmopolis.

Carmen Souza (Cape Verde) – Decolonise our minds!
(2024)

Early British imperialists like Francis Drake and Walter Raleigh kidded history by profiling themselves as 'explorers.' Here's a brilliant singer with her roots in Cape Verde, who, in her songs, often with an incisive wit and passion, explores their brutal pathfinding and exposes the origins of 400 years of colonial oppression.

Carmen Souza was born to Cape Verdean immigrant parents in Lisbon in 1981. Her father worked in shipping cargo, her mother was a housekeeper. 'There was a lot of music and singing around me at home,' she says. 'My father played guitar, my mother sang and my grandfather played violin. Growing up in Lisbon, I played my father's many Cape Verdean records, so all that was the sound of my childhood, a full immersion in the culture of the islands. I ate the food, spoke the Creole and listened to traditional music. It was all passed on to me naturally. My dad didn't have many singing records, except for songs about independence and Amilcar Cabral, father of our nation. Then he bought some Cesaria Evora albums. The power and beauty of her voice was incomparable, and hearing her made me want to search for my own voice.'

'Our Creole language is very musical and I like to mix all the islands' different accents. Creole itself is an instrument of expression, and I use different island Creoles to express different or more profound emotions. And because I didn't grow up in Cape Verde, my own Creole is very personal.' Carmen moved to London in 2008. 'Experience here has given me so many things as an artist, access to different cultures and ways of life. London is a melting pot and a fast-paced city that never stops. So I had to find my own pace, but it's becoming harder to live here. More and more there's a big divide between the wealthy and poor, with people working at two or three jobs to earn a bare minimum and rarely spending time with their families. Isn't this a form of slavery too?'

In her album, Port'Ingles, she sings of a duality in the history of the relationship between Britain and Cape Verde. Her opening song, St Iago, tells warmly about the time Darwin spent in Cape Verde in 1832, after his ship The Beagle set sail from Woolwich Dockyard. That's followed by Pamadi, telling of the 'chains and whips' of imperialism and, for the few, the colonial 'prosperity that is stained with blood and pain' of the many. 'The imperialist perspective was always there,' she reminds me. 'We grew up hearing stories of Sir Francis Drake [the theme of her song Francis Drum], how he was a hero of Britain. But in Cape Verde he is known for piracy, pillage, rape and arson. We all need to decolonise our minds so we can take informed steps to a better future.'

Her love and joy with language comes out humorously yet ruefully in her song Ariope! as she remembers how phrases of English found their way into Cape Verdean Creoles. 'I am passionate about languages. I love to explore different intonations and how our Creole has incorporated anglicisms. Growing up speaking Creole. I always heard the word 'Ariope!', but I never knew its imperial beginnings, derived from 'Hurry up!' and the orders given to men working under scorching temperatures, making them work as if they were machines.'

Her songs and tunes dance with their rhythms and have a powerful jazz heartsblood. 'Jazz influenced me because it means, first and foremost, freedom. I was amazed by its musicians' individuality and dedication: Thelonious Monk's personality and creativity; the pain in the voice of Billie Holiday which ultimately shapes her sound; Horace Silver with his Cape Verdean origins in his groovy piano playing; Ella Fitzgerald's voice bringing me joy; Bill Evans' quiet piano fire and soulful melodies; Mingus's daring arrangements. Jazz has taught me to use my voice not as a conventional singer, but as an instrument that can shape, shift and mould itself in the moment.'

Port'Ingles unifies the joy of the human voice with its huge power to educate and criticise for young and old. Did you know, for example, how Cape Verdeans raised money and resources to buy aircraft to fight against the Nazis in the second world war? Souza tells us all about it in her song Amizadi. Listen closely, dance gleefully and see what you think!

(Port'Ingles is available on Galileo Records)

Larry Stabbins (England) - Thunderous tenor of a superb sax

Working Week - Working Nights (Cherry Red Records)
Larry Stabbins - Monadic (Eminem)
Larry Stabbins - Transcendental featuring Zoe Rahman (Noetic) (2013)

When I met the thunderous tenor saxophonist Larry Stabbins after his powerful gig at the London Jazz Festival last November, we talked about one of his heroes, Sonny Rollins, whom we had both heard the night before at his memorable Barbican concert. 'I love Rollins because of the strength and beauty of his sound, his astonishing invention and the chances that he takes,' declared Stabbins, and hearing his own horn sound, you might say something very similar about him.

Stabbins was born in Bristol in 1949, the city that was the birthplace of two British jazz giants of the same generation, saxophonist Evan Parker and pianist Keith Tippett. It was clarinet at eight, saxophone at 11 and his first enthusiasms were James Brown and Junior Walker, but at 16 he met and played with Tippett before moving to London and supporting himself with club and studio work. He also threw himself into free jazz and improvising circles with .John Stevens, Eddie Prevost, Tony Oxley, Louis Moholo-Moholo and Chris McGregor's Brotherhood of Breath.

By 1983 Stabbins had teamed up with guitarist Simon Booth to create Working Week and their first record was Booth's Venceremos, specially geared to Latin soul-jazz club dancers and dedicated to the murdered Chilean singer/guitarist Victor Jara for a benefit for the Chile Solidarity Campaign.

The new double CD compilation of Working Week music, Working Nights, has been issued by Cherry Red Records and carries in its sounds a vibrant spirit of its age, with interventions from some prime British jazz soloists. Hear trumpeter Guy Barker launch his horn from the ensemble jazz-rock mist of Thought I'd Never See You Again, Moholo-Moholo pounding through Stella Marina or Harry Beckett's trumpet touching the peaks on No Cure, No Pay. And Stabbins pierces through the melee with a ferocious tenor on Pepe's Samba and a joyous soprano on Autumn Boy and the jazz-dance special version of Venceremos.

In 2002 Stabbins recorded an album of solo soprano and tenor improvisations, Monadic. He had first played solo at Ronnie Scott's Upstairs venue in 1972, during Keith Tippett's small group Ovary Lodge's tenure, and at various times and venues through the '70s and '80s. In his sleeve notes Martin Davidson reminds us that 'monadic' means 'like a monad, or Isolated single unit of being,' the antithesis of the hugely collectivised and communal sound of Working Week.

Every track is titled as a present participle, beginning with Breathing, the saxophone like a steamship horn, but in a becalmed yet menacing sea. His tenor rocks and vibrates in Singing while in the long Thinking the notes ever-surprising, several times seeming to be on the cusp of melody. Loving employs the soprano saxophone with tenderness and grace, exquisite in its phraseology. Monadic is a wondrous, surprising and beautifully birdlike album - listen to Chirruping, the testimony of a true and unsung British master of the saxophone.

In 2012 Stabbins, now known as 'Stonephace' Stabbins was leading a quintet which cut the album Transcendental with Karl Rasheed Abel on bass, Crispin 'Spry' Robinson on Afro-Cuban percussion, Pat Illingworth on drums and the marvellous Zoe Rahman featuring on piano. 'She is amazing,' he told me. 'I'm very lucky that she plays with me.' Their mutual empathy is impressive. His oft-times volcanic sound seems to make her hit her keys harder, and her astonishing inventiveness inspires, he suggests, greater complexity and subtlety within his own musicianship.

He met his four bandmates in the ranks of Jerry Dammers's very large Spatial AKA Orchestra, and the five-some often carry timbral echoes of a big band, nowhere more than on the opener, Coltrane's Africa, where Stabbins's huge surge, Rahman's percussive keys and Robinson's conga undertow create a titanic and ancestral sound, taking the hornman back to his 13th birthday in 1962 when he bought Coltrane's epochal Africa Brass album.

Immanence is a short but telling flute/piano duet, Abel's earthen bass delves beneath the tarmac on Yellow Brick Road and Transcendental Euphoria is a salute to Coltrane's great tenor confrere Pharaoh Sanders, with Stabbins's muscular solo anticipating a volley of anthemic notes from Rahman, before Robinson's hand-pounded drums preface Stabbins's final roaring chorus.

There is a sense of summation in Transcendental, a unity of generations and genres centreing around Stabbins's unique musical life's journey. From Coltrane to free improvisation to R&B and soul jazz to the effusive meeting place of this fine album, a staging post to the future for five always adventurous musicians.

(Working Nights is available on Cherry Red Records, Monadic on Eminem & Transcendental featuring Zoe Rahman on Noetic)

Larry Stabbins (England) - Aurora and Cup And Ring
(2025)

'I played in a local dance band in my early teens, but got thrown out for trying to sound like John Coltrane. I played a solo and thought it sounded great, but the bandleader said: 'Don't you ever do anything like that again!''

The insurgent saxophone sound of Larry Stabbins, born in Bristol in 1949, has marked his life in music. 'My Mother was a primary school teacher from the Welsh valleys, and my Dad worked in the Filton Aerospace factory, although he'd been a percussionist in silent picture houses before the war and carried on playing drums until well into his seventies.'

'I started on clarinet when I was eight - for long enough to put me off clarinet and classical music in general. It was the trad jazz boom so I preferred Acker Bilk and the great Sidney Bechet. My Dad had a soprano sax so I started on that at nine, and as soon as I was big enough to play tenor, propped up on the arm of a sofa, I started to play that. Dad had a 78 rpm record of Charlie Parker playing Lover Man and many of his friends were jazz musicians who played me their records. One gave me some lessons and told me to listen to the pioneer tenor saxophonist Coleman Hawkins. My Dad took me to lots of concerts - Ellington, Basie, Ella Fitzgerald, Tubby Hayes, and the great Hawkins who made a big impression on me.'

'On my twelfth birthday I bought Coltrane's Africa Brass and that blew me away. The bass player in our school jazz club played me Ornette Coleman, then from the mid-Sixties it was mainly Archie Shepp and Albert Ayler - but Junior Walker too. I left school at seventeen and went straight into a Mecca dance hall band for six months, then went off to London to join a soul band. By 1978 I was playing more and more free music after meeting John Stevens. I decided I didn't want to play any more commercial music by making a living in

London night clubs. So I moved back to Bristol to concentrate of free music and paid the rent by repairing instruments.'

Fellow Bristolian, pianist Keith Tippett, brought him into his largescale orchestral recordings of Septober Energy (1971) and Frames (1978), and he made a key album, Terns, with Tippett and South African drummer Louis Moholo-Moholo in 1982. Between 1985 and 1989 he made five albums as the co-leader of Working Week (formerly Weekend) with guitarist Simon Booth, playing a fusion of Latin, dance rhythms, soul, jazz and funk.

Now, many years on in 2025, are two new albums simultaneously released: a duo album, Cup and Ring, with drummer Mark Sanders, and a trio album, Aurora, with Sanders and bassist Paul Rogers. Throughout both records, spontaneous melodies teem from his saxophone, and in Cup and Ring, his flutes too. 'I was musically brought up playing melodies, so a lot of them must be stored somewhere inside me. When I started writing for Weekend and Working Week I realised I had a flair for it and I was getting fed up with that type of improvisation where anything resembling melody or rhythm is beyond the pale. I wanted the freedom to play simple melodies again.'

I asked him about the special musical qualities of Rogers and Sanders. 'The music just happens naturally. We hadn't even discussed what we might do - we've known each other a long, long time and have done all kinds of improvising in different situations. We have a tremendous respect for each other's playing. For myself, I could just listen to the other two for ages. They both have experience of playing a vast range of music and wonderful creative imaginations.'

'Paul supplies an endless stream of melodic and textual ideas to inspire me. Apart from being a whole string section in himself on his seven-string bass, he brings both references to contemporary chamber music and folk music. Virginia Woolf called it 'thickening the soup'. I also think we both absorbed a lot of influence from Keith Tippett in our many (overlapping) years of playing with him. Mark has a particularly fine sense of sound and texture. He really listens and responds, and not all drummers do that, that's why he's in demand in so many situations. And if you want driving power, he has loads of it. But above all, I love the way he can play so much rhythm, layers of overlapping rhythmic patterns, without overtly stating time.'

'In Cup and Ring I wanted to do something with more space. In a duo there's nowhere to hide. I had to come up with a more melodic dimension, and make a break from tenor and soprano sax and do something new with flutes, rather than recreate the past.'

How does he think his music can seek to challenge and change the violent and disruptive times we are living through? 'It serves as a focal point to bring people together with similar views on the world and how we'd like to change it. There's a quotation I like and I don't know where it comes from: 'We make art in order to know we are not alone.'

Listening to both these musical outings and their brilliant communal creators who we can hear live on our ears in our own front rooms or in live performances, you certainly feel Morris' words, 'Fellowship is life', but more too, because you want to add: 'Art is fellowship'.

(Aurora is available on Jazz in Britain Records and Cup And Ring on Discus Records)

Larry Stabbins (England)/Mark Sanders (England/Belize)/ Alexander Hawkins (England)

The Vortex, Dalston, London N.16
(2025)

Veteran saxophonist Larry Stabbins announced this trio's opening set by recalling the greatness of the late Cape Town drums griot, Louis Moholo-Moholo, saying how he had first played with him in the Brotherhood of Breath in 1971. As pianist Alexander Hawkins was Louis' final piano partner and drummer Mark Sanders is a devotee of his artistry, this was an ideal threesome to play what Stabbins described as 'a celebratory lament' for the recently passed percussive genius.

Stabbins began on tenor with a huge blast of reedsong. The decibels of his immensely powerful, elegiac and blisteringly beautiful notes raged up the shopfronts and cosmopolitan food booths of Kingsland Road and shuttered stalls of Ridley Road Market - scene of concentrated anti-fascist activity in 1947 - while the romping, swinging, pounding lyricism of Hawkins' piano remembered on his every key a great African drums virtuoso. Sanders' polyrhythmic fire, snares crashing, his bass drum booming, his cymbals a synchronised rattle like a giant hob full of boiling saucepan lids, made this a trio performance like no other.

When Stabbins picked up his soprano sax his rasping old man river of sound was gradually transformed into a serene and rippling rivulet, like the Thames becoming the Lea, yet still full with the same relentlessly flowing mystery of London waters so close to the venue.

The passionate song of Stabbins' tenor returned, with each musician raising the volume of sound even more, so the power of their musicianship did not hide its melodism, nuances and spontaneous complexity but only magnified it, so the African spirit of the legendary Louis lives again in their once-for-always sounds.

Tomasz Stanko (Poland) - Last refrains of love and longing from jazz trumpet great

Tomasz Stanko's New York Quartet - December Avenue (2019)

Aurally and visually, Tomasz Stanko's New York Quartet live was startling. The tiny Polish-born trumpeter, who died last year, produced notes that were sometimes terse, sometimes tender and his unique tone was full of a troublesome power as he stood out front of his confreres, his horn pointing outwards under a cloth cap.

With him on his final album was drummer Gerald Cleaver, pianist David Virelles and bassist Reuben Rogers and on opener Cloud, Virelles's numinous Cuban notes preface the dark, breathy and beautiful Stanko horn, floating over Rogers's pulsating bass and Cleaver's distant-sounding brushes.

Blue Cloud is overcast by Stanko's melancholic and fretful tone, his sound like no other trumpeter. Cleaver's flickering cymbals lift the delving bass heartbeat and Virelles makes soft and beguiling keyboard patterns beside them. The quartet's final notes make a sound which brings Europe and the Americas together, all their histories in an aspiring road to peace.

Rogers's deep-plucked strings create the foundation for Stanko's swift aural essay in Burning Hot, with a Caribbean fire to Virelles's solo, a preface to the high-pitched trumpet volley. These neighbours from Cuba and St Thomas palaver in the conversational David and Reuben, as if the stretch of sea between them were but an illusion.

There's an ominous yet loving lyricism in Stanko's tribute to the Polish-Jewish writer, Ballad for Bruno Schulz. He was shot dead by an occupying nazi SS officer in Poland in 1942 and the stark and personal tenderness of Stanko's notes for a countryman of powerful creative genius murdered by fascism is both elegiac and deeply moving.

The connections to Schulz by Stanko's three musical compadres of another generation from Cuba, the Virgin Islands and Detroit are fused by the community of the jazz cosmopolis.

Stanko's homage to Schulz continues in The Street of Crocodiles, the title of one of the writer's works. Its theme brings echoes of Ellington's All Too Soon and Stanko's tune has sadness and pathos too but also a grandeur and pride, his lingering last note one of love and longing.

(December Avenue is available on ECM)

John Stevens (England), Paul Rutherford (England), Evan Parker (England) & Barry Guy (England) - A fantastic foursome

John Stevens, Paul Rutherford, Evan Parker and Barry Guy – One Four and Two Twos
(2014)

In August 1978 they came together again for a recording at London's Riverside Studios. A British quartet of powerful pioneer improvisers - drummer John Stevens, who organised the session, bassist Barry Guy and the two monster horns, saxophonist Evan Parker and trombonist Paul Rutherford. They prepared themselves with a lengthy sound check for a date which never, in truth, actually happened. As Parker remembers it: 'We went to the pub and never got back.' As is so often the fortuitousness of jazz, the sound check itself was well-recorded, becoming the real thing and being issued as an album in 1980.

All four musicians knew each other's sounds intimately, and had played together before on many occasions, particularly 10 years before when as a quartet they were one formation of the pioneering Spontaneous Music Ensemble (which first recorded in 1966). Stevens and Rutherford had first met and played together while they were both members of the RAF. Guy and Rutherford had both been partners - with Sheffield guitarist Derek Bailey - of the revolutionary trio Iskra 1903, whose recorded concert at the Institute of Contemporary Arts in 1970 became the pathbreaking album Chapter One. Stevens and Rutherford, both born in 1940, and Guy (born 1947) were Londoners and Parker was a Bristolian born in 1944. The union of four profound innovators was bound to create a ceaseless musical combustion.

The album with the quizzical numerical title One Four and Two Twos is made up of five quartet pieces and five more from two different duos all named in mixed numbers. The versatile foursome includes Stevens's drumset and voice, Rutherford's euphonium and trombone, Parker's tenor and soprano saxophones and Guy with his bass and electronics.

1,4,4, begins the proceedings with Stevens's scuttling drumplay and exclamations and Guy's scraping bass. Rutherford enters below them, his unstoppable slides ricocheting across a forest of sounds. The much longer 2,4,4, gives Parker's squelching tenor a more prominent place in a fevered horn colloquy, with Rutherford moving up and down the fullness of his sound as if he were now being blown to unknown places in the midst of a typhoon. 3,4,4, - which follows - has a haunting timbre, with Guy's ghostly artistry everywhere in the soundscape and Rutherford's low, low notes creating a strangely spectral blues pitch.

In the ever-changing world of jazz the unified sound of these four Englishmen was unique in its time. Their music was entirely their creation. Nothing like it was being conceived or played on either side of the Atlantic, except by their other British confreres playing in related formations. It was a very specific territory of jazz improvisation that had been birthed in post-war English cities like London, Bristol and Sheffield. Through the 18 astonishing minutes of 4,4,4, - with all four musicians playing out of their skins with the deepest of empathies with each other - the listener begins to realise the true scope of their artistic achievement. The speed, agility and invention of Stevens's drumming is ear-dazzling as he lays out the earth beside and below his three bandmates. Parker's huge wasp-like buzzing phrases, Rutherford's continuous and smoothly growling commentary and Guy's flickering genius gyrate in all the spaces around the drumplay to make an amalgam of sound that is peerless.

As for the duos, the Guy/Rutherford colloquy - beginning with a seething Rutherford howl and continuing with excitation of a debate of sounds on 1,3,2, and the more delving 2,3,2, is like two voices in call, response and dialogue of sheer surprise, with the unexpected falling from every note and managed by two master musicians with life-dedicated technique. Rutherford's infusion of electronics adds an even more modernistic vein. Parker and Stevens are head-to-head on 1,2,2, and 2,2,2, - a giants' pathway of sound with the Bristolian's tenor sounding like no other horn in jazz, chuntering, gossiping, declaring and confessing.

Thanks to Martin Davidson and Emanem records for enabling such sounds to enter our lives, ears and homes some 40 years later. They don't grow stale.

(One Four and Two Twos is available on Emanem)

John Stevens (England) – Monk at school

John Stevens and Evan Parker - Corner to Corner & The Longest Night (2008)

Let me tell you a story of the pathfinding London drummer, John Stevens (1940 - 1994), and his seething Yorkshire alto saxophonist compadre, Trevor Watts, both pioneers of British free improvisation. I first met them both in 1974 when they were invited into the backward Church of England secondary school in Stepney, East London, where I was teaching, by the school's progressive music teacher, to give our students a taste of jazz - all paid for by the Inner London Education Authority. I was teaching poetry in the next door classroom in morning school, when I heard thirty twelve year old children blowing and tapping out the very familiar theme of Blue Monk. There was something pristine, free and soulful about their sound, for these were Blake's children as well as the children of Monk. Their spontaneous notes resonated through classroom walls and along the sterile corridors of this 'dim and dull' school (which was how one of my students described it in a telling poem.) By that date, the great Thelonious was locked into his long late-life silence in his New York

apartment, and I remember thinking, 'If only he could hear this! He would marvel at the sound.'

As I walked outside the school during the lunch hour, I met John and Trevor standing disconsolately opposite the school gates. After I thanked them for conjuring what I'd heard, they told me, angrily and frustratedly, that some senior teachers had complained about the disturbing 'noise', and they had been told not to come back for the already arranged afternoon classroom sessions. I could believe it: it was in complete accord with the nature and culture of the school and those who controlled it, and as we talked outside its walls, they pointed me in the direction of a different note in jazz - then to me unknown until that day, of free improvisation, which led to John, Trevor and the Ornette Coleman confrere Bobby Bradford - who was visiting England and staying with John at the time, accompanying my efforts at poetry and Joe Hill-inspired songs at the now demolished Half Moon Theatre, in an ex-synagogue in Whitechapel.

So what a delight to savour the drums of Stevens again, playing in a duo with the Bristolian saxophonist Evan Parker. Two sessions are included on a double CD, The Longest Night, from 1976, and Corner to Corner, from 1993. By 1976, Stevens and Parker had been playing together for a decade as members of the Spontaneous Music Ensemble, with other path-finding musicians such as Watts, Derek Bailey and Paul Rutherford. They knew each other's music intimately and empathetically, creating their own improvisational dialogue with a pioneering commitment and daring.

Parker plays soprano saxophone, Stevens plays drums without a bass drum, percussion and cornet. As soon as the opening track, 19.11, begins, there is a unique amalgam of sounds. Although Stevens could play volcanic drums like an Art Blakey or Elvin Jones, here, he plays with fluttering cymbals and gently rolling snares, tapping his skins while Parker's gurgling reed converses with the percussive density. All through the 73 minutes of the recording, there is a quiescent intensity of jazz comradeship intuitively realised and, when one or the other artist takes solo flight, as Parker does with an adenoidal sublimity in 19.44, part-spitting, part-screeching, part-burbling, part-babbling out his sounds, you can feel his silent confrere willing him forward.

Waxed some 16 years later, Corner to Corner may sound more competitive, even gladiatorial, by its title, but the two contenders' musical embrace is even more telling. Parker's playing is beautifully fluid, as lucid as spring water as he plays many more phrases in a high, leaping register. Stevens plays as if the world is full of percussion, as if he is prepared to test and sound any surface to make music, to touch, to tap, to strike, to scrape, to tinkle.

It made me think that this was a part of the lesson that he and Watts were teaching those engrossed Stepney children in their classroom three-and-a-half decades ago - that music comes from real sounds, real instruments, real objects, real connections and real lives. That is also the enduring message of this unique record.

(Corner to Corner & The Longest Night are available on Ogun)

Karen Street (England) – Now-times accordion
(2025)

As a boy I always loved the familial, old-worldly sound of the accordion, and when my brother-in-law bought one to while away his national service time at Catterick Camp, he brought it home and its bellows seemed to give it lungs like a human. The first and rare time I heard it in a jazz context was when I bought a Duke Ellington LP with vintage tunes like the 1929 Accordion Joe, in which Ellington's arrangement of the accordion's quasi-fairground sound fitted into his orchestra brilliantly. So when I heard the new Mike Westbrook Band of Bands' album with accordion virtuoso Karen Street an integral part of the Westbrook sound, I loved it, and wanted to know more about her life in music.

Born in 1959 in Burton on Trent, her parents were teachers, with her maternal grandmother 'a very good pianist who played by ear.' Her brother played accordion (a colleague of her dad ran an accordion school), 'and I kept trying to play it too, so Mum thought I should have lessons. I learned clarinet at school and at 15, Dad, who liked Oscar Peterson and big band music, bought me a saxophone as I wanted to play in a local music centre jazz band. Looking back at some old accordion music I used to play, I now realise it was quite jazz-oriented, so from a young age I was playing quite advanced jazz harmony without knowing it.'

'After university at Bath and Wales I moved to London. I played sax in Don Rendell's education big band and listened to a lot of jazz funk - Weather Report, The Brecker Brothers and the amazing John Serry, whose father was an accordion player.'

I ask her how playing with Westbrook had affected her. 'Mike has been an enormous influence on me. When I joined his Big Band Rossini I was suddenly thrown in amongst the most amazing jazz players. As for the Band of Bands, Mike was interested in using the accordion as a front-line instrument, blending with the two saxes. 'I don't know if anyone else has done this - it's a unique sound and it isn't obvious there's an accordion there. Ellington used the accordion (played by Hungarian Cornell Smelser) as part of the rhythm section as well as playing melody, which is what Mike does a lot in Band of Bands.'

What about her bandmates? 'Drummer Coach York is solid as a rock, generous and unflappable; bassist Marcus Vergette is mischievous, bringing lots of joy to the bandstand and saxophonist Chris Biscoe plays outstanding solos - where do they come from? Fellow saxophonist Pete Whyman has amazing technicality and emotional depth, and as a singer and lyricist Kate Westbrook is utterly unique, as well as a warm and generous friend.' She loves accompanying Kate: 'Many of her songs are theatrical-like in delivery, so there's often lots of space. Having listened to her voice for so long, I feel I can follow what she's about to do with a song.'

'As for Mike, he is a true bandleader; inspiring, clever and he never stops writing music to challenge us. His catalogue is so diverse, he never sticks to one genre. This is his strength. His music is timeless. When you hear his compositions from the '60s onwards they could have been written today, they sound so fresh even though they're rooted in the jazz tradition.'

Her favourite track on the album is Mike and Kate's composition Gas, Dust, Stone: 'It has a simple but powerful driving rhythm - the subjects they create are always meaningful. It's about the end of our world, with the idea of hanging a 19th century fairground alongside the world wide web - modern technology in the form of a fairground attraction. It's a blues for the planet - when the ride is broken, nature is defeated and just gas, dust and stone remain.'

It's what the Westbrooks write: parables of our time in the most original sonic settings, and it's what Karen Street loves to play with her ever-surprising yet erstwhile sound. 'Jazz is inclusive of many different backgrounds and cultures and can go a small way to heal divisions. Like music in general, it can take us to a different place, finding us beauty and solace.'

(Band of Bands is available on Westbrook Records)

John Stubblefield (USA) - Immense artistry

John Stubblefield – Prelude
(2013)

I used to earnestly look forward to the yearly visits to Ronnie Scott's of the Mingus Big Band, mainly because of the prospect of hearing the mighty tenor sax of John Stubblefield. And when he rose from the crush of saxophones in the reed section on Ronnie's small stage to blow his monstrous solo on Mingus's cold war anthem Oh Lord! Don't Let Them Drop Their Atomic Bomb On Me! something elemental was definitely afoot - human, fierce and deeply beautiful. So the reissue of Stubblefield's classic 1976 album Prelude on the Danish Storyville label filled me with memories of his intense power and brilliance.

Stubblefield was born in Little Rock, Arkansas, in 1945 and spent his boyhood through the stirring years of the Civil Rights movement. He moved to Chicago in the '60s and studied with the Association for the Advancement of Creative Musicians's founder Muhal Richard Abrams and tenor giant George Coleman before arriving in New York in 1971. There he joined the Collective Black Artists band and played with an array of legends, from Mary Lou Williams, Mingus and Tito Puente to Anthony Braxton, the Thad Jones/Mel Lewis Orchestra, Abdullah Ibrahim and Miles Davis, with whom he recorded Calypso Frelimo on the Get Up With It album of October 1974.

Prelude finds Stubblefield within a sextet of vibrant jazz ground breakers including pianist Onaje Allan Gumbs and tenorist Jimmy Heath's percussionist son Mtume, Max Roach's long-time trumpeter Cecil Bridgewater and the great post-bop bassist from Tulsa, Oklahoma, Cecil McBee, whose brilliance has added to the bands of hornmen such as Sonny Rollins, Jackie McLean, Sam Rivers, Charles Tolliver, Pharaoh Sanders and Chico Freeman and who even now holds the bass for The Cookers. The drummer is Joe Chambers, veteran of many a prime Blue Note session.

Stubblefield composed four of the selections of Prelude and the vaunting Song for One is his opener. His tenor guffaws out above McBee's dancing beat and Bridgewater's high, note-splitting chorus follows before the bassist's fullness of solo sound reverberates through the New York studio. Little Prince is an opportunity to hear Stubblefield's soprano saxophone dexterity, weaving through Gumbs's reflective notes and Chambers's almost hushed cymbals. Stubblefield's salute to the bop trumpeter and Charlie Parker partner Kenny Dorham, Twelve for KD, begins with a very pacy tenor chorus with Gumbs leaping to keep up with Stubblefield's onrush of sound. Bridgewater joins in the romp, followed by a breathless Gumbs and McBee's irrepressible pulse pulling all his confreres forward. Four minutes passes in a sonic instant.

Stubblefield is back playing a caustic soprano on Gumbs's tune If You Ever Knew, dynamised by the girdling percussion - perhaps deliberately referred to as 'concussion' in the sleeve's personnel notes - of the relentless Mtume. Bridgewater blows a zealous chorus and Gumbs offers a slice of electric keyboard before the members' colloquy calms into silence. Bridgewater leaves his composing mark with the slow and almost statuesque What's Gonna Be Is. Stubblefield's tenor creates a sound of serene beauty over Gumbs's keyboard, McBee sounds exalted in his pure depth of sound and the trumpeter's solo has Ellingtonian echoes with sudden allusions to Satin Doll, as if jazz's great tradition is essential to Stubblefield and his men.

The album's closer is Stubblefield's Minor Impulse, led by the tenorist's stomping solo urged on by the incandescent McBee's subterranean lead. Stubblefield's sheer power of sound is hugely affecting and catches Bridgewater's spirit too as his chorus soars to a zenith in its final note. Gumbs careers along his keys with renewed excitation and Chambers's valedictory solo makes its own earthen mark of seven musicians in full accord.

Stubblefield died in the Bronx in 2005. Immediately before the last time that I heard him I was sitting at the pavement coffee shop outside Ronnie's in Frith Street, Soho, when this large, black, moustachioed man slowly walked by with his grandiose tenor saxophone case and ponderously stepped into the club. Later, as his horn roared, murmured and sang, speaking of his own life and that of his people, I fully realised again his immense artistry.

(Prelude is available on Storyville)

Sun-Mi Hong (South Korea) - Meaning Of A Nest
(2025)

A jazz musician's life is often a wandering, ever-transient existence and such a state of living, no matter how creative and cooperative at its core, leads to a powerful and effusively constant dream of home. South Korean and Amsterdam-based drummer, composer and bandleader Sun-Mi Hong expresses this dilemma with a moving truth and inventiveness all through her album Meaning of a Nest with her quintet of fellow South Korean pianist Chaerin Im, Scottish trumpeter Alistair Payne and two Italians, Nicoli Ricci from Milan and Alessandro Fongaro from Valdagno.

When I heard these young musicians at Dalston's Vortex, I was deeply moved both by their musicianship and their ability to express life stories of the urge of outward and inward striving for peace, roots and home. I asked Sun-Mi about her life in music and what had created this hunger for home, which so movingly finds its apogee in her album's final track, Heart stone. Born in Incheon, near Seoul in 1990, her mother was a hairdresser and her father worked in housing construction. 'I started on piano at six and drums at seventeen. As a teenager I loved K-pop,' she told me. Her family were regular churchgoers and in church she would play piano and sing hymns.

'I got into jazz in 2010 after listening to great U.S. drummers like Tony Williams, Brian Blade and Jeff Tain Watts.' By 2011 she wanted 'to step away from the Korean jazz scene' and moved to Amsterdam. 'I found it a welcoming city, although challenging too for a female Korean drummer. After my Master's degree in Jazz Studies I focused on gigging and formed my own band. Yes, I found my nest in Amsterdam, while realising that my roots are in Korea with my family. Meaning of a Nest is about finding a new way to live in a foreign place while honouring your roots.'

I asked her about the cosmopolitanism of her band. Did she see it as an affirmation of internationalism in music? 'Absolutely! It shows that nationality doesn't matter when connecting through music and humanity.'

Her mellow melodies are beautifully played on the album and were even more affective live at the Vortex. Payne's trumpet, seething with vibrato and incisiveness rang through the Dalston air and fomented a true horn harmony with Ricci's much calmer saxophone timbre. Chaerin's pianism seemed to chime out from the very edge of her keys, particularly in the Never Wilting Petal trilogy, turning 'brilliant corners' like a Korean Monk, and Fongaro's bass underscored his bandmates with a plunging, dancing beat.

How did Sun-Mi describe her bandmates? 'Nicolo is intelligent and funny; Alessandro is strongly supportive and emotionally grounded and Chaerin brings a great vibe to the band and is a sweetheart! Alistair is a true champion, from his album production to giving me confidence as a bandleader.' They are a solid collective unit, playing off each other while inspiring true communal joint endeavour.

The album has a strong compositional and melodic foundation, with all tunes written by Sun-Mi. I asked what track did she warm to most? 'A Never Wilting Petal is my favourite. It tells my Mum's life story and I tried to re-imagine it from different angles.' and 'angles' is the word as her tunes seem to turn towards new directions at expressive moments so many times, at mid-phrase and mid melody. But was there a sense of lamentation about the album, a jazz musician's life of regret at what seemed to be a life of continuing compelled wanderlust? 'It's about finding a nest wherever you are. Touring helps you grow your network and connect with others, which can sometimes lead to further unexpected journeys.'

From Korea to Dalston via Amsterdam playing music which began more than a century ago in New Orleans, Louisiana: unexpected journey yes, but profoundly beautiful too.

(Meaning Of A Nest is available on Edition Records)

Monty Sunshine (England) - Stepney Boy
The Full Monty Sunshine (Upbeat Recordings)
(2003

There was once a Stepney boy who played New Orleans clarinet like a dream. Once, in 1959, he recorded a creole tune written by one of the Crescent City's great clarinet masters with a group of British jazzmen and sent it to the top of the Hit Parade, alongside records by Elvis, Buddy Holly, Adam Faith and the Everley Brothers. Yet this record was under another man's name who didn't even play on it. Such was the 'Chris Barber' version of Sidney Bechet's Petite Fleur, a million-seller played rhapsodically by Monty Sunshine, an East Londoner of Romanian heritage.

At the time he was a teenage hero of mine, with his rich and liquid clarinet tones, sounding like Johnny Dodds reborn in the London docklands. But in 1960 Sunshine left the Barber outfit to form his own band, collecting together some of the best New Orleans-inspired players of the day, including the young trumpeter Rod Mason, pianist Johnny Parker from the Humphrey Lyttelton band, trombonist Graham Stewart from Ken Colyer's Jazzmen and an ex-Barber guitar and banjo man Dickie Bishop, who had been a skiffle pioneer with Lonnie Donegan.

The Full Monty Sunshine CD includes a 1962 BBC session with this band in strong fettle, made finer by the inclusion of British blueswoman Beryl Bryden, who sings Bessie Smith's Young Woman's Blues with ironic relish and feeling. Bryden's own larger-than-life musical career had also touched the charts as washboard player on Donegan's number-one bestseller Rock Island Line. Her crashing washboard, infectious laughter and raucous vocal bursts out of a very lively version of Joe 'King' Oliver's Doctor Jazz, with bassman Gerry Salisbury switching to tuba.

Sunshine's love of Ellington is expressed in his own Manhattan Blues, a beautiful track which plays homage to the Duke's great New Orleans clarinettist, Barney Bigard, with Stewart too showing his mellow melodism. Then stalwart George Melly sings his way through Cakewalkin' Babies, leaving Sunshine to lead the band into Bye and Bye with a stirring second-line clarinet opening.

The second part of the CD was recorded five years later in Hamburg, with a completely different band. Sunshine was very popular in Germany and his Crescent City style had followed the artistry of the regular European visits of George Lewis, immediately apparent on his lucid and birdlike opening solo on Just a Closer Walk with Thee. Bigard's Saratoga Swing is very close to the small-band Ellington arrangements that the Barber band, including Sunshine, were playing in the mid-1950s. On this track, as with the other full-band selections, Sunshine gets rousing support from Ian Hunter-Randall on trumpet and Charlie Galbraith's trombone.

But it is on the final four tracks, comprising clarinet and rhythm section only, that Sunshine expresses his true reed artistry in the path of the masters. The Old Rugged Cross, Philip Street Breakdown and Burgundy Street Blues were all marked by George Lewis' brilliance, but Hushabye was all Sunshine, his own composition and a feature much loved by listeners all over Europe.

After Sunshine's virtually anonymous success with Petite Fleur, Bechet as composer was the recipient of more than a little bit of surprise royalty prosperity. He sent the Stepney man a precious signed photograph with the inscription: 'To Monty, who made Petite Fleur in the Sunshine.' A warm enough thought, but many jazz lovers will want to thank Sunshine for a lifetime of beautiful notes from the Mississippi levees to the Thames lapping on Shadwell stairs.

(The Full Monty Sunshine is available on Upbeat Recordings)

The Sun Ra Arkestra (USA) - Make earthfall in East London

Café Oto, Dalson

(2015)

Playing music out of their interplanetary skins, the Sun Ra Arkestra touched down at Café Oto in Dalston last week.

Sun Ra of Birmingham, Alabama, died in 1993, but under the staunch leadership of 91 year old alto saxophonist Marshall Allen, the eleven Saturnians who constitute the Arkestra have continued touring the Earth with their rampaging galactic sounds. The whole of jazz history is in their timbre. Cecil Brooks' searing trumpet cuts loose like Buddy Bolden's New Orleans horn, George Burton's piano is the ghost of Earl Hines and Knoel Scott's storming tenor blows echoes of the rumbling saxophone engine of Coleman Hawkins and the sublimity of John Coltrane.

Their sparkling, sequinned robes reflected the golden sweat trickling from their faces under the Café Oto's spotlights, and when Tara Middleton sings: 'Folks been walking, walking, walking on the moon', you can believe it. Yet there's nothing unworldly about the Arkestra's power as Middleton calls out: 'They say that history repeats itself, but history is your story.' The Arkestra is the greatest of jazz metaphors, yet these space sonics are definitely of our world and all its heterogeneous peoples.

The familiar chant: 'May you like it in space, in some far place', is also a commentary of Ferguson, Watts, Brooklyn, Calais, Palestine, Western Sahara or the seething streets outside this Hackney venue. The veteran Allen plays some astonishing solos as he conducts and provokes his bandmates and strums his valves as if they're guitar strings, accompanied by the pounding Afro-Latin drums of Elson Nascimento and Wayne Antony Smith, the relentless subterranean bass of Tyler Mitchell and Danny Ray Thompson's gurgling baritone.

Gone for now to some other planet, but not for long. They'll be touching terra firma again at Café Oto soon enough. Don't miss them.

John Tchicai (Denmark/Congo) - A jazzman of precious unity's beautiful saxophone songs

Christopher Dell, Jonas Westergaard, Christian Lillinger and John Tchicai – Dell, Westergaard, Lillinger featuring John Tchicai (2018)

The tenor saxophonist John Tchicai was born in Copenhagen in 1936 to a Danish mother and Congolese father, who had met when they were both waiters at the city's Aarhus Pleasure Gardens. He studied at the Royal Danish Music Conservatory, heard the touring avant-garde jazzmen Archie Shepp and Bill Dixon at a festival in Helsinki and pursued them to New York, where he played alongside them as a member of New York Contemporary Five. In 1965 he played with John Coltrane on the epochal Ascension album session. He also recorded with Albert Ayler, and in 1969 found himself in Cambridge, performing and recording with John Lennon and Yoko Ono: altogether, a beginning in professional music of many sides.

During the next two decades, Tchicai spent much of his career in Europe, teaching full time. In 1982 he joined Pierre Dorge's New Jungle Orchestra in Copenhagen and made some powerful records with them. In the '90s he returned Stateside to southern California, but kept a presence too in France. Always a free spirit who bonded closely with young musicians, he died in October 2012. One of his final recordings was the live 2010 session at the Jazzwerkstatt Café in Berlin, which, combined with a studio session three days later, composes this album, with Tchicai blowing with his compatriot Jonas

Westergaard, a bassist of a new generation and two Germans; vibist Christopher Dell, born in Darmstadt in 1965 and the young drummer Christian Lillinger, born in Lubben in the German Democratic Republic in 1984.

Lillinger's dazzling percussive power is prominent on the opener Fortune at Zou Feet, and is followed by Traveller, which could have been Tchicai's life story. His tenor, full, authoritative and resonating, simmers alongside Dell's trickling vibes, ending in long, seemingly life-reflective, almost hushed notes. Tchicai was 76 when he recorded this album, but plays with an astonishing youthfulness. On the age-defying track Share the energy and crystalline lucidity of his sound meshes with the vigour, vitality and range of ideas of Lillinger, some 50 years his junior, so much so that they could be sonic brothers.

Dell is the solo voice of the following track, Fond, his mallets seeking 'time blocks in the improvisation' as his notes cascade and climb up and down the Café walls. Tchicai enters chunteringly on Wet, beside Lillinger's battery of drums. On A Double Mescal he blows a breathy flute while Westergaard's bass delves out a springing riff and Lillinger clips the rhythm forward.

Double Exposure is the album's longest track, its 14 minutes full of the Tchicai-Dell duo. There are two complex mind-processes here inventing the notes. Both men dig deep and Tchicai's rare artistry pours out of his horn: all those years, all those virtuosi who crowded round his youth. You hear echoes of Ayler and Coltrane, a cluster of notes from Shepp - but mostly his timbre is his own, airy, clear, ever-inventive, sounds you can see through to the truth about life and its music, with Dell, the other voice of the palaver, receiving and responding, even during a final sublime Tchicai burst.

Who is the Intangible Doorman who gives the title to the next track? He's sprightly and lively and Westergaard gives him an agile gait before Tchicai springs in to characterise his cordiality in a human sketch of humour and reality which may be a remembrance of his father, who, among many jobs before he met his mother, was a nightclub doorman.

Strange, almost heroic, that a septuagenarian saxman should be casting his horn into a piece of music called New!!!, composed by a drummer still in his 20s, and still sounding as if he is an essential part of the new wave. Through the last track, Venus, Tchicai sounds like a bird, a travelling bird like one of the millions that journey and migrate every year between Africa and Europe, bringing the sounds of two continents together, while his European companions play next to him, embracing and enhancing his beautiful saxophone song. A pioneer of musical concord was John Tchicai: a jazzman of precious unity.

(Dell, Westergaard, Lillinger featuring John Tchicai is available on jazzwerkstatt)

Don Cherry (USA), John Tchicai (Denmark/Congo), Irene Schweizer (Switzerland), Pierre Favre (Switzerland) and Leon Francioli (Switzerland) - Musical Monsters
(2025)

At the end of August 1980 at the Willisau Jazz Festival in Switzerland, an extraordinary quintet of free jazz virtuosi assembled for a one-off performance. They called themselves, with ample justification, the Musical Monsters, and the live recording of their 'odious' concert conclave lay in the festival's archives for 46 years. Now this fiendish tryst is available on the Zurich-based Intakt label and the Monsters are reborn in full and wild sonic fettle.

So who were these five jazz ogres in a frenzied palaver? There was the Oklahoma-born pocket trumpeter Don Cherry, late of the Ornette Coleman Quartet and one of the great free spirits of jazz and founders of 'world music'. famed for playing with anyone, anytime, anywhere. His comrade horn was the Danish/Congolese saxophonist John Tchicai, born in Copenhagen in 1936, who had played with John Coltrane on his Ascension album of 1965, and with Cherry and Archie Shepp as part of the New York Contemporary Five in 1963.

The other three Monsters were all Swiss. The pianist was Irene Schweizer, also a drummer and one of the founding mothers of European free music, whose trio had been accused by a prominent Swiss music critic of creating sounds like 'dying pigs in a hail of bullets'. Little did he understand and predict the next four decades of her brilliance and sheer originality. The drummer was Pierre Favre, who as a young man had played and recorded with Louis Armstrong and other U.S. touring giants, and had turned towards freer forms in the late Sixties. The bassist was the Lausanne-born Leon Francioli, who despite being less renowned than his bandmates, also played like a fully-fledged Monster.

The four tracks are improvisations around themes written by Cherry, Tchicai and the Danish guitarist Pierre Dorge. Musical Monsters 1 is based on a riff by Cherry and Tchicai's tune Real Kirsten. It begins with some sizzling ensemble and the horns carping above Schweizer's percussive keys. Cherry's fanfarish brass and Francioli's dancing bass are prominent before Tchicai re-enters with a sharp-edged, blistering series of phrases and Schwieizer slows down the pace as if her notes are conducting her compadres, each one a hammer blow. Tchicai's horn howls as if he were playing Flee as a Bird at a New Orleans funeral, and the piece concludes.

The second track gradually moves to the cusp of Tchicai's tune, Transportation of Noodles, and both his alto saxophone and voice move into unaccompanied eloquence, with Francioli and Favre building up the boiling heat while Schweizer pounds her piano as if she were assaying a second set of drums. Tchicai's alto weeps before Favre's blocks ground the spontaneous upsurge of sound and the folkloric repetitions of the childlike Three Blind Mice riff holds the music to infantile memories. Favre sounds like a master drummer playing toy drums before he lets loose on a thunderous solo and his multiplicity of melodic cymbals.

The third track grows from the Dorge theme Xongly, and Cherry leads the way, his miniature horn creating a sawing, naked sound. Tchicai's alto creates a whirl of notes before he duets with his own voice and Schweizer's keys march beneath him. Then it's Francioli's solo turn, his bowed bass incantation touching every listening ear. Cherry and Tchicai share an expressive colloquy before Schweizer's lightning hands provoke her piano to move like the quaking earth.

The flesh and blood of three continents are making these sounds in the heart of Europe, and the final track, including Tchicai's theme Pa Tirstag is another blast of freedom and unity born from a repeated eight-note riff, which seems to drill even deeper into a common earth, until Tchicai's volley of liberating notes send the music skywards. Perhaps it is such passages of a coalescence of bold audacity, instant and uncanny creation and sheer collective free beauty that make these Monsters such defiant enemies of silence.

(Musical Monsters is available on Intakt Records)

Clark Terry (USA) - World Citizen

Clark Terry And The Toronto All-Star Big Band,
George Weston Recital Hall, Toronto
(2005)

Clark Terry, who was born in St Louis in 1920, is one of the greatest trumpeters of jazz. Blowing a horn for all genres of the music, he is the living truth of a treasured message that he was once given by Louis Armstrong - 'keep playing that trumpet, boy, because you can blow your arse off!' And so he can. From his earliest days as a brassman in a local band called Dollar Bill and his Small Change to his forays into post-bop with fellow trumpeter Hugh Ragin, Terry is up for just about anything across the entire panorama of jazz.

His multifaceted approach has also seen him voyaging up and down the Mississippi with Fate Marable's Riverboat Band, playing for many years in the big bands of Charlie Barnet, Count Basie and finally Duke Ellington between 1951 and 1959 and recording with Monk, Lester Young, Oscar Peterson and Ben Webster. His unique vocalese approach to both trumpet and flugelhorn recalling Rex Stewart and anticipating Lester Bowie, the phenomenal, almost magical speed of his solos and improvisations, the sheer wit and humour of his phraseology have attached a uniqueness to his artistry. Not for nothing did Ellington cast him as Puck in his Shakespeare suite, Such Sweet Thunder.

He has inspired some of the greatest modern horns, in particular the young Miles Davis, also a citizen of St Louis. So, to hear him in Toronto at the age of 85 on a Saturday afternoon, playing with some powerful young musicians, is an ear-feast indeed. The Toronto Big Band is made up of music students and Terry, who set the standard for jazz educators many decades ago, is in his element, using every opportunity to encourage the 'wonderful soloists' and joke with them too. 'When I was their age,' he quips, 'I wasn't playing pretty music like this - I was out stealing hubcaps.'

Perched on a high chair with his legs relaxed on a wooden footrest, Terry declares: 'Golden years are hard ones, aren't they?' There are many in the audience who agree. For this is a matinee concert, organised so to attract jazz-loving Canadian senior citizens - 97 come from the Honeywell Retirees Association outside of Toronto, for example, and it is full of friendliness and good humour. Halfway through the proceedings, Terry is presented with the Honorary Award of the International Trumpeters' Guild - previous holders include late great hornmen like Louis Armstrong, Miles Davis and Clifford Brown - and guests and journalists are introduced with warm welcoming applause. Yours truly is introduced as 'Chris Earl, a jazz journalist from London, England, of the Morning Star' and I feel very honoured.

But what about the music? After a few big band pre-war and wartime numbers, including Benny Goodman's Don't Be That Way and a couple of Glenn Miller nostalgia-jerkers, on comes Terry and immediately plunges in to Easy Does It, his muted trumpet surging over the combined blast of five trumpets, three trombones and six saxophones.

For the rest of the concert, he plays flugelhorn and the legendary speed of attack, high-note clusters and felicitous clarity of notemaking are all present. In Cold Tater Stomp, he interpolates the phrases of the famed High Society New Orleans clarinet solo and, in his solo during the ballad Sheba, his flugelhorn sings with a pristine flair, breaking into a brief but beautiful coda at the end of the tune.

He includes Basie and Ellington number, two Ernie Wilkins numbers associated with the Count, A Penny for Your Thoughts and Big Bad Band, which are shot through with Terry's wit and swing. The Duke's proud anthem from Black, Brown and Beige, Come Sunday, is played with a telling and moving dignity, ending with a beautiful dipping cadence.

His sheer speed of notes seems undiminished in CT's Express and, as he scats and blows his miraculous sound through Mumbles, you marvel how Terry's 85 years are the history of a man, but also the history of a music, born in the US, but, like this man's life, a part of the world.

Art Themen (England) - It's great to be anywhere at my age!

Art Themen Trio: Live In Soho

(2025)

As I listened to Art Themen, the octogenarian tenor and soprano saxophonist with his organ trio in the warm basement of Soho's Pizza Express, I marvelled that here was a lifetime jazz musician, who has also spent his working life as a National Health Service orthopaedic surgeon. Two lives! 'I love them both!' he exclaimed: 'They grew together in me, almost subconsciously. I express them both as I'm playing. If I lived my life over again, I wouldn't change a thing!'

He was born in Oldham in 1939, his mother the daughter of an Irish lodging house keeper, his father an immigrant doctor from Surinam. 'My Father died when I was four, and we had very little money. We lived over a fish and chip shop in Salford. My council school headteacher saw something in me, and managed to get me into Manchester Grammar School.'

An aunt had given him tin whistles as a child, then he learned the recorder, and then the clarinet at school and eventually tenor sax. 'I loved traditional jazz and was inspired by clarinetist Monty Sunshine, playing Bobby Shaftoe with Chris Barber's Band.' He studied Medicine at Cambridge from 1958, carrying on with his music with the University's jazz band, and learned more modern sounds listening to records of Sonny Rollins and Dexter Gordon, and hearing John Coltrane playing with Dizzy Gillespie at a concert in the Gaumont State, Kilburn. 'I was learning from the masters in a form of educated plagiarism!'

In 1964 he qualified as a surgeon, and also found himself playing with Alexis Korner and Jack Bruce in Blues Incorporated. It seemed that every step he took in medicine, he took another in music. By 1968 he was a recognised session musician, playing on Joe Cocker's top hit, With a Little Help from my Friends. In 1974 he began a two-decade relationship with pianist Stan Tracey, after playing with prime British maestros like Ian Carr, Graham Collier and Michael Garrick. 'Stan was the source, the real thing. Playing with him was an amazing experience. I loved the camaraderie I found with fellow musicians like Barbadian trumpeter Harry Beckett and Jamaican bassist Coleridge Goode. All the British Council tours to Hong Kong, Beirut, Australia - on the same bill with McCoy Tyner in Melbourne or Stanley Turrentine in New York. It was all like a jazz family and I loved it!'

But how had he managed his time, also working as a surgeon in a district general hospital? 'I had wonderful, understanding colleagues. We swapped shifts and I worked by day, not often at nights, and I paid them all back with my time. And as a musician I wasn't a composer, arranger or bandleader, so all my musical time was spent playing. I was a sideman for fifty years, playing at nights and then in the mornings I was ready to work expeditiously on my operations.'

His organ trio album, Live in Soho, was recorded at the Pizza Express with organist Pete Whittaker and drummer George Double. 'Pete swings, he's sensitive - a wonderful player, so strong, uniting the bass with the keyboard. George is the real bandleader, I'm just titular! He's a human dynamo and very versatile. He's resurrected me!'

The album has some beautiful tracks - Abdullah Ibrahim's African Market Place and Keith Jarrett's Country are jewels, and exemplify Art's eclecticism, with Horace Silver's Cape Verdean Blues and Zoot Sims'

Brahms... I Think. Another tune the trio played live and very movingly was Ballad of the Sad Young Men. When I told Art that as a lifelong schoolteacher it brought to my mind the loss and grief of the predominantly black working class families of the young victims of knife crime, he told me: 'I'm touched by your interpretation. As we played it, the venue was silent, respectful, and I wondered what the listeners were thinking.'

I asked him, as a fellow octogenarian, did playing his saxophone with such optimism and energy, keep him keeping on, now in his mid-eighties? 'It's profoundly important to be doing what you love doing at any time of life,' he replied in a warm bedside manner. 'As for me, it's great to be here, but then it's great to be anywhere at my age!'

(Live In Soho is available on Ubuntu Records)

Omar Thomas (USA/Guyana) - Sounds of optimism and human outreach

Omar Thomas Large Ensemble: Griot Songs (2025)

Omar Thomas' parents came from Guyana to find work in Brooklyn, where Thomas was born in 1984. He learned trombone at school and played in school assemblies, but his life in music since then has been one of protean accomplishment. His composing has straddled jazz and classical genres, and has been performed by Dionne Warwick to the Colorado Symphony Orchestra, from the San Francisco and Boston Gay Men's Choruses to Chaka Khan and the Showa Wind Symphony. His 2014 album, We Will Know: An LGBT Civil Rights Piece in Four Movements was described by epochal drummer Terri Lyne Carrington as 'a thought-provoking, multi-layered masterpiece.' A musical polymath in every sense, his new album Griot Songs, he describes as 'a cohesive story that I'm telling to the listener. Rather than just doing a flyover of this planet, I really wanted to land on its surface and explore it.'

Yet there is much, much more than a mere surface to his music. As the West African griot keeps safe, tells and is the holder of legends, history, ways of living and wisdom, so Thomas expresses all through his unbridled consciousness and musical narratives of Africa, the Caribbean and South and North America.

His compelling orchestrations are matched by the creative virtuosity of powerful soloists, beginning with the beauty of Lihi Haruvi's soprano saxophone introduction and Jason Palmer's searing trumpet on the opening track, The Sun in September, dedicated to trombonist Bob Brookmeyer. Nothing There has a long, searching and radiant tenor saxophone solo by Jon Beam.

The longest track of seventeen minutes is The Path, a tribute to a friend of Thomas, a doctor who cared for sick children in orphanages in Zimbabwe, China and Guatemala. It has a cosmic yet earthly sound, full of echoes of human striving across the world, with the featured guitar power of Mark Cocheo.

In the track closest to his own Guyanese roots, Obeah Woman, the rhythmic propulsion ramps up Josh Reed's skyward trumpet, which bursts from the ensemble undergrowth. It is as if Thomas' orchestrations are sharing Guyana's forested and riverine reality with its own literary masters like Jan Carew and Wilson Harris, as Evan Amoroso's muted trombone spills its revelations. It is a profoundly awakening sound, as if its people were realising new consciousness, new actions.

Griot Songs is an album of the sounds of optimism and human outreach and his music fuses with the words of Guyana's own laureate, Martin Carter: 'We do not sleep to dream/ But dream to change the world.'

(Griot Songs is available on Omar Thomas Music Records)

Pat Thomas (England/Antigua) - Elemental sounds of the creation

Pat Thomas – Nur
Thomas/Strid/Thomas – Wazifa
(2013)

Down in the gut of a deep basement bar in a derelict Sheffield cinema he strolled to a battered old upright piano, undemonstratively sat down, stared at the keys and began to play to some 80 transfixed listeners who forgot their drinks and found their focus on his every note.

In that shadow-filled subterranean room and within a 10-minute sonic foray the whole of jazz's century of history poured from his miraculously deft hands. I heard the Crescent City echoes of Jelly Roll Morton and the galvanising stride of James P Johnson and Fats Waller, the intellectual swing of Mary Lou Williams and Monk's sudden careering corners alongside Bud Powell's bopstorms and the timbral power of Cecil Taylor. Suddenly, from the density of his phrases and the ever-new pathways of his improvisation, I thought I heard the strains of Tiger Rag. And all on an ordinary Sunday night in South Yorkshire. The pianist was Pat Thomas, and with all his astonishing technique and sense of tradition in his musical universe, as avant garde as you can get.

He was born in 1960 and studied classical piano from the age of eight, fascinated too by the reggae sounds around him. At 16 he happened to see Oscar Peterson on the television and he started to play jazz, eventually fixing his concentration upon free improvisation. In 1990 he was invited by the guitarist Derek Bailey to join him at the first International Symposium for Free Improvisation in Bremen. Through the '90s he played with the Tony Oxley Quartet and Oxley's Celebration Orchestra, the US bassist Sirone, Larry Stabbins and trumpeter Manfred Schoof, as well as creating a lasting partnership with the soprano saxophonist Lol Coxhill.

In 1990 he cut his album Nur - an Arabic word meaning 'light' - for the Emanem label, which was recorded in the superb acoustic concert setting of the Cheltenham and Gloucester College of Education Chapel. And a rare unity of potent sound and spirit is afoot here. Christian context, Islamic muse, human beauty and serenity peal from the, in turns, quietude, reflection, assertiveness and splendour of the 26-minute title piece. It is the first of four pieces 'completely improvised.' Thomas continues in his sleeve note: 'I came to the concert with no paper, and had not made any predetermined plan about what areas to cover. It is unlikely the music I played could have been made in any other way.'

The second track, Mubarak ('blessed'), celebrates Ramadan, played during the holy month. The notes spin and gyrate through the chapel at the astounding speed and with boundless invention and pitch. Variation on Two Themes is the amalgam of melodies, one 'very well known in the west, while the second theme is very well known in the east.'

Is the 'western' theme the tune from the Chaplin film Limelight? Did I also hear Swing Low, Sweet Chariot? And while you listen and guess, a challenge of a concord is created.

Then finally there is The Analogy, dedicated to the music of Thelonious Monk of Rocky Mount, North Carolina, 'which I feel is found throughout the music I played that night.' Playful, full of the unexpected, the tightrope, the melodies and patterns of surprise and incredulity - who else could be Thomas's prime musical inspiration?

A very different sound-scape is built in the 2009 album Wazifa, another Arabic word meaning 'assignment,' 'duty' or 'daily ration,' with bassist Clayton Thomas and the scuttling Swedish percussionist Raymond Strid. Pat moves between piano stool and an adjacent seat for the synthesiser to forge his notes. There are three separate but entirely related tracks. The first and longest at some 22 minutes is called Perceptive. There is a world of grating, lacerating sounds here with Clayton's whining bowed bass, Strid's bell-like cymbals and scratching drums and Pat's dancing steps along his keys - a trio's birth-song of elemental sounds at their very moment of creation.

The much shorter Preceptive follows. The tinkling drops of Pat's piano notes mutate to brawny chords through the body of the piece and dive into Perspective, where Clayton's plucked basslines leap through the opening sequence beside Strid's twitching vibrations before Pat's piano enters in rampant fruition.

It is as if the trio is all - not one, not two, but all three humanities in coalesced musical voice, which you think is how Pat Thomas would best like it.

(Nur is available on Emanem & Wazifa on psi)

Pat Thomas (England/Antigua) - Truly an act of musical transformation

Pat Thomas Plays The Music Of Derek Bailey And Thelonious Monk (2020)

How does an astonishing pianist of Caribbean roots embrace the music of that most atonal of guitarists, Sheffielder Derek Bailey, on the same album as playing the starkly beautiful and deceptively simple melodies of Rocky Mount, North Carolina-born pianist Thelonious Monk? The answer is fundamental, even easy: he finds intimate kinship with both - so much so that it is often difficult to discern where Bailey ends and where Monk begins, for both are internalised by Pat Thomas' huge musical intelligence and wayward, explorative imagination.

I first heard Thomas play live in a derelict cinema basement in the neighbourhood where Bailey was born and spent his early years. I lived there and often imagined his wartime boyhood years, scrumping apples from some of the large Nether Edge gardens near the terraced Sharrow streets that he knew so well. Thomas struck out his own music on a battered upright piano, and as I listened I thought how much Bailey would have empathised with him, playing in that cinema just up the road from where he was born and where he must have sat and watched films dozens of times.

His Bailey tracks on the album begin with transcriptions of some of the guitarist's early recordings, as a starting point for Thomas' own striking improvisations. He does something similar with Monk's melodies. They were all recorded live in two Oxford venues, so Thomas was performing in his own home city, which seems to give them an even sharper edge. When he moves on from Bailey's Extract 4 to a wondrously tuneful rendition of Victor Young's 1949 melody, My Foolish Heart, he does what Monk did to the tenderest of ballads, balancing wit and gentleness with the same timbral truth. Then it is directly back to Bailey's Extract 5, which begins and is sustained with the same restrained and chiming beauty as he seems to be thinking out each single note, before he dives back into the Monkish corners and complexities of In Walked Bud, played with brilliant keyboard runs and multi-rhythmic flourishes. And how he swings too, as if he is playing at least two pianos.

Thomas' love of melody is profound. I remember hearing his sublime interpretations of Ellington tunes at the Café Oto in 2019, and how he struck his keys with such strength and lucidity - I had never heard Prelude to a Kiss or Solitude played with such serene yet tranquil power. He does something not dissimilar with Benny Golson's Along Came Betty, recreating a hard bop anthem into a warm, restrained air of love.

To bring Bailey's unique, scratching, blood red guitar sounds to the piano and to give Monk's tunes a second birthing on the same record, is truly an act of musical transformation. Hear Monk, hear Bailey and then play this album, and you will know what I mean.

(Pat Thomas Plays The Music Of Derek Bailey And Thelonious Monk is available on FMR Records)

Pat Thomas (England/Antigua), Rachel Musson (Wales)
& Mark Sanders (England/Belize)
Shifa - Ecliptic
(2025)

A Welsh saxophonist, an English pianist and drummer of Antiguan and Belizean heritage respectively, improvising as a trio with an Arabic name - Shifa, meaning 'healing', and recorded in February 2023 at Café Oto, Dalston, East London, play a 46 minute sound creation called 'Ecliptic' - the path of the sun.

The powerful music of Rachel Musson, Pat Thomas and Mark Sanders spans the world of sound with an astonishing and emotive virtuosity. I listened to their album immediately after watching a horrific newscast from the Gaza genocide and reading the words of Dr. Nidal Jboor from the blitzed al-Shifa Hospital in Gaza City, 'bombed into ash, doctors and nurses killed in their white coats, and patients - children, elders. the wounded - left to die on the floors of ruins that once promised healing. More than 25,000 children exterminated, hospitals and schools flattened, doctors executed, patients burned alive, aid turned into bait, starvation used as weapons, cities erased.'

We hear the cry and the ordeal of the Palestinian people all through Shifa's music, sometimes calm and serene, sometimes caustic and rasping, sometimes mollifying, sometimes irascible, always brilliantly played with instant, ever-inventive improvising, a musicianship which moves into every vein of the listener's blood. The listener listens, imagines, interprets and understands in what dramatist Edward Bond called 'the art of the audience'. Sanders' riveting introduction is soon fused with Musson's belching notes and Thomas' first chinking, bell-like phrases. Then a hushed pause, some scuttling Sanders and Musson's sustained tenor saxophone at its most piercing and pained alongside Thomas' unbridled runs and Sanders' omnipresent drums. We are away and the world of healing is upon us.

Somewhere amongst the multi-rhythms, the beauty of the quasi-melodic infusions, the spontaneous soundscape of real life from agony to hope, light and healing, Palestinian wilfulness, like this music, never gives up. 'We are always scared that any reconstruction in Gaza is a target,' says Dr. Karameh Hawash Kuemmerle, a paediatric neurologist, yet he talks too of active plans to re-build al-Shifa so its healing can take new life, including a new 80-bed West Wing, even in the very crux of Israeli bombardment and deadly drones.

The Shifa trio comprises a pianist, drummer and hornplayer. In the poem by the late Palestinian laureate, Mahmoud Darwish, the protagonist is a 'wandering guitar player' and Darwish writes of him:

'I almost see him,
Almost smell the blood on his strings.
I almost hear him
Shouting like a storm:
Listen:
That's the music of human flesh.'

All the oxymorons of sound rise and fall in Ecliptic's sunlit passages, in the storytelling eyes of the beautiful children of Gaza - skeletal, foodless and maimed. Yet still Shifa's music, theirs and ours, cries out to every different ear in hope and love for them and the healing of their future in their Palestine, their own life-land, their own hereafter signalled by Shifa's healing sounds.

(Ecliptic is available on Discus Records)

Malachi Thompson (USA) - In praise of Chicago
Malachi Thompson - 47th Street
(2014)

Throughout the century of jazz, there have been those musicians who have always wanted to tell their stories about their cities and the neighbourhoods where they lived, worked and played their music. There was the host of New Orleans pioneers whose almost every tune was a praisesong to the streets of Storyville, Duke Ellington's sonic poems to Harlem and Basie's to Kansas City, Yusef Lateef's album-hymn to Detroit - and in our own days in our own land, Soweto Kinch's evocations of the crowded estates and tower blocks of Birmingham 19. But one of the most powerful and streetwise urban jazz troubadours was the Chicago trumpeter Malachi Thompson, who between 1991 and 2003 cut a series of vibrant freebop albums that sang out the black glory of his city and its people, in particular those who lived in the 47th Street community.

Most of the album 47th Street was recorded in the city in 1996, but there are three earlier tracks which go back to 1993, which included two superb and cruelly underestimated Chicago horns, both long-time confreres of Thompson, Joe Ford and tenorist Carter Jefferson, with the rampaging CJ's Blues being the latter's last ever recording.

Thompson was born in Chicago in 1949. When he was a boy his mother took him to a Count Basie concert which hooked him for life. During his teens he blew with R&B bands, but involvement with the Windy City's Association for the Advancement of Creative Musicians invited him towards experimentation and serving the local musical community.

He left for New York City in 1974, worked in Washington DC and Vienna, and returned to Chicago in 1989, diagnosed with a rare form of lymphoma. Back in his home city, he hurled himself into its music, and threw off his disease. He also campaigned to restore historical performance venues of the South Side, like the Sutherland Hotel where Gillespie, Miles Davis, Gene Ammons and John Coltrane had played in the '50s, and 47th Street is both a celebration of those years and an affirmation of a jazz future.

The album's title tune comes from a play by Charles White, The Sutherland, part of the movement to restore the hotel as a jazz centre. Thompson's raw notes rasp abrasively over the group vocal before he lets himself loose with a searing chorus and the muscular sound of Ron Bridgewater's tenor takes over, while Kirk Brown's piano rocks relentlessly over lyrics about 'big business and the black economy.' Thompson blows forcibly through It Is Not True Simply Because You Cannot Believe It, vitalised too by tenorist Billy Harper's gravelly solo. X gives prominence to Ford's cruising alto before Thompson's horn bursts in, and in CJ's Blues, now muted over Harrison Bankhead's plunging bass, he prefaces Jefferson's final solo, musical soulmates together in the studio for the last time.

Some Freebop For Monk has a bigger-band sound with Brown's dancing piano beneath it all and Thompson's penetrating notes cutting through the theme, pursued by Steve Berry's growling slides. When it is Harper's time his huge sonic patterns boom over Lake Michigan. Thompson's beautifully lucid sound blows, as if effortlessly, through Wayne Shorter's Miyako and African Sun Dance, with Nassar Abadey and Dr Cuz sharing the drums and other percussion, and Ford's soprano saxophone resonating though a long and vibrating solo before Thompson returns to take the track home.

The final three tracks of the album make up a suite called The Mystery of Jaaz. Thompson researched the Hebrew meaning of the word 'jaaz' and discovered three associations - 'the creator listens,' 'a bold statement' and 'harmony.' The are all vibrantly expressed in the music of the suite, along with poetry and song. Thompson's high-pitched wails are at the centre of An Elevated Cry before Harper brings the depth of his chorus back to the earth and the South Side streets, throbbing with life and noise. Dee Alexander's ear-splitting vocal begins the concluding track, Lamentation, and it leaves you with the sense that this music will never die, that there is nothing nostalgic about Thompson's music, so racked with the present and the future is it.

And the Sutherland still grooves, still pours out its sounds, with Thompson's emphatic spirit.

(47th Street is available on Delmark)

Keith Tippett (England) - Timeless music

Keith Tippeth, Harry Miller, Julie Tippetts & Frank Perry - Ovary Lodge (2008)

Ovary Lodge is just 47 minutes long, yet it represents one of the most distinctive and beautifully strange sonic statements in the entire recorded canon of jazz. First released in 1973, perhaps it could only have come out of that era, when then nakedly new was so often the everyday. So, to hear it again three-and-a-half decades on when musical audacity is far less common brings back memories of an age of jazz bravery, when free improvisation took risks that, these days, are not often even contemplated and combinations of sounds rocked their genres with such daring innovations.

Keith Tippett, a Bristolian born in 1947, played piano harmonium and recorder. Harry Miller, a South African, played bass. The percussionist who surrounded himself with drums, cymbals, bells, Buddhist gongs and other Eastern percussion was Frank Perry. The woman whose haunting voice swept over the music and who played the sopranino recorder and a Chinese bow and string instrument called the erhu was the astonishing Julie Tippetts. Their music pushed hard at the frontier of what at the time was seen as the freest of free jazz. Nobody, not even the musicians themselves could categorise it. These were unprecedented sounds. Tippett played maracas, Perry played hsiao and sheng - so was this genuinely 'east-west' or authentic 'world music' in a jazz setting?

And yet the musicians made no compositions, eschewed any discussion before embarking on their sounds and depended absolutely on the improvisational moment, putting their complete trust in spontaneity and their free collective empathy. I suppose that you could argue that, if all this were authentically born, why record it, why give it a permanence and then why reissue it at the beginning of the next century? Yet, when you listen and you hear, you are so glad and relieved that this revelatory music still exists and that you can hear it again and again.

The opening track, 14 minutes long, is called Gentle One Says Hello. The solitary chime of a bell begins the piece, followed by others and the tapping of a metal vessel. Tippetts' wordless voice hovers over the percussion, anchored by Miller's bowed and moaning bass and Keith Tippetts' yearning vocalisms. An uncanny greeting, for sure. Fragment No 6 begins with the deep, surging spring of Miller's bass and Tippett's dark passages along his keys. The Cecil Taylor-like keyboard charges and arpeggios struck in alliance with Tippett's wailing crescendos create perplexing sounds ambivalently pitched between joy and sorrow. Then there is the mere five minutes of A Man Carrying a Drop of Water on a Leaf through a Thunderstorm, introduced by the erhu backed by Perry's throbbing percussion and Miller's heartbeating bass. It is a picture visualised by momentary sounds, appearing and gone again almost in an instant. Man, leaf and storm all come and gone, from darkness briefly into light and sound and into darkness again.

. Communal Travel is the album's core, all 18 minutes of it. A bass and erhu duo begins the track, the dialogue picking up speed and direction as it moves, taking with it first Tippetts' recorder, then Perry's drums and whistles and the contrasting pitches of the voices. Travel it is, with a congruent unity - the essence of Ovary House's keening music, hitching the listener to its movements.

Of its era, yes. But of all time? Yes too. In a true and real sense, the music is indescribable. You have to hear it, not read about it - and hear it many more times than once.

(Ovary Lodge is available on Ogun)

Jean Toussaint (Virgin Islands) - Lyrical lessons in brotherly love

Jean Toussaint Allstar 6tet - Brother Raymond (2018)

Most of the eleven tracks on Jean Toussaint's album Brother Raymond are dedicated to people he has known, loved, admired and emulated and, at its heart, is his brother Raymond, whom he lost in 2016. A powerful presence and teacher in British jazz, despite being born in the Virgin Islands, Toussaint was nurtured by the founder and leader of the Jazz Messengers, Art Blakey, with whom he played in one of the legendary drummer's last bands from 1982.

In Brother Raymond he brings together some of his dearest musical friends and longstanding bandmates to play 10 of his own compositions in an intimate and entirely empathetic London studio setting. He starts with Amabo - turn its letters around - on which Alec Dankworth's earthy bass, Shane Forbes's hustling drums and the congas of Williams Cumberbatch Perez lay down a pulsating beat before Ashley Henry's stomping piano chorus, some jubilant tenor from Toussaint, Dennis Rollins's jumping trombone and Byron Wallen's joyous trumpet contribute to a throbbing opener.

Major Changes was written at the time of Trump's election and the aftermath of the EU referendum and on it Wallen's horn soars and crackles, driven by Andrew McCormack's stomping piano and Daniel Casimir's pulsating bass. Letter to Milena is dedicated to Toussaint's wife and his saxophone salutes her with streaming cadences, together with Rollins's tender slides.

His homage Brother Raymond borrows from two giants of jazz, Duke Ellington and Wayne Shorter. McCormack has another inventive chorus, Forbes shows more of his mettle on the drums and Toussaint's solo is as gentle and powerful as a brother's love, exemplifying the sense of family and friendship that radiates from this album's every note.

Then it is Mingus Fingers, a tribute to bassist Charles Mingus, one of the great jazz warriors, on which Wallen is full of fire and piercing notes, while trombonist Tom Dunnett holds onto the passion before Toussaint's incendiary entry and drummer Mark Mondesir and pianist Henry stoke up the rhythmic groundswell with Casimir's throbbing bassline.

Casimir's quasi-subterranean notes also open Toussaint's Wonder Where, his salute to the mercurial Stevie Wonder. Troy Miller and Perez combine for a rich percussive underlay to his tune and there is a swinging alto saxophone chorus from Tom Harrison before Uganda-born trumpeter Mark Kavuma, Toussaint himself and Ashley Henry all take ebullient solos.

The album closes with a second version of Amabo which, Toussaint reminds us, is also Latin for 'I shall love.' It's a jam full of verve and joy, celebrating Toussaint's role as one of British jazz's great mentors, unifiers and forces of progress.

(Brother Raymond is available on Lyte Records)

Jean Toussaint (Virgin Islands) – Caribbean muse

Jean Toussaint - Live in London and Paris (2013)

Born in St Thomas in the Virgin Islands in 1960, Jean Toussaint grew up with calypso stomping in his veins. As a teenager he was as student at the Berklee College of Music in Boston, and at 22 the sound of his tenor saxophone attracted the attention of the veteran drummer Art Blakey. Between 1982 and '86 he was a member of one of Blakey's final versions of the Jazz Messengers, touring the world with confreres like trumpeter Terence Blanchard, pianist Mulgrew Miller and altoist Donald Harrison. He decamped to Britain in 1987, where he has both performed and taught at Birmingham Conservatory and Trinity College of Music.

Not a prolific recording artist, so this very live album, cut partly in Paris at the Sunside in 2004 and partly at the 606 Jazz Club on the Fulham Road in 2008, is a welcome boost to his canon. With him are his regular piano confrere Andrew McCormack, with bassist Larry Bartley and Troy Miller on drums.

Jerome Barde employs his own invented 'Bardophone,' a modified guitar, on two of the Paris tracks and Benet McLean takes the piano stool for the final track Round Midnight. Toussaint leaps into the album on his soprano for the opener The Bean Counter, which according to the accompanying notes, is 'a negative tribute to the greed and heartlessness of the international banking system,' and the new millennium's equivalent of Duke Ellington's ironic Wall Street Wail of 1929, which put into the jazz consciousness the terrible social consequences of that year's financial crisis. Toussaint unleashes some fiery torrid lines with subliminal pain in their timbre, while Miller simultaneously propels and answers them beside Bartley's relentless pulse. It is a sound of our fiscal times with capital on its edge, and McCormack's choruses with their piled-up cadences tell us that something large is falling.

Toussaint's unaccompanied tenor at the outset of Random Discourse has echoes of another powerful hornman with his provenances in the Virgin Islands, the 80-year-old Sonny Rollins. Toussaint shakes off his notes like an earnest prophet while McCormack's repeated chords build up a wall of fevered sound.

Chubby Rain is McCormack's jaunty tune, full of life and optimism and includes a ringing solo from Barde's bardophone, weaving intricacy and springing movement. The 14 minutes of Heian Yondan are Toussaint's sonic tribute to the Shokotan form of martial arts, and his tenor spurts a sense of proud defiance, his long solo gurgling with a muscled artistry while Miller stokes up the rhythmic engine. McCormack takes over and the thinking energy of his chorus stretches far inside the listening ears, his notes chiming like besotted bells.

Toussaint returns to more blessed and Caribbean-edged ground to find the dedicatee of his own moving praise-song, Hymn (For Mother). Switching back to soprano, he etches endearment and admiration in every note, often with a soaring peal of birdsong-like sound hover over bass and drums. McCormack's tenderness of phrase and inventiveness sound almost classical in its realisation and beauty, reminding us of his recent performances with the London Symphony Orchestra, before Toussaint returns with his own loving theme.

On to a remembrance of a great trumpeter and fellow ex-Jazz Messenger, Mirage - a salute to the recently passed Freddie Hubbard, which is Toussaint's composition based upon Ellington's classic theme, Caravan. Hubbard's horn excitation and all-out musical commitment is well recalled in the authoritative and bold flight of Toussaint's soprano and McCormack's own rampaging choruses. Miller's percussive volleys towards the close of the piece arouse a feeling of joy in a jazz life powerfully lived, and prompted me to remember Hubbard's signal anti-Vietnam war message of his 1971 album Sing Me A Song of Songmy.

The finale of many fine albums is also the finale of this one - Monk's Round Midnight, hauntingly comforting, smarting yet warmly humane. Toussaint plays it as a rhapsody, with the beating heart of Bartley's bass close beside him, and followed by a pounding, echoing solo from McLean. It's a resonating and enduring album, bringing Toussaint radiantly out of the shadows.

(Live in London and Paris is available on Space Time Records)

Colin Towns (England) - John Lennon reimagined

Colin Towns & the NDR Big Band - John Lennon: In My Own Write Provocateur (2011)

Three decades after John Lennon's murder in New York, you might not have predicted that 18 of his tunes and others written with Paul McCartney would turn up on a marvellous jazz album by a German big band. But arranger Colin Towns and the Hamburg-based NDR Orchestra have achieved just that, with '60s and '70s melodies and soundscapes given new life and dynamism.

Towns, an East Londoner born in 1948, surrounds himself with grippingly fluent and powerful musicians, eloquent soloists and ensemble sections. Yet his true instrument - like Ellington, Basie, Gil Evans and Mike Westbrook - is the huge fullness of a jazz orchestra itself, and in the NDR he has found his own and Lennon's true high-point.

Those of us who shared the Liverpudlian's astonishing years and dazzling sonic universe - once the Beatles had left the sounds of normality behind - will be pricked into remembrances that are anything but nostalgic, so skilful and contemporary are these arrangements. Take Give Peace a Chance, originally composed and recorded when the US imperial war against Vietnam was at its cruel height. Towns recreates the simple sloganism of Lennon's song as a cry of indignation against Bush and Blair in Iraq. The track begins with the sounds of 'shock and awe' being inflicted on Baghdad, the flute and piano showing the fragility of human life beneath such a blitzkrieg and martial drums proclaim invasion as a trumpeter opens the theme of peace. Then the telling of the consequences: '850,000 dead, 1.5 million seriously injured and no weapons of mass destruction found,' as Blair's words resonate from the 2009 inquiry - 'I'd do it again!' The trombones of Dan Gottshall and Stefan Lotterman testify as Lennon's words echo into 2011: 'You either get tired fighting for peace or you die.'

There are more than two hours of Lennon, Towns and the NDR virtuosi on this double album and it is all engrossing. For me the key moments were in the contrasts: vibrant rampaging ensembles in familiar stomping themes and the tender lyricism and balladry of melodies such as Woman, Jealous Guy, Beautiful Boy and the sublime finale of Imagine with Lutz Buchner's sumptuous tenor saxophone blowing the beloved theme, making a jazz classic of Lennon's opus just as Coleman Hawkins immortalised Body and Soul as the tenor's classic rhapsody in 1939.

Across the Universe is another beautifully orchestrated track which would have enthused that sojourner from Saturn, Sun Ra. Held on its interplanetary course by the NDR's reed and brass sections, with tenorists Frank Delle and Sebastian Gille keeping the tune earthed, and a felicitous trumpet solo from Ingolf Burkhardt takes the track into outer space.

Following straight on is Nowhere Man, fired by Marcio Doctor's ubiquitous percussion and Roland Cabezas's strident guitar, with it Stephan Meinburg's trumpet testing the stratosphere. Lennon's endpiece to Sgt.

Pepper, the psychodelic oblivion of A Day in the Life, is given an enigmatic piano intro by Vladyslav Sendecki before Fiete Felsch's alto peals out over Gary Husband's crashing drums. Towns's long-time veteran English horn brother Alan Skidmore has his telling tenor moments with a reverberating, skin-tingling chorus after a menacing ensemble. The final full-orchestral blast and fading coda is simply enormous and finds huge comradeship with Lennon's sonic cosmos.

Woman's serene melody tingles with Burkhardt's magnetic horn, I Want You (She's So Heavy) has a full-on impassioned tenor colloquy between Skidmore and Buchner, while Jealous Guy has more pristine Burkhardt to carry its narrative - and Tomorrow Never Knows sounds almost anthemic when ushered into a jazz context by Towns's riveting orchestration.

Potent big-band arrangers and virtuoso soloists have frequently transformed pop into jazz, and in doing so often created permanence out of the transient. Lennon's works were never that, and Towns has shown again how, even though they were essential to their epoch, they were never locked or trapped within it. Rather they transcend it and sweep forward into our own era, and this compelling album shows that note after note, again and again.

(John Lennon: In My Own Write is available on Provocateur)

Stan's the Man at Ronnie's - Stan Tracey (England) with Sonny Rollins (USA). Johnny Griffin (USA). Rahsaan Roland Kirk (USA), Jimmy Witherspoon (USA) and Ronnie Scott (England)
(2006)

That marvellous cavern of hot music, Ronnie Scott's Jazz Club on Frith Street, Soho, opened again this week after a long re-fit. So it's an apt time to reflect on some of the historic early sessions that were recorded in the club's previous premises in Gerrard Street. During three years of the mid-1960s, jazz journalist Les Tomkins got Scott's permission to take his Ferrograph Mk2 tape recorder into the club and record what he wanted. This was the time when many of the great musicians of the US jazz scene were regular visitors and Tomkins' labours waxed them all. Some of the best of these sessions have been gradually released on the London-based Harkit label and they are precious albums indeed, full of some of the great moments of British jazz history, re-lived for us as they were being made in a small room in London's Chinatown.

These were also golden nights for Stan Tracey, the nonpareil of British jazz pianists and the house pianist at Ronnie's all through these recordings. We hear him in all guises, accompanying the hyper-unpredictable Sonny Rollins through his marathon solos, keeping pace with the sprinting Johnny Griffin and responding like a brother to Rahsaan Roland Kirk as he blows three horns simultaneously, then playing his own south London version of the blues as he teams up with the Arkansas blues of Jimmy Witherspoon. 'Does anybody here really know how good he is?' Rollins asked the Soho audiences during his first visit in 1965. Coming from the brilliant Rollins, there could hardly have been a greater compliment paid to a British jazz virtuoso, and Tracey himself remembered Rollins' musical generosity, how much he eschewed the egocentricity of stardom and made his music 'a four-way thing' with Tracey, drummer Ronnie Stephenson and bassist Rick Laird.

Rollins' 1950s creative surge including albums like Saxophone Colossus (1956) and his solidarity statement with the Civil Rights Movement, Freedom Suite (1958), had been followed by a period of musical reflection and retreat, broken in in 1962 by his first Bluebird album The Bridge and later, his 1964 album with the first great fellow-master of the tenor saxophone, Coleman Hawkins. So by January 1965 he was in full, unabashed creative revival and these London sessions show that in all its fullness. London listeners had never heard live anything like his Blue' n 'Boogie before - the seemingly eternal flights of invention with notes spinning everywhere. They certainly inspire Tracey's confidence and piano audacity as Rollins prompts and nudges him through his early choruses, doing the same for Laird as he springs into solo action.

Then he dialogues with Stephenson's drums for a long, stirring colloquy before, with quiescent beginnings, he launches himself into a series of melodic patterns which defy any kind of audience expectation, bursting in all directions and returning to occasional familiar snatches of tunes like Oh Susannah or Where or When. And just as you are marvelling at his apparently breathless virtuosity, he changes tempo with an unaccompanied sweep into the ballad, Where are You? Its melody becomes the canvas for dozens of improvisational themes. Left to himself, he ends with a final coda including phrases from God Bless the Child and Do Nothing Till You Hear from Me, all woven into his own internalised extempore tunemaking.

The appropriately titled Four is leaped into by Rollins with the other three chasing him hard. This is a mere 23 minutes long, includes some compelling Tracey choruses, catching the inspiration of Rollins' innovation. His own Sonnymoon for Two follows for 27 more minutes, his tireless tenor horn surging into the boppish theme. With every successive musical pathway an exploration, he travels through the performance breaking unknown territory all the way - gurgling, soaring, spluttering, floating.

Chicagoan Johnny Griffin, born in 1928, already had some classic recordings behind him when he arrived in London in 1963, as well as a reputation for being 'the world's fastest saxophonist'. Tracey was waiting at Gerrard Street for him, along with bassist Malcolm Cecil and drummer Jackie Dougan, who, as Scott announces, was 'deputising for our regular drummer who has unfortunately been taken suddenly drunk.' In the interview with Tomkins at the end of Johnny Griffin Live in London, Griffin describes himself as a romantic, playing with his customary fire, feeling and excitation 'as an unconscious thing'. He hurtles through All the Things You Are - which includes a long, enigmatically Monkish solo by Tracey at his finest and some sprightly Cecil; makes a breathless dash of Wee Dot after Tracey's opening solo emulates a runaway train, and puts the brakes on for Exactly Like You, still sprinkling notes all along Gerrard Street.

Griffin's time with Monk is invoked through the pianist's Straight, No Chaser, presenting a particular challenge to Tracey, for whom Monk was always a hero. Neither saxophonist nor pianist shows the slightest trepidation - Griffin has absolute confidence in the Londoner's understanding of Monk's music, and Tracey's angular phraseology, his unexpected keyboard quirks and pathways are all provocations to Griffin's own luminous playing.

The October 1964 visit of Rahsaan Roland Kirk to Ronnie's was also momentous. Born in Columbus, Ohio in 1936 and blind from birth, he was already a jazz legend - a powerful tenorist who played three reed instruments simultaneously, not to any freakish or superficial effect but with an astonishing artistry and self-ensemble sound. Tracey was there to join him with Laird and drummer Allan Ganley and, very swiftly, a powerful jazz relationship grew. On Roland Kirk: Live in London, you can hear Rahsaan urging Tracey on during his solos and the pianist seems completely unperturbed by the American's brilliance, from the moment that the opener, Oleo, begins with a wondrous unaccompanied tenor passage. Rahsaan introduces tenor, manzello - something like a soprano saxophone, and stritch - closest to alto saxophone, on Green Dolphin Street, and Tracey sounds in his element with Rahsaan's encouraging shouts of 'Git it on! Git it on!' as he flies off in a solo.

You Did It! You Did It! is an exploration of Rahsaan's flute/voice duality and tenor and manzello are to the fore on a rapid Lover Come Back to Me. He takes hold of the stritch for RK Blues in an adventurous excursion, with Tracey strolling at first in his solo, then picking up spirited pace with Rahsaan's sighs of delight beside him.

Tracey's Ellington and Monk allegiances hardly made him the obvious accompanist to Arkansas bluesman Jimmy Witherspoon, but such was his protean adaptability. and astonishing versatility that he created a very special Soho blues sound for the visitor. Witherspoon loved it. 'I dig Stan!' he exclaimed, 'he's got his own thing going. He's my running buddy! He plays some things you don't hear from no young piano player.' He was right enough there. Tracey's accompaniment on songs such as Trouble in Mind or Nobody Knows You When You're Down and Out is entirely empathetic as Witherspoon squeezes out the feelings and historical realities that provoked the blues as a mass phenomenon.

Jimmy Witherspoon Live in London was recorded from two sets in Gerrard Street in May 1966. Freddie Logan is on bass, Bill Eyden on drums and Ronnie Scott himself blows his tenor saxophone throughout. But despite being essentially bop musicians, they give Spoon a version of the blues that excites his voice in this faraway London setting. Tracey's percussive technique finds a kindred timbre in Spoon's vocals, and his reflective intros to numbers like In the Evening or See See Rider set the mood for the bluesman's elegiac lyrics. In Mean Mistreater, Tracey's soft blues undertow makes a startling contrast to Spoon's raw blues story, and in Everyday Scott excels himself in a strange idiom for him, blowing with a full, chunky, quasi-Texas sound. His horn carps harshly on St. Louis Blues, letting rip on a brief, howling chorus and in I'm Gonna Move to the Outskirts of Town his gruff tone is perhaps remembering his own East London roots.

As the session winds up with Roll 'em Pete with Ronnie's saxophone charge, Tracey's romping piano and Spoon's raucous words, we also thank the conscientious work of Tomkins for his waxing of jazz history during an era of some of its most riveting and memorable sessions.

Niwel Tsumbo (Congo) – Milimo
(2025)

It's more than a little like first hearing the guitar of Django Reinhardt, or Lonnie Johnson, Wes Montgomery, John McLaughlin, Derek Bailey, Lionel Loueke or even Jini Hendrix: the guitar and its revolutionary sound. Now Congolese master Niwel Tsumbu certainly has it as he struts and frets his way through Milimo, his debut album, the title meaning, quite justifiably, 'good works'.

Niwel was born in Kinshasa in 1982. 'My Father was a mining engineer but was poisoned and passed away when I was three. I never got to know him. My Mother suffered from depression. She didn't work, but hustled hard to raise me with my four siblings. It was a very difficult childhood, to say the least. I never learned any other instrument before the guitar. As kids we always played hand drums, bells and shakers in church. I was attracted to a diverse range of sounds. I loved all traditional African music as well as Afro-pop, and I loved listening to the classics and movie music on the radio'

'I was self-taught for a year, then my mentor introduced me to jazz, as well as opening my mind to other music I wasn't familiar with. I had a tape of George Benson and Wes Montgomery which I listened to as I created my own path. I played a lot of their licks. I also loved Salif Keita, Lokua Kanza, Pepe Kale, Mory Kante, Youssef N'dour and Tshala Mwana, to name a few.'

So where did his own very singular technique and style come from? 'From the very beginning I was told my style was unique, but to me it's just like the sound of my voice. I don't know why it sounds the way it does. I'm constantly learning new things and am open to new ideas - even now, while I'm touring America. I've put in lots of time over the years to develop my technique and express the ideas in my mind as best I can.'

Why did he choose to emigrate to Ireland? 'I wanted to go to Paris, as most Congolese people do, but a friend who lived in Dublin said I should come there instead and check it out. It didn't take me long. I met my girlfriend there and now we have three kids. I soon met other musicians and quickly became a professional. There was already a Congolese community there and a band that played soukous and rhumba, so I started playing with them while I worked with a friend painting houses. I'd stop anybody carrying a musical instrument in the street. That's how I got involved with Irish musicians, and rather than jazz, I ended up playing in the traditional and contemporary Irish music scene, which was good because it made me develop my music in the way I play today.'

Milimo isn't a long album. Its 28 minutes are full of wondrous sounds and moments, sometimes flamenco-like, other times radiating a soulful lyricism in its improvisations and spontaneous melodies with the ghosts of African blues hovering within the notes. The traditional song Masta has Niwel's vocal accompaniment in its hurrying beauty, and at the outset of Gracias Paco he strikes his guitar like a drum.

'My music is always rooted in the music I grew up with, and I bring my personal experience into it. I really like the track L'Afrique Moderne. It came to me after listening to an old Congolese band called Choc Stars. Tears of Joy is my favourite track. The superb virtuosity brings a listener's response which is just that - its brilliance an alignment with pure happiness. Whereas, The Silence Within, that directly follows it, exudes a sense of reflective loneliness and exclusion. In the album's brevity there is a kaleidoscope of aural moods and patterns.

When I asked him who were the musicians who, over a century of jazz, he would have most liked to have played with, he surprised me with the extremities of his choice, 'Charlie Parker and Ella Fitzgerald!' he retorted. Perhaps you can find echoes of Bird's bebop surprises and Ella's melodism in his record, and much more too - almost an emancipation of multiple sounds released from the prisons of their genres and brought together in Niwel's strings.

And is he coming across the Irish Sea soon? 'We're working on something for the UK. It'll be announced soon. I can't wait to come and share my music with the people over there. I'm on tour in America now and feel very inspired. I'm planning to record again when I get home.'

Listen and look out for him and don't miss him when he comes. You won't have heard the guitar, from the very heart of Africa, played anything like it.

(Milimo is available on Diatribe Records)

McCoy Tyner (USA) – An orchestra of piano

The McCoy Tyner Trio, Jazz Café, Camden Town (2000)

Of all the great and gifted jazz pianists, there have perhaps been but three whose power over their instrument have made it sound like an orchestra in itself. One was the ivory powerhouse and nonpareil of the jazz keyboard, Art Tatum. Another was Erroll Garner, whose massive, many-textured notes sounded like six pianos being place simultaneously. The third, live in London at the Jazz Café this week, is the extraordinary McCoy Tyner. Tyner was, of course, the pianist of the epochal John Coltrane Quartet between 1960 and 1965. To have played and recorded five years with such a giant would have overwhelmed most pianists. But Tyner was never a mere accompanist or sideman. He was always an immense musical force in himself and added his own whole dimension to Coltrane's artistry.

Perhaps there was a sense of the inevitable that a boy growing up in Philadelphia with close musical neighbours of the likes of Bud and Richie Powell would play piano like the masters, but Tyner struck out on his own path with solo, trio, quartet and big band combinations while sucking in deep internationalist influences from Africa, the European classical tradition and Latin America. After the Coltrane years and 25 years with his own groups, his playing retains all its cumulative massiveness, while still expressing a delicacy, lyricism and freshness which finds its ideal setting in the trio context alongside his long-time bassist and drummer, Avery Sharpe and Aaron Scott - two hugely accomplished, mature and underestimated musicians to whom the heart of jazz belongs,

I found myself sitting on the edge of the Jazz Café stage, literally within a yard of Scott's bass drum, hi-hat and four large cymbals. He played, by turns, with a tempestuous power and with gentle yet supportive brushwork, but, through all his percussive fullness I could hear every lucid note of Tyner's piano, even as they fell in such complex and profusive clusters.

As the trio began with Mellow Minor and Tyner moved into sections of unaccompanied power, then fell back again into the union of the trio, you wondered how just three men could make such an awesomely beautiful sound of such proportions, as Tyner's climactical cascades of notes came down upon the listeners' ears like Niagaras.

As he moves through his 60s, he begins to sound as if Tatum is reborn within him, revisiting, yet bringing back with him Powell, Garner and the whole history of jazz on piano at the side of the free genius of Coltrane.

As I write this, the trio's astonishing versions of Will You Still Be Mine? and the St Louis Blues still ebb and flow in my head - Sharpe playing his bass like a drum with Africa burning in his fingers, Scott's huge range of drum and cymbal thunder beating and caressing through the brain. As for Tyner, you marvel that a piano can make so much sound and so much beauty too in one small and throbbing venue in Camden Town.

James Blood Ulmer (USA) - Brilliant blood brother of the blues

James Blood Ulmer Café Oto, London
(2017)

Sometimes the sound of James Blood Ulmer's slashing guitar is like a man at the crossroads playing a revelatory duet with himself. At others, his harmolodic blues are as if Leadbelly were playing In the Pines simultaneously with Ravi Shankar plucking a Mississippi raga. In this solo gig the 75-year-old from St Matthew's, South Carolina, reveals his extraordinarily eclectic jazz and blues range.

Ulmer grew up singing in his family gospel group but moved to New York as a young man to play with organists Larry Young and John Patton, then with Art Blakey and Joe Henderson. Crucially, he then joined forces with his hugest influence Ornette Coleman - the inventor of harmolodics - in 1972, before cutting a string of rampaging albums from Tales of Captain Black (1978) to his critical masterpiece Are You Glad To Be In America? in 1980.

Worried that his audience might not fathom his lyrics, he declares: 'Hey a minute, I'm in England. You understand what I'm saying?'

But the powerful message of his riotous notes is crystal clear. He sings BB King and Muddy Waters but when he declares: 'It's a damn shame, people calling each other names,' suddenly he is very much a contemporary blues commentator.

And when he sings the repetitive line: 'Devil, who do you think you are?' you see the young white man twisted in the ways of his KKK antecedents gunning down nine people in a Charleston church.

The blues speak of today through the truth of his implacable guitar.

Chucho Valdes (Cuba) - Comanche exile songs

Chucho Valdes and the Afro-Cuban Messengers – Chucho's Steps & Border-Free (2017)

Born in Quivican, Cuba, in 1941 and the son of celebrated pianist Bebe Valdes, Chucho began playing the home piano aged three and by the time he was a teenager he was leading his own band. In his twenties he formed the Orquesta Cubana de Musica Moderna and in 1973 he founded the most luminous of Cuban jazz groups, Irakere, while also building a formidable reputation as a solo artist. In the nineties he began to record for the classic US label Blue Note and the albums that emerged - like the solo session at the Village Vanguard (Live in New York) or the superbly innovative New Conceptions - showed his eclectic brilliance, fusing his Afro-Cuban roots with the traditions of hard bop, Coltrane, Miles Davis and Horace Silver.

Chucho's most recent band, the dynamic sextet the Afro-Cuban Messengers, has much of the elemental spirit of their rampant forebears, Art Blakey's Jazz Messengers, with a hugely Cuban verve and rhythmic pulse. Their 2010 album Chucho's Steps begins with a hard-struck, stomping passage from Valdes in the opener, Las dos Caras (Both Sides) before Reynaldo Melian Alvarez takes a fiery trumpet solo and Chucho bounds out of his keys and the percussive fury of Yaroldy Abreu Robles makes its testimony.

The rhythm of the authentic Danzon runs through the blood of the next track, with its repeated changes of pace and a balladic tenor saxophone message from the beautifully toned Carlos Miyares Hernandez. Zawinul's Mambo is a salute to the Austria-born pianist of Weather Report, with both Alvarez and Hernandez blowing songfully over the surging rhythm and Chucho leaping into a blustering solo. Bassist Rivero Alarcon marks out the path for Begin to Be Good, where the lyricism of Alvarez's horn tells its story with a powerful lucidity.

New Orleans is dedicated to the Marsalis family of the Crescent City, and is Chucho playing off the horn ensemble and rampaging down his keys, with a street parade simulation at the end. The echoes of West Africa pulsate through the Yoruba origins of Yansa with the added bata drums and Dreiser Durruthy Bombale's compelling vocals. Chucho's pounded piano is one more complex drum in a forest of sound.

Julian is back to the sextet and expressively wrought solos all round and Chucho's hands hitting his keys with even greater weight. The closer is a loving nod to Coltrane, whose Giant Steps has been transmuted to Chucho's Steps. Hernandez is within 'Trane's spirit and Alvarez's trumpet sings out its joyous Cuban message before Chucho's choruses put him abreast of the master.

His 2013 album Border-Free has a photo of Chucho with a full Comanche head-dress on its sleeve, and its title track Afro-Comanche holds the narrative of the rebellious Comanche native Americans who were deported to the eastern side of Cuba during the 19th century, where they lived and founded families with Cubans, creating an Afro-Comanche heritage. Cuban griot Chucho and his drum-piano tell their story of a wearisome journey to a faraway island of exile, servitude and release, and Angel Gaston Joya Perellada's pungent bass tells of more insurgent history.

Border-Free is an album of eloquent tributes, to his father (Bebo), his mother (Pilar), his grandmother (Caridad Amaro) and the beloved Cuban composer Margarita Lecuona (Tabu). On three tracks Chucho is joined by tenor saxophonist Branford Marsalis, and their union reaches a particular splendour on the closing track (Abdel), dedicated to a prominent Moroccan musician and seething with the triangular musical life-force of Africa, Cuba and New Orleans. The colloquy of drums, Perellada's plunging beat, the heat of Chucho's pianism and the final uplift of Marsalis's soprano saxophone coda burn your ears and melt into your consciousness.

(Chucho's Steps & Border-Free are available on World Village)

Kid Thomas Valentine (USA) - I loves to play for dancing

Kid Thomas Valentine - Sonnets from Algiers & The Dance Hall Years (2017)

I remember him at Oxford Street's 100 Club in the summer of 1973, a small and wiry man of nearly 80, standing on a table and blasting out his trumpet with an astonishing power and verve in front of a band of British New Orleans jazz musicians who played behind him, nonplussed and amazed - like all of us there were - that such an aged man could blow with such frenzy. This was Kid Thomas Valentine, born in 1896 in Reserve, Louisiana, a small town across the Mississippi River from New Orleans.

He started performing in 1915 and by 1926 he was leading his own band, as he would do for the rest of his musical life. With the New Orleans 'revival' of the 1940s, he achieved a second recognition, with the opening of more tourist-orientated venues like Preservation Hall in the Crescent City and the creation of new recording labels, and he toured and performed until his death in 1987. The American Music recordings of the early '60s are powerful evidence of Valentine at his most strident and pugnacious. As lead horn, he attacked his tunes with uncompromising assurance, and his confreres took fierce inspiration from his vanguard sound.

This is particularly true on the album Sonnets from Algiers where he is at the centre of a four-horn front line, with trombonist Louis Nelson, Paul Barnes on clarinet and tenor saxophonist Emanuel Paul, veteran of the Eureka Brass Band. Joe James is the pianist, Sammy Penn the drummer with 'Creole' George Guesnon, one of New Orleans' most renowned banjoists. The band play a succession of Storyville classics, starting with Put on Your Old Grey

Bonnet, in which the beautiful reed lyricism of Barnes and Paul's velvet tenor contrast starkly with the searing edge of Valentine's lead.

Nelson begins the chorus of the parade hymn Just a Closer Walk with Thee, and Barnes's soft-edged clarinet seems to be pleading, before Valentine's searing vibrato takes the band home. A very relaxed Milneberg Joys looks to be sauntering along before it suddenly changes to the chorus of Dippermouth with Valentine's reprise of King Oliver's famous solo. Nelson's slides break free over Penn's clicking beat before Barnes's delicacy of sound on In the Shade of the Old Apple tree and Guesnon plays a purring banjo solo in I Can't Escape from You. The session starts to really move from S'il Vous Plait with Paul's rocking solo, and on the spiritual Sing On, all members radiate a sense of joy and pride of sound when tenor and clarinet palaver in a dancing duet, the soul of New Orleans becomes truly manifest.

Nelson's trombone tells the story of When You And I Were Young, Maggie with Paul's beautifully lucid tenor, Valentine's horn cuts through Dinah and Barnes brings the album's finale with his rendition the test-piece clarinet solo on High Society, played with a sublime softness as a serenade to Paul's tenor.

In March 1964, two slightly different bands assembled across the river at Kohlman's Tavern in Algiers to cut another album, The Dance Hall Years. New Orleans jazz was made for dancing and Valentine was sure of it: 'I loves to play for dancing,' he declared. 'It puts good in you and you feel better.' And he goes off roundly with Anytime, this time with alto saxophonist Ruben Roddy, who plays a fine solo on Bb Blues followed by a jumping piano chorus from Joe James. Valentine is on the edge all the way, as if a cracked tooth could strike your ear-buds.

For the second session, it is back with Nelson, Paul and Penn, plus pianist 'Sing' Miller and bassist Joseph Butler. On the Bayou swings melodiously, its familiar theme echoing across the dance floor, prefacing Big Bill Broonzy's In the Evening, which gives Miller an appealing horn. Paul exchanges tenor for clarinet all through The Bells of St Mary, and plays it with an effusive, almost sacred, beauty - very different from the good-times song Blueberry Hill which gives Nelson's slides an outing, and choric interlude for Paul, now back on tenor.

The bassman takes his opportunity on Joe Butler's Blues, as do all three horns, and the band leaves us playing Je Vous Aime as if it were the most natural sound in the world - as it was, of course, signalled always by Valentine's terse and laconic trumpet.

(Sonnets from Algiers & The Dance Hall Years are available on American Music)

David S Ware (USA) - An astonishing creative power

David S Ware Quartet - Corridors and Parallels, David S Ware - Saturnian & Onecept
(2016)

When the great tenor saxophonist David S Ware died in late 2012, his longtime bass partner William Parker said of him that 'he was someone who can play music that will cause human revolution through means of the soul and the spirit.' Ware was born in Plainfield, New Jersey, in 1949 and began playing saxophone when he was nine, and during his mid-teens met and was mentored by Sonny Rollins, the powerhouse tenorist of the previous generation.

He played with groups led by pianist Cecil Taylor and drummers Andrew Cyrille, Milford Graves and Beaver Harris before recording a series of mighty albums for the Japanese DIW label, including Flight of I (1992), Third Ear Recitation (1993) and Earthquation (1994). Afflicted by kidney disease throughout the last decade of his life, he began dialysis in 1999 and received a kidney transplant in 2009. Despite this he continued to blow and create with astonishing creative power, as these four albums evince.

Corridors and Parallels was recorded in 2001, with Ware in a quartet setting including the omnipresent Parker, Matthew Shipp playing organ and synthesiser and drummer Guillermo E Brown. Both Parker and Shipp played on Ware's DIW masterpieces, but here Shipp, always super-subtle and unexpected, creates entirely different timbres. On Straight Track he innovates on a chirping organ behind Ware's tongue-induced sounds while on Jazz Fi-sci his notes are like droplets of falling water. Parker, as always, keeps the ever-changing heartbeat.

Brown stokes up a Latin groove on Superimposed and Ware, breathlessly with vaunting breath, begins an endless sonic search. During the album's title tune his tone becomes gruffer, more acerbic, contrasting with Parker's humming bow strokes, and through Spaces Embraces, with Shipp's shimmering synthesiser, he enters depths of tenderness. But the album's climax is the salutation and elegy within Mother May You Rest in Bliss, where his saxophone speaks and sings out a love as supreme as that of his great horn forebear, Coltrane.

The albums Saturnian and Organica are both recordings of solo concerts, the former in October 2009 in New York City, with Ware playing a track each on saxello, stritch and tenor saxophone, and the latter a concert at Park Slope in Brooklyn in 2010 and another in the same year at the Umbrella Music Festival in Chicago. In the brief note to Saturnian, Ware declares: 'There's a voice inside each saxophone, expressing different orders of Being. When you listen, learn to open your third ear. Listen for the voice inside the music. It will expand who you think you are.' The saxello performance is Methone and the horn's sharpness creates a strangely beautiful angularity of pitch. It is followed by solo stritch on Pallene, which Ware blows in boppish staccato phrases that revive memories of the great stritch pioneer Roland Rahsaan Kirk. Third up is Ware on tenor and Anthe, with more kinship with Coltrane and an abiding spirituality which permeates every note.

Lucky those listeners sitting on Park Slope who heard both Ware's sopranino rhapsody Minus Gravity 1 and the tenor artistry of Organica 1. For Ware, a solo performance is never an act of aloneness. He brings with him ancestors and others who came before, and here, as in the Chicago set, you hear saxophonists from Coleman Hawkins to the contenders of 2012, as well as those he thanks, all who have given their donations from a few cents to a life-saving kidney, to help his recovery.

By 2010 Ware was celebrating 50 years of playing the saxophone and he was determined to mark this with 'a special recording project.' His kidney transplant the year before made the project even more propitious. The result was the summative trio album Onecept, with Parker again and the veteran free drummer Warren Smith.

Ware begins with his astonishing thunder cracking on Book of Krittika. Smith beats tympani and Parker's bow is everywhere. In his sleeve notes Ware writes: 'The intent of the music is for people to listen to what it is I do - and to make them think.' A surprising statement for such a profoundly spiritual player perhaps, but as he stormed through Wheel of Life on his tenor, I thought more than momentarily of Lear on the heath and his own 'wheel of fire.'

But that is what great music like that of Ware makes you do - cross boundaries, categories, genres and forms to find that unity and 'onecept.'

(Corridors and Parallels, Saturnian & Onecept are available on AUM)

Ray Warleigh (Australia) - Rue Victor Masse
(2025)

The brilliant alto saxophonist and flautist Ray Warleigh (1938 - 2015), born in Sydney and an arrivant in London in 1960, spent much of his musical life making a living in manifold studios as a lauded session musician, alongside stars of pop like Dusty Springfield, Marianne Faithfull, Stevie Wonder and Scott Walker. Simultaneously, in another musical life, he was exploring incandescent blues, melodies and free improvising sounds with, amongst many others, Alexis Korner, Georgie Fame, Ronnie Scott, Humphrey Lyttelton and John Stevens. The last time I heard him he was playing alongside Evan Parker in one of Kenny Wheeler's last concerts on the South Bank.

As Wheeler had come from Toronto, Canada to find an incomparable destiny in London's multifarious jazz scene, so Warleigh had come from even farther afield. Like Wheeler he was a modest and self-effacing perfectionist. 'The reason I've made so few recordings is that I've always thought what I'd done wasn't good enough. I've made a couple of albums and found myself thinking: I can do so much better.'

The venue for Warleigh's rare and beautiful 2009 duo album with the luminous drummer Tony Marsh wasn't a plush studio with all the attributes, but Marsh's girlfriend's Paris flat in Rue Victor Masse. Both musicians play with an undiminished spontaneity, and the intimacy of the recording only amplifies their cooperative musicianship. In the floating, buoyant drift of Warleigh's flute, you can almost sense the music flying through the apartment windows and winging over the Paris skies, and it is only the solidity of Lancaster boy Marsh's grounding drums that pulls the music back to the single stereo microphone. Thank Warleigh's own basic recording acumen that the album even exists, for it is a jewel of jazz duo artistry.

For a nonpareil of improvisation, Warleigh loved and was a prime player of melody, as was his partner. Evan Parker admired Marsh's melodic percussionism, and that too came powerfully to the fore that day in Rue Victor Masse. The two melodists play only one composed tune - the Cahn and Style songbook theme of I Fall in Love too Easily - but instantaneous melodies constantly spin off the duo's improvised sequences, as in the reflectively serene track Inner Ray, and Warleigh's own commentary on his improvising seem to express this musical truth: 'What I play is absolutely unpremeditated. There are no soundscapes or pictures in my head. But I like melody very much, and I've thought about it a lot.'

Perhaps the final flute track, Standards and Blues, depicts the roots of Warleigh's creative power. A London apprenticeship in the blues, and a studio career backing vocalists singing standards and pop gave him a broad musical foundation which he turned to an uncommon artistry. More than an ocean separates the two marine cities of Sydney and New Orleans, yet Warleigh's musical soul flows out from the soundscape of both, and through the Thames and Seine too.

(Rue Victor Masse is available on psi records)

Bobby Watson (USA) - Hard act to follow

Blakey's protégé emulates his master's genius in more ways than one

Bobby Watson - From the Heart

(2009)

I have to admit that of all the alto saxophonists I have ever heard live, along with the great Johnny Hodges, Bobby Watson, who was born in Lawrence, Kansas in 1953, edges it for me. In 1977, Art Blakey, ever a superb judge of young talent, brought the young graduate in music from the University of Miami into the Jazz Messengers as a virtual unknown. Watson spent five years with Blakey, eventually becoming the band's musical director, before he left to form his own band, Horizon.

A reedman of outstanding versatility, he has played everything from hard bop to free jazz. These include a marvellous tribute album to Ellington's nonpareil alto saxophonist Johnny Hodges (The Year of the Rabbit, 1980) a solo alto album (This Little Light of Mine, 1991) and a quartet album of high artistry and beauty which contains the memorable tribute to the imprisoned Mandela, Love Remains (1986) with pianist John Hicks, drummer Marvin Smith and his long-time Miami confrere bassist Curtis Lundy.

His new album, From the Heart, features his Live and Learn band, a sextet with Lundy's bass at its rhythmic centre, Harold O'Neal on piano, trumpeter Leron Thomas, Warren Wolf on vibes and drummer Quincy Davis. Watson, now almost a veteran, plays with his customary technical brilliance and emotional release, drawing some inspired improvisation from his bandmates.

Take the opener Wilkes BBQ, where the ensemble near the end takes fire from the horns and Wolf 's stirring vibes after Thomas's burnished notes have empowered the sound with their purity and ringing tone. Purple Flowers shows Watson at his most rhapsodic and Hodges-like. He alternately embeds himself within and skims the melody, achieving a singing, winsome tone before Thomas enters with another pellucid chorus. All the while, O'Neal's sprinkling notes splash the theme forwards.

The sassy Deep Pockets has Thomas bending his notes assuredly and Wolf spurting fire before Watson soars away like a migrating bird, his notes proclaiming the trajectory of his travels. Climbing the Stairs suggests an aged ascent, with Lundy's twanging solo offering sonic images of experience and longevity.

Whether Watson, ever a musician's musician, is delivering a tribute to another, the late vibist Milt Jackson, in For Milt is not explicit, but the altoist provides an elegiac and spacious melody with Wolf 's vibes entering on the bridge and then following with a blues-laden solo worthy of the master.

There's a more fluent Wolf on Peace, Love and Carrots, while O'Neal takes a stomping chorus and Lundy adds his eternal rhythmic lift. Thomas's horn has a fanfarish timbre during his solo on Del Corazon, a Latin- tinged version of the title tune.

Timeless releases Watson for a hovering chorus and the outstanding Wolf adds a surprising and stuttering vibrato to his notes. From the Heart is played pacily and first Watson, then O'Neal responds to the buoyant and airy foundation of Davis and Lundy.

With Davis's compelling drumming sounding right through the band in the final track Marcus Vein, the listener begins to reflect on how Watson has emulated his old thunderous leader in assembling a notable team of young confreres, inspiring them with an emboldening confidence and setting them free to express the sheer quality of their musicianship. That is what Blakey did for more than three decades as mobiliser and inspiration of the Jazz Messengers.

Watson is continuing that same achievement, and in doing so, further expressing his own brilliance.

(From the Heart is available on Palmetto)

Trevor Watts (England) - Old and new combine in celebrations of infinite variety

(2019)

From the very first minutes of this year's London Jazz Festival, it was the jazz elders who were celebrated. Yorkshire's 80-year-old saxophonist Trevor Watts introduced his quartet's opener at the South Bank's Purcell Room by dedicating it to 'all the musicians who have left us, who never got the chance to play here.'

Perhaps he was remembering his brilliant free-playing confreres of the past like trombonist Paul Rutherford or drummer John Stevens. But their spirits were hovering all around his seething soprano saxophone, Veryan Weston's chiming piano, Mark Sanders's ricocheting drums and John Edwards's diving, echoing bass. It was a powerfully moving and inventive challenge to all who were to follow in the ensuing 10 days.

Three of these were Joe Lovano's Trio Tapestry at Queen Elizabeth Hall - saxophonist Lovano, pianist Marilyn Crispell and drummer Carmen Castaldi - created a jazz garment of darkly subjective texture, with Lovano's beautiful tone and the complex figures of Crispell's keys weaving sounds and dreams together.

At Omnibus Theatre, the anguished joy of Albanian vocalist Elina Duni and Rob Luft's lucid electric guitar, sounding sometimes like an orchestra in one instrument, created Kosovan and Dalmatian heart songs of migrant sorrow and joy, while in the grandiose lobby of Cadogan Hall drummer Clark Tracey's band of brilliant young contenders with trombonist Daniel Higham and altoist Mark Payne, played Ellingtonian standards like Take the 'A' Train as if born to it.

In Wigmore Hall, the Liberetto Quartet of bassist Lars Danielsson, drummer Marcus Ostrom, guitarist John Parricelli and pianist Gregory Privat, played a version of jazz chamber music where passion broke through, especially in Privat's scintillating keyboard runs and Ostrom's furious brushwork.

At the Art Blakey celebration in Cadogan Hall saxophonist Jean Toussaint and his band led off the tribute, with trumpeter Byron Wallen's pellucid solo embellishing his tune The Gatekeeper and trombonist Dennis Rollins providing rumbustious choruses on Major Changes. Toussaint's own serenely modulated tone sang through bassist Daniel Casimir's melody The Missing of Sleep.

There was Blakey-like thunderous drumming of Ralph Petersen in the Messenger Legacy concert that followed. As soon as the US band of ex-Jazz Messengers roared into Tell it Like it Is and the notes came surging out of Bill Pierce's tenor saxophone, Brian Lynch's blistering trumpet or Robin Eubanks's creamy trombone in Lover Come Back, you knew time was reversing to a place where the groove was all.

At Café Oto, two powerful jazzwomen, alto saxophonist Matana Roberts and bassist Joelle Leandre, were a sisterly duo of improvisation of improvisation. Leandre's scything bow sawed through her wordless vocals, while a musical belligerence attacked her notes and Roberts, like a griot of old, blew and sang her sound-stories above her partner's groaning, subterranean bow-sound.

A festival of infinite varieties indeed.

Trevor Watts And The Eternal Triangle at Café Oto

(2025)

Trevor Watts and all of his 86 years was at it again last night at Dalston's Café Oto. With his alto and soprano saxes, compadres Veryan Weston with his Nord Keyboard and Jamie Harris with four conga drums and crashing cymbals, The Eternal Triangle performed a succession of Watts compositions, all powerfully rhythmic and full of melodic fire to a transported audience with the keenest listening ears.

Yorkshireman Watts is a pioneer of free improvisation, one of the founders of the Spontaneous Music Ensemble of the1960s, but is also the sharpest and most sinewy of tunesmiths. How this trio rocked and swung through Watts' often quite brief compositions, fired up by his internalised love of African rhythms and artistry.

Harris is a hand-drummer whose Afro-Cuban mastery is astonishing, while Weston explained to me why he chooses to play the Nord. 'It has three zones, which means I can divide the keyboard up into a bass area, a more melodic piano area and an ensemble-sounding chordal area. Each has the potential to be layered with combinations of sounds, giving many possibilities to shape the texture and colour of each zone.'

As for Watts, his ageless sound is a sheer validation of breath itself, as such an affirmation of life everywhere. For starting in Halifax, he has played across the world, always inspired by the West African drummers who were such consummate rhythm-makers in his longtime band Moire Music, and as he makes his miracle ascents and plummeting cadences, his notes falling from his horns and cutting off the moment they are created, so that the next note and the next and the next are always discoveries, piercing high notes, importunate birdsong of Pennine sound.

In tunes like Gravity, Organics, Afroism, or Timbala, Weston's stomping keys and Harris' pounding drums find rhythmic and melodic flesh and unity with Watts' quicksilver fingers as they dance blurringly up and down his horns.

But not always joyous. For me his most moving piece was his Ballad for Lost Friends, which Harris introduced as 'a ballad, but it may not be a ballad'. It was an elegy, with his confreres' rhythmic undertow and Watts exerting tremendous Bechet-like power, as if it expressed the beauty and solace of many lives in music, a cosmos of lives that play on in the muscles of his marvellous notes, here in the very global heart of London.

Bobby Wellins (Scotland) and Adrian Kendon (England) – Scottish rebel sounds

Bassist Adrian Kendon on Bobby Wellins's epic Culloden Suite (2024)

50 years ago I was living in Blackwall, east London and teaching in the local comprehensive school. Our street was a part of the Aberfeldy Estate, where all the streets and council blocks had Scottish names: Oban, Portree, Nairn, Currie. The local pub was the Aberfeldy and the primary school down the road was named... Culloden. I remember thinking then, how could such a cursed name, signifying such atrocious English royalist slaughter and no-quarter-given bloodshed of April 1746, ordered directly by the King's son, the Duke of Cumberland, be attached to a school?

Strange how now, in 2024, such ancestral voices call out from the heartsblood of the tenor saxophone sound of the late Glaswegian, Bobby Wellins (1936-2016) from his Culloden Moor Suite, first recorded in 1979, duetting with the Portsmouth-born, insurgent soprano saxophonist Lol Coxhill (1932-2012), accompanied by the blind Newcastle pianist Pete Jacobsen (1950-2002), bassist Adrian Kendon, Spike Wells on drumset, and Bryan Spring on military percussion.

Wellins's haunting introduction begins Gathering, the First Movement, while Jacobsen's rolling keys move into March, with the Wellins and Coxhill horns palavering. The Battle interactions are expressed starkly, with Spring's martial snares and Kendon's bass ascending and descending menacingly. The final episode, Aftermath, is solemn, almost hymnal, as Jacobsen's ice-cold notes accompany the horns locked in mourning for the slain, and Wellins's final coda holds fast in listeners' memories.

I asked Kendon, now 81, how he first came to play with Wellins. The son of a poet and a Froebel schoolteacher, he had begun on tea chest bass in skiffle days and trumpet. He went to university in Brighton, where he became involved in the jazz scene and established a club where Spike Wells would often play. He heard that Wellins was living nearby in Bognor Regis, recovering from drug addiction and working in a refrigerator factory.

'When Bobby came to play with us it was soon obvious he was in a different league,' he told me. 'One day I called Spike and told him that Bobby would guest with us, bringing with him a pianist, Pete Jacobsen. So that was how our quartet came together.'

'Our first album was cut by a friend who operated a recording machine; the second was made in a studio in Eltham. The Culloden Moor Suite was introduced to us by Bobby as a project for an Arts Council tour, with Bobby proposing that we create a sextet with the addition of Lol Coxhill on soprano sax and Bryan Spring on Scottish snare drum which he was very skilled at playing - and also the madingum, a west African hand drum. Bobby told us about the battle and later I went to visit the site when I went on holiday to Scotland. He made us aware of the brutal nature of English colonialism, which he was also trying to tell us through the suite.'

'Its central part was Pete's improvised piano solo segment. Being blind from birth he was extremely sensitive to sound. I remember a gig in Basildon where there was a fruit machine at the back of the hall and somebody started playing it while we were playing. Pete immediately incorporated its sounds into his solo, much to our amusement.'

What about the two drummers? 'Bryan was extremely talented, a fairly eccentric individual who practised his snares insistently with a pair of sticks, on his knees or on a table. Spike is a wonderful and thoroughly musical drummer with a prime sense of time, always listening to his fellow musicians, providing the complementary conversational response to what everyone in the band is doing. I've never heard or played with a better drummer.'

The Homage to Caledonia album, although centred around the Culloden suite, begins and ends with other powerful tracks, with the reed partnership of Bobby and the maverick Lol, playing with real comradeship and aplomb.

Right after the suite and changing the mood completely is Dizzy's Blues, full of the saxophone pair's exultation of improvised sound and scintillating duetting. It is a finale of joyous relief for all members. The album is a brilliant 'find' by Jazz in Britain and a prime example of how jazz can be the chronicler of sustained and truly eloquent history.

(Homage to Caledonia is available on Jazz in Britain Records)

Best of 2020 jazz albums
Lafayette Gilchrist - Now
Mikkel Ploug – Balcony Lullabies
Kate Westbrook – Earth felt the Wound
(2020)

Three albums of 2020 are not only powerful jazz artefacts that challenge and break through many musical norms and genres but are also resonating commentaries on today - the year's key moments expressed in raw and beautifully inventive sounds.

Pianist Lafayette Gilchrist is from Baltimore, a city steeped in resistance to racism, and that experience is starkly intoned on his trio's double album Now in such tracks as the rampaging Assume the Position.

"When you come to Baltimore," he says, "you need to show some respect for the struggle within the town and how strong the people are on the ground here."

Gilchrist's pianism is a compendium of jazz history and you can hear Jelly Roll Morton's New Orleans Joys in his notes, along with James P Johnson's New York stride and echoes of Thelonious Monk, Bud Powell and Cecil Taylor.

An Everyman of jazz piano, driven on by his trio confreres, drummer Eric Kennedy and bassist Herman Burnie, there's a lyrical beauty to many of his tunes.

Love ballads such as Say a Prayer for Our Love or Newly Arrived show the indivisibility of love and struggle, evincing again how Gilchrist is a pianist for all seasons.

(Now is available on Lafayette Music)

A very different record is Balcony Lullabies by Danish guitarist Mikkel Ploug.

During the months of lockdown, he has played solo guitar on his apartment balcony every evening for his Copenhagen neighbours. "Maybe I was trying to send a message to the world," he says.

Amid the succession of melodic Danish folk tunes and ballads are also You Are My Sunshine, Over the Rainbow and the deeply affecting John Lennon tune Julia, dedicated to his mother.

(Balcony Lullabies is available on Stunt Records)

Kate Westbrook's album with her Granite Band turns to Milton's epic Paradise Lost for her title, Earth felt the Wound, and never has she sung with such protean power.

Lyricism, blues, prophecy, exhortation, admonition and menace are all in her octogenarian voice, as if life's fullness and forebodings pour out of her words. In Storm Petrel she envisages a catastrophe of a deluged world: "Do you hear the drowned band/Playing in deep water street?" she sings, alongside Billie Bottle's bass like a flat stone skimming across an ever-rising seascape.

She leaves the warnings of Weltende Begins to Roz Harding's eloquently free saxophone or the ominous pathos of husband Mike's piano intro to Once Upon a Time.

Her voice, in unison with Matthew North's guitar, "wise up" blues in Bathing Belles and Fiscal Analysts and on Irving Berlin's Let's Face the Music and Dance, embellished by Coach York's buoyant drums, captivates. And she has her moment of augury with: "Before they ask us to pay the bill and while we still have the chance."

Cabaret and truth have rarely found such an amalgam.

(Earth felt the Wound is available on Westbrook Records)

Mike Westbrook (England) - A tasty spice of life

The Mike Westbrook Band - Fine 'n Yellow (2012)

The many diverse tones of humanity in Kate Westbrook's powerfully livid voice, the complex multilayered dimensions of the expressively ambivalent saxophones of Chris Biscoe and Pete Whyman and the throbbing heartbeat of Steve Berry's bass with Jon Hiseman's pulsating drums are long and often-heard companions of Mike Westbrook and his ever-inventive keys.

They sound again all through Fine 'n Yellow, where Kate's lyrics become the true provocateurs of Mike's notes and arrangements. 'I will write love as a girdle round the globe,' wrote Kate in My Lover's Coat, as one group of a group of songs without music she composed for and dedicated to John and Margery Styles, two late friends who founded the Smith's Academy Informer, a newsletter committed to the Westbrooks' music. Mike took Kate's words as his musical starting point and allowed 'the shape of the texts to determine the musical form rather than coercing the words into existing structures,' a sequence he wrote that he found 'liberating.'

The result is a beautifully honed musical essay which creates a living harmony with the words, most of which speak of love , friendship and union - as Kate sings in What I Like. 'Bless us with friendship/ Bringing hearts ease/Warmth and kindness/The gift to please.' And the music brings the same sensations, played by six veteran jazz troubadours.

The tension is raised by 34 seconds of Kate singing Billie Holiday's Fine And Mellow and as she passes into Yellow Dog, she tells the harrowing story of Margery's father, who died as a prisoner of war in 1942, working on the Burma railway, as the sun 'Burns the ground, burns the gully dry/Burns my burgeoning surprise/Burns my weeping eyes.' Berry's booming bass beneath Hiseman's skittering cymbals preface Kate's words of lives blasted by fascism and war and Biscoe's withering moving alto solo, his pealing notes that follow Kate's lines. 'No-one will whisper Blaydon Races' for this Geordie lad, all prefacing his mournful yet life-lived coda on Dollarbird.

My Lover's Coat tells of Margery wearing John's jacket after he died 'On all the great land masses and/Over all the mighty oceans.' Berry's sound is huge again - as huge as love itself and the word Margery speaks with the blackbird in her hedge: 'Did you read what I wrote my love, love, love? Did you spell out love?'

The passage of time and life itself is the theme of Yellow Fig Leaf as Kate reflects on the last autumnal leaf hanging in the Westbrooks' Devon yard. 'Yellow gold, it seems lit from within' and it breathes her friend's name. Berry's bass and Hiseman's drums dance inside Kate's beautifully sung words. Biscoe's soprano horn and Whyman's bass clarinet find unity and harmony within the promises of 'fleshly green buds' given new life.

A rare piano feature from Westbrook himself is the body and soul of Through The Dark, each note dropping on the ears like water, yet full of depth and experience of a jazz lifetime. It precedes the Creole echoes of Whyman's pure clarinet on Yellow Tracery which takes jazz back to its Crescent City beginnings before it swings onwards to My Lover's Heart, where Kate digs low in her notes as she 'writes 'love' as a star burst through the dark' and her own dark timbre contrasts so starkly with the startling clarity of Whyman's revelatory clarinet. The track vibrates with subterranean fire as Berry's everlasting bass beats its enormous sound.

The final song What I Like is a praise song to pleasure and to all its humane dimensions, to 'desires, humour and grace' to love and wisdom all in harmony. 'Bless us with song', sings Kate with the saxophones of Whyman and Briscoe whirling around her in 'a yellow room of life's enjoyment.'

She invokes 'comedy, tragedy, anything absurd,' a world and its achievements to learn and to savour, sung and played with verve and a storm of creativity and energy by six life-filled musicians.

This is an album that makes you proud of life, pleased to be human, played by jazz musicians whose endless music has made them into griots of sound, melody and improvisation.

And a word for the Westbrooks, in particular for Kate's lucidity of voice and message, always wrapped in reality, always positive and Mike taking his cues from her words, making notes of meaning, warning and celebration and so often reaching and staying with beauty.

One day this country will realise their greatness.

(Fine 'n Yellow is available on Gonzo)

Mike Westbrook (England) - Great last night at the old place

The Mike Westbrook Concert Band – The last Night at the Old Place (2021)

It was a prime expression of jazz musicians' generosity on the 1968 London scene that, when Ronnie Scott moved to new premises in Frith Street, Soho, from the 'old place' in Gerrard Street, he encouraged new bands to use it, responding to the upsurge of brilliant young musicians making their mark on the new music and the genius of the Blue Note exiles from South Africa, shortly to form the Brotherhood of Breath.

Many of this powerful musical generation found their way into the Mike Westbrook band, giving precious opportunity for young virtuosi like saxophonists Mike Osborne, John Surman and George Khan, trombonists Paul Rutherford and Malcolm Griffiths, trumpeter Dave Holdsworth, South African bassist Harry Miller and drummer Alan Jackson.

For Westwood, it was an 'almost unlimited opportunity to experiment and to push boundaries and gave us the chance to find our individual voices.

We were fully aware of American jazz but no longer in thrall to it. As a composer, having a ready platform to present new work and an influx of marvellous musicians to play it, was a great opportunity.'

This record documents the last-ever music heard at Ronnie's Scott's 'old place' and opening track The Few is an outing for Surman's rumbling and dancing baritone saxophone, with Jackson's flashing cymbals crashing beside him. The freedom mode of the music, its repeated riffs and percussive joy expresses the South African impact of the Blue Notes and the heartfelt unity that they created.

There are no intervals between the tracks and the sounds segue into the wonderful solo alto saxophone of Osborne and his gradual steps into Lover Man, with Miller's plangent bass accompanying Osborne's sweeping horn as he moves into the melodic phrases inside and outside of For Ever and a Day.

In We Salute You, the pealing trumpet is played by Dave Holdsworth, so often Osborne's horn partner, while Khan comes belching in with a growling and sustained tenor saxophone blast. Folk Song is an anthem for the peerless free trombonist Paul Rutherford, a multisonic magician combining lifelong revolutionary politics with music. His twisting, ever-inventive sonic gait, his uniquely perplexing slide technique and his ability to mesh with all who played with him - here, mainly Jackson and Miller - are all in joyous evidence.

Lionel Hampton's swing classic Flying Home has Surman's gushing baritone pushed on by Jackson's drums and the opening clamour is carried on by Griffiths's rumbustious slides, blowing like a tailgate horn man on the back of a cart in New Orleans, until Khan comes blasting in. Hampton would never have known the like.

There are some precious Westbrook solo piano doodles on Sugar before the full ensemble enters, then it is a delving Miller introducing Who's Who and Surman's gurgling baritone, with Khan's rasping, belligerent tenor in the full glory of a succession of epochal horns. Osborne comes forward again, this time rising above the riffing ensemble, pouring out his notes as if they were sonic wine throughout Can't Get it Out of My Mind amid the excitation of Jackson's drums.

This is indeed a precious record, pitched absolutely within its own 1968 times, yet creating universal sounds that rise right out of their era to reach us now, particularly in the everlasting instrumental song of those musical geniuses that have since left us like Osborne, Miller and Rutherford. Long live their artistry.

(The last Night at the Old Place is available on Cadillac Records)

Mike Westbrook (England) - Blakean bliss

Mike Westbrook - Glad Day Live: The Poetry of William Blake (2017)

Emerge from Toynbee Hall on Commercial Street, London E1, the venue where the works of this album were performed and recorded, and you walk into the streets of William Blake's real life and imagination. You see, feel and hear the same places that Blake knew, loved, hated and dreamed of being transformed into an earthly paradise and revolutionary Jerusalem.

It is still Blake's city, cut through by the streets where he listened to every sound: 'In every cry of every man / In every infant's cry of fear, / In every voice in every ban / The mind-forg'd manacles I hear.'

Mike Westbrook's notes in this live version of his homage to Blake, Glad Day (first waxed in 1997 with a seven-piece brass band and singers Kate Westbrook and Phil Minton) hold Blake's insurgent spirit, his love for humanity and his understanding of its oppression, and with his tunes and musical brain, Westbrook brings Blake's words into union with the life-force of the blues.

For if Blake had been born in the US South he would have hollered the blues and breathed the breath of jazz. Read Holy Thursday again, know the injustice that it describes and feel its truth: 'Is that trembling cry a song? / Can it be a song of joy? / And so many children poor? / It is a land of poverty!' Or in the Con-Dem land in which we live: 'Is this a holy thing to see / In a rich and fruitful land, / Babes reduced to misery / Fed with a cold and usurous hand?'

Blake in a land of Wonga and X-Factor, where the gulf between rich and poor widens every day, where learning about the world is not circumscribed by curiosity, compassion and a human urge for betterment, but by school and examination league tables and the worst culture of obedience and copy-catting. Adrian Mitchell wrote of Blake that he was 'unfashionable but politically dangerous. Frankly opposed to all kings, warriors and priests, he was tried for sedition in 1804 and was lucky to escape with his life.'

For this performance Minton and Kate are with Westbrook and his piano, Karen Street plays accordion, Billy Thompson violin and Steve Berry bass with the London College of Music Choir, conducted by Paul Ayres. The arrangements are by Mitchell and Kate.

On London Song the humming choir and Westbrook's almost doodling piano subside to a haunting duet between Street and Berry, all a prelude to Kate's icily lucid vocal truly running 'in blood down the palace walls.' Thompson's violin cries out in outrageous beauty as Minton sings of the freed slave, 'his chains are loose, his dungeon doors are open... for empire is no more.'

Kate and Minton's voices turn to tenderness and Street's accordion sways through Lullaby. Pain and empathy rise through Westbrook's solo piano through the long introduction to Holy Thursday before Kate's vocal of cool anger and Street's singing and airy keys take us directly into Blake's world of 2014.

Blake's contrasts are harmonised in The Tyger and the Lamb firstly by Berry's pulsating, delving bass and then by a host of women's voices and the power of Street's astonishing accordion. She is there too at the outset of A Poison Tree, spectral, menacing and full of portent before Kate's own ominous vocal and Thompson's grim, dancing solo.

The blues are in Whitechapel and all through Long John Brown and Little Mary Bell. Minton's growling voice and Westbrook's aching piano tell the story of the Devil's spoliation of love before Thompson's bow adds its shimmering tailpiece.

Berry's long, thudding then mercurial solo and Thompson's wailing violin introduce the key opening lines of The Human Abstract: 'Pity would be no more / If we did not make somebody poor,' then straight on to The Fields and Blake's clearest vision of a socialist Jerusalem in the very heart of London's rare green spaces: 'Mutual shall build Jerusalem / Both heart in heart and hand in hand.'

It makes me remember the Westbrooks, Minton, the great trombonist Paul Rutherford and the Brass Band playing at the E1 Festival on Bigland Green, Stepney E1 in 1975. Blake would have loved it and would have joined in too, with children singing, dancing and writing poems. Long live his vision, insights and the beautiful sounds of the Westbrooks - all interlaced, all of a piece, all one.

(Glad Day Live: The Poetry of William Blake is available on Westbrook Records; Last Night at the Old Place is available on Cadillac Records)

Randy Weston (USA) - A great sound of Africa

Randy Weston African Rhythms Quintet and
The Gnawas Of Morocco, Barbican, London
(2001)

Born in Brooklyn, in 1926, and tutored by his neighbour Thelonious Monk in the latter's small New York apartment, Randy Weston's life-commission has been to explore and explain through his jazz the origins and continuing revelation of Africa through music. In 1961, a visit to Nigeria began his musical devotion to Africa and, later, in the same decade, a long sojourn in Morocco.

Now, 40 years later, his towering six-feet seven-inch frame ambled onto the Barbican stage and, in his introductory solo piano piece, you could hear the continent redolent in his notes, along with Monk and Bud Powell's New York streets, touches of Harlem stride and subliminal echoes of Ellington.

His quintet went through their brilliant paces in Weston's own African Cookbook, with the bass growls and the silken beauty of trombone veteran Benny Powell, Talib Kibwe's muscular, discovering alto saxophone, the twanging, percussive bass of Alex Blake and the four gleaming red drums of Neil Clarke accompanying Weston's Monkish perturbations.

'You can't have a civilisation without a spiritual music base,' declared Weston before introducing African Sunrise. And the elemental mysteriousness of Powell's muted slides duelling with Kibwe's shimmering flute musically manifest his words, before Kibwe switched to alto to concoct a Parkerian fanfare and the trombonist surged into a striding, marching solo. Suddenly, his horn is snorting, farting and exclaiming as Weston rises from his piano, taking a proprietorial strolling around the backs of his musicians, as if beholding the African waterhole, hosting ardent, thirsty animals. Africa in sound, in nature, in fauna, in spirit - huge, rebellious and alive with wonder.

Ranging from the Atlas Mountains to the Zambesi and the Cape, this music is a commentary on Weston's words that 'our music is a talking to Africa's nature and in the diversity of the continent's nature is the diversity of the music and the spirit of the people.'

A convincing introduction indeed to the compelling and visceral sound of six Moroccan musicians who comprise the Gnawas Of Tangier and Marrakech. The Gnawas are an Islamic brotherhood directly descended from Africans brought across the Sahara and sold into slavery by Arab traders.

The two separate trios each played metal castanets and traditional gimbri, a goatskin lute which, when strummed with great force, made a sound uncannily close to Alex Blake's hugely resounding and vibrating bass. In these moments, the listeners caught the true provenances of jazz, in the heart and sounds forged within the life histories of the African people.

In an image of antiquity as the present, Blake stayed on stage closely watching, fixating - entranced by the ecstatic and joyous cries and dances of the Gnawas, as if his own artistry was being created at that moment and passed forward in history, to be transmuted from animal hide to gleaming wooden orchestral bass. As he plays it, he still plays with the strength, vision and sound of the ancestors.

But that is what those lucky enough to be there take from a Randy Weston concert - an empathy with Africa and its people and their music. It gets taken into the streets of London, Brooklyn or anywhere where the genius of the great continent can be understood and enacted.

Veryan Weston (England) – Trio of fire
(2024)

Gravity is the powerful new album by The Eternal Triangle, composed of octogenarian soprano and alto saxophonist Trevor Watts, septuagenarian pianist and multi-keyboard virtuoso Veryan Weston, and the much younger percussionist Jamie Harris.

Born in Uckfield, Sussex, in 1950, Weston's father was a judge advocate in the RAF, his mother a dancer and actor. One of his two sisters became a jazz singer, the other sang opera. 'There was a beat-up upright piano at home, and I got to just stand and play it in a kind of open way which I picked up from records lying around. My mum loved Spanish flamenco and if I played anything she liked she'd shout 'Ole!' from the kitchen. Later I borrowed my sister's blues records of Otis Spann, Sonny Boy Williamson and Mose Allison. I failed most of my O-levels, lived with my parents in Cornwall and did retakes at the local poly. I worked on farms and as a hotel dishwasher in Truro and started buying records from a Café in Falmouth. I was listening to Bartok chamber music, Booker Ervin and Dexter Gordon's Setting The Pace and John Cage's Fontana Mix, hearing all kinds of music from all over the world in my upstairs room.'

'When I was 16 I hitch-hiked to the Edinburgh Festival. I met and stayed with the folk and blues singer and amazing guitarist Davey Graham. The nights were getting colder and I remember him putting a blanket over me as he left the room we were all sharing. It took me three days to get back to Cornwall, with my last night spent vertical in a Bodmin Moor telephone box, with the rain pouring down outside.'

'I moved to Stoke Newington in north London. I got an old upright from Finsbury Park and wheeled it on a trolley to my flat and put it in the kitchen. I met my future wife Jill on a bus coming back from a gig. We moved back to Cornwall where I met Frank Charlton, who had a cottage in the hills and loads of books and records. He played trumpet and I started playing jazz and blues with him in local clubs, restaurants and military bases. He became my mentor and I loved him. Then it was back to London again, and Brixton Hill. We'd regularly go to The Plough in Stockwell to hear Stan Tracey's Trio with John Stevens and Scottish bassist Lindsay Cooper. Stan gave me a piano lesson and I got an artist-in-residence opportunity at Digswell House in Hertfordshire and did regular improvisation workshops with younger local musicians. We formed a band called Stinky Winkles and won the Young Jazz Musicians of 1979 award, and played in festivals in Dunkirk, San Sebastian and Wroclaw in Poland. I made my first record with Lol Coxhill, played with drummer Eddie Prevost and finally met Trevor again, who asked me to be part of his new project with west African drummers, Moire Music. We toured America, Europe and Australasia. It was a truly fruitful time for me.'

Veryan and Trevor reunited in the 2000s and improvised saxophone/piano dialogues. After Trevor's 80th birthday they formed a trio with Jamie Harris, and The Eternal Triangle was born. Harris's percussion retains the power of the superb African drummers of Moire Music. 'Jamie is powerfully rhythmic and Trevor has worked with him for many years. They live close to each other and regularly work out ideas and rhythms. They work beautifully as a duo - I'm lucky to be there too!'

What about Trevor's astonishing skill in creating melody out of improvisation? 'Trevor discovers new melodic phrases, always sudden and fresh-sounding. It's the way he practises. He finds scale material that can be turned into characterful phrases and these can be extended into shaped melodies. It's a very organic way to work. I like this and feel I can do it as well. Nothing is set in stone, we make frames that can be shaped, allowing us to instantly respond to each other, but within the shape and character of the piece.'

What is it about the Watts/Harris partnership that expresses such unity? 'Trevor and Jamie share a real depth and love for rhythm. Trevor first suggested that Jamie play drums and soon realised that he was a 'natural.' He passes on many ideas from his own musical wisdom and ability to adapt to playing situations, and Jamie and I have learned to be adaptable. To me, this feels like a microcosm of natural communism, where we, as three people, think of our music and work together as a shared collective. Nobody is the boss or paymaster, we share and support each other.'

And how does Trevor, now in his mid-eighties, still keep creating such hugely energetic music and performances, so imbued with the Moire spirit of Africa? Listen to the track called Ghana Friends. 'He's worked day-in, day-out on his music. Each of his two saxophones now show symbiotic connections that are aged with his body into more or less one item. The sounds flow from him as one. Nothing can be separated any more. That's all there is! Whoever gets a chance to hear this will have the opportunity to have one of the most memorable listening experiences of their life.'

(Gravity is available on Jazz Now Records)

Veryan Weston (England) - A unification of sonic traditions

Veryan Weston - Mercury Concert, Gateway to Vienna,
Five Shadows & Tessellations For Lutheal Piano
(2017)

The free pianism of Veryan Weston has something very special to it. Born in Sussex in 1950, he was named after his piano-playing mother's Cornish village, renowned for its round houses. Migrating from Cornwall to London in 1972, he soon fell in with pioneering free jazz spirits at the Little Theatre Club, collaborated in the formation of a band called Stinky Winkles and earned a music fellowship at a college in Digswell, Hertfordshire. He made his first record with the busking saxophonist Lol Coxhill - the prelude to a life in free improvising jazz in many contexts over 40 years.

A series of albums recorded for the pioneering Emanem label has ensured that Weston's succession of many diverse musical settings has been waxed, including the prime albums cut with the regular British duo of brilliance, arch-bassist and arch-drummer John Edwards and Mark Sanders. The first of these is Mercury Concert, an unedited cut of a trio performance at the Mercury Theatre in Colchester in June 1998.

There are three tracks, with the Longer Piece as opener, lasting for almost 36 minutes and as audacious a piece of threesome sonic exploration as you would encounter, with beauty as the harmony of detailed effrontery and crafted courage.

At the basement of all is the remarkable Edwards, whose tireless fingers and perturbing bow are the true tools closest to the earth in which this singular music grows as an undersong to his mates' startling virtuosity. At one moment during this marathon of sound his bass resembles an eternally buzzing bee fomenting the wild honey of their unity. I doubt if this garrison city has ever known the like, before or since.

As for the quicksilver percussion of Sanders, I closed my eyes and through his artistry I thought I heard a child experimenting with a ghostly Meccano set, before Weston's lonesome, echoing solo notes opened up the sky. Then towards the end came the pianist's long rush of sprinted notes, leaving the listener's ears breathless, yet still eager for the Shorter Piece and Slightly Longer than Shorter Piece.

One of the two CDs of the enigmatically titled double album Gateway to Vienna was recorded in the Gateway Studios, London, in December 2003, the other in Vienna in May 2002. There are six Gateway excursions which continue to make you marvel at how three men making vibrantly different sounds can achieve such oneness on the same journey - one imagination in three with the touch of Weston on keys and Sanders's astonishing agility on drums seemingly to be stemming from the same hands. As the trio rise to a crescendo on Gateway 2, the empathy is boiling.

As for the two lengthy Vienna tracks (35 and 39 minutes), they have the tingling atmospherics of a live concert audience with Sanders in particular superbly recorded, his every sound and percussive flicker entering the ears like fire.

The album Five Shadows introduces Weston with a horn partner, the San Francisco-born alto saxophonist Caroline Kraabel, used to organising and playing with the 20-piece all-women saxophone orchestra, Mass Producers. Between December 1999 and May 2000 the duo explored different acoustic settings in England, from Colchester again in the Arts Centre, to Liverpool, St Mary's church in Cheltenham to The Standard pub in Walthamstow, east London, usually a rock venue. It's a very different sound from the fullness of the trio, a music full of pause, space, transcendant rises and sudden halts in Colchester, deep-throated birdsong and galloping keys in Liverpool, the scintillating edge of Kraabel's reed within the haunted echoes of long-aching pews in Cheltenham and saloon bar flourishes in Walthamstow.

Who would have thought that an English pianist from the free jazz and improvising traditions, accompanied by Jennifer Pike, a silent dancer, would record an album on the only existing Lutheal piano, made by the Belgian Georges Cloeteus in 1918, a working exhibit in Brussels's Museum of Musical Instruments? And after just 51 minutes of trials and a 25-minute rehearsal on the recording day?

Tessellations for Lutheal Piano, the album's called, and the sometimes harpsichordal timbre of his so rarely borrowed instrument and the sheer inventiveness of Weston's musical brain create a unique and timeless amalgam which unifies a whole miscellany of sonic traditions - Celtic, African, the Americas and European, within and without the rubric of jazz.

(Mercury Concert, Gateway to Vienna, Five Shadows & Tessellations For Lutheal Piano are available on Emanem Records)

Kenny Wheeler (Canada) - Knocking us for six with a fiery beauty

Kenny Wheeler - Six For Six

(2013)

A colloquy of veterans here, a palaver of experience and musical beauty by lifeworn artists expressing decades of jazz discovery. And led by a trumpeter born in Toronto who has spent a life making music in England since his arrival in London as a young man in 1952, who blew with swing pioneers like Buddy Featherstonhaugh, bop-influenced jazzmen like John Dankworth and early free improvisers like John Stevens and the Spontaneous Music Ensemble. A long jazz lifetime has taken him through the Azimuth trio with John Taylor and Norma Winstone, the Anthony Braxton Quartet (1971-76) and the Globe Unity Orchestra among thousands of other diverse jazz formations.

A Glaswegian, Bobby Wellins, born in 1936, a tenor saxophonist of a host of quartets, most notably that of Stan Tracey, and a Londoner, Stan Sulzmann, born in 1948 and a veteran tenorist and soprano saxophonist of the Gil Evans Orchestra, the Hamburg-based NDR Band and the stomping Kenny Clarke/Francy Boland Big Band, are the sextet's other two horns. Manchester-born John Taylor, an ex-confrere of Ronnie Scott, Jan Garbarek, Enrico Rava and Lee Konitz, is the pianist.

The drummer, big band specialist Martin France, born in Rainham, Kent, in 1964 started at the age of 12 backing crooners in working men's clubs, played with great jazz figures like Evan Parker and Wheeler and became principal percussionist with the Halle Orchestra and the London Sinfonia, while bassist Chris Laurence, another Londoner, was drummer Tony Oxley's long-time bassist and has made a series of momentous albums with baritonist John Surman. Together they are a true amalgam of British - and Canadian - jazz genius at the apex of their musicianship, and this album is their combined testimony, led by an ever-excellent and ever-young 83-year-old.

France's resonating tympanic solo announces the opener Seven, Eight, Nine (Part 1) before Wheeler and the two saxophones begin a call-and-response sequence. Wheeler shines through his solo, Wellins's tenor sings over France's thrashing drums and Sulzmann brings in his soprano, gyrating through his horn story with clarity and relish.

Canter N6 begins with Wellins's gurgling tenor over Laurence's delving notes, making the beginnings of ever-forming, curling melodies which grow like ballads of pure surprise. Wheeler's trumpet peals and suddenly touches the skies. The Long Waiting was written for Wheeler's big band in which Laurence,

France and Sulzmann are regular members. It begins with some beautiful duo sounds between Taylor and Sulzmann before Wheeler's brass chorus sails through the Ludwigsburg studio, searching high reaches but kept close to the Earth by Taylor's comradeship.

When the pianist moves into his own solo outing it is as if he is marking out the trail for his bandmates, who follow him and Wheeler resolutely into Four, Five, Six with the brother saxophones in full exchange and sharing messages, and the juice pouring from these virtuosi horns as if they are squeezing their lifetimes to tell us everything, all the way from a Glasgow boyhood to another in Harold Hill, the huge Essex estate where Sulzmann grew up as a young post-war rehoused Londoner.

As for Wheeler, his own long transatlantic jazz life pours out in Ballad No 130, the serenity of its melody scooping up the reeds too and Taylor's reflective chords. Sulzmann's soprano sings like a homecoming bird. The second part of Seven, Eight, Nine follows, with Wellins's tenor spinning on its own sonic axis and France's rattling snares behind him. Taylor voyages out full of fire and exploration, his keys ever-searching, and Wheeler's soaring solo has the contrariness of strength and fragility in every note.

Then there comes The Imminent Immigrant, and whether this is Wheeler's autobiographical tale, an act of musical empathy with east London neighbours or perhaps both, which edges the listener's imagination onward. His solo is one of a fiery beauty and inspires Taylor's pianism to reach a rare plane of emotive complexity, setting off Sulzmann's soprano rhapsody. Then back to Wheeler's delicacy and finally a concluding ensemble for the wisest musicians.

The last track, Upwards, begins with Wheeler and his old piano partner Taylor inside each other's notes and successively each member adds their timbral witness. France and Laurence's brotherly pulse beds down the unified sound, and as a listener you come out of this hour's recorded music earnestly thanking and blessing your ears, as well as such superb and seasoned musicians.

(Six For Six is available on Cam Jazz)

Annie Whitehead (England) – Blessed sonic oneness

Annie Whitehead's World Music Workshop, Vortex, London (2017)

Standing in front of the 15 horns of her 18-piece World Music Workshop orchestra, trombonist Annie Whitehead's shining slides thrust straight towards the centre of the Vortex. The combined surge of these musicians, largely amateurs who make music together every Monday night in London's King's Cross, is a sound of love and dedication to the musicians of the world whose music they play.

They're evidently inspired by the Oldham-born Whitehead, a superb practitioner who learned her instrument at school and in local brass bands.

They begin with August One, written by South Africans Dudu Pukwana and Adam Glasser and the rhythms of solidarity are immediate, as are the solos of David's eloquent bass clarinet, Peter's piercing trumpet and Justin's earthy, slashing guitar. Only their first names are announced - another expression of the intimacy and bond between the London musicians and faraway composers. I didn't get the names of the pounding drummer and the vibrant soprano saxophonist - while the founding beat of basswoman Alison and Rachel's vocalised tenor sax also make their mark.

Then it is Jibubi, written and played by the late US tenor saxophonist George Adams. The pulsating horn ensemble roars against the Vortex's steel roof and when Whitehead's wondrous trombone peals into the Trinidadian calypso Matilda, the melody rocks the venue, soon charged by Ros's bouncing accordion solo.

Whitehead tells us that Nonto Sangoma was written by Johannesburg composer Zakes Nkosi and it went on to become a regular number of the African Jazz Pioneers, Mandela's favourite band. This is music played for sheer pleasure and union between musicians and listeners and these troubadours and their blessed sonic oneness with music-makers worldwide cause you to have faith in the universal joy of music.

Barney Wilen (France/USA) - Parisian lustre

Barney Wilen - Premier Chapitre 1954-1961 (2016)

His mother was French, his father was an American. He was born in Nice in 1937, but grew up in Arizona where his family found a wartime refuge. He returned to France in the late '40s and became a teenage saxophone prodigy.

Bernard Jean 'Barney' Wilen's remarkable early jazz years are compellingly captured on this three-CD set, years in which he found himself performing and recording with some of the touring US jazz icons of the age: drummers Roy Haynes and Kenny Clarke, trumpeters Miles Davis and Kenny Dorham, pianists Bud Powell and John Lewis and fellow reedmen Coleman Hawkins and Don Byas, and as a member of Art Blakey's luminous Jazz Messengers: quite a Paris apprenticeship.

The marvellous bop drummer Roy Haynes is not a bad bandmate to be next to you on your debut recording on a November day in Paris when you're 17, and on Subscription, Barney's tenor sax rocks confidently alongside Jimmy Gourley's guitar. By 1956 he was recording Bags' Groove with Lewis and bassist Percy Heath, both of the Modern Jazz Quartet, and the sharp French guitarist Sacha Distel, and in Afternoon in Paris in comes the MJQ drummer Connie Kay while Wilen plays a lustrous tenor solo.

By January 1957 he was leading his own quartet recording standards, classic Monk tunes and his own compositions. On Blue Monk he follows the familiar theme by a burning melodic chorus, while Nature Boy is an opportunity for him to show his effective balladeering chops. By December 1957 he was partnering Miles Davis at major venues like the Olympia in Paris and the Concertgebouw in Amsterdam, where Miles flies on Monk's playful Well, You Needn't, and Wilen, chasing him hard, blows a powerful addendum buoyed up by Clarke's urgent drums.

The four tracks, Jazz sur Seine have Wilen playing with Heath, Clarke and Milt Jackson on piano. Heath's booming bass pounds through Charles Trenet's Que reste-t-il de nos amour? before Wilen enters for a lucid chorus and Django Reinhardt's Nuages, slow and ponderous, reveals the full beauty of his mellow and crystalline tone.

Five tenors, three from the US (Don Byas, Stan Getz and the great saxophone pioneer Coleman Hawkins) and two from France (Wilen and Guy Lafitte) jam and take turns to solo on a TV airing of Indiana / Donna Lee in a joyous expression of transatlantic jazz unity, and Wilen is joined by Japanese pianist Toshiko Akiyoshi, Haynes and US bassist Tommy Bryant for a broadcast from the 1959 Newport Jazz Festival. Wilen plays soprano saxophone on Monk's Round Midnight as if he were born to it and Akiyoshi's chiming notes reinvent the tune.

Then come two film soundtracks. First there are the duets with New York pianist Duke Jordan from Un temoin dans la ville, including a tenderly etched Melodie pour les Radio-Taxis and then the extracts from Les Liaisons Dangereuses of 1960, recorded with Blakey's Messengers - including trumpeter Lee Morgan, pianist Bobby Timmons, Jordan and bassist Jymie Merritt. Prelude in Blue has a poised and melancholy Wilen on soprano and the faster-moving Valmontana No 2 has Blakey's drums aflame behind some incendiary Morgan and Wilen's more temperate tenor.

The tracks with the great Bud Powell, resident in Paris at the time, have their own electric ambiance, with How High the Moon having Dizzy Gillespie's horn blowing hot next to Barney. When Clark Terry brings his flugelhorn to the November 1959 session he follows a self-confident, swinging Wilen with his super-agile, puckish brass phrases on No Problem. Bud himself is full of inventive zest on Miguel's Party.

There are two 1961 dates in Milan, playing with bands including the Swiss pianist George Gruntz, and extracts from the soundtrack of the film Mental Cruelty recorded in Zurich later that year.

By 1969 Wilen's extraordinary prolific youthful decade and a half was over, and it was as if he had become saturated with the Parisian jazz scene. Heading to Africa, perhaps to escape what he called a 'bop monoculture,' he travelled widely, absorbing its rich and complex musical diversity, lived with the Touaregs of upper Niger and eventually recorded his album Moshi which brought his jazz experience together with the sonic richness of sounds that he encountered in many parts of the continent. But that was another chapter, written far from the clubs and venues of the Paris groove.

(Premier Chapitre 1954-1961 is available on Fremeaux & Associes)

Immanuel Wilkins (USA) - Blues Blood
(2025)

In April 1964 in an infamous case, six young black men, shortly to be called the Harlem Six, were wrongfully arrested by New York police, and accused of attempted murder. They had intervened when they saw police beating children, and once detained were themselves continually badly assaulted by the same police, and envisaged before them a life in prison.

One of the Six, Daniel Hamm, sought to expose his battered flesh and obtain medical treatment, by cutting open his bruises: 'I had to open the bruise up and let some of the blues blood come out to show them.'

Now sixty years on, the alto saxophonist Immanuel Wilkins has created his powerful musical testimony through his album called Blues Blood, to show the present in the past and attest to the continuing racist violence in the streets around him in now-times America.

Wilkins is a Philly boy, born in 1997. His first musical experiences were in his local church, and when his prodigious talent took him to the Juilliard School of Music in New York City, he was tutored by prime saxophonists, Bruce Williams, Steve Wilson and Scotland's Joe Temperley. From the 2010s he led his own band, specialising in his own compositions. His first Blue Note album, Omega, was released in 2020.

The quartet on Blues Blood includes some new names of youth and budding talent: pianist Micah Thomas, Rick Rosato on bass and drummer Kweku Sumbry. They are joined by vocalists Cecile McLorin Salvant, June McDoom, Ganavya and Yaw Agyeman. Throughout the album these voices often become obligatos to Wilkins' very vocal horn, and merge as if the combined sounds were coming from the same unified instrument. Wilkins' floating, featherweight lyricism of sound creates calls and answers between him and the singers, whose words often skip, like children at play, over the pain-sourced notes.

Thomas' apparent sonic tenderness gains a sudden earnestness in the track Afterlife Residence Time. Rosato's shimmering basslines in Dark Eyes Shine meet Wilkins' tranquil timbral beauty, revealing, combatting and defeating black suffering next to Salvant's mollifying beauty. It is as if the brutality of street racism is exposed even more pungently by musical delicacy, even quasi-quietude of sound and story. In this sense the album is uniquely powerful, the calm excitation contradictorily manifesting in note after note, sound after sound, that 'the storytelling is in my bloodline' and deep in the musicians' soundscape too.

James Baldwin, also born and raised there, had much to say about the Harlem Six. In his 1966 essay, 'Report from Occupied Territory', he wrote: 'I know in my own flesh, and know, which is worse, the scars borne by many of those dearest to me, the thunder and force of the belly club, the paralyzing shock of spittle in the face, and I know what it is to find myself blinded, on one's hands and knees, at the bottom of a flight of steps down which one has just been hurled... where is the civilisation and where indeed is the morality which can afford to destroy so many? ... one cannot possibly arrive at a more surefire formula for cruelty.'

In a post-George Floyd America Wilkins' album rings out in challenge, even eight decades after the terror of the Harlem Six. Blues Blood is a part of the great insurgent tradition of jazz protest, stemming back to the Civil Rights era, with flashbacks and echoes of Mingus' Fables of Faubus, Roach's key album We Insist!, Coltrane's Alabama and Shepp's Attica Blues. The album has much to tell us here in Britain too, and it makes you look forward to hearing Wilkins here in London, and hearing him live with his message of struggle and hope.

(Blues Blood is available on Blue Note Records)

Chris Williams (England) - From Spurs to Sound Waves

LEDLEY - a bold fusion of Jazz, football, and community spirit (2025)

The extraordinary electro-acoustic album LEDLEY, by three Tottenham Hotspur fans and friends, saxophonist Chris Williams, trombonist Raph Clarkson and electronics wizard Riaan Vosloo, shows how sport, friendship, community activism and jazz improvisation can be united in powerful and perceptive musical sounds.

Ledley King is a Spurs' fans' icon, a one-club defender and international, plagued by injury through much of his career. The musicians are local and loyal Spurs supporters since childhood, who see the club as a focus for community cohesion and strength. I asked Williams about his life in music and football.

'I was born in Edmonton, north of Tottenham, in 1983. My mum's Tottenham-born English and my dad settled in Tottenham when he came from Jamaica as a young boy.'

'He built up his own cleaning company and mum did clerical work. Dad played bass in bands, but I never saw him play. I was surrounded by musical sisters, but it wasn't until I heard a kid playing sax at school that I found something I really wanted to play.'

'I started at 11. We were eligible for free lessons so I got 15 minutes a week. I bottled it the first two weeks then the third week the tutor brought with him a tape of Charlie Parker playing My Little Suede Shoes. It was like a switch had gone off in my head. I never knew music like this existed. Its life and freedom blew my mind.'

'I sang the tune the whole way home so I wouldn't forget it, then got out my sax and butchered it! That was the real start of it, how music felt and what it meant to me had been permanently shifted.'

'My sax tutor Nick Stevenson gave me so much, pushing me to get into the borough-wide jazz band and making me cassettes of albums to check out, exposing me to so much. My mum and sisters also inspired me, I'd be nowhere near the person I am now without them.'

'My first playing gig was with a Nigerian singer who wrote his own tunes. I'd lay down sax tracks for him and we'd do gigs at a Nigerian restaurant in Tottenham - my first experience of Afrobeat. A pastor spotted me and got me to play in his church. Looking back, playing by ear, learning tunes on the fly in random keys was great training, and it felt grand to be earning money through music.'

I first heard Chris in 2011, playing with Bolton-born clarinettist Arun Ghosh. I remember surging versions of Ghosh's tunes Intifada, dedicated to the Palestinian struggle, and Longsight Lagoon, written about the working-class neighbourhood of Manchester, dear to Arun's heart.

'He's an extremely soulful musician, with a way of connecting and resonating with people, caring deeply how moods and feelings are expressed through music. Going on this journey with him, finding a way to retain my voice within it, while fully being a part of it, certainly contributed to how I approach collaboration.'

'I got into teaching after getting my degree at Middlesex University, and still teach to this day. It meant a lot to work in my old school for a while. Teaching in schools for 17 years near where I grew up has meant so much to me, teaching young people who lack the opportunities compared to those in other areas.'

What about the new album, LEDLEY?

'It comes from the friendship between Raph and I. Football and music brought us together and laid the foundation for this band. We used to go to the matches at White Hart Lane with Raph's dad, and these bonds stretch out and connect with the wider community. Every home match day you see these connections, these moments of togetherness, a sort of pilgrimage, a sense of belonging.'

'Ledley King epitomises so many positive traits: resilience, determination, loyalty - a one-club player who continues to give to the community. He was stalwart and captain while Raph and I were teenagers and young adults. For both of us he embodies so much about what is good about following your childhood club. The record represents passions and friendships we share: it could only be called LEDLEY.'

'Raph has a real gift of being a wonderfully empathetic musician while also playing with an absolute, full commitment: all heart! He means what he plays, a stellar musician and a joy to play with. Riaan's post-production electronics feel as if they were in the room with us - astounding!'

And how does the sound truly reflect North London and its people?

'There's a constant hum in London, something buzzing, tapping, whirring - connections being made, brief moments existing in the haze. The range of influences Raph and I have as improvisers was shaped by these sounds growing up in Tottenham with all the cultural mixes, different sounds, accents, languages. I don't bat an eyelid hearing multiple languages on a bus, wherever I'm going. This melting pot shapes our lives as people, musicians and football supporters, taking in rock, jazz, improv, SE Asian, Afro-Cuban, South African, embracing electronics as part of this sound-world, and finding a means to interweave them all.'

'But there's also a hardness here, life being tough. I still feel an element of hardness in my playing. Life can still be a bit of a scrap. I feel incredibly lucky to have the opportunities to make the music that we do. So many others miss out on these chances, or didn't get the support at vital moments. But you've got to care about what you do, be behind it, otherwise what's the point? I take pride in being committed when improvising on records like this, and I know Raph does too, and taking pride in what we do is something we should all claim.'

'So following Spurs and going to home matches lets me feel connected to my local community, my childhood, both sides of my family. It's the same for Raph and it feeds into how we play music together, our personal connections to Tottenham and what these relationships mean in shaping our music.'

What's your favourite track on the album?

'It has to be 'One Club,' the record's culmination, as if it all points to this. It felt special in the recording studio at the time. The moment where Raph and I come together with our lines is one of my key moments of the record.'

Has Ledley heard it yet?

'Not too sure, but he's said he'd like to meet us. Hopefully, he's intrigued enough to give it a listen, see where it takes him!'

And what impact will this community-loving music have on those racist elements who seek to divide, in football and community?

'After reflection, us being out there doing what we do, not shying away, is a statement in itself - not to be silenced by a minority that feels greater than it is, seeping into any silence that is left.'

No silence in LEDLEY though. It peals out for the vibrant, many-cultured and generous community that walks the streets and cheers on the terraces of Tottenham and every urban centre of Britain, and finds its true expression in the soundscape of this audacious record.

(LEDLEY is available on Impossible Ark)

Steve Williamson (England) - Sax sensations
Steve Williamson Trio, Pizza Express Soho, London
(2018)

Born in West London in 1964 of Jamaican parents, Steve Williamson began playing saxophone at 16 and blew reggae with Misty in Roots before attending the Guildhall School of Music and joining the Jazz Warriors in 1984.

In 1988, he played with Courtney Pine at the Nelson Mandela 70th Birthday concert at Wembley and in the South African-led bands of Louis Moholo-Moholo and Chris McGregor's Brotherhood of Breath.

The Verve label released his marvellous Waltz for Grace album with Abbey Lincoln in 1990 and Rhyme Time two years later.

Then he became much less prominent for two decades, so it was tremendous to hear him at full pelt in Soho again with two powerful confreres, bassist Larry Bartley and drummer Rod Youngs.

His mercurial spirit shone through the trio's rendition of Thelonius Monk's Evidence, with his breathy tenor saxophone timbre planting the theme deep in jazz earth and his startling improvisation inventing multi-dimensional note-patterns over Bartley's ever-dancing bass and his raw cadences tumbling over Youngs's rattling snares.

He took to soprano saxophone for the songbook ballad What Is This Thing Called Love? and tore into its melody with a Sidney Bechet-like attack, while Youngs used his palms on toms and snares as a gentle underlay.

But true horn glory came with Williamson's very free interpretation of the tenor saxophonist test-piece Body and Soul, a reminder of Pablo Picasso's words: 'You start a painting and it becomes something altogether different.'

The same is true of Williamson, as the cusp of the tune became the launching of new, astonishing and unique notes.

It was the signal of true creation and artistry, a beautiful sound.

Buster Wilson (USA)
Buster Wilson: 1948 – 49
(2025)

Thank you the London Co-op in Romford Shopping Arcade, for it was from their record counter that I bought my first jazz record in 1959. It was an extended play (E.P.) of Kid Ory's Creole Jazz Band, with the virtually unknown pianist, one Buster Wilson, comping as part of the rhythm section, but never taking a solo behind the New Orleans horns of Ory's creole trombone, Omer Simeon's liquid clarinet and Mutt Carey's deliciously muted cornet, as they played tunes like Get Out of Here, Creole Song, Blues for Jimmy Noone and South.

Wilson became a mystery man for me. I used to wonder what he was like as a soloist, how he played when he was given his head, where he came from and what happened to him after the golden Ory years of the New Orleans revival in Los Angeles, where the tunes were recorded.

Albert Wesley 'Buster' Wilson was born in Atlanta in 1897, but as a boy was brought to L.A. with his family, where he grew up to a hard life as a jobbing pianist. He replaced Lil Hardin in King Oliver's band in 1921, became one of Dink Johnson's Five Hounds of Jazz in 1922 and played with Mutt Carey and New Orleans clarinetist Jimmy Noone, before a stint with Lionel Hampton's band in 1936. In 1941 he played with Jelly Roll Morton, and was at the heart of the New Orleans revival in L.A., when in 1944 Orson Welles brought him into his 'All-star Jazz Group' for his CBS radio show, a band which under Ory's leadership became the Creole Jazz Band, performing, broadcasting and recording to great acclaim until 1948.

Wilson has this one album to his name, compiled from obscure sessions he made in the last two years of his life, before he died of pneumonia in Los Angeles in 1949. In the first of these he plays with three trumpeters, including Carey, the master of mutes, who takes lyrical solos on the sentimental songs River of Roses and Goodbye, Pretty Baby, on which Buster sings appealingly.

Another unusual 1947 session features a fellow Dink Johnson alumnus, trombonist Ash Hardy, with guitarist Prince Stansel, who really digs into his strings in Emaline, with a vibrant Hardy and Buster's hard-struck notes, and the anonymous blues where Buster's Southern origins gush out as he sings of 'having the blues so long, they're turning red.' The sound of No, No Nora has a speakeasy ethos, with a gruff Hardy and more startling guitar from Stansel.

In 1949 Buster recorded five tunes alone in L.A., two of them Jelly Roll Morton compositions. He thumps the keys on Ballin' a Jack like a Crescent City parade drummer, and his affinity for melody pours out of his fingers on the 'untitled pop song'. On the Jelly Roll tunes his emotions are stirred on Winin' Boy and the solo piano of The Pearls is played with an inventive zest that would have tickled the huge ego of its composer.

Ten days before he died Buster recorded a 'demo' tape in his apartment with the local young trumpeter Ron Ronnei. Its sound quality is surprisingly good, and the hornman is clearly inspired by his veteran companion. Buster is playing with strength and a warm sense of empathy with his junior partner, and the two men find a warm unity on Egyptia, and when they join for New Orleans tunes like Weary Blues - where Buster really jives in his notes, and Dippermouth Blues - written by another of his maestros, King Oliver, they could both be dancing down Bourbon Street. When Buster calls out 'Oh, play that thing!' he is already there. He sings a little plaintively on None of My Jelly Roll before turning to scat, while all the time the notes are dancing off his keys.

The album's sleeve photograph shows a sharply-suited Buster at his piano with stiff collar and tie, gesticulating to his bandmates. It's 66 years since I first met him in the Romford Co-op, and hearing this record, I now at last feel that I know a little more about his life and artistry. Long live his marvellous keyboard sound!

(Buster Wilson: 1948 - 49 is available on American Music Records)

Gerald Wilson Orchestra (USA) - Mythical City of Sound
Detroit
(2010

As a young emigrant to Canada in the mid-1960s, I would stare with a certain wonderment from Windsor on the Ontario side of the Detroit River over at the skyline beyond, and marvel at what music had come from between those giant buildings.

Like New Orleans, Chicago, Kansas City, New York and Los Angeles, Detroit was for me a mythical city of sound - not only of the Motown tradition that had deluged the British pop charts during the early 1960s, but of its jazz and the marvellous musicians of the second bop generation that it had produced while I was growing up in London. Pianists like Tommy Flanagan and Barry Harris, hornmen like Donald Byrd, Sonny Red Kyner and Pepper Adams and guitarists like Kenny Burrell. Altoist Yusef Lateef had even produced an album called Detroit: Latitude 40 Degrees, Longitude 83 Degrees. Yet more than four decades on, when I listened to now-times Detroit as I did when I returned two years ago, I could hear only emptiness, desolate unpopulated streets that were virtual soundless canyons of a musical world passed by.

When Gerald Wilson from Shelby, Mississippi - savaged by Jim Crow racism, arrived as a sixteen year old in 1934 Detroit to attend its Cass Technical High School, it seemed like another world. 'I had dreamed to live in the North, so the day I arrived in Detroit, staying with family friends, was a day I had dreamed of. Unlike other places where I had lived, Detroit was racially integrated. So for me, Detroit was freedom.' He stayed until 1939, when he joined the touring Jimmy Lunceford Orchestra as trumpet replacement for Sy Oliver, finally settling in Los Angeles and organising his own big band. He moved to San Francisco in 1952, recording several successful albums for World Pacific in the 1960s and writing arrangements for Ella Fitzgerald, Nancy Wilson, Julie London and Bobby Darin.

He has never slowed down and at the age of 90 in 2009 he was commissioned to write a suite in honour of the Detroit Jazz Festival on its 30th anniversary. This led to his new album, Detroit, played in a broad pan-U.S. spirit with the first six tracks by his LA-based orchestra and the final two tracks by his New York-based big band. Named after the park on the Detroit River, the opener, Blues on Belle Isle features Brian O'Rourke's rocking piano, a rasping violin chorus by Yvette Devereaux and Sean Jones' burnished trumpet. Relaxed and joyous, here is the portrait of a city populace enjoying themselves.

Wilson remembers his invaluable study years in Cass Tech, with vibrant ensemble passages that bear more than a passing resemblance to Philly boy Benny Golson's hard bop classic Along Came Betty. Tenor saxophonist Kamasi Washington digs deep and Jones' solo is flowing and fluent. Then Washington's powerfully moving tenor traces the balladic theme of Wilson's melody named after the city. Jones then switches to flugelhorn with the reed section humming behind him, before Randall Willis' flute returns to blow again the thematic notes which sing out the name with memory and love: 'De... troit!'

The heavy trombone riffs of Before Motown prelude a Latin-emphatic solo by trumpeter Bobby Rodriguez. Wilson's West Coast years prompted his fascination with Latino life and music, and he developed an intense admiration for bullfighting. Latin notes permeate this tune too, even as far north and east as Detroit, and there are some stirring choruses from trombonist Les Benedict to mix up Motown with Mexico. 'It's a kind of wild thing,' declared Wilson of his tune The Detroit River. As the watery frontier with Canada flows rough, the moment Jones soars away for his opening solo, you begin to understand why. Jack Kelso's soprano sax is swift and riverine, Eric Jorgensen's trombone seems to be navigating the straits with difficulty and Devereaux's violin is rocking in the rapids.

A different Detroit is portrayed in Wilson's suite to the savagely de-industrialised post-Motown city of 2010. It's fine music though, recalling a vibrant metropolis, a seething city of musical brilliance and hope, set down in groove through one veteran jazzman's irresistible skill.

(Detroit is available on Mack Avenue Records)

Norma Winstone (England)

Pizza Express Jazz Club, Dean Street, Soho
(2025)

Soho's Pizza Express jazz grotto has a special location. Across the road, through St. Anne's Court William Blake was born. Did he wander the Soho streets thinking and rhyming in ways close to the blues:: 'In every cry of every man,/ In every infant's cry of fear,/ In every voice, in every ban,/The mind-forg'd manacles I hear.' Shelley lived around the corner, contemplating his words 'for the many, not the few', and along Dean Street itself outside this basement chamber, Marx lived and passed mornings and evenings going to and from the Reading Room in the British Museum, creating his greatest works.

Today it's a voice from Bow, the other end of London, that of 84 year old Norma Winstone, that swings through the tables full of pizza, their crusts curling in time to her song. This cellar room, with its cabaret ambiance, is the perfect setting for her. As she begins, her body gently swaying, her fingers clicking with 'Isn't it a lovely day to be caught in the rain?', with her instinctive melodic sense, sudden surprising ascents and cadences and perfect diction, she sings the American Songbook like a song-thrush, with Nikki Isles' sisterly piano, Mark Lockheart's warm tenor saxophone solos and obligatos, and Steve Watts' steadfast bass.

She extracts all the lyrical poetry from Guess I'll Hang My Tears Out to Dry and Gershwin's I Love You Porgy, and when she sings Brubeck's Meadow Lark and 'your wings have brushed against the stars', so does Norma's voice, so full of joy and hope. Her version of Randy Newman's I Think it's Going to Rain Today is ageless like her voice which rises movingly with the words 'human kindness overflowing' like an oracle.

Through Joni Mitchell's Two Grey Rooms she tells a love story like no other, and as she recounts how Clifford Brown's Joy Spring was the first song she ever sang on the radio in 1967, and then sings it with sheer octogenarian meaning and happiness, it touched many a listening nerve.

She remembers Coltrane's sound of Out of this World, and as she sang it, I thought of Brother Karl walking past on the pavement outside, above our heads, thinking of 'the heart of a heartless world' and the now-times heartlessness of Trump, Musk, Netanyahu, Putin, of Gaza and Ukraine, and the truth brewing in Norma's words and wordless improvisations: sing on, Norma!

Nate Wooley (USA) – Columbia iconoclast

Ancient Songs Of Burlap Heroes

(2025)

When I heard the iconoclastic trumpeter Nate Wooley play at Dalston's Café Oto in September I was drawn into his horn sounds, sometimes clear and icy, other times muffled, snorting and growl-toned.

Born in Clatskanie, a small Oregon city in 1974, his parents were teachers. I asked him about his new album Ancient Songs Of Burlap Heroes with the Columbia Icefield sextet. 'I grew up in the mouth of the Columbia. Its violent confluence with the Pacific always seemed wonderful. People spoke of the Columbia Bar, one of the most dangerous stretches of water in the US, with reverence, awe and a kind of anthropomorphism. When I was older I visited the Columbia Icefield, finding the same sense of awe in its quiet power.'

'I've been pretty much a professional musician since 12, as it's defined by being paid to play. I needed supplemental work if I was going to play the way I wanted to, so I worked in bookstores and restaurants, did some office work and used my horn-on-the-face time to try to achieve the sound in my head.'

I asked him how much the Burlap Heroes album says about the US attitude towards impending ecological disaster of retreating glaciers and rising sea levels and their consequences for the US. 'I don't believe in the music saying something specific. All the ephemera around the album - my liner notes,

Aaron Munson's brilliant sleeve photographs tell you about that... I wanted to bring attention to the beauty and power of the Columbia, one of the strongest, largest and most shackled rivers in the world. I see the Columbia as a great serpentine god that is woefully under the thumb of a 20th-century vision of humanity's defeat of nature.'

'Its main stem contains at least 14 major dams, some of which are completely unnecessary for power production or flood mitigation. Some create reservoirs for recreation, others were simply good political projects for whoever was in power at the time. If anyone listens to the album or reads this interview, it may open the eyes of people not living near the river to the complexity of the situation there.'

What about the unique sound of his trumpet? 'On any of my records there is the idea of the trumpet as a voice unlimited by our conception of what is beautiful, but including every small and large thing a human voice can do. Sing and scream, yes, but also cough and mumble and sigh. I want the trumpet to exist outside of its limiting historical framework in jazz or classical music, and become something that emulates a full human experience with all its beauty, ugliness as well the mundanity in between.'

Who are the 'Burlap Heroes' of the album's title? 'It's a phrase cribbed from novelist Saul Bellow, referring to persons struggling just to exist. Everyone has inner and outer battles to deal with at every moment. The Burlap Heroes are those who have a little more to overcome than most, who maybe aren't always succeeding, but find a way to rise to their own challenges and find the strength to get out of the house or talk to another human being - the small victories that can mean a lot to certain existences.'

Wooley speaks proudly and warmly about his bandmates. Guitarist Mary Halvorson 'is one of my oldest New York friends. I'm so happy she still surprises me with her playing.' Pedal guitarist Susan Alcorn's 'artistry is more organic than most, with more blood, guts, passion and humanity.'

Drummer Ryan Sawyer 'is the rock of a lot of my groups, and the world at large should know what he can do on the drums.' Viola virtuoso Mat Maneri 'has been a long-time hero and I have nothing but respect for his years of honing a language very specific to him.'

As for bassist Trevor Dunn, 'I've been an admirer of his playing ever since I was living in Oregon.' Together they make intense musical heat out of the depth of ice, in a way which is rare and pregnant with meaning.

He's a unique musician with new sounds, and a new world!

(Ancient Songs Of Burlap Heroes is available on Pyroclastic Records)

Nate Wooley (USA) - Seven Storey Mountain V1
(2021)

In this insurgent album, Oregon-born trumpeter and composer Nate Wooley creates a harrowing musical tableau as an accompaniment to the lyrics of Peggy Seeger from her song Reclaim the Night: 'If we choose to walk alone/For us there is no safety zone.'

No music could be more relevant to the mass protests after the murder of Sarah Everard. Wooley uses synthesisers, pianos, organ, drums, guitar and women's choral voices to create a powerful overtone of defiance. 'I was fucking angry watching the government attempt to wrest control of women's bodies and black people incarcerated and killed with impunity,' he attests.

The final repeated Seeger stanza ends with the spurning phrase from Bobbie McGee's Union Maid above a boiling ocean of turbulent sound: 'You can't scare me!'

This imperative listening experience is an open provocation to protest and resist for 'the right to live, the right to walk alone.'

(Seven Storey Mountain V1 is available on Pyroclastic Records)

World Saxophone Quartet (USA) - Four with the horns
World Saxophone Quartet - Yes We Can
(2012)

'Today isn't about the black struggle any more. It's about the class struggle. The poor urgently need to form an alliance against the greedy rich.' These aren't the kind of words you would expect to read within the sleeve notes of a jazz album, even if they were spoken by David Murray - probably the prime tenor saxophonist of his generation - a successor and true inheritor of Coleman Hawkins, Lester Young and John Coltrane. They accompany the newest album of the World Saxophone Quartet, Yes We Can, the title words which were of course the war words of the massive campaign to elect Barack Obama to the US presidency in 2008. And this album follows the 2005 record Political Blues, full of direct and damning criticism of the Bush years in the White House and a presidency of war, imperial arrogance and domestic neglect of the poor and those assailed by natural catastrophe. In the same sleeve notes Murray is still hopeful about Obama as 'someone we can trust,' although many among his people are not, as they contemplate the present administration's actions and inactions across the world stage and the disappointments and deflated hopes from Palestine and Guantanamo to Venezuela and Afghanistan. The quartet was created in 1976 and made many of its empowering and pioneering albums in the Reagan years, when it consisted of Murray, altoist Oliver Lake, baritonist Hamiet Bluiett and altoist Julius Hemphill. In this incarnation Bluiett and

Murray come together with the astonishing Detroit tenor and soprano virtuoso James Carter.

Coming in as a guest star is the veteran New Orleans altoist Kidd Jordan, who was originally instrumental in bringing the quartet together all those years ago. He plays as if he has been a fixture all through his musical life.

The group's whirling ensembles bring in the opener Hattie Wall, after Bluiett's baritone riffs provide the foundation for some mesmeric reed acrobatics, with Carter and Murray brandishing tenor broadsides simultaneously, and Jordan's higher flourishes sweep between, around and above them.

It is a unique jazz sound from a unique formation which flies in every conceivable direction like the scattering of a flock of piping birds. Carter's soprano is prominent through Jordan's tune The River Niger, until Murray comes howling and squirming in as if Africa was afire with sound, union and hope. Jordan's solo alto spits and sucks its solo notes before cessation is all. Bluiett's grounding baritone and Carter's soprano sound out the bold theme of Murray's title tune. Anthemic and bursting with echoes of people's organisation and power, it is as if these four saxophones represent the US millions - a sonic mobilisation is happening within our ears.

The conclusion - Minguslike in its burlesque and with a pastiche of pseudo-patriotic song tune extracts - perhaps suggests that the election of the US's first black president does not mean that ties have been anything like cut between Obama and the most reactionary Pentagon and White House powerbrokers of previous administrations, from Hillary Clinton to Robert Gates. Murray's haunting opus The God of Pain is a long, and mournful draught of the blues with three horns in unison and Murray's tenor reaching out beyond them in agonised, crescendo phrases that culminate in a lingering, wounded coda. Then comes the more jaunty Angel of Pain, bringing relief and - it seems - some sonic optimism.

Bluiett's The Guessing Game is the longest track, in which his clear-toned clarinet duets with the undertow of Murray's bass clarinet for a full five minutes before the other confreres enter. Bluiett's clarinet is a revelation - full-voiced, sometimes with a New Orleans liquidity, at other times searing and transcendent, giving the quartet a transformed sound.

Then, before the final reprise of Hattie Wall, is Murray's Long March To Freedom, introduced by a howling tenor fanfare as if the saxophone itself is the black US's resurgent and true horn of liberation, from Hawkins and Coltrane, all the way to Murray and Carter. And as it blasts out of this Berlin concert hall, far from its arena of struggle, you can hear within it the voices of Douglas, Tubman and Dubois, Robeson, King and Malcolm propelling it forward towards its summation, well beyond Obama.

(Yes We Can is available on jazzwerkstatt)

Seymour Wright (England) - The struggle made sonic

Seymour Wright, Steve Noble, Pat Thomas and John Edwards, Café Oto, Hackney, London
(2024)

Just outside Café Oto, along Dalston Lane, is the huge and marvellous mural of a Hackney Carnival; all musicians soaring, all people dancing, all colours coalescing. So I was hearing music in my head as I passed the momentous image, preparing me for the sounds I was to hear inside the Café Oto's old industrial walls.

It was Derby alto saxophonist Seymour Wright, Hounslow-born bassist John Edwards and drummer and pianist from the Thames Valley, Steve Noble and Pat Thomas; all in powerful creative fettle.

How much is the unfettered sound of the saxophone like human life struggling to free itself? Wright's horn exploded with snorts, howls, cries of release, suspirations, shrieks and wailing guffaws of the search for sonic freedom, all in the joyous agony of his hornsound.

Noble's meteoric wrists of fire scorched his drums and melted his cymbals with sticks, brushes and mallets: Edwards's plucking fury was a visual and timbral blur as his fingers leapt up and down his strings, and Thomas's storms of strikes along his keys and strumming of the piano's innards preceded a succession of chimes which took its listeners' ears back a century to New Orleans and Joe King Oliver's Creole Jazz Band's pioneering Chimes Blues, now ringing through the Hackney night.

Full of the present in the future, but never far from tradition, and as I walked to get the bus and stared at the mural high above me again, I knew that what I had heard and what I was seeing was the same human struggle.

Eri Yamamoto (Japan) - Unforgettable stories

Eri Yamamoto - Redwoods, In Each Day, Something Good, The Next Page & Duologue
(2013)

Eri Yamamoto, Osaka-born and trained as a classical pianist since she was three, left Japan when she was a young woman to spend some time with her sister in New York in 1995. 'I had no ideas about jazz, 'she remembers.

Without knowing anything about him, she went to hear the veteran bop pianist Tommy Flanagan at a concert in Central Park. She was astonished to see that he needed help to climb the bandstand and reach his piano. 'I thought 'Oh my gosh! I paid $40 to see that old guy? 'But once he started playing it was so strong. That moment, I knew I wanted to be like him.' She managed to find another piano giant, Junior Mance, and took some lessons from him. She listened intently to the records of the genius Bud Powell, who lived through racist and mental agony.

Then in 1996, she found intense empathy with the Paul Bley Trio and it was as if the way they played started to set her own pianism free. 'I knew I wasn't going to be a musician like Bud Powell. His life was so different from how I'd grown up. But Paul Bley's music reminded me of my own roots. I didn't have to be the next Bud Powell fake. I could play what I wanted.' Then the free jazz pianist Matthew Shipp saw her play. 'Move your finger a half-step,' he said, 'and you might find a different world.' She did, and she did, and since 2000 she has been performing in Greenwich Village and recording with her two bandmates, bassist David Ambrosio and drummer Ikuo Takeuchi.

Yamamoto has a uniquely narrative way of playing piano, as if her sounds tell stories of the everyday, capturing common moments and rendering them unforgettable. It is excellence in the ordinary taken from the heart of jazz, when the mundane becomes special, becomes brilliant. Her trio's recent album for the AUM Fidelity label, The Next Page, expresses this with an intense beauty and apparent simplicity. The clouds through her Manhattan window, sensations walking the sidewalks of New York City, the first green leaves from trees in Central Park, watching her eight-year-old nephew swimming, a whiskey-coloured river in the Wicklow Mountains - all painted with such evocative sonic lucidity and virtual quietude.

Or read her sentence sleeve note to the quivering tune Waver - 'Sometimes I wonder, what shall I do? ' And she does it too in her album Redwoods of 2008 with her true sound brothers Ambrosio and Takeuchi whose string heartbeat, brushes, skins, sticks and cymbals never leave her.

'It is wonderful when you can feel our stories through our music,' Yamamoto writes in her sleeve notes, and whether she tells of the glory of Californian redwoods, a bumpy bike ride on Cape Cod, or with 'This Is An Apple' - one of the first sentences in English she learned in Japan, which, as she jokes, proved prophetic since she made her home in the Big Apple. Her tunes grab at your consciousness like parables of the real, and my special one on this album is Magnolia, which very tenderly radiates a promise of betterment in 'a flower of light pink colour which tells me spring is coming to town soon.'

Her sophomore AUM album, In Each Day, Something Good, is just as fine with each track reflecting the title's customary optimism. They are all her compositions, and five of them were written for the soundtrack of a classic Japanese film by Yasujiro Ozu, I was Born, But.... which was made in1932. Ambrosio and Takeuchi are in perfect concord with the pianist's inventive melodism on tunes like Attraction Of The Moon or the sheer enhanced normality of Every Day. Ambrosio's dancing bass on the jaunty We'll Figure Out Blues creates an undertow of joyous enigma.

Duologue (2008) is a very different album, not a trio at work, but Yamamoto paired with some freer musical comrades of huge stature and experience, including bass-man William Parker, drummer Hamid Drake and saxophonist Daniel Carter. She is never intimidated or outdone though - hear her assurance all the way through, especially with the arch-resonant Parker on the ebullient Subway Song, with Carter's buoyant tenor on Violet Sky or with Drake's frame drum on the tarred and concrete reality of the overtly down-home opus Midtown Blues.

Tommy Flanagan, her first accidental inspiration, graced with a gentle keyboard touch himself, would have loved the lyrical beauty and subliminal power of Yamamoto's notes and would have instantly recognised a kindred sound in the heart of a great cosmopolis.

(Redwoods, In Each Day, Something Good, The Next Page & Duologue are available on AUM Fidelity)

Jason Yarde (England) and Andrew McCormack (England) – Powerful duo, a potent mix

Andrew McCormack and Jason Yarde - MY Duo (2010)

At last an opportunity to review an album on which the name Jason Yarde features, particularly as the London-based saxophonist is playing in partnership with another very fine and inventive young musician - the pianist Andrew McCormack. For a decade Yarde has been blowing with powerful fire in bands like Jazz Jamaica and Tomorrow's Warriors, and in groups led by Soweto Kinch and Louis Moholo-Moholo. Late last year he was a member of Charlie Haden's Liberation Music Orchestra in an Ornette Coleman Meltdown concert.

As for McCormack, he was a part of the Jazz Jamaica line-up on their tribute to Motown, Motorcity Roots, and has played on albums by Denys Baptiste and Abraham Wilson. He has a particular skill in the duo context too, as I discovered at the 2008 London Jazz Festival where he partnered another saxophonist of Caribbean roots, the Virgin Islands-born and veteran of Art Blakey's Jazz Messengers, Jean Toussaint.

The MY Duo album gives both musicians ample opportunity to exercise their solo chops as well as showing how two jazz musicians, black and white, can empathise and perform with a potent creative unity. All the album's tunes have the performers' stamp all over them. McCormack is the composer of four, Yarde of six, with one written jointly. McCormack's arrangements frame the other two from other composers.

The opener, McCormack's Obsessive, is a prime example of how the duo attack a tune. Yarde's soprano is vibrant and vocalistic while the pianist, ever-conscious and confident of his other half's sonic vision, joins him not in accompaniment but in shared dialogue and artistry. Yarde soars on his own ballad How Long Will You Hold Me? and climaxes in one long, pealing and beautiful note near the end while McCormack caresses his keys with a tenderness that entirely befits his partner's theme. The only immediately recognisable tune on the album is Bernstein's Something's Coming from the parable of migration West Side Story. McCormack chimes out the opening before Yarde dances in boldly with the theme.

The track is another example of how two powerful jazzmen can create drama around an expressive melody. McCormack's solo is tense, dense with menace and the future in the present, while Yarde follows with echoes of the great soprano players - of Bechet and Coltrane, and of Steve Lacy too - in the scope of his pictures and narrative. When they combine, the story of danger and hope also coalesces.

Yarde turns to his tenor for McCormack's Tunnel Vision. Beginning with a solo exposition, Yarde joins with McCormack before the pianist unleashes a pounding lone chorus. Yarde sweeps back in, bursting with ideas and rhythmic intensity. Apart from the co-operatively composed Float Away, the rest of the tunes are all Yarde's, beginning with his own ballad No Time Can Tell - another essay in poised soprano artistry transforming into sheer musical breath in the concluding notes.

Yarde's Lullaby follows, so full of life and energy that you know that it would cause a baby to wake and dance rather than sleep. Its melody and lucid notes might make it a lullaby for this reviewer - yes, a lullaby for the old!

The 14 minutes of Yarde's Breezabeth set you wondering about the person it was named for, both musicians stretch out but they are always in vital connection with each other, signifying the most profound truth about this duo - they never detach themselves from their union, their considerable individual strengths are continuously meshed to create a greater musical and human power. And as Yarde's soprano birdsong hovers in Breezabeth, it never leaves McCormack's grounding notes.

A pairing of great equality, beauty, hope and surprise, and that is the black and white of it.

(MY Duo is available on Joy and Ears)

Gloria Yehilevsky (USA) and Jason Yarde (England) – Scoop it up!
Gm?R at the Vortex
(2025)

Gloria Yehilevsky is a young vibraphonist from San Diego, California, where her immigrant parents came from Russia. She began her music in a local drum and bugle corps, before moving to university in Kentucky, then Orebro University in Sweden and the Royal Birmingham Conservatoire. Then on to Chicago, back to San Diego and now in London, studying for a doctorate in Music at Trinity College.

Constant movement, like her music, and now playing her xylosynth in Dalston, at the Vortex with bassist Aram Bahmaie and the superbly weathered saxophonist of Jamaican roots, Jason Yarde. Sneaking in to hear the warm-up, past the relaxing hubbub of jerk chicken eaters and Red Stripe drinkers of

Gillett Square, I found Gloria was practising her xylosynth. I'd never heard or seen one before. Conjuring all kinds of drumsound and percussive effects from its electronic innards, she swung her mallets like a sorceress while Yarde blew long, swirling notes on his golden alto.

She introduced the session, saying the trio would begin by invoking 'real time', then move on to 'off the grid' and 'out of time' sounds. Yarde blew tersely with his long, quasi-nightmarish notes above the xylosynth's phantom drums, then with tumbling clusters and cadences, as he stalked the venue, along the bar, past the exit doors, under the stairs, instantly provoking with his improvised responses. When Bahmaie eventually joined them, digging deep with his electric bass, it was as if the trio became awesome tunnellers of time and harmony, delving below the tar and concrete of Dalston, while outside in Gillett Square the communal drinking and merriment carried on.

Yarde is a protean musician who can play anything. Guffawing on his black and shining baritone sax, then in an instant, blowing a yellow plastic policeman's whistle into the centre of the xylosynth's virtual AI representations, which were now suddenly transformed to the sound of vibes, as Yehilevsky picked up her handfulls of mallets and played like another Californian, the great maestro of vibes past, Bobby Hutcherson.

I was literally nonplussed by sound as I walked back to Dalston Kingsland Station to catch the train home, my ears still burning, all my old flesh quivering. Was it jazz? Did this come out of what was born in New Orleans more than a century ago? How would you define it? What does it matter: just let all your senses scoop it up!

Miguel Zenon (Puerto Rico) - An abiding love

Miguel Zenon – Tipico & Miguel Zenon featuring Spektral Quartet – Yo Soy La Tradicion
(2019)

Miguel Zenon's musical heart has never left his country of birth and it beats powerfully through all his performances and albums like the 2016 album Tipico, on which he is joined by Austrian bassist Hans Glawischnig, Venezuelan Luis Perdomo and fellow Puerto Rican compatriot, drummer Henry Cole.

Zenon has written all the album's tunes and every track shows the Caribbean roots of his artistry. Folk-inspired, they provide tremendous zest and a sense of hope to Zenon's horn and to Perdomo's fast-flowing, rippling piano runs which extend and harmonise the sounds of Latin American freedom.

Sangre de mi Sangre is a melody which Zenon plays with simplicity and an uncomplicated lucidity, his notes falling in cadences like sonic petals. Glawischnig's bass tunnels below Cole's tapping drumsticks, while on Corteza Zenon's notes drop like gentle rain. Entre las Raices has the pianist's notes running like a wild stream and Las Ramas begins with a whistled melody - like a labourer returning home from work – which is repeated and developed by Zenon's saxophone, a fitting way of ending the album.

The album Yo Soy la Tradicion is even more folk-inspired and draws on jazz, Puerto Rican folklore and New Music in what Zenon describes as a 'chamber-like context.' To help him create it, he's joined by Spektral String Quartet, to make a band of five expressing the 200 years of musical and cultural traditions from Zenon's native land.

On Cadenas, with its origins in folk poetry and dance, Zenon's horn rises out of the repeated strings riff in joyous choruses and dances on his reed. Yumas, one of several tunes with origins in the Jibaro 10-line rhyming stanza tradition, unifies poetry and sonic lyricism, with Zenon turning words into notes with beautiful aplomb as the quartet pluck their strings in showers of sound.

The album ends with Villabeno, named after the town, with its slower, cello-emphatic opening. Zenon plays with a deeply reflective, blues-tinged sadness, raising his horn to a buoyant serenity, concluding a brilliant and loving jazz-inflected insight into Puerto Rican folklore.

(Tipico & Yo Soy La Tradicion are available on Miel Music)

Louis Armstrong in London
(2025)

This book goes from A to Z, Abrams to Zenon, yet it must end back at A, and still the greatest and most luminous name in jazz: Armstrong. In 2024 the long-unreleased July 1968 sessions of Louis in London were finally set free, recorded with his All-Stars at a BBC 'Show of the Week', after his live appearances at the Batley Variety Club in West Yorkshire and the Odeon, Hammersmith. It is Satchmo at his most populous, a compilation of many of his most commercially successful songs, from Helly Dolly and When it's Sleepy Time Down South to Mack the Knife and What a Wonderful World.

The recordings were made in an epochal year for America, while Armstrong and his band were touring abroad, a year of profound loss with the murder of Martin Luther King and intense protest against racism, war and poverty. I had been teaching in western Canada, and crossed the frontier and came east to take part in the Poor People's Campaign in Washington and the mass rally before the Lincoln Memorial, where Resurrection City, a town of wooden shanties made in the rain and mud from duckboards, shuttering wood, corrugated iron and plastic sheets had been hastily built by demonstrators who had come from all over the USA and beyond - soon to be destroyed by police who attacked the encampment with tear gas, driving out the protesters.

The 1968 version of the All-Stars was far from Louis' greatest line-up, but there was still the great Texan trombonist and Ellington alumnus Tyree Glenn, the clarinetist of Hungarian roots, Joe Muranyi, and drummer Danny Barcelona from a Filipino family and born in Waipahu, Hawaii. Along with pianist Marty Napoleon and bassist Buddy Catlett, these were the 'tireless road warriors' (as Ricky Riccardi, Director of the Louis Armstrong House Museum, called them), who toured the world with Satchmo in his final years. They went everywhere - my Chilean friend Pedro, a refugee from a Pinochet prison after the 1973 fascist coup, remembers going to a Santiago concert when he was a teenager, and as Armstrong makes clear on the record, his mind was still on his nation's hostile military presence in Vietnam as he dedicates You'll Never Walk Alone, now forever an anthem of Liverpool Football Club and the 1989 Hillsborough tragedy, to the mothers of U.S. soldiers drafted to fight along the Mekong.

The album is racked in musical sentiment - there was no 'sleepy time down south' in 1968 for those fighting Jim Crow racism in Alabama, Mississippi, Arkansas or Georgia - neither does it have the brilliant horn artistry of Armstrong's Hot Five and Seven recordings of 1925-26 or his orchestral tracks of 1932-33. Yet it is still the great showman Armstrong with his wonderfully endearing voice and short bursts of brass fire, and as he sings the final verse of What a Wonderful World:

I hear babies cry
I watch them grow,
They'll learn much more
Than I'll ever know ....

you feel and know that he believes it, as I do too as a lifelong teacher.

The album made me remember when I first became conscious of the greatness of Armstrong. I was ten in 1955 when my teenage sister took me to the Odeon Cinema in Romford to see the film High Society. She was more interested in Grace Kelly and Frank Sinatra, but I was enraptured by Armstrong. When the first sequence of the film came on the screen, with Satchmo and his band playing on a bus, and his announcement: 'End of tune, beginning of story!' I was pulled into his person and his music, and that of those who came after him, for life. And his beautifully soaring notes on I Love You, Samantha, later in the film and his performance of Now You Has Jazz! with Bing Crosby, including some brief choruses from trombonist Trummy Young and clarinetist Ed Hall, and the glory of Armstrong himself's high note phrases left me. even as a boy, crazy for more of him and the music he played.

So thank you Louis, for everything that you and those who emulated you all over the world have given to me and millions of others, all stemming from a boy who found himself playing cornet in the New Orleans Colored Waifs' Home in 1913, and whose first job was pulling sacks of coal from a horse-drawn wagon, out of which in 1925 came the wondrous Coal Cart Blues by the pioneering Clarence Williams Blue Five, with the young Armstrong and the astonishing clarinetist, Sidney Bechet. For all the jazz and improvised sounds that we have, come and still come from such sources: real life, real work, real struggle, real human artistry and the brilliance of nature and life itself.

(Louis Armstrong in London Is available on Verve Records)

Chris Searle has been jazz correspondent of the Morning Star, Europe's only socialist daily newspaper, for nearly three decades. During that time he has written hundreds of reviews of recorded and live jazz performances and interviewed numerous musicians.

'Global Groove' is his fourth book on jazz, following 'Forward Groove' (2008), 'Red Groove' (2013) and 'Talking The Groove' (2024). Throughout its pages he mixes his reviews with dozens of interviews with jazz veterans, established virtuosi and younger musicians - who Art Blakey called 'new stars of the jazz firmament'. He shows how through more than a century of its existence, jazz has grown hugely in its internationalism and inclusiveness, always remaining a campaigning and evolving music with its aims rooted in a quest for freedom, popular justice and astonishing, boundary-breaking artistry.

Chris Searle was born in Romford in 1944. Fifty years a working teacher and educationalist, he has written or edited over fifty books on education, language, poetry, cricket and jazz. His book 'The Forsaken Lover' won the Martin Luther King Award in 1972, and he has written four autobiographical accounts: 'Isaac and I', 'We're Building the New School! Diary of a Teacher in Mozambique', 'Grenada Morning' and 'The World is in Our Words'.

Chris Searle by Paul Dash, Barbados-born artist, educator and writer who in 1957 migrated to Britain, where he was a part of the 1960s Caribbean Artists Movement.